Read What Others Are Saying
About This Amphibious Operations Series...

"Bill McGee, a prolific author and veteran of naval service in the South Pacific, has written a book that will do any 'Amphibian' proud. He has managed by dint of exceptional research and extensive interviews to perfectly blend the historical development of naval amphibious forces with humorous anecdotal references.

"You'll find yourself chuckling and nodding in the affirmative as you recall your own moments of terror, mind-numbing boredom and outrageous pranks. It is a compelling story of 'green' crews, 'green' officers, 'green' dragons, and 'green' camouflage.

"If your children or grandchildren have ever asked, 'What did you do in the war?' then point them to this book. Throughout the book you will find yourself saying, 'Yup, that was us,' and I guarantee you'll have a renewed respect for the guy you see in the mirror every morning."
—**Howard "Tiny" Clarkson**, USS LCI National Association

"Bill McGee, himself a veteran of the World War II navy, has not only done some exhaustive research into the documentation of how the amphibious forces were built, but has added the words of the men who took the theory of the amphibious doctrine and the new machines to sea. His dedicated work will surely help keep the day-to-day naval record of the 'Greatest Generation' from being lost."
—**John Lorelli**, author of *To Foreign Shores,*
U.S. Amphibious Operations in World War II

"Just finished *The Amphibians Are Coming!*—a fascinating and accurate history on the landing ships and craft of WWII and a welcome addition to the short list of books on the subject. It brought back many memories, even tears to my eyes. I look forward to your next two volumes on the Pacific War. For me it's a long-awaited dream, since they deal with my kind of war. You've brought great pride and joy to thousands who were there, and to future generations who will learn how America fought in the Forties."
—**John McNeill**, USNR, Officer-in-Charge, LCT-159

"*The Amphibians Are Coming!* is a great read. I am very impressed with the overall scope of your projected effort. Sandra Maguire's comment in the press release, 'Bill McGee...became a serious naval historian...' is clearly an understatement. As they say in the Navy, 'Well Done!'"
—**W. C. Hilderbrand**, Capt CEC, USN(Ret.)
Executive Vice President, CEC/Seabee Historical Foundation

"Having personally experienced a full measure of life at sea during World War II, in both Atlantic and Pacific Oceans, I found *The Amphibians Are Coming!* a 'must read' and not just for veterans. It is detailed, vivid and accurate."
—Anthony P. Tesori, USNR, Gunnery Officer, LST-340

"*The Amphibians Are Coming!* is a 'must read' for all shipmates of the 'Gator Navy. Whether your landing craft duty was the European Theater or you helped push the Japanese off the Pacific islands, this is an excellent chronicle of your participation. McGee's book combines the testimony of the amphibians that witnessed the terrible costs of combat, with the hindsight of scholars. The book unrolls the images of 'our war.'

"No matter why you turn to the pages—for reference, enlightenment or nostalgia—you will immediately rediscover your own life and the lives of ordinary guys who helped save the world from becoming the domain of mad men. A 'must' addition to our libraries."
—Charles J. Adams Jr., USS LST-281

"Bill, you have done a masterful job in dealing with the wide range of *Amphibians* in your Volume I. I enjoyed every minute re-living those South Pacific days. I particularly liked hearing the stories of the other classes of amphibs, in addition to our own LCIs. You included just the right amount of detail to make the book very readable."
—Alfred J. Ormston, Skipper, LCI-334

"Congratulations! I'm impressed with the scope of your *Solomons Campaigns*. The struggle for control of the Solomons was certainly a critical turning point in the Pacific war. You have managed to blend the amphibious operations with anecdotal references, while achieving a difficult objective: compressing all Solomons operations into one sweeping and compelling narrative. Many a Marine will enjoy this read."
—John M. Brigham, USMCR

"My own feeling in reading Bill McGee's book, is that it describes *miracles*. I'm serious. First, the miracle of bringing LSTs and other landing vessels into high production only a short time after the original designs were created. Then the miracle of bringing together untrained officers and men to perform tasks which should have required months of training and experience. Finally, there was the miracle of making all this work under unbelievable combat conditions. One wonders if the same achievements could be possible today."
—Mel Barger, Director, U.S. LST Association
author of *Large Slow Target*

Admiral Chester W. Nimitz USN
Commander in Chief United States Pacific Fleet

AMPHIBIOUS OPERATIONS IN THE SOUTH PACIFIC IN WORLD WAR II

VOLUME II

THE SOLOMONS CAMPAIGNS
1942 – 1943

FROM GUADALCANAL TO BOUGAINVILLE

PACIFIC WAR TURNING POINT

WILLIAM L. McGEE

PART I BY
Samuel Eliot Morison

BMC PUBLICATIONS
Santa Barbara, California
2002

LIBRARY OF CONGRESS Card Number: 2001117767
McGee, William L., 1925-
The Solomons Campaigns. 1942-1943.
From Guadalcanal to Bougainville: Pacific War Turning Point/
William L. McGee
   Includes appendices, bibliographical references, notes, and index
   ISBN 0-9701678-7-3 (Volume II)
   ISBN 0-9701678-9-X (3-Volume Set)
   1. World War, 1939-1945—History.   2. World War II
Amphibious Operations in the South Pacific—1942-1943.
3. 1942-1943 Solomons Islands Campaigns—Guadalcanal,
Tulagi, New Georgia, Vella Lavella, Bougainville, Treasury Islands.
4. United States Navy—History, 1939-1945.
5. United States Marine Corps—History, 1939-1945.
6. United States Army—History, 1939-1945.
7. United States Air Force—History, 1939-1945.
I. Title.

Printed in the United States of America on acid-free paper

Third printing

Published by BMC Publications
(A BMC Communications Company)
           98 Main Street, #337
           Tiburon, California 94920
           Tel: (415) 435-1883   Fax: (415) 435-1893
           E-mail: BMCpublications@aol.com
           website: www.BMCpublications.com

Front Cover Illustrations, clockwise from top center: TBF Avenger Navy torpedo bomber; LCI (L)
335 Infantry Landing Craft bucket brigade at Rendova, Central Solomons; Hand-to-hand unloading of small arms on Solomons Beach in 1943. LCT-159 skipper was Ensign John A. McNeill;
PT-77 cuts through the wake of sister PT boat during 1943 action; Ship burning following Japanese air attack as 40-mm gunners search for other bogies; Vought F4U-1A Corsair fighters of VF-
17 over Bougainville in Northern Solomons. Plane #29 is flown by Lt (jg) Ira Kepford, the Navy's
then leading Ace with 16 "kills." (All photos courtesy U.S. National Archives, Washington, D.C.)

DEDICATION

To the many brave men who served on land, on sea,
and in the air during the Solomons Campaigns
—especially those who made the ultimate sacrifice—
and to their families.

Books by William L. McGee

Bluejacket Odyssey 1942-1946—Guadalcanal to Bikini.
Naval Armed Guard in the Pacific

First printing, 1997
Revised Edition, 2000

Amphibious Operations in the South Pacific in World War II

Vol. I: *The Amphibians Are Coming! Emergence of the 'Gator Navy and its Revolutionary Landing Craft*

First printing, 2000
Second printing, 2001

Vol. II: *The Solomons Campaigns 1942-1943*
From Guadalcanal to Bougainville—Pacific War Turning Point

First printing, 2002

Vol. III: *Pacific Express—America's World War II Military Supply System*

First printing, 2003

Meet the Author

Bill McGee, a Montana country boy, joined the U.S. Navy in 1942 on his 17th birthday, after serving six months as a welder in Kaiser's Vancouver, Washington Shipyards building Liberty ships and LSTs. He was assigned to the Naval Armed Guard, the navy branch that protected Merchant Marine ships and their valuable cargo and crews from enemy attacks and sabotage.

After gunnery training, McGee's "Kid's Cruise" threw him in the middle of air attacks at Guadalcanal and torpedoings in the South Pacific; carried him through the action in the Western Pacific; and ended in peacetime on the cruiser USS *Fall River* with the atomic bomb tests at Bikini.

After his "Kid's Cruise" (1942-1946), McGee attended Montana State College, established an import-export company, and later began a long and successful career in broadcasting. He is also the author of nine books on retail advertising and broadcast advertising sales. He and his wife Sandra live in Santa Barbara, California.

His first book, *Bluejacket Odyssey,* "a memoir within a naval history," is now available in paperback. It is a close-up view of a defining period in our nation's history, as experienced from the unique perspective of a volunteer enlisted man. McGee is already deep into his third book on amphibious operations in the South Pacific during WWII.

Acknowledgments

Many people have contributed to the completion of this work, either by information, suggestions or critique.

Lists of interviewees and contributors of privately published memoirs are included in the Bibliography, but I would especially like to thank the following amphibians who shared their memories with me:

Charles Adams, Herb Alhgren, Jim Cogswell, Read Dunn, Harry Frey, Walter B. "Bo" Gillette, Gerhard Hess, Bill Jayne, Jack E. "Cookie" Johnson, Bob Kirsch, John McNeill, Martin Melkild, "Monty" La Montagne, Tom Mulligan, Al Ormston, Elmo Pucci, Rogers Aston*, Bob Sahlberg, Don Sterling*, Anthony Tesori, and Austin Volk.

A special thanks to the trustees of the Samuel E. Morison Trust and their publisher, Little Brown, for granting me permission to excerpt portions of Volumes IV and V of Samuel Eliot Morison's *History of United States Naval Operations in World War II* for Part I of this book.

I am also indebted to Samuel Loring Morison, accomplished naval historian and non-pareil researcher who not only condensed and edited his distinguished grandfather's work, but also provided me with invaluable war diaries, action reports, and numerous other documents from our nation's archives.

Thanks also to Richard F. Cross III, Washington, D.C.-based historian and photo consultant, and to the Still Photo Sections of the National Archives and the Naval Historical Center.

I want to express my appreciation to Jan Adelson for the many long hours of typing and retyping of manuscripts, and to the talented Jaye Carman who edited and designed this book.

A very special thanks to my friends Lee Mourad and Spencer Boise, and to my beautiful wife, Sandra, for the hundreds of hours of copy-editing and proofing they endured on my behalf.

William McGee
Santa Barbara, California

* Sad to report, these men have crossed over the bar since our interviews.

Contents

Preface

World War II was the largest and most violent armed conflict in the history of mankind. However, with almost sixty years now separating us from that conflict, time has taken its toll on our collective knowledge. While World War II continues to absorb the interest of its veterans as well as historians and military scholars, two generations of Americans have grown to maturity largely unaware of the political, social and military implications of a war that, more than any other, united us as a nation with a common purpose.

World War II was waged on land, on sea, and in the air over several diverse theaters of operation for approximately six years. Highly relevant today, it has much to teach us about global strategy, military preparedness, and joint operations against totalitarian governments and so-called rogue nations.

This book zeros in on the Solomons campaigns in the South Pacific for several reasons. First and foremost, I consider Japan's defeat in the bloody struggle for Guadalcanal the KEY turning point of the Pacific War. Granted, some historians are equally convinced that the Battle of Midway deserves this honor because its results were so far-reaching.

But code-breaking, luck, and skill were on the American side at Midway. Consider this: The intelligence available to Admiral Chester W. Nimitz, Commander in Chief, Pacific Fleet, regarding where and when the enemy would strike was conclusive. When the Japanese carrier attack force approached within launching distance of the Midway atoll on 4 June 1942, it ran into a whirlwind of American planes. Nimitz had brought up all his available carriers, had added long-range bombers staging from Hawaiian airfields, and had given the Midway garrison's Marine Aircraft Group 22 new planes to meet the enemy threat. The result of these preparations was electrifying: all four of the Japanese carriers were sent to the bottom, and the invasion force streaked back to the relative safety of home waters.

The Battle of Midway was certainly a major U.S. victory, but it was a three-day carrier air fight that turned in a matter of minutes, when American pilots in their SBD Dauntless dive bombers destroyed the four large Japanese carriers.

In contrast, the Guadalcanal campaign was the first amphibious operation undertaken by the United States since 1898. It took twenty-six weeks of hard fighting by Navy, Marine Corps, and Army Forces to secure what had been occupied in little more than a day.

The Japanese, through night actions at sea, were able to land reinforcements and supplies onto the island by transports and barges. The result: almost continual ground fighting by U.S. Marine and Army troops against a tenacious enemy in the Battles of Tenaru River, Matanikau River, Bloody Ridge, Henderson Field, Point Cruz, Gifu and Galloping Horse—all worthy of recounting in any military history.

During the course of all this ground fighting, the U.S. Navy fought six major engagements in the Solomons, more bitter and bloody than any naval battle in American history since 1814. Four of them were night gunfire actions of a kind that we may never see again, and two were carrier-air battles of the pattern set at Coral Sea; all significant in the history of war.

Other reasons for focusing on the Solomons amphibious operations include the opportunity to:

•   Chronicle all campaigns—from Guadalcanal to Bougainville—under one cover. Many books have been written on Guadalcanal, but this is the first, to my knowledge, to include all campaigns.

•   Continue to follow the new shore-to-shore landing ships and craft as they earn their battle stars in the Central and Northern Solomons—considered by many as "the forgotten wars."

Part One of this book is devoted entirely to the Guadalcanal Campaign (7 Aug 1942 – 9 Feb 1943), in which the U.S. Navy experienced more fighting than in any three previous wars. The relationship between ground fighting and naval warfare, a significant feature of this campaign, is described in considerable detail. In addition, numerous naval actions are recorded, as well as the sufferings of the supply train, and the almost daily air fighting.

Major naval actions covered include the severe defeat of the U.S. in the Battle of Savo Island, and the three-day Naval Battle of Guadalcanal in which two rear admirals were lost.

Part Two chronicles the Russells, New Georgia, and Vella Lavella campaigns in the central Solomons between February and October 1943. The five separate New Georgia landings at Rendova, Segi Point, Viru Harbor, Wickham Anchorage, and Rice Anchorage are recorded as well as the naval battles of Kula Gulf, Kolombangora, and Vella Lavella. (We also follow the action of the APDs and the Flotilla Five LCTs, LSTs and LCIs featured in *Volume I, The Amphibians Are Coming!,* as they move up the Slot in subsequent campaigns.)

Part Three covers the seizure of the Treasuries, the Choiseul Diversion and the Bougainville landings in the northern Solomons, as well as the naval battles of Empress Augusta Bay and Cape St. George between 27 October – 25 November 1943. The many valuable lessons learned during the Solomons amphibious operations, ranging from logistic support and shore bottlenecks, to force requirements and night landings, are summarized in the final chapter.

The Solomons Campaigns is based on archival research and hundreds of interviews and correspondence with men who have *been there and done that.* Welcome aboard!

William L. McGee
Santa Barbara, California
June 2001

Abbreviations and Acronyms plus Ship and Aircraft Designations

The military has a language all of its own. This list includes most of the commonly used World War II acronyms, code-words and abbreviations as well as aircraft, ship and landing craft designations. (Abbreviations frequently used in footnotes by our sources have also been included.)

1. World War II Acronyms, code-words and abbreviations

AA — Anti-aircraft
AAA — Antiaircraft Artillery
AAF — United States Army Air Force
ABDA — American-British-Dutch-Australian
Adm — Admiral
AE — Ammunition Ship
AF — Stores Ship
AGC — Amphibious Force Command Ship
AH — Hospital Ship
AirSols — Air Solomons Command
AK — Cargo Ship
AKA — Attack Cargo Ship
ANZAC — Australia New Zealand Area
AO — Oil Tanker
AOG — Gasoline Tanker
AP — Transport
APA — Attack Transport
APD — Fast Destroyer Transport
APc — Coastal Transport
AR — Action Report
AR — Repair ship
ARL — Landing Craft Repair Ship
Arty — Artillery
AS — Submarine Tender
ATF — Ocean Tugs, Fleet
ATS — Army Transport Service
BB — Battleship
BAR — Browning Automatic Rifle
BGen — Brigadier General
BLT — Battalion Landing Team
Bn — Battalion
Btry — Battery
Bu — Bureau
Buord — Bureau of Ordnance
Bupers — Bureau of Naval Personnel
Budocks — Bureau of Yards and Docks
Buships — Bureau of Ships
BuSandA — Bureau of Supplies and Accounts
CA — Coast Artillery
CA — Heavy cruiser

Cactus — Guadalcanal code name
Cal — Caliber
Capt — Captain
Cardiv — Carrier Division
CB — Large Cruiser
CCS — Combined Chiefs of Staff
Cdr — Commander (also Cmdr)
CG — Commanding General
CinCPOA — Commander in Chief, Pacific Ocean Area
CIC — Combat Information Center
CinCPac — Commander in Chief, Pacific Fleet, (Admiral Nimitz)
CL(AA) — Light Cruiser (antiaircraft)
CL — Light Cruiser
CLEANSLATE — Code name for occupation of Russell Islands
CMC — Commandant of the Marine Corps
Cmdr — Commander (also Cdr)
CNO — Chief of Naval Operations
Co — Company
CO — Commanding Officer
Col — Colonel
COM — Commander
ComAirSoPac — Commanding Aircraft (land based) South Pacific Force
ComAirWing I — Commander Genocide 1st Marine Air Wing
ComAmphibForSoPac — Commander, Amphibious Force, S. Pacific Force
ComGenSoPac — Commander General, U.S. Army South Pacific Force
COMNAVBAS — Commander Naval Base(s)
ComServonSoPac — Commander, Service Squadron, South Pacific Force
ComSoPac — Commander, South Pacific Force
ComSowesPac — Commander, Southwest Pacific (also CinCSWPA)
Cpl — Corporal
Crudiv — Cruiser Division
CT — Combat Team
CTF — Commander, Task Force
CTG — Commander, Task Group
CTU — Commander, Task Unit
CV — Aircraft Carrier
CVE — Escort Carrier
CVL — Light Carrier
DD — Destroyer
DE — Destroyer Escort

DMS — Destroyer Minesweeper
DOW — Died of Wounds
DRYGOODS — Code name for assembly of supplies
for New Georgia Offensive, February, 1943
DUKW — Amphibious Trucks
Ens — Ensign
ExO — Executive Officer
FA — Field Artillery
FAdm — Fleet Admiral
Flex — Fleet Landing Exercise
Flot — Flotilla
FMF — Fleet Marine Force
Gar — Garrison
Gen — General
GHQ — General Headquarters
GO — General Order
GQ — General quarters
HMAS — His Majesty's Australian Ship
HMS — His Majesty's Ship
HMNZS — His Majesty's New Zealand Ship
HQ — Headquarters
IJA — Imperial Japanese Army
IJN — Imperial Japanese Navy
Inf — Infantry
Is — Island
JCS — Joint Chiefs of Staff
Lant — Atlantic (Fleet)
LC (FF) — Landing Craft, Flotilla Flagship
LCC — Landing Craft, Control
LCI (G) — Landing Craft, Infantry (Gunboat)
LCI (L) — Landing Craft, Infantry (Large)
LCI (M) — Landing Craft, Infantry (Mortar)
LCI (R) — Landing Craft, Infantry (Rocket)
LCM — Landing Craft, Mechanized
LCdr — Lieutenant Commander (also LCmdr)
LCol — Lieutenant Colonel
LCP (L) — Landing Craft, Personnel (Large)
LCP (R) — Landing Craft, Personnel (Ramp)
LCR (L) — Landing Craft, Rubber (Large)(also Small)
LCS (L) — Landing Craft, Support (Large)
LCT (5) and (6) — Landing Craft Tank
LCV — Landing Craft, Vehicle
LCVP — Landing Craft, Vehicle and Personnel
LSD — Landing Ship, Dock
LSM — Landing Ship, Medium
LST — Landing Ship, Tank
Lt — Lieutenant
LtCol — Lieutenant Colonel
LtGen — Lieutenant General
Lt (jg) — Lieutenant, junior grade
LVT — Landing Vehicle, Tracked (Marks I-IV)
LVT (A) — Landing Vehicle, Tracked (Armored)
MAC — Marine Amphibious Corps
MAG — Marine Aircraft Group

MAINYARD — Code name for Guadalcanal Island
Maj — Major
MajGen — Major General
MARAD — Maritime Administration
MarCor — Marine Corps
MAW — Marine Aircraft Wing
MD — Marine Detachment
MI — Military Intelligence
MIA — Missing in Action
MOB — Mobile
Mm — Millimeter
MSgt — Master Sergeant
MSTS — Military Transportation Service (later Military
Sealift Command)
MTB — Motor Torpedo Boat
NAD — Naval Ammunition Depot
NAS — Naval Air Station
NGF — Naval Gunfire
NOB — Naval Operating Base
NSD — Naval Supply Depot
OB — Order of Battle
O-in-C — Officer in Charge
ONI — Office of Naval Intelligence
OOD — Officer of the Deck
OPlan — Operations Plan
PC — Sub-Chaser (steel hull)
PC — Patrol Craft
PCE — Patrol Craft Escort
Pfc/PFC — Private, First Class
Phib — Amphibious
Pion — Pioneer
Pl — Platoon
Plt Sgt — Platoon Sergeant
POA — Pacific Ocean Area
POW — Prisoner of War
PT — Motor Torpedo Boat
Pvt — Private
PTO — Pacific Theater of Operations
RAAF — Royal Australian Air Force
RAdm — Rear Admiral
RAF — Royal Air Force
RAN — Royal Australian Navy
RCT — Regimental Combat Team
Rdr — Raider
Reinf — Reinforced
RING BOLT — Tulagi code name
RLT — Regimental Landing Team
RN — Royal Navy
RNZAF — Royal New Zealand Air Force
RNZN — Royal New Zealand Navy
SC — Submarine Chaser (Wooden hull)
SEC NAV — The Secretary of the Navy
SFCP — Shore Fire Control Party
SoPac — South Pacific Area, South Pacific Force

SoWesPac — Southwest Pacific Area (SWPA)
Sgt — Sergeant
SM — Submarine Minelayer
Sqn — Squadron
SS — Submarine
SSgt — Staff Sergeant
TBS — (Talk Between Ships) Voice radio
TF — Task Force
TG — Task Group
TOENAILS — Code name for New Georgia operation
TSgt — Technical Sergeant
TU — Task Unit
UDT — Underwater Demolition Team
USA — United States Army
USAFISPA — United States Army Forces in the South Pacific Area
USAT — United States Army Transport
USASOS — United States Army Services of Supply
USCG — United States Coast Guard
USN — United States Navy
USNR — United States Naval Reserve

USNS — United States Naval Ship
USMC — United States Marine Corps (also United States Maritime Commission)
USSBS — United States Strategic Bombing Survey
VAdm — Vice Admiral
VF — Navy Fighter Squadron
VMF — Marine Fighter Squadron
VMSB — Marine Scout-Bomber Squadron
VP — Navy Patrol Squadron
VS — Navy Scouting Squadron
WATCHTOWER — Code name for the Guadalcanal-Tulagi Operation
WD — War Diary
WIA — Wounded in Action
WO — Warrant Officer
WPB — War Production Board
XO — Executive Officer
YMS — Motor Minesweeper
YP — Patrol Vessel
1st Sgt — First Sergeant

2. Aircraft Designations of the U.S. Navy, Marine Corps and Army, circa 1942-1943

A-20 — Boston, Army (2) light bomber ; A-29 — Hudson, Army (2) light bomber*

B-17 — Flying Fortress, Army (4) heavy bomber; B-24 — Liberator, Army (4) heavy bomber (called PB4Y by Navy)*

B-25 — Mitchell, Army (2) medium bomber; B-26 — Marauder, Army (2) medium bomber*

B-26 — Marauder, Army (2) medium bomber

B-29 — Superfortress, Army (4) heavy bomber

Black Cat — PBY equipped for night work

C-47 — Skytrain, Army (2) transport*

Dumbo — PBY equipped for rescue work

F4F — Wildcat; F4U — Corsair; F6F — Hellcat; all Navy (1) fighters*

P-38 — Lightning, Army (2) fighter; P-39 — Airacobra; P-40 — Warhawk, Army (1) fighters*

PBY — Catalina, Navy (2) seaplane; PBY-5A — amphibian*

PV-1 — Ventura, Navy (2) medium bomber*

SBD — Dauntless, Navy (1) dive-bomber*

SB2C — Helldiver; Navy (1) dive-bomber*

TBF — Avenger, Navy (1) torpedo-bomber*

3. Japanese Aircraft Designations, circa 1942-43

"Betty" — Mitsubishi Zero-1, Navy (2)medium bomber*

"Emily" — Kawanishi Zero-2, Navy (4) patrol bomber (flying boat)*

"Helen" — Nakajima, Navy (2) medium bomber*

"Judy" — Aichi, Navy (1) torpedo-bomber*

"Kate" — Nakajima 97-2, Navy (1) high-level or torpedo-bomber*

"Pete" — Sasebo, Zero-o, Navy (1) float plane*

"Sally" — Mitsubishi 97, Army (2) medium bomber*

"Tojo" — Nakajima, Army (1) fighter*

"Val" — Aichi 99-1 Navy (1) dive-bomber

"Zeke" — Mitsubishi Zero-3, Navy (1) fighter (called "Zero" in 1942-43)

* Numerals in parentheses indicate number of engines.

MILITARY MAP SYMBOLS

SIZE SYMBOLS

• • • Platoon

I Company

I I Battalion

I I I Regiment

x Brigade

x x Division

UNIT SYMBOLS

Basic Unit

Marine Unit(serving with units of other services)
usmc

Enemy Unit

Antiaircraft

Artillery

Cavalry

• DB Defense Battalion

Engineer

UNIT SYMBOLS

Infantry

Prcht Parachute

Rdr Raider

• SW Special Weapons

Tank

EXAMPLES

• • •
9DB Tank Platoon, 9th Defense Battalion

G(+) 2Prcht Company G (reinforced) 2d Parachute Battalion
usmc

2 141 2d Battalion, 141st Infantry Regiment (Japanese)

19 19th Marines

2 I 2d Brigade, 1st Cavalry Division

3NZ 3d New Zealand Infantry Division

Source: U. S. Marine Corps.

Amphibious Force Ships and Craft [1]

	DISPL.[2]	TOTAL VESSELS[3]	TOTAL LOST[4]	COMM. or CONV.[5]
Ship-to-shore Cargo Ships & Transports				
AK Cargo Ships	1600-8900	160	3	'41-'45
AKA Attack Cargo Ships	4087-8045	108		'43-'45
AP Transports	1745-43,407	129	8	'21-'45
APA Attack Transports	4247-13,529	227	2	'43-'45
APc Coastal Transports	147-186	69		'42-'43
APD High Speed Transports				
-Converted Destroyers or Seaplane Tenders	1020-1190	32	8	'40-44
-Converted Destroyer Escorts	1400-1450	95		'44-'45
Shore-to-shore Amphibious Landing Ships & Craft				
LCT Landing Craft, Tank (Mark V & VI)	123-143	1,435	75	'42-'45
LST Landing Ship, Tank	1490	913	41	'42-'45
LCI(L) Landing Craft, Infantry (Large)	178-209	905	16	'42-'44
LCI(G) Landing Craft, Infantry (Gunboat)	210-230	218	8	'44-'45
LCI(M) Landing Craft, Infantry (Mortar)	235	60		'45
LCI(R) Landing Craft, Infantry (Rocket)	215	52		'45
LSM Landing Ships, Medium	513-520	474	9	'44-'45
LSM(R) Landing Ships, Medium (Rocket)	760-1187	50	3	'44-'45
LC(FF) Landing Craft, Flotilla Flagship	234	49		'43-'44
LCS(L) Landing Craft, Support (Large)	123	130	6	'44
LSV Landing Ships, Vehicle	4626-5177	6		'44-'45
LSD Landing Ships, Dock	4490-4546	18		'43-'45

[1] Morison, *History of United States Naval Operations in World War II,* Vol. XV, pp. 79-109; Principal reference works cited include: *Ships Data US Naval Vessels,* editions of 1943, 1945 and 1949; *United States Naval Vessels* (ONI 222-US) 1 Sept. 1945; Comairpac *Index of United States Fleet,* 1 Dec. 1944; and K. Jack Bauer's manuscript, "Ships of the United States Navy, 1775-1945."
[2] DISPL. - Light displacement, i.e., ready for sea but without consumable or variable items or crew.
[3] Ship counts will vary somewhat due to ship conversions and/or transfers under Lend-Lease. *Note:* ship losses have not been deducted from ship totals.
[4] Number of ships or craft lost in combat or by accident, 27 Jun.1940–2 Sept.1945 when data available.
[5] Year commissioned or converted.

LST (3) Landing Ship, Tank (class 3). A British adaption of the American design shown with LCT and Army MTLs carried on deck. ONI/226.

LSM Landing Ship, Medium. An oceangoing tank landing ship designed to operate with LCI(L) convoys. ONI/226.

LSM(R) Landing Ship, Medium (Rocket). Converted LSMs serve as rocket support ships in amphibious operations preparatory to landings. ONI/226.

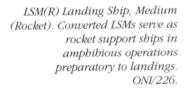

LCS(L)(3) Landing Craft, Support (Large)(Mark 3), designed to provide close-in fire support for landing operations and to intercept and destroy inter-island barge traffic. ONI/226.

LSV Landing Ship, Vehicle designed to transport large numbers of LVTs, DUKWs, and troops in a fast amphibious task force to the landing area; disembarking vehicles over a stern ramp. ONI/226.

Amphibious Force Ships and Craft [1]

	LENGTH	DISPL.[2]	TOTAL VESSELS[3]
Small Ship-to-shore Landing Craft			
LCC Landing Craft, Control	56'	30-50	99
LCM Landing Craft, Mechanized (Mks II-IV)	45'-56'	23-26	11,496
LCP(L) Landing Craft, Personnel (Large)	36'8"	5.8	2,193
LCP(R) Landing Craft, Personnel (Ramp)	35'10"	5.8	2,631
LCR(L) Landing Craft, Rubber (Large)	16'	395 lb.	10,123
LCR(S) Landing Craft, Rubber (Small)	12'5"	210 lb.	8,150
LCS(S) Landing Craft, Support (Small)(Mks I-II)	36'8"	9-10	558
LCV Landing Craft, Vehicle	36'3"	7	2,366
LCVP Landing Craft Vehicle, Personnel	36'3"	9	23,358
LVT Landing Vehicle, Tracked (Mks I-IV)	21'6"-26'1"	7.5-12.5	15,501
LVT(A) Landing Vehicle, Tracked (Armored)(Mks I-IV)	26'1"	11.4-17.0	2,850
TOTAL:			**79,325**
Amphibious Trucks			
DUKW	31'8"	5.8	NA[4]
Jeep	15'7"	1.6	NA

[1], [2], [3] *(Footnote information is given below chart on page XXI.)*
[4] NA - Not Available.

LVT(A)(4) Landing Vehicle, Tracked (armored) (Mark 4) with an army 75-mm Howitzer. Capacity: 5,000 lbs ammunition and gear. ONI/226.

LCC(1) Landing Craft, Control (Mark 1) Lead-in navigational craft for landing boats; to mark line of departure; for traffic control; for preliminary hydrographic surveys. Not intended to beach. ONI/226.

LCR(L) Landing Craft, Rubber (Large). A BAR man in the bow of the rubber landing craft provides covering fire as the 10-man boat crew reaches the undefended beach of Pavuvu in the Russell Islands. U.S. Marine Corps Photo.

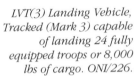

LVT(3) Landing Vehicle, Tracked (Mark 3) capable of landing 24 fully equipped troops or 8,000 lbs of cargo. ONI/226.

DUKW 21/2-ton, 6x6 amphibious army truck for ship-to-shore transport. ONI/226.

LSD Landing Ship, Dock. Transports loaded landing craft to the landing area, where the hold is flooded and the small craft move out under their own power. ONI/226.

Partial List of Maps and Charts

Prelude to War 1931-1941

For America, World War II began on December 7, 1941 when the Japanese planes bombed Pearl Harbor. Americans who remember that Sunday can summon up the exact moment when they heard the news. It shattered the leisure of listening to a football game or concert on the radio: *We interrupt this broadcast to bring you a special news bulletin. Pearl Harbor has been attacked by the Japanese.*

The war had already begun for the valiant, long-forgotten, thirty-seven man merchant crew of the unarmed tanker, *Astral*. They lost their lives on 1 December 1941 when torpedoed and sunk by German submarine U-43, while en route to Portugal. For the crew of U.S. destroyer *Reuben James*, the war began even earlier, on 31 October 1941 when a U-boat sank their ship.

For Americans eager to fight as volunteers, the war had begun at other times. Some became pilots for the Flying Tigers to fight the Japanese invaders of China, the first country to fall victim to aggression in the war that would engulf the world.

Impatient young Americans in 1939-1940—using false names to avoid prosecution under U.S. Neutrality Acts—went off to fight for England by joining the British Army or the all-American Eagle Squadrons of the Royal Air Force.

For millions of other young American men, the war began on October 29, 1940, when blindfolded Secretary of War, Henry L. Stimson, reached into a ten-gallon glass bowl and started drawing numbers assigned by lottery to those who had registered under the Selective Service Act for America's first peacetime military draft.

For the benefit of the younger reader, let's flashback to the pre-World War II era for a brief review of events leading up to the beginning of World War II for America.

First, we'll review Japan's empire expansion and armed forces buildup prior to Pearl Harbor. Second, we'll examine America's early War Plans as they evolved in the 1930s and early 1940s, and then review the U.S. Armed Forces buildup. Third, we'll highlight the Japanese mostly uncontested Pacific and Far East campaigns prior to facing the U.S. Marines in the Solomons.

Finally, we'll position the Anglo-American Combined Chiefs of Staff, profile the top Pacific Commands, and summarize the South Pacific plans and preparations immediately prior to Operation WATCHTOWER—the seizure of Guadalcanal and Tulagi in the Southern Solomons.

Japan's Empire Expansion, 1931-1941 – Japan began expanding her empire on September 18, 1931 when Japanese troops, claiming that Chinese saboteurs were tampering with the Japanese-owned South Manchuria Railway, seized the Chinese city of Mukden (now Shenyang). The bogus "Mukden incident" launched a swift conquest of northeastern China, where the Japanese set up the state of Manchukuo. When the League of Nations belatedly condemned Japan in 1933, Japan simply quit the League.

Japan again moved against China in 1937, when another staged event was used as a pretext for attacking Chinese troops near Peking. The undeclared war, which Japan called the "China Incident," was envisioned by the Japanese militarists as a way to create another puppet state similar to Manchukuo.

Japanese Troops posed in the streets of Shanghai. The Japanese had been fighting in China since the early 1930s. Courtesy of U.S. Army.

By this time, realization had grown in Washington that U.S. forces in the Philippines could not hold out long enough against a serious Japanese attempt to take the islands, until the U.S. Fleet reached the area. Increasing the defenses there was out of the question, for appropriations were still low, and other demands had priority on limited resources.[1] (See p. XLV for notes.)

After the Germans won the battle of France and installed the Vichy France regime, Japan, about to sign the Tripartite Pact and become a member of the Axis, got German approval to occupy French Indochina, from which supplies had been flowing to China. In Indochina, Japan would have bases for further expansion and acquisition of Southeast Asia's oil, rubber, tin, quinine, and timber. Japanese military and political leaders plotted the seizure of the Pacific colonial territories of the Dutch and British, particularly the oil-rich Dutch East Indies. Japanese occupation forces in China intensified an anti-foreigner campaign, focusing particularly on British subjects.

President Roosevelt reacted to Japan's militarism by notifying Japan that the United States would terminate the 1911 U.S.-Japanese commercial treaty, cutting Japan off from vital imports.

The military-dominated Japanese Cabinet expelled the remaining moderates, and in July 1941 ordered a Japanese invasion of the rest of Indochina and the call-up of more conscripts. President Roosevelt responded by freezing all Japanese assets in the United States and cutting off all oil exports to Japan.

Prime Minister Konoe was replaced by the Minister of War, General Hideki

General Hideki Tojo. Courtesy U.S. Army.

Tojo. With the military primed for war, he reiterated Japanese demands: the United States must end aid to China, accept the Japanese seizure of Indochina, resume normal trade, and not reinforce U.S. bases in the Far East. He publicly maintained that the demands were not negotiable and set a deadline for U.S. acceptance.

Talks began between U.S. Secretary of State Cordell Hull and Japanese Ambassador Nomura, but the two nations were at an impasse. Tojo saw Hull's position as an "ultimatum" and cocked the gun of war. He ordered a Japanese task force, secretly assembled off the Kuril island of Etorofu, to sea. The ships were to carry out the attack on Pearl Harbor Sunday morning, 7 December 1941, Hawaii time.

To Americans, the raid on Pearl Harbor was "a sneak attack," and Japan became a synonym for treachery. Japan's political strategy called for the United States to soon propose talks for a negotiated peace. But the attack infuriated U.S. citizens, who girded for revenge and a decisive defeat of Japan.

Mandated Islands – The Japanese also controlled the Pacific islands that were taken from Germany and ceded to Japan under the Versailles Treaty at the end of World War I. They included the Marshall Islands, the Caroline Islands, and all of the Mariana Islands except Guam, which the United States had acquired after the Spanish-American War. When Japan quit the League in 1933, the fortifying of the islands intensified. (As the world would soon learn, Japan had transformed the mandate into a license to convert many of the islands into air and naval bases.)

Japan's Military Buildup, 1937-1941 – A major buildup of Japan's armed forces was undertaken from 1937 to 1941, as preparations were being made for war.

Army: By the fall of 1941, the Japanese Army had about 1,700,000 men in 51 divisions, of which 28 were engaged in operations in China and 13 were stationed in Manchuria and Korea for defense against the Soviet Union. The Army was experienced and hardened by its fighting in China. The troops were also vicious. (Army Minister Tojo had published a field service code in 1941 that stated, "Do not be taken prisoner...." This may explain not only the tenacity of the Japanese fighting man, but also his treatment of POWs with such hatred and savagery.)

Navy: The Imperial Japanese Navy, at the beginning of the Pacific War, was large and highly innovative, especially with respect to submarines and aircraft carriers. Further, Japanese naval aviators had combat experience from the war in China. At the start of the war, the Japanese Navy ships outnumbered the combined U.S., British Empire, Dutch, and Free French forces in the Pacific, except for capital ships, light cruisers and submarines.

Naval Aviation: The Japanese naval air arm was the largest and most capable in the world when the war began. Japanese carrier planes and naval land-based aircraft had seen extensive action in China. There were six large and four light aircraft carriers in service. The navy counted some 1,250 aircraft on 7 December 1941, including the new A6M Zero fighter and G4M Betty twin-engine bomber. These planes alone totaled more than many of the world's air forces.

The bold Japanese naval strokes upon the opening of the war were totally victorious. At the cost of relatively few aircraft (only 27 at Pearl Harbor), and no warship larger than a destroyer, the Japanese effectively destroyed U.S. and British naval power in the region (including the eastern Indian Ocean). Successful assaults quickly followed on the Philippines, Malaya, the Dutch East Indies, and numerous smaller island groups.

The Japanese Navy suffered a minor setback after five months, in the Battle of the Coral Sea. But at Midway, one month later, the Japanese suffered a major defeat with the loss of four carriers, and even more importantly, their planes and most of their trained pilots.

America's War Plan[2] – In the 1930s, America's plans were concerned primarily with courses of action to be taken in the event of a conflict in one theatre and against one nation, or a contiguous group of nations. In these so-called "color plans," each probable enemy was assigned a separate color designation; Japan became Orange.

With the advent of the Axis coalition, American military men began thinking in terms of a true world war. As these new plans evolved, they were given the name "Rainbow" to signify their concept of a multi-national war.

On 29 January 1941, ranking British and American staff officers met in Washington to discuss joint measures to be taken if the United States should be forced into a war with the Axis Powers. It was regarded as almost certain that the outbreak of hostilities with any one of the Axis partners would bring immediate declarations of war from the others. By insuring action on two widely separated fronts, the Axis could expect, at the very least, a decreased Allied capability to concentrate their forces. The American-British conversations ended on 27 March with an agreement (ABC-1) which was to have a profound effect on the course of World War II. Its basic strategical decision, which never was discarded, stated that:

> Since Germany is the predominant member of the Axis Powers, the Atlantic and European area is considered to be the decisive theatre. The principal United States military effort will be exerted in that theatre, and operations of United States forces in other theatres will be conducted in such a manner as to facilitate that effort...If Japan does enter the war, the Military Strategy in the Far East will be defensive. [3]

The defensive implied in the war against Japan was not to be a holding action, however, but rather a strategic defensive that contemplated a series of tactical offensives with the Pacific Fleet as the striking force.

A new American war plan, Rainbow 5, was promulgated soon after the end of the American-British talks. Almost the whole of the Pacific was made an American strategic responsibility and the Army's primary mission under the plan was cooperation with and support of the fleet.

The success of the Japanese raid on Pearl Harbor forced a drastic revision of strategy which effectively postponed amphibious assaults in the Central Pacific. Certain defensive measures which were mentioned in the plan, however, were implemented prior to the outbreak of war.

The Rainbow 5 plan called for the development of bases, primarily air bases, at Midway, Johnston, Palmyra, Samoa, and Wake. All of these islands, which were under control of the Navy, were to have Marine garrisons with defense forces sufficient to repel major attacks. Some of the Marine defense battalions, tailored to

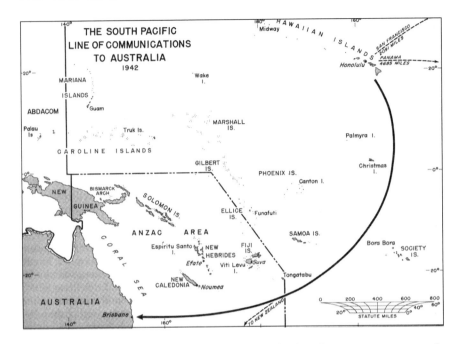

meet the needs of garrisons for isolated island outposts, were already in the Pacific by the time Rainbow 5 was published.

The purpose of establishing bases on these islands was two-fold: Samoa was to help protect the routes of communication to the Southwest Pacific; Johnston, Palmyra, Wake, and Midway were to serve as outguards for the Pacific Fleet's home port at Pearl Harbor.

U.S. Armed Forces Buildup – During the summer of 1940, Congress passed the Two Ocean Navy Bill, authorized procurement of thousands of planes and tons of army equipment, and passed the Selective Service Act to provide more men to use the arms in defense of the nation.[4]

When the war began, the United States had three fleets: Atlantic, Pacific and Asiatic. The Atlantic Fleet consisted of 4 aircraft carriers, 1 escort carrier, 8 battleships, 5 heavy cruisers, 8 light cruisers, 87 destroyers, and 60 submarines.

The Pacific Fleet consisted of 3 aircraft carriers, 9 battleships, 12 heavy cruisers, 9 light cruisers, 71 destroyers, and 22 submarines. (The most significant losses at Pearl Harbor were battleships and patrol aircraft.)

Finally, the Asiatic Fleet consisted of only 1 heavy cruiser, 2 light cruisers, 13 destroyers, and 29 submarines.

Large numbers of U.S. warships were also under construction or on order—15 fast battleships, 11 large aircraft carriers, and scores of cruisers, destroyers, and submarines.

U.S. yards would also produce thousands of cargo ships, troop transports, and tankers as well as thousands of antisubmarine craft, minesweepers, motor torpedo boats, and amphibious landing ships and craft during the war.

Massive recruiting efforts were undertaken to man these ships and the U.S. Navy, Coast Guard, and Marine Corps grew from 203,127 officers and enlisted personnel on 1 July 1940 to 843,096 on 30 June 1942. (The grand total, including the naval air arm, would reach 4,064,455 by 31 August 1945.)[5]

About 55,000 merchant seamen and officers were sailing in December 1941. The personnel system administered by the War Shipping Administration resulted in a peak seagoing force of 250,000 merchant mariners by war's end.[6]

Beyond ship and personnel numbers, the U.S. Navy was able to develop a large air arm and continue innovative developments in anti-air and anti-submarine weapons, radar, and sonar. The major Navy technical failure was in torpedoes. (Not until early 1943 were the torpedo problems fully solved and submarines able to demonstrate their effectiveness. By that time, Japanese warship losses had drastically curtailed Japan's anti-submarine capability.)

In some respects the most important aspect of the war was the ascendancy of the aircraft carrier over the battleship. This direction was understood by the U.S. naval leadership even before the war, as evidenced by the extensive carrier-building program. Admiral King, CinC U.S. Fleet and Chief of Naval Operations, was himself an experienced aviator and aviation planner.

In the European war, the U.S. Navy had a major role (albeit at times subordinate to the Royal Navy) in the anti-submarine campaign in the Atlantic and the various Mediterranean and European landings. But in the Pacific the Navy had the principal role, carrying and supporting Army and Marine units in their assaults on various Pacific atolls and islands, and in destroying the Japanese Fleet.

Naval Aviation: The U.S. naval air arm, which predated World War I, was fully integrated into the fleet. It expanded more than tenfold during the war, from just under 4,000 aircraft at America's entry into the war, to more than 40,000, including Marine aircraft, when Japan surrendered.

Naval pilots (including Marine and Coast Guard) were trained by a large naval air training establishment. Also, the Naval Air Transport Service provided long-range delivery of mail, spare parts, and personnel to the fleet throughout the world.

Early Japanese Pacific Campaigns, 1940-1942 – While Japan's war with China raged on, Japanese troops marched into French Indochina in September 1940 without opposition from the Vichy French government. The Japanese move illuminated part of Japan's plan for a Greater East Asia Co-Prosperity Sphere, a version of Hitler's European "New Order."

By the fall of 1941, diplomatic relations between Japan and the United States had reached an impasse. With only a six-month supply of petroleum available in Japan, and fearful of further U.S. political-economic actions, the Japanese Cabinet, under Premier Tojo, agreed that it had to choose between a war with the United States and dissolution of the empire.

The Japanese Navy, under the direction of Admiral Yamamoto, undertook the sneak attack on Pearl Harbor to prevent the U.S. Fleet from interfering with the Japanese conquest of the Philippines, Malaya, and the Dutch East Indies. Yamamoto, CinC of the Japanese Fleet, estimated that the attack on the U.S. fleet—if successful—would give the Japanese six months of freedom from attack to secure its goals in the Far East.

Hours after attacking Pearl Harbor, Japanese bombers struck U.S. bases in the Philippines, and on the islands of Guam and Wake. They also hit Singapore. Guam fell to the Japanese in a day; Wake and Singapore in a few weeks. The Japanese invaded the Philippines in massive numbers. (The U.S.-Filipino forces, led by General Douglas MacArthur, made a stand on Luzon's Bataan Peninsula, but it fell on 9 April 1942.)

Japanese forces overran the Malayan peninsula, and after long and heavy fighting, the island fortress of Singapore fell on 15 February 1942.

*Aerial view of Naval
Operating Base, Pearl
Harbor, looking west.*

*Hickam Field disaster,
7 December 1941.*

*Sneak attack, 7 December 1941.
All courtesy U.S. Navy.*

The Japanese landed troops on the southern tip of Burma on 8 December 1941. After heavy fighting to hold Mandalay and the Burma Road, the British defenders began a long retreat to the borders of India. The Burmese end of the Burma Road fell on 29 April and Mandalay on 2 May.

Japanese troops also overran New Britain and New Ireland in the South Pacific, as well as the Admiralty and Solomon Islands. By the spring of 1942 Japan had gained control of the entire Western Pacific, and had a massive foothold in China, Indochina, Malaya, and Burma, and threatened Australia and British interests in the Indian Ocean. Japanese losses had been minimal—a few dozen planes, a few hundred troops, and several warships, the largest of which were destroyers. The success was beyond the expectations of Japanese military and political leaders, and beyond the greatest fears of Allied leaders.

Japanese Troops on Bataan during the spring of 1942. The Japanese commander insisted upon unconditional surrender of all the troops in the Philippines and was furious when he learned that only the U.S. forces of Bataan Peninsula had surrendered. The forces on Corregidor held their fire until the captured Bataan troops were removed from the area. U.S. Army.

Admiral Halsey's *Enterprise* group TF 16 made a number of successful hit-and-run raids in the Central Pacific during the early months of 1942, but all paled in comparison with the Halsey-Doolittle raid on Tokyo.

Since the Fleet had no carrier bombers with enough range to operate from outside the limits of the Japanese air patrol, the Army Air Force provided sixteen B-25 Mitchell medium bombers, which made a deckload for carrier *Hornet* (Capt Marc A. Mitscher). Halsey's

B-25s on flight deck of aircraft carrier USS Hornet (CV-8) before taking off to bomb Tokyo on 18 April 1942.

Admiral Halsey and Flag Staff. Both courtesy U.S. Navy.

Enterprise (Capt George D. Murray) provided combat air patrol; RAdm Raymond A. Spruance commanded the cruisers; and Capt Richard Conolly, the destroyers of the screen.

Although B-25 pilots could be trained to take off from a carrier, the deck was too short for recovery; the planes had to fly 668 miles from *Hornet's* launching point to Tokyo, bomb the city, and then fly another 1100 miles to friendly Chinese airfields.

The strike group, led by LtCol James H. Doolittle, USA, was airborne by 0824 April 18, and over the city by noon. They completely surprised the Japanese, and not one B-25 was lost over Japan; but some made crash landings in China or splashed off the coast, and two pilots picked up by the Japanese were executed.

This "answer to Pearl Harbor" inflicted relatively little damage on the enemy's homeland, but it gave the American public, which had nothing but bad news for nineteen weeks, a great lift. And, what is even more important, the event expedited plans for an overextension that led to the Japanese defeat at Midway.

In May, Admiral Yamamoto had hoped to bring the U.S. carrier force to a decisive battle in the central Pacific, but instead, agreed to support an assault on Port Moresby, New Guinea. The port would be the launch site for Japan's thrust to Australia. The U.S. Navy,

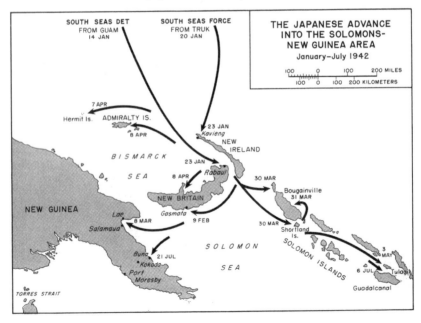

thanks to American code-breaking efforts, had been warned of the approaching Japanese landing forces, and attacked first. The ensuing Battle of the Coral Sea, on 7-8 May 1942, marked the first Japanese defeat of the war. Adm Yamamoto had been absolutely correct in his estimate that Japan could have six months of freedom from U.S. attack in the Pacific.

Frustrated in their attempts to take Port Moresby, and suffering the loss of the light carrier *Shoho* and damage to two larger carriers, the Japanese took a different approach to the capture of Port Moresby. Troops were landed on the Solomon Islands of Guadalcanal and Tulagi to establish airfield and seaplane bases.

Battle of the Coral Sea, May 1942. Japanese light carrier Shoho is torpedoed by U.S. Navy planes on 7 May.

USS Lexington (CV-2) sinking after being abandoned 8 May. Both courtesy Naval Historical Center.

But the principal Japanese forces were steaming eastward, for the decisive carrier battle to be fought near Midway.

The Japanese Midway operation had two objectives: The first was the seizure of Midway Island as an advance base to help provide early detection of U.S. aircraft carriers seeking to raid Japan, as had occurred in the Doolittle raid of April 1942. The second was an attack on the Aleutians, a diversion to draw out what was left of the U.S. Pacific Fleet so that it could be engaged and destroyed. With these objectives achieved, the invasion of Hawaii itself would become possible. The plan of Adm Yamamoto depended upon secrecy and good fortune—both of which would be denied in the battle.

USS Enterprise (CV-6) at Midway.

Battle of Midway, June 1942. USS Yorktown (CV-7) after first attack. Both courtesy Naval Historical Center.

Admiral Chester Nimitz, CinC of the U.S. Pacific Fleet, knew of Yamamoto's plan in advance through American decrypts of Japanese naval codes. Nimitz's problem was how to obtain sufficient forces to intercept the approaching Japanese fleets. Yamamoto had assembled 4 large and 2 medium carriers, 11 battleships, 16 cruisers, and 55 destroyers plus a large submarine force to engage the U.S. Pacific Fleet and support the invasion of Midway. Simultaneously, the assault on the Aleutians was to be carried out by 2 medium carriers, 6 cruisers, and 13 destroyers.

In contrast, Nimitz could assemble but 3 carriers, 8 cruisers, and 17 destroyers plus submarines to stop the Japanese.

But code-breaking, luck, and skill were on the American side. Nimitz knew of the Japanese plans and that Yamamoto had dispersed his forces into several separate task forces that were not mutually supportable. The tide of battle was turned in a few moments at Midway, when U.S. SBD Dauntless dive bombers smashed and left three of the Japanese large carriers sinking. A short time later the SBDs destroyed the fourth large carrier. Sunk on 4 June 1942 were the *Kaga, Akagi, Soryu,* and *Hiryu*—all veterans of the Pearl Harbor attack—along with hundreds of their veteran pilots and skilled mechanics, and all of their aircraft. The U.S. Navy lost one carrier, the *Yorktown,* plus many valiant pilots and their land-based bombers and carrier-launched torpedo planes.

Although the Japanese failed to seize Midway, they did take the remote Attu and Kiska Islands in the Aleutians chain, which they would occupy until the spring of 1943, having relatively minimal effect on the course of the war.

Anglo-American Plans and Responsibilities

At their Arcadia Conference in Washington in December 1941-January 1942, President Roosevelt and Prime Minister Churchill decided to create the Anglo-American Combined Chiefs of Staff. The British component already existed as the Chiefs of Staff, consisting of the heads of the British services. There was no comparable U.S. body of senior military officers. Without specific executive action or congressional legislation, the senior U.S. military officers met as a body for the first time with their British colleagues to form the *Combined* Chiefs of Staff on 23 January 1942.

U.S. Joint Chiefs of Staff – The JCS membership experienced some early changes, but finally stabilized in July 1942 at four members for the remainder of the war. The JCS line-up:

Adm William D. Leahy, Chief of Staff to the Commander
in Chief (Roosevelt) and de facto chairman of the JCS

Adm Ernest J. King, Commander in Chief, U.S. Fleet

Gen George C. Marshall, Chief of Staff, Army

LtGen Henry H. Arnold, Chief of the Army Air Forces

U.S. unified and Allied commands consisted of forces from more than one military service and from more than one nation, respectively. World War II saw the unification of forces in the field—ground, air, and naval—on an unprecedented basis. And, on a practical basis, the U.S. and Allied components were often indistinguishable within Allied commands.

U.S. Pacific Commands – Numerous high-level conferences took place in early 1942 between Allied heads of state, military staffs and their planning committees before decisions could be reached on these all-important commands. In the end, two unified commands were established. On 18 April 1942, General MacArthur officially took charge of the Southwest Pacific Area and on May 8, Admiral Nimitz assumed command of the Pacific Ocean Areas. Both men controlled all U.S. and Allied forces within their areas of responsibility. Historian Grace P. Hayes:

> Each of the commanders was assigned tasks in consonance with the basic strategic policy of the governments concerned, 'although no policy was defined.'

The Supreme Commander, Southwest Pacific Area, was directed to:

> a. Hold the key military regions of Australia as bases for future offensive action against Japan, and in order to check the Japanese conquest of the SOUTHWEST PACIFIC AREA.

> b. Check the enemy advance toward Australia and its essential lines of communication by the destruction of enemy combatant, troop, and supply ships, aircraft, and bases in Eastern Malaysia and the New Guinea - Bismarck - Solomon Islands region.

> c. Exert economic pressure on the enemy by destroying vessels transporting raw materials from the recently conquered territories to Japan.

> d. Maintain our position in the Philippine Islands.

e. Protect land, sea, and air communications within the SOUTHWEST PACIFIC AREA, and its close approaches.

f. Route shipping in the SOUTHWEST PACIFIC AREA.

g. Support the operations of friendly forces in the PACIFIC OCEAN AREA and the INDIAN Theatre.

h. Prepare to take the offensive.

The Commander in Chief, Pacific Ocean Areas, was directed to:

a. Hold the island positions between the United States and the SOUTH-WEST PACIFIC AREA necessary for the security of the line of communications between those regions; and for supporting naval, air, and amphibious operations against Japanese forces.

b. Support the operations of the forces in the SOUTHWEST PACIFIC AREA.

c. Contain Japanese forces within the PACIFIC Theatre.

d. Support the defense of the continent of North America.

e. Protect the essential sea and air communications.

f. Prepare for the execution of major amphibious offensives against positions held by Japan, the initial offensives to be launched from the SOUTH PACIFIC AREA and SOUTHWEST PACIFIC AREA.[7]

The line between the two theaters was the 160th degree of east longitude; almost immediately, however, it changed to the 159th degree to put Guadalcanal under Adm Nimitz's command, because Navy and Marine units were to be used in that operation.

In general, the dual command scheme worked well, although there was continued debate between the Navy and MacArthur, as well as between the JCS and MacArthur.

South Pacific Plans and Preparations [8]

Scarcely had Admiral Yamamoto pulled his Combined Fleet away from its defeat at Midway, before the U.S. Joint Chiefs of Staff began reconsidering basic Pacific policy. They wanted an offensive which would aid containment of the Japanese advances toward Australia and safeguard the U.S. communication lines to the ANZAC[9] area. As early as 18 February, Admiral Ernest J. King, Commander in Chief of the U.S. Fleet and Chief of Naval Operations, told Army Chief of Staff George C. Marshall that he considered it necessary to garrison certain South and Southwest Pacific islands with Army troops in preparation for launching U.S. Marines on an early offensive against the enemy.

Shortly after the Battle of the Coral Sea, General MacArthur advanced plans for an attack against the Japanese at Rabaul. For this move he requested aircraft carriers, additional troops, and more planes. But Nimitz rejected this plan. His carriers were too precious for commitment in waters so restricted as the Solomon Sea, he told the general. Besides, the admiral had a plan of his own. He wanted to capture Tulagi with one Marine raider battalion. Admiral King's reaction to this plan was initially favorable, but on 1 June he sided with Marshall and MacArthur that the job could not be done by one battalion.

By now time and the victory at Midway had improved the U.S. position in the Pacific, and on 25 June, Admiral King advised Nimitz and Vice Admiral Robert L. Ghormley, Commander of South Pacific Forces, to prepare for an offensive against the lower Solomons. Santa Cruz Island, Tulagi, and adjacent areas would be seized and occupied by Marines under CinCPac, and Army troops from Australia then would form the permanent occupation garrison. D-Day would be approximately 1 August.

The task seemed almost impossible. Ghormley had just taken over his Pacific job after a hurried trip from London; the 1st Marine Division, slated for the Solomon landing, was making an administrative move from the United States to New Zealand; and Marshall and King continued to debate matters of command.

The Joint Chiefs resolved this conflict on 2 July with issuance of the "Joint Directive for Offensive Operations in the Southwest Pacific Area Agreed on by the United States Chiefs of Staff." The directive set the seizure of the New Britain-New Ireland-New Guinea area as the objective of these operations, but it broke this goal down into three phases designed to resolve the dispute between MacArthur and Nimitz.

Phase One, labeled Operation WATCHTOWER, would be the seizure of the islands of Santa Cruz and Tulagi, along with positions on adjacent islands. Nimitz would command this operation, with MacArthur concentrating on interdiction of enemy air and naval activity to the west. And to remove MacArthur's geographic claim on the Phase One target area, the Joint Chiefs shifted the boundary between the General and Admiral Nimitz to place the Lower Solomons in the Admiral's South Pacific area.

MacArthur then would take command of Phase Two, seizure of other Solomon Islands plus positions on New Guinea, and of Phase Three, the capture of Rabaul and adjacent bases in New Britain and New Ireland.

Questions of timing, establishment of task organizations, and arrangements for command changes from one area to another would be governed by the Joint Chiefs. But, valid as was the Chiefs' of Staff determination to lose no time in launching this first offensive, problems facing Ghormley and Nimitz were so grim that the pseudo code name for the undertaking soon became "Operation Shoestring."

That brings us up to date with where things stood just prior to Operation WATCHTOWER. You now know a lot more than any World War II veteran did at the time, since most of the preceding data were highly classified.

Santayana wrote, "Those who cannot remember the past are condemned to repeat it."[10] I hope this close-up look at America's first amphibious operations in World War II will help both present and future generations remember.

William L. McGee
Santa Barbara, California
June 2001

---

[1] Lt Grace P. Hayes, USN, *The History of the Joint Chiefs of Staff in WWII – The War Against Japan*, Vol. I Pearl Harbor through TRIDENT, 1953, p. 5 (hereafter "History of the Joint Chiefs").

[2] Unless otherwise noted, the material in this section is derived from *Pearl Harbor to Guadalcanal – History of U.S. Marine Corps Operations in WWII*, pp. 62-64 (hereafter "From Pearl Harbor to Guadalcanal").

[3] Para. 13 of ABC-1 quoted in *Hearings Record*, Part 33, 958.

[4] "History of the Joint Chiefs," p. 7.

[5] Annual Report of the Secretary of the Navy, 10 January 1946, pp. A14-15.

[6] The United States Merchant Marine at War—report submitted to President Truman by VAdm E.S. Land on January 15, 1946.

[7] "History of the Joint Chiefs," p. 141-142.

[8] "From Pearl Harbor to Guadalcanal," pp. 235-237.

[9] ANZAC refers to the geographic area of Australia and New Zealand.

[10] George Santayana, 1863-1952, American philosopher.

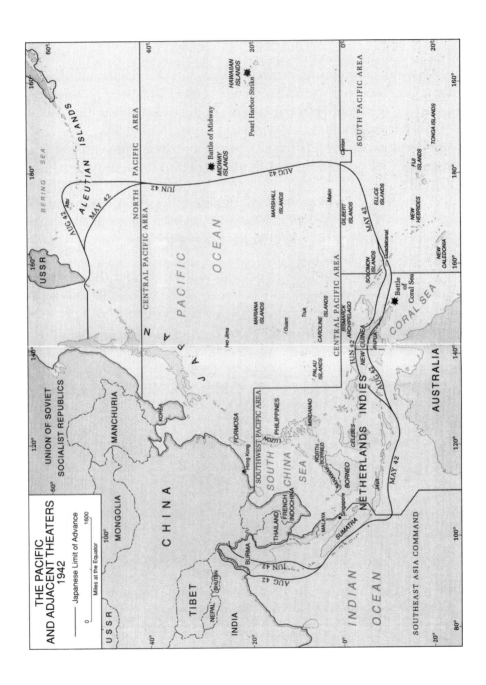

THE PACIFIC
AND ADJACENT THEATERS
1942

PART I

The Southern Solomons Campaigns

Part I covers the bloody six-month struggle for Guadalcanal. The relationship between ground fighting, naval warfare, and air combat is described in considerable detail, as first one side and then the other gains the advantage. Seven major naval engagements are recounted, including America's severe defeat at Savo Island and decisive victory in the three-day Naval Battle of Guadalcanal—another dramatic turning point.

Part I is an abridged version of Volumes IV and V of the History of United States Naval Operations in World War II *by distinguished historian RAdm Samuel Eliot Morison. It has been condensed and edited by the author's grandson, Samuel Loring Morison.*
(Excerpting privileges have been granted by the trustees of the Samuel E. Morison Trust and the publisher, Little Brown.)

Samuel Eliot Morison, Professor Emeritus of American History at Harvard, was convinced that too many histories were written from the outside looking in. He felt that more was to be gained by writing in contact with the events, while most of the participants were alive, than by waiting until the ships were broken up and the sailors had departed.

Just after Pearl Harbor, Professor Morison went to President Roosevelt with his idea. The President was enthusiastic; so was Secretary of the Navy Frank Knox. Before he knew it, Professor Morison was Lieutenant Commander Morison, USNR, with the active writing assignment that he had suggested.

For the remainder of the war, Morison spent more than half of his time at sea, with active duty on eleven different ships, emerging a Captain with seven battle stars on his service ribbons. He was present at Operation TORCH (the North African invasion); he served on Atlantic convoys, and his journeyings took him through most of the combat areas of the Pacific during the height of the conflict. He retired from the Navy with the rank of Rear Admiral, and died in 1976 in his 89th year.

CHAPTER **1**

Strategic Decisions,
Plans and Preparations
March – July 1942

The Guadalcanal operation was the first in the Pacific War—excepting the operations of submarines—in which the United States took the strategic offensive. Earlier carrier strikes and sharp backlashings on the enemy like those on Balikpapan and Badung Strait were offensive only in a tactical sense. Moreover, they were hit-and-run affairs; this was a hit-and-stay proposition. Since it was initiated by the United States, the discussion among top-level planners which led to the strategic decision to occupy the Solomons goes back almost to the very start of the Pacific War, and the objectives of that decision were not fully attained until 1944.

Although the decision to "beat Hitler first" to which the American Chiefs of Staff had agreed even before America entered the war[1] imposed a strategic defensive in the Pacific, that decision never implied mere passivity. It did not preclude raids, attrition tactics by submarines or the exploitation of favorable opportunities for limited offensives. Admiral King, eager from the first to seize such opportunities, germinated the Guadalcanal operation in a memorandum to General Marshall dated 18 February 1942.

King requested the Chief of Naval Operations (Admiral Stark) and his opposite number on the Joint Chiefs of Staff (General Marshall) to approve the establishment of an American base in Efate Island of the New Hebrides, 300 miles northeast of Nouméa and 600 miles southeast of Guadalcanal. Marshall, with his usual perspicacity, replied that such a step had far-reaching implications; air power commitments in other theaters would seem to preclude expansion in the Southwest Pacific for sometime to come; but if the Admiral wanted it, "the entire situation must be considered." King developed his thoughts further on 2 March. The occupation of Efate would provide a bastion to the United States-Australia lifeline; but, more important, would be the first of a series of strong points, near enough for mutual air support, "from which a step-by-step general advance could be made through the New Hebrides, Solomons and Bismarcks." In other words, he anticipated the entire course of the war in the South Pacific to the middle of 1944.

Three days later the Admiral expressed the same concept in a memorandum to the President. By that time, 5 March, the situation in the Southwest had further deteriorated. The surrender of Java was a matter of hours and General MacArthur had been ordered to retire to Australia. Nobody seemed able to stop the Japanese, and in Washington there was even serious talk of abandoning Australia and New Zealand to the enemy. But, as King told the President, "We cannot in honor let Australia and New Zealand down. They are our brothers, and we must not allow them to be overrun by Japan." And the President agreed.

As Admiral King saw it, the approaches from Japan to Australia should be actively and continuously probed in order to hamper the enemy's southeasterly advance and prevent his consolidation of conquered areas. The Allies already possessed strong points in Samoa, Suva and Nouméa, and the Navy was about to set up a base at Tongatabu. The time was ripe to occupy and fortify Efate in the New Hebrides and Funafuti in the Ellices. When reasonably secure in these new bases the Navy could cover the West Coast-Australia sea route more effectively, and also "drive northwesterly from the New Hebrides into the Solomons and Bismarcks."

Accordingly, on 14 March 1942, the Joint Chiefs of Staff reconsidered the entire situation. Wherever the Joint Chiefs turned, the situation seemed urgent. In their opinion the United Nations "would constantly be on the verge of ultimate defeat during 1942." Faced by this dilemma, the Joint Chiefs recommended a limited deployment of American forces into the Southwest Pacific, with the object of securing the antipodes and putting such pressure on Japan as to prevent any further westward or southward offensive on her part.[2] They estimated that 416,000 United States troops would be required in overseas positions in the Pacific to secure Australia and New Zealand; 225,000 were already there or en route. As for naval forces available then or during 1942, this table tells the story:

DEPLOYMENT OF UNITED STATES SHIPS, 1942

	Available 15 March		Expected Additions	Recommended Deployment	
	Atlantic	Pacific	1942	Atlantic	Pacific
Battleships*	2	7	3	2	10
Large Carriers	2	5	–	1	6
Escort Carriers	1	–	10	7	4
Heavy Cruisers	4	13	–	4	13
Light Cruisers	8	12	6	13	13
Destroyers	78	92	44	106	108
Submarines	50	61	13	28	96

*Exclusive of the old *Texas, New York* and *Arkansas* in the Atlantic.

On 17 March (East Longitude date) General MacArthur arrived in Australia. The ANZAC Command was now obsolete; ABDA had ceased to exist. After about two weeks' negotiations, conducted mostly in London among representatives of the American, British, Australian, New Zealand and Netherlands-in-exile governments, a new division of Pacific Ocean areas and assignment of commands was decided upon, about 1 April 1942. This delimitation endured with little change for two years, and, in its main division between the Nimitz and MacArthur commands, until the end of the war. Vice Admiral Ghormley,[3] whose long and varied naval experience qualified him for this important command, arrived in Washington from London on 17 April, to be informed that he was to command the South Pacific Force and Area. Next day he saw Admiral King who said, as he remembered:

"You have a large and important area and a most difficult task.

I do not have the tools to give you to carry out that task as it should be done. You will establish your headquarters in Auckland with an advanced base at Tongatabu. In time, possibly this fall, we hope to start an offensive from the South Pacific."

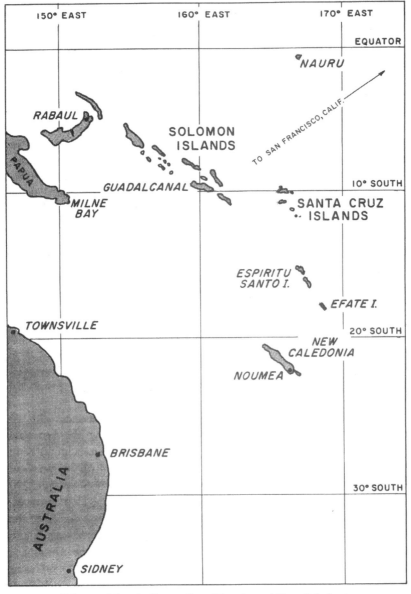

Solomon Islands, Santa Cruz Islands and New Caledonia.

Admiral Ghormley left Washington with his staff on 1 May, and spent about a week conferring with Admiral Nimitz and staff at Pearl. At his request Rear Admiral John S. McCain, who later won fame as a carrier task force commander, was appointed Commander Aircraft South Pacific Area. McCain set up headquarters on board U.S.S. *Tangier* in Nouméa Harbor shortly after, and exercised operational control of all Allied planes, with a few exceptions, in the South Pacific.[4]

In the meantime the Battle of the Coral Sea had been fought. The Japanese lunge at Port Moresby had been thrown back, but their seaplane base at Tulagi in the southern Solomons, facing Guadalcanal, had survived its bombing by Admiral Fletcher's carrier planes on 3 May. Tulagi was a new threat to the line of communications which it was Ghormley's prime duty to defend. If King's long-deferred plans to move into the Solomons were to be carried out, it was high time a start should be made.

The military situation at Nouméa was satisfactory. Major General A. M. Patch was there in command of the "American" (America-Caledonia) Infantry Division United States Army which had started arriving from Australia in March; and Brigadier General Chamberlain, an old cavalry officer who became a tower of strength to Ghormley, commanded the small garrison at Efate. Sixteen Catalinas were based on tender *Tangier* in Nouméa harbor, four Flying Fortresses and 34 Army fighter planes were on the Gajacs field at the center of the island, and the advanced base at Efate was already operating under difficulties imposed by malaria, terrain and lack of bare necessities.

This was not enough. The two Generals and the Admiral promptly decided that, in order to counter the new Japanese base at Tulagi, another advanced air and naval base must be set up at Segond Channel, Espiritu Santo. Washington replied that no airfield should be constructed there until adequate defense forces were available, but that Ghormley could start a seaplane base at any time. General Chamberlain, who (said Ghormley) would have taken troops up in fishing boats if necessary to get started, released the original Efate garrison, which went up to Espiritu Santo to start Base "Button" on 28 May.

On 28 May Admiral Nimitz proposed to General MacArthur that the 1st Marine Raider Battalion, then at Tutuila, pull off a raid on Tulagi. MacArthur rejected the plan on the ground that we had insufficient strength to hold Tulagi if captured, and Ghormley agreed.[5] Many in the Navy, however, believed that we missed a golden opportunity to slip into Tulagi and Guadalcanal when the enemy's back was turned, for at that time almost the entire Japanese Navy was converging on the Aleutians and Midway.

On 19 June, the date when the South Pacific Force and Area were formally activated, the New Zealand light cruisers *Achilles* and *Leander,* two destroyers at Samoa, and all the other auxiliaries in the area, were placed under Vice Admiral Ghormley's command.

The logistics problem did not become acute until the plan of operation came out. Captain M. C. Bowman, with the best sort of cooperation from the Dominion authorities, managed to set up a system whereby a large part of the fresh provisions consumed by the South Pacific Force as it marched up the Solomons was furnished by the farms of New Zealand. In Nouméa, facilities for handling military cargoes were even less than at Auckland, and supply ships sometimes swung around the hook for weeks before they could get unloaded. The absolute necessity of sending up cargo-handling equipment, stevedore personnel, cranes, tugs and the like ahead of the fighting forces was a lesson we learned the hard way in Operation "Watchtower."[6]

On the Glorious Fourth of June the Battle of Midway dispelled Japanese dreams of further conquest. Operation plans for the occupation of New Caledonia, Fiji and Samoa had been issued on 18 May; now they were shelved and on 11 July were formally canceled. The center of enemy effort shifted to Rabaul, where the garrison originally intended for Port Moresby was waiting. Formerly the Bismarcks, Papua, the Solomons and the Coral Sea had been the responsibility of Admiral Inouye's Fourth Fleet based at Truk, but on 10 June a new Eighth Fleet was created to take care of that area. Vice Admiral Gunichi Mikawa, the first commander in chief, arrived with his staff at Rabaul in heavy cruiser *Chokai* on 29 June. His initial combat force of five heavy and three light cruisers and a number of destroyers was soon augmented, and the program of airfield construction and air-power concentration was intensified. By the end of June, Rear Admiral Yamada's 25th Air Flotilla at Rabaul comprised 24 land-based bombers and 30 fighter planes, together with ten seaplanes and ten float-plane fighters at Tulagi." Besides two large airstrips at Rabaul (eventually expanded to five or six) the Japanese were building others on New Ireland, at Gasmata on the south coast of New Britain, at Lae and Salamaua in New Guinea and on Buka, the little island at the north end of Bougainville. They were determined to make the Bismarck-Solomons area a bastion against American advance through Dampier Strait, as the Central Pacific route was already blocked by the Marshalls and Carolines.

The Japanese had no plan as yet for an offensive from Guadalcanal south. That would doubtless have come in good time; but for the present the role of Guadalcanal was to assist the Tulagi-based seaplanes in preventing Allied interference with the Buna-Port Moresby thrust. Now turning our attention to Pearl Harbor and the Central Pacific, we see that the Pacific Fleet after the Battle of Midway enjoyed a brief period of upkeep, rest and training. Rear Admiral Spruance now became chief of staff to Admiral Nimitz. Carrier *Wasp,* having completed her Malta ferry duties, the new battleship *North Carolina,* heavy cruiser *Quincy,* light cruiser *San Juan,* and seven destroyers passed through the Panama Canal on 10 June. This was the first substantial reinforcement to the Pacific Fleet in 1942. Cincpac therefore reorganized his carrier striking forces as follows on 15 June:

TASK FORCE	11	16	17	18
C.O.	R.Adm. Fitch	R.Adm. Fletcher	R.Adm. Mitscher*	R.Adm. Noyes
CVs	*Saratoga*	*Enterprise*	*Hornet*	*Wasp*
CAs	*Minneapolis*	*Louisville*	*Northampton*	*Quincy*
CAs	*New Orleans*	*Portland*	*Salt Lake City*	*Vincennes*
CAs	*Astoria*	*Chester*	*Pensacola*	*San Francisco*
CLs		*Atlanta*	*San Diego*	*San Juan*
DDs	*Desron 1*	*Desron 6*	*Desron 2*	*Desdivs 15, 23*

*Pending Admiral Halsey's return to duty.

Fletcher's and Mitscher's forces were placed on 48-hour notice at Pearl for rest, reorganization and training. "Sara" was then on a plane-ferrying mission to Midway, and Task Force 18 would be formed at San Diego shortly.

The busiest American naval officers, other than those engaged in training, were the higher command. What would happen next? What should be our next move?

One basic condition that limited possibilities in the Pacific was Atlantic priority. Although our African adventure, Operation "Torch" of November 1942, was not formally adopted by the Combined Chiefs of Staff until 25 July, it had been on the cards since June, and the preparations for it absorbed a major part of new naval construction, as well as all combat-ready divisions of the United States Army. Admiral Nimitz and the Pacific Fleet planners, therefore, had no hope of getting additional ships, planes and men for a strategical offensive during the ensuing twelve months. They must do with what they already had, together with the forces that had been promised to the Pacific Fleet on 14 March.

Yet the question remained, What should we do with what we had? The sanguine General MacArthur had a proposition ready, immediately after Midway. Give him one division trained in amphibious warfare, a naval task force including two carriers and a few score big bombing planes, and he would jump off next month to recapture Rabaul. That sounded fine; even in retrospect the General's strategy appeals to one as bold and incisive, sparing the long agony of conquering the Solomons island by island.

But the Joint Chiefs (greatly to the relief of the Navy) turned down this proposal for several reasons. No transports were yet available for troop lift. Rabaul, at the end of an "air pipeline" from Japan, could be readily and steadily reinforced by the enemy, yet was beyond fighter-plane range from the air bases then in Allied possession. There is no doubt that the decision against moving into Rabaul was wise. In June 1942 the balance of naval power in the Pacific was too delicate to warrant an attempt to seize and hold a position so exposed to Japanese counterattack. Rabaul had to be left in enemy possession, a formidable barrier to MacArthur's advance, until Allied forces became much stronger; and, by the time they were strong enough, it seemed better strategy to beat down, encircle and neutralize rather than to assault Rabaul.

Thus, the one promising target left was Tulagi. That, too, had the advantage of leading somewhere — toward Rabaul, for the capture of which the forces under MacArthur's command might ultimately be employed.

Admiral King, who had never given up his concept of a gradual advance up the line of the Solomons, returned to it in a memorandum to General Marshall on 25 June. He predicted that the enemy would not stay still in the South Pacific, or permit us to do so. It was urgent that we take the initiative. Using the 1ˢᵗ Marine Division, then en route to New Zealand, an offensive could be mounted in the South Pacific about 1 August. Admiral Nimitz in fact had already suggested this: an amphibious operation to retake Tulagi, covered by the two carrier task forces he had in readiness at Pearl.[7]

General Marshall thought well of the idea, but suggested that it be entrusted to MacArthur rather than to Nimitz. King replied (26 June) that in his opinion any such operation "must be conducted under the direction of Cincpac and cannot be conducted in any other way." One can readily understand why: the only amphibiously trained troops available were Marines; the only troop lift available was Navy transports; the only covering and supporting force (other than Ghormley's tiny force) was the Pacific Fleet. And the only assistance that MacArthur could render would be land-based air cover from distant Australian fields. King believed that, after the amphibious phase was completed, MacArthur with Pacific Fleet support should take charge of troop movement into the southern Solomons and of consolidating the area. Marshall agreed, and King then flew to San Francisco to consult with Nimitz, bringing with him the Joint Chiefs of Staff directive which, with some modifications, governed Allied movements in the South Pacific for the next eighteen months.

Nimitz's plane crash-landed at Alameda 30 June, but fortunately the Admiral was only slightly injured. Cominch and Cincpac quickly agreed on the broad lines of the operation.

On 5 July Admiral Nimitz received a bit of news that sparked off the whole operation. An American reconnaissance plane observed that the Japanese were starting to build an airfield—the future Henderson Field—on Guadalcanal. This news had very different effects on the Ghormley-MacArthur team and on the King-Nimitz team.

Admiral Ghormley flew to Melbourne to confer with General MacArthur, General Sutherland, his chief of staff, and Vice Admiral Arthur S. Carpender, about to be appointed Commander Naval Forces Southwest Pacific under General MacArthur. They liked neither the proposed operation nor the target date of 1 August. MacArthur voiced his and Ghormley's views in protesting to King and Nimitz on 8/9 July against a premature and possibly disastrous beginning. In view of the recently developed enemy airfields, and the shortage of Allied planes, airfields, transports and troops, they warmly urged that Operation "Watchtower" be deferred until adequate means were available for a quick seizure and rapid follow-up.

To Marshall, when he received this discouraging opinion, King observed, "Three weeks ago MacArthur stated that, if he could be furnished amphibious forces and two carriers, he could push right through to Rabaul. . . . He now feels that he not only cannot undertake this extended operation but not even the Tulagi operation." Nevertheless, King felt it necessary to stop the enemy's southward advance without delay. An airfield in his possession in Guadalcanal "will hamper seriously if not prevent our establishment in Santa Cruz," would put him "in a position to harass Espiritu Santo." To MacArthur he wrote the same day (10 July) that he could not sanction any delay. Even if additional demands for Operation "Torch" or elsewhere should postpone the follow-up into the Solomons, the Tulagi operation must go on.

He was right. The Tulagi-Guadalcanal operation was indeed a perilous undertaking at that time; the armed forces involved liked to refer to it as "Operation 'Shoestring.'" But the risk had to be taken. This new Japanese spearhead had to be cut off then and there, lest it sever the lifeline between the United States and "down under." In accepting the grave responsibility for ordering the seizure of these islands, Admiral King made one of the great decisions of the war.

In July Admiral Ghormley received Admiral Nimitz's operation order for the seizure of Tulagi, Guadalcanal and Ndeni (Santa Cruz), including a list of available ground and air forces and ships. A day or two later he observed that enough ships and men had been given him to do the job, provided General MacArthur could interdict interference by enemy planes based at Rabaul and near-by fields. "I desire to emphasize," he said, "that the basic problem of the operation is the protection of ships against land-based aircraft attack during the approach, the landing and the unloading." General MacArthur remarked that his air force would need heavy and quick reinforcement to accomplish that. It certainly did.

The movements of forces had already begun. Nimitz informed McCain on 11 July that he was building up the number of Flying Fortresses in the South Pacific Area to 35, and that a thousand men of Army Air Force ground crews and 1500 tons of freight were being sent to him in the *President Tyler*. Ghormley and Nimitz were already thinking ahead to Task 2. Assault troops cannot be used for garrisons; where were these garrisons to come from? King warned him that no new troops were available; neither the Hawaiian Army command nor MacArthur could spare any; Ghormley would have to roll up garrisons from Samoa and the other South Pacific bases.

Nimitz, with prophetic insight, pointed out that once we had occupied Guadalcanal our forces on land and in air would be in close contact with the enemy, who would be in a position to move up amphibious forces under cover of land-based aircraft to recover his lost positions. It must be assumed that the Japanese would exert every effort to do that, and the process was bound to be costly for both sides. Unless provision were made for a steady flow of replacements from the United States, "not only will we be unable to proceed with Tasks 2 and 3 but we may be unable to hold what we have taken." But, alas for Operation "Watchtower," no such provision would or could be made. Operation "Torch" was getting all the gravy; even the 3rd Infantry Division, amphibiously trained by the Marines at San Diego, had sailed away in several large transports en route to Africa via Norfolk.

The movement of the 1st Marine Division to New Zealand had

long been planned, but not with a view to their immediate employment in combat. One of its regiments, the 7th, had been sent to Samoa as early as March 1942. Of the other two regiments, about one half were embarked in two large passenger transports *(Wakefield* and *Ericsson),* and stores and equipment in nine cargo ships— "commercial-" rather than "combat"-loaded,[8] because as recently as May it had been assumed that the Marines would have at least six months to train at New Zealand. This echelon, with Major General Vandegrift the division commander, arrived at Wellington 14 June. The General did not know what he was in for until the 26th. By that time most of the transports had been un-loaded and were on their way back to the Atlantic to participate in Operation "Torch." Captain Reifsnider then brought up a division of Pacific Fleet transports. All supplies had to be reloaded during the cold and rainy southern winter, and with inadequate ware-house space so that thousands of tons of supplies in cardboard containers were spoiled. Fortunately there was a good, high camp area about 35 miles from Wellington where the Marines kept in fine physical condition and trained in the near-by forest.

This first echelon reembarked and reloaded its equipment and supplies in transports *American Legion, Fuller, Bellatrix* and *Neville,* beginning 2 July, in order to leave port facilities available for the second echelon when it arrived. A working team of 300 Marines to each vessel did practically all the reloading, since New Zealand labor was found to be lazy, expensive and inefficient.

The second echelon reached Wellington on 11 July and sailed on the 22nd; the third, in six transports, combat-loaded at San Diego, sailed thence 1 July escorted by the *Wasp* carrier group; stopped off two days at Tongatabu to wait for the carrier, which had had an engineering accident and sailed on the 20th for the grand rendezvous south of Fiji.

If there is one factor more important than surprise for the suc-cess of an amphibious operation, it is Intelligence. Exact informa-tion is wanted, both hydrographic and topographic, so that the ships may know where to anchor and the troops where to land and where to go when they get ashore. Admiral Ghormley's turn-of-the-century charts of the Solomons were distressingly vague.

He did not need a prompting from Nimitz on 4 July to fly an "Intelligence team" to Australia to obtain more information from evacuated planters, skippers of coastal craft and the like. MacArthur's command and the Australian Navy helped; but the amount of new information thus obtained was disappointing both in quantity and quality. Data imparted orally by former residents of the Solomon Islands proved to be of slight use in many cases and misleading in others. For instance, Mount Austen, one of the principal landmarks near the future Henderson Field, was assigned as a D-day objective on the basis of an old resident's information. Actually it was located nine miles WSW of the landing beach across thick jungle.

In the planning of an amphibious operation, there is no substitute for an intensive study of the area by military people in time of peace (which nobody had even thought of doing here) or aerial reconnaissance just before the operation. For Guadalcanal, the most useful sources of information were aerial photographs and an observation flight undertaken on 17 July by two Marine Corps officers, Colonel Twining and Major McKean, in one of General Brett's Army Air Force B-17s. They checked up on the installations Tulagi-side, but, before they were ready to inspect enemy activities on Guadalcanal, the float-fighter planes from Tulagi got after them and the Flying Fort had to vamoose. She made Port Moresby all right, with fuel tanks almost dry.

A third product of Intelligence, important for any military or naval operation, is knowledge of the movements of enemy forces. At about the time of Midway the Japanese generally tightened up on their security and appeared to be on their guard to such an extent that, in July and August, Naval Intelligence was largely deprived of its best sources and had to rely almost wholly on the observations of reconnaissance planes.

A certain number of local pilots and former residents volunteered to accompany the task force, in order to identify landmarks and pilot the ships through unfamiliar waters. These men, mostly Australians, gave excellent service.

On 16 July it seemed impossible to meet D-day, only two weeks off. Admiral Ghormley therefore postponed it six days, to 7 August.

This important and salutary decision was made after consultation with Rear Admiral Richmond K. Turner,[9] newly designated commander of the amphibious force, who called at Auckland 15 July en route to Wellington. Turner took command of the Amphibious Force of the South Pacific at Wellington 18 July. Promptly he and his small staff began intensive planning for the landings, working day and night. This admiral, like President Roosevelt, had an equal capacity for broad views and for minute details; and, although his was the first amphibious operation of the war, he carefully planned it down to the employment of every landing craft and the exact times and amounts of naval gunfire support. For, as Turner often remarked, he "hated above all things to see soldiers swimming."

Readers who are allergic to Task Force Command Organization and ship lists will be glad to know this detail is included in the "Appendix" to this book. However a brief review of the command setup and the components of the force is highly recommended before starting the next section on the Guadalcanal and Tulagi Landings.

Admiral Ghormley as Comsopac was the overall strategic commander charged with the general direction of the campaign; but the O.T.C., the officer in tactical command, was Admiral Fletcher. Turner, commander of the amphibious spearhead and the embarked Marines, was in the command echelon below Fletcher, but actually he had complete autonomy from the moment of sailing. The command setup was such that General Vandegrift's landing force remained subordinate to Turner, even long after it had been engaged in battle. Admiral Fletcher limited his command in practice to the three carrier groups, whose function was to provide air cover for the landings.

Admiral Crutchley RN, in command of the small Australian and United States cruiser and destroyer force formerly known as Task Force 44, was second in command to Turner and actually in command of the ships that furnished gunfire support and anti-aircraft protection to the amphibious operation.

CHAPTER 2

The Landings[10]
7–8 August 1942[11]

Rendezvous, Rehearsal and Approach

The landings were only three weeks away when Admiral Ghormley issued his operation plan and made final assignments of ships and troops within his command.

Admiral Turner was responsible for the detailed operation plan for the landings. Nineteen large transports and cargo ships were to carry the major load of the landing force, supplemented by four of the tiny converted destroyer transports. Cruisers *Quincy, Vincennes, Astoria* and *San Juan* and six destroyers must blast the enemy away from the landing beaches. If enemy mines lay in the narrow approaches, five converted destroyer minesweepers would cut the unseen hazards adrift. Rear Admiral Crutchley RN was to command a group composed of H.M.A.S. *Australia, Canberra* and *Hobart,* U.S.S. *Chicago* and nine United States destroyers; his task was to protect the other groups from air, submarine and sea attack. His own fighter director augmented by two carrier teams controlled Fletcher's carrier planes when they arrived over Savo Sound. The landing force was split into a Guadalcanal Group under the overall commander Major General Vandegrift and a Tulagi Group under Brigadier General Rupertus.[12]

Rear Admiral Richmond Kelly Turner USN.

Rear Admiral McCain's land- and tender-based aircraft had to reconnoiter the Solomons for several days before the landings. This essential function could be performed only if sufficient planes and bases were available in the outward fringes of Allied territory. So the month of July was a busy one for the birdmen and their servicing components; airfields were hacked out of jungles in the New Hebrides, New Caledonia and the Fijis; planes bearing the insignia of Army, Navy, Marine Corps and New Zealand air forces were ferried to the jumping-off points. By 25 July the seven air task groups were ready to go. The Army's 69th Bombardment Squadron sent scouts winging 400 miles north of New Caledonia. Long-stepping B-17s flying from Efate kept the southern Solomons under observation. Aircraft tender *Curtiss* (Commander Maurice E. Browder) of Pearl Harbor fame prepared to shift berth from Nouméa to Espiritu Santo, her flock of patrol seaplanes to base in both places and Efate as well. Tenders *McFarland* and *Mackinac* stood by to provide Catalina bases in Ndeni, Santa Cruz Islands, and Maramasike Estuary, Malaita. Marine Corps fighter and scout planes took over the local defense of the vulnerable New Hebrides bases. General Kenney dispatched his Southwest Pacific planes on far-ranging searches west of 158° East Longitude.

Invasion rehearsals for the Marines and Army troops always included debarking down the nets with full packs and combat gear.

Ghormley's small planning staff deserves no small credit for a successful rendezvous, right on time, of a number of task forces which started out from places as wide apart as Wellington, San Diego, Nouméa and Sydney. He gave all subordinate flag commands an opportunity to confer by designating a rendezvous 400 miles southeast of the Fiji Islands. Forenoon watch 26 July found Admirals Turner, Kinkaid, Noyes, McCain and Callaghan and General Vandegrift boarding Admiral Fletcher's flagship *Saratoga* for this mid-ocean forum.

Admiral Ghormley, the top commander, was already flying up to Nouméa to his flagship, the hybrid vessel-of-all-work *Argonne,* and had no opportunity to view this South Pacific Force, so recently swollen from ANZAC remnants and assorted oddments to fleet dimensions. But every man in the force enjoyed the sight of a sea sprinkled with fighting ships to the horizon's rim—the great flattops lunging into the wind to launch and recover planes, the cruisers briskly maneuvering to keep step, the destroyers in their never-ending quest for sound contacts, the transports stolidly zigzagging, their topsides green with Marine "zoot suits" (the herringbone twill coverall of that era), the bright signal hoists constantly being run up, answered and lowered, and the drone of Wildcats and SBDs overhead.

Fletcher's expeditionary force was small in comparison with later ones which set out to take the Marianas and the Philippines; but it was mighty impressive to sailors of the Pacific Fleet in 1942. Particularly did they welcome recent arrivals from the Atlantic Fleet (three of them, alas, destined to sink in these waters)—carrier *Wasp,* heavy cruisers *Quincy* and *Vincennes* and, most of all, *North Carolina,* first new American battlewagon to roll over the Pacific surges, bringing a 16-inch main battery to blast the Japs, her topsides bristling like a porcupine with the new allowance of anti-aircraft guns, double or treble what her elder sisters had had at Pearl Harbor. A brave sight altogether; but, after all, a scratch team. None of them, except two of the carrier groups, had ever operated together before. Admiral Crutchley did not even have an opportunity to meet the captains of the American cruisers suddenly placed under his command.

The operation had been planned so hurriedly that there were a thousand details to be worked out at this mid-ocean conference, and worked out they were, in about forty-eight hours. Fletcher already had his own plan for air support of the landing, but arrangements had to be made for the B-17s based at Efate and New Caledonia to help out. He told Turner that he had been ordered not to hold his carrier force within supporting distance of Guadalcanal for more than two days and Turner protested in no uncertain terms that he would need air protection while the AKs —cargo ships—were being unloaded; but his protest was unavailing. "Everyone deplored lack of time to plan carefully and thoroughly," reported Admiral Ghormley's representative, "but saw no way out except to whip plans into shape as rapidly as possible."

Turner's Amphibious Force rehearsed the landings at Koro Island in the Fijis between 28 and 31 July. These exercises were useful in teaching Marines, carrier planes, naval gunners, transport and landing craft crews to cooperate in a large-scale, ship-to-shore boat movement, but were a failure as far as landing was concerned because a coral reef prevented all but a few boats from going ashore.

Troops practice using Hunter Liggett landing nets then go back up and over the side to their quarters.
U.S. Coast Guard Photo.

Rehearsal completed, the Amphibious Force and its escorts formed up according to Admiral Turner's approach plan, steered westward to about lat. 16° 36' S, long. 159° 06' E, and then due north for Cape Esperance, Guadalcanal. At 2000 August 6 the van, led by Admiral Crutchley's flagship *Australia,* had reached a position 60 miles southward of the nearest shores of Guadalcanal. So far as anyone knew—and so far as we now know—even the existence of this force was unknown to the enemy. It had been assembled so quickly and secretly, and had been so favored by a weather front which thwarted enemy plane search, that surprise was complete. Early in the morning the Japanese radio station at Tulagi reported: "A large force of ships of unknown number and types is entering the Sound. What can these ships be?" They would soon find out.[13]

Now it was D-day, with H-hour coming up. This was the first amphibious operation undertaken by United States forces in World War II; the first, indeed, since 1898. It cannot be said, in that favorite phrase of military writers, that "the atmosphere in the force was one of sober confidence." Even the Marines, who had studied and practiced amphibious warfare for many months, felt a little queasy when they reflected that this time they were not going to meet dummy opposition but the famous jungle fighters who had run us out of the Philippines and the British out of Singapore and the Dutch out of Java. As for the naval officers, some had taken part in exercises at Culebra or San Clemente, but most of them knew nothing of amphibious warfare except theory, and the more of that they knew the less confidence they felt in this operation. For the whole history of war from Syracuse to Gallipoli proves how difficult amphibious warfare is at all times and how disastrous it may be to a force unfamiliar with its practice; how easily such a force may be thrown into confusion by stout opposition, want of exact timing, foul weather or even ordinary bungling. The time would come when both fleet and ground forces were at home with this work, schooled by experience and fortified by success; when Admiral Turner's "V 'Phib" with the alligator shoulder patch would become a proud and confident force, making web-footed operations so formidable that the enemy would flinch from

Amphibious forces off Guadalcanal on D-day, 7 August 1942. Four transports (AP) and a large number of small landing craft are present. National Archives.

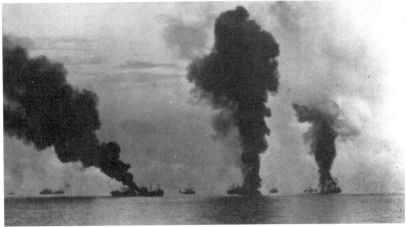

Burning Ships off Guadalcanal on 7 August 1942 after a Japanese air raid. In left center is the USS George F. Elliot (AP-13), which is afire amidships. Naval Historical Center.

defending his own beaches. But that time seemed far, far away on 7 August 1942.

Furthermore, there is something sinister and depressing about that sound between Guadalcanal and Florida Islands, from which the serrated cone of Savo Island thrusts up like the crest of a giant dinosaur emerging from the ocean depths. It is now hard to dissociate this feeling from events and from the remembrance of those who there met death in its most horrible forms. Yet there is that which eludes analysis; one never felt so, for instance, about the blood-soaked ashes of Iwo Jima. Men who rounded Cape Esperance in the darkness before dawn of 7 August insist that even then they felt an oppression of the spirit—"It gave you creeps." Even the land smell failed to cheer sailors who had been long at sea; a rank, heavy stench of mud, slime and jungle arose from the faecaloid island of Guadalcanal.

A brief lift was given by a fine message from Admiral Turner that was read over the loud-speaker of every ship before the landings began:

> On August seventh this force will recapture Tulagi and Guadalcanal Islands which are now in the hands of the enemy.
>
> In this first forward step toward clearing the Japanese out of conquered territory we have strong support from the Pacific Fleet and from the air, surface and submarine forces in the South Pacific and Australia.
>
> It is significant of victory that we see here shoulder to shoulder the United States Navy, Marines and Army and the Australian and New Zealand Air, Naval and Army services.
>
> I have confidence that all elements of this armada will in skill and courage show themselves fit comrades of those brave men who already have dealt the enemy mighty blows for our great cause.
>
> God bless you all!
>
> R. K. TURNER

Landings at Guadalcanal

Transport Group "Yoke" destined for Tulagi separated from Group "X-ray" destined for Guadalcanal about 0300 August 7, when the cruising disposition was about ten miles northwest of the big island; the one steered north of Savo Island, the other between it and Cape Esperance, to parallel the north coast of Guadalcanal. It was a silent night and a silent dawn; no sign of life could be seen afloat or ashore as the ships' bows hissed through the calm waters of that sound where so many of them would find their graves. We shall follow the fortunes of the X-ray group first. This was much the larger of the two, in view of the expectation that the enemy on Guadalcanal was some 5000 men strong. As far as can now be ascertained, there were actually no more than 2230 Japanese then on the island, and 1700 of these belonged to naval construction units.

First Division Marines storm ashore across Guadalcanal's beaches on D-Day, 7 August 1942, from the attack transport Barnett (AP-11) and attack cargo ship Fomalhaut (AK-22). The invaders were surprised at the lack of enemy opposition. National Archives.

Guadalcanal landings, August 1942. Marines land on Tulagi Island. National Archives.

At 0613 cruiser *Quincy* broke silence to begin her scheduled bombardment of the coast west of Lunga Point, where there was supposed to be a coastal battery. A few minutes later an auxiliary schooner was sighted, carrying gasoline from Tulagi to Guadalcanal; a carrier's Wildcat promptly sank it. The other fire support ships began seeking out gun emplacements and storehouses along shore, and presently 44 planes from *Saratoga* and *Enterprise,* arriving on schedule, began doing their part in the shore bombardment. At 0647 the 15 transports coasted to their assigned positions in the debarkation area off the beach designated "Red," a thousand yards of black sand just east of the Tenaru River,[14] and at 0650 Captain Reifsnider made signal from *Hunter Liggett,* "Land

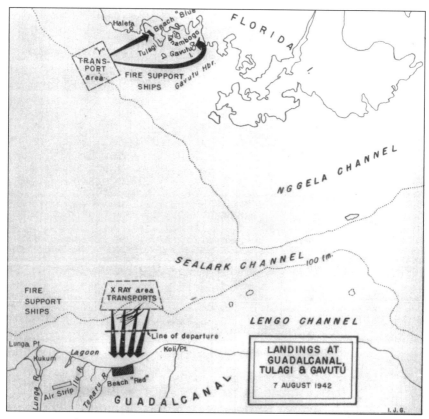

Landings at Guadalcanal, Tulagi and Gavutu, 7 August 1942.

the Landing Force!" The sun was just rising to a fair morning with partial overcast; temperature was 80° Fahrenheit, and it only rose two or three degrees during the day.

As this was the first full-scale American amphibious operation of the war, it followed very closely the prewar doctrine worked out by the Navy and Marine Corps at Culebra, and it differed from the landings in North Africa, which came three months later, only in being made in full daylight.[15] At Guadalcanal the operation proceeded fairly smoothly because of lack of opposition; the Japanese, mostly labor troops and concentrated at Kukum several miles to the westward, appear to have been dazed by this great panoply of force. The landing craft employed were the old, blunt-nosed 36-foot Higgins boats for the Marines and the 36-foot ramped LCPR, together with a few 45- and 56-foot LCMs capable of carrying a

Landing craft at Beach "Red," Guadalcanal.*

small tank or 15 tons of cargo. Preceded by a short but superfluous shore bombardment, the first wave gathered at the line of departure, 4000 yards from the inner line of transports and 5000 yards from the beach, and at 0913 the first troops were ashore.

The Marines landed two battalions abreast. In view of the lack of resistance and the minesweepers' report "negative" after a preliminary sweep, the transports moved in nearer to the beach at 1100. All day the ship-to-shore movement continued, interrupted only by the noon air attacks; by nightfall about 11,000 Marines were ashore. The only untoward feature of this landing was the failure to provide an adequate working party, understandable since an immediate fight had been anticipated. By late afternoon, supplies were stacked high on Beach "Red," laden landing craft circled offshore for hours waiting for a clear spot to ground; and, although the work continued well into the night under artificial light, it had to be called off because of beach congestion. This slow-up turned out to be very serious for the Marines because no transports were completely discharged when forced to retire on 9 August.

While a part of the first combat team to land occupied and organized the immediate beachhead, the second marched west along

* *All photographs in this chapter not otherwise credited are Official United States Navy.*

the water's edge and a third pushed southwesterly through dense jungle into the interior, hoping to capture the rugged, nine mile distant Mount Austen, which had been located much nearer on the maps. Both prongs of the advance continued early on 8 August without encountering any Japanese except a few stragglers who were taken prisoner. As these reported that the enemy had retreated to Kukum near Lunga Point, where his major installations were, General Vandegrift made a quick change of plan, abandoned the hopelessly remote Mount Austen objective, and sent Colonel Hunt's team along the coast road to seize Kukum and the Lunga River mouths. Crossing the Lunga at noon, Hunt's men encountered their first opposition—light rifle and machine-gun fire which was quickly silenced—and entered the main Japanese encampment at 1500. In the meantime Colonel Cates' team overran a small enemy patrol and by 1600 had occupied the 3600 foot Japanese airstrip, soon to be renamed Henderson Field. According to the Japanese it was ready to handle 60 planes,[16] but none were yet there.

The Marines were now in possession of an airfield, machine shops, two large radio stations, two large electric light plants, an air-compressor plant for torpedoes, and great stores of rice, soybean sauce, canned vegetables and beer which came in very useful during the lean days ahead. The rest of 8 August was spent in relieving the supply congestion at Beach "Red" and shifting the landing place to a beach some two miles nearer to Kukum, just west of the Tenaru River. So far so good; but it never remains good long on Guadalcanal.

Landings Tulagi-side [17]

The landings Tulagi-side were a different story. Planned as the lesser of the two, Group "Yoke" had only four large transports and four destroyer-transports (APDs) as against 15 big ones in Group "X-ray," and carried only three battalions of Marines—but the enemy opposite proved to be in sufficient strength to fight back viciously. The terrain, too, was complicated.

Tulagi, a narrow island only 4000 yards long, lies in a bight of Florida Island, 18 miles across the sound from the landing beach on Guadalcanal. The southern third of the island had been developed

Coast Guardsman directs traffic on beach at Guadalcanal as landing craft unload supplies and equipment from AKs. U.S. Coast Guard.

Logistics problems. National Archives.

LCM (2) Landing Craft, Mechanized (Mark 2). ONI/226.

as the capital of the Solomon Islands Protectorate, with the usual Residency on a hill, cricket field, golf links, courthouse, jail, wharves and cluster of Chinese shops and native dwellings. These had been taken over by the Japanese in May, almost intact. The harbor is on the northeast side of the island. Across the harbor mouth, some 3500 yards east of the southern point of Tulagi, lies the small, high island of Gavutu connected by a causeway with the even smaller Tanambogo Island to the north. The two resemble a weight-lifter's bar bell and are only 1200 yards long from north to south. On Gavutu the Lever firm had built its offices, stores, machine shop and wharves, before the war; and there in May the enemy established his seaplane base. Both Tulagi and Gavutu-Tanambogo had to be taken. The Japanese expected an attack, although not now; they had about 500 troops well dug in on the larger island (we buried 427) and 1000 on the two smaller ones (we buried 980). Brigadier General Rupertus commanded all the Marines Tulagi-side.

This terrain required a complex landing plan, which Admiral Turner's and General Vandegrift's staffs had worked out to the last detail; and it worked surprisingly well. The Tulagi landing was

Wrecked seaplane at Tanambogo Island, near Tulagi, after it was bombed by U.S. Navy planes. Photographed on 8 August 1942. National Archives.

effected on Beach "Blue" on the northern, unsettled part of that island, since it could be expected that the enemy would be prepared to defend the better beaches farther south. Gavutu was so reef-ringed that the only possible landing beach lay inside the harbor, by a long and complicated approach. As the boat lanes both to Beach "Blue" and to Gavutu passed close under the Florida Island shore, two small Marine units landed early at Halevo and Haleta to prevent firing on the boats. The Japs had not thought of that, and these Marines had no trouble.

For landing on Beach "Blue," Tulagi, the inner line of four destroyer-transports carried most of Lieutenant Colonel Edson's 1st Raider Battalion. No finer officer than Merritt A. Edson ever wore the Anchor and Globe; no tougher Marines existed than the 1st Raiders. As they were waiting to enter their landing craft, Edson read them a remark made by "Tokyo Rose" the previous day: "Where are the United States Marines hiding? . . . No one has seen them yet!"

The first wave of raiders waded ashore on Beach "Blue" at H-hour, 0800 August 7, and nobody was there to meet them; but the boat movement had been observed, for at 0715 Radio Tulagi sent off a dispatch: "Enemy has commenced landing." They promptly plunged into the jungle, crossed the island ridge to Sesape—soon to be our motor torpedo boat base—and worked cautiously south along the eastern shore. The second wave, which landed a few minutes later, advanced along the island crest and along the western shore, with a battalion landing team of the 5th Marine Regiment close behind. "Enemy strength is overwhelming," radioed Tulagi to Rabaul at 0800, its last message before a salvo from cruiser *San Juan* smothered the radio station.

Before noon the Marines on both flanks found the going very rough. The scheduled naval bombardment, as usual at this stage of the war, was too brief to be of much assistance to the ground troops. *San Juan, Monssen* and *Buchanan* had fired about 1500 rounds of 5-inch shell into Hill 208[18] but had succeeded only in driving the defenders underground. Dive-bombers from the carriers, directed by Lieutenant Commander Beakley in a TBF, pounded positions on the eastern shore. There were plenty of Japs topside, too; it was here that the Marines first encountered enemy snipers tied up in the fronds of coconut palms. "If they had been good shots, few of us would have survived," said Major Chambers of the raiders. More naval fire support was requested, but for some reason the word did not get through, and the Marines had to take the hill with rifle fire and hand grenades.

By nightfall only Hill 281 on the southeast end of Tulagi was in enemy hands. During the midwatch the enemy made four or five separate counterattacks, one penetrating even to battalion headquarters in the Residency, but the Japs made no effort to consolidate and were thrown back. Infiltration, sniping, shouting and whistling went on all night. "The Japs practically slept with us," said Major Chambers. But the Marines held. Soon after daylight on 8 August two battalions of the 2nd Marine Regiment, one of them originally earmarked for Guadalcanal, were landed on Beach "Blue" with orders to help sweep Tulagi clean. They found Edson's Raiders already doing that. In the morning, with the capture of Hill 281, Tulagi was practically secured. "Each Jap fought until he

Attack on Solomon Islands, August 7, 1942. Guns and planes of the Pacific Fleet blast tiny Tanambogo Island, enemy strongpoint in the Solomons, just prior to its capture by the Marines. In foreground is the famous causeway to Gavutu Island, which the Marines crossed under heavy enemy machine gun fire. National Archives.

was killed," reported General Vandegrift, "each machine-gun crew to the last man, who almost invariably killed himself rather than surrender." Only three prisoners were taken, but about 40 escaped by swimming to Florida Island.

Tiny Gavutu and Tanambogo were tougher than Tulagi. Early in the morning of 7 August, planes from Admiral Fletcher's carriers bombed and strafed the Japanese seaplane base, destroying its entire complement of aircraft—19 float planes and two 4-engined flying boats. After that, the two small islands received all the attention that fire support ships and air bombers could spare from Tulagi, but no great damage was done to the caves and dugouts where 1000 Japs were waiting to sell their lives dear. That was the situation at noon when the 1st Parachute Battalion of the Marine Corps (Major R. H. Williams) moved in to take these islands by assault.

The paratroops were boated from transport *Heywood* in the Yoke area, which meant a rough trip of seven to nine miles off a lee shore with wind and sea making up; the men were two hours afloat, cramped, drenched, and many seasick. Owing to the reefs around Gavutu, they almost had to circle the island before reaching the

Solomon Islands Raid, 7 August 1942. Tanambogo Island in foreground, Gavutu Island in background, and Florida Island in the distance. National Archives.

only possible landing place, the seaplane ramp. Although *San Juan* and two destroyers delivered a brisk bombardment just before the landing, and one destroyer followed the boats in, shooting, the three boat waves met scattered rifle fire before landing and a severe machine-gun fusillade rattled out of the hills as they debarked a few minutes after noon. These hills were lined with earth-and-coconut-log dugouts, which the Japanese always built very cleverly. Before two hours had elapsed, one Marine in ten had become a casualty and the majority were pinned down to the beach. But on the left flank the paratroops overran Hill 148 on Gavutu and at 1800 raised the American flag on its summit.

Tanambogo, still full of live and angry Japs, remained to be dealt with. During the afternoon it was pounded both by naval guns and air bombs until the trees were completely stripped of leaves and most of the trunks were down too; but the defenders could still deliver such a murderous fire on the causeway leading from Gavutu that there was no question of taking it that way. As all other Marines were well occupied, General Rupertus had the bright idea of reembarking the unit that had gone ashore at Haleta in the early morning, and sending half of it to take Tanambogo from the rear, and the other half to reinforce Gavutu. The first three boats reached the smaller island at dusk, hoping to land under cover of darkness. Unfortunately the preliminary bombardment by the destroyers exploded a gasoline tank that lit up the scene brilliantly. The Japs opened fire and killed or wounded every occupant of one boat and decimated the other two. These Marines were forced to retire and join the other three boatloads at Gavutu. Thus, at midnight 7 August, Tanambogo, like Tulagi, was still in enemy hands.

In view of the easy situation on Guadalcanal, transports *Adams* and *Hayes,* carrying the 2nd and 3rd Battalions of the 2nd Marine Regiment, were sent Tulagi-side and Lieutenant Colonel Hunt's 3rd Battalion was given the job of cleaning up Tanambogo. It landed on Gavutu in seven waves shortly before noon 8 August; but the problem of getting men across that fire swept causeway remained. Fortunately, the Colonel had two tank lighters from *Adams* at his disposal. Well on in the afternoon, each LCM carried one tank and a number of ground troops from Gavutu around the reefs to the inside of Tanambogo, covered by vigorous and effective bombardment at point-blank range from destroyer *Buchanan*.[19] One tank landed safely but got ahead of its supporting troops, the Japs rushed out of their dugouts, stalled the tank track with an iron bar and killed all but one of the crew with hand grenades. But the other tank, aided by perhaps 60 infantry, worked around the little island, blasting out the dugouts until the Marines on Gavutu could cross the causeway in safety, as they promptly did. By 2200 August 8 the two ends of the bar bell were in American hands.

The taking of Tulagi, Gavutu and Tanambogo had cost the lives of 108 Marines, with 140 wounded; but the force of about 1800 Japanese was wiped out, except for isolated snipers in holes and caves, who made trouble for a week or more.

Air Counterattacks, 7–8 August [20]

Admiral Ghormley well said that a basic problem of the operation would be to protect ships from land-based air attack during the landing and the unloading. Rear Admiral Yamada, Commander 25th Air Flotilla, had some 48 long-range bombers ready on 7 August as well as 12 to 15 big flying boats based on tender *Akitsushima* in Simpson Harbor. A staging field for land-based planes was already in use at Buka Passage between Buka and Bougainville. It did not take Admiral Yamada long to react to the report of our landing at Tulagi. At 0900 August 7 his orders went forth to the 5th and 6th Air Attack Forces under his command, and at 1045 an Australian coastwatcher in Bougainville sighted many twin-engined bombers flying southeasterly, and passed the word to Admiral Turner at Guadalcanal. At 1315, the radar in *Chicago* picked up this flight 43 miles away; five minutes later, about 27 of them covered by fighter planes were seen coming in high over Savo Island. The attack was a high-level one that did no damage. At about 1500, two unheralded groups, of 16 dive-bombers, singled out the X-ray group off Guadalcanal and scored a hit on destroyer *Mugford* that killed 22 men but did slight damage.

Both counterattacks would undoubtedly have been more effective but for the work of the combat air patrol furnished by

Scene on the bridge of USS Wasp (CV-7) during operations off Guadalcanal, 7 August 1942. Naval Historical Center.

Ordnancemen of Scouting Squadron Six load 500-lb. demolition bomb on a SBD bomber, aboard USS Enterprise (CV-6), during the first day of attacks on Guadalcanal and Tulagi, 7 August 1942. Naval Historical Center.

carriers *Enterprise* and *Saratoga,* then operating with *Wasp* south-west of Guadalcanal. These were directed by the fighter-director team in *Chicago.* Considering that almost all the carrier-plane pilots were naval aviators of the latest crop, with a little leaven from the victors of Midway; that this was the first American amphibious operation to be covered by carrier-based air, and that the enemy was energetic and relentless, these American pilots did exceedingly well. They certainly saved the transports from damage, and paid for it by the loss of eleven F4Fs and one SBD. As usual, their claims of planes shot down were excessive, owing to duplication; but Admiral Yamada admitted the loss of 14 out of 43 bombers and two out of 18 "Zekes" in the two attacks. He was not at all pleased with the results of this attack, especially as his planes had been unable to find the carriers.

When the enemy delivered a torpedo attack next day, the Task Force was better prepared to meet it. Admiral Turner, tipped off some 80 minutes in advance by the faithful coastwatcher on Bougainville, had both transport groups in cruising disposition, screened by cruisers and destroyers and maneuvering at 13.5 knots by simultaneous turns, in which he had vigorously drilled the transports en route to Guadalcanal.

A few minutes before noon August 8, a large formation of enemy planes was sighted swinging over the eastern cape of Florida

Japanese Navy G4M "Betty" bombers come in low through anti-aircraft fire to attack U.S. Navy ships off Guadalcanal, 8 August 1942. Naval Historical Center.

Island. The majority of them were low-flying "Bettys" armed with the deadly Japanese aerial torpedo. Three fighter planes from *Enterprise*, patrolling over Nggela Channel, took out four of them. One peeled off to strafe Beach "Red," but the rest had to pass the gauntlet of the screen's anti-aircraft fire and then that of the transports. They came in very low, some only 20 feet above the water; and those that got as far as the transports were so groggy with machine gun hits as to remind one officer of heifers loose in city streets. Only nine out of 26 torpedo-bombers were seen to pass

USS Enterprise (CV-6). View taken 24 July 1942, prior to the Guadalcanal operations. Douglas SBD Dauntless is in the foreground. National Archives.

Japanese "Betty" bomber floating off Tulagi after being shot down during air attack 8 August 1942, Naval Historical Center.

through the transport formation; the Japanese admitted that 17 were shot down. The only hit they obtained was on destroyer *Jarvis.* A few minutes later, a small formation of the "Bettys" came in. They too took a bad beating, but two of them when lethally hit tried suicide tactics, one with success. The Japanese pilot just managed to steer his burning plane into transport *George F. Elliott,* with deadly effects.

If the air battle of the 7th was won by the carrier planes, this defeat of a major threat by the torpedo-bombers was largely due to the ships' anti-aircraft gunners and to excellent ship handling. Admiral Turner always turned his transports to parallel the line of the planes' approach; and, as torpedo-bombers have to come in on a wide angle in order to drive their "fish" to a target, this quick maneuver baffled them and gave the anti-aircraft gunners a chance. Ship losses might have been nil had damage control been up to par. What happened on board *Elliott* is not entirely clear; but it seems that a fair part of the crew abandoned her prematurely, the one destroyer which helped the fire fighting was insufficient, an attempt to smother the fire below by the time-honored method of closing all hatches proved unsuccessful, and by the time darkness set in the transport was a mass of flames. A destroyer sent to sink her fired four torpedoes at close range without effect and *Elliott* became a burning derelict which made a handy mark for the enemy that night. She was a total loss.

Thus during the first two days of Operation "Watchtower," the enemy had managed to inflict a few losses without accomplishing anything more than a slight delay in the American time-table. Before midnight August 8 the beachhead, airfield and enemy encampment on Guadalcanal, and the three islands wanted on Tulagiside, were secured; everything looked rosy. But the critical period in an amphibious operation, under World War II conditions, was not the actual landing; the crisis came when the enemy counterattacked in strength. That moment had now arrived. A few minutes after midnight, the Battle of Savo Island opened.

CHAPTER 3

The Six-Month Struggle for Guadalcanal
7 August 1942 – 9 February 1943

1. KING SOLOMON'S ISLES, 1567 – 1942 [21]

On 8 August 1942 the American public, who had been starved for good war news for two months, read in their morning papers that United States Marines had landed on Guadalcanal and Tulagi, islands in the South Pacific of which few had ever heard. For the next year, hardly a day passed when Guadalcanal was not in the news. That mountainous island, of the Solomons group, only ninety miles long by twenty-five wide, was bitterly contested by the naval, air and ground forces of the United States and Japan for almost six months. In the Pacific war, Leyte and Okinawa may have been as stubbornly fought for as Guadalcanal; but this Solomon Island has had the distinction of being the scene of numerous pitched battles and the occasion for six major naval engagements within a space of four months.[22] In addition, there were some half a hundred ship-to-ship and air-sea fights, only one of which, in this super-abundance of heavy slugging, attained the dignity of a battle name.[23] Costly they were, too, both in ships and in men. You may search the seven seas in vain for an ocean graveyard with the bones of so many ships and sailors as that body of water between Guadalcanal, Savo and Florida Islands which our bluejackets named Ironbottom Sound.

The Japanese promised great benefits to the Melanesians, now that they were in the "Co-prosperity Sphere," and handled very roughly those who refused to accept paper "occupation shillings" for labor, or who otherwise failed to show proper gratitude for liberation from white imperialism. The effect was to make most of the natives eager to have the white men back.

One important institution outlasted the Japanese invasion—the Australian "coastwatchers." They were a network of small radio stations through the Bismarcks and Solomons, established several years earlier and taken over by the Australian Navy in 1939. Only eight or nine coast-watchers remained in all the Solomons after the evacuation of Tulagi, but many others were brought back by American boats or planes. These coastwatchers, whom the natives generally aided and abetted, were of inestimable value throughout the Solomons campaign. They relayed to Allied headquarters the movements of enemy ships, planes and ground forces. At a time when American air power was worn thin, their reports of southward-flying enemy aircraft, received as much as fifty minutes in advance, made it possible for American planes to take off and gain altitude in time to swoop down on the enemy. And, in less than a year, coastwatchers succored 120 crashed Allied airmen.

For some time after their occupation of Tulagi on 2 May, the Japanese paid no attention to Guadalcanal except to send over parties to round up and kill the wild cattle. But before the end of

Guadalcanal and Adjacent Islands.

June a convoy of 13 ships put in, bringing a substantial force of labor troops, engineers and heavy equipment to build the landing field. It was the discovery of this by an Allied reconnaissance plane on 4 July that put the heat on Operation "Watchtower."

There was little time for planning this important operation, but almost the entire Expeditionary Force managed to assemble at a mid-ocean rendezvous on 26 July, at a point about 400 miles south of the Fijis. Some 75 ships were there, "loaded with rude human-ity, trained only for fighting and destruction," as Parkman said of Wolfe's force that captured Quebec in 1759. What better phrase for United States bluejackets and marines! Lucky indeed for America that in this theater and at that juncture she depended not on boys drafted or cajoled into fighting but on "tough guys" who had volunteered to fight and who asked for nothing better than to come to grips with the sneaking enemy who had aroused all their primitive instincts. Fortunate, too, that they had a commander of the Stonewall Jackson breed; a quiet, unassuming man who had learned the fighting trade in the hard Marine school, who had a paternal regard for his troops, but never forgot what they were there for, Major General Alexander A. Vandegrift USMC.[24]

Before dawn on 7 August, while Turner's Expeditionary Force rounded Cape Esperance, Guadalcanal, Fletcher's carrier group maneuvered restlessly south of the island and prepared to furnish air support for the landings. These landings were the least part of the long drawn out Guadalcanal operation. The first amphibious operation undertaken by the United States since 1898 went off fairly smoothly because the enemy was taken completely by sur-prise and overwhelmed. Landing craft from 15 transports took 11,000 Marines ashore on a beach at Guadalcanal, about four miles east of Lunga Point, by nightfall. By the following afternoon the Marines were in possession of the partially completed airstrip and of the principal Japanese encampment at Kukum on the west side of Lunga Point. The enemy, not more than 2000 in number and mostly labor troops, retired after only token resistance.

During the afternoon of 8 August, Lieutenant Commander Dwight H. Dexter USCG and 25 coastguardsmen were set ashore from *Hunter Liggett* with their landing craft, as nucleus of naval operating base on Lunga Point, and Dexter assumed the duties of beachmaster.[25] These men proved both courageous and resource-ful; indispensable in moving small bodies of Marines along the coast.

On the Tulagi side, where the lesser part of the troops were discharged, the Marines ran into stout opposition. Tulagi was not secured until the afternoon of 8 August, nor did the Japanese sea-plane base on the small islands of Gavutu and Tanambogo fall into American possession until just before midnight of the same day. In the meantime, the transports and their escorting destroy-ers, with effective aid by fighter planes from the three carriers, beat off several heavy attacks by Japanese bombing and torpedo planes that flew down from Rabaul. Transport *George E. Elliot* and, indirectly, destroyer *Jarvis*, were lost as a result of these air attacks; but on the whole the landings at Tulagi and Guadalcanal were very successful. Not the most pessimistic old chief petty of-ficer in the Expeditionary Force could have predicted that it would take twenty-six weeks' hard fighting by Navy, Marine Corps, Army and Air Forces to secure what had been occupied in little more than that number of hours.

2. THE BATTLE OF SAVO ISLAND (9 August 1942) [26]

The Setup, 7–8 August

From Nouméa, on 8 August, Admiral Ghormley greeted all hands in and around Guadalcanal, declaring that the "results so far achieved make every officer and man in the South Pacific area proud of the task forces." Yet, even before the sun dropped be-hind Cape Esperance, the enemy was setting the stage for an out-standing victory. The Battle of Savo Island placed the occupation of Guadalcanal in jeopardy and delayed the completion of Op-eration "Watchtower" for several months. It was one of the worst defeats ever inflicted on the United States Navy.

Early in the morning of 7 August news of the American land-ings reached Vice Admiral Gunichi Mikawa, Commander Eighth Fleet and Outer South Seas Force, at Rabaul. Shortly after 0800 came the last message from his countrymen in Tulagi, "We pray for enduring fortunes of war," promising resistance "to the last man." The Japanese Admiral had already decided to supplement

Savo Island from the north shore.

prayer by gun power. His first effort was unsuccessful. Troops were hastily collected at Rabaul and embarked in six transports to reinforce the garrison at Guadalcanal. While one of these transports, the 5600-ton *Meiyo Maru,* with an escorting destroyer, was steaming about 14 miles west of Cape St. George at midnight August 8, she encountered U.S. submarine S-38 (Lieutenant Commander H. G. Munson), a veteran of the Asiatic Fleet. Using sound tracking instead of periscope sight, she fired two torpedoes. Both hit and the transport sank with a loss of 14 officers and 328 men.

When the bad news started to come in from Tulagi around 0700 August 7, it happened that five heavy cruisers had just departed Kavieng, three of them bound for the Admiralties, two for Rabaul. In accordance with an urgent message from Mikawa at 0800, all five headed for Rabaul at top speed. In the early afternoon *Chokai* and destroyer *Yunagi* peeled off to enter Simpson Harbor for orders, while the rest steamed at reduced speed toward a rendezvous in St. George Channel.

Admiral Mikawa broke his red and white striped flag in *Chokai* and at 1628 August 7, led out light cruisers *Tenryu* and *Yubari,* already under his command, to join the four heavies. By the end of the second dogwatch, his task force of seven cruisers and one destroyer had taken departure from Cape St. George; course E by N to pass to the northward of Buka Island.[27]

While United States Marines were spending the first of many uneasy nights ashore in the Solomons, and Admiral Turner's ships were patrolling off shore, Admiral Mikawa and staff considered how to deal with the invaders. The attack must be delivered by stealth if possible, by night for certain; for the Emperor's sailors had been well trained in night gunfire and torpedo action, and they knew that few American aviators were trained for night flying. So the plan was made to strike into the Sound in the small hours of 9 August. But the 8th would have to be passed mostly in the open, where search planes might rob them of surprise.

Sure enough, at 1026 August 8 a Hudson plane of the Royal Australian Air Force located the cruisers and trailed them briefly. Mikawa ordered evasive courses, to deceive the pilot. He was not deceived but anti-aircraft fire kept him at a distance that prevented accurate identification. He reported the force as consisting of "three cruisers, three destroyers, two seaplane tenders or gunboats, ..." At 1101 a second Australian Hudson sighted the Japanese still milling about in the same location north of the strait between Bougainville and Choiseul. The pilot reported two heavy cruisers, two light cruisers and one unidentified vessel.

In every Japanese ship sailors busied themselves with preparations for battle. Inflammables and depth charges were stowed below, ordnance and ammunition were inspected. During their cruise down the Slot the only craft they sighted, either air- or water-borne, was seaplane tender *Akitsushima* en route to northern New Georgia.

At 1640 Mikawa drew up a brief battle plan and sent it by signal blinker to every ship. The gist of it was, first, to make a torpedo attack on the United States ships at the Guadalcanal anchorage; then to cross to Tulagi-side and shell and torpedo the enemy there; then to retire north of Savo Island.

As a double check on American shipping, two planes from cruisers *Chokai* and *Aoba* took the air at 1612 for a final daylight look at the enemy.

Satisfied that everything was in readiness, Admiral Mikawa in Nelsonian fashion at 1840 sent a semaphore signal that spelled out to his delighted sailors:

"Let us attack with certain victory in the traditional night attack of the Imperial Navy. May each one calmly do his utmost!"

Failures in ship identification and communications are enough to explain why Admiral Mikawa managed to make his approach undetected. Yet there were still other factors to make happy Japs and sorry Allies. One was the complete withdrawal of Fletcher's three carriers from waters where they could be of any help to Turner or Crutchley.

At the ocean conference of 26 July on board *Saratoga*, Admiral Fletcher had announced that he would not remain within supporting distance for more than two days. Admiral Turner protested vehemently, remarking that he could not possibly unload the transports in less than four days, during the whole of which they would need air cover; but he failed to convert Fletcher. Admiral Ghormley, superior to both in chain of command but capable of exercising only a general strategic direction from Nouméa, was in no position to resolve this important difference of opinion.

At 1807 August 8, after recovering all his planes from the day's strikes and patrols, when he had been in the area only thirty-six hours, Fletcher sent this important dispatch to Ghormley: "Fighter-plane strength reduced from 99 to 78. In view of the large number of enemy torpedo planes and bombers in this area, I recommend the immediate withdrawal of my carriers. Request tankers sent forward immediately as fuel running low."

It is easy to understand Turner's consternation when he intercepted this dispatch, even though Fletcher had warned him he would pull out before 10 August. It must have seemed to him then, as it seems to us now, that Fletcher's reasons for withdrawal were flimsy. Supposing his fighter-plane strength had been reduced 21 per cent? His air groups still numbered one more Wildcat than the three American carriers had before the Battle of Midway. Supposing the Coral Sea to have been infested with Japanese night-flying bombers (which was by no means true) and that they threatened the safety of fast-stepping, well-defended carriers; were not these planes an infinitely greater threat to anchored transports? Turner could not presume to judge the oil situation; but it can now be ascertained from ships' logs that at noon 8 August the destroyers still had enough fuel for several days' operations, and they could have been refueled from the cruisers and carriers, as well as from fleet oilers.[28] No Japanese search plane had yet found the carrier force, and Fletcher had no

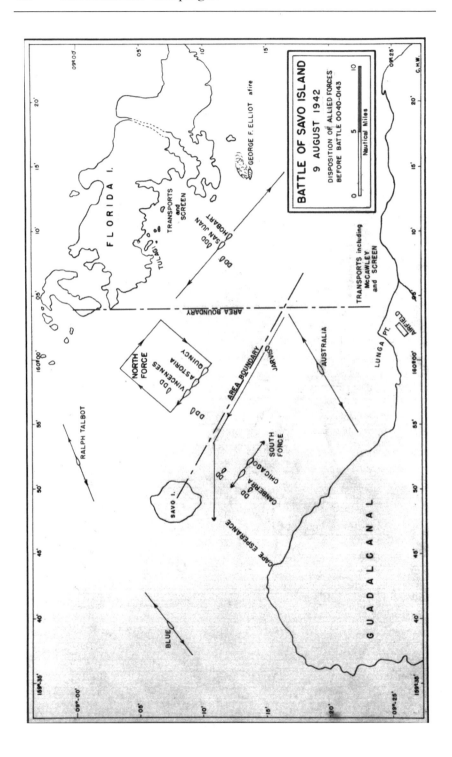

BATTLE OF SAVO ISLAND
9 AUGUST 1942
DISPOSITION OF ALLIED FORCES
BEFORE BATTLE 0040-0143

Nautical Miles

evidence of having been "snooped"; his force could have remained in the area with no more severe consequences than sunburn. But Fletcher, who had lost *Lexington* at Coral Sea and *Yorktown* at Midway, apparently was determined to take no risks this time. In the carrier task force his retirement request was greeted with dismay by senior officers, especially when they learned that the Australian Hudson's report of Mikawa's force had been received on board before 1900, and guessed that the Japanese Fleet was about to show its hand.

At 1807 when he originated the "recommend withdrawal" dispatch, Fletcher was off the northwestern cape of San Cristobal, about 120 miles from Savo Island. Instead of waiting for a reply, the commander of this powerful, mobile force built around three carriers, changed course to the southeastward, leaving Turner (in his own picturesque phrase) "bare-arse."

While Fletcher was retiring and Mikawa was advancing at 26 knots, Crutchley's cruisers and destroyers assumed their night dispositions. In order to protect the transports off Tulagi and Guadalcanal, the Sound was divided into three sectors to be patrolled by a Northern, a Southern and an Eastern Force. Crutchley took immediate command of the Southern Force with cruisers *Australia* (Captain F. E. Getting RAN), *Canberra* (Captain H. B. Farncomb RAN) and *Chicago* (Captain Howard D. Bode), and with destroyers *Patterson* (Commander Frank R. Walker) and *Bagley* (Lieutenant Commander George A. Sinclair). These ships had operated together for months in the old ANZAC Force and at the Battle of the Coral Sea. They patrolled south of a line running 125° from the center of Savo Island, to block the entrance between it and Cape Esperance. The Northern Force, which covered the area north of that line to block the entrance between Savo and Florida Islands, comprised cruisers *Vincennes, Astoria* (Captain William G. Greenman) and *Quincy* (Captain Samuel N. Moore) with destroyers *Helm* (Lieutenant Commander Chester E. Carroll) and *Wilson* (Lieutenant Commander Walter H. Price), under the tactical command of *Vincennes's* skipper, Captain Frederick L. Riefkohl. For early-warning purposes, destroyers *Blue* (Commander Harold N. Williams) and *Ralph Talbot* (Lieutenant Commander Joseph W. Callahan), which carried SC radar, were assigned patrol lines to the westward of Savo Island, supposedly to cover both western entrances to the Sound. The sector east of the meridian of Lunga Point, covering the eastern approaches by Lengo and Scalark Channels, was covered by Rear Admiral Norman Scott with light cruisers *San Juan* and H.M.A.S. *Hobart* and destroyers *Monssen* and *Buchanan.* Turner had tactical command of all the vessels off Guadalcanal, and Scott of all those off Tulagi. The remaining 18 transports *(Elliott* being then on fire and sinking), intended to continue unloading all night.

This four-way division of forces proved to be very unfortunate, although in view of the Admiral's ignorance of enemy deployment and intentions, it was the natural thing to do. All three passages leading into the Sound had to be defended against submarine as well as surface attack. *San Juan,* the one ship with the new SG surface search radar, would have been more useful elsewhere; but the eastern approaches, where Japanese heavy ships would be unlikely to enter, was the place to post a light-hulled anti-aircraft cruiser. It would have been well to have sent Admiral Scott on board *Vincennes,* but 8 August was a busy day that left Turner no time to shuffle commands and shift flags. The separation of the Northern and Southern Forces, and the disposition of the two radar picket destroyers were both unnecessary and faulty; cruisers in single column would have covered both entrances more effectively and given a better account of themselves if surprised.

No battle plan or instructions were signaled to either of these two forces. Presumably *Ralph Talbot* and *Blue* would give adequate warning of approaching enemy ships, but as Admiral Crutchley had never found opportunity to confer with the captains of the three northern cruisers, they had no idea how he expected them to fight a battle that might be forced upon them. Their situation was not improved by the fact that Crutchley, for no fault of his own, was absent during the battle.

At 2032 Admiral Turner urgently summoned Admiral Crutchley, already on patrol, and General Vandegrift, ashore at Guadalcanal, to report on board amphibious force flagship *McCawley,* then lying off Lunga Point. Turner's desire for an immediate conference was prompted by his concern over the departure of Fletcher's carriers and by the information that little or no cargo had yet been unloaded from the transports at Tulagi. Fletcher's retirement placed the amphibious force commander in a distressing dilemma, either to leave the Marines hungry and short of ammunition, or take a beating from enemy air power augmented by big bombers from the assumed seaplane base at Rekata Bay.

Crutchley, upon receipt of the summons, directed Captain Bode of *Chicago* to take charge of his Southern Force, and at once left the formation in cruiser *Australia* to join *McCawley* in Lunga Roads.

Turner bluntly proposed that the transports depart next morning. All three agreed they had better do so, although Vandegrift was dismayed at the prospect of his 18,000 Marines being left with inadequate supplies and no naval support. But he could arrange to discharge the most urgently wanted items at Tulagi and Guadalcanal during the night. Crutchley took occasion to ask Turner's opinion as to the belated report of an enemy force of cruisers, destroyers and "seaplane tenders or gunboats." Turner reiterated his belief that this force would hole up in Rekata Bay, thence to launch torpedo-carrying float planes against the amphibious force. To anticipate them, McCain's land-based planes had been requested to bomb the shipping in Rekata Bay next morning. Turner admitted the possibility of a surface raid, but was satisfied that all was in readiness to meet it.

At about 2330 a heavy rain squall began making up on the slopes of Savo Island. As it drifted slowly to the southeastward it drew a wet, opaque curtain between the two cruiser groups. At 2345, just as the midwatch was gulping down "jamoke" and stumbling up to relieve the "eight to twelvers," came the first disturbance of the night—three reports of one or more unidentified planes. These were two scouts launched from Mikawa's cruisers at 2313 to check upon the night locations of the Allied ships and to illuminate them at the proper time. *Ralph Talbot,* the northern picket, sighted one of them, identified it as a cruiser type and broadcast an alarm: "Warning – Warning: Plane over Savo headed east." Despite numerous repetitions of this report, it failed to reach Admiral Turner's flagship, only 20 miles distant. *Blue,* the southern picket, heard *Ralph Talbot's* call and subsequently picked up a plane on her radar; but the radio warning was received by only a few ships present and those who did get it failed to grasp its significance, even though they sighted the planes themselves. *Quincy,* for example, made radar contact on a plane and several minutes later disregarded it as of no consequence. *Vincennes's* captain was deceived into the belief that the planes were friendly because they showed running lights. Other commanding officers assumed that Turner had received the report and knew the planes to be friendly; otherwise he would have sent out an alarm. So, for the next hour and a half, the Japanese aircraft continued to drone unmolested over the American ships, and to send exact information of their movements that was very interesting to Admiral Mikawa.

The first hour of 9 August was disarmingly quiet. Admiral Crutchley, leaving *McCawley* five minutes before midnight to return to his flagship, could see very little. Low water-burdened clouds hung sullenly overhead, barely drifting in a light air from the northeast. Rain blotted out the western horizon toward Savo. Winking flashes of distant lightning occasionally limned the dark-hulled transports. To the northeast a fitful red glow marked the burning shell of *George F. Elliott.* The Admiral had offered to set General Vandegrift on board minesweeper *Southard* for passage to Tulagi; it took time for his barge to find *Southard* and, by the time Crutchley was back on board his flagship and clear of the transport area, only the butt of the night remained. He decided to patrol seven miles west of the Guadalcanal transports, rather than attempt rendezvous with *Canberra* and *Chicago.* By this decision the Southern Force was shy a much-needed heavy cruiser; but that heavy cruiser would probably have arrived at the same time as the enemy and added to the existing confusion.

The Battle South of Savo, 0054 - 0150

On the flag bridge of *Chokai* Admiral Mikawa was eagerly assimilating the reports of his scout planes. One American ship burning brightly—a good guide to the location of the other transports off Tulagi and Guadalcanal—the prime objective; Allied cruisers to the west of the beach area—a hazard to be met and brushed aside before reaching the fat transports. The Admiral had his force in a long column: heavy cruisers *Chokai, Aoba, Kako, Kinugasa* and *Furutaka;* light cruisers *Tenryu* and *Vubari* and destroyer *Vunagi.* Several of these had never operated together before, but with a generous 1300 yards between ships they had ample sea room. Their total armament was 62 torpedo tubes (all but ten of them 24-inch), 34 eight-inch guns, ten 5.5-inch guns and 27 five-inch and 4.7-inch guns. The force had orders to steam single file into the Sound, tackling first the American ships off Guadalcanal, next those off Tulagi; a lightning strike at the enemy and a quick getaway to be beyond carrier-plane range by daybreak. "Battle Warning" was signaled to every ship at 2230; "Three Heavy Cruisers South of Savo" and "Prepare to Fire Torpedoes" at 0025; "Battle Stations Alerted" at 0045.

No Japanese ship mounted radar, but at 0054 *Chokai* sighted destroyer *Blue* on her starboard bow, heading southwesterly. Anxious moments followed. While the force tore by at 24 to 26 knots, some fifty guns were trained on *Blue,* waiting for her to act. But the American destroyer steamed slowly away, giving no indication that she had seen the Japanese; nor had she. Her SC radar was not good enough and her lookouts must have been looking everywhere but astern—a common failing of lookouts.

Nevertheless, Admiral Mikawa feared that *Blue* had reported him and so ordered a small course change left to pass north of Savo Island. Shortly after making the turn, his lookouts reported a destroyer bearing NE by E. *Ralph Talbot* actually was out there but (according to her log) she must have been a good ten miles away—too far to be seen, even by a cat's-eyed Japanese lookout. Mikawa, however, believed the report and returned to his original plan to enter the Sound between Savo and Cape Esperance. At 0505 he ordered course 150° and 26 knots to leave Savo on the port hand. As it rounded the island, the Japanese column swung more to the eastward; at

Rear Admiral Gunichi Mikawa.

0132 to course 95°. One minute later, Mikawa spat out his battle order, "All Ships Attack!" It was the time, no doubt about that. At 0134 his port lookouts vaguely discerned the outline of an American destroyer moving slowly westward, only 3000 yards to the northward. Detection seemed inevitable, but this was the damaged destroyer *Jarvis,* who had no means of communication.[29] Two more minutes passed, and the starboard lookouts chimed in, reporting ships ahead. These were *Patterson* and *Bagley* of the Southern Force, then nearing the northwestern extremity of their patrol course, closing the Japanese on a collision heading at 36 knots. Lookouts on other Japanese ships sighted *Jarvis,* mistook her for a cruiser and launched torpedoes, all of which missed; but they did not open gunfire because the flagship did not, and their good discipline served the Emperor well, as gunfire would have alerted the Southern Force, which was unable to observe the oncoming Japanese ships because a heavy rain cloud to the south of Savo Island blended with their silhouettes.

Japanese lookouts were sending a continuous stream of reports to bridge and gunnery stations; now two destroyers sharp on port and starboard bows respectively; now *Chicago* and *Canberra* in view, distant 12,500 yards, closing fast. The Admiral now ordered speed reduced to 18-20 knots—so he said in 1949; but promptly built up again to 26 knots—as his track chart proves. "Independent Firing!" ordered Mikawa at 0136. Target angles were hastily cranked into torpedo directors and at 0138 hissing "fish" leaped out of their tubes, one salvo bound for *Bagley,* others for the cruisers. *Chokai* was soon a mere two miles from them, still closing, still undetected. Suddenly, at 0143, from the only American ship that was properly awake, came the long-delayed tocsin. *Patterson* sighted the loom of a ship 5000 yards ahead and broadcast a radio alarm:

WARNING – WARNING: STRANGE SHIPS ENTERING HARBOR!

It was too late. At that very moment—only seconds before or after *Patterson's* warning—Japanese float planes dropped brilliant flares over the transports at Lunga Point which silhouetted *Chicago* and *Canberra;* at that very moment *Chokai,* only 4500 yards away, *Aoba,* 1000 yards farther, and *Furutaka* at 9000 opened fire with main batteries. At that very moment, too, a sharp-eyed lookout on *Canberra's* bridge was trying to point out a strange ship, dead ahead, to the officer of the deck. As the two Australians peered intently into the gloom, torpedoes came slashing in on both sides of the ship. These had been fired five minutes earlier, but the 8-inch and 4.7 inch salvos did not take many seconds to arrive. The fateful minute 0143 had not elapsed, General Alarm was still sounding, and *Canberra's* guns were still trained in, when two torpedoes sundered her starboard side and the first of 24 shells hit her high hull. Captain Getting was mortally wounded and his gunnery officer killed instantly. The Australian cruiser got off two torpedoes and a few 4-inch shots from her secondary battery before power and propulsion died. Fires spread topside, and a ten-degree starboard list developed. In less than five minutes this fine ship was out of the war.

Patterson, after repeating her radio warning by blinker, commenced a hard left turn to unmask her batteries. Gunners laid a spread of star shell; Commander Walker shouted, "Fire Torpedoes!" The enemy replied in kind. Walker, noting that the Japanese column had come left to a northeasterly heading, conned his destroyer a high-speed zigzag course and engaged in a vigorous gunfire duel. Yet *Patterson* escaped the usual fate of a David in modern warfare. A shell hit near her No. 4 gun, igniting ready-service powder and putting two guns out of action. She came full circle, parallel to the enemy course, clawing at the aftermost cruisers with her remaining guns until they could no longer be seen. Only then did the captain discover that his order to fire torpedoes had not been heard. So brief and sudden was the action that the executive officer, then off watch, had no time to arrive at his battle station before the shooting stopped. He rallied the crew aft and put out the fire quickly.

Destroyer *Bagley,* screening on *Canberra's* starboard bow, saw the Japanese cruisers only a few seconds after *Patterson* did. A sharp left turn brought her starboard torpedo batteries to bear faster than torpedomen could insert firing primers. Lieutenant Commander Sinclair did not wait for them but made a tight circle to the left until the port torpedoes bore; then he fired. The few moments lost were fatal because the enemy column was disappearing so fast to the northeastward that the best-aimed torpedoes could not catch up with it. Although Japanese vessels passed within a mile of *Bagley,* they did not fire on her, as their gun sights were already on bigger game.

Chicago's turn came next. She had been favored with three warnings. Orange flashes were seen at 0142, then the aircraft flare over the transports; then a sudden right turn by *Canberra* ahead; but not until two black objects loomed out of the darkness did Captain Bode, just awakened from a sound sleep, direct his 5-inch guns even to prepare to illuminate with star shell. At 0146 a lookout saw a torpedo wake to starboard. Bode gave the order for full right rudder, then shifted helm when he saw torpedoes approaching his port bow. He did his best to comb the bubbling wakes but, at 0147, one of the warheads smacked into *Chicago's* bow and knocked off a part of it. A tall pillar of water rose into the air, then deluged the ship from bow to No. 1 stack. *Chicago's* gunners caught their breath, sputtered and gasped, went into action. Star shell was fired on both bows to spy out the enemy, but as all were duds the gunners groped blindly for targets. A Japanese cruiser made one shell hit of little consequence on her foremast. *Chicago* did not turn away like the destroyers, because at this juncture a vessel to the westward illuminated what appeared to be two targets ahead and gave her something to strike at for two minutes.

Admiral Mikawa, concerned about leaving his rear uncovered to the attention of *Blue* and *Jarvis,* at 0136 had directed his one destroyer, *Yunagi,* to reverse course and block the southwestern entrance to the Sound; she is the ship that attracted *Chicago's* attention. After the cruiser had fired 25 rounds, *Yunagi's* searchlight went out; *Chicago* snapped on her own searchlights at 0151 and swept the water to port and ahead but found nothing. The main battle had moved to the northeast, leaving Captain Bode's bewildered cruiser alone, slowly steaming in the wrong direction.[30] And, what was even worse, the Captain failed to alert the *Vincennes* group.

Hitherto, Mikawa's cruisers had been steaming in a single column. Now, at 0144, probably because he had briefly glimpsed the *Vincennes* group to the northeastward, Mikawa changed course almost 30° left, to 69° (ENE). The other ships were expected to follow *Chokai,* but the maneuver was badly executed. Cruiser *Furutaka,* fifth in column, perhaps to avoid collision with *Kinugasa* ahead, sheered off to starboard and charged directly at the Allied formation; at about 0147, she came hard left to 11° (N by E). Light cruisers *Tenryu* and *Yubari* turned simultaneously and in the same direction as *Furutaka*. Thus Mikawa's force was divided into two separate groups: a western one of three cruisers in line of bearing; an eastern one of four cruisers led by flagship *Chokai*.[31]

At 0146 *Tenryu* sighted the *Vincennes* group bearing 60 degrees, distant over seven miles. Mikawa's ships had fired 17 torpedoes for only three hits, yet by 0149 they had finished the Southern Force as an effective fighting unit, without receiving a single hit. All in six minutes!

Mikawa's swing northward was decisive. It meant three more Allied cruisers in the bag. His column, at this point, resembled a vicious prehistoric monster, deadly at both ends. The battle south of Savo was only a tail-lashing. Now with two heads, hydra-like, the beast would put the bite on the Northern Force.

The Battle East and North of Savo, 0143 - 0230

At the very moment (0143) when *Patterson* was broadcasting her "Warning – Warning: Strange ships..." Japanese float planes loosed a string of brilliant and long-burning parachute flares over the two transport areas off Tulagi and Guadalcanal. Flares and warning, seen and heard simultaneously, were the first inkling of danger to Captain Riefkohl's Northern Force.

The action east and north of Savo commenced only five minutes after the action south of Savo began, at 0148, when flagship *Chokai* fired four torpedoes at the Northern Force, then ahead of her and less than 20,000 yards distant. *Astoria,* as the aftermost of the Northern Force was, however, the first to be hit, and by shellfire. This second half of the battle was such a mêlée that we can only clarify it by relating the experience of each American ship in turn.

On *Astoria's* bridge at 0143 the officer of the deck was intent on maintaining station. The gunnery officer tested the forward fire control radar, which had been acting cranky; the radar technician had just replaced some defective tubes. Captain Greenman was worn out by the exertions of the past two days. Three bells of a quiet "graveyard watch" had passed.

Nobody on board had yet reacted to the flares or to *Patterson's* warning when, about 0145, Topper felt a slight tremor in *Astoria's* hull. It was *Chokai's* torpedoes exploding after their run past the *Chicago* group. Topper called the damage control watch. Yes, they had felt a slight shake and were very much on the alert. Suddenly a shout from the port wing of the bridge—"Star shell on the port quarter!" Topper dashed out on the wing, to see a string of aircraft flares over Guadalcanal casting reflections on clouds and water. What could that mean? Lieutenant Commander Truesdell, the gunnery officer, also saw the bright lights and told the bridge to go to General Quarters. High time, too, for out of the darkness at 0150 came searchlights and, less than a minute later, a salvo of Japanese shells, short and ahead. Main battery spotter announced that there were enemy cruisers on the port quarter. "Guns" ordered Commence Firing, and at about 0152$\frac{1}{2}$ six 8-inch guns roared out at Mikawa's flagship.

Although *Chokai* had fired four salvos at *Astoria,* she had not yet made a hit. Presently an 8-inch salvo ripped into her superstructure, turning the midships section into a flaming torch. Now the Japanese had a nice point of aim. *Astoria,* blazing in her own consuming fires, was an easy and a close target. Shell after shell, accurate and deadly, plowed into the cruiser from 6000 down to 5300 yards' range. Captain Greenman, in order to unmask what was left of his main battery, altered course slightly to port and rang up full speed, keeping a seaman's eye on *Quincy* next ahead. But loss of communications, destruction of men and material topside, and the effects of choking smoke and blinding flame fatally lowered *Astoria's* battle efficiency. Eleven salvos of varying quantity left her 8-inch guns. One of *Quincy's* burst in Mikawa's staff chart room in *Chokai.* It was easy to keep station on the two cruisers ahead, since both were burning amidships. Captain Greenman maneuvered on a zigzag course, slightly on *Quincy's* port quarter, for several minutes while his ship received a steady rain of blows. Both forward turrets were knocked out, aircraft amidships spouted flame, the 5-inch gun batteries became mangled and useless, the navigator and chief quartermaster were killed. At about 0202, when the navigator was struck down, the Captain realized that his ship was in line of fire between *Quincy* and the enemy. The black gang were being driven from their stations below by the heat and smoke from main deck conflagrations, and *Astoria* slowed down. Her propellers still thrashed the water but gave only a feeble seven knots. Enemy shells sprinkled her with their fragments and ignited fires over her entire length. Proud *Astoria* was becoming little better than a funeral pyre for American sailors. But she was still fighting. Lieutenant Commander Davidson, communications officer, climbed into undamaged turret No. 2, coached its guns onto a searchlight to the eastward, and this, twelfth and last salvo, hit a forward turret on *Chokai*.

Quincy, next ahead of *Astoria,* received the worst beating of all on this terrible night. As in other ships, the low-flying Japanese aircraft were heard, reported and discussed on several occasions; but the assertion of a junior officer that they must be enemy was regarded by his seniors as mildly hysterical, so the last two contacts were not even reported to the Captain. Enemy aircraft flares were the first signs accepted as ominous. Immediately after they were seen, *Patterson's* "Warning – Warning…" was heard on the bridge. The gunnery control officer, Lieutenant Commander Andrew, was still trying to figure out the flares when the general alarm sounded. The bridge reacted promptly to *Patterson's* warning, calling Captain Moore from his emergency cabin off the chart house, but in the confusion nobody informed the gunners. As the enemy closed from astern, *Aoba* snapped open her searchlight shutters and illuminated *Quincy* so brightly that the Japanese lookouts could see that her guns were trained in, fore and aft. "We continued the battle very easy minded, without any worries," recalled the executive officer of *Chokai*. But Admiral Mikawa snorted at this: "We had plenty of worries; target selection, shortage of time, use of torpedoes, running aground, etc., etc."

The same searchlight beam that proved so soothing to Japanese nerves was a horror to the startled crew in *Quincy*. Lieutenant Commander Heneberger, gunnery officer, arrived in the gun control station just as shells began to fall in the water ahead. Men were still dashing to battle stations when the 8-inch turrets turned to port. "Fire at the ships with the searchlights on!" came from Captain Moore on the bridge. Two quick 9-gun salvos were pumped out at 8000 yards' range, but immediately after these the Captain, who had not seen the dim silhouettes of the enemy cruisers, decided that he was firing on friendly ships and ordered recognition lights turned on. While junior officers were trying to argue him out of it the officer of the deck, fearing a collision with *Vincennes* ahead, ordered a change of course and committed the error of turning right with an enemy shooting at him from the port quarter, which masked the fire of his forward turrets. Before the completion of this turn a Japanese shell touched off a plane resting on the catapult. Thereafter no searchlight was needed to see *Quincy*.

Caught in a crossfire between the *Chokai* group and the *Furutaka* group, unable even to see her antagonists, the cruiser was doomed. Turret No. 2 was hit, and exploded. The Captain telephoned to the gunners: "We're going down between them—give them hell!" Immediately after this an enemy shell wounded him fatally and snuffed out almost every life in the pilot-house. A torpedo hit the port side at No. 4 fireroom, bashing it in. Last words from gun plot were a telephoned message giving news of the explosion. The engineer officer, Lieutenant Commander Elmore, sent a messenger to tell Captain Moore that his ship would have to stop—last words again. For the engine rooms, though yet undamaged, had lost communication and become sealed deathtraps. In mess compartments, repair stations and bunk rooms, men struggled hopelessly with fire and explosions. The sick bay was wiped out. On anti-aircraft batteries, guns and men were flattened down, chopped up and blown to bits. At No. 4 five-inch gun a shell neatly removed the bases from several cartridge cases and ignited them, "causing them to burn like a Roman candle and killing all hands on the left side of the gun." There was no doubt now among surviving officers that *Quincy* was doomed; the only question was whether she would succumb to fire or water.

"Guns" Heneberger ordered Abandon Ship upon receiving word Captain Greenman was dead. The forecastle was now completely awash with water coming over the gun deck. Life rafts and flotsam were cast overboard in the nick of time; at about 0235 *Quincy* capsized to port, twisted completely around in her agony with stern high in air, and slid under the black waters—first of many fighting ships whose shattered hulls would justify the name "Ironbottom Sound" for that body of water.

There is this consolation for *Quincy* survivors. Admiral Mikawa and his chief of staff recalled in 1949 that the "center ship of the Northern Group" returned the heaviest fire of any American cruiser, and expressed great admiration for her commanding officer's gallantry.

Leading the northern cruiser column and first to be sighted but last to be engaged was *Vincennes,* "Vinny Maru" as her crew called her. Captain Riefkohl had retired to his emergency cabin on the bridge less than an hour before; Commander Mullan, his executive officer, was on the bridge and Lieutenant Commander Craighill at gun control. These officers had heard *Talbot's* radio warning of the enemy plane sighting at 2345 and had been cautioned in the Captain's night order book to exercise extreme vigilance. Yet *Vincennes* too was not alerted until enemy flares fell on her port quarter. It is not clear whether *Patterson's* "Warning – Warning" of 0143 reached the Captain; he was called to the bridge after the flares were seen but before he reached it General Quarters sounded. Riefkohl and Mullan were still speculating on the significance of the flares when they felt two underwater explosions, heard gunfire and even saw a few gun flashes through the rain squall to the southward; but they assumed that this was the *Chicago* group shooting at planes. Oh the stupendous optimism of that night!

Captain Riefkohl decided to continue on his course after increasing speed to 15 knots. At 0150 searchlights from three ships abaft the port beam fastened each to an American cruiser. The Captain, assuming they came from the Southern Group, sent out a request by voice radio that they be shut off, while his gunnery officer, Lieutenant Commander Adams, as a precaution trained on the nearest one. Doubts were quickly resolved by a salvo from *Kako* that fell 500 yards short of *Vincennes.* She replied at 0153 with a full 8-inch salvo (range about four miles) after her 5-inch had fired star shell for illumination. "Vinny" drew Japanese blood with her second salvo by hitting *Kinugasa* but, simultaneously, enemy shells hit her amidships and planes on the catapults went up in fire. Japanese searchlights snapped shut, as no longer necessary, and their gunners and torpedomen commenced a methodical destruction of this easy target.

Captain Riefkohl now decided to close the enemy by turning left; but more hits on his brightly illuminated ship prevented it.

One on the port side of the bridge killed several men. Hits throughout the superstructure demolished guns, destroyed communications and kindled blistering fires. Main battery gunfire was resumed in local control but with little hope of success. The concentrated fire from both enemy groups was so devastating that Riefkohl turned his ship hard right in an effort to escape. During this turn, two or three torpedoes from *Chokai* penetrated No. 4 fireroom on the port side. The eviscerated cruiser shuddered in agony. Below decks the No. 2 fireroom crew were smothered in smoke and showered with debris. In the after engine room men watched with dismay the steady drop in steam pressure and tried in vain to call the bridge. At 0203½ a torpedo from *Yubari* hit her No. 1 fireroom, killing everyone there. Now *Vincennes* floundered to a halt, still under concentrated fire. The Captain, deprived of communications, mobility, sight and organization, had only a chaotic picture of what was happening. A submarine was rumored to be close aboard. Two enemy searchlights which leisurely inspected *Vincennes* were identified as friendly, because they came from her hitherto unengaged side, so the Captain ordered a large set of colors raised to the fore. The enemy, mistaking this big battle ensign for an admiral's flag redoubled his efforts to sink *Vincennes.*

IJNS Kako class heavy cruiser in the Battle of Savo Island.

Riefkohl ordered funnel smoke to conceal his blazing hull, but all surviving water tenders and firemen had been driven from their boilers.

So it went, from one horror to another. The Captain sent a messenger to the gunnery officer asking for fire on the two searchlights still focused on the ship; "Guns" himself came down to the bridge to announce that no guns remained. Both forward turrets had received direct hits and the 5-inch batteries were nothing but twisted metal and flame. *Vincennes* was now listing heavily to port, with enemy gunfire still aggravating her many grievous wounds. The Captain was seriously considering whether he should order Abandon Ship to save lives when at about 0215 the Japanese guns ceased fire and the searchlights blinked out. The enemy had moved on, leaving *Vincennes* dead in the water, burning and helpless.

Commander Mullan strove to put out fires and jettison ammunition but was shortly felled by an explosion which broke his leg. He and several other wounded were lowered into a life raft. In the coding room Acting Pay Clerk Willess ordered his men to don gas masks as smoke filled the compartment. As minutes went by and no communications could be established, he opened the door to find the ship ablaze. His men jettisoned the coding equipment while he went out on deck with the disbursing records, a paymaster's sacred trust. He was still looking for a floating object on which to stow them when the rising water floated him off the deck, minus his box of records. Captain Riefkohl, his Marine orderly Corporal Patrick, and Chief Yeoman Stucker stayed with the ship to the last; even when in the water the Captain swam from one group to another, rendering what aid and encouragement he could after his ship went down. It was about 0250 when *Vincennes* heeled to her beam-ends, hesitated briefly, capsized and sank. Water and fire mixing in angry swirls of steam and smoke marked her end.

Wilson and *Helm,* screening destroyers of the Northern Force, were eager to help their cruisers, but to them the battle appeared a confused jumble with Japanese ships everywhere you did not want them and nowhere when you did want them. Lieutenant Commander Price of *Wilson* was duly alerted by the aircraft flares and *Patterson's* radio warning. At about 0150 he sighted a three ship Japanese column illuminating and attacking his cruisers. At once he opened fire, his four 5-inch guns shooting over the Americans at the enemy searchlights some five miles away. At the same time he tried to conform to the cruiser movements, turning first left and then hard right, firing continuously whenever his guns would bear. Fire was interrupted when *Helm* materialized out of the darkness ahead. Price rang up 30 knots, turned hard left and passed clear. *Wilson* continued to toss out 5-inch shells at *Chokai.* The enemy, intent on sinking cruisers, took little notice beyond firing a few salvos at her, all of which missed. Destroyer *Helm,* on the port bow of *Vincennes,* never did lend a hand.

Admiral Mikawa and staff had been watching the battle's progress with relish. At 0200, for reasons which to the present writer are inexplicable, the Admiral turned flagship *Chokai* away from the northerly course, whether to port or to starboard cannot now be determined. Apparently he expected the column to follow, but they kept right on to the northward. Mikawa, accordingly, made another quick change, returned to the original course and fell in at the rear of *Kinugasa.* This move was a fortunate break for us. It not only saved the transports, but got *Chokai* into trouble. At 0205, two shells from *Quincy* hit the Japanese flagship. One shell wiped out the Admiral's staff chart room and a second scored near the aviation crane. A third shell hit a forward turret, but inflicted no damage of consequence. At 0220 Mikawa signaled his captains, "All ships withdraw." Still steaming in two columns, they turned westward to leave Savo Island on the port hand. *Chokai* turned left and increased speed to 35 knots and cut the corner to regain the lead position. At the same time the *Furutaka* group ran into destroyer *Ralph Talbot,* who, single-handed, took on the lot.

Ralph Talbot was the picket destroyer that patrolled the channel between Savo and Florida Islands. *Patterson's* first radio warning had sent her scurrying southwest at 25 knots. Lieutenant Commander Callahan and everyone else topside watched the battle within the Sound, wondering what the score was. At 0215 they began to find out when *Tenryu,* moving westward, focused a searchlight on them and shells began to come their way. *Furutaka,*

Tenryu and *Yubari* opened up on *Talbot* from a range between 4500 and 6000 yards, and in about seven salvos scored one hit on her torpedo tubes. Callahan, seeing a single searchlight and colored splashes like those from American shells, thought he was being fired on by friends, flicked on recognition lights and shouted his identification over voice radio. This unexpected procedure appears to have puzzled the enemy, who checked fire momentarily. But *Ralph Talbot* had little respite. *Yubari,* the rear Japanese cruiser, less than two miles away, turned searchlights on the destroyer's bridge and fired several more salvos. Callahan replied, but after his second salvo the enemy got the range. One shot hit the destroyer's charthouse and knocked out part of the automatic gun control system, a second exploded in the wardroom, a third demolished a torpedo tube and a fourth struck the after 5-inch gun. *Talbot* launched four torpedoes at her antagonist without success. *Talbot* entered a rain squall and the battle ended abruptly, leaving the destroyer in flames and listing 20 degrees to starboard. Yet *Ralph Talbot's* plucky fight may have convinced Admiral Mikawa that there were more American ships about than met his eye, and so furthered his decision to retire.

While battle raged around Savo Island, American ships in the transport area were baffled but busy. The first enemy parachute flares, expertly placed to silhouette the Guadalcanal transport area, were quickly followed by another cluster over the Tulagi group. Thoroughly alarmed, all ships discontinued unloading, got under way and milled around in uneasy expectation. Admiral Turner from *McCauley's* flag bridge could see occasional gun flashes and the sudden flare of explosive hits. Rain squalls directly in line with Savo Island drew a curtain of uncertainty. The situation was even more obscure to Admiral Scott's *San Juan* force, which continued its routine patrol between Florida Island and Guadalcanal. Admiral Crutchley in *Australia,* patrolling to seaward of the Guadalcanal transports, ordered the seven destroyers he had earlier designated as a striking force to close his flagship, if not in contact with the enemy. But this order, too, got fouled up and its only effect was to pull four destroyers out of the battle and send them hot-footing toward their assigned rendezvous five miles northwest of Savo Island. In the amphibious force the situation was touch-and-go.

Each transport was blacked out, apprehensive, with no guide and in no formation; one over imaginative gunner might have sparked a battle of friend against friend. On the other hand, observing that the battle was moving away, transport sailors were convinced that their side had won. And as far as they were concerned it had; Admiral Mikawa was going home.

After Mikawa had cleared the passage between Florida and Savo Islands, he showed indecision. His flagship, as we have seen, was now at the rear of the heavy-cruiser column. The *Furutaka* group was scattered, out somewhere in the darkness. Mikawa thought three hours would be needed to whip his ships into battle formation again, and by that time it would be almost daybreak. If he then ventured into the Sound with weather clearing, as it always did around sunrise, he would lay himself open to a carrier air attack; Fletcher's departure was unsuspected.

It is always difficult to assign exact motives to a decision like this, where some criticism of the commanding officer is involved. Admiral Yamamoto was displeased with Mikawa for not carrying out his explicit orders to destroy the transports, and his Commander in Chief's displeasure put Mikawa on the defensive. In 1949 both he and his chief of staff insisted that Mikawa personally wished to return to the fray, but that the staff dissuaded him for two reasons: the fact that all torpedoes had been expended, and fear of a daylight carrier air attack. This may well be true; but the present writer suspects that the Admiral and staff simply did not want to go back and tempt luck a second time; felt they had done enough.

By about 0240 all Mikawa's ships had increased speed to 30 knots for a hasty run up the Slot.

Picking Up the Pieces, 9–10 August

Savo Island was the first large surface action since Santiago to be fought by a predominantly United States force. Unlike Java Sea, here the command as well as the major part of the force was American. Unlike Pearl Harbor, here the United States Navy had been at war eight months, operating in a combat area. The enemy was little superior in strength—inferior in destroyers—yet one side was all but annihilated and the other escaped virtually unscathed.

The violent repercussions within the Navy and later among the American people[32] brought about an investigation. In December 1942 the Secretary of the Navy ordered Admiral Arthur J. Hepburn, former Commander in Chief of the Fleet, to conduct an inquiry to determine the "primary and contributing causes of the losses and whether or not culpability attaches to any individual engaged in the operation." The Admiral, with Commander Donald J. Ramsey, traveled all over the Pacific to talk with the principal officers involved and to obtain their statements. He concluded that "the primary cause of this defeat" was "the complete surprise achieved by the enemy." The reasons for this surprise he listed as follows, in order of importance:

(a) Inadequate condition of readiness on all ships to meet sudden night attack.
(b) Failure to recognize the implications of the presence of enemy planes in the vicinity previous to attack.
(c) Misplaced confidence in the capabilities of radar installations on *Ralph Talbot* and *Blue*.
(d) Failure in communications which resulted in lack of timely receipt of vital enemy contact information.
(e) Failure in communications to give timely information of the fact that there had been practically no effective reconnaissance covering enemy approach during the day of August 8.

As a contributory cause . . . must be placed the withdrawal of the carrier groups on the evening before the battle. This was responsible for Admiral Turner's conference... [and] for the fact that there was no force available to inflict damage on the withdrawing enemy.

Admiral Nimitz agreed with Admiral Hepburn that complete surprise was responsible, but listed the causes of it in a somewhat different order: communication weaknesses, poor air search, erroneous estimate of enemy intentions, dependence on ineffective radar, disregard of the unidentified planes, want of a flag officer in the Southern Force, and "the probability that our force was not sufficiently 'battle-minded.'" Admiral King, in general, concurred, and all three agreed that blame for the defeat was so evenly distributed that it would be unfair to censure any particular officer. That was wise and just. Some of the commanding officers concerned were broken by the defeat, but Admiral Crutchley later made a creditable record in command of Allied forces in the Southwest Pacific, and Admiral Turner went on from Guadalcanal to become a master of amphibious warfare.

The present writer has little to add. Lack of "battle-mindedness," faulty radar and communications, basing decisions on the enemy's probable intentions (as at Pearl Harbor) and premature withdrawal of carrier forces (as at Wake) are painfully evident to anyone who has read the sad story. But let us remember, too, that Luck—the constant and baffling major factor in naval warfare—was with the Rising Sun this time. We may deem it fortunate that the capricious lady smiled once on the Allies at the end, in persuading Mikawa not to come back.

Despite the grievous losses that night,[33] some consolation could be gleaned from the battle. As Admiral Crutchley later declared, "Our forces did achieve our object, which was to prevent the enemy from reaching the transports." Defeat taught the United States Navy many lessons; planners of later operations put them to good advantage. Americans gained a new and healthy respect for Japanese night fighting and would eventually beat the enemy at this game. Important, if minor, technical improvements came about as a result of the battle: the removal from all ships of wooden furniture and other inflammable material, such as "battleship linoleum" and paint, which had burned like dry brush; provision of fireproof covers for bedding; improved fire-fighting equipment such as a fog nozzle, which poured a cooling, quenching mist on flames, far more effective than solid streams of water; a more reasonable battle-readiness condition that relieved sailors from continual tension; improvements in communication methods and equipment; the development of adequate air-search systems.[34] Savo Island was not a decisive battle, although it might have been if the Japanese had followed it up with energy instead of committing forces piecemeal. Savo was the inaugural engagement of a bloody and desperate campaign and the 9th of August was the first of many terrible days when commanders on either side might well have raised their hands to Heaven like the Psalmist, to cry out, "For all the day long have I been plagued, and chastened every morning."

3. THREE WEEKS ON GUADALCANAL [35]
(9 August – 1 September 1942)

The Marines' Problem and Initial Skirmishes

As the transports that had brought the Marines to this unpleasant island disappeared over the horizon on the afternoon of 9 August, escorted by all combat ships still afloat, General Vandegrift knew that he was in for a rough, tough time. No ground force, not even United States Marines, can long hold a remote island against an enemy who commands the surrounding seas and the routes to its own bases. Mahan's axiom needed no fresh proof after what had happened at Wake and Corregidor. It is true that Admiral Mikawa had not made a clean sweep; but, by forcing all combat shipping that he did not sink to retire, he had opened the watergates through which Japan could reinforce her small garrison on Guadalcanal at will. Kelly Turner had made no promise to "return," but Vandegrift knew he would send supplies, reinforcements and fighting ships at the earliest possible date and that McCain would fly in planes as soon as an airfield was ready. The only question was whether he could hold out that long. While the Marines in general felt that the Navy had let them down badly, Vandegrift, a man of iron, uttered no complaint and let no doubt enter his mind that the Corps would hold Guadalcanal, with or without help from the Navy.

The Marine problem on Guadalcanal was threefold: fending off enemy counterattacks, supplying the garrison and completing the airfield. If one failed, all failed. To meet a possible counter-landing, Vandegrift set up a five-mile defense line from the Ilu (Tenaru) River to Kukum. Since no coast defense guns had been landed, the largest weapons along the waterfront were mobile 75-mm "half tracks," 37-mm field pieces and a captured Japanese 3-inch gun. To the rear and on their inland flanks the Marines main-

tained separate strong points manned by small security detachments until the enemy commenced night infiltration. After that a
thin outpost line was set up. At Tulagi the defense was simplified
by quick elimination of the Japanese, but for some time the commanding general, William H. Rupertus USMC, felt he had to be
prepared against an amphibious counter-landing on the back of
Florida Island.

In addition, there was the constant peril of aerial and naval
bombardment. Defense had to be passive until the airfield could
be used. The 90-mm anti-aircraft batteries could and did keep en-

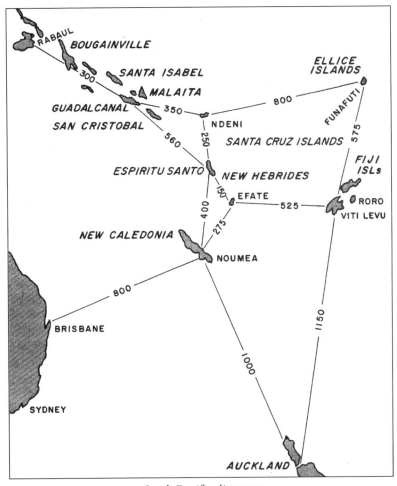

South Pacific distances.

emy planes at a respectful altitude—say 27,000 feet—but even from that height the Japanese high-level bombers, who were unprovided with the Norden bombsight, managed to lay their "eggs" with care and no mean accuracy. The captured 3-inch gun was turned against surfaced submarines; but most of them flaunted the Rising Sun impudently out of gun range, as did the Japanese destroyers whose guns outranged anything the Marines had. One of the submarines, *I-123*, ventured too near the converted minesweeper *Gamble*, which disposed of this boat very neatly in Indispensable Strait on 28 August.

Supplying Guadalcanal was a tough problem. The unloading so rudely interrupted on 9 August had deprived the troops of many coast defense guns, heavy construction equipment and half the required ammunition. Food supplies, husbanded by serving only two meals a day and using Japanese rice, could last but a month. There was not enough aviation material to operate a combat airstrip. Yet the transports and cargo ships, of which the South Pacific Force had few, were too vulnerable and valuable to be risked. Old converted destroyers with high speed and maneuverability were selected to do the job.

On 15 August the first destroyer-transport echelon—*Colhoun, Gregory, Little* and *McKean*—brought in aviation gas, bombs and ammunition, proving that it could be done. Their most important passengers were Major Charles H. Hayes USMC, the first operations officer of Henderson Field, Ensign George W. Polk and 120 men of "Cub One" to service the daily expected planes. Again, on 20 August the first three APDs brought in 120 tons of rations, enough for about three and a half days, and retired safely. Another vessel impressed into the lifeline was not so lucky. This was the old China river boat *Lakatoi*, acquired by the Navy and loaded at Nouméa with 400 tons of rations and ammunition. She might have made it had she not been fitted with a machine gun and a concrete shield to the wheelhouse, which made her top heavy. Three days out, after consuming several tons of the diesel oil that served as ballast, *Lakatol* "just turned over and sank." Her volunteer naval crew made land safely after two weeks in a lifeboat and rubber rafts.[36]

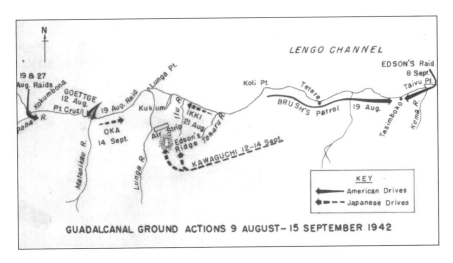

GUADALCANAL GROUND ACTIONS 9 AUGUST– 15 SEPTEMBER 1942

Putting the airfield into operation was a back- and heartbreaking task for the 1st Marine Engineer Battalion. The Japanese had merely cleared the ground and made a flat surface, which General Vandegrift wished to lengthen by another thousand feet. The tough, saw-toothed kunai grass resisted burning, and most of it had to be mowed by bayonets. A large hole in the center of the runway had to be filled by hand-loaded Japanese trucks and dump carts. Tropical rainstorms beat the field into a wallow of viscous mud which sucked at men's feet and swallowed up truck wheels. Even so, by 12 August the first plane, an amphibious Catalina, made a trial landing; and on the 17th Vandegrift informed Ghormley that Henderson Field, named after a Marine hero of Midway, was ready for use in dry weather. Hideouts were ready for the SBDs, an operations station was set up in the Japanese-built control tower known as the "Pagoda," Cub personnel organized fueling details and an air warning system; but barracks, mess halls, fuel tanks and the like were wanting and conditions were still embarrassingly primitive on 20 August when the first flight of Marine Corps planes alighted on Henderson Field.

In preparing his ground defenses, General Vandegrift wished to know where the enemy was concentrated. Patrols threading through the jungle to the west of Lunga River reached the Matanikau on 10 August, where they found the answer from numerous Jap automatic weapons that cut loose. But there was still doubt as to where the main enemy body was encamped. First Sergeant Stephen A. Custer of Division Intelligence proposed that a reconnaissance party be taken by boat to a position west of the Matanikau River, there to land and thence to probe the interior for enemy spoor.

A Japanese naval warrant officer taken prisoner admitted that the main body of his countrymen lay beyond the Matanikau and, on being pressed, admitted that "perhaps" they might be persuaded to surrender. This tied in neatly with a report of a white flag being displayed in the vicinity. Colonel Frank B. Goettge, division Intelligence officer, jumped to the conclusion that the enemy was starving and ripe for surrender, and took command of the reconnaissance party, which landed somewhere west of the Matanikau in pitchy darkness during the night of 12 August. Within a few minutes of landing they were ambushed and only three men escaped. Goettge, Custer, and many other valuable men were killed. As for the white flag, it had been an ordinary Japanese banner with the "meat ball" concealed in drooping folds. No treachery had been intended; but from that time on it was hard to persuade Marines to capture live Japanese, who in any case preferred death to capture.

U.S. Marines resting in the field before fighting the Japs on Guadalcanal.
National Archives.

A week later, on 19 August, another jab was made on the Matanikau sector, to keep the enemy off balance. Three companies of the 5th Marine Regiment, covered by artillery, made a three-pronged assault: from seaward, from the east and from the south. The villages of Kokumbona and Matanikau fell after a brief but spirited skirmish in which 65 Japanese and 4 Marines were killed. But Vandegrift had insufficient troops to extend his lines thither, so the three companies retired to the perimeter.

Battle of the Tenaru River, 21 August [37]

There were bigger doings on the Marines' eastern flank, the result of decisions made in Tokyo and Rabaul; Shortly after the American landings, General Tojo transferred the conduct of ground operations on Guadalcanal from Navy to Army. Lieutenant General Harukichi Hyakutake, commanding the Emperor's Seventeenth Army with headquarters at Rabaul, studied the situation and decided that 6000 troops would be sufficient to recapture the island. And, since that many soldiers were not available, he decided to commit what he had, fewer than 1000; for he estimated that there were only 2000 Americans on Guadalcanal, instead of the 17,000 actually there.

U.S. Marines reloading their howitzer. National Archives.

Colonel Kiyono Ichiki, originally slated to occupy Midway, was given the honor of retaking Guadalcanal. He embarked 916 men at Truk in six destroyers which entered Savo Sound on the night of 18 August and, unseen from the shore, passed eastward of the American perimeter to land unopposed in the vicinity of Taivu Point. His scheme was simply to move westward along the coast and destroy the Americans by flank assault. The day before, units of the Special Naval Landing Force landed at Tassafaronga.

The six destroyers indulged in a brief bombardment of Guadalcanal and Tulagi after landing the troops. They caught and destroyed a Higgins landing boat plying between the two bases, and plopped a few salvos onto the airfield and the Tulagi docks. This gave the Army's Flying Forts based at Espiritu Santo a chance to bomb the enemy in broad daylight. Hitting a squirming destroyer by horizontal bombing methods is a difficult business, and the B-17s did well to lay one egg on the after gun mount of destroyer *Hagikaze*. She got away, but the bomb was a clear warning to the Japanese that daylight operations around Guadalcanal were unhealthy.

The Marines were not completely in the dark about Ichiki. Major Martin Clemens and 60 native troops of the British Solomon Islands Defense Force went scouting to the eastward, as did a Marine patrol under Captain Charles Brush, on 19 August. Shortly after noon that day, Brush encountered an Ichiki patrol hiking westward and heedless of danger. The Marines neatly ambushed this force and wiped out 31 of the 34 men. A careful examination of the dead revealed that these Japanese were sleek, clean-shaven and well-dressed Army troops. Their pockets and dispatch cases bulged with charts, codes and diaries, which said very clearly that fresh enemy troops were ashore and that an offensive was in preparation on the east flank. They even had accurate maps of the Marines' positions. Fortunately the battalions of the 1st Marine Regiment had dug in on the left bank of the Ilu (Tenaru) River. They now laid wire, spread out a net of listening posts, installed a 37-mm gun and sat back to await developments. Early in the evening of 20 August a white flare seared the dark eastern sky, and individual Marines in listening posts reported Japanese patrols. Ichiki was on the move.

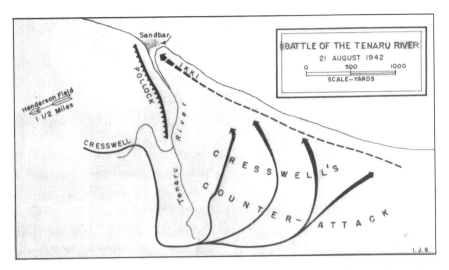

At 0130 on the 21st the battle broke on a dry sandbar, when the first Japs to arrive encountered the trip wire. Along this narrow 45-yard-long spit at the mouth of the river poured 200 Japanese infantrymen, shouting and screaming, with bayonets fixed, guns blazing and hand grenades popping. Lieutenant Colonel Pollock's battalion, strongly entrenched at the west end of the bar, turned rifles and machine guns against the attackers, while gunners of the Special Weapons Battalion gnawed away with 37-mm canister shot. Saber-waving officers in the van fell, but their men did not falter; some even overran the American positions, throwing giant firecrackers behind the Marines' lines to make them think they were surrounded. The Marines refused to be rattled. Riflemen stood toe-to-toe with the attackers and killed them with rifle butts, bayonets, machetes and knives. One private stripped a jammed machine gun and reassembled it while two pals kept the Japanese out of his emplacement with bayonets. Colonel Pollock brought up the battalion reserve and before daylight every Japanese who had forded the stream was dead.

As immediate victory had been assumed in Ichiki's plan, his men now milled aimlessly around in small groups which made convenient targets for the Marines. The survivors by daybreak were holed up in a coconut grove on the east bank of the river, well defended by water on two sides of a small triangle. Marines smothered the position with all kinds of fire and at the same time started envelopment from the south. Lieutenant Colonel Cresswell led his battalion upstream, crossed the river and by 1400 had the enemy squeezed tightly between the river on the west and the sea on the north.

The Japanese reacted viciously to envelopment by mounting a determined bayonet attack against the Marines on their southwest flank. Captain Stevenson's "C" Company held firm, then closed in with a successful bayonet charge of their own. Cresswell's next move was a full battalion assault which drove the desperate enemy from cover. Flight followed a frantic resistance; many took to the sea and drowned, others tried to slip through to the east. But the majority died from Marine bullets. About four in the afternoon a platoon of light tanks waddled over the stacked-up bodies on the bar and got to work. It was a great sight seeing them weaving through the coconut grove, knocking down snipers from the palms by butting at the trunks, and chasing survivors on the run. By nightfall Ichiki's force was virtually exterminated; the Colonel and some of his officers took leave by the suicide route. Thirty-five Marines lost their lives and 75 were wounded, many of them in the last mop-up—when some of the enemy, who had simulated death by

Japanese soldiers killed in the Battle of the Tenaru River, 21 August 1942. National Archives.

smearing themselves with blood, rose up with gun or grenade for a final effort. But the Marines had sent almost a thousand Sons of Heaven to the wrong address.

This Battle of the Tenaru River, a model of perfectly coordinated effort, fire and movement, freed the eastern flank. And its effects were far reaching. The Marines' first stand-up fight with the much touted jungle-fighting Jap proved to the Corps and to their countrymen that the American was the better fighting man, even on the enemy's chosen terrain. From that time on, United States Marines were invincible.

Henderson Field and the Seabees

An American motorship named *Mormacmail* had plied a drab but respectable trade of cargo and livestock transport between North and South America during the ten months following her completion in May 1940. Then came the national emergency. The Navy could not wait to build aircraft carriers from the keel up, so *Mormacmail* was acquired, a flight deck slapped on her topsides and a few guns mounted, and in June 1941 she was commissioned as the escort carrier *Long Island,* first of her kind in the U.S. Navy. Here she was, on 20 August 1942, carrying 19 Wildcats and 12 Dauntless dive-bombers of two Marine Squadrons,[38] with their crews.

From a position southeast of San Cristobal, *Long Island* catapulted the planes and retired. Coconut palms were pointing long shadows eastward when Lieutenant Colonel Charles L. Fike, executive officer of Marine Air Group 23, led his planes in for a landing on Henderson Field. The Colonel would have liked another six weeks' training before being turned loose on the Japanese air force, but the very next day his planes were mixing it with the enemy. Major John L. Smith, leader of his fighter squadron, chalked up Henderson Field's first kill, a "Zeke." Eighteen more planes would fall to the Major's guns in days to follow. And on the 25th Lieutenant Colonel Mangrum's SBDs bombed the ships that were hurrying in a second echelon of Ichiki's regiment, and postponed another enemy landing effort. It looked as if command of the sea would go by default if we commanded the air; but one needed both to hold Guadalcanal.

After the Battle of Tenaru River. The coconut grove.

The river mouth.

Within five days of their arrival at Guadalcanal, one third of the planes sent in by *Long Island* were washed out for one reason or another, and on 30 August only five of the original 19 Wildcats could fly. But help had come.

On 22 August, Henderson Field welcomed a portion of the Army's 67th Fighter Squadron composed of P-400s, a bastard version of the P-39 originally intended for export. These planes were practically useless as fighters since it was impossible to fly them high enough to catch the Japanese. But, as they were well armed with a 37-mm cannon and six guns each, they afforded the Marines close ground support by strafing enemy positions.

The Naval Air arm was first represented on Henderson Field on 24 August when the *Enterprise* contributed her dive-bombers. From that time on there was an irregular flow of all types of planes from every imaginable source. Nobody cared about lineage. If it had wings it flew; if it flew it fought; and if it fought very long, something was certain to happen to it. The trouble might come from a Japanese plane's machine guns, a concealed rut or bomb hole on the field, an enemy bomb hitting the parked plane, anti-aircraft fire, naval bombardment, bad weather, or just hard usage.

Henderson Field, Guadalcanal, shortly after the American occupation.

By the end of August, 19 more Wildcats and 12 SBDs had arrived. Colonel Wallace, commander of the group, took over from Colonel Fike while "Scat" (South Pacific Combat Air Transport) brought in a big bear of a Marine major general, Roy S. Geiger, as commander of all Allied planes flying out of Henderson Field.[39] There was nothing formal about command relation-ships. Marine, Navy and Army fliers flew on missions together, lived through bombing raids together, and many died together aloft or in foxholes.

On 1 September 1942 Marines posted on the Lunga waterfront observed Higgins boats, loaded to the gunwales with men and gear, putting off from transport *Betelgeuse* and heading for the beach. Curious leathernecks strolled to the water's edge, hoping to meet old friends among the newcomers. No such luck; these faces were those of "old men," frequently framed by gray hair. But their owners wore a quiet air of competence, as of men who had confronted life and bested its problems. These were the first Seabees, men of the Naval Construction Battalions, to reach an action area; and their good works would be a vital factor in the Guadalcanal campaign.

Rear Admiral Ben Moreell, Chief of the Bureau of Yards and Docks, was responsible for the organization of the Seabees[40] two months before Pearl Harbor. Shortly after, experience of unarmed civilian workers at Wake, Midway and Cavite, inefficient and useless in case of attack, proved that Moreell had the right idea. A large proportion of petty-officer ratings, a special insignia[41] and, most of all, the promise that they would be an integral part of the fighting Navy and provided with weapons, attracted skilled and patriotic artisans. Their officers, largely obtained from the Navy's Civil Engineer Corps or commissioned from the engineering professions, were granted full autonomy, a departure from the peacetime practice of allowing only line officers to command. The result of this effort was a military organization composed of carpenters, plumbers, metalsmiths, surveyors, road builders and the like, solid citizens of the average age of 31; men who could have stayed at home and earned high pay. All received basic military training, and so in case of need could substitute guns for tools, as they later proved both to delighted friend and discomfited foe.

The cadre which landed on Guadalcanal on 1 September consisted of a portion of the 6th Seabee Battalion, 387 men and five officers. Two bulldozers and other equipment came with them, and, they promptly took over from the Marine Corps engineers the maintenance and improvement of Henderson Field. In addition they tackled road, wharf and bridge construction, electric power installation, building tank farms and fuel lines, developing camps, base and raid shelters, and they brought in six 5-inch guns.

The Seabees found many enemies besides Japanese. The soil, for instance, was an elastic and unstable muck which stimulated the toughest former road boss to new heights of profanity. Daily tropical rains taxed drainage ditches and kept the mud from drying. Equipment was long in arriving, so Japanese trucks and power rollers were pressed into service along with the American bulldozers, half a dozen dump trucks, a grader and an excavator. But the worst enemy was the almost daily Japanese naval and artillery bombardment.

Yet no challenge remained unanswered by the Seabees. The existing portion of Henderson Field was put in shape by adding to the base material quantities of gravel, coral and clay and by raising a crown along the center. An extension was constructed by blasting coconut palms with Japanese powder and surfacing the new runway solid. Then a grid of Marston mat— perforated metal strips or "pierced plank"—was laid over the field to support planes in every kind of weather. A supplementary fighter strip, quickly constructed, handled all air traffic in October when Henderson Field was knocked out. Later, a second fighter strip was built. Work stopped only while bombs or shells were actually falling. Then the Seabees retired to foxholes and waited for the last explosive to "crump" before dashing back to the job. Trucks stood loaded with earth ready to fill new craters, but the Seabees also used their helmets as buckets. Commander Joseph P. Blundon USNR, Seabee skipper, described the task:

> We found that 100 Seabees could repair the damage of a 500-pound bomb hit on an airstrip in forty minutes, including the replacing of the Marston mat. In other words, forty minutes after that bomb exploded, you couldn't tell that the airstrip had

ever been hit. But we needed all of this speed and more. In twenty-four hours on October 13 and 14, fifty-three bombs and shells hit the Henderson airstrip! During one hour on the 14th we filled thirteen bomb craters while our planes circled around overhead waiting to land. We got no food during that period because our cooks were all busy passing up the steel plank. There were not enough shovels to go around, so some of our men used their helmets to scoop up earth and carry it to the bomb craters. In the period from September 1 to November 18, we had 140 Jap raids in which the strip was hit at least once.

Our worst moments were when the Jap bomb or shell failed to explode when it hit. It still tore up our mat, and it had to come out. When you see men choke down their fear and dive in after an unexploded bomb so that our planes can land safely, a lump comes in your throat and you know why America wins wars.

Shell craters are more dangerous to work on than bomb craters. You have a feeling that no two bombs ever hit in the same place; but this isn't true of shells. A Jap five-inch gun lobs a shell over on your airstrip and blasts a helluva hole. What are you going to do? You know, just as that Jap artilleryman knows, that if he leaves his gun in the same position and fires another shell, the second shell will hit in almost the same spot as the first one. So a good old Jap trick was to give us just enough time to start repairing the hole and then fire a second shell. All you can do is depend on hearing that second shell coming and hope you can scramble far enough away before it explodes. But this is a gamble which is frowned upon by life insurance companies.[42]

Life for sailors and Marines alike on the borders of Henderson Field was a hodgepodge of horror and discomfort. Foremost in nastiness were the constant attentions of the enemy, dropping air bombs day and night, sending naval shells crashing through palms and men and planes, firing field artillery from concealed positions at anything that moved. Marines who had occasion to spend a night at Henderson Field were always glad to get back to the comparative quiet of the front lines. Then there was the business of keeping the "crates" flying. There was never enough of anything—gasoline, starter cartridges, spare parts, tools, men or time.

Fliers even borrowed engine starter cartridges from the crews of Marine tank battalions. Rest was impossible. Air raid warning flags on the Pagoda kept men leaping in and out of foxholes at all hours. Just for variety, an earthquake one night helped murder sleep. Rain drenched them every night, and the heat roasted them every day. Anopheles mosquitoes squirted a man full of malaria while gastroenteritis sneaked into his guts and racked his bowels with enervating dysentery. Officers and men, pilots, ground crews, anti-aircraft gunners and Seabees were brothers in misery.

The exploits of the pilots who flew from Henderson Field will appear as the story of Guadalcanal unfolds, but we must also keep in mind the men of courage and good will who defended and developed the field. It was alike the target and the prize of sea battles, jungle assaults and bombardment missions. If we kept Henderson Field we would keep Guadalcanal and, someday, go roaring up the Slot toward Rabaul. If we lost it, our first Pacific offensive would have to be written off as a costly failure.

4. THE BATTLE OF THE EASTERN SOLOMONS (24 August 1942) [43]

The American landings in the Solomons had generated a typhoon of enemy reaction. The advance semicircle of this hurricane was the destructive Battle of Savo Island. On it swept, leaving a restless turbulence — the eye of the storm, promising more disaster when the rear and more dangerous half of the tempest broke. On 24 August it came: the Battle of the Eastern Solomons.[44] Japan had recovered naval initiative with the Battle of Savo Island; there was no doubt about that. The war lords at Tokyo were annoyed by the Marines' hold on Guadalcanal but confident that control of the surrounding waters would give them the island at their convenience. At Rabaul commanders of the Eighth Fleet, the Seventeenth Army and the Eleventh Air Fleet put their heads together to plan a Marine ouster before the end of August.

This Rabaul get-together resulted in the Japanese landings on 28 August which were expected to win the island in three days.

As we have seen, the Marines shot this plan and its executors full of holes at the Ilu River. Another conference must be called; more forces must be brought up.

The conferees decided on a new all-out effort, Operation "KA,"[45] commencing 24 August. A reinforcement of only 1500 troops would be supported by the entire Combined Fleet, a flexible organization which Admiral Yamamoto could expand or contract at will. Ships of all types were drawn from far corners of Greater East Asia. In preparation for the big push, planes of the Eleventh Air Fleet would hammer the Marine positions with daily bombings while the Eighth Fleet harassed them nightly with naval bombardment. The planes of two big carriers and one light carrier would dispose of United States surface interference. Finally the troops would be landed under cover of carrier planes and ships. This naval set-up seems elephantine in comparison with the small troop contingent, but it proved to be too little rather than too much. Scheduled operations in New Guinea would go forward as planned; the Japanese still considered Guadalcanal a side show, but not for long. Mobilization for Operation "KA" was speedy. By 21 August Admiral Yamamoto could place his stubby forefinger on the chart near Truk and cover the position of 3 carriers, 3 battleships, 5 cruisers, 8 destroyers, one seaplane carrier and numerous auxiliaries, all ready to move south at his command. And at Rabaul Admiral Tsukahara had 4 cruisers and 5 destroyers together with 100 planes of the Eleventh Air Fleet.

Japanese preparations did not escape the notice of Australian coastwatchers and American reconnaissance planes. [But,] no serious effort was made to drive off Mikawa's nightly surface raiders, who came so regularly down the Slot as to be named the "Tokyo Express" by disgusted Marines.

At daybreak 23 August, when the American carrier force was about 150 miles east of Henderson Field on the other side of Malaita, the Japanese Combined fleet was advancing from Truk in five main groups. First there was Admiral Nagumo's Carrier Striking Force, now shorn of the four flattops sunk at Midway, but still formidable, with two veterans of Pearl Harbor and the Coral Sea — *Zuikaku* and *Shokaku*. Slightly ahead of the carriers, Rear

Admiral Abe of Wake fame led the Vanguard Group composed of battleships *Hiei* and *Kirishima* and three heavy cruisers. Ready to be detached from the Striking Force was a Diversionary Group baited with small carrier *Ryujo* under the leadership of Rear Admiral Hara, who must have remembered somewhat uneasily what had happened to *Shoho,* the corresponding Yank-bait at Coral Sea. Vice Admiral Kondo, overall tactical commander of the Supporting Forces, had under his visual control[46] six cruisers and a seaplane carrier, which steamed far in advance of the Striking Force. Six fleet submarines swept ahead of him in line-abreast to act as scouts and weapons of opportunity, while three more took station in the Coral Sea west of the New Hebrides. The troops were carried in *Kinryu Maru* and four old destroyer-transports escorted by the famous Desron 2, Rear Admiral Tanaka commanding in light cruiser *Jintsu*. Yamamoto, unshaken in his basic strategy, intended to pull the old gambit of tempting the enemy to gang up on the insignificant *Ryujo* group, while planes from his big flattops struck the American carriers and Henderson Field was bombarded with heavy gunfire and 1500 troops got ashore.

One of Admiral McCain's patrol planes flying from tender *Mackinac* at Ndeni, Santa Cruz Islands, sighted enemy transports at 0950 on the 23rd and passed the word—two cruisers and three destroyers covering the troop vessels, speeding at 17 knots for Guadalcanal. This contact caused a flurry of excitement in Admiral Fletcher's task force. Captain DeWitt C. Ramsey passed on Flag's orders to the *Saratoga* air group—Attack with 31 SBDs and 6 TBFs. "Sara's" planes zoomed aloft at 1445, circled to gain height, formed in orderly ranks and sped over the northwest horizon. An hour and a half later, the Guadalcanal Marines launched a 23-plane strike at the same transports.

[Both were unsuccessful in locating the enemy forces.] By the end of the first dogwatch on 23 August, Admiral Fletcher had no positive intelligence of the enemy. "Sara's" planes had brought none; Pacific Fleet Intelligence believed the enemy carriers to be well north of Truk; no word had reached Fletcher of the recent course change of the Japanese transports. He was now beset by two familiar problems: fueling, and finding the enemy. Reasoning that a major clash would not occur for several days, Fletcher sent

Admiral Isoruku Yamamoto

Vice Admiral Nobutake Kondo

Noyes' *Wasp* group south to a fueling rendezvous as the destroyers were reported to be running short of oil. This was a bad guess; because Yamamoto had ordered a nonstop run to the Solomons, fueling at sea. The American force was thus deprived of one of its three carriers in a crucial battle.

At Guadalcanal the temporarily grounded *Saratoga* airmen were treated in mid-watch to a nuisance bombardment by destroyer *Kagero*. It was ineffective, but the guests passed an uncomfortable night, stimulated only by an occasional shot of "jamoke" tendered by the hospitable Marines. The carrier planes were held in readiness pending reports from the dawn search. When Marine scout aircraft reported no contacts, they flew back to *Saratoga,* landing on board at 1100 August 24.

See Appendix B for composition of Japanese and United States Forces.

The Battle Joined, 24 August

While *Saratoga's* planes were coming on board from Guadalcanal, four of her Wildcats led by Lieutenant David C. Richardson were chasing a Japanese snooper located by radar some 20 miles from the carrier; Richardson got the first "Emily" (a four-engine flying boat) to be encountered. There was great jubilation in *Saratoga* over this, the first kill made as a result of her fighter-director crew vectoring out combat air patrol.

At 0905 August 24, an American PBY spotted carrier *Ryujo,* about 280 miles northwest of Fletcher's now two-carrier force. At 1345 Fletcher took the offensive, launching 38 bombers and torpedo planes to snap at the bait. Within one hour, his search planes discovered *Shokaku* and *Zuikaku,* some 60 miles farther north than *Ryujo.* Fletcher attempted to divert his strike to the big carriers; but communications that afternoon were abominable and he could not reach the pilots. Commander N. D. Felt's air group attacked *Ryujo* successfully, and at 2000 she was swallowed up by the sea.

Admiral Nagumo decided that the hour had come to avenge Midway. At 1507 and 1600, two attack groups rolled off the decks of *Shokaku* and *Zuikaku.*

Poseidon and Aeolus had arranged a striking setting for this battle. Towering cumulus clouds, constantly rearranged by the 16-

knot southeast tradewind in a series of snowy castles and ramparts, blocked off nearly half the depthless dome. The ocean, two miles deep at this point, was topped with merry whitecaps dancing to a clear horizon, such as navigators love. The scene—dark shadows turning some ships purple and sun illuminating others in sharp detail, a graceful curl of foam at the bow of each flattop, the long bow of *North Carolina* (a recent arrival from the Atlantic), *Atlanta* bristling like a porcupine with antiaircraft guns, heavy cruisers stolid and businesslike and the destroyers thrusting, lunging and throwing spray—was one for a great marine artist to depict. To practical carrier seamen, however, the setup was far from perfect. Those handsome clouds could hide a hundred vengeful aircraft; that high equatorial sun could provide a concealed path for pouncing dive-bombers; that reflected flare of blue, white and gold bothered and even blinded the lookouts, and made aircraft identification doubtful. Altogether it was the kind of weather a flattop sailor wants the gods to spread over the enemy's task force, not his own.

As at Midway and Coral Sea, each carrier group, in a tight circle about two miles in diameter, was independent of the other. *Enterprise* operated ten miles northwest of *Saratoga*.

Fletcher was ready for Japanese bombers with 51 Wildcats, mostly from *Enterprise,* stacked in three layers as Combat Air Patrol. At 1629 August 24 the attack group was only ten miles away. Dive-bombers and torpedo planes helped C.A.P. to intercept it. About 24 dive-bombers got through, one diving about every seven seconds. *Enterprise* took three bombs—which killed 74 men, ruptured her decks and wrecked the 5-inch guns; but good damage control saved the ship. *North Carolina* also attracted enemy attention, but she drove off or shot down 14 bombers that got through C.A.P. By 1647 this main attack was finished, and *Enterprise* at 1749 headed into the wind to recover planes. But "Big E's" troubles were not over; delayed effects of two bombs stifled the steering engine and jammed her rudder. By amazingly quick and courageous work this was brought under control at 1859, just when the second Japanese attack wave should have come in; but it missed the carriers altogether.

None of the attackers got through to *Saratoga,* but she hit back at the enemy. Five TBF and two SBD under Lieutenant Harold H. Larsen were scrambled to counterattack. At 1745 they attacked Kondo's Advance Force, badly damaging seaplane carrier *Chitose,* and were back on board "Sara" by 1930. They had no fighter cover, and they were only seven, on a mission for which tenfold the number of planes would have been assigned later in the war. Gallant lads these; none braver.

Admiral Fletcher now decided to call it a day, and turned southward toward a fueling rendezvous. His two carriers, amazingly, had lost only 17 planes. Kondo sent his van of battleships and cruisers in pursuit, but gave it up and retired before midnight.

Neither commander regarded the battle as finished, but to all intents and purposes it was, except for Admiral Tanaka's reinforcement unit. His destroyers pranced up and down off Lunga Point that night, bombarding the Marines' perimeter. Next morning, 25 August, the Marines' own air group from Henderson Field badly damaged Tanaka's flagship *Jintsu* and a transport; while a B-17 actually sank a destroyer, which caused amazement on both sides. The Battle of the Eastern Solomons was over.

The Battle of the Eastern Solomons, third of the great carrier

USS Enterprise under attack during the Battle of Eastern Solomons

engagements of the war and second of the naval actions center-
ing around Guadalcanal, was not a decisive battle. But it did prevent the 1500 Japanese troops from landing and, as Admiral Nimitz
wrote, "The Japanese had shot their bolt and with air forces seriously reduced were retiring." And the diary of a Japanese officer
at Guadalcanal remarked pertinently, "Our plan to capture
Guadalcanal came unavoidably to a standstill, owing to the appearance of the enemy striking force." [47]

5. ATTRITION TACTICS (28 August – 5 September) [48]

Colhoun Sunk, *Sara* Smacked

The six weeks following the Battle of the Eastern Solomons
was the one period in the Guadalcanal campaign when gnawing
at the other fellow's extremities was more fashionable than slashing at his vitals. Admiral Ghormley initiated a continuous movement of cargo ships from Noumea to supply the Marines, and in
order to protect these ships from air attack he established carrier
patrols covering the main approaches. To augment and cover this
defensive employment of naval vessels, he planned to harry the
enemy at sea and in harbor with land-based aircraft from
Guadalcanal, the New Hebrides, New Caledonia, New Guinea and
Australia. At the same time several submarines were stationed
where they could do the most harm. But Commander South Pacific wisely refused to commit his ships piecemeal, knowing they
would still have to reckon with the Japanese Fleet. And the enemy, since the Henderson Field bombers were not numerous
enough to stop him, accepted his losses at the Battle of the Eastern Solomons and kept reinforcing his Guadalcanal garrison by
"Tokyo Express."

Although Lieutenant General Hyakutake in Rabaul still regarded
the Guadalcanal campaign as secondary to taking Port Moresby,
he decided to commit some 3,500 more troops, under Major General Kiyotake Kawaguchi. The first echelon, in four destroyers,
entered Indispensable Strait on 28 August. Toward evening two
Dauntless scouts spotted them, shouted for help and made an in-
effectual bombing attack. At 1800 eleven of Mangrum's Marine

Corps dive-bombers arrived over the enemy, then some 70 miles north of Guadalcanal, and did a very workmanlike job. Destroyer *Asagiri* blew up with a terrific explosion after being hit by a 500-pound bomb and sank almost immediately. Destroyer *Shirakumo* was stopped but left afloat; *Yugiri's* superstructure was well burned. The landing was called off and the one undamaged destroyer took *Shirakumo* in tow for a painful return trip to the Shortlands. Only one American plane was lost in this highly successful raid.

It took more than that to discourage Hyakutake. Next day five destroyers sortied from the Shortlands and landed 450 soldiers on Taivu Point, east of the American perimeter, after dark. On 30 August, elements of General Kawaguchi's detachment were again embarked for a southward dash, in destroyer *Yudachi,* and a diversionary air attack not only protected her but exacted revenge for the loss of *Asagiri.*

The victim was fast transport *Colhoun*, converted from a four-stack destroyer. She and sister ship *Little* were covering a small auxiliary ship, *Kopara*, that was discharging stores at Guadalcanal. At 1415, in response to an air alert, the three vessels got under way for Tulagi. At 1512 a formation of twin-engined bombers appeared almost overhead, directly in the glare of the sun. *Colhoun's* men had but a short glimpse of 18 planes flying in two large Vees, when the enemy disappeared into the clouds. Lieutenant Commander Madden rang up full speed while his gunners prepared to shoot at any plane within range of *Colhoun's* pitifully inadequate anti-aircraft guns.

Those guns never had a chance. The enemy had already released two sticks of bombs which, with phenomenal accuracy for horizontal bombing, hit all around and upon the little ship. On so thin-shelled a vessel the effect of several near-misses, exploding in the water only 50 feet away and evenly spaced from bridge to fantail, was devastating. The hull lurched violently to port, the foremast toppled, 4-inch guns were twisted from their mountings, main engines, boilers, pumps and piping were torn from their fastenings, and the ship began to sink rapidly by the stern. Chief Quartermaster Saunders tried to work his way aft to the steering-engine room but was stopped when two more bombs struck, one on the after deckhouse, the other on the after engine room. Fuel oil burst into flames and prevented repair parties from approaching the damaged areas. Madden, realizing his command was a sinking shambles, ordered his executive officer to place the wounded in boats, but the boats were shattered. Within two minutes of the time the enemy planes were discovered, *Colhoun* went down with 51 men; the rest were picked up by tank lighters from Guadalcanal.

That night *Yudachi* landed her troops safely at Taivu.

On 31 August, the same day that *Sara* was hit, the Japanese successfully ran the aerial blockade with seven or eight destroyers, which discharged 1200 more troops—including engineers, artillerymen, anti-tank units and General Kawaguchi himself— on the west flank of the Marines' perimeter. The attempts of General Geiger's airmen to hold up these "Tokyo Express" runs were as a rule unsuccessful. Their SBD-3s were only good for a 200-mile radius of action and for months there were not enough of them, or enough fuel, to launch an attack group every day. The Japanese were able to plan their reinforcement echelons, in the twelve-

USS Colhoun APD-2 sunk.

hour nights of that latitude, so as to start a fast run-in within an hour of darkness, debark troops and supplies in a few minutes, and be 175 miles or more up the Slot when day broke. Thus they were visible and vulnerable to air bombers only for a short time coming and going, and the SBDs had to figure on bucking a tropical thunderstorm at least one way. Efforts to hit vessels unloading were fruitless, except on the rare unclouded moonlit midnights, because the blacked-out Japanese ships soon learned not to give away their position by gunfire. And the primitive form of radar with which Catalinas tried to find them could not distinguish ships from an adjacent shore.

Situation, 1–6 September

A curious tactical situation had developed at Guadalcanal; a virtual exchange of sea mastery every twelve hours. The Americans ruled the waves from sunup to sundown; big ships discharged cargoes, smaller ships dashed through the Sound, "Yippies"[49] and landing craft ran errands between Lunga Point and Tulagi. But as the tropical twilight performed its quick fadeout and the pall of night fell on Ironbottom Sound, Allied ships cleared out like frightened children running home from a graveyard; transport and combat types steamed through Sealark Channel while small craft holed up in Tulagi Harbor or behind Gavutu. Then the Japanese took over. The "Tokyo Express" of troop destroyers and light cruisers dashed in to discharge soldiers or freight, and, departing, tossed a few shells in the Marines' direction. But the Rising Sun flag never stayed to greet its namesake; by dawn the Japs were well away, and then the Stars and Stripes reappeared. Such was the pattern cut to fit the requirements of this strange campaign; any attempt to reshape it meant a bloody battle. The Japanese rarely, and then only disastrously, attempted daytime raids with ships; the Americans more frequently interfered with the night surface express, but any such attempt proved to be expensive.

Little and *Gregory* Lost, 5 September

During the night of 4–5 September an event occurred that recalled the tribulations of the Asiatic Fleet. Destroyer transports *Little* and *Gregory*, sister ships to sunken *Colhoun*, were still acting as water taxis for Marines and their supplies. Following an unconfirmed rumor that the enemy had occupied Savo Island, they ferried the 1st Raider Battalion from Tulagi to deal with the situation. But no Japs were on Savo. The Raiders reembarked and were taken to Guadalcanal, where they landed at dusk. Under normal circumstances both ships would have returned to Tulagi Harbor, but the night was unusually dark and no landmarks were visible. Commander Hugh W. Hadley, division commander in *Little*, decided to patrol off Lunga Point during the night, steaming two to six miles off shore and parallel to the beach.

It so happened that the Japanese chose that night to land another group of Kawaguchi's detachment and, in addition to troop-carrying APDs, sent three destroyers, *Yudachi*, *Hatsuyuki* and *Murakumo* to provide diversionary bombardment.

On entering Savo Sound in the opening hour of the midwatch, the Japanese bombardment force passed well to seaward of *Little* and *Gregory*, so that neither force sighted the other. At 0100 September 5, just as *Little* was reversing course from 130° to 310°, occasional gun flashes were observed to the eastward; destroyer *Yudachi* and friends had opened fire on the beach. The deck watch in both American ships jumped to the reasonable conclusion that the gunfire came from a Japanese submarine conducting a nuisance bombardment. Both officers of the deck went to general quarters and called their skippers, in anticipation of an anti-submarine skirmish. Weary sailors, routed out of their bunks by the clamor of the general alarm, dressed hastily, sharing the feeling of one boatswain's mate that it was just routine gunfire "a good piece off."

But *Little's* radar showed four distinct contacts almost dead astern and only two miles distant. A tough choice lay before Commander Hadley. He could turn and run while still undetected, a logical but distasteful decision for any skipper; or, relying on his radar and on surprise, he could try a hit-and-run battle which might scare the enemy off. As ill luck would have it, neither choice could be followed.

The fatal agent in this case was a Navy Catalina flying over

Savo Sound and trying to be helpful. The pilot, probably unaware of the presence of *Little* and *Gregory*, also believed that the gun flashes came from a surface submarine, and decided to show it up. Scarcely a minute after *Little's* radar had indicated the real enemy, Helpful Harry released a string of five flares only half a mile ahead of the two destroyer-transports. It was like one of those bad dreams where you find yourself naked on Broadway. Japanese gunners, at first startled by the illumination, soon spotted the APDs and shifted their guns and searchlight accordingly. *Little* struck out at the enemy with every gun that could bear: one 4-inch, some 20-mm, .50-caliber and .30 caliber machine guns—all woefully ineffective against modern destroyers. The Japanese in the meantime were feeling for the range. Their first two salvos were over, the third short, but the fourth connected with the American's stern. One shot penetrated the steering-engine room, one entered the after fuel tanks, and another put the after 4-inch gun out of action. Fuel oil burst into brilliant flames. *Gregory* drew attention of another searchlight and accurate 5-inch salvos followed. Explosions shredded her bridge, knocked down the after stack, pried open the galley deckhouse, burst a boiler and killed seamen with jagged hunks of metal. Flames pranced from stem to stern; *Gregory's* fighting days were over.

On board *Little*, Lieutenant Commander Lofberg decided to beach his ship. But the hit in the steering-engine room had jammed her rudder; other hits knocked out the few remaining weapons, ruptured the main steam line and ignited the Higgins boats. There was only one course open, to abandon ship. But before he could carry out his order, Lofberg and Commander Hadley were killed on the bridge.

Gregory, too, had to be abandoned, but a boatswain's mate and a coxswain[50] helped their badly wounded skipper, Lieutenant Commander Harry F. Bauer, over the side. They were pulling him clear of the suction and burning oil, when he heard through the darkness a sailor cry out that he was drowning; Bauer ordered his would-be rescuers to go to the man's assistance, and he was never seen again.

Both ships were already lifeless and burning hulks, but the Japanese, to make certain of their kill, steamed between them at high

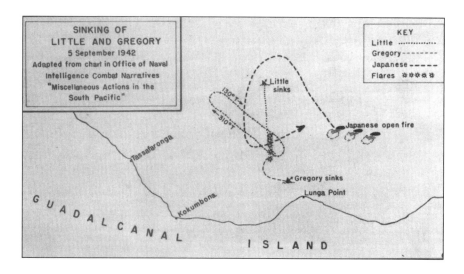

speed firing shells, some of which killed floating survivors; finally satisfied, they left the area at about 0135 September 5. The survivors spent a miserable night in shattered boats, overturned life rafts and shrapnel-torn life jackets. Planes sighted them at daybreak from Guadalcanal and directed landing boats to the rescue.

Admiral Turner in his report justly said: "The officers and men serving in these ships have shown great courage and have performed outstanding service. They entered this dangerous area time after time, well knowing their ships stood little or no chance if they should be opposed by any surface or air force the enemy would send into those waters. On the occasion of their last trip in they remained six days, subjected to a daily air attack and anticipating nightly surface attack." [51]

6. THE SEPTEMBER CRISIS

Raid on Tasimboko, 7–8 September

Events were building up to another crisis. Toward the middle of every month from August to November inclusive, the Japanese made a major effort to recapture Guadalcanal. Their pattern in every instance was the same; only the forces varied. First, for a week or ten days, the "Tokyo Express" made nightly runs landing reinforcements; owing to the excellent work by American airmen

based on Henderson Field, the Japanese would not commit capital ships to Savo Sound in daylight. In the meantime Admiral
Yamamoto mustered the Combined Fleet at Truk and drew up an
operation plan which would be sparked off when the Emperor's
ground forces captured the airfield; but he was also ready to
accept a sea battle whenever challenged. For the September show,
Yamamoto provided a carrier-battleship-heavy cruiser force, similar
to the one engaged in the Battle of the Eastern Solomons, with
orders to await developments north of Santa Isabel and Malaita.

General Kawaguchi, who, as we have seen, landed before the
end of August with his first echelon at Taivu, east of the Marines'
perimeter, had the mission of capturing Henderson Field. His plan
involved three separate attacks against each flank and the rear of
the Marine lines, to be followed by an amphibious assault on the
beachhead.[52] D-day was to be 12 September, and Kawaguchi
promised his superior officer, Hyakutake, that by 10 October the
Marines would be eliminated and he could shift his headquarters
from Rabaul to Henderson Field. This strategy was a curious re-
versal of principles that had come down from the pre-air age. Instead of counting on a fleet to secure command of adjacent waters
before pressing a land assault, the Japanese decided they must
capture the air base before challenging their enemy's fleet. Billy
Mitchell would have approved, but it didn't work.

Kawaguchi's engineers on 2 September began hacking a trail
from Taivu through the jungle to a chosen point of attack southeast of Henderson Field. In the meantime, Allied native scouts
and aerial reconnaissance caught occasional glimpses of
Kawaguchi's main body of troops. The natives reported correctly
that they were several thousand in number; but the Marines discounted Melanesian arithmetic and estimated enemy strength at
about 500. Deciding that a full battalion of fresh troops would be
sufficient to deal with them, Vandegrift ordered over from Tulagi
the 1st Raider and 1st Parachute Battalions, amalgamated under the
command of Colonel Edson. Tulagi could hardly be called a health
resort, but it was a paradise compared with the sodden coastal
plain of Guadalcanal, and Edson's men were both rested and
eager. They were first brought to Kukum and there embarked at

1800 September 7 in destroyer transports *McKean* and *Manley, YP-346* and *YP-289*.

Edson's raiders landed east of Taivu Point at dawn 8 September. A lucky break gave them a pushover. Transports *Fuller* and *Bellatrix* happened to be steaming along the coast on other business, but Kawaguchi thought they were going to pull a major landing and withdrew his entire force inland. *McKean* and *Manley* made a second trip with reinforcements, and as the Marines moved westward, covered by strafing planes from Henderson Field, the enemy retreated, losing a battery of artillery. He made a desperate stand at Tasimboko village, then fled into the jungle. Tasimboko turned out to be a main supply depot stocked with artillery, ammunition, rice, medical supplies and equipment which the raiders gleefully destroyed. Late in the afternoon Colonel Edson reembarked his men, taking a fine haul of interesting enemy documents as well as General Kawaguchi's wardrobe of white full-dress uniforms with silk facings. "The bastard must have been planning to shine in Sydney society," was the comment of a Marine. Only two men were killed and six wounded out of nearly 600 in this successful foray.

The only flareback occurred because of the unconscious transport ruse. Admiral Kusaka ordered an air raid that gave *Fuller* and *Bellatrix* a few bad moments, and Admiral Mikawa dispatched cruiser *Sendai* and eight destroyers down the Slot after them. Failing to locate the transports that night, this force bombarded Tulagi Harbor and hit *YP-346,* wounding three men and driving the little craft aground.

The Battle of the Bloody Ridge, 12–14 September

General Kawaguchi, like so many of his compatriots, followed a pattern. His original plan with its devious complications was so pretty that he clung to it even after the Tasimboko tip-off. So on he went to his destruction.

In the Marine command post, General Vandegrift and staff studied the terrain map with misgivings. As there were not nearly enough troops properly to defend the entire perimeter, he decided to beef up the sectors most likely to receive the blow. The

Ilu (Tenaru) River was one such, and to it went Lieutenant Colonel McKelvy's 3rd Battalion 1st Marine Regiment, which extended the eastern flank to a length of two miles inland. The western flank was deemed strong enough for anything that might come that way, but in the rear there was a weak two-mile stretch between the Lunga River and the western flank, open except for two strong points, one held by the 1st Pioneer, the other by the 1st Amphibian Tractor Battalion. Since every Marine receives basic training as an infantryman, Vandegrift was confident that these specialists could hold their own until reserves could be brought up.

East of the Lunga River there was another two-mile hole in the perimeter, occupied only by knots of artillerymen, engineers and pioneers. Yet something could be done to thwart the enemy. Studying the map and the ground itself, Colonel Edson called Vandegrift's attention to a grass-covered ridge which ran south from the airfield. This is the feature that came to be known as "Edson's Ridge" or "Bloody Ridge." Higher than the surrounding jungle trees, it commanded the airstrip and would be a natural assault channel to Henderson Field, particularly as the jungle-covered flats on either side afforded excellent cover. Edson's combined Raider-Paratroop Battalion, returning from the Tasimboko affair, prepared positions on this ridge. Flank support on the right rear was furnished by the 1st Pioneer Battalion, and on the left rear by the 1st Engineer Battalion. And, right after the mêlée began, Brigadier General Pedro del Valle of the Marines' artillery regiment sighted his 5th Battalion's 105-mm howitzers and his special weapons battalion's automatic weapons, in positions to render direct support.

September 12 was supposed to be Kawaguchi's day of victory. He had picked out the same ridge, just as Edson had anticipated, and committed the main body of his men to advance both alongside and on top of it. A small detachment took position still farther east. Daylight on the 12th saw numerous skirmishes between patrols; but, when evening fell, Kawaguchi began probing for weak spots in the Marine line. One group even broke through, cut off a company of Marine raiders and disrupted communications; but still Kawaguchi refrained from an all-out drive.

Meanwhile, the Japanese air force based at Rabaul delivered a bombing attack which cost them 4 "Zekes" and 10 bombers, shot down by intercepting Wildcats and Marines' anti-aircraft fire, but placed a stick of bombs right down the center of the Ridge. Fortunately they inflicted little damage. One of Mikawa's cruisers and three destroyers chimed in with a haphazard night bombardment which failed to distinguish between friend and enemy. In this "rest area," as Colonel Edson jokingly described the Ridge when another officer asked where the Marines were going next, there was little sleep on the night of 12–13 September. When the Japs were not jabbering down on the jungle flats, they were charging the Ridge in bayonet attacks. By morning the Marines were worn out and General Vandegrift was worried, since he had few reserves. Edson's men dug in and prepared for another scrap. The 13th passed with a series of small raids; the Marines were too few to take the offensive, and the Japanese waited for night. A relief battalion under Colonel Whaling camped south of the airfield, ready to relieve the raiders.

Kawaguchi's soldiers were tired, too, after a long march through

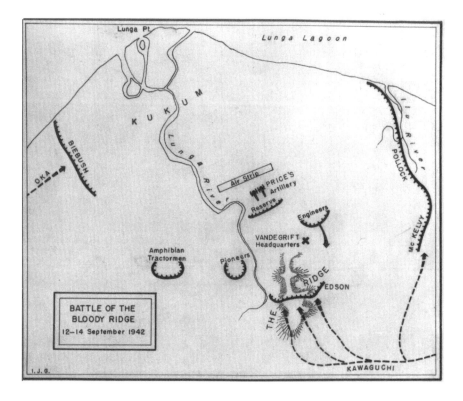

the jungle and successive charges; but they still felt confident when they saw their "Eagles" make raid after raid on Henderson Field. As night fell on the 13th, the last Nip plane left for Rabaul and Kawaguchi's soldiers whetted bayonets for the charge. They had no artillery preparation, because most of their big guns were on the bottom of Sealark Channel, where Edson's men had dumped them after their raid on Tasimboko.

A red rocket flared over the jungle, and the Japanese began to scream and drop heavy mortar fire into the Marine line. It held, but the enemy managed to find a hole in the jungle to the west of the Ridge, where he pushed back one raider company and out-flanked another, while pressing heavily against the fronts of the rest. The outflanked company fought its way clear, then took up defensive position again. At 2100 General del Valle's 105-mm how-itzers, commanded by Colonel Price, opened up and fired furi-ously all night long, slinging shells over the Ridge at the attackers. Communication was broken between the three batteries and their observers on the Ridge; the gunners then fired wherever the Japa-nese sent up rockets, their signal for each fresh attack.

At 2230 the Emperor's men delivered a howling charge on Edson's left flank. Hoping to demoralize the paratroops, enemy soldiers shouted in English: "Gas Attack! Marine, you die!" and laid down a covering smoke screen. The Marines were not fooled, but the ferocity of the assault pushed them out of position and exposed the flank. Edson now had his center company, 60 men under Captain John B. Sweeney, sticking out like the prow of a ship into a sea of maddened Japs. In the swirling darkness it was imperative to maintain contact, so the Colonel ordered his forward troops back to the last knoll of the Ridge, only 1500 yards short of Henderson Field. There they stayed while the Japs literally beat their brains out against a wall of steel from artillery, mortars, machine guns, rifles and grenades. General Vandegrift watched and listened from division headquarters only a quarter of a mile away, and a few intrepid men ventured near enough to be killed by his headquarters staff. Time and again a rocket flowered red, rallying the enemy to brave and bloody action. Time and again they were driven back. On each occasion some of the Japanese

The Bloody Ridge after the battle.

pressed resolutely through the dreadful barrage, halted briefly to illuminate the Marines with calcium flares, then swept up the last few yards of the slope, screeching defiantly before crumpling under the impact of close-range automatic fire.[53] By 0230 September 14, Colonel Edson and his executive officer, Lieutenant Colonel Griffith, were certain their men's lines would hold. And at dawn the last charge flickered out.

Day broke silently except for bird calls and the shrilling of insects, but it uncovered a grisly scene. Those tumbled hillocks, soon to be named the Bloody Ridge, were littered with Japanese bodies sprawled in the pitiful and repulsive attitudes of death. Now every plane that could fly took the air, and with their strafing machine guns herded Kawaguchi's survivors back into the jungle.

Kawaguchi's two other attacks were more easily repulsed. His eastern prong also pushed in during the night of 13–14 September, choosing the inland flank of McKelvy's Ilu River defenses. Two companies attacked positions protected by barbed wire, skillfully placed machine guns and determined riflemen. They accomplished nothing. The western prong attacked a day late. Lieutenant Colonel Biebush's 3rd Battalion, well wired-in on a small grassy ridge south of Kukum and supported by 105-mm pack howitzers, fended it off easily.

Forty Marines died on Edson's Ridge and 103 were wounded, one fifth of all Americans engaged. But, of the 2000 or more Japs who participated, 600 fell on the Ridge and hundreds more died of wounds on their long, roundabout retreat to the coast. An estimated 200 more were lost in the fight with McKelvy. About 400 of those who straggled westward, cutting trails behind the perimeter, eventually staggered into Kokumbona. When Kawaguchi counted noses, almost half of his 3450 troops were no longer present or accounted for.[54] It would be another month before he could resume the offensive.

The Battle of the Ridge was one of the crucial ground actions of the Pacific War. It was won by Edson's inspired leadership, and the skill and courage of individual Marines. If this battle had been lost, Henderson Field would have been lost, and the Marines would have been hard put to hold the island.

Wasp's Sacrifice, 15 September

On 14 September, when the Marines were engaged in burying enemy dead, a convoy of six transports carrying the 7th Marine Regiment sailed from Espiritu Santo, covered by cruisers and destroyers. It was well known that enemy battleships and carriers were lurking north of the Santa Cruz Islands, that other formidable forces were poised in the central and northern Solomons, that eager enemy bombers were nested on Rabaul and Bougainville fields, and that nearly a score of submarines were waiting for targets in Solomon Islands waters. But Guadalcanal had to be reinforced. To protect the transports against carrier or big-gunned opponents, Ghormley committed his two sound carriers, *Hornet* and *Wasp;* the latter had already run a plane-ferry mission to reinforce Henderson Field on the 12th. The task force built around them steamed in distant support, out of sight of the transports and their screen. In the hope of keeping knowledge of the troop convoy from the enemy until it was ready to land, Turner plotted a course well to the east of the normal approach. All day long on the 14th, the air was blue with reports of plane contacts on carriers and battleships to the north and "Tokyo Express" groups to the northwest. *Hornet* launched a search attack group but the enemy carriers retired before being found.

By the morning of 15 September Kelly Turner's mind was weighed down with responsibility and apprehension. The 7th Marine Regiment, the only one available in the South Pacific for reinforcement of Guadalcanal, could not be exposed to attack in the defenseless state before or during disembarkation. When, at noon, one of the lumbering Kawanishi bombers was detected snooping his formation, Turner felt certain of an ugly reception if he kept going. He made the hard decision to retire temporarily and await a more favorable opportunity, but held the convoy on its course until nightfall to deceive the enemy into thinking it was still closing Guadalcanal.

The carriers, meanwhile, were cruising from a position south of the 12th parallel of latitude and about a hundred miles from the Turner transports.Exploratory flights in quest of enemy forces developed nothing, and the two carrier groups ambled along at

16 knots on a westerly course, occasionally swinging to a south-easterly heading for flight operations. September 15 was a perfect South Pacific day, with a fresh 20-knot southeast tradewind, a white plume on every wave and hardly a cloud in the sky. Four cruisers and six destroyers surrounded *Wasp,* flagship of Rear Admiral Leigh Noyes, while five or six miles distant steamed *Hornet,* squired by battleship *North Carolina,* three cruisers and seven destroyers. Since early morn there had been but one brief flurry of excitement: a snooping "Mavis" detected by radar had been shot down by combat air patrol beyond visual range of the task force. On flight decks planes were gassed and fully armed, but there was no indication as yet of anything to attack.

Wasp, responsible that day for combat air and anti-submarine patrol, turned into the wind at 1420 and slowed down to launch and recover planes. In short order, 18 SBDs and eight Wildcats took the air from the flight deck; three of one and eight of the other landed on board. This operation was watched with keen interest by a submerged enemy submarine, *I-19,* one of those sent into the area to knock off the 7th Marine transports. None of the six destroyers around *Wasp* had yet picked up the boat on their sound gear when the carrier's commanding officer, Captain Forrest P. Sherman, sounded the routine whistle signal for a turn, bent on 16 knots, and brought rudder right standard for a return to her base course, W by N. While the ship was swinging in the turn, her lookouts shouted a warning of torpedoes on the starboard side. *I-19* had just fired a spread of four "fish" from a position to the southwest of *Wasp.* They were approaching from three points forward of the starboard beam, running "hot, straight and normal" and already very, very close. Captain Sherman ordered the rudder full right but it was too late. Two racing warheads struck deep, forward on the starboard side; a third broached, then dove under to hit the hull about fifty feet forward of the bridge; a fourth missed ahead and ran harmlessly under destroyer *Lansdowne.*

The ferocity of the explosions buffeted men and gear like a Kansas twister. Planes on flight and hangar decks took the air vertically only to fall back and smash their landing gears. Planes suspended from the hangar deck overhead ripped loose to fall on other planes and on men. An engine-room switchboard tumbled over; generators were pulled from their foundations. Fire broke out, spreading to ready-ammunition and to airplanes full of fuel and bombs. Oil and gasoline—the gasoline pumping system was in use—spread the scurrying tongues of fire. The writhing of the ship's hull broke all forward water mains, which boded ill for fire fighting. Decks canted crazily as the ship took a heavy starboard list.

Captain Sherman discovered that he still had telephone communications with the engines, the damage control center and the after steering station. By telephone he ordered engines slowed to 20 knots and rudder full left to get the wind on the starboard bow; then he rang up "back" on all engines and ordered right full rudder until *Wasp* had the wind on her starboard quarter, blowing the fire away from her undamaged portion. The pilothouse was filled with smoke and flying fragments.

On watch in the engine room at the time of the hit was Chief Machinist Chester M. Stearns, who immediately took steps to correct the heavy list. At his direction Chief Watertender Coffee, the "oil king," shifted fuel from low to high side. Shortly thereafter, the engineer officer arrived and relieved Stearns. In a brief time the list was reduced to 4 degrees, the engines answered all bridge orders and repairmen busily worked on generators and switchboard. That was most important, for if electrical power failed steering would be impossible, the ship's head would fall off and smoke would suffocate the men throughout the ship. Machinist's Mate Holmes put an after generator in operation and furnished precious "juice" to the steering engine where Seaman Cornell followed the captain's telephoned instructions to the helm.

Wasp's troubles were bad enough for one afternoon but the Japanese were not yet through. Submarine *I-15,* keeping company with *I-19,* observed the success of her companion and attempted to duplicate the performance, selecting *Hornet* as the prospective victim. A spread of torpedoes slithered out of her tubes and headed for *Hornet's* position some five miles NNE of *Wasp.*

These torpedoes were not unheralded, for the sight of *Wasp* as a pyramid of flame had given rise to much conjecture. Had one of the carrier's planes caught fire, or was the trouble a result of enemy activity? *Lansdowne* squawked a warning by voice radio when the one torpedo which missed *Wasp* passed beneath her, but not every ship got the word and it remained for destroyer *Mustin* on *Hornet's* port bow to arouse the task force. She sighted a torpedo wake ahead and to port, turned hard left to avoid it, hoisted the torpedo warning signal and repeated the alarm by voice radio. She was lucky; the "fish" passed under her keel without touching. But it had only a 500-yard run from *Mustin* to *North Carolina* and, despite evasive measures instantly taken, the ponderous ship was unable to dodge. At 1452 the characteristic pillar of water and oil marked a score for *I-15*.[55]

North Carolina demonstrated that new battleships could take it as well as dish it out. The torpedo, striking forward on the port side and 20 feet below the waterline, killed five men, opened a wound 32 feet long by 18 high, caused flooding through four bulkheads from the skin of the ship and sent a flash into No. 1 turret handling room. The captain ordered the forward magazines flooded. But none of the damage kept "Carolina" from holding her station in formation, even at 25 knots. Damage control removed a 5.5-degree list in as many minutes.

That was only one of *1-15's* torpedoes. At 2454 *O'Brien,* a few hundred yards on *North Carolina's* quarter, sighted a torpedo to port and continued her swing to the right so that the warhead

Wasp burning; O'Brien hit.

passed a man's length astern. Meanwhile the gunnery officer from his post above the bridge sighted another torpedo and shouted a warning. There was no time for the skipper to duck this one; with a resounding roar the explosion jerked open a section of the bow from keel to hawsepipe, leaving the destroyer looking like a huge fish with its mouth agape. The ship vibrated like a coach whip, dislodging machinery and hull fittings and throwing men to their knees; happily there was no fire.

Wasp in the meantime was being eaten alive by fire. Faster, and faster the swirling yellow flames moved, taller and taller they flared. Around 1500 a terrible explosion shook the entire ship, propelling gases into the bridge and island structure. Several men on the port side of the bridge were killed and Admiral Noyes had a close call when he was thrown onto the signal bridge deck, with singed face and burning clothes.

Captain Sherman and his assistants now evacuated the bridge to take control of the ship from Battle II, the after station. They were just in time, for another severe explosion on the hangar deck lifted the No. 2 flight-deck elevator into the air, crashing it down all askew.

Although nobody would then have believed it, there were still living men on *Wasp's* forecastle. Officers in the wardroom country and steward's mates taking their midafternoon siesta in their bunk rooms, both directly below the hits, were slaughtered. But many individuals, in forward staterooms, on gun stations and in bow compartments, were able to make their way forward. Asphyxiating gas billowed around these men and it soon became apparent that encroaching fires would drive everybody into the sea. But the water offered perils too, a film of burning oil and gasoline ringed the bow completely and it was not until several hardy souls had led the way by plunging in and swimming under the fires that the majority were convinced that salvation required the hazardous jump. On the hangar deck Lieutenant Raleigh C. Kirkpatrick could see nothing forward except an opaque wall of fire. He noted little knots of men vainly trying to use the various sprinkling systems, but no water came. A continuous din of popping machine-gun ammunition, bursting gas tanks and exploding bombs prevented orders from being given other than by gesture. A canvas curtain was pulled across the hangar deck and moistened in order to confine the fire; fire hoses were led from aft, but weak water-pressure made them of little use. The explosion which swept the Admiral off his feet tossed the hangar deck fire fighters aft, like chaff before the wind. The forward elevator pit was now an active volcano.

Captain Sherman held a conference with officers from the hangar deck and came to the reluctant conclusion that the fire was completely out of hand. He expressed this opinion to Admiral Noyes and with the latter's approval ordered Abandon Ship at 1520.

Strangely little of the ship's sore troubles was known in the engineering spaces. There were electrical difficulties, and escaping steam from a split condenser shell made conditions uncomfortable but not unbearable. The engineer officer, Lieutenant Commander Ascherfeld, and his assistants were somewhat startled when the word came to leave, and it was not until they reached the inferno of the hangar deck that they realized how far gone the carrier really was.

The conduct of the crew while leaving the ship was marked by courage and good will. The badly injured were tenderly lowered over the stern, to be given space on life rafts and floating mattresses. Chief Carpenter Machinsky, one of the last to leave, searched the hangar deck for lumber and mattresses to assist the men in the water. Finally, at about 1600, Captain Sherman left his ship.

Wasp survivors were picked up by escorting destroyers, but not before several depth-charge attacks on suspected submarines had given them some uncomfortable belly jolts. Rear Admiral Norman Scott in *San Francisco,* assuming from *Wasp's* inflamed appearance that Admiral Noyes was lost, took over command of the task force, and when Noyes was picked up by *Farenholt* he directed Scott to retain the command. It was obvious that *Wasp* could not be saved, so the sooner she went down the better. *Lansdowne,* selected to deliver the *coup de grace,* fired five torpedoes. All hit and three exploded. At 2200 September 15 the carrier, which had survived all attempts by U-boats in the Atlantic and the Mediterranean and which had saved Malta, succumbed at last. [56]

Of the 2247 souls on board, 193 were killed, 366 wounded. All but one of 25 airborne *Wasp* planes were safely recovered by *Hornet*. That evening radio operators of the task force had the humiliation of hearing from Radio Berlin "Enemy 22,000-ton carrier has been sunk." *1-19* had escaped and passed the word.

In *Hornet's* task group, *O'Brien* reported that she could make 15 knots and at 1600 she was detached with orders to proceed independently to Espiritu Santo, where she arrived the next day. At dusk *North Carolina* with two escorting destroyers was detached and directed to Tongatabu. She was repaired in Pearl Harbor, acquiring at the same time more and better anti-aircraft guns. *O'Brien*, temporarily patched in Espiritu Santo, made passage to Nouméa, where the crew of a tender made further repairs and a naval constructor passed her as fit to proceed to the West Coast. He made a bad mistake. The shock of the torpedo detonation had caused such a violent flexural vibration of the principal ship girder that her longitudinal strength was insufficient for a long voyage. She steamed 2800 miles before a temporary strengthening member let go. Then despite reduced speed the hull began to work, more cracks opened up, leakage got out of control, and on 19 October, off Samoa, she broke in two and sank.

Not one of the three ships torpedoed on the afternoon of 15 September could be easily spared. In the seven weeks since the first Americans had stepped ashore on Guadalcanal, Pacific Fleet carrier strength had dwindled from four to one; but the enemy, even after his carrier losses at Midway, could still muster two big ones and a number of light carriers. The damage to *North Carolina* left only one new battleship, *Washington,* operating in the Pacific. *O'Brien,* specially fitted with extra anti-aircraft firepower, carried guns which *Hornet* would miss in future battles.

Admiral Turner and his six transports were still at sea awaiting a favorable chance to deliver the 7th Marine Regiment to Guadalcanal. He felt that their situation was hazardous but not hopeless, and on 16 September decided to push on so as to be off Lunga by dawn on the 18th. "Stout hearts make safe ships," the old adage in days of sail, was again tested by this bold amphibious commander; and he won through. Hazy weather concealed his convoy from lurking subs; MacArthur's fliers crashed through with some handsome bombing raids on Rabaul airfields; the Japanese task force that had been prowling about north of Guadalcanal withdrew. The convoy made Lunga Roads without further incident and, at 0550 September 18, the 7th Marines began flowing ashore in the most orderly fashion of any American debarkation to date. Tanks, vehicles, weapons, bullets, food, fuel and assorted supplies along with nearly 4000 men were landed in twelve hours. Destroyers *Monssen* and *MacDonough* paraded up and down the enemy-held sections of the beach, throwing 5-inch shells ashore —to the vast delight of the Marines and distress of the enemy, as he himself reported.

Admiral Turner's ships departed in the evening of 18 September for Espiritu Santo and Nouméa. No attack of any description occurred on the entire round trip. For that happy ending Turner could thank the American carriers, which had discouraged Yamamoto from taking positive offensive action.

Wasp was not vainly sacrificed.

A group of Marine Officers. August 1942.

7. FIGHTING ALONG THE MATANIKAU
(23 September – 9 October 1942) [57]

The 18th of September, when Admiral Turner brought in Colonel Sims' 7th Marine Regiment, was a big day for Vandegrift's men. Although they had given the Japs a thorough whipping on the Bloody Ridge only four days before, they wanted reinforcements badly, and the arrival of the 7th Marines made it possible to draw up a plan which the General called "active defense." It was now known that the enemy's strength lay west of the Matanikau River, in a part of Guadalcanal made to order for defense: steep, jungle-clad hills, kunai grass ridges commanding every approach, and deep woody ravines running down to the sea. As a "cross corridor" advance would be very expensive and probably unsuccessful against an enemy in such terrain, Vandegrift's staff planned an enveloping movement from the interior; this they planned to start promptly in order to keep the Japanese off balance. Edson, now Colonel of the 5th Marine Regiment, was in overall command.

This operation made a bad start on 23 September. Lieutenant Colonel Lewis Puller's 1st Battalion of the 7th Marines was given

Night action. Courtesy National Archives.

the inland route along the slopes of a series of hills (Grassy Ridge or Mount Austen) six miles southwest of Henderson Field. The land, furrowed like a crumpled wad of foolscap and matted with jungle growth like barbed wire, slowed the men to an exhausting crawl and the Japs rushed down on them from Mount Austen. Unable to cross the Matanikau in the time allotted, Puller turned north to parallel the stream and reached the mouth at night on the 26th. The 1st Raider Battalion, now commanded by Lieutenant Colonel Griffith was sent upstream from the mouth of the river that day, to make a crossing at the Nippon Bridge. Lieutenant Colonel McDougal's 2nd Battalion 5th Marines was poised at the river mouth, ready to assist either of the others. Before the raiders reached the bridge the enemy, from the other side of a clearing, let loose a vicious fire which killed Major Kenneth Bailey, one of the heroes of the Bloody Ridge. The only way to get at the enemy was to mount a steep, jungle-clad hill which commanded his position. It was a tough, four-hour climb up the hill, and after reaching the top Griffith was severely wounded and the raiders were recalled to the mouth of the Matanikau. It was now 27 September.

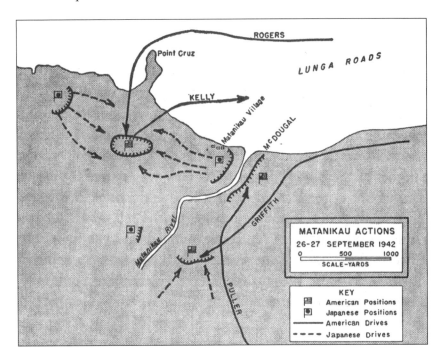

In order to solve the impasse at the river, three companies of Puller's 1st Battalion under Major Otho L. Rogers embarked in Higgins boats the same day, to land west of Point Cruz where, owing to a garbled transmission by portable radio, they supposed Griffith to be. They landed after a rough trip dodging air bombs, but had advanced only a quarter of a mile when Japanese troops got between them and the beach and killed Major Rogers. The Marines deployed in a circle on a kunai-grass knoll to fend off attack from all directions, laying their undershirts on the ground to spell the word HELP. A friendly plane spotted the improvised ground panel and reported by radio to division headquarters, but a bomb had just plumped into headquarters and knocked out communications. Colonel Puller, suspecting that his men were in difficulties, boarded the destroyer *Monssen* at Kukum and steamed right over to Point Cruz that afternoon. When the beleaguered Marines sighted her, Sergeant Raysbrook stood in full view of the enemy and arm-signaled their situation to the ship. Puller ordered them to move down to the coast while *Monssen* covered their withdrawal with a naval barrage. The two companies fought their

Point Cruz, Guadalcanal.

way to the beach and established a tight defense ring. A Coast Guard petty officer, Douglas A. Munro, led in from *Monssen* five Higgins boats, occupying the Japs long enough with his two small boat guns to get the Marines clear, and in so doing lost his own life. Withering fire met the boats when they went in for a second load, so Henderson Field sent an SBD to make a strafing run and cover the retreat.

This four-day exchange of unpleasantries near the Matanikau had cost the Marines 60 killed and 100 wounded, and gained nothing except experience. As one of the officers involved in it remarked to the writer, "high commanders of ground forces are apt to lose their appreciation of time and distance; they forget how long it takes a column to move over tortuous ground, to climb rugged hills, and how long it takes for orders to be disseminated to the echelons that do the fighting."

For the next ten days the Marines strung barbed wire, sowed land mines and sighted artillery in order to release men for a second attempt to secure the Matanikau.[58] Six battalions were ordered to jump off on 8 October.

The Japanese chose the same day to start a similar drive, a warming-up for the monthly big show. General Hyakutake, in order to overwhelm the Marines, whose numbers he now estimated at 7500, reverted to his original plan of throwing in 25,000 men, including Lieutenant General Maruyama's 2nd Division. Part of another division was left at Rabaul in readiness to move into New Guinea as soon as Hyakutake should receive Vandegrift's surrender. His operation order even named the spot on the Matanikau where Vandegrift was to appear with a white flag on or about 15 October.

"This is the decisive battle between Japan and the United States," read Maruyama's address to his troops on 1 October," a battle in which the rise or fall of the Japanese Empire will be decided. If we do not succeed in the occupation of these islands, no one should expect to return to Japan alive." Apparently some of his men were becoming skeptical of this fanfaronade, judging from entries in captured Japanese diaries of a day or two later. For instance: "Where is the mighty power of the Imperial Navy? . . . The strength of the enemy is increasing . . . the morale of our forces is going down. . . . How long can we live on in this sort of a condition? When I think of it, the tears come out."

The first step was to secure both banks of the Matanikau for the use of Maruyama's artillery. Colonel Nakaguma, commanding the 4th Infantry Regiment, brought his battalions into line on the west bank ready to thrust across the river in two prongs, one inland and the other along the beach. But the Marines took the initiative. On 7 October two battalions of Colonel Edson's 5th Regiment swept forward along a front whose right flank rested on the shoreline. Before they reached the river they flushed an advance enemy force and backed it into the bend a few hundred yards upstream from the river mouth. The raiders were brought forward on the 8th to deal with this group. In the meantime Colonel Whaling's 3rd Battalion 2nd Marine Regiment marched upstream and bivouacked near the coconut-log Nippon Bridge.

During 8 October, a day of heavy rain, both sides were bogged down in jungle mud. At nightfall the Japs, cooped up on the east bank, came out of their foxholes screeching, shooting and hurling grenades, mauled the raiders severely in hand-to-hand fighting and broke through to a river sand spit where they were held up by a wire barricade and finally wiped out.

Vandegrift, seeing signs of the impending full-scale drive, decided to keep his reserves in the perimeter and ordered Edson to

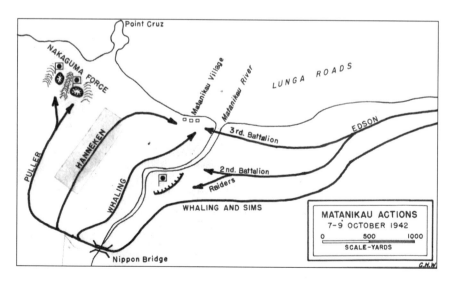

conclude his operation in a hurry. On 9 October, as the hot sun made the jungle steam and the Marines sweat, Whaling's battalion crossed Nippon Bridge and marched down the west bank unopposed. Lieutenant Colonel Hanneken's 2nd Battalion 7th Marines followed, pushed a little farther to the westward and then struck north to Matanikau Village on the coast. They too found no Nips. Where were they? Puller's battalion, which crossed third, probed along a trail about half a mile west of the river. As his men struggled over rugged ground they suddenly came upon two ravines filled with Nakaguma's troops, whose weapons enfiladed the coast road but afforded them no protection inland. Puller by radio asked Del Valle's artillery to lay down a barrage on a group directly in his path, and at the same time turned his own mortars on a group farther west. The resulting shower was more than Japanese flesh could bear. Panic-stricken soldiers scrambled wildly up the slopes, where Puller's machine-gunners sprayed them relentlessly, the survivors sliding back into the ravines to be chased up again by mortar and artillery fire. This grim routine continued until Puller had exhausted his ammunition and most of the human targets. A captured diary later revealed that 690 of Nakaguma's men had perished, most of them in the cul-de-sac.

Late in the afternoon of 9 October the attack force returned to the American lines, having lost 65 killed and 125 wounded. Vandegrift left his 5th Regiment guarding the east bank of the lower Matanikau as the key to his western defenses, since the shore road was the only possible approach for enemy tanks and wheeled vehicles. His good judgment was later confirmed.

Across Ironbottom Sound, the 2nd Marine Regiment had been enjoying a relatively quiet tour of duty on Tulagi. The only operation of consequence began on the same day as Puller's victory. About 45 officers and men, under Lieutenant Colonel R. E. ("Bunker") Hill, were ferried to Aola Bay, Guadalcanal, 30 miles east of Lunga Point where, in a two-day operation, they wiped out a small Japanese base at the mouth of the Gurabusu River at small cost to themselves. Vandegrift could now disregard any enemy threat from the east.

Despite Nakaguma's reverses, Japanese preparations for the

big push continued. On 9 October General Hyakutake landed on Guadalcanal to direct the campaign, and on the 11th ships came down the Slot carrying heavy artillery and protected by a covering group of heavy cruisers. But they encountered Task Force 64, commanded by Rear Admiral Norman Scott; and the ensuing Battle of Cape Esperance was one of the most interesting of the campaign.

8. THE BATTLE OF CAPE ESPERANCE
(11–12 October 1942) [59]

This campaign of attrition was indecisive and unsatisfactory to both competitors in the bid for Guadalcanal supremacy. The American Navy in the South Pacific, still smarting from the sting of Savo Island and the loss of valuable carriers and destroyers, daily plagued by the submarine denizens of "Torpedo Junction,"[60] longed for active retaliation. The Marines, embittered by the nocturnal hammering of the "Tokyo Express" and the apparent paucity of the supply and reinforcement effort, grew increasingly restive. On board Japanese ships and around their campfires there was an even stronger feeling of "On to Victory!" since they disliked war in less than blitz tempo. At the very depth of this winter of our discontent came the battle off Cape Esperance—which, if far short of glorious summer, gave the tired Americans a heartening victory and the proud Japanese a sound spanking.

Unwitting occasion of this naval battle was the 164th Infantry Regiment of the Americal Division, a former National Guard outfit from the Dakotas, now reinforced to about 2837 officers and men. The 164th constituted the next echelon of reinforcement for the hard-pressed Marines. Admiral Ghormley, assuming that the Japanese would take a hostile view of the passage of this regiment from Nouméa to Lunga Point, marshaled naval forces to give them constant protection and cover. The distant covering forces, three in number, consisted of Rear Admiral Murray's *Hornet* carrier group, Rear Admiral Lee's *Washington* group and Rear Admiral Norman Scott's cruiser group. It was this last on which fell the onus of blocking for Admiral Turner, who brought up the soldiers in *McCawley* and transport *Zeilin,* with eight destroyer-type escorts.

On 9 October this transport group sailed from Nouméa. Course was set to pass north of San Cristobal, head west through Lengo Channel and anchor in Lunga Roads on the morning of the 13th. Of the distant support forces, *Hornet* took station off Guadalcanal some 180 miles southwest of Henderson Field, *Washington* maneuvered about 50 miles east of Malaita, and Norman Scott's team (TF 64) was poised in the vicinity of Rennell Island. Admiral Scott,[61] flying his flag in *San Francisco,* considered himself lucky. He had orders from Admiral Ghormley to protect the convoy by offensive action, to "search for and destroy enemy ships and landing craft." It was the perfect assignment for an aggressive sailor. His staff was small and to his liking: four young and ambitious lieutenants.

Scott in three weeks had given his task force intensive training for night action, simulating battle conditions by keeping crews at stations from dusk to dawn; a Spartan procedure which taught them how to take it. He was ready to accept a night action, in which the enemy had hitherto shown superiority, and he intended to be master of the situation. His scheme was to stay outside the enemy's air range until noon and then turn north to a position whence he could reach Savo Island before midnight. Scott, moreover, was one of the first task force commanders in the Pacific to enter combat with a carefully drawn battle plan. According to this plan his ships were to steam in column with destroyers both ahead and astern; destroyers were to illuminate with searchlight, fire torpedoes at large targets and guns at

Rear Admiral Norman Scott USN.

small targets; cruisers were to open fire whenever they saw a target without waiting for orders; cruiser planes would locate and illuminate the enemy with float lights; if the Japanese proved to be strong in destroyers, the force would be divided to reduce torpedo hazard.

On 9 and 10 October Admiral Scott made tentative advances toward Cape Esperance only to turn back when aerial reconnaissance reported no suitable targets.

Admiral Mikawa's scheme required that troops be landed off the northwestern cape of Guadalcanal every night, while the Marines were heckled with naval gunfire or aerial bombing. So far he had been successful: destroyers, carrying an average of 150 soldiers each, had on several occasions discharged as many as 900 men a night. But on the afternoon of 8 October, bombs from Henderson Field fliers derailed the "Express" so effectively that traffic down the Slot was snarled for twenty-four hours; but on the 9th, about midnight, *Tatsuta* and five destroyers landed General Hyakutake and troops at Tassafaronga, despite a bombing by American aircraft en route.

These attacks by Henderson Field fliers sorely tried Admiral Mikawa's temper. He appealed to Vice Admiral Kusaka, Eleventh Air Fleet commander at Rabaul, to do something. Kusaka offered to neutralize Henderson Field on the 11th if Mikawa would run express that day, and he was as good as his word. On the afternoon of 11 October Henderson Field suffered a visitation of some 35 Japanese bombers protected by 30 fighters; but the former dumped their loads harmlessly in dense jungle and the latter shot down only two American planes at a cost to themselves of 4 "Zekes" and 8 bombers. Yet they kept the American airmen so busy defending their base that Mikawa's southbound surface force was not molested.

Fortunately the long-legged patrol planes were not affected by this raid. It was a B-17 of Colonel L. G. Sounders' 11th Bombardment Group that first reported two cruisers and six destroyers tearing down the Slot. Two more air contacts were made that afternoon; at 1810 the enemy force was less than a hundred miles from Savo Island.

Admiral Scott received this intelligence eagerly. He signaled his approach order, and at 1600 throttlemen commenced building up speed to 29 knots. The enemy might reach Guadalcanal before midnight but Scott would be there first.

The search reports were correct as to enemy heading but short as to strength. Mikawa had sent a bombardment group consisting of heavy cruisers *Aoba, Kinugasa* and *Furutaka* (which we have already met off Savo Island) with two destroyers, and a reinforcement group, comprising seaplane carriers *Nisshin* and *Chitose* with six destroyers, to bring in troops and supplies.[62] The bombardment ships, like Scott's, had just completed several days' tactical and target practice in the Shortlands. Mikawa considered this a routine mission and let the cruiser division commander, Rear Admiral Goto, take the command.

See Appendix C for the Task Organizations for each side.

Crossing the "T," 2100 – 2400

On board Scott's speeding vessels sunset was marked by bugles and boatswain's pipes, followed by "All hands man your battle stations!" Sailors moved to their action posts on the double. Steel doors clanged shut. Over the complex telephone circuits reports streamed to the department heads, and from them to the quiet bridges:

> "Bridge! Bat Two, manned and ready for General Quarters."
>
> "Bridge! Gunnery Department, manned and ready for General Quarters."
>
> "Bridge! Damage Control, manned and ready for General Quarters, Condition Zed set throughout the ship."
>
> "Bridge! Engineer Department, manned and ready for General Quarters, Condition Zed set. Boilers 1, 2, 3 (etc.) on the line."

As the tropical darkness shut down, Admiral Scott swept his eyes upward and around the horizon. Sky slightly overcast; the sliver of a new moon just setting; a smooth sea ruffled gently by a 14 knot southeast breeze, a dark horizon brightened at intervals by flashes of distant lightning.

Ships in the Battle of Cape Esperance: USS Duncan (at top), USS San Francisco.

Good weather for surprise. He knew his radar would be handicapped by the proximity of land, but the enemy had no radar. On the other side of the world, at New York and Norfolk, mighty forces were starting for North Africa. They had so much and he so little! Well, he'd show those fat boys of the Atlantic Fleet that SoPac could win victories "on a shoestring."

For a week or more, the Japanese had been running nightly Tokyo Expresses to northwestern Guadalcanal, and a particularly strong one was due on the night of 11–12 October: two seaplane carriers and six destroyers carrying troops and a vast amount of ammunition and materiel, commanded by Rear Admiral Joshima. In addition, Rear Admiral Goto brought down the Slot a bombardment group of three heavy cruisers and two destroyers. These

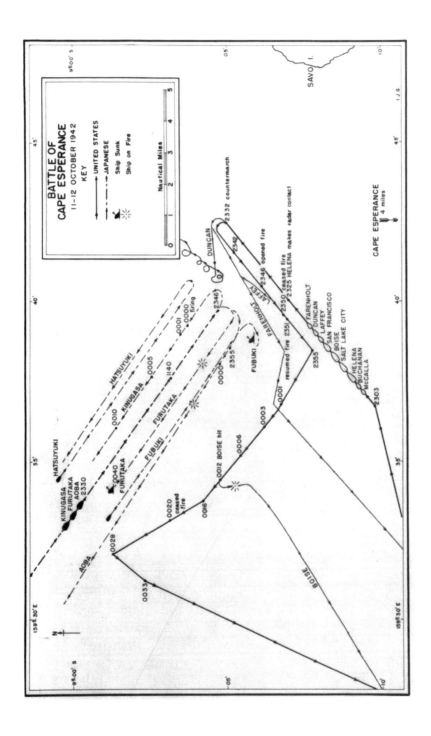

were reported by a B-17 to Admiral Scott in the early afternoon of the 11th. He built up speed to intercept them west of Savo Island, launched his cruisers' floatplanes to track them, and Goto was completely surprised when Scott's cruisers opened gunfire at 2346.

The American task force (five destroyers, heavy cruisers *San Francisco* and *Salt Lake City,* and light cruisers *Boise* and *Helena*) was just executing a countermarch, southwest of Savo Island and north of Cape Esperance, Guadalcanal, from which this battle is named. The range of *Aoba* at the head of the Japanese column, to *Helena,* was only 4800 yards.

So far, so good; but this might have been called the Battle of Mutual Errors. Scott, fearing that his cruisers were firing on van destroyer *Duncan,* ordered Cease-Fire only one minute after firing began. Fortunately the American cruiser commanders, emulating Nelson at Copenhagen, turned deaf ears to this order and their gunners continued to pump shells into the enemy ships. Admiral Goto, thinking that Scott's column was Joshima's Reinforcement Group (then safely within the Sound), did the same, and ordered his column to turn right. A few seconds later the Admiral was mortally wounded by a shell explosion near his flag bridge. By that time, both *Aoba* and *Furutaka* were burning brightly. At 2351 Scott discovered his error and ordered Resume Firing. Four minutes later he swung his column northwest to parallel the Japanese. Partly as a result of Goto's bad guess and sudden death, the enemy never returned an effective fire, and lost cruiser *Furutaka* and destroyer *Fubuki* to gunfire and torpedo hits. On our side, *Duncan* was mortally wounded and *Farenholt* badly so; *Boise* was badly pounded by two enemy cruisers, her No. 1 turret breached and a magazine exploded. But the luck of the Irish and good damage control saved the "Galloping Ghost," as the men called Captain "Mike" Moran's cruiser, to fight another day. The main action was over at 0020 October 12.

In the meantime Admiral Joshima was setting ashore the contents of his Reinforcement Group. At 0250 a floatplane from *Boise* sighted his formation steaming out of the Sound. Bomber planes summoned from Henderson Field sank two of his destroyers which were combing the scene of the action for survivors.

Scott's Score

Norman Scott fought the Battle of Cape Esperance with a cool, determined courage. Despite the trouble caused by an intricate countermarch, he never let the situation deteriorate into a mêlée. His ignorance of the varying capabilities of different types of radar was almost universal in the United States Navy in 1942. Later commanders learned that proper use of radar could eliminate the searchlights and recognition lights which attracted enemy gunfire as a candle attracts moths. [63]

Unfortunately, because it is human to conclude that the result justifies the means, some fallacious conclusions were drawn from this battle. Thus, Scott was convinced that his long single-column formation was all right and that American gunfire could master any night battle situation. Actually his disposition was dangerously unwieldy and prevented the destroyers from exploiting their proper weapon, the torpedo. And because the surprised enemy did not get off his usual torpedo attack, that was assumed to be no longer a serious threat. So, because we won the Battle of Cape Esperance, serious tactical defects were carried over into subsequent engagements with unfortunate results. One learns more from adversity than from success.

Savo Island was a victory for the Japanese, but the American transports were not touched; Cape Esperance was an American victory but the Japanese accomplished their main object. Not only did fresh troops get ashore at Tassafaronga while Goto and Scott were fighting, but seaplane carriers *Nisshin* and *Chitose* unloaded heavy artillery, which meant trouble for the Marines. Nor did Scott's victory prevent the Japanese from inflicting a heavy air raid on Henderson Field on 12 October (fortunately with very bad aim) or the heaviest bombardment yet two nights later (unfortunately with very good aim).

Cape Esperance helped American morale, spared the Marines one night of bombardment, and punctured Japanese confidence in their superiority at night fighting. "Providence abandoned us and our losses mounted," says one of their official reports." But the decisive naval battle of the Solomons was yet to be fought.

9. MID-OCTOBER MISERY (13–17 October 1942)

"The Bombardment," 14 October

Sunrise 13 October revealed the gray hulls of Admiral Turner's transports bringing up the 164th Infantry Regiment of the Americal Division; a heartening sight for Marines, particularly for the 1st Raider Battalion which was scheduled to provide these transports with return passengers. Out on the fringes of the perimeter things were looking much better; patrols pushed to the west of the Matanikau River without hindrance. On Henderson Field also there was cause for optimism. Ninety operational aircraft, about equally divided between dive-bombers and fighters, were scattered in the dispersal areas; and though the gasoline supply was low replacement prospects were good.

Events shortly proved that American optimism was premature. At noon about 24 Japanese bombers, flying nearly six miles high, made an unexpected and accurate bombing run over Henderson Field. Two hours later, while American fighter planes were fueling, 15 more bombers came in and left the field looking like a slice of Swiss cheese. No sooner had the Seabees filled the holes than a new and disgusting Japanese character made his bow with a shrill whine followed by an explosive thud, smack in the middle of the airstrip. This was "Pistol Pete,"—the heavy field artillery unloaded on the 11th, and now laid on Henderson from well-concealed positions beyond the Matanikau. When he opened up again on the evening of 13 October, destroyers *Sterett, Gwin* and *Nicholas,* covering the unloading, took him under fire and silenced him, though not for long.

While this was going on Japanese naval officers were talking on the darkened flag bridge of battleship *Kongo,* headed for Guadalcanal. Vice Admiral Takeo Kurita, Combatdiv 3, discusses with his staff gunnery officer, Commander Yanagi, the details of an interesting operation planned for that night. Over nine hundred 14-inch bombardment shells are ready in battleships *Kongo* and *Haruna,* but less than three hundred of them are the thin-skinned HE (high explosive) kind especially designed to tear Marines and their planes apart. The rest, all AP (armor-piercing) may not even explode against soft ground and yielding coconut palms, and at best will only blow a big hole in the ground. The two officers review their plan carefully. Four destroyers, already sweeping ahead of the battleships, will give warning of any ships in the area, then torpedo them. The battleships, screened by light cruiser *Isuzu* and four or five destroyers, will pass between Santa Isabel and Florida Islands, leaving Savo Island on the port hand, and catapult float planes for gunfire spot. Then watch the fireworks!

Shortly before midnight the drone of a low-powered observation plane is heard over Henderson Field, and at a few minutes after 0100 October 14, sixteen 14-inch guns break the silence with monstrous thunder which echoes from the mountains of Guadalcanal. A bright, unwinking flare descends from the observation plane, affording the aviator and Japanese observers in the hills a sharply defined picture of the airfield. The first shells plant orange-red seeds of flame to mark the target. Kurita's fire control parties calculate range data and apply corrections radioed in from plane pilots and land observers. The Admiral and his gunnery officer note with growing elation how each salvo starts new blazes until the entire airfield is a field of fire.[64]

Marines crouch in their foxholes and speculate. There is something disturbingly different about this bombardment. The ground shakes as the shell pattern walks back and forth, shattering planes and storehouses, setting off fuel dumps, knocking down trees, killing men or tearing their bodies with jagged fragments. One 14-inch shell bursts in General del Valle's command post. Newly arrived soldiers of the 164th Infantry wonder if this is what life on Guadalcanal is always like.

On the beach at Lunga Point, searchlights waver to and fro seeking the source of this misery; star shell daubs the darkness with flickering yellow splotches. Five-inch naval guns ashore bark savagely but ineffectively; the battleships are outside their range. Over on Tulagi, Lieutenant Alan R. Montgomery is awakened by the thud of distant explosions. He can do something. Only the day before he had brought four motor torpedo boats to Tulagi for just such an emergency. Montgomery calls his four young skippers— all junior grade reserve lieutenants: Henry S. Taylor of *PT-46,* Robert C. Wark of *PT-48* and the Searles brothers, John M. of *PT-*

60 and Robert L. of *PT-38.* Go get 'em!

All four pile in eagerly. A spirited but baffling action is joined with the Japanese destroyer screen, the PTs firing torpedoes, shooting machine guns and receiving plenty of near misses from 5-inch shells. The PT men are certain they are making hits but what they probably see is the flash of enemy gunfire. The brawl has its effect, however, in helping Admiral Kurita decide to break off. American searchlights have picked up his battleships; he knows not what may develop behind the PTs; he has already been shooting for 80 minutes and his initial ammunition allowance is expended. So at 0230 he orders Cease-Fire and retires according to plan. *Kongo, Haruna* and escorts, untouched by a single hit, slip around Savo Island and head northward for the fleet rendezvous. Kurita knows that his colleague Kusaka will have bombing planes over the field next day, so he has little fear of retaliation from the air.

Kurita is right. In the morning the Marines crawl out of foxholes to find yawning chasms spotting the airfield and dispersal areas. Only 42 planes (35 fighters and 7 dive-bombers) remain operational out of 90. The aviation gas supply, critically low before, is nearly all gone. Forty-one men are dead, others wounded. And every 15 minutes "Pistol Pete" spits up geysers of dirt around the field. Then at noon, without warning, an air raid hits the field hard, followed by another an hour later. Henderson Field is through for the time being. Whoever flies must use the new grass-covered fighter strip.

A Marine colonel from division headquarters appears at the field and delivers a short pronouncement to the Army aviators:

"We don't know whether we'll be able to hold the field or not. There's a Japanese task force of destroyers, cruisers and troop transports headed our way. We have enough gasoline left for one mission against them. Load your planes with bombs and go out with the dive-bombers and hit them. After the gas is gone we'll have to let the ground troops take over. Then your officers and men will attach yourselves to some infantry outfit. Good luck and good-by."

On board *Kongo,* now well to the northward, an orderly hands the Admiral a copy of an intercepted Marine dispatch: "Last night we received a terrific bombardment from surface ships." Kurita grunts with satisfaction and thinks of the tremendous victory to follow.

Rebound, 14–15 October

Admiral Kurita's punitive visit bore down heavily on Marine morale; the more so because, following hard on the Battles of the Matanikau and of Cape Esperance, it seemed to prove that the enemy's resources were unlimited. The men knew that they could not stand many more such drubbings. For the rest of the war Guadalcanal veterans would talk of Kurita's shelling as "The Bombardment," as if there had never been any other.

On 14 October the last echelon of General Hyakutake's troops was on its way down the Slot in six transports, escorted by destroyers on the surface and overhead by "Zekes." Four Dauntless dive-bombers (all that would fly at the moment) and seven Army fighter planes armed with bombs took the air in a pathetic effort to stop this reinforcement. They did their best, but the only ship to suffer, and that lightly, was destroyer *Samidare*. When darkness set in, she was still heading south.

The night of 14–15 October was another bad stretch for the Marines. Admiral Mikawa personally entered "Sleepless Lagoon" (as the Marines were beginning to call it) in cruiser *Chokai*, followed by lucky *Kinugasa*, to churn up the Henderson Field community with 752 eight-inch shells. Four PT crews looked on but could do nothing; one boat had been damaged by grounding the night before, one was out of torpedoes and the other two were compelled to remain with a small-craft convoy moving between Tulagi and Guadalcanal. Dawn of the 15th revealed a spectacle highly humiliating to the Marines who saw it, and to the Navy that did not. In full view were enemy transports lying-to off Tassafaronga, unloading troops and supplies with as much ease as if they had been in Tokyo Bay. Hovering around and over them were destroyers and planes.

General Geiger, Marine air commander, was told there was no gas at Henderson Field. "Then, by God, find some!" he ordered. Men scoured the dispersal areas, collected some 400 drums of aviation gas from swamps and thickets where they had been cached and trundled them to the field. Even the two disabled B-17s had their tanks siphoned dry. By these pint-pot methods enough fuel was procured to enable the planes to make the ten-mile hop to the targets and back. And by mid-morning, Marine and Army transport planes began to fly in gasoline from Espiritu Santo.

Off Tassafaronga, Army, Navy and Marine pilots bombed and strafed the transports all day long 15 October, fighting off "Zekes" and dodging the darting tongues of anti-aircraft tracers. Flying Forts flew up from Espiritu Santo and lent a hand. A visiting PBY, General Geiger's personal "hack" piloted by Lieutenant Colonel Jack Cram, contributed a pair of torpedoes, and returned to Henderson Field full of holes, with swarms of enemy fighters on its tail, but safe. High over the revitalized airfield, Wildcat bullets and anti-aircraft shells brought down twelve Nip bombers and five fighters. Everybody who flew claimed damage that day, and for once they were right. Three large transports not yet completely unloaded (*Azumasan Maru, Kyushu Maru* and *Sasako Maru*) had to be beached and became a total loss. By 1550 things had become so hot that the Japanese task force commander decided to withdraw with the other three transports.[65] Not one transport escaped damage, not one troop unit landed without casualties and loss of equipment. This field day cost the Americans three dive-bombers and four fighter planes.

That night, breathing was a bit easier for all hands. Even a downpour of 1500 eight-inch shells from cruisers *Myoko* and *Maya* failed to quench the spark of hope kindled by the feeling that the enemy had done his worst. But, alas, he had not.

Carrier *Hornet,* keystone of Task Force 17 under Rear Admiral George D. Murray, also lent a hand. On 16 October she launched an air raid on Rekata Bay, Santa Isabel, which chewed up twelve enemy seaplanes. On the same day her planes flew over Guadalcanal, socking beached Japanese transports and troop and supply concentrations.

United States submarines in these waters were not very successful in October, but *Sculpin* and *Gudgeon* between them sank three freighters amounting to 13,500 tons; and *Sturgeon* sank a large aircraft ferry, *Katsuragi Maru.*

Supply-train Sufferings

On October 15 Admiral Nimitz expressed his estimate of the situation in three sober sentences: "It now appears that we are unable to control the sea in the Guadalcanal area. Thus our supply of the positions will only be done at great expense to us. The situation is not hopeless, but it is certainly critical."

The Nimitz-Ghormley-Vandegrift team were determined to hold on; but they staggered under a multitude of afflictions, number one being the Japanese Navy; Nimitz had no doubt whatever that it was making an all-out effort. He and his service force had to provide the South Pacific with the tools of war at a time when the North African operation acted as an absorbent sponge for ships, planes and fuel, beans and bullets. Fortunately Admiral King in Washington never for a moment forgot Guadalcanal. Ghormley was harassed by the need for doing too much with too few ships. Vandegrift was plagued with the problem of hanging onto valuable acres of jungle-surrounded airfield in the face of air bombs, naval and heavy artillery shells, supply deficiencies, fanatically fighting Japs and enervating diseases. It could hardly be expected that such a doubtful issue could be quickly resolved. The battles of October were not decisive but they defeated the second serious attempt of the Japanese to retake Guadalcanal and afforded the Americans a much-needed opportunity to catch their breath and strike back.

The extremity of the American situation in mid-October is illustrated by gallant if pitiful efforts to keep the lifeline intact. The twin-engine Douglas Skytrooper became a flying workhorse, bringing in enough aviation gas from Base "Button" (Espiritu Santo) each trip to keep twelve Wildcats aloft for an hour. Submarine *Amberjack*, fitted to carry 9000 gallons of gasoline together with ten tons of bombs, did her part. To swell the trickle, a barge-towing expedition was made up, to arrive at Lunga Roads on the 16th. It comprised cargo ships *Alchiba* and *Bellatrix,* motor torpedo boat tender *Jamestown,* ex-minesweeper (now fleet tug) *Vireo* and destroyers *Meredith* and *Nicholas,* each towing a barge carrying 2000 barrels of gasoline and 500 quarter-ton bombs.

On 15 October, 75 miles from Guadalcanal, these lucrative targets were sighted and reported by a Japanese search plane.

The American ships, with the exception of *Vireo* and *Meredith*, hastily retired. At 1050 these two beat off a two-plane attack. At the same time word was received that two enemy ships were close at hand. Course was reversed and at noon *Meredith* ordered the slow and vulnerable *Vireo* to be abandoned and sunk, after taking off her crew. At 1215, just as *Meredith* was about to torpedo *Vireo*, a 27-plane raid from the big Japanese carrier *Zuikaku* plastered the destroyer with bombs, torpedoes and machine-gun fire, and sank her almost instantaneously.

Vireo, abandoned but still undamaged, was drifting so rapidly to leeward that only one life raft from *Meredith* succeeded in boarding her, and those men were saved. The other life rafts became floating horrors. Horribly burned sailors lay on the sea-washed gratings while able-bodied survivors clung to the rafts' lifelines, fighting off sharks until the death of a wounded man released a place for them inside. Lt Commander Harry E. Hubbard, *Meredith's* skipper, was one of many who so died. One shark even boarded a life raft and gouged a chunk from a dying man's thigh before his exhausted raft mates could heave the beast over by the tail.

After three days and three nights of suffering, 88 men were rescued by destroyers *Grayson* and *Gwin*, but *Meredith* lost 185 and *Vireo* 51 officers and men.[66] The tugboat and both gasoline barges were salvaged.

Destroyer seaplane tender *McFarland* and destroyer mine-

USS Meredith at Guadalcanal.

sweepers *Southard* and *Hovey* also were drafted for the "B., T. & B." (Button, Tulagi and Back). Literally a floating ammunition and fuel dump, *McFarland* stood into Lengo Channel on the morning of 16 October carrying twelve torpedoes, a quantity of 37-mm ammunition, crates of aircraft flares and 40,000 gallons of gasoline in tanks below and drums topside. That kind of cargo robbed her skipper (Lieutenant Commander John C. Alderman) and his crew of all peace of mind. At 1320 they anchored off the beach at Lunga and began discharging cargo with great alacrity. Passengers were taken on board—160 ambulatory hospital patients and "war neurotics," an emotionally inflammable cargo. At 1700 the sighting of a submarine periscope convinced Alderman that he was too good a target at anchor, so he got under way with the gasoline barge alongside still taking fuel from *McFarland's* tanks.

Then, at 1750, out of the sky plunged nine enemy dive-bombers. The ensuing action lasted only a couple of minutes during which *McFarland's* bridge rang up full speed, her gunners shot down one "Val" and damaged another, and the gasoline barge was cast off, exploding furiously. The last "Val" scored a hit on the depth-charge racks which made a shambles of the fantail and threw the poor neurotics into uncontrolled panic. While *McFarland's* bluejackets calmly carried out damage control and defense measures, these unfortunate passengers stampeded the passageways, tried to take weapons and life jackets from the crew, and otherwise added tension to an already taut situation. But the ship's company were determined to save *McFarland*. Rudderless, leaking aft, engines damaged and passengers demoralized, the ship was a problem. Yet the black gang in the engine room soon found that they could give her five knots on a generally straight course by running the damaged port engine astern and the intact starboard engine ahead. It was nearly midnight before this tough little ship anchored in Tulagi, towed the last few miles by *YP-239*. She had lost 27 men with 28 wounded.

That was only the beginning of *McFarland's* improvisation. Next day (17 October) her crew moved her up the narrow Maliali River mouth on Florida Island, covered her with a camouflage of jungle greenery and began repairs. This involved raiding the former

Japanese seaplane base for steel and fashioning a jury rudder out of telephone poles. During a three-week period Alderman and his hearties not only repaired the damage but established the new U.S. Naval Base, Tulagi. Thanksgiving Day found *McFarland* once more on her own, steering for Espiritu Santo. Her experience was an inspiration, but she could deliver no more liquid gold to hungry planes at Gaudalcanal. Admiral Nimitz was right; supply was very expensive.[67]

Enter Halsey

Admiral Nimitz was confronted with many problems of which the question of leadership in the South Pacific was the most pressing. Admiral Ghormley, a meticulous and conscientious man with a long record of achievement, apparently lacked the personal qualities needed to inspire American fighting men in a tough spot. As area commander, he received blame for many things beyond his control, for employing too many ships around "Torpedo Junction," for landing too few American troops and supplies on Guadalcanal and letting too many Japanese soldiers get there, for supply bottlenecks at Nouméa and Espiritu Santo.[68] Yet, could any new leader do as well; would not a change at this time create even more confusion? Admiral Nimitz weighed the matter scrupulously. On the evening of 15 October, after a conference with his staff, he decided that "the critical situation requires a more aggressive commander," and that he wanted Vice Admiral William F. Halsey. Next day Admiral King granted authority for the change, and Nimitz acted at once.

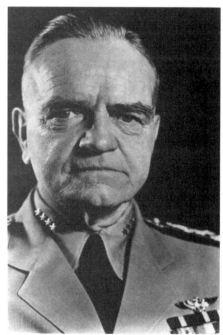

Vice Admiral William F. Halsey USN.

Since May Admiral Halsey had been on the binnacle list with aggravated dermatitis, but mid-October found him in the South Pacific on an inspection tour preparatory to taking over command of a carrier task force. In health and spirits he was "back to battery," but he had no inkling of the load about to be dumped into his lap. On 18 October he landed at Nouméa to be confronted with a terse order: "You will take command of the South Pacific Area and South Pacific Forces immediately." That same day with feelings of "astonishment, apprehension and regret," he relieved his old friend Ghormley. "Bill" Halsey had won golden opinions in the Fleet for his aggressiveness and his character. The announcement was received on board ships of the South Pacific Fleet with cheers and rejoicing.

Besides replacing the top commander, Admiral Nimitz considered and took other positive measures. A task group powered by new battleship *Indiana* was ordered through the Panama Canal to the South Pacific. The 25th Infantry Division U.S. Army at Oahu was given word to pack its gear for a voyage to the southern seas. A flock of 50 Army fighter planes was told to migrate from the Central to the South Pacific. A plan was devised to infest enemy-held waters in the Solomons with an additional 24 large submarines. A similar number of Army B-17s droned across the Equator to join Admiral Fitch's brood.[69] Most important, carrier *Enterprise,* recovered from her 24 August wounds, rushed pell-mell to the Solomons.

Insistent demands of the South Pacific were met as far as possible, but Nimitz could not allow himself or his forces to become too absorbed with one locale.

In Washington Admiral King had his hands full. Our predicament in the Solomons was more than matched by that caused by the German submarines, which, during the month of October, sank 88 ships and 585,510 tons in the Atlantic. The North African venture was already at sea; British forces in Egypt still had to be supplied by the Cape of Good Hope and Suez route. Guadalcanal had to be fitted by the Joint Chiefs of Staff into a worldwide strategic panorama, but Guadalcanal could be reinforced only by drawing on forces originally committed to the build-up in the United

Kingdom (Operation "Bolero") for a cross-channel operation in 1943. General Arnold wished to concentrate air forces in Europe for the strategic bombing of Germany; Admiral King and General MacArthur argued against risking disaster in the Solomons and New Guinea in order to provide for the eventuality of a future operation in Europe. President Roosevelt broke the deadlock on 24 October by sending a strong message to each member of the Joint Chiefs of Staff, insisting that Guadalcanal must be reinforced, and quickly.[70]

The nerve center of this campaign was not, however, at Washington or Pearl Harbor but at Nouméa, where Admiral Halsey and his chief of staff Captain Miles Browning, with about 15 seasoned staff officers and 50 bluejackets, ran the entire South Pacific Force of Navy, Army, Marine Corps; ships, boats, freighters, net tenders; search radars, anti-aircraft batteries and barrage balloons; N.A.S. and N.O.B.; service of supply and repair stations; Flying Forts, Cats, SCAT, Cubs, Acorns, Seabees; camps, hospitals, officers' and enlisted men's clubs; a hundred other groups, units and forces; not to mention the thousands of men who were just passing through, and the unwanted and troublesome "do-gooders" who were occasionally flown across from the States.

10. THE BATTLE FOR HENDERSON FIELD
(19–26 October 1942)

The Japanese Plan and the Matanikau Drive

While the Americans were counting their several woes and infrequent blessings, the Japanese high command concluded that the time had come to unsheath a myriad Samurai swords and chase the enemy out of the Solomons. Preliminary to this great joint operation were General Maruyama's attacks on Henderson Field, the Combined Fleet's sailing from Truk 11 October, the successive night bombardments, the landing of 4500 troops on the 15th, and the accelerated tempo of air raids. The new fighter strip at Buin in southern Bougainville was being pushed to completion, and as early as 20 October thirty of the one hundred "Zekes" at Rabaul were advanced to the new field, to escort Rabaul-based bombers to Guadalcanal.

The Japanese plan stemmed from an Army-Navy agreement for operations in mid-September, revised as the situation altered. In this agreement Guadalcanal was given top billing by the Emperor's chiefs of staff, and the Papua operation dropped to second place. The substance of the Tokyo order was contained in its opening paragraph:

> After reinforcement of Army forces has been completed, Army and Navy forces will combine and in one action attack and retake Guadalcanal Island airfield. During this operation the Navy will take all necessary action to halt the efforts of the enemy to augment his forces in the Solomons Area.

This plan was a sincere compliment to Henderson Field and its fliers. The Emperor's high military advisers would not risk another battle until the field was captured. But, as it turned out, they would better have stuck to Mahan, because unexpected delays by the Japanese ground forces gave Admiral Kinkaid time to bring up carrier *Enterprise* to take a decisive part in the sea action. We are accustomed to sea battles deciding a land campaign; in this instance, Japan lost a naval engagement because her army bogged down.

Marine camp near Henderson Field.

By 15 October the Japanese reinforcement phase was completed. The third week of October was to be devoted to softening up the Marines in preparation for "Y-Day," the 22nd, when the Rising Sun was to be planted on Henderson Field by General Maruyama. The Combined Fleet, impatiently circling north of the Solomons, would then "apprehend and annihilate any powerful forces in the Solomons area, as well as any reinforcements."

The Marines and their fellow soldiers of the 164th Infantry Regiment United States Army declined to soften. Despite breakages in the supply train, food was now sufficient for almost everyone to have three meals a day. Japanese thrusts had been tossed back wherever made. Henderson Field fliers were daily demonstrating their combat superiority. On the other hand, the nocturnal ship bombardments and diurnal air attacks continued. There was also the certain knowledge that the enemy was shoving in troops at the rate of 900 a night, not to mention the 4500 who had come ashore from the transports on 15 October. These troops could, in theory, be deployed all over Guadalcanal while the Marines were pinned down to their perimeter around Henderson Field. But the hated 'Canal jungle now turned American ally, thwarting neat Japanese plans for envelopment.

General Hyakutake made the assignments, as before; fortunately he still underestimated both the strength and quality of his antagonists and had very inaccurate information on the nature of the terrain his troops were to traverse. To Major General Tadashi Sumiyoshi, commanding Seventeenth Army artillery, was given the honor of making a frontal attack on Marine positions along the Matanikau. This

Signal Tower at Henderson Field, Guadalcanal.
John Case, 1st Special NCB.

Henderson Field, Guadalcanal. Courtesy John Case, 1ˢᵗ Special NCB.

was to be coordinated with a two-pronged assault on Henderson Field from the south, the eastern prong to be directed by Major General Kawaguchi, the western one by Major General Yumio Nasu, both under Lieutenant General Masai Maruyama, Commanding General 2ⁿᵈ Division. Air strikes and surface bombardment were to be provided as softening agents.

Sumiyoshi jumped off against the Marines' defensive sectors along the Matanikau on 20 October. Colonel McKelvy's battalion, stationed near the river mouth, became the recipient of heavy mortar and artillery fire. On the 21st, nine light tanks tried to force a crossing by the coast road but were easily repulsed by Marine Corps artillery. Next day destroyer *Nicholas,* which had just escorted a small supply echelon to Guadalcanal, saw her charges safely anchored (as she thought) at Lunga Roads, and pranced over to make four bombardment runs on enemy shore positions, firing over a thousand rounds of 5-inch shell by 0830. A Japanese shore battery retaliated by opening up on one of *Nicholas's* charges, the small freighter *Kopara,* but *Nicholas* scurried back to pump an additional 181 rounds into the offending battery, which silenced it. After severe artillery preparation on 23 October, Sumiyoshi just before midnight 23 October sent in his tanks with infantry support for another try. The 11ᵗʰ Marines' 105-mm howitzers took care of the tanks, destroying twelve, and McKelvy's battalion disposed

Mouth of the Matanikau River.

of several hundred soldiers at small cost to themselves. Thus, the western attack was a complete failure, and the occupation of Henderson was already two days overdue.

Next morning, 24 October, the enemy unexpectedly appeared upstream on the Matanikau. Marines of Colonel Farrell's 3rd Battalion 7th Regiment sighted a strong Japanese force on a ridge to their left and rear. They shouted for artillery fire and air support, and got both, together with Hanneken's 2nd Battalion of their regiment, which during the previous night had shoved off from its defensive position south of the airfield.

Coffin Corner (24–25 October)

This withdrawal of the 2nd Battalion forced Colonel Puller's 1st Battalion of the same regiment to "single-up its lines"[71] along the U-shaped perimeter south of Henderson Field. An action, which for bloody devilment came close to the earlier Battle of the Ridge, was fought here on the edge of the woods, only half a mile south of the Ridge.

Puller's lines lay in the jungle, partly along the south edge of a large field of kunai grass that sloped up to a grassy knoll 2000 yards away. On his left, the lines bent back along the course of the river which the troops called the Tenaru, and this sector was guarded by Lieutenant Colonel Timboe's battalion of the 164th

Infantry. A second battalion of the same regiment was posted to the rear, as reserve. The lines were prepared for assault with barbed wire on which shell fragments and other metal oddments were hung to jingle a warning if a Jap tried to cross them at night. Fields of fire were cut with bayonets through the seven-foot-tall kunai grass and pickets were connected with their outfits by strings—two jerks to mean "Japs coming." A detachment of 48 Marines was posted on the summit of the grassy knoll, 3000 yards from the lines.

All day on the 24th signs of an approaching Japanese force were observed. This was General Nasu's prong; Kawaguchi had been delayed in the jungle. After nightfall at 2130 the Marine outpost on the grassy knoll was overrun, and half an hour after midnight Nasu's men poured down through the kunai into the Marines' lines. It was raining buckets. Colonel Hall's reserve battalion of the 164th Infantry was ordered up from the rear in support, and made it in spite of rain and darkness.

Along "Coffin Corner," as the soldiers named this point where their lines came out of the woods, the Japs tried all their tricks and fought savagely all night; but the Marines and GI Joes had their weapons properly sighted and slaughtered them as fast as they came. By daylight General Nasu (or his second in command, for he was killed at some time during the action) withdrew to reform.

Five smashed Japanese tanks lie on a sand spit across the mouth of the Matanikau River, Guadalcanal. They were destroyed by U.S. Marine artillery on 23 October 1942. Savo Island is in the background. National Archives.

The Marines and the 164th spent daylight of the 25th readjusting their lines, as soldiers of the two outfits were completely commingled by morning; and many found time to walk across the field and bathe in the river.

At nightfall the attack was renewed with the aid of part of Kawaguchi's brigade which had found its way there. "Coffin Corner" still held, and the only result was more piles of bodies added to those heaped up in the grass, and along the edge of the woods. Puller's and Timboe's outfits together buried 941 of the enemy in that small sector.

In the meantime Hanneken's 2nd Battalion, 7th Marines, whose departure for the Matanikau had caused the 1st to "single-up its lines," had taken an east-west position along an irregular line of grassy ridge parallel to the coast, facing a steep-sided and heavily-wooded valley. There they were attacked by Colonel Oka's unit with heavy artillery support, subjected to sniping fire from tall trees on the other side of the valley, and infiltrated at night. One company of Marines was almost wiped out, and when the survivors withdrew the enemy employed two machine guns on the ridge and enfolded the rest. Dawn 26 October revealed this unpleasant fact to the battalion command post, only a few yards distant. Major Odell M. Conoley, the battalion "exec.," formed his communication personnel, company runners, cooks and mess-boys, to the total number of 17, into an assault force which knocked out the two machine guns with hand grenades and cleared the crest.

Skirmishes in the Sound and the Strait, 25 October [72]

On the 25th, while Marines and soldiers were preparing for the next night assault, a small Japanese bombardment force was tangling with four little American ships out in Ironbottom Sound. An "assault unit," consisting of three destroyers of the Eighth Fleet, *Akatsuki, Ikazuchi* and *Shiratsuyu*, had come down that morning to try a daylight surface raid.

That same morning destroyer-minesweepers *Trever* and *Zane* entered the Sound laden with good things for the PT boys at Tulagi. Piled high on the decks of these erstwhile four-stackers were torpedoes, ammunition and gasoline; astern of each were towed two new motor torpedo boats. Then, at 1000, the Japanese destroyers appeared. Lieutenant Commander Agnew of *Trever*, the senior skipper, decided to escape via Sealark Channel. At 1018, with the range under ten miles, the hostile group commenced a high-speed approach on Agnew's old-timers. At a range under five miles the Japs opened up. *Trever* and *Zane* fired back, although their 3-inch shells could not carry more than four miles. The Japanese salvos began slapping the water "feet, not yards" from *Zane*.

Lieutenant Commander Agnew decided there was no escape by way of Sealark Channel and headed for the shoal-studded waters south of Nggela Channel and signaled *Zane* accordingly. Before the skirmish ended, the Japanese drew first blood, a hit on the *Zane* that killed three men and knocked out a gun.

At this critical juncture help came from the heavens in the shape of an American air attack on the Japanese. The enemy commander, perhaps remembering orders to bombard the airfield, turned abruptly away and headed toward Guadalcanal, fighting off the bombing planes as he went. However, the only other American shipping then in the Sound, tug *Seminole* and "yard bird" *YP-284* weren't so lucky.

U.S. Army Transport President Coolidge beached in sinking condition after striking mines, Segond Channel, near S.E. corner Espiritu Santo Island, 25 October 1942. Her merchant skipper blundered into the protective mine field. She was carrying the 172nd Infantry 43rd Division. Although it cost but two lives, the big Army transport was a total loss. All the troops' equipment and heavy weapons were destroyed and their reinforcement for the Guadalcanal garrison was delayed for weeks. USNCB.

These two craft of the "Cactus Navy" had made a routine ferry run from Tulagi to Lunga loaded with troops, ammunition, gasoline and weapons and were in the process of discharging cargo when *Akatsuki, Ikazuchi* and *Shiratsuyu* were sighted.

At 1050 *YP-284* was hit; the cargo caught fire, and a few minutes later the engine room was holed. Dead and defenseless, the patrol craft quickly sank, with the loss of three Marine passengers. And at 1120 *Seminole*, with gasoline cargo blazing, followed *YP-284* to the bottom. As most enemy shells had passed through her thin hull without exploding, only one life was lost.

The enemy destroyers next let go at the Lunga Point shore batteries but accurate return fire scored a hit on *Akatsuki* at 1055 and persuaded the trio to retire behind a smoke screen.

Thus, the Battle for Henderson Field ended shortly after daylight 26 October with the sinking of a bombardment force flagship by Henderson Field fliers and the repulse of Japanese land attacks at all three points—Matanikau, Hanneken's Ridge and Coffin Corner. Japanese ground force casualties were numbered by the thousands, and on our side they were heavy. The 7th Marine Regiment lost 182 killed; the 164th Infantry Regiment, 166 killed and wounded. Marine-Army-Air Force cooperation had been well-nigh perfect under Generals Vandegrift and Geiger;[73] GIs had proved they could fight Japs as well as could the Leathernecks.

As the sounds of battle faded out on land, the two Navies were hurling planes against each other's ships in the great Battle of the Santa Cruz Islands.

11. THE BATTLE OF THE SANTA CRUZ ISLANDS
(26–27 October 1942)[74]

Preliminary Maneuvers, (23–25 October)

Yamamoto's orders to his subordinate naval commanders, all poised for action awaiting word of the capture of Henderson Field, were "to apprehend and annihilate any powerful forces in the Solomons area, as well as any reinforcements." Yamamoto had every confidence that the word "annihilate" would mean just that, for he could deploy against Halsey no fewer than 4 carriers, 5 battleships, 14 cruisers and 44 destroyers. These were divided as usual into several groups, spotted over that part of the ocean between the Marianas and the Solomons in a manner difficult to follow. The giant battleship *Yamato* lay at Truk, flying the flag of Admiral Yamamoto. Under him Admiral Kondo commanded all surface forces that it was the Commander in Chief's intention to commit: Kondo's own Advance Force of battleships *Kongo* and *Haruna* (which had just had search radar installed) and four heavy cruisers, including two carriers under Kakuji Kakuta of Aleutians fame; Nagumo's Striking Force containing his own carrier group, ahead of which operated Hiroaki Abe's vanguard of battleships and heavy cruisers. About 220 land-based planes were at Rabaul, where also lay Mikawa's workhorse Eighth Fleet of two heavy cruisers and 16 destroyers. A submarine screen completed the setup. There were no transports because Yamamoto, taking heed from the Eastern Solomons battle, had sent them down in advance—unsuccessfully, as we have seen.

The first brush occurred on 23 October about 650 miles north of Espiritu Santo. One of Admiral Fitch's PBYs spotted an enemy carrier and radioed the alarm. That night several torpedo-toting Catalinas went after the flattop. Lieutenant (jg) George A. Enloe USNR was the only pilot lucky enough to locate an enemy ship, a large cruiser which his torpedo missed.

October 24 passed quietly at sea, as far as enemy contacts were concerned. The best news was the arrival of the "Big E" accompanied by the new, fast battleship *South Dakota*. The latter, on her way out in early September, had had her bottom sliced open by a coral pinnacle near Tongatabu. But this accident proved a blessing in disguise because the Pearl Harbor Navy Yard, not content with patching her bottom, installed dozens of new 40-mm anti-aircraft guns that stood her in good stead in the forthcoming battle. No ship more eager to fight ever entered the Pacific, for Captain Gatch, by constant target practice, neglecting the spit-and-polish things that vex bluejackets, and by exercising a natural gift for leadership, had welded his green crew into a splendid fighting team.[75]

Admiral Halsey now had two carriers, two battleships, nine

cruisers and 24 destroyers organized into three teams: Kinkaid's *Enterprise* group (TF 16), Murray's *Hornet* group (TF 17) and Lee's battleship-cruiser group (TF 64). The rendezvous of the two carrier groups was set at a point 273 miles NE by E of Espiritu Santo, and Halsey gave them explicit and daring routing instructions. They were to make a sweep north of the Santa Cruz Islands and then change course to the southwest in order to be in a position to intercept enemy forces approaching Guadalcanal.

The Santa Cruz archipelago, lying to the north of the New Hebrides and to the east of the southern Solomons, includes four volcanic islands of which the better known are Ndeni and Vanikoro. They are so infested with malaria of the malignant cerebral type that few white men have succeeded in surviving, and their inhabitants are more primitive than those of the Solomons. The original plan for Operation "Watchtower" provided for the occupation of these islands in order to guard the supply route and provide another airfield; but the terrain proved to be too rugged for airfield construction, and many of the Army Engineers sent in to survey died of malaria. In late October the islands were a no man's land.

Combined Fleet was losing its edge, and the ships were running out of fuel, waiting for the Japanese ground forces to take Henderson Field. A premature paean of victory—later retracted—from the liaison officer on Guadalcanal, at 0126 October 25, sparked off the naval battle. Yamamoto did not know where the American carriers were; but a far-ranging Catalina from Espiritu Santo sighted Nagumo's spoiled children of victory, carriers *Shokaku* and *Zuikaku*, at noon. Kinkaid acted on this contact by launching a combined search-strike from *Enterprise* that afternoon. But they located nothing, as the Japanese had cagily reversed course, again waiting for certain news of victory ashore.

In the small hours of 26 October Admiral Kinkaid, who had been steering northwesterly at 20 knots, began to receive plane contacts on enemy carriers 200 miles away. In the gray hours before dawn Admiral Halsey on Nouméa riffled through the dispatches, glanced at his operations chart, and sent out these words: "ATTACK—REPEAT—ATTACK!"

See Appendix D for United States and Japanese composition of forces.

The Carrier Plane Battle, 26 October

The sun rose at 0523 on a fair South Sea day, low broken cumulus clouds apportioned haphazardly to about half the sky, the soft belly of the ocean rising and falling in a gentle swell, a languid 8-knot breeze from the southeast scarcely raising ripples on the sea's smooth skin. It was weather to the taste of dive-bomber pilots who could lurk in the clouds, but to the distaste of anti-aircraft gunners—no cloud has a silver lining for them.

Already *Enterprise* launched a search mission, each SBD armed with a 500-pound bomb "just in case." At 0740, two bomber pilots sighted light carrier *Zuiho,* used their bombs, and knocked her out so far as this battle was concerned.

One hour earlier a Japanese search plan had sighted *Hornet.* Admiral Kondo, again Japanese O.T.C., ordered strikes to be launched at her immediately from his three viable carriers. Twenty minutes later *Hornet* followed suit. The two hostile groups passed one another in the air, each eyeing the enemy and wondering which would find a flight deck on its return. Half *Enterprise's* group was shot down 100 miles short of its target by a dozen "Zekes," which had peeled off especially to get them.

Now came the most tense moment for the opposing commanders, Kinkaid and Kondo. Each had found the other, each was lashing out at the other.

Flagship *Enterprise* was the hub of a tight little circle rimmed by battleship *South Dakota,* heavy cruiser *Portland*, anti-aircraft cruiser *San Juan* and eight destroyers. Ten miles to the southeast cruised Rear Admiral George D. Murray's flagship *Hornet*, similarly surrounded by floating gun platforms. Stacked in layers overhead were 38 fighters of Combat Air patrol, all under *Enterprise* fighter-direction.

The Japanese strike, first to depart, was also the first to arrive at its target. At 0859 the American C.A.P. sighted "Val" dive-bombers at 17,000 feet. At about the same moment *Enterprise* entered a local rainsquall, which concealed her from the approaching enemy; but *Hornet* was in the clear and the enemy concentrated on her, commencing at 0910. "Vals" dove down, loosing a series of explosive bombs. *Hornet* and her protectors blackened the sky with shellbursts. One bomb hit the starboard side of the flight deck aft.

The Japanese squadron commander, crippled by a shellburst, made a spectacular suicide crash. His plane hit the stack, glanced off and burst through the flight deck, where two of its bombs detonated. Even more deadly were the torpedo-carrying "Kates," which bored in low from astern slugging nastily at *Hornet's* tender groin. Two torpedoes exploded in the engineering spaces. The carrier, in a thick cloud of smoke and steam, lurched to starboard, slowed to a stop, lost all power and communications. She was now immobile—deaf, dumb and impotent. Three more quarter-ton bombs hit the flight deck. She was still writhing from this onslaught when a flaming "Kate" with a doomed pilot, made a suicide run from dead ahead, piled into the port forward gun gallery, and blew up near the forward elevator shaft. In all, some 27 Japanese planes jumped this carrier, and only two got home; but that was a cheap price to pay for depriving the Pacific Fleet of one third of its carrier strength.

At 0925, when *Hornet* looked like a bad risk, 52 planes of her air group led by Lieutenant Commander "Gus" Widhelm were approaching the Japanese force. Eleven bombers under Lieutenant James E. Vose fought their way through to the pushover point, drew a bead on *Shokaku,* and roared down through flak with "Zekes" still on their tails. It was worth the risk. Three to six 1000-pound bombs ripped the Japanese carrier's flight deck to shreds, destroyed the hangar and ignited severe fires. *Shokaku* was out of the war for nine months. *Hornet's* second wave missed the Japanese carriers, but exploded two bombs on cruiser *Chikuma* and knocked her out—for a time.

Thus, by 1030 October 26, one large and one small Japanese flattop had been scratched, and *Hornet* almost finished; but *Zuikaku* and *Junyo* were still intact, and Admiral Kondo had already ordered their planes to go get "Big E." His earlier strike would have done so, but for superb ship handling by Captain Hardison, and magnificent shooting by the "wild men" of *South Dakota.* She in this action secured for battlewagons the place of honor that they occupied during the rest of the war—defending carriers from attack. *Enterprise* took three bombs which killed 44 men but inflicted no lethal damage on the ship.

Forty minutes later, at 1101 *Junyo's* dive-bombers tumbled out of the low overcast. One of them planted a bomb on *South Dakota's* No. 1 turret; an armor-piercing bomb went right through the thin skin of anti-aircraft cruiser *San Juan,* exploding below her keel and jamming her rudder.

Enemy planes kept dogging *Hornet,* when under tow by cruiser *Northhampton;* she took three more hits, and had to be abandoned. Two Japanese destroyers then sank her. Had the later expedient of attaching powerful fleet tugs to each carrier group been in effect, she would have been towed out of enemy range and salvaged.

Kondo now shaped a retiring course northward, hoping to renew battle on the 28th, but Kinkaid by that time was too far away for him to make contact.

The Santa Cruz set-to was the fourth carrier battle in six months. Something of a pattern had been established and little new occurred. There was much criticism of the poor fighter-direction. The standard doctrine of carrier tactics, operating each flattop as the center of a special group, came up again for discussion; and the older practice was abandoned during sorties of the carrier task forces in early 1943.

American pilots and gunners remarked that the Japanese flier was losing his touch. Possibly so, owing to five months' heavy losses; but the main reason why the enemy seemed less efficient in the air was an improvement in American fighting technique, both in the air and on deck.

What effect did the battle have on the situation? Was it still "not hopeless but certainly critical," as Nimitz had said? Measured in combat tonnage sunk, the Japanese had won a tactical victory; but other losses forced them back to the Truk hideout. The land assault against the Marines had ended in a fizzle; the sea effort had dangerously reduced Japanese air strength. Tokyo claimed "three carriers, one battleship, three cruisers and one destroyer," but the Imperial Rescript that followed suggested that the Emperor was not too sure he had won.

American claims for the battle were moderate and accurate.

The loss of an aircraft carrier was promptly made known to the public. Several days after the battle Admiral Nimitz observed, "The general situation at Guadalcanal is not unfavorable" —a much more hopeful view than his mid-October statement. But he well knew that the Japanese were more determined than ever to retrieve Guadalcanal. All right, let 'em try; the Battle of Santa Cruz Islands had gained priceless time for the Americans—days in which to reinforce and prepare.[76]

Torpedo bomber approaching USS South Dakota.

USS San Juan repelling air attack.

12. THE NAVAL BATTLE OF GAUDALCANAL
(12–15 November 1942)[77]

Great Expectations

At the end of October a feeling of frustration respecting Guadalcanal pervaded both Japanese and American high commands. Allied ships afloat and aircraft aloft had failed in their efforts to seal off Guadalcanal from enemy access, or even to ensure the safe arrival of American reinforcements. Admiral Halsey, after two weeks as Commander South Pacific Force, felt exasperated. On shore an alleged irresistible force, the Imperial Japanese Army, had met a demonstrably immovable object, the United States Marine Corps. Something had to give soon. The break came in the great three-day Naval Battle of Guadalcanal.

Each side decided to attack the other during November, each believing that his strength was sufficient to hammer the issue into a favorable and final shape. In Nouméa, Admiral Halsey and staff prepared to accelerate the movement of supplies and reinforcements and, at the same time, disrupt the enemy's efforts. In Truk, Admiral Yamamoto completed an operation plan designed to secure supremacy in the Solomons.

On 30 October anti-aircraft cruiser *Atlanta* and destroyers *Aaron Ward, Benham, Fletcher* and *Lardner* escorted to Guadalcanal the transports bringing General del Valle's 155-mm artillery—a welcome present for the Marines, who now had something with which to outshoot the Japanese "Pistol Petes." Shortly after sunrise on the 30th, while the big guns were being unloaded, the escort gave rousing bombardment support to a westward push of the Marines which carried them to Point Cruz by 3 November.

The night of 2–3 November, the enemy pulled his old trick of sneaking through the Sound to land 1500 troops and some artillery near Koli Point, east of the American lines. However, cruisers *San Francisco* and *Helena* and destroyer *Sterett* drenched the new enemy positions with a destructive bombardment. The Marines followed up relentlessly and by 9 November had practically exterminated the Koli Point force.

Nevertheless, between 2 and 10 November the enemy brought

in 65 destroyer loads and 2 cruiser loads of troops to western Guadalcanal. Seabees worked overtime to repair and enlarge Henderson Field, and planes based there inflicted major damage on destroyers *Takanami* and *Naganami* on the 7th.

Execution of American plans was still in the hands of Rear Admiral Richmond K. Turner, Commander Amphibious Forces South Pacific. Incorporated under his command were two task groups of transports loaded with troops, food, ammunition and aviation material; and a support group of cruisers and destroyers. Three attack cargo ships (AKAs), escorted by Rear Admiral Norman Scott in *Atlanta* with four destroyers, left Espiritu Santo 9 November and arrived Lunga Point on Armistice Day. The second transport contingent, commanded by Rear Admiral Turner in *McCawley*, sailed 8 November from Nouméa and made Lunga on the 12th. Escorting Turner's four transports were two cruisers and three destroyers from the support group commanded by Rear Admiral Daniel J. Callaghan. The rest of this group, three cruisers and five destroyers, rendezvoused with the transports off San Cristobal on 11 November.

Intelligence reports indicated such a press of enemy shipping at Truk, Rabaul and the Shortlands that American commanders

Landing craft lowers ramp on beach so Marine reconnaissance vehicle can move out to join others in showdown fight, 4 November 1942. National Archives.

were not sanguine of discharging their own transports safely and at the same time preventing the enemy from landing heavy reinforcements. So Admiral Halsey sent a formidable team of troubleshooters to the area, with Rear Admiral Kinkaid in command.

Indirect support for Turner, Callaghan and Kinkaid was provided by the 24 submarines deployed in the Solomons, and by Rear Admiral Fitch's South Pacific planes in Espiritu Santo. General Geiger's First Marine Air Wing at Henderson Field gave direct support.

As the American transports steamed northward, D-day dawned on the other side of the world in North Africa. An auspicious event for Allied fighting men everywhere, it was particularly welcome to those of the South Pacific, so long inured to delay and disappointment.

At daybreak on the 11th when anchor chains roared down the hawsepipes of transports *Zeilin, Libra* and *Betelgeuse,* the Marine passengers lost no time landing; and their shore movement was expedited by a dive-bombing attack delivered by about a dozen enemy planes from carrier *Hiyo,* then northwest of Guadalcanal. Ample warning from a coastwatcher and from radar resulted in a vigorous anti-aircraft reception for the bat-winged "Vals," few of which escaped.

Landing craft clustered offshore, during landing operations at Lunga Point, Guadalcanal in November 1942. National Archives.

Marines unload bombs at Guadalcanal. National Archives.

Meanwhile, Turner's four transports had been pushing north-ward, closely covered by Callaghan's Support Group. Turner or-dered the troops ashore immediately upon their arrival at 0540 November 12, carrying only one unit of fire and two days' rations per man. During the previous midwatch Callaghan's group had searched Ironbottom Sound and found it empty of enemy ship-ping. For protection of transports during the unloading, cruisers *San Francisco, Portland* and *Helena* steamed in a close semicircle while *Atlanta, Juneau,* eleven destroyers and two large mine-sweepers afforded anti-submarine protection about three miles out.

The unloading proceeded at accelerated pace, anticipating an air attack. And at 1317 November 12 a coastwatcher in Buin sent word that enemy bombers and fighters were coming.

Admiral Turner immediately broke off unloading, got his ships under way and formed anti-aircraft disposition. During the eight-minute period of action, anti-aircraft batteries averaged one kill per minute, while the fighters accounted for all but one of the remaining "Bettys." Other fighter planes disposed of a flight of dive-bombers as well as nine high-level bombers who had been making holes in the landscape around the flying field.

On the debit side there were two serious incidents. Destroyer

Buchanan received so much topside damage from friendly anti-aircraft fire that she was ordered out of the area at nightfall. A wounded enemy plane deliberately crashed cruiser *San Francisco* on the after control station, knocking out a fire control radar, disabling an anti-aircraft gun director, and inflicting casualties on some 50 men including the executive officer, Commander Mark H. Crouter. The wounded were transferred to *President Jackson,* but Commander Crouter, eager to return to duty at the earliest moment, insisted on remaining on board, a decision that shortly cost him his life.

Prologue, 12 November

A tense calm followed the afternoon's elimination shoot. As Turner's ships steamed back to the unloading area through floating remains of downed planes, they realized that the enemy had just begun to show his hand. Five cruisers of varying capabilities and eleven destroyers of assorted origin were available to chop it off.

An abundance of aircraft intelligence, routed to all flag bridges during the day, indicated the convergence of heavy surface forces north of Guadalcanal that night. Morning observation revealed two battleships or heavy cruisers, one cruiser and six destroyers 335 miles to the northward. Another group of five destroyers lay less than 200 miles to the NNW. In mid-afternoon two carriers and two destroyers were reported 265 miles to the westward. That was bad enough, and Admiral Turner suspected that it was not all. Since no troop ships had been sighted, he guessed that the enemy was intent on attacking the American transports or else bombarding Henderson Field and adjacent troop positions. Since 90 per cent of their lading was already on the beach, these vulnerable targets could be sent away; but a bombardment could be countered only by a night battle.

In his appraisal, Turner listed enemy strength as two battleships, two to four heavy cruisers, two light cruisers and ten to twelve destroyers—obviously too large a bite for Callaghan's two heavy and three light cruisers and eight destroyers. Yet, with Kinkaid's carrier-battleship force too far away to help, there was nothing else to be done but for Callaghan to block, and block hard.

Admiral Turner's decision was embodied in a dispatch to Admiral Callaghan, which confirmed his earlier written orders. Transports would retire and Callaghan's Support Group, after shepherding them safely to sea, would return to Guadalcanal that night and strike enemy ships present. Turner left Callaghan to work out the tactics of this desperate effort.

Dusk of 12 November found the four transports (with Adm Turner embarked in *McCawley*) and the two cargo vessels of Scott's group (*Zeilin* had already departed)—escorted by the damaged *Buchanan*, destroyers *Shaw* and *McCalla* (selected because they were short of fuel) and minesweepers *Southard* and *Hovey*—hauling out for Espiritu Santo, where they safely anchored on 15 November.

Rear Admiral Callaghan[78] was now on his own, faced with an urgent situation. His two-starred flag now flew in the ship he had commanded six months earlier before serving on Ghormley's staff. Austere, modest, deeply religious; a hard-working and conscientious officer who possessed the high personal regard of his fellows and the love of his men, who called him "Uncle Dan," Callaghan had reached the acme of his career.

Included in Callaghan's force were anti-aircraft cruiser *Atlanta* flying the flag of Rear Admiral Norman Scott, and two of his destroyers. Scott, the victor of the Battle of Cape Esperance, was junior to Callaghan, who thus became O.T.C.

Callaghan ordered his group to assume battle disposition B-1, a snakelike column, the van consisting of destroyers *Cushing, Laffey, Sterett* and *O'Bannon;* the center, of cruisers *Atlanta, San Francisco, Portland, Helena* and *Juneau;* and the rear, of destroyers *Aaron Ward, Barton, Monssen* and *Fletcher.*[79] This disposition, resembling the old line-of-battle of sailing ship days, was chosen because it appeared to have worked well under Scott at the Battle of Cape Esperance. A long column helped one to navigate restricted waters and facilitated communication between ships. Unfortunately, the three cruisers and two destroyers that mounted the latest search radar were not placed in lead positions; anti-aircraft cruiser *Atlanta* with inferior radar steamed ahead of flagship *San Francisco* and the rear destroyers were in no position to join the van in a torpedo attack.

Takeoff. National Archives.

Japanese Navy G4M ("Betty") bomber skims the waves while under attack by one of VB-106's PB4Y-1 Patrol bombers, in the South Pacific. Naval Historical Center.

A Japanese twin-engine bomber missed this U.S. Pacific Fleet Carrier in a dramatic crash dive. Naval Historical Center.

At 2200, after seeing the transports safely away, Callaghan reversed course and passed back through Lengo Channel into Ironbottom Sound. A 9-knot easterly breeze scarcely rippled the surface. The stars shone brightly and jagged flashes of lightning over the islands fitfully illuminated low-lying clouds. The new moon had vanished below the dark horizon. Sailors peered from darkened bridges, waited in crowded plotting rooms and sweated in stifling engine rooms, wondering what the score would be. Few of these ships had operated together before that afternoon; yet no intelligence of enemy movements was distributed to commanding officers and no battle plan was issued.

Enemy forces were heading southward, planning to leave Santa Isabel Island on their starboard hand, pass south of Savo and round up on an easterly bombardment course parallel to the Guadalcanal shore. The battleships and destroyers which had departed Truk 9 November, and the additional destroyers which left Shortlands on the 11th, were the elements reported by American air patrols on the morning of the 12th. At 1530 that day they rendezvoused 70 miles north of Indispensable Strait and became Vice Admiral Hiroaki Abe's Raiding Group, consisting of two battleships, light cruiser *Nagara* and 14 destroyers. Their mission was to knock out Henderson Field completely. Shell hoists were crammed with thin-shelled, quick-fused bombardment projectiles. Special flash-less powder was on hand to assure concealment during action.[80] If challenged on the surface, the destroyers could brush off the intruder with torpedoes.

The core of Abe's formation was a bombardment unit of two battleships, *Hiei* leading *Kirishima,* with six destroyers and *Nagara* screening. On both advanced flanks rode destroyers (two on one side, three on the other) prepared to deal with motor torpedo boats. Both the disposition chosen and his lack of armor-piercing projectiles indicate that Abe was not looking for a major surface encounter. This miscalculation cannot have been caused by lack of Intelligence, because the Admiral had been informed that nine United States cruisers and seven destroyers were near Guadalcanal; it must rather have been based on the assumption that the Americans as usual would be gone with the sun, leaving Dai Nippon to prowl the Sound at will.

The first deviation from plan occurred at midnight. Abe's Raiding Group entered a squall northwest of Savo Island and the Admiral reversed course, apparently fearing lest the weather prove too thick in Ironbottom Sound for a shore bombardment. Upon obtaining a favorable weather report from Japanese headquarters on Guadalcanal, he put about again for Lunga; but he had lost 40 minutes and set forward to 0130 the time for the bombardment to commence. In maneuvering, the right-flank destroyers *Asagumo, Murasame* and *Samidare* fell out of position and were now far back on the starboard quarter instead of on the port bow of the battleships.

The Night Action of Friday the Thirteenth

It was now Friday the Thirteenth, last day of life for eight ships and many hundred sailors, including two American admirals.

See Appendix E for composition of U.S. and Japanese forces.

Early in the midwatch a *Helena* radar operator detected a suspicious "blip" on his scope. Then appeared two traces that were neither friendly ships nor neutral landmasses. The report went out at 0124: "Contacts bearing 312 and 310, distant 27,000 and 32,000 yards." Obviously one was a group of ships screening another 5000 yards behind it.

Three minutes after this first contact, Admiral Callaghan ordered his 13-ship column to change course two points to starboard, to course 310°. Apparently he desired a head-on clash rather than the more subtle run-around accompanied by torpedo launchings from the flanks. At 0130 *Helena* informed all ships that the enemy disposition was on their port bow distant 14,500 yards, steaming at speed 23 knots on course 105°. Opposing forces were closing at a rate of over 40 knots, and as the range decreased, the initial American advantage of radar vanished. Fire control men, intent on the complicated controls of range-keepers, watched the relentless spinning of the range dials, heard the drone of the range talker's voice, "Range one three 0 double 0 — range one two 0 double 0," wondering why no word came to let fly "fish" or commence gunfire. For ten long minutes their questions remained unanswered. Course was changed to due north, speed upped to

20 knots. On board *San Francisco* Admiral Callaghan, blind for want of adequate radar, was continually and urgently calling on his seeing-eye dogs, *Helena* and *O'Bannon,* for vital ranges, bearings, courses and composition. Yet this same voice radio (TBS) channel was the tactical control circuit; imperative directions for course, speed and gunfire had to be sandwiched between information requests. The outlets of the "squawk box" (voice radio) on the ships' bridges delivered a confused medley that baffled listeners and fast typists alike.

The fast-approaching Japanese did not listen in on this circuit; they were unaware of an enemy in the Sound. But they were not to be caught with defenses down. In anticipation of the scheduled shore bombardment, stocky gunners waited in their turrets while torpedomen, secondary battery gun crews, and searchlight operators stood alert at battle stations. Without radar, Admiral Abe realized that any surface action would be quick, close and decisive.

Inexorably the range closed. Commander Stokes of Desdiv 10, embarked in van destroyer *Cushing,* suddenly sighted Japanese

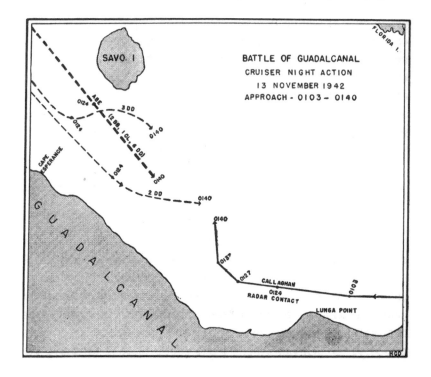

destroyers crossing ahead, port to starboard, at the uncomfort-
ably close range of 3000 yards. A flash radio report was passed
down the line as *Cushing's* skipper, Lieutenant Commander Parker,
turned left from a northerly heading at 0141 in order to unmask
his torpedo batteries. His quick turn avoided collision with the
enemy but resulted in a pile-up of the van, in which every ship
struggled to keep station while swinging to the new course 315°.
Atlanta, heavier than the destroyers, had to swing hard left. "What
are you doing?" asked Callaghan over voice radio. "Avoiding our
own destroyers," answered Captain Jenkins.

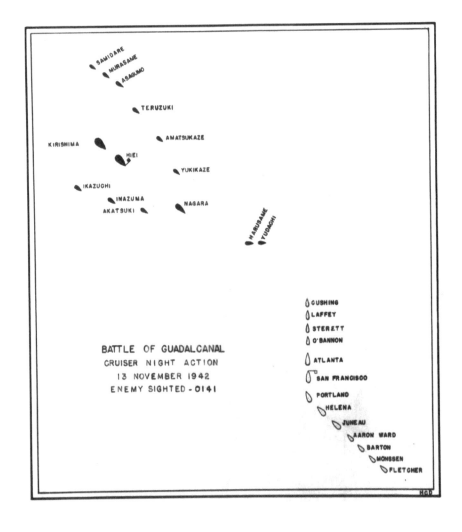

BATTLE OF GUADALCANAL
CRUISER NIGHT ACTION
13 NOVEMBER 1942
ENEMY SIGHTED - 0141

The ships seen by Stokes were destroyers *Yudachi* and *Harusame,* whose skippers may have been startled but were certainly not asleep. By 0142, a minute after first sighting, the entire Japanese force knew of the contact, surprise was lost, and the American delay in opening fire gave Admiral Abe's ships eight good minutes to prepare for action.

The United States ships were doubly confused by the sudden left turn and the resulting press of voice radio transmissions. Nobody could be certain whether reported target bearings were true or relative to the reporting ships. Nobody knew which target to take under fire, or when. Commander Stokes could stand it no longer. "Shall I let them have a couple of fish?" he asked. Permission was granted, but by this time the enemy destroyers had scudded into the darkness. Finally, at 0145, Admiral Callaghan gave the word, "Stand By to Open Fire!"

The prologue was now over and the principals in place; Americans confused, Nipponese surprised. Through the darkness Japanese night glasses picked up the loom of ships almost within their own formation, *Atlanta's* high superstructure standing above the

Rear Admiral Daniel J. Callaghan USN.

low destroyer silhouettes. At 0150 Japanese searchlight shutters clicked open; beams shot out, feeling right and left; one probably from *Akatsuki* quickly came to rest on the port wing of *Atlanta's* bridge, bathing the whole superstructure with the kind of light that sailors rightly fear. The cruiser's gunnery officer shouted two orders, "Commence Firing! Counter-illuminate!" The range was a scant 1600 yards, with solution already set on the range-keeper; the cruiser's 5-inch guns spewed forth a stream of shells which extinguished the offending light, but not quickly enough. While *Atlanta* sent salvo after salvo crashing into the Nips on both bows, they and their sister ships concentrated on her. Enemy shells crunched into the misnamed "Lucky A." One of them killed Admiral Scott, all but one of his staff, and others on the bridge. Simultaneously, from *San Francisco* came the long-awaited order: "Odd ships commence fire to starboard, even ships to port."[81]

Atlanta's participation in the battle was brief. Japanese destroyers, ever ready to exploit torpedo opportunities, dispatched several salvos at the confused American column. One, perhaps two, hit *Atlanta*. Their explosion lifted her bodily from the water, then set her down shuddering and crippled. In the plotting room, fire control men watched the needle on the pitometer log (the ship's speed indicator) slide down the scale until it rested against zero.

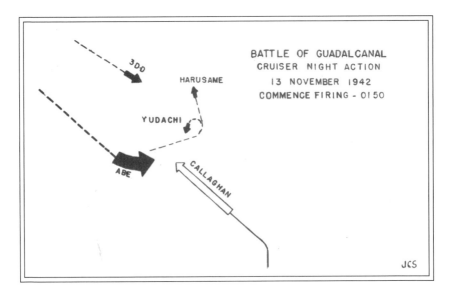

BATTLE OF GUADALCANAL
CRUISER NIGHT ACTION
13 NOVEMBER 1942
COMMENCE FIRING - 0150

300
HARUSAME
YUDACHI
ABE
CALLAGHAN

JCS

Atlanta was dead in the water, and the battle scarce begun. The ship's mascot terrier, misnamed "Lucky," whimpered pitifully in a corner of the damage control station, while the officer in charge telephoned vainly for reports from damaged areas.[82]

General Mêlée

From now on, Japanese and American ships mingled like minnows in a bucket. It is impossible to reconstruct their tracks; we can only relate what happened to each. Van destroyer *Cushing* sent several salvos screaming after a destroyer to starboard, but within two minutes received shell hits amidships which severed all power lines and slowed her down. Her bow was pointing almost due north when her skipper sighted *Hiei* on his port beam, on a collision course. Using hand steering control and what little way remained, he swung *Cushing* right and, by local control, fired six "fish" at the enemy battlewagon less than half a mile distant. None hit *Hiei*, which was also the target of destroyer and cruiser gunfire; but she didn't like it and turned slowly away to the westward. *Cushing* had only a few moments to exult like David. A probing searchlight beam picked her out and enemy gunfire reduced her to a sinking wreck in short order.[83]

Laffey, directly astern of *Cushing*, also entered a disastrous argument with *Hiei*, passing so close that collision was barely averted. Her torpedoes, launched at too short a range, failed to arm and bounced harmlessly off the battleship's sides. Topside machine gunners sprayed the pagoda-like bridge with 20-mm and 1.1 bullets as *Hiei* passed, shooting. Then two large-caliber gun salvos and a torpedo in the fantail put *Laffey* out of action for all time. She was promptly abandoned, the third to go. Many swimming survivors were killed when the burning hull exploded.

Destroyers *Sterett* and *O'Bannon*, respectively third and fourth in column, had better luck. The former, as an odd-numbered ship, ordered Action Starboard and took an enemy vessel under rapid fire at 4000 yards' range. Although the *Hiei* fracas on her port had rendered visual fire control difficult, radar and early fire-igniting hits on the target solved the problem. Three minutes after *Sterett* had opened fire, an enemy salvo found its mark in her port side aft, disabling her steering gear. This was followed by a hit on her foremast which destroyed the radar. But *Sterett* and her wiry little skipper, Commander Jesse G. Coward, were still full of fight. Maneuvering her with the engines, Coward turned his attention to *Hiei* and pumped out four torpedoes at 2000 yards' range. Simultaneously *O'Bannon* was getting in a few licks; she had opened fire when the first searchlight burst out and so continued throughout the battle. The illuminating Jap took a pummeling from her guns before *O'Bannon* turned on *Hiei,* then some 1200 yards on her port bow. Commander Wilkinson, in the midst of a maneuver to avoid collision with *Sterett,* ordered fire on the big battleship.

At that moment came a puzzling order from Admiral Callaghan: "Cease firing own ships!" *O'Bannon's* skipper checked fire momentarily and then launched two carefully aimed torpedoes at *Hiei.* He thought they had scored, but actually they either failed to hit or did not explode. The range was so short that the battleship was unable to depress her guns sufficiently to hit back. As her 14-inch salvos shrieked harmlessly over their heads, *O'Bannon's* sailors had the pleasure of seeing this enemy ship of the line completely enveloped in sheets of incandescent flame. A moment later, *O'Bannon* sheered left to avoid the sinking *Laffey's* bow, and tossed lifejackets to survivors as she passed. Torpedo wakes

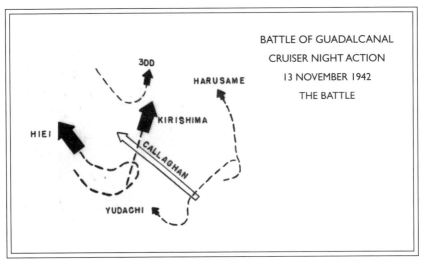

BATTLE OF GUADALCANAL
CRUISER NIGHT ACTION
13 NOVEMBER 1942
THE BATTLE

3DD

HARUSAME

KIRISHIMA

HIEI

CALLAGHAN

YUDACHI

Movements of Principle Japanese Units relative to American Formation.

crossed her bow. Suddenly an enormous underwater explosion jolted the ship, disrupting light and power and rattling the teeth of all on board. This quake may have been *Laffey's* explosive death rattle or it may have been an enemy torpedo exploding at the end of its run.[84]

Admiral Abe had already disposed of a light cruiser and two destroyers; but his position on the flag bridge of *Hiei,* cynosure of American gunfire, blinded him to the actual progress of the battle and he ordered a change of course in order to get clear. The American column had actually penetrated the center of his formation between his van destroyers, and between his two battleships. This was not according to book, and the Admiral did not like it. While *Hiei* was bearing the brunt of American fury, her sister battleship *Kirishima,* about 800 yards on the flagship's quarter, was dishing out 14-inch punishment but receiving only near-misses in return. She was nicked but once during the entire engagement, by an 8-inch shell. Both battleships turned left in compliance with the retirement order; *Hiei* so slowly that she was rapidly left behind, but she had not yet been torpedoed and was in not too bad a shape.

Flagship *San Francisco,* sixth in the American column and astern of *Atlanta,* had entered the fray promptly, taking under fire an enemy vessel on her starboard beam less than two miles distant. For illumination she used 5-inch star shell, fired to burst above and beyond the target. The unblinking beam of a searchlight, originating on her starboard quarter, wavered and then settled on her; and the illumination of American ships astern served to silhouette her to the enemy. After delivering seven hefty salvos, *San Francisco* shifted to a target described as a "small cruiser or a large destroyer." Two full main-battery salvos were pumped into the vessel, "setting her on fire throughout her length."[85] It will be recalled that *Atlanta* was now dead in the water and ahead of *San Francisco;* the crew of *Atlanta* believe that she was the victim.[86] How else can one explain Admiral Callaghan's order to cease fire? Before he gave that order, however, the flagship's main-battery control officer had sighted *Hiei* and contributed some well-placed salvos toward the devastation of that ship. When the Cease Firing

USS President Jackson and San Francisco under air attack 12 November 1942.

USS Atlanta.

order took effect, *San Francisco* was the first to suffer. *Kirishima* on her starboard hand dealt out heavy blows; another enemy ship on her starboard quarter employed searchlight illumination and gunfire to good effect; a destroyer darting down her port side raked the superstructure. Steering and engine control were temporarily lost, and as she slowed down, an avalanche of shellfire from three different ships snuffed out the lives of Admiral Callaghan and his staff, of Captain Cassin Young and of nearly every man on the bridge.

At this juncture, cruisers astern of *San Francisco* rallied to her support. *Portland,* seventh in line, had closed firing keys when the enemy illuminated. Her shells located a starboard-hand target whose return fire registered but one hit, which wounded the executive officer. Five minutes after the battle's start, Captain Laurance DuBose received the Cease Firing order but disregarded it except for an incredulous inquiry addressed to the flagship: "What's the dope, did you want to cease fire?" Callaghan had time to answer "Affirmative," and to order a course change to the northward. *Portland* checked fire briefly while turning, then picked up a target three miles to starboard and commenced gnawing away at it with her turret guns. A Japanese torpedo tore through the water toward her. A terrific wallop rocked the cruiser as the explosion ripped a huge chunk from her stern, bending the structure so that projecting hull plates acted as an unwanted auxiliary rudder and she made an involuntary complete circle. As she came out of it *Hiei* loomed up in her sights, range 4000 yards, and *Portland* let her have it from both forward turrets. This concluded the evening's main-battery performance for the "Sweet Pea," as her crew called this happy ship.

Helena, next astern, was favored by fortune. Opening fire at the same instant as the ships ahead of her, she directed her tracers at the inquisitive searchlight on her port beam some two miles away. Enemy shell splashes reared up in ugly gouts astern but *Helena* received only minor superstructure damage. During the next few minutes Captain Hoover made strenuous efforts to avoid the damaged ships ahead while his guns shifted from target to target. Almost simultaneously his 6-inch main battery lashed out at a ship that was pummeling *San Francisco,* his 5-inchers went after a destroyer on the starboard quarter, and his heavy machine guns worked over a ship of unfriendly contour only 3000 yards distant, probably *Nagara.* When the enemy's retirement opened the range, bullets from *Helena* hastened him on his way.

Juneau, last cruiser in column, fired along with the rest of the task force during the hectic quarter-hour between 0148 and 0203. In common with other ships, she had difficulty in identifying targets; Callaghan's Cease Firing order belayed a brief spraying of

Helena. An enemy torpedo sundered *Juneau's* forward fireroom with a shock which put the ship completely out of action, dead in the water and probably with a broken keel. From that moment her main concern was to clear out and keep afloat.[87]

Bringing up the rear, and thus late for the initial slugfest, were destroyers *Aaron Ward, Barton, Monssen* and *Fletcher.* Captain Robert G. Tobin, the squadron commander who flew his pennant in the first-named, was handicapped by lack of orders and an ineffective radar. His opening ranges were considerably greater than the side-scraping distances at which the van destroyers fought, and the jumbled state of the column rendered target selection and station keeping almost impossible. *Aaron Ward* opened up on a target 7000 yards on her starboard bow, discharged 10 salvos and then checked fire because friendly cruisers fouled her range. Commander Gregor was forced to stop and back engines to avoid collision with a ship ahead—probably *Helena.* Ten minutes elapsed before he could feel certain that an enemy target was in the optics, and then *San Francisco* charged into his line of sight. A target showing unfamiliar recognition lights sharp on the starboard bow was next taken under fire at a mile-and-a-half range, and firing continued until the ship appeared to explode and sink. *Aaron Ward* then used enemy searchlights as points of aim. She received one hit in the director which occasioned a shift to local control of gun batteries.

Destroyer *Barton,* commissioned as recently as 29 May, had a total combat life of exactly seven minutes. She opened fire, launched four torpedoes to port, stopped to avoid collision and, when almost dead in the water, received a torpedo in the forward fireroom which was followed almost instantly by another in the forward engine room. She broke in two and sank in a matter of seconds, taking with her all but a handful of the crew.

Monssen, her conning party eagerly listening to the jabber of the voice radio, trailed *Barton.* She had lost the use of her fire control radar during the afternoon air fight and was forced to rely on radio information and optics. Her knowledge of the situation was slight but her interest was great, particularly after a torpedo passed directly under her keel. *Monssen* fired a 5-torpedo salvo at a battleship on her starboard bow, then turned her attention to another vessel two miles on the starboard beam, launching a spread of five more torpedoes. The 5-inch guns meanwhile went after targets on the port side while the 20-mm guns raised havoc on the topside of a destroyer a quarter of a mile to starboard. Star shell began to burst over and around *Monssen,* lighting up the ship like a nightclub floor show. Lieutenant Commander McCombs, believing the star shell to be friendly, switched on his fighting lights; and the click of that light switch was the death knell of his ship. Two blinding tentacles of light grasped her, a deluge of explosives followed, torpedoes hissed by. Some 37 shell hits reduced *Monssen* to a burning hulk.

Destroyer *Fletcher,* despite her station in the very rear of the column, had excellent information from a superior search radar. When the enemy first illuminated *Atlanta,* Commander Cole triggered his firing keys at the offending ship, then some 5500 yards on his port bow. Next, observing that many other ships had chosen the same target, *Fletcher* shifted to a more distant target and had the satisfaction of starting some bright blazes. The order Cease Firing caused her to check momentarily and then resume firing at a third target still farther back in the enemy formation. Eight minutes after the first shot, *Fletcher* sailors witnessed the sudden disintegration of *Barton* and the riddling of *Monssen.* Now that the column was in complete disorder, Commander Cole decided to leave this cluttered area, make another evaluation and return to launch his yet unused torpedoes. Aided by a constant flow of information from the radar room, he threaded his way through the maelstrom of friends and foes, turned south, bent on 35 knots and rounded up to a firing position ahead of the enemy. Torpedo wakes swirled under and around her, gun salvos bracketed her, but *Fletcher* had a charmed life; she emerged without even her paintwork scratched.

Four bells of this sinister midwatch had struck during these fifteen minutes of raw hell. A literally infernal scene presented itself to the participants. The struggle had deteriorated into a wild and desperate mêlée. The greenish light of suspended star shell dimmed the stars overhead. Elongated red and white trails of shell

Consolidated PBY-5 "Catalina" Flying Boat of a "Black Cat" night patrol squadron. National Archives.

tracers arched and crisscrossed, magazines exploded in blinding bouquets of white flame, oil-fed conflagrations sent up twisted yellow columns. Dotting the horizon were the dull red glows of smoldering hulls, now obscured by dense masses of smoke, now blazing up when uncontrolled fires reached new combustibles. The sea itself, fouled with oil and flotsam, tortured by underwater upheavals, rose in geysers from shell explosions.

By 0200 November 13, the main issue had been decided by Admiral Abe's order to *Hiei* and *Kirishima* to turn left and steam north. Henderson Field and its precious planes were safe for that night at least, but nobody on the American side knew it.

Exeunt Fighting

Fighting continued with little respite after the battlewagons retired, *Hiei* to the south of Savo, *Kirishima* to the north. A short lull gave *Cushing* opportunity to fight fires on board, but just as they were brought under control several enemy salvos came her way. The flames then took charge and finally, at 0315, with magazines in volcanic action, the skipper ordered Abandon Ship. *Laffey* was already on the iron bottom. *Sterett*, with steering gear disabled, encountered an enemy destroyer 1000 yards on her starboard bow at 0220 and launched two torpedoes which appeared to hit and sink her; but, shortly after, *Sterett* was peppered with 5-inch shells and forced to retire southeastward, slowing down periodically to reduce the windage on the flames.

Commander Wilkinson in *O'Bannon* decided, since the scene was utterly confused, to haul off to the southeastward in an effort to locate friend or foe. At 0215 he sighted a smoking vessel on the port bow but wisely withheld torpedo fire on what later proved to be *San Francisco*. Thinking that enemy transports might have entered the Sound, *O'Bannon* turned south and investigated the shoreline. Saint Christopher, Saint Barbara and the luck of the Irish must have been with plucky *O'Bannon* on this fearful night.[88]

Atlanta's fighting men by 0200 were mere spectators, a status which they had neither time nor inclination to enjoy. Their ship was ravaged by more than 50 large-caliber shell hits, holed by torpedoes and consumed by fire. Survivors found devastation behind every bulkhead and in almost every compartment. Below decks men groped in complete darkness through acrid smoke and sloshed heavily in oily waters on flooded decks. Cursing and coughing, they labored to seal hull ruptures, succor the many wounded and bring fires under control. The main deck was a charnel house. Burned and eviscerated corpses, severed limbs and chunks of flesh mixed with steel debris, littered it from stem to stern. Blood, oil and seawater made a nasty, slippery slush through which one could move only on hands and knees. The "spud locker" amidships had burst open, strewing the decks with potatoes; no joke to groaning men who slipped on the treacherous tubers.

Muzzles of useless guns drooped silent over the motionless dead. Seven out of the eight 5-inch turrets had been hit, all but four of the machine guns were smashed. Flames ate greedily into the superstructure, belching out as burning ammunition detonated. Shadowy figures, the only living part of this macabre setting, moved perilously back and forth as bucket brigades or to jettison the cumbersome weights which threatened to capsize the ship, or to carry the wounded to improvised dressing stations. Admiral Scott was dead but Captain Jenkins and his executive officer, Commander Campbell D. Emory, were spared serious injury. They were able gradually to establish communications with the little knots of survivors around the ship and to direct a coordinated effort to save *Atlanta*. Gasoline handy-billys were rigged to fight fire, a damage control party worked to get one fireroom back into operation, the remaining guns were manned, the injured were taken to comparative safety aft.

As the battle drew to a close, *San Francisco's* topsides were in almost as bad shape as *Atlanta's*, but three circumstances saved the flagship from annihilation. The close range had prevented the enemy from depressing his guns sufficiently to score hits below the waterline; thin-skinned bombardment shells, fatal to human lives and damaging to superstructure, had been deflected by armor; she had suffered no torpedo hits. On the navigation bridge Lieutenant Commander Bruce McCandless, communications officer, found himself the only able-bodied survivor. In central station, Lieutenant Commander H. E. Schonland, acting first lieutenant, learned that he had succeeded to command. Realizing that his knowledge of damage control was vital to the ship's survival, he elected to lead the fight against the twenty-five fires then raging, and ordered McCandless to conn the ship out of harm's way. That he did very well, skirting the coast of Guadalcanal.

Portland, with her warped stern, continued to steam in tight circles for the remainder of the night. Captain DuBose at one time counted nine burning vessels in the Sound. *Helena* ceased firing at 0216 and, except for brief searchlight scrutiny, received no more attention from the enemy. Captain Hoover, unable to contact either Scott or Callaghan and believing his to be the senior undamaged command, called all ships (only two answered) and at 0226 ordered them to follow him and retire via Sealark Channel. *Juneau* got under way by the end of the midwatch and moved toward Indispensable Strait.

Meantime, Captain Tobin's three remaining destroyers of the rear were acting individually. *Aaron Ward* with guns in local control lashed out at enemy searchlights that were guiding salvos her way. She cleared out after being pierced by nine medium-caliber shells. The damage was cumulative and progressive, so that by 0235 she lay dead in the water with a flooded engine room, and spent the rest of the night in efforts to get way on. *Monssen* burned and exploded with such fury that she was hastily abandoned. The crew, clinging to life rafts, watched their ship flame and erupt throughout the remaining hours of darkness.

Fletcher, the apparently untouchable Shadrach of the American task force, was now in an excellent position to reënter the contest with torpedoes. A large target was selected and radar commenced tracking as the ship stalked her prey. The enemy vessel, on an easterly course, was shooting to the northward, probably at her friends, when *Fletcher* dispatched ten "fish" on a three-and-a-half-mile run at 36 knots. Having shot her bolt, *Fletcher* retired in the general direction of Sealark Channel.

On the enemy side, it is probable that most torpedo tubes were emptied during the first ten minutes. At any rate, after 0200 the Martian display diminished rapidly. *Hiei* steered an erratic northwesterly course, limping from damage to steering and communication systems and loss of firepower. She had taken over 50 topside hits. Destroyer *Akatsuki,* one of the forward screening vessels, had gone down. *Yudachi* of the advanced flank, emerging from a penetration run through the American forces, underwent a severe explosion at 0220 which stopped her dead some five miles south of Savo Island. Three destroyers had been hit but not stopped: *Ikazuchi*, forecastle gun damaged; *Murasame*, forward boiler room out; *Amatsukaze,* minor scars. These three retired to the north in company with undamaged ships, *Samidare* took off *Yudachi* survivors and followed them later, and the Patrol Unit of three destroyers stood by the stricken battleship.

Daylight Disasters

A glassy, metallic sea, stippled by the floating litter of death and destruction, reflected the sun's first rays. The mountains of Guadalcanal turned from black to purple and then to lush green. Sailors on crippled warships of both nations stood by their damaged guns, grimly aware that between ship and ship no quarter would be given. Early birdmen could see eight crippled ships scattered without order between Savo Island and Guadalcanal. Five were American: unsteerable *Portland,* shattered *Atlanta*, immobile *Aaron Ward,* burning and abandoned *Cushing* and *Monssen.*

The Rising Sun was still flying on rudderless *Hiei* and her loyal protectors and on flaming and abandoned *Yudachi*. It was inevitable that more compliments would be exchanged.

Portland still churning in circles, embraced *Yudachi* 12,500 yards distant, with six salvos. Enough of these 36 projectiles hit to produce a magazine explosion which completely erased the destroyer, a cheering sight to many a swimming American.

On board *Atlanta* all efforts were concentrated on saving the ship. Captain Jenkins, wounded painfully in the foot, urged his bedraggled seamen to superhuman efforts. By 1400 the cruiser was anchored off Kukum, but she could not be kept afloat. No salvage facilities were available, she was listing heavily to port and the enemy was expected again that night. So the crew was ordered to scuttle the old girl with a demolition charge. *Atlanta* went down three miles off Lunga Point shortly after dark on Friday evening, the Bloody Thirteenth.

Cushing and *Monssen* continued to burn but did not sink until late in the afternoon.

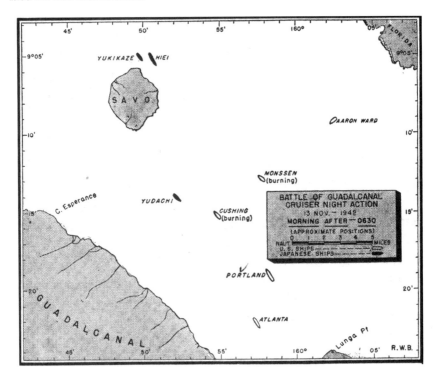

All day *Portland* continued her efforts to recover steering control. Every conceivable maneuver and gadget were tried. "Sweet Pea" finally anchored in Tulagi Harbor at 0100 November 14.

The American vessels which had retired from the hot spot around Savo found themselves at dawn in a formation proceeding southeasterly down Indispensable Strait. Captain Hoover of *Helena,* now senior officer present, took charge of *San Francisco, Juneau, O'Bannon, Sterett* and *Fletcher*—three of them lame ducks. Zigzagging through a smooth sea at 18 knots, they set course for the New Hebrides.

In order to provide anti-submarine protection, *Fletcher* and *Sterett* were placed 4000 yards ahead of the heavy ships. As *O'Bannon's* sound gear had been damaged by the previous night's underwater explosion, she was sent ahead to transmit a radio message to Admiral Halsey. At 0950 *Sterett* made a sound contact and delivered an urgent depth-charge attack with indeterminate results.

An hour later, this task force touched the nadir of its fortune. *Helena* was steaming 1000 yards ahead of *San Francisco; Juneau* was 1000 yards on the latter's starboard beam. Submarine *1-26,* cruising at periscope depth, drew a bead and fired a spread of torpedoes. Two of them shot past *San Francisco* but she, with no means of rapid communication left, could not broadcast the alarm. Straight and true, one enemy torpedo traveled toward *Juneau,* and at 1101 detonated against her port side under the bridge. Horrified sailors in *San Francisco* saw the light cruiser disintegrate instantaneously and completely, sinking with apparently no trace except a tall pillar of smoke and a little debris. Nobody waited to look for survivors. A Flying Fortress, attracted thither by the force of the explosion, was informed of the disaster and asked to relay a rescue request to Admiral Halsey's headquarters.[89]

Unfortunately this message never got through. Of more than a hundred men who miraculously survived the eruption and who clung pitifully to the flotsam that marked their ship's end, all but ten perished. Three paddled their raft to a small island where friendly natives and a European trader brought them back to life, and a Catalina carried them home. Another PBY rescued six; *Ballard* picking up the sole survivor of one raft on 20 November.

Almost 700 men, including the five Sullivan brothers, went down with *Juneau* or died in life rafts.[90]

So ended the wildest, most desperate sea fight since Jutland, one that recalls the Anglo-Dutch battles of the seventeenth century. Ship losses were fairly well balanced; two light cruisers and four destroyers as against two destroyers and a battleship so badly damaged that airmen could sink her next day. Casualties on the American side were many times those of the enemy. But the Japanese bombardment mission was completely frustrated—Yamamoto admitted as much by relieving Abe and depriving him of any further sea command. Callaghan, on the other hand, completed his mission; he saved Henderson Field from a bombardment which might well have been more serious than "the" bombardment of mid-October, and certainly would have stopped the American air operations, which next day disposed of eleven troop-laden transports.

Thus, in the end, all mistakes were canceled out by valor. While the shells that were to strike him down were being loaded into enemy gun breeches, Admiral Callaghan called out over voice radio, "We want the big ones!"—meaning Japanese battleships. His men stopped one; on the following night Admiral Lee consigned another to the iron bottom. Let none deny praise, glory and honor to those who fell on Friday the Bloody Thirteenth with two great seamen and gallant gentlemen, Daniel J. Callaghan and Norman Scott.

Kinkaid Moves Up, Nishimura Bombards, (13 November)

Abe's failure in no way softened Admiral Kondo's determination to land troops and supplies on Guadalcanal. His cruisers and destroyers, idling off the coral reefs of Ontong Java some 250 miles to the northward, were summoned to save *Hiei* at 0630 November 13. At the same time, Vice Admiral Mikawa in *Chokai* sallied forth from the Shortlands with four heavy cruisers, two light cruisers and six destroyers to bombard Henderson Field. That left Rear Admiral Tanaka with eleven destroyers to escort eleven troop-laden transports to Guadalcanal. This Reinforcement Group had departed Shortlands at nightfall 12 November, prudently retired to its Faisi base early on the 13th, and that day made preparations to dash into Guadalcanal and discharge troops after sunset on the

14th. In preparation, Kondo's Main Body would assimilate un-damaged remnants of Abe's Raiding Group—*Kirishima, Nagara* and four destroyers—to make way for the Emperor's transports. Air cover would be provided by two carriers, supported by two Kongo class battleships and cruiser *Tone.*

After a foul night, American prospects looked fair on the morning of the 13th. Henderson Field still supported an aggressive brood of aircraft. Admiral Kinkaid's Task Force 16 with carrier *Enterprise* and two new battleships, which had departed Nouméa on the 11th, was boiling up from the south. "Big E" rang day and night with hammer blows and the sputter of welders' arcs as she steamed north, but still the forward elevator refused to operate. Cruiser *Pensacola* and destroyers *Gwin* and *Preston*, detached from Callaghan's command before the night action, were on their way down from the Solomons to beef up Kinkaid's screen.

Admiral Turner had discounted the contact report of two enemy carriers 150 miles west of Lunga at 1450 November 12. Admiral Kinkaid could not afford to ignore it—he knew to his cost what carrier planes could do to carriers. So, at dawn 13 November, when Task Force 16 was still 340 miles SSE of Guadalcanal, *Enterprise* launched ten planes to search 200 miles out over a 120-degree northerly sector. An attack group was readied on "Big E's" flight deck, but the questing planes found nothing; *Junyo* and *Hiyo* were well beyond their range. Kinkaid then decided to contribute some *Enterprise* planes to Henderson Field, for his carrier was still incapable of her usual fast flight operations. Accordingly, nine Avengers and six Wildcats took off with orders to report to General Vandegrift, after searching for enemy ships en route and attacking any that might be sighted.

The first target encountered by these planes was the long-suffering *Hiei*. Lieutenant John F. Sutherland, leading the TBFs, sighted this wounded battlewagon with her attendant destroyers about ten miles north of Savo Island, approached through a protective cloud blanket, made runs on both bows simultaneously and, at 1020, emerged unscathed by anti-aircraft fire. The Avengers made two hits, one of which disabled the rudder so that *Hiei* steamed in circles; but the "unsinkable old so-and-so," as the aviators were beginning to call her, needed more punishment than that.

Sutherland had his planes reserviced at Henderson Field and took the air again at 1330 in company with eight Marine Corps SBDs and two additional Wildcats. This time the Avengers launched torpedoes at 90-degree angles to the almost stationary battleship. Two bounced harmlessly off the armored sides and a third ran wild, but two exploded; and these, although they did not sink *Hiei,* left her dead in the water at 1430 so that other planes could work her over. The next to do so flew up from Espiritu Santo. Fourteen Flying Fortresses dropped 56 bombs, only one of which possibly hit. By 1800 *Hiei's* crew had been taken off by three destroyers, who left her going down stern-first, about five miles NNW of Savo Island.

Other land-based aircraft of Admiral Fitch's from Espiritu Santo were active on 13 November. Scout planes ran into more than their share of excitement. Flying Forts, snooping Admiral Kondo's ships near Ontong Java, on two occasions were attacked by "Zekes." Another B-17, cruising up the Slot, reported four cruisers, six destroyers and twelve transports. These were Tanaka's group, whose schedule had been delayed as a result of Callaghan's night action. Navy Catalinas, too, had several brushes and sighted enemy ships. But *Enterprise* had only one brief flurry of excitement. About noon a 4-engined Kawanishi reported her location and was shot down by her combat air patrol. Apparently the Japanese were too busy to make any use of the plane's contact report.

Admiral Halsey from Nouméa had ordered Admiral Kinkaid to cover the retirement of American ships damaged in the night action by remaining south of lat. 11° 40′ S; but information of enemy movements that flowed in during the day indicated more important work to be done. In mid-afternoon Halsey ordered Lee's heavy gunfire component of Task Force 16 (*Washington, South Dakota* and four destroyers) to be readied for a quick run to Guadalcanal, when he gave the word. Halsey had determined to keep *Enterprise* south of Guadalcanal, whatever happened.[91] So it was up to the battlewagons.

At about 1700 November 13, Kinkaid turned his entire task force due north, to close Guadalcanal at 23 knots. About an hour and a half later, during the second dogwatch, word came from Halsey to send Lee's group ahead to prevent a bombardment of Henderson Field. Unfortunately, Kinkaid's northward advance had been slowed by emergency turns to avoid submarine contacts, and by flight operations which had required fast steaming into a gentle southeast breeze; and by the time Halsey's order reached the task force it was still 350 miles from Savo Island. No battleship could get there that night. Kinkaid sent destroyer *Mustin* 50 miles to the eastward to let Halsey know by radio that it would be impossible for Lee to reach Savo before 0800 November 14. So, as a result of poor staff work at Nouméa, there was nothing to put between Henderson Field and the Japanese bombardment ships except the Tulagi motor torpedo boat contingent.

Admiral Mikawa's cruisers and destroyers, after taking the long way north of Choiseul and Santa Isabel to escape detection, arrived off Savo Island shortly after midnight. Mikawa then detached Nishimura's bombardment group to enter the Sound, while he patrolled to the westward as a precaution against interference. Star performers for the scheduled fireworks were Nishimura's flagship *Suzuya* and another heavy cruiser, *Maya*, each carrying some 500 rounds of high-capacity 8-inch shells destined for Henderson Field. Covered by light cruiser *Tenryu* and four destroyers, the two heavies steamed south of Savo, turned to parallel the Guadalcanal coast, and let fly off Lunga.

On the receiving end of this lethal deluge was Henderson Field, whose aviators and ground crews were playing host to several hundred survivors from *Atlanta* and the sunken destroyers. Sleepy and indignant, these weary Americans groped their way to the familiar muddy foxholes to sit out the show. All hands had hoped that Callaghan's last fight had put a stop to such doings; yet here was another "Tokyo Express" right in the old groove. For thirty-seven minutes the Japanese shells whistled, screamed and caromed through the coconut palms while soldiers and sailors, furious at their inability to strike back, ran the gamut of profanity and prayers. "Washing-Machine Charlie," the Japanese aerial spotter, added insult with bright flares as he sent corrections to the cruisers' fire control teams. When losses were counted in the morning, they were much less than had been anticipated: one dive-bomber

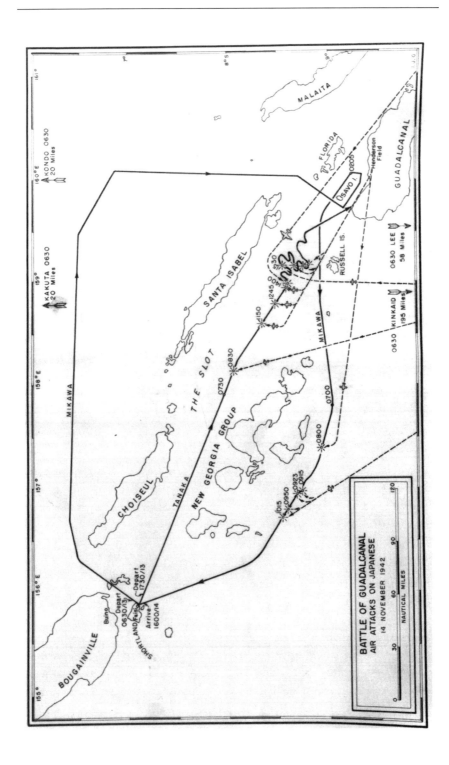

BATTLE OF GUADALCANAL
AIR ATTACKS ON JAPANESE
14 NOVEMBER 1942

and 17 fighter planes destroyed and 32 more fighters damaged, but the field was still operational. Nishimura's bombardment was a poor show compared with what Abe's big boys might have staged the previous night, if let alone.

During the bombardment two motor torpedo boats bravely sortied from Tulagi, made three runs at the heavy cruisers and launched six torpedoes. They made no hits but possibly influenced the enemy to hurry up and get out. At 0205 November 14, when Nishimura had expended his allowance of bombardment ammunition, he led his ships around the north end of Savo, and rendezvoused with Mikawa's patrol group; both retired toward the Shortlands.

Smacking the Transports, 14 November

As the sun rose over Sealark Channel, airmen and ground crews at Henderson Field rolled out of their foxholes. Reinforcements from *Enterprise*, missing their good Navy chow, shared an exiguous breakfast with Army aviators, Marines and Navy survivors, and Henderson warmed up to one of the busiest days in its hectic history.

Search planes from Henderson and Espiritu Santo were out scouring suspected waters by daybreak, and shortly after 0700 their reports started to roll in: two large groups of combatant ships and transports up the Slot 150 miles northwest of Henderson Field and headed southeast; Mikawa's retiring Support Group bearing W by N, distant about 140 miles. Six Avengers, 7 Dauntless and 7 fighter planes took to the air, hot after the nearer contingent; found it at 0800 and attacked. Torpedo planes, visitors from *Enterprise*, and others of the Marine Corps, holed heavy cruiser *Kinugasa*, while dive-bombers zipped through anti-aircraft fire to plant bombs on light cruiser *Isuzu*. The jubilant pilots left the leading cruiser burning vigorously, and the other emitting clouds of smoke. The entire American flight returned safely to base by 1015; a good early morning's work.

Enterprise, now some 200 miles SSW of Guadalcanal, was eager to get in on the fight. Bad weather delayed her dawn search until 0608 when two planes were launched to cover a northwesterly sector for 200 miles out and eight planes to cover a northerly sector for 250 miles out. Ten fighters and 17 dive-bombers armed with 1000-pound bombs were ready on the flight deck. At 0708 one of the search planes reported ten unidentified planes 140 miles to the northward, flying toward *Enterprise*. What these planes were never was ascertained, but the report caused Captain Hardison to head into the wind and launch his attack group with instructions to head north, look and listen. Their early departure served them well when an exciting contact report came through: "Two battleships, two heavy cruisers, one possible converted carrier, four destroyers, position 8° 45´ S, 157° 10´ E, course 290°." That group again was retiring Mikawa's, to the southward of New Georgia; it included no battleships, however. While the two search planes which had made the contact report trailed Mikawa, and at 0915 took a crack at *Kinugasa* which started flooding and gave the heavy cruiser a 10-degree list, Lieutenant Commander James R. Lee in command of the *Enterprise* attack group was making a beeline for the enemy.

At 0950 Mikawa's disorganized command hove into sight. After searching the area carefully for carriers, the bomber leader selected cruiser targets. Planes went into their dives and were rewarded with two apparent hits. A near-miss ruptured *Kinugasa's* gasoline tanks and started another fire and, a few minutes later, the pilots had the satisfaction of seeing this heavy cruiser take the plunge.

Admiral Mikawa, whether he intended it or not, was serving his country somewhat expensively as a decoy, leading American air power away from the crowded troopships. In a series of attacks over a period of two hours he lost *Kinugasa* and suffered damage to heavy cruisers *Chokai* and *Maya*, light cruiser *Isuzu* and destroyer *Michishio*. But the cripples and undamaged ships reached Shortland safely.

Admiral Tanaka's heavily escorted Reinforcement Group, following the direct route down the Slot, had been sighted at 0700 and identified at 0730 by Henderson scout planes when north of New Georgia; but it was not until an hour later that two *Enterprise* SBD pilots found these ships in the Slot midway between New Georgia and Santa Isabel. The planes selected a fat transport and scored one near-miss and one probable hit. As they pulled out, strafing, they encountered a buzz-saw of seven furious "Zekes" which had flown down from carrier *Hiyo*, then operating to the northward. One SBD was shot down but the other managed to escape, returning to *Enterprise* with tanks almost dry after nearly five and a half hours airborne.

Guadalcanal-based airmen now turned their entire attention to the transports approaching Savo Island. A mixed group of Marine Corps and Navy planes—7 torpedo and 18 dive-bombers escorted by 12 fighters—rose from runways still scarred from the night bombardment. They picked up Tanaka's convoy at 1150, attacked, and opened gaping holes in several transport hulls.

The next relay—17 dive-bombers with a fighter escort of mixed antecedents—drew a bead on the transports at 1245, zoomed down from 12,000 feet to drop bombs, pulled out strafing and had the satisfaction of seeing at least one enemy ship break in two. Fifteen Flying Fortresses started out from Espiritu Santo at 1018. Their turn arrived at 1430 when, from an altitude of three miles, they loosed 15 tons of bombs over the transports, scoring one hit and several near-misses. "Zekes" were present in equal number to the Forts, and a lively aerial skirmish ensued, six of the enemy falling victim to the American gunners.

In Task Force 16 Admiral Kinkaid made the sound decision to shoot the works. *Enterprise's* 8 bombers accompanied by 12 fighters and led by skipper Flatley of "Fighter Ten," skimmed skyward at 1310, "pouring on the soup" in an effort to reach the targets before they were all gone. Flatley had his first glimpse of Tanaka's disordered ranks about 60 miles northwest of Savo Island at 1530. The Japanese admiral was attempting to reform his ships. Some seven or eight transports and five or six destroyers were turning southeast again, leaving three or four others dead in the water and on fire. The attendant "Zekes," much diminished in number, actually flinched from attacking Flatley's Wildcats. Each SBD selected a target and peeled off from 15,000 feet while the Wildcats guarded its tail and then came in strafing. Some bombs hit their marks; fighter-plane bullets whipped troop-crowded decks. Every one of the *Enterprise* planes was safely grounded at Henderson Field by 1600.

Tanaka was in a dilemma. If he retired, his mission would be a failure and he would lose face; if he continued he might possibly deliver some troops to Guadalcanal but would certainly lose his ships. He chose the bolder alternative. Bringing his eleven destroyers close aboard the burning and sinking transports, he succeeded in transferring between 600 and 1000 men to each, and at the same time organized such transports as were still navigable to continue doggedly on their advance.

It was too much to expect that American planes could continue the slaughter all day without cost. Lieutenant Commander Thomas, commanding *Enterprise* "Bomber Ten," departed Henderson Field at 1530 leading a seven-plane flight without fighter escort. That gave the "Zekes" guarding Tanaka their chance. They shot down three of the unprotected SBDs, seriously damaged and turned back two others, and gave a hot reception to the two which penetrated the fighter curtain. One of these played hide-and-seek with a Nip, up through the clouds and down through the Russell Island jungles, finally shaking him off to return to base with 68 holes in his Dauntless and a firm belief in the merits of fighter protection. And two more Marine flights were dispatched from Henderson before nightfall.

Thus, in one day Tanaka lost seven transports, with all their supplies and many of their troops, to air attack alone.[92] Four transports and eleven destroyers remained afloat, still boldly steaming toward Guadalcanal.

To the south of the island *Enterprise*, with only 18 fighter planes remaining on board, passed into a weather front at 1400. An enemy snooper's error in reporting her position resulted in a large flight of would-be attackers passing far to the westward while Kinkaid snuggled into the squall. Next day, Halsey ordered the carrier and her screen back to Espiritu Santo and Nouméa.

The 14th of November offered a striking illustration of what happens to lightly protected ships that venture under enemy-controlled skies. At a cost of only five planes the Americans had sunk a heavy cruiser and seven transports and inflicted serious damage on several others. Both sides learned much that day. The Japanese observed that a destroyer screen with fighter cover was not enough to protect feebly armed ships; they must have close support from heavily gunned men-of-war. And they also learned the need of an additional airfield to help protect the "Tokyo Express." The Americans noted how greatly the effectiveness of carrier planes was increased when they were provided with an optional land base.

Joust of Giants, 14-15 November

These pulverizing air blows against Mikawa and Tanaka obscured the activities of Lee's heavy gunfire group and Kondo's Emergency Bombardment Group, both of which had missions of great import.

Task Force 64 was the first flag command of Rear Admiral Willis Augustus Lee. Behind his lined and weather-beaten face was one of the best brains in the Navy. As director of fleet training just before the war he had been responsible for many improvements in the equipment of combat ships and "he knew more about radar than the radar operators." In addition he had the quality of imperturbability, the capacity to keep in mind the details of a complicated and rapidly changing situation, and the gift of quick and accurate decision that characterized Spruance at Midway. The Navy would need everything he had in the rough night action ahead.[93]

It will be recalled that Lee's group peeled off from Kinkaid's carrier task force on the evening of 13 November, the two battleships and four destroyers hightailing northward. Unable to reach Savo in time to thwart Nishimura's cruiser bombardment, Lee stood off during the 14th, about 100 miles S by W of Guadalcanal, hoping to avoid detection. The enemy did snoop him, but Lee on his side was picking up everything that went on elsewhere. Reports of what was being done to Mikawa and Tanaka, though encouraging, were not nearly so interesting to him as other contacts which crackled in from the north: enemy battleships in Ontong Java waters, big combatant force southbound some 150 miles north of Guadalcanal at 1600. That was Kondo's. It confirmed Lee's suspicion of a forthcoming "Tokyo Express" run that night. His sailors checked their big guns and armor-piercing shells with the certainty that both would find employment.

Admiral Kondo's Emergency Bombardment Group — battleship

Kirishima, heavy cruisers *Atago* and *Takao,* two light cruisers and an entire destroyer squadron, started south from its stand-by position near Ontong Java at about 1000 November 14 to enter the Slot east of Santa Isabel. During the afternoon this group was attacked by U.S. submarine *Trout,* three of whose torpedoes passed underneath a destroyer and almost nicked the flagship. *Trout* sent an urgent plain-language report of the episode, which Kondo overheard and from which he concluded that a warm reception would await him off Lunga Point. His intention was to brush off American air and surface interference and carry out the devastating airfield bombardment originally assigned to Abe but frustrated by Callaghan.

Early in the evening of 14 November, Lee began prowling around the western end of Guadalcanal, within nine miles of the shoreline. Leading his six-ship column were destroyers *Walke, Benham, Preston* and *Gwin,* followed by battleships *Washington* and *South Dakota.* He was suffering from the same lack of practice in teamwork that had plagued Callaghan. The four destroyers, from four different divisions and with no division commander on board, had been assigned to him because at the moment they had more fuel than any others under Kinkaid. The battleships had not operated together before leaving Nouméa. Admiral Lee had no opportunity to prepare a formal operation order, but signaled his intentions by visual dispatch. Many at Comsopac headquarters doubted the wisdom of committing two new 16-inch battleships to waters so restricted as those around Savo

Rear Admiral Willis Augustus Lee USN.

Island, but Admiral Halsey felt he must throw in everything at this crisis. And he granted Lee complete freedom of action upon reaching Guadalcanal.

Lee's task force, sweeping to the west of Savo, made no contact but saw the distant flares from Tanaka's burning transports on the western horizon. Shortly after 2100 November 14 the Admiral signaled a course change to 90° to take the ships into Ironbottom Sound. He intended to intercept the enemy bombardment group first and early, then deal with the covering group. With Savo on the starboard beam at 2148, course again changed to 150°, SE by S. Now they were steaming over the hulls of ships lost in the battles of 9 August and 13 November, as one could ascertain by watching the needle deflect on the magnetic compass. Ironbottom Sound was flat and calm. A light 7-knot breeze sharp on the port bow hardly ruffled the surface. The first-quarter moon, due to set at 0100, was now and then obscured by low clouds which cast dark shadows on the water. Lookouts could pick up looming heights of land on every side; shore outlines appeared on the radar screen; but neither eyes nor radar discerned any trace of Nips. A rich, sweet odor like honeysuckle floated out from the land over the calm waters, a pleasant change from the normally fecal smells exuded by the Guadalcanal jungle. It seemed a good omen to sailors topside.

Lee badly wanted exact intelligence of the enemy. As he had been assigned no radio call sign in the hurry of departure, he tried to contact radio Guadalcanal ("Cactus"), asking for any late information and signing with his last name. To this he received the snub, "We do not recognize you!" As a last resort he signaled again, "Cactus, this is Lee. Tell your big boss Ching Lee is here and wants the latest information"—for he was a personal friend of General Vandegrift, who knew him by his old Naval Academy nickname. Before "big boss" could be reached, flagship *Washington* picked up voice radio chatter between three motor torpedo boats that were patrolling northeast of Savo. Someone was saying "There go two big ones, but I don't know whose they are!" Admiral Lee, believing it highly desirable to resolve their doubts, at 2230 called Guadalcanal headquarters: "Refer your big boss about Ching Lee;

Chinese, catchee? Call off your boys!" The PT's immediately chimed in that they knew Lee and were not after him. Shortly after, "Cactus" called and said, "The boss has no additional information."[94] So all that Lee knew before the battle opened was that the Japanese were coming down in force.

Admiral Kondo's express was now running in three sections: a distant screen consisting of light cruiser *Sendai* (Rear Admiral Hashimoto) and three destroyers; a close screen composed of light cruiser *Nagara* (Rear Admiral Kimura) and six destroyers; and the big bombardment group, Kondo's flagship *Atago*, her sister ship *Takao* and battleship *Kirishima*. Hashimoto's ships were two or three miles ahead as pickets. Kimura's were steaming close to the bombardment ships. Admiral Kondo had scheduled his bombardment to commence simultaneously with the landing of reinforcement troops from Tanaka's tough remnant, the four transports and accompanying destroyers which also were approaching Savo.

Sendai, leading Hashimoto's pack, first sniffed trouble at 2210 when she sighted "two enemy cruisers and four destroyers" north of Savo, heading into the Sound. Destroyers *Ayanami* and *Uranami* were detached to reconnoiter south of Savo, passing to the westward of the island, while *Sendai* and *Shikinami,* unknown to Lee, took off in eager pursuit of him. *Sendai's* report caused instant action on the flag bridge of *Atago*. Kondo issued his attack order. He divided Kimura's group into two elements: cruiser *Nagara* and four destroyers as an advance guard, destroyers *Asagumo* and *Teruzuki* remaining with the firing unit to lead it west and north of Savo. The *Nagara* group was to enter the Sound at full speed south of Savo Island behind *Ayanami* and *Uranami*. Kondo's plan could be considered the ultimate in the Japanese tactical pattern of dispersion. Fourteen ships were split four ways in a ten-mile-square area which had to be shared with the antagonist.

At 2252 as the moon set behind the mountains of Cape Esperance, Admiral Lee, at the limit of the southeasterly leg, executed a column movement to the right to course west. *Washington* had barely settled on this course when her radar picked up a target distant nine miles, a point and a half west of north. This, cruiser *Sendai*, was tracked until 2312 when the main battery director actually saw her through his telescopes. *South Dakota* also saw her but none of the destroyers did. At 2316 Lee ordered his captains to open fire when ready. A minute later 16-inch projectiles were burning up the air toward Admiral Hashimoto's flagship. *Sendai,* alarmed by this dubious welcome, laid down a blanket of smoke, and at high speed doubled back to the northward in company with destroyer *Shikinami,* pursued by battleship salvos out of radar range.

Destroyers' Slaughter

Fortunately this indecisive bout had not distracted the leading American destroyers sufficiently to cause them to relax vigilance in other quarters. Enemy destroyers *Ayanami* and *Uranami,* sneaking along the south shore of Savo, were by this time within visual, gunfire and torpedo range. *Walke,* at the head of the American column, sounded the alarm with a 5-inch salvo at 2322. *Benham* and *Preston* followed with rapid gunfire. *Gwin,* which had been firing star shell in the direction of the battleship targets, attracted by the rumpus on the starboard bow, swung optics and trained guns at 2326, just in time to pick up Admiral Kimura's advance guard cruiser *Nagara* and four destroyers. A private gun duel started between *Gwin* and the Kimura contingent. The enemy, concealed by the overhanging mountains of Savo, replied heartily with gunfire, and was not slow in employing his customary equalizer, the torpedo. *Ayanami* and *Uranami* laid their tubes carefully, the ugly shark-shaped engines swooshed overboard at 2330; others from Kimura's force five minutes later.

At about this time *Walke* was struck by enemy shells and began to fall off to port, shooting furiously and endeavoring to get onto the target with her torpedoes. *Benham,* 300 yards astern of her, continued to fire whenever a target could be seen but refrained from shooting torpedoes at what were thought to be destroyers. *Preston* shot at a ship, probably *Nagara,* but like *Walke* received more than she gave, one salvo putting both firerooms out and toppling the after stack. Shortly thereafter, shells coming in from the quarter practically demolished her topsides from amidships aft; *Preston* was out of action with torpedoes still on board. *Gwin,* tailing her, also was a mark for Japanese destroyer guns; one shell detonated in an engine room, another struck the fantail, and the shock disrupted her torpedo safety links so that the "fish" slid harmlessly out of the tubes. By the time enemy torpedoes began to boil around the destroyers, only *Benham* had escaped serious damage by gunfire. And at 2338 enemy warheads began to find their marks. *Walke* had her forecastle blown off as far aft as the bridge; *Benham* had a large chunk of her bow destroyed in one massive eruption.

While the destroyers were bearing the brunt of enemy attention, the battleships were striving to lend a hand, their secondary batteries hammering away at vessels in the shadow of Savo. But *Washington* had trouble sorting out the numerous targets on her radar screen and, at 2333, *South Dakota* had a stroke of bad luck: electrical circuit breakers jumped out and caused loss of electrical power throughout the ship. Faith in radar had become so great that the loss of both SG and SC equipment had a most depressing effect on officers and men; it gave all hands the feeling of being blindfolded.

If Kondo's intention was to confuse by splitting his forces, the ruse was certainly succeeding. Milling about in the narrow channel between Savo and Guadalcanal at 2335 were three separate groups. Kimura's advance guard was retiring close to Savo after firing torpedoes; *Ayanami* was damaged and with *Uranami* was striving to extricate herself from a hot spot less than two miles from the Americans; and, finally, Hashimoto's pugnacious cruiser *Sendai* and destroyer *Shikinami* were resuming action with a stealthy attack from astern. Small wonder that American radar screens made no sense to the puzzled operators and that American commanders were confused by reports of motor torpedo boats, flares, lightning, phantom contacts and completely contradictory "dope" as to enemy movements. Even after the battle many gunners were convinced that their targets were shore batteries on Savo. But the Japanese, aware that their enemy was in one concentrated formation, were able to follow Lee's movements and disregard the comings and goings of their own various groups. By 2335 all four American destroyers were out of action without having launched a single torpedo; one battleship was blinded by power failure and the other handicapped by floundering cripples ahead and confused by radar echoes against Savo Island. *Ayanami* alone of ships flying the Rising Sun was injured, and *Uranami* stood ready to rescue her crew or protect her against further attack.

In the individual American destroyers conditions were sickeningly similar to the horrors of Friday the Thirteenth. *Walke,* dismembered and blazing, was down by the head and sinking fast. Commander Fraser ordered Abandon Ship in the nick of time; the after two-thirds of the ship sank at 2342 and depth charges previously reported as "safe" exploded directly under the survivors. *Benham,* her bow partially destroyed, limped painfully clear of friendly ships, then turned to a westerly course, passing through swimming and shouting survivors. *Preston,* gutted by an internal fire, was ordered abandoned at 2336. Seconds later she rolled heavily on her side, hung ten minutes with bow in air and then sank. *Gwin,* least damaged of the destroyer quartet, passed through the swirling water marking *Preston's* grave, shaken by exploding depth charges. She continued to fire at the enemy as long as anything remained within range. *Washington's* sailors found time to toss life rafts overboard as the flagship tore past the stricken destroyers.

Round One ended at 2335 when Admiral Lee changed course left from 300° to 282° in order to pass to the southward of burning destroyers. *South Dakota* started to follow in her wake but had to turn to starboard to avoid *Benham* and so got herself silhouetted by the burning *Preston* and *Walke.* At 2336 all hands in the battleship heaved a sigh of relief as steady power flowed back once more to operate gyros, radars, guns and motors. Gunners took advantage of their rejuvenation to pour out a few main battery salvos at *Sendai* astern. At 2342 *South Dakota* was again in trouble of her own making; a turret gun blast set fire to planes on the fantail catapults. Fortunately, a succeeding salvo blew the planes overboard and the fires out.[95]

Battlewagon Duel

At 2348 Admiral Lee, recognizing that his destroyers were no longer capable of offensive action, ordered them to retire while he altered his own course slightly to the northward. The time was now at hand for *South Dakota* to pay dearly for her electric power failure earlier in the game. When she turned to starboard instead of to port to clear the burning destroyers, she inadvertently closed the range on Kimura's retiring advance guard and completely lost track of her own flagship. Kimura sighted *South Dakota*, shouted an alarm to Kondo and at 2355 launched a swarm of 34 torpedoes. Fortunately, all missed.

Kondo's bombardment unit had been tacking back and forth on the sheltered northwest side of Savo throughout the entire first phase of the battle. At 2348 his ships were in column on a westerly course eight miles due north of Cape Esperance; order of ships: destroyers *Asagumo* and *Teruzuki*, heavy cruisers *Atago* and *Takao*, battleship *Kirishima*. Upon hearing Kimura's warning, Kondo swung this column completely around to a southeasterly course in order to join the fight.

South Dakota, with the radar picture incomplete as a consequence of that untimely power loss, continued to close both Kimura and Kondo. The former, making a complete loop after delivering his torpedo attack, fell back and somehow lost sight of both American battlewagons. At the same time Kondo's leading destroyers picked them up. At a scant 5000 yards searchlight shutters were snapped open to expose *South Dakota* to the combined fury of the entire bombardment force. Again the torpedoes missed, but large-caliber shells plowed into the battleship's superstructure. She replied with everything she had, directed against the offending beams of light. She was in a tough spot, the primary target of three heavy ships.

Lee was of no mind to let this situation deteriorate further. With radar humming accurately, *Washington* had tracked a big target for several minutes but had refrained from shooting for fear it might be her sister ship; *South Dakota* actually was in the "blind spot" of *Washington's* radar on her starboard quarter. All doubts were resolved when the Japanese illuminated, and at midnight Lee's flagship opened fire. Selecting *Kirishima*, the fattest target, bearing almost due north, the 16-inch main battery cut loose at a range of 8400 yards. The 5-inch mounts divided their attention between her and the ship that was illuminating *South Dakota,* while one 5-inch gun sent up star shell which showed Lee what the big fellow was. One of the few actions of World War II between line-of-battle ships was joined.[96]

In Kondo's ranks there was a general rush to get at the brightly illuminated *South Dakota*. *Asagumo* fruitlessly launched torpedoes. Other ships spat out rapid-fire salvos of large-and-medium caliber shells. So intent were they on this obvious target that they failed even to locate the American flagship. The results were fatal to *Kirishima*; 9 out of 75 sixteen-inch shells from *Washington* scored, as did about 40 fast-shooting 5-inchers. Within seven minutes *Kirishima* was out of the fight, steering gear hopelessly wrecked, topsides aflame. Meanwhile *South Dakota* and *Washington* had registered a few hits on cruisers *Atago* and *Takao,* revealed by their own searchlights.

South Dakota took numerous hits topside, from 14-inch down to 5-inch. She had lost track of *Washington;* her radio communication had failed; only one radar in the entire ship was unhurt; radar plot was demolished; one main battery turret was damaged in train; gunnery control stations were depleted by casualties; many small but dangerous fires were creeping throughout the superstructure. The redoubtable Captain Gatch, finding his ship no longer under fire and without means to reënter the engagement, moved to retire; course was set at 2350 and the battered ship drew clear at full speed.

Washington Wins

Admiral Lee tried without success to raise *South Dakota* by radio; he could only hope that she was retiring, not sinking. In an effort to draw enemy fire away from her and to encounter any Japanese ships that might be coming down from the north, he turned his flagship to a northwesterly course. *Kirishima* and the rest of the bombardment group were left behind on her starboard quarter as *Washington* pushed on alone. At 0020 November 15 the Admiral changed course to 340°, a move which (judging from the radar screen) set the entire enemy force in motion to the northward. The Japanese were hastening to protect their transports. Their bombardment unit (minus *Kirishima*) roughly paralleled Lee, with Kimura in hot pursuit; Tanaka, justifiably concerned about his remaining transports, detached destroyers *Oyashio* and *Kagero* to make a torpedo attack on any American that approached them.

At 0025 Admiral Kondo thought better of his decision to pursue and ordered all ships not actively engaged to withdraw. Led by *Atago*, the bombardment unit turned sharp right to course NNE, laid down a smoke screen and retired. Admiral Lee observed this move with satisfaction. Convinced that the enemy troopships would now be delayed until daylight, when Henderson Field airmen could take care of them, and that *South Dakota* was out of harm's way, he ordered an abrupt right turn at 0033 and commenced retirement. With Chinese cunning he charted a course far to the westward, at one point only 4000 yards from one of the Russell Islands, in order to draw trailing enemy destroyers away from the tracks of damaged American ships. This decision was good joss, for at 0039 *Kagero* and *Oyashio* of Tanaka's screen and Kimura's advance guard destroyers launched torpedoes at *Washington,* some of which exploded on entering her troubled wake. Through moonless darkness keen lookouts sighted the torpedo tracks and Captain Davis' clever maneuvering dodged their embarrassing caresses as nimbly as a young girl eluding a sailor on a park bench. At 0040 she changed course again to 210° and speeded up to 26 knots in order to shake off these persistent destroyers.

While *Washington* was acting as a lone-ship task force, *Benham* was struggling to survive with her bow shattered and keel damaged. *Gwin,* although making sluggish recoveries from dangerous rolls, was in no immediate danger. *South Dakota* was out of the battle zone, heading at high speed for a prearranged rendezvous. Admiral Lee, apprised of *Benham's* woes, directed *Gwin* to escort the noseless destroyer to Espiritu Santo, and further authorized *Benham's* skipper to abandon ship if necessary. Necessity arrived next afternoon and abandoned she was by 1724 without loss of life. *Gwin* sank *Benham* by gunfire and made Espiritu Santo without further incident.

South Dakota fell in with *Washington* at 0900 November 15, and the two ships proceeded in company toward Nouméa. *Washington* had come off unscathed; but *South Dakota*, with superstructure badly damaged by 42 large-caliber hits, 38 men killed or missing and 60 wounded, returned to the States for refitting.[97]

The battle was over. Admiral Kondo abandoned his bombardment plan and faced the problem of succoring the burning and exploding *Kirishima*. *Sendai* and *Shikinami* had previously been ordered to stand by the wounded queen, and three destroyers were added to her ladies in waiting. In addition to her steering gear, the engines had been slightly damaged. But her skipper wanted no repetition of *Hiei's* daytime ordeal and so lost little time in ordering the abandonment and scuttling of his ship. Destroyers closed to take off her crew, sea valves were opened, and the ship settled slowly, sinking northwest of Savo Island at 0320 November 15.

One more Rising Sun had set. Destroyer *Ayanami*, in hopeless shape after running close aboard the American ships, was given the deep six by her skipper after the crew had been transferred to *Uranami*.

For sheer tenacity of purpose, every sailor owes a salute to Rear Admiral Raizo Tanaka. When the sea was finally cleared of dueling warships, Tanaka resumed his "Cape Esperance or Bust" mission with four remaining transports escorted by eleven troopladen destroyers. By 0400 the transports had been grounded on the beach off Tassafaronga, and the soldiers were joining their unfortunate fellows in the Guadalcanal jungle. It is doubtful whether the destroyers disembarked their passengers because, according to the Japanese, only 2000 troops in all got ashore. At any rate, the destroyers scampered back to the Shortlands, arriving at midnight on the 15th.

Fork in the Road

When *Meade* entered Tulagi with her cargo of survivors on the afternoon of 15 November, curtain fell on the Naval Battle of Guadalcanal. Both fleets retired from the field of battle; both countries claimed a tremendous victory. In view of what each was trying to do, and in the light of future events, who really won?

Both objectives were similar: to reinforce one's own garrison on Guadalcanal but deny it to the enemy by air and sea. With that yardstick the conclusion is unmistakable: Turner got every one of his troops and almost all his materiel ashore, while Tanaka the Tenacious managed to land only about 2000 shaken survivors,

260 cases of ammunition and 1500 bags of rice.[98] The Americans dominated the air from start to finish and kept possession of Henderson Field. On the surface, Callaghan chased one force out of Ironbottom Sound, losing his life and several ships in the process, and Lee disposed of Kondo's second attempt to follow Mahan doctrine. Air losses were far greater on the Japanese side. Of combat ships the United States Navy sustained the greater loss, but the elimination of two battleships and transports from the Japanese Fleet was far more serious. The enemy could accept a heavy loss of troops because he had plenty of replacements, but he could not replace battleships or transports, and he depended on air and surface fleets to stop any American offensive against Greater East Asia.

The Battle of Guadalcanal was decisive, not only in the struggle for that island, but in the Pacific War at large. The Imperial Army did not give up Guadalcanal for another ten weeks, but the Navy performed its ferryboat duties with increasing reluctance and made no further bid to rule the adjacent waves.

In torpedo tactics and night action, this series of engagements showed that tactically the Japanese were still a couple of semesters ahead of the United States Navy, but their class standing took a decided drop in the subject of war-plan execution.

The conclusion of this great battle was marked by a definite shift of the Americans from the defensive to the offensive, and of the Japanese in the opposite direction. The United States Navy felt that it could never again be defeated; the Marines and soldiers, confident at last of real naval support, fought with greater vigor and lighter hearts; the airmen had won a definite ascendancy over and around Ironbottom Sound. And during the first two weeks of November, fortune for the first time smiled on the Allies everywhere: North Africa, Stalingrad, Papua, Guadalcanal. President Roosevelt, while mourning the loss of his friend Dan Callaghan, announced, "It would seem that the turning point in this war has at last been reached."[99] Churchill chose this moment to proclaim "the end of the beginning." And a captured Japanese document admitted: "It must be said that the success or failure in recapturing Guadalcanal Island, and the vital naval battle related to it, is the fork in the road which leads to victory for them or for us."[100]

From 15 November 1942 until 15 August 1945 the war followed the right fork. It was rough, tough and uncharted, but it led to Tokyo.

13. THE BATTLE OF TASSAFARONGA
(30 November 1942) [101]

The Americans were quick to profit by mid-November victories, but there was plenty to do before Guadalcanal could be converted from a precarious foothold into a solid platform for the long overdue advance up the Slot. First, the island must be tidied up; the enemy must be destroyed or pushed into a corner where he would be impotent.

A fair start for this clean-up would be the relief of the long-suffering 1st Marine Division. For 15 long weeks and twenty-four-hour days—these stout fighters had taken all that the enemy offered, and the jungle as well. They were enervated with malaria and combat fatigue after double the tour of duty that medical officers considered possible under such conditions. For the last month they had had the help of the 164th Infantry Regiment and, since 4 November, of the 8th Marine Regiment (Colonel Jeschke's). Plans were completed for bringing the 6th Marine Regiment up from New Zealand and the 182nd Infantry, Americal Division, from New Caledonia.

Much could be done and was done to better the condition of troops who stayed and of those coming. Improvements were effected in sanitation and care by sending up the 101st Medical Regiment United States Army, which landed at Guadalcanal 13 November just in time to help the victims of the great three-day battle. They collected 1156 casualties in two nights and a day. But of these the battle casualties were very much less than those from fatigue and disease.[102]

General Vandegrift wished to follow up the naval victory of Guadalcanal by pushing forward to new lines westward. The ensuing action was called the Battle of Point Cruz, a small cape between the Matanikau River and Kokumbona where Mendaña had landed in 1568. At this point the shores of Guadalcanal rise steeply from the sea, leaving only enough flat land for the dirt road;

numerous defiles and ravines gave the defense ample opportunity to enfilade any advancing force. The hills and ridges, in fantastic shapes, are covered with kunai grass.

This operation proved that the Japanese on Guadalcanal, though disappointed of their expected reinforcements, still had plenty of fight and savvy. Vandegrift pushed his forces ahead in three prongs. The 1ˢᵗ Battalion 182ⁿᵈ Infantry Regiment took the coast road, and by 19 November cut off the Japanese on Point Cruz from their fellows in the interior, and pushed about 300 yards beyond. On their left marched a company of Marines; some 1000 yards to the Marines' left, the 2ⁿᵈ Battalion 182ⁿᵈ Regiment, which took position on a grassy knoll. Between this battalion and the Marines, the Japanese strongly held another grassy knoll and were not completely dislodged until the 1st Battalion 164ᵗʰ Regiment was called up to help on the 21st. The entire enemy front was very strongly held; the 182ⁿᵈ and the Marines found Nips on three sides of them and suffered a very harassing mortar fire. They had little artillery and no naval support, as every ship left whole after the battle had retired. On the 22nd the American troops had to fall back to a position a little in advance of Point Cruz, which they proceeded to clean out. And the lines which they then occupied were substantially unchanged for the next fifty-four days.

In the meantime, Lieutenant Colonel Carlson's 2ⁿᵈ Raider Battalion went on a manhunt in early November which afforded them a good dozen fights in which over 400 of the enemy were killed at the cost of only 17 Marines. The route chosen by these colorful Raiders carried them through some of the most forbidding country on Guadalcanal: the upper valleys of the Tenaru and Lunga Rivers and a long detour around Mambulo (Mt. Austen), a hilly mass on the central part of the coast. It was December before they returned to the perimeter, lean from a diet of rice, bacon and tea.[103]

Air strength on Henderson Field increased during the last fortnight of November from 85 single-engine planes to 124 aircraft, including 5 New Zealand Hudsons and 8 Flying Fortresses. At the same time, Seabees were grading and laying steel mat on the mile-long bomber strip and the two fighter strips. Logistics could barely keep pace; on 30 November only four days' supply of aviation gasoline was on hand.

Afloat there were changes, too; the motor torpedo boat flotilla by 30 November mustered 15 PTs and tender *Jamestown.* Antisubmarine patrol boats and aircraft put in their first appearance at Tulagi. Eight destroyers were assigned to escort duty between the Solomons and South Pacific bases. Base "Ringbolt" (Tulagi) was becoming solidly embedded.

However the American supply train continued to suffer. Naval freighter USS *Alchiba* was torpedoed by Japanese midget submarine No. 10 while unloading a much-needed cargo of aviation gas, bombs and ammunition off Lunga Point 28 November. She was beached and burned for four days as unloading and fire fighting continued simultaneously. She also survived.

The attrition of naval power incident to five big naval battles forced Admiral Halsey to reorganize his South Pacific Force. Nouméa and Espiritu Santo were the bases for these revamped forces. No more would task forces mill around "Torpedo Junction;" henceforth ships entered the Coral Sea only with a destination to reach or a combat mission to perform.

There were also administrative changes in the South Pacific Force. Halsey was promoted to Admiral on 26 November in recognition of his success and the growing importance of his command. And, since the majority of ground troops on Guadalcanal were henceforth to be of the Army, it was decided to relieve Major General Vandegrift USMC by Major General Alexander M. Patch USA of the Americal Division.

American commanders still had to consider the possibility of another Japanese attempt to win back Guadalcanal. Yet, confident that any such effort could be thwarted allowed bolder planning than heretofore. Assurance was justified. The enemy carriers were refitting in Japan, and the rest of the Combined Fleet was held in readiness to serve Yamamoto's ambition for one big decisive battle with the entire Pacific Fleet, a battle that was not to occur until after Yamamoto's death. As for Guadalcanal, the very name was anathema to the Nipponese; an evil place like quicksand, where ships and men sank out of sight without ever finding *terra firma* for victory. Tojo's planners began to shift interest to the middle Solomons. Perhaps New Georgia, a potpourri of irregular islands, could be blended into a stew unpalatable to the

Americans. In the meantime, Tanaka the Tenacious must employ destroyers to supply the unhappy troops on Guadalcanal. No more nightly naval bombardments, however.

After losing the Naval Battle of Guadalcanal in November, the Japanese Navy proposed to abandon the island. Tojo, having switched his major South Pacific objective from New Guinea to the Solomons, refused to change back. So the struggle continued.

Captain Morton L. Deyo of Cincpac staff wrote a trenchant memorandum to Admiral Nimitz on 10 October. Commenting on the defeat at Savo Island and the far from satisfactory events that followed, he declared that unrealistic training of our destroyers and cruisers and the almost exclusive employment of them in escort of convoy had prevented the development of a tough, offensive spirit. He suggested the formation of a cruiser-destroyer group in the South Pacific, to be given a solid month of training, especially night fighting, and then thrown up the Slot to break up the Tokyo Expresses.

Belatedly, Admiral Halsey did just that, about a week after the Naval Battle of Guadalcanal. He appointed Rear Admiral Kinkaid commander of a new striking force, composed of heavy cruisers *Minneapolis, Pensacola, New Orleans* and *Northampton,* light cruiser *Honolulu* and four to six destroyers, based at Segond Channel, Espiritu Santo. Kinkaid took command 24 November, before the task force had all been collected, worked up an operation plan, conferred with the officers—and then was detached by Admiral Nimitz. Cincpac wanted Kinkaid to command the North Pacific Force based on Dutch Harbor, where "Fuzzy" Theobald was making a mess of things. As commander of the striking force, Kinkaid was relieved by Rear Admiral Carleton H. Wright, to whose unhappy lot it fell, on the second day of his command, to lead his yet untrained task force against a Tokyo Express led by the redoubtable Tanaka.

This Japanese reinforcement plan was comparatively modest. Tanaka's force, consisting of destroyers only, would dash into Ironbottom Sound and off Tassafaronga would jettison rubber-wrapped drums of provisions, shove troops overboard to be recovered by small craft operating from the shore, and quickly retire. On this particular night Tanaka had six destroyers crammed with troops and supplies, and two more not so encumbered. At 2225 November 30, before arriving off Tassafaronga, he encountered Admiral Wright's much stronger task force. The ensuing battle reflected slight credit on the United States Navy, but great luster on the Imperial Navy of Japan.

See Appendix F for composition of U.S. and Japanese Task Organizations.

The surface of Ironbottom Sound that calm night was like a black mirror, and the American float planes detailed to illuminate Tokyo Express were unable to rise from the water. But Wright had the advantage of radar, and destroyer *Fletcher* in his van had the latest kind. At 2316 she picked up Tanaka's force, broad on the port bow, steaming slowly along the Guadalcanal shore toward the dumping-off place. The squadron commander in *Fletcher* asked permission for his four van destroyers to fire torpedoes; Wright hesitated for four minutes before granting it, and so lost the battle. For, by the time the torpedoes were launched, about 2321, the Japanese column had passed the Americans on a contrary course and the range was too great for American torpedoes to overtake them. Immediately after his last torpedo smacked the water, Wright ordered cruisers to open gunfire, and the flashes of his guns sparked off Tanaka's reaction. Despite initial handicaps of surprise, cluttered decks and enemy gunfire, Tanaka's disciplined

Rear Admiral Raizo Tanaka.

crews in the first moments of battle managed to launch more than twenty fast-running torpedoes. And a large share of the American gunfire concentrated on one Japanese destroyer, *Takanami,* the only enemy ship sunk in this battle.

Not one American torpedo found its target, but at 2327 the Japanese "long lances" began to rip the bowels of Wright's cruisers. *Minneapolis* took two violent explosions and was out of the fight. *New Orleans,* maneuvering to avoid her, ran smack into another torpedo that sliced off her bow and everything up to No. 2 turret. *Pensacola,* turning to port to avoid her two burning sisters, became silhouetted by them for the enemy's benefit and took a torpedo hit directly below her main mast, which became a torch blazing with oil from a ruptured fuel tank. *Honolulu* escaped by smart seamanship on the part of the officer of the deck, Lieutenant Commander George F. Davis. *Northampton,* after firing 18 salvos from her 8-inch battery, took two torpedo hits, and sank, after more than three hours' frantic efforts by Damage Control to save her. By 0130 December 1, all Japanese ships except sinking *Takanami* were hightailing out of Ironbottom Sound, undamaged.

The three stricken heavy cruisers, saved by remarkable energy and ingenuity of their crews, were sent to major bases for repairs, and joined the Fleet again by next fall. But it is painfully true that the Battle of Tassafaronga was a sharp defeat, inflicted on an alerted and superior cruiser force by a surprised and inferior destroyer force whose decks were cluttered with freight. Tanaka was prevented from delivering the goods, and that was held against him by the higher command.

Japan had good reason to be proud of her destroyers; and their success was well earned. For forty years the Imperial Navy had put much thought and great effort into improved torpedoes, night fighting, and torpedo tactics. The 2300 ton *Fubuki* class destroyer, such as those of Tanaka's squadron, were equipped with nine torpedo tubes fitted for the deadly "long lances," the crews were trained to reload them in a matter of minutes, and the C.O.s were all torpedo experts. American and British destroyers enjoyed no comparable materiel, technique, or training. Nevertheless, faulty tactics and stupid strategy doomed to failure Japan's effort to hold Guadalcanal.

USS Minneapolis in Tulagi Harbor.

It is a painful truth that the Battle of Tassafaronga was a sharp defeat inflicted on an alert and superior cruiser force by a partially surprised and inferior destroyer force.

Every flag officer concerned—Tisdale, Wright, Halsey and Nimitz—sought an explanation for the disaster to Task Force 67, but each was hard put to find a simple answer.[104]

It must be remembered that the United States force, though larger than the enemy's, had never before steamed together, even in daylight, and that it was strictly a "scratch team;" while Tanaka's force had been well trained and long practised under the same commander.

Tassafaronga ended four months of vicious hull-to-hull slugging the like of which neither the Americans nor the Japanese had ever seen. No man who fought in those bloody waters can forget the apprehension, the exultation and the terror that he experienced, the hideous forms of death that he witnessed, or the self-sacrificing heroism that gave him a new respect for his fellow seamen. "Savo," "Guadalcanal," "Tassafaronga" and the rest are not mere battle names to the survivors; they are flaming banners of deathless deeds by ships and men whose bones forever rest in Ironbottom Sound.

14. SECURING GUADALCANAL
(1 December 1942 – 29 January 1943)

It took the Japanese a long time to adjust themselves to their strategic defeat in the lower Solomons. An occasional tactical victory like Tassafaronga blinded them to the fact that the American hold on Guadalcanal was tight and permanent. Like exhausted salmon trying to ascend an impassable stream, the fanatic Nipponese continued to hurl themselves at the American barrier in suicidal frenzy. On 1 December the Cincpac analyst noted, "It is still indicated that a major attempt to recapture 'Cactus' is making up." He was right.

Up from Java in December came General Hitoshi Imamura, and by the year's end some 50,000 troops of his Eighth Area Army had joined him in Rabaul. Imamura was under orders from Imperial Headquarters to recapture Guadalcanal.

Meanwhile, in Nouméa, Halsey's staff made plans to break up this last serious effort to recapture Guadalcanal. Replacement of depleted Marine regiments with Army infantry was given high priority. Henderson Field still suffered from effects of rainy weather and traffic congestion, so work was pushed forward to improve the original strips, to construct a new field at Koli Point and to build storage tanks for a million gallons of gasoline.

Want of facilities and manpower kept the local naval base a somewhat rickety affair manned partly by uninterested survivors from sunken ships. One expected to wake up some morning to see it disappearing into the mud. Not until the close of the year were base projects given adequate equipment and personnel.

American air and naval actions in early December were directed largely toward thwarting the enemy's reinforcement.

Munda Built, Bombed and Bombarded

Loss of valuable destroyers was making the Japanese wince, and for the rest of the month, while the moon waxed full and then waned to last quarter, they refrained from sending anything but submarines to relieve the Guadalcanal garrison. But they were shoring up their crumbling foothold on New Guinea and at the same time building a launching platform in the central Solomons for later thrusts against Guadalcanal. This put the burden of the Solomons offensive on American land-based aircraft; the Japanese project gave them a new target within comfortable flying range, Munda Point airfield.

The Japanese had originally by-passed New Georgia in favor of Guadalcanal. That was one of their big mistakes, for Guadalcanal was beyond range of their fighter planes and a bomber unaccompanied by a fighter in those days was about ten times as vulnerable as a bomber-fighter team. Buin field in Southern Bougainville shortened the range so that "Zekes" could fly to Guadalcanal and back but had no time to linger. A new airfield on New Georgia was the answer.

On a few acres of flat land bordering the southern bight of New Georgia, ten miles south of Kula Gulf and ten miles north of Rendova, an Australian planter had grown long rows of coconut palms. Here was the ideal spot, only 175 miles from Henderson Field. "Zekes" based there could orbit over Lunga all day; big-bellied "Bettys" could stage through and carry double their previous bomb loads. So on 24 November 1942 a convoy put in at Munda Point, New Georgia island, and commenced work on the new "Munda Emergency Airfield."

As early as 28 November Admiral Halsey suspected that airfield development was under way, but American pilots who swooped over Munda saw only a few new buildings and the disciplined rows of coconut palms. It remained for the prying lens of an airplane's camera to disclose the truth on 3 December. The Japanese, like termites, were building under the coconut grove; when it became necessary to remove a tree, palm fronds were laid on overhead wires in its exact position. Next day P-39s from Henderson Field fired the opening gun in what was to be a long campaign against that pesky airstrip. The busy Japs kept right on working; and when they were good and ready down came both real and false palm trees, holes were promptly filled up, and there was a nice airfield!

On 9 December the first major air strike against it was carried out by 18 B-17s, and from then on planes of all types made Munda a routine daytime bull's-eye. On the 13th a PBY inaugurated a series of night harassing runs on the strip. By mid-December the

"Black Cats" on Prowl.

Japs were being pasted at all hours with heavy bombs, fragmentation bombs, incendiaries, strafing bullets and even empty beer bottles, whose banshee-like whistles when falling were presumed to be a prime sleep-robber. Even so, the field was finished and nesting "Zekes" by the second fortnight of December.

During this period the "Tokyo Express" ran a spur line to Munda, but soon discovered that overhead was eating up profits.

Coastwatchers, airmen and natives also reported ship and troop movements into the northern islands of the New Georgia group. At Rekata Bay on Santa Isabel, the Japanese had a flourishing barge-staging point and seaplane base which American air power could never seem to knock out. It seemed clear that only fast work could prevent New Georgia from becoming the Japanese answer to Guadalcanal.

In past experience, any concentration of Japanese shipping meant something. Consequently, when in late December the number of combat and supply ships at Rabaul rapidly increased to 70 or more, Admiral Halsey became intensely interested. By New Year's Eve nearly a hundred ships swung at anchor in volcano-rimmed Simpson Harbor, Rabaul.

After Tanaka's battle with motor torpedo boats on 11 December, three weeks passed without any Japanese reinforcements reaching Guadalcanal. The trickle of supplies sent in by submarines and barges was not enough even to keep the troops fed. Captured Japanese diaries of this period reflect discomfort and discouragement. Troops at the front eked out scanty rice and soybean rations with grass, roots, ferns and even, on occasion, human flesh. The malaria rate was practically 100 per cent; dysentery ditto, spread by flies feeding on unburied corpses and exposed refuse.

Now was the time for Halsey to try a night bombardment of the new Munda airstrip. The character selected for the conductor role on this new north-bound express was the ruddy, genial Rear Admiral Walden L. Ainsworth, better known as "Pug."[105] A former destroyer squadron commander in the Atlantic Fleet, Ainsworth in July had been given flag rank and the administrative job of Commander Destroyers Pacific Fleet. In December, when on an inspection tour to Nouméa, he was willingly "shanghaied" by Halsey and placed in command of Task Force 67, the cruiser-destroyer force that had just taken a beating off Tassafaronga.

Since another U.S. infantry echelon was due to make Lunga Roads on the morning of 4 January 1943, Halsey decided to raid Munda the following night, and to make a triple play of bombardment, diversion and cover. Light cruisers *Nashville, St. Louis* and *Helena,* and destroyers *Fletcher* and *O'Bannon* were selected to deliver the bombardment, for which the rapid-firing 6-inch cruiser guns were well suited.

Fletcher led the column but flagship *Nashville* in second place was to shoot first. The approach on a northeast course paralleled the west coast of Rendova. Just before commencing fire the column slowed to 18 knots and in a few minutes changed course to NW to bring guns to bear. Shortly after 0100 January 5, with fire control radars using a prominent black rock as a reference point, the first salvo flew out. "No change!" radioed the spotter. A second and a third salvo followed, and then the gunners shifted to continuous rapid fire. It was a magnificent sight; each cruiser, continually wrapped in muzzle flashes, seemed a ball of fire. Spotting aviators aloft stared at the bridge of tracers arching onto the field and mushrooming like sheet lightning all over the target. They

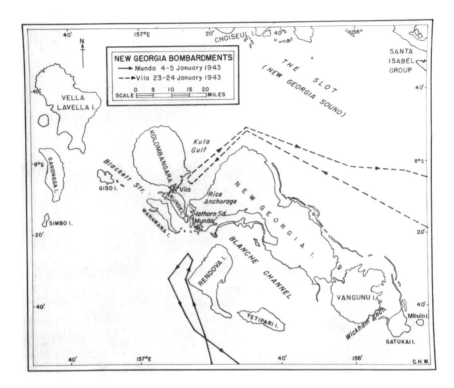

shook their heads in amazement—this was really the stuff! Occasionally a large and sustained flash would indicate that some of Tojo's ammunition or gasoline was afire.

During less than an hour Munda had been treated to nearly 3000 rounds of 6-inch projectiles and 1400 rounds of 5-inch. It had been a remarkable demonstration of the American Navy's favorite weapon, the naval gun. To this day it is not known how much damage the enemy suffered during this first trip of the "Ainsworth Express," but next morning scout planes reported the airfield and environs well chewed up and no anti-aircraft fire.

December Doings Ashore[106]

Ever since losing the Naval Battle of Guadalcanal in November, the Japanese Navy had been in favor of abandoning the island. To this frank proposal the Army opposed a decided negative. Tojo, having switched his major South Pacific objective from New Guinea to the Solomons, would not change again if he could help it. But he could not help it. The attrition of men, planes and ships, especially of destroyers, finally convinced him at the turn of the year that the island could not be taken. Accordingly, on 4 January 1943 word went forth from Tokyo that Guadalcanal must be evacuated within a month.[107] The Japanese characteristically imparted this decision only to their top commanders, while their forces on the island had to fight as though victory were around the corner.

As Allied Intelligence obtained no hint that evacuation was even being discussed, the new ground force commander at Guadalcanal, Major General Alexander M. Patch USA, prepared to push the enemy off the island by force. He had relieved General Vandegrift on 9 December 1942; and on that very day the 5th and 11th Regiments, 1st Marine Division, after completing a four months' tour of duty on the island, filed down to the beach, climbed on board

This photo, taken on Guadalcanal in 1942, captured three men who figured prominently in the brief history of the Raiders. LtGen Thomas Holcomb, left front, authorized the activation of the Raiders in February 1942. Col Merritt A. Edson, right rear, played a major hand in creating the Raider concept. MajGen Alexander A. Vandegrift, left rear, relied heavily on the Raiders in winning the Guadalcanal campaign, then disbanded them in early 1944 when he became Commandant. Courtesy of U.S. Marine Corps.

transports and sailed for Australia and a well merited rest. The 1st and 7th Regiments followed on 22 December and 5 January, respectively. But virtually the entire 2nd Marine Division remained, to represent the leathernecks. Plenty of Army reinforcements were on their way,[108] but until they arrived General Patch was constrained to take it easy.

One Japanese strongpoint demanded immediate removal. General Patch decided to take Mount Austen, both to wipe out the observation post and to start an enveloping movement.

While the 2nd and 8th Marine Regiments cleaned out resistance pockets in the lower Matanikau sector, the 132nd Regiment United States Army prepared to assault the mountains. This time the enemy got the jump. On the night of 12 December a raiding party stole through the American lines and wrecked a plane and a gasoline truck on Fighter Strip No. 2. On the 14th, American reconnaissance of Mount Austen's northwest slopes met enemy rifle, machine-gun and mortar fire. General Patch's Intelligence still underestimated enemy strength on the mountain. Colonel Oka had two infantry battalions and a mountain artillery regiment perched on the hilltop, and a ridge to the southwest contained a 1500-yard pillbox line manned by 500 men. The Japanese named this the Gifu, after a homeland prefecture.

Colonel John M. Arthur USMC, in command of the operation, slated Lieutenant Colonel Wright's 3rd Battalion to lead off. Both

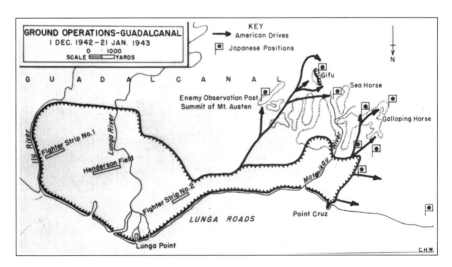

Marines unloading supplies on Guadalcanal Beach. National Archives.

Marine and Army artillery were to lend support at the same instant. The bout began on 17 December with an advance which slowed as soon as the troops entered the jungle and became exposed to fire from cleverly placed machine guns and rifles, one of which killed Colonel Wright. The enemy's favorite infiltration tactics worked well; supply lines were cut, the battalion command post was brought under fire, and at night his noise-making ruses raised a general hullabaloo. Meanwhile most of the 1st Battalion 132nd Infantry was moving up to help.

December 20-24 were spent in patrolling and sporadic jungle fighting, with the supply people and litter-bearers constantly under attack; but on Christmas Eve the Japanese observation post on Mount Austen's highest point fell to the 3rd Battalion. Further advance was halted when the soldiers ran into a withering fire from the Gifu strongpoint, but the enemy could no longer keep Henderson Field and Lunga Roads in his sights.

Frontal attacks against Gifu were launched on Christmas Day and the next, while destroyers *Mustin* and *Perkins* fired almost 2000 rounds of 5-inch ammunition in a diversionary bombardment of enemy supply columns and rear areas to prevent reinforcement. But the Gifu's dirt-covered pillboxes were hard to find and harder to stamp out; the clean-up had to be postponed. On the other side, General Sano assured his men that their patience under attack and starvation would soon be rewarded by all kinds of reinforcement.

On New Year's Day 1943, Colonel Ferry's fresh 2nd Battalion 132nd Regiment moved into a jump-off position to the southeast of the Gifu, and at daybreak 2 January the drive began. The 1st and 3rd Battalions plunged in from the east and north respectively, keeping the enemy occupied while the 2nd Battalion made a flanking climb from the southeast—a hot, grinding march through dense undergrowth and sawtooth kunai grass. Their efforts paid off handsomely. At 1100, two companies reached the summit of the Gifu ridge where they caught a Japanese artillery crew lolling in the shade. The gunners, completely surprised, were killed with looks of astonishment frozen on their features. But their fellows soon recovered and began a desperate series of counterattacks. Six times Colonel Oka's infuriated soldiers charged with blazing rifles; six times they were driven back. Only a welcome and accurate interdiction by artillery fire saved the 2nd Battalion from being completely surrounded.

As the Gifu was now menaced by American guns on every side except the west, Colonel George of the 132nd Regiment felt he could afford to wait. His soldiers dug in and held on until 9 January, when infantry men from the 25th Division climbed the hill and relieved them in preparation for greater doings.

On the night of 14–15 January Tanaka brought down the Slot in nine destroyers a 600-man rear guard destined to cover the Japanese evacuation. Sighted too late for a dusk air attack, this echelon still had to run a gauntlet of motor torpedo boats.

Early in the morning of 15 January, Henderson Field fliers roared up the Slot to collect toll on the "Express." Fifteen SBDs squired by fighter planes attacked the retiring foe. A near-miss damaged *Arashi's* rudder, and strafing bullets holed *Urukaze*. But all destroyers had delivered their goods and all returned.

This was not the last, but one of the best field days of Marine Fighter Squadron 121, who helped their fellow airmen make a day's score of 30 planes. Major J. J. Foss USMC got three "Zekes" to bring his total score to 26; but his runner-up, Lieutenant Eugene

Marontate, was shot down. VMF-121 was credited with 164 Japanese planes destroyed in 122 days' fighting ending 29 January, at the cost of less than 20 pilots.

Patch's Push, 10–26 January

The tenth of January was D-day for an American westward drive of unprecedented magnitude, all in ignorance of the Japanese decision to evacuate Guadalcanal. General Patch's command was now dignified by the title of XIV Corps; the 25th Army Division, arriving in late December and early January, was groomed for frontline fighting; and the 6th Marine Regiment, landing on 4 January, brought the 2nd Marine Division to full strength.[109] He now commanded nigh 50,000 men, including those in the air forces and the naval bases at Lunga and Tulagi. Objectives of the four-pronged attack were the Gifu, the "Sea Horse" series of hills one mile to the westward, "Galloping Horse" hill,[110] and the coast westward from Point Cruz. The coastal objective was given to the 2nd Marine Division; the other three to units of the 25th Division under Major General J. Lawton Collins USA.

Cracking the Gifu was a tough job. Assaults on 10, 11 and 12 January were stopped by Colonel Oka's 40 well-hidden machine guns. Destroyer *Reid* contributed a shore bombardment on 12 January, expending 360 rounds of 5-inch ammunition on Japanese shore positions between Kokumbona and Visale on Cape Esperance. An assault on the 15th netted only a hundred yards to angry Americans. Major Inagaki, out of rations, completely surrounded, hopelessly outnumbered and without artillery support, decided to fight it out despite his colonel's orders. A loud-speaker broadcast urging the Japs to surrender brought in only half a dozen starved soldiers. So the loud-speaker was replaced by Army 105-mm and 155-mm howitzers, which on the 17th dropped over 1700 rounds in the 1000 square yards of the strong point. The break came on the 21st when a Marine tank, manned by troopers and supported by infantry, snorted up the hillside. That night Major Inagaki, with a hundred followers, charged madly and hopelessly into the American lines. Every one was mowed down. Next day Colonel Larsen's battalion of the 35th Infantry Regiment overran

U.S. Marine unit marches back from the Guadalcanal front after being relieved following months of continuous fighting in 1942. National Archives.

Army unit moving toward the front, on Guadalcanal, 30 January 1943. National Archives.

the Gifu and ended a month-long campaign which had employed over five American battalions.

The drive to capture the Sea Horse also began on 10 January. Fortunately there was neither a fanatical major nor a Gifu to oppose the line of advance, but this group of ridged, wooded and gullied hills made an ideal terrain for Japanese-style defense. Two battalions of the 35th Infantry Regiment, assigned the job of lassoing the Sea Horse, made fair progress; the principal problem was to supply them. Three hundred native bearers, an impromptu barge line on the Mantanikau River (known as the "Pusha Maru"), and air drops by B-17s helped, and by the 16th the Sea Horse was safely corralled, together with 600 more dead Japanese. Galloping Horse, believed to be an enemy strong point, was taken by the 27th Infantry Regiment on the evening of 13 January.

General Patch now had enough elbowroom on his western front to undertake a further advance without fear of being flanked on the south or crowded on the west. The next step was to capture the Japanese base at Kokumbona, three miles west of Point Cruz.

Two factors thwarted Patch's scheme to catch this sizable Japanese force. The lesser was the difficulty of supplying front-line troops; the greater and more significant was the decision of 4 January by the Imperial War Council at Tokyo to abandon Guadalcanal and let Imamura salvage what he could of the garrison.

On 22 January the American troops were sufficiently supplied with ammunition and food to resume their advance. A unit of the 25th Division under General Collins marched across the hills to the west of Galloping Horse; a composite Army-Marine outfit, newly formed under General DeCarre, pushed along the coastal road with the 6th Marine Regiment to seaward, the 147th Infantry in the center and the 182nd Infantry on the left flank. Despite enthusiastic support by their own artillery, destroyer gunfire and aerial bombardment, the Marines ran into some very aggressive Nips and had to kill about 200 of them in order to reach Kokumbona late on 23 January. Occupation of the village won the Americans a new landing beach for staging supplies, as well as a radar station, trucks, artillery, landing craft, and about 400 dead Japanese for the burial detail. But the main enemy force had flown the coop.

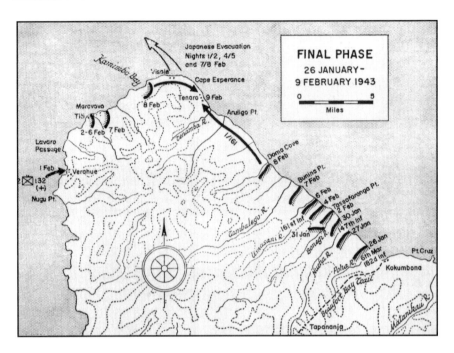

[The Japanese retreat from Kokumbona toward embarkation points on Cape Esperance began the night of 22–23 January.]

The Americans took off in pursuit and, by 1 February, were at the Bong River just below Tassafaronga. Here the rear guard made a brave stand, covering Hyakutake's evacuation.

15. THE BATTLE OF RENNELL ISLAND [111]
(29–30 January 1943)

By 23 January, aerial reconnaissance had reported a large number of transports, freighters and destroyers at Rabaul and Buin, and carriers and battleships milling around Ontong Java, north of Guadalcanal. These were preparations for the final evacuation; but Admiral Halsey, assuming that they meant another major attempt at reinforcement, sent up four loaded transports powerfully covered and escorted, in the hope of tempting Yamamoto to another naval battle. C. in C. Combined Fleet declined the gambit; but, with the new Munda airfield as base, he laid on two successful bombing attacks which cost us the only heavy cruiser which had survived the Battle of Savo Island.

Rear Admiral Robert C. Giffen's covering group for the reinforcement echelon comprised heavy cruisers *Wichita, Chicago* and *Louisville,* three light cruisers, eight destroyers and two of the *Sangamon* class escort carriers, which had demonstrated their worth off Casablanca.

See Appendix G for composition of Admiral Giffen's Task Force 19.

"Ike" Giffen, a tough, colorful officer, had had slight experience in dealing with enemy aircraft. Thus, when Japanese torpedo-bombers jumped his task force in the twilight of 29 January, he was in a bad formation to meet air attack, his ships had no orders what to do, and (worst of all) he had left his escort carriers behind in order to meet an unimportant rendezvous, so had no air cover. He plugged doggedly ahead, trusting to anti-aircraft fire alone, while the Japanese aviators pressed their attacks repeatedly. At 1945 *Chicago* was hit and went dead in the water. Giffen then countermarched, *Louisville* (Captain C. Turner Joy), took the stricken cruiser in tow, and, escorted by six destroyers, headed south at slow speed. At 1600 January 30, the Japanese caught up with them. Crippled *Chicago* now had air cover from *Enterprise*, which Admiral Halsey had ordered up; but the Combat Air Patrol provided by "Big E" was not strong enough to protect an almost stationary target. At a point a few miles east of Rennell Island, nine torpedo-toting "Bettys" ganged up on *Chicago* and put four "fish" into her already damaged starboard side. She sank in twenty minutes.

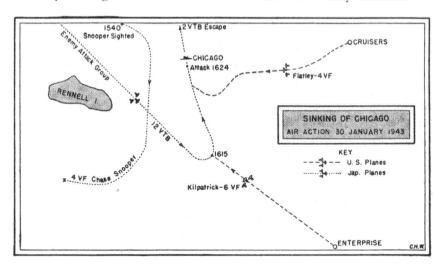

SINKING OF CHICAGO
AIR ACTION 30 JANUARY 1943

KEY
------ U. S. Planes
.... Jap. Planes

USS Chicago going down.

The Battle of Rennell Island was over. Japan made extravagant claims of sinking one battleship (*Chicago*, as usual) and three cruisers and damaging others. The official propaganda, snatching eagerly at something to divert the people's attention from the imminent evacuation of Guadalcanal, even predicted that this would be considered the decisive battle of the war.

This defeat was due not only to a combination of bad luck and bad judgment, as at Tassafaronga, but to Admiral Giffen's inexperience and his determination to make the rendezvous with Briscoe on time. Halsey's endorsement on Giffen's Action Report was a scathing indictment of mistakes in judgment; that of Nimitz was more tolerant.

Japanese flares and float lights soon became familiar to American sailors, but it was not until the Pacific Fleet developed carrier-based night fighter techniques that the menace of twilight and moonlight air attacks was effectively met.

There was one consolation; owing to Giffen's diversion of Japanese air forces, the American transports unloaded their troops and materiel at Lunga Point without molestation, as did a second convoy of five transports which left Espiritu Santo 31 January and arrived 4 February 1943.

16. GUADALCANAL EVACUATED [112]
(1–9 February 1943)

Operation "KE"

Back in December, General Patch wished to land a regimental combat team on the southwest coast of Guadalcanal to plug the enemy's reinforcement channel near Cape Esperance and, at the same time, pinch him in the stern. That plan fell through because the Navy was unable to furnish either troop lift or support. But six LCTs (landing craft, tank) that arrived at Tulagi in January were sufficient for a shore-to-shore amphibious operation, and Captain Briscoe's "Cactus Striking Force," the four Tulagi-based destroyers, were deemed adequate support.

General Patch selected the 2nd Battalion 132nd Infantry for this interesting task. Since very little was known about that part of Guadalcanal, a reconnaissance party marched across the island by the Kokumbona trail and at Beaufort Bay embarked in *Kocorana,* a small Solomon Islands schooner, in the early hours of 1 February, to set up an observation post at Verahue. At the same time, destroyer transport *Stringham* and 5 LCTs were being loaded with troops, trucks, artillery, ammunition and rations at Kukum. At 0400 February 1, they shoved off for the seven-hour trip around Cape Esperance. Well screened by destroyers *Fletcher, Radford, Nicholas* and *DeHaven,* and by Henderson Field fighter planes, the troops and their gear were safely deposited on Verahue beach. Japanese bombers on the "milk run" to Henderson Field never even fluttered an aileron at the sight, but one of them was shot down by the destroyers.

Unknown to the Americans, the enemy had chosen the night of 1–2 February to begin his big evacuation, and his aviators were instructed to prevent any interference with the sea lane of retreat. It doubtless looked to them as if the secret of Operation "KE" had leaked out, and that Briscoe was trying to break it up.

Destroyers *DeHaven* and *Nicholas,* escorting back to Ironbottom Sound three LCTs which had completed unloading, had reached a point about three miles south of Savo Island. *Radford* and *Fletcher* were still t'other side Cape Esperance escorting the other two landing craft and, by some unexplained mismanagement, they had all the fighter escort, leaving *DeHaven* and *Nicholas* bare. Enemy dive-bombers winged in over Florida Island at 1450 and turned toward Savo Island. Guadalcanal radio hastily broadcast a warning which put both destroyers and LCTs very much on the alert. Within a few minutes the formation of 14 "Vals" appeared. On board *DeHaven* there was a delay in getting permission to shoot, and it was not until six of the enemy peeled off from low altitude—5000 feet—that the destroyer fought back. Three bombs hit *DeHaven* and a near-miss mined the hull. Commander Charles E. Tolman was killed by a direct hit on the bridge; the ship settled quickly by the bow and, within two minutes, was on her way down to the Ironbottom graveyard with 167 of her crew. During this brief action the machine guns of LCT-63 and LCT-181 shot down a plane, and after it was over, the landing craft rescued 146 survivors including 38 wounded. Destroyer *Nicholas* (Lieutenant Commander Andrew J. Hill), which attracted the attention of eight Japanese planes, got out of it with only near-misses that damaged the steering gear and killed two men.

Naval commanders around Guadalcanal soon had something else to worry about. In the early afternoon, coastwatchers and scouting aircraft reported a score of enemy destroyers, north of Vella Lavella, coming down the Slot at high speed. This was the first echelon of Operation "KE." It looked like another drive to land troops; it must be stopped. At 1820, 17 SBDs and 7 TBFs covered by 17 F4Fs swooped down on the destroyers when passing Vangunu Island and met a hot reception from a combat patrol of 30 "Zekes." At a cost of four American planes, destroyer *Makinami* was stopped by a bomb hit; but the other nineteen, after some adroit dodging, continued toward Guadalcanal.

It is to their credit that the Japanese destroyers, in the face of varied opposition, managed to carry out their evacuation mission. Even after the start of Operation "KE" the Japanese kept it secret. The only indication of retreat was our capture of an abandoned base near Tassafaronga on 2 February. A powerful radio station, a large undamaged machine shop and ten pieces of artillery fell to the Americans. But this might still have indicated consolidation

USS DeHaven (DD-469) passing north of Savo Island off Guadalcanal on 30 Jan. 1943. She was sunk on 1 Feb. 1943 in these waters by a Japanese air attack. Photo taken from USS Fletcher (DD-445). National Archives.

USS LCT-181 coming alongside USS Fletcher (DD-445), with survivors of USS DeHaven (DD-469) aboard. DeHaven had been sunk by Japanese air attack on 1 Feb. 1943, the day this photo was taken off Guadalcanal. National Archives.

for a renewed offensive. The hectic events of 1–2 February only increased the apprehension that another reinforcement similar to that of mid-November was under way.

The second Japanese evacuation echelon was scheduled for 4 February, but this time there was little excitement off Cape Esperance. Early in the afternoon one cruiser and 22 destroyers weighed anchor at Faisi and commenced a rugged run down the Slot. Again Henderson Field airmen went halfway to meet them with bombs. Thirty-three SBDs and TBFs covered by 31 fighters were met by swarms of "Zekes" and seasoned ships' gunners. In the resulting mêlée 10 American and 17 Japanese planes were lost. *Maikaze* was disabled by flooding from near-misses; *Shiranuhi* took a bomb on an after gun mount, and two other destroyers were slightly damaged by near-misses.

On 7 February the third evacuation echelon comprising 18 destroyers was sighted on its way down the Slot. Because of rain squalls only 15 dive-bombers got through. They made two hits on *Isokaze* and one on *Hamakaze* but neither destroyer fell out of formation. Compared with the night of 1–2 February, the rest of that run was a lark for the Nips. Japanese troops at Cape Esperance and the Russells ferried themselves to the waiting destroyers in landing barges. When the last barge was unloaded and cut adrift, this final run of the "Tokyo Express" hastened up the Slot crowded with high-ranking officers, rear-echelon soldiers and sailors. And the Rising Sun never rose again over Ironbottom Sound.

During these three nights of evacuation, 11,706 men were pulled out of Guadalcanal; an amazing performance which elicited praise from Admiral Nimitz: "Only skill in keeping their plans disguised and bold celerity in carrying them out enabled the Japanese to withdraw the remnants of the Guadalcanal garrison." [113]

General Patch's ground forces, slogging along jungle trails during the first week of February, were bemused. What were the Japanese up to? By 7 February Colonel George's western pincer, operating from Verahue, was about three miles from Cape Esperance, organizing for a decisive thrust. His eastern tentacle, composed of the 161st Infantry and the 10th Marines as supporting artillery, was already a mile west of Tassafaronga and going strong. On the

Japanese freighter destroyed and beached on Guadalcanal, 1942-1943.
Courtesy Claude Gulbranson, 1ˢᵗ Special NCB.

Japanese minisub beached and abandoned on Guadalcanal, 1943.
Courtesy Claude Gulbranson, 1ˢᵗ Special NCB.

morning of 8 February, nothing could be found on the Cape Esperance beaches but empty boats and abandoned supplies. And that was the General's first certain knowledge of an evacuation.

The troops now redoubled their efforts to close the gap. At 1625 February 9, in a village on the Tenamba River, the 2nd Battalion of the 132nd Infantry coming from the west met the 2nd Battalion of the 161st Infantry coming from the east.

General Patch radioed to Admiral Halsey: "Total and complete defeat of Japanese forces on Guadalcanal effected 1625 today… Am happy to report this kind of compliance with your orders… 'Tokyo Express' no longer has terminus on Guadalcanal."

The Cost and the Return

There it was—2500 square miles of miasmic plain, thick jungle and savage mountains in American hands, after exactly six months of toil, suffering and terror. What had it cost? What was the return? Where were we going next?

In war's brutal scale of lives lost against lives risked, the bloodletting from 60,000 Army and Marine Corps troops committed to Guadalcanal, had not been excessive; 1592 killed in action. Navy losses were certainly in excess of that figure, and several score fliers of all three air forces had given their lives.[114] But the Japanese had lost about two thirds of the 36,000 men who fought on Guadalcanal— 14,800 killed or missing, 9000 dead of disease and 1000 taken prisoner. Many thousand more soldiers went down in blasted transports or barges, and the number of Japanese sailors lost in the vicious sea battles will never be known, because such matters do not interest the Japanese.

American Cemetery at Lunga Beach, Guadalcanal. John Case, 1st Special NCB.

On the material side the tallies of combat ships lost by each side in the Guadalcanal campaign are surprisingly even:

| | ALLIED | | JAPANESE | |
	Number	Tonnage	Number	Tonnage
Battleships	0	0	2	62,000
Aircraft Carriers	2	34,500	0	0
Light Carriers	0	0	1	8,500
Heavy Cruisers	6	56,925	3	26,400
Light Cruisers	2	12,000	1	5,700
Destroyers	14	22,815	11	20,930
Submarines	0	0	6	11,309
Totals	24	126,240	24	134,839

Table compiled by Mr. W.L. Robinson. It does not include transports (AP, AK or APD) of which the Japanese had far the heavier loss, or auxiliaries such as *Seminole,* or patrol craft.

Author's Note: To compare above losses with total U.S. Navy combatant ship losses during WWII, see Appendix M, page 593.

Tactically—in the sense of coming to grips with the enemy—Guadalcanal was a profitable lesson book. The recommendations of Guadalcanal commanders became doctrine for Allied fighting men the world over. And it was the veteran from "the 'Canal" who went back to man the new ship or form the cornerstone for the new regiment. On top level, mark well the names of Halsey, Turner, Vandegrift, Patch, Geiger, Collins, Lee, Kinkaid, Ainsworth, Merrill. They would be heard from again.

Strategically, as seen from Pearl Harbor or Constitution Avenue, Guadalcanal was worth every ship, plane and life that it cost. The enemy was stopped in his many-taloned reach for the antipodes. Task One in the arduous climb to Rabaul was neatly if tardily packaged and filed away.

There were more subtle implications to Guadalcanal. The lordly Samurai, with his nose rubbed in the mud and his sword rusted by the salt of Ironbottom Sound, was forced to revise his theory of invincibility. A month previously Hirohito had issued an imperial rescript stating that in the Solomon Islands "a decisive battle is being fought between Japan and America." Radio Tokyo gave out that the Imperial forces, "after pinning down the Americans to a corner of the island," had accomplished their mission and so departed to fight elsewhere. There was a laugh for Americans in that; but Guadalcanal never inspired much laughter.

For us who were there, or whose friends were there, Guadalcanal is not a name but an emotion, recalling desperate fights in the air, furious night naval battles, frantic work at supply or construction, savage fighting in the sodden jungle, nights broken by screaming bombs and deafening explosions of naval shells. Sometimes I dream of a great battle monument on Guadalcanal; a granite monolith on which the names of all who fell and of all ships that rest in Ironbottom Sound may be carved. At other times I feel that the jagged cone of Savo Island, forever brooding over the blood-thickened waters of the Sound, is the best monument to the men and ships who here rolled back the enemy tide.

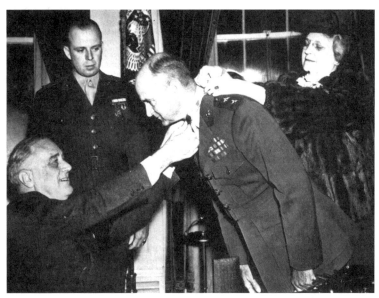

President Franklin D. Roosevelt presents General Vandegrift the Medal of Honor for his heroic accomplishments against the Japanese in the Solomons. Looking on are Mrs. Vandegrift and the General's son, Major Alexander A. Vandegrift, Jr. National Archives.

PART II

The Central Solomons Campaigns

Part II chronicles the amphibious operations in the New Georgia Islands group, including the five separate landings at Rendova, Segi Point, Viru Harbor, Wickham Anchorage, plus three more significant naval battles and the occupation of Vella Lavella.

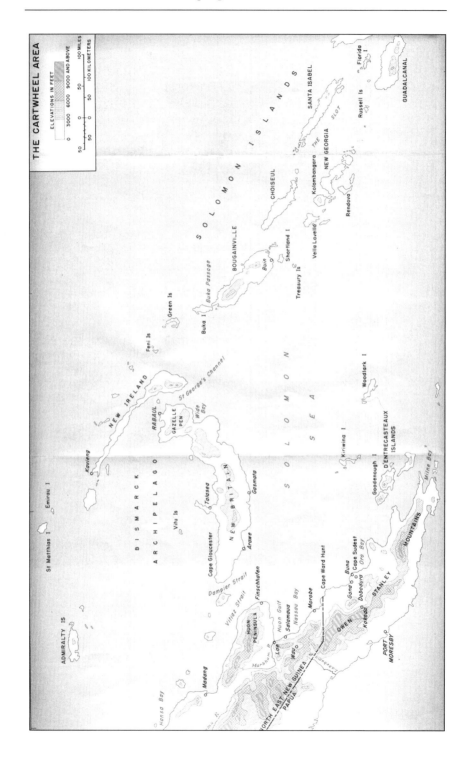

CHAPTER 4

Amphibious Rehearsals
in the Russells
21 February 1943[1]

The last of the Japanese troops evacuated Guadalcanal on 7-8 February 1943, at which time WATCHTOWER could be marked in the books as completed. The pressure was immediately on the amphibians to get moving.

The first real move north was to Rendova Island in the New Georgia Group about 180 miles northwest of Lunga Point, but this most worthwhile step was preceded by an advance a stone's throw away to the nearest Russell Island lying only 30 miles northwest of Guadalcanal Island.

The Amphibians had learned a lot from the August 1942 landings at Tulagi and Guadalcanal, and they continued to learn a great deal more during the long, six-month struggle to maintain logistic support for these two important toe holds in the Southern Solomons. By January 1943, marked changes had occurred in their thinking about the techniques of support through and over a beachhead as documented in the new January 18, 1943 "Amphibians Bible." [2] Also, the revolutionary new amphibious craft were just becoming available. They were anxious to test these changes and the new craft on a foreign shore.

On 21 February 1943, the amphibious forces of the South Pacific Area landed in major strength on the Russell Islands. This landing, if it did not do anything else, fulfilled Major General Vandegrift's requirement that "...landings should not be attempted in the face of organized resistance if, by any combination of march or maneuver, it is possible to land unopposed and undetected."

The Planning Stage

Admiral Nimitz visited the South Pacific in late January 1943 in company with Secretary of the Navy Frank Knox. At a COMSOPAC (Halsey) conference of principal commanders and their planning officers on January 23, 1943, Adm Halsey received from CINCPAC (Nimitz) a tentative and unofficial approval meaning "go ahead with the planning while my staff back in Pearl takes a hard look at the proposition."[3]

Shortly thereafter, on 28 January, COMSOPAC informed CINCPAC that if the reconnaissance then underway indicated the Russell Islands were undefended, he planned immediate occupation. After CINCPAC gave his formal approval (29 January) and despite somewhat misleading information received from the coastwatcher intelligence organization about "enemy activity Russell Islands increasing," COMSOPAC issued his preliminary operational warning order to the prospective commanders involved on 7 February 1943. COMSOPAC issued his dispatch Operation Order first and then his plan for the landings, code named CLEANSLATE, on 12 and 15 February 1942.

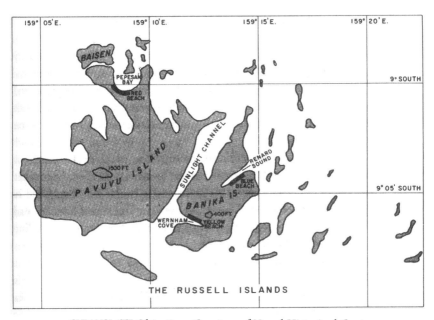

CLEANSLATE Objective. Courtesy of Naval Historical Center.

The Russell Islands are 60 miles west-northwest of Henderson Field on Guadalcanal. The two main islands of the Russells are Pavuvu and Banika, the former being about twice the size of the latter, which is nearer Guadalcanal. Pavuvu is about 7 x 8 miles and Banika is about 8 x 2 miles slotted by two comfortable inlets, one on its east coast, the other on its west coast. While there is a 400-foot high knob in the southern part of Banika, the rest of the island is low and in 1943 was clear of jungle although with many beautiful coconut trees. It was judged suitable for an airfield.

These two main islands, separated by Sunlight Channel half a mile wide, are surrounded by dozens of small islands extending ten to twelve miles off shore, particularly to the eastward.

When Adm Halsey issued his final CLEANSLATE Operation Plan, he initiated an action resembling its predecessor in that there would be no long-term planning available to RAdm Turner's staff prior to the actual landing just nine days away.

The major purposes assigned by COMSOPAC for the operation were:

1. To strengthen the defense of Guadalcanal, and
2. To establish a staging point for landing craft preliminary to further forward movement.

The mission also included establishing an advanced motor torpedo base, an advanced air base, and radar installations.

RAdm Turner, COMPHIBSOPAC, was named Commander of the Joint Force designated Task Force 61, with Commanding General 43rd Division, MGen John H. Hester, U.S. Army, Commander Landing Force.

Task Force 61 was tailored for a "shore-to-shore" amphibious task. In the language of the amphibians this meant that the assault movement of personnel and materiel would move directly from a shore staging area to the landing beaches of the assault objective, involving no further transfers between types of landing craft or into landing boats during the assault movement. The shore staging area designated for CLEANSLATE was Koli Point, Guadalcanal. Gavutu Island in Purvis Bay would handle the overflow.

A desire to effect complete surprise if the Japanese were still in the Russells, or if they were not, a desire to deny the Japanese knowledge of the occupation of the Russells for as long as possible, prompted the decision to carry out a shore-to-shore operation.

Such a "shore-to-shore movement" meant that the long distance over-water movement to Guadalcanal of the amphibious troops participating in the D-Day initial landings of the CLEANSLATE Operation had to be carried out prior to the final embarkation at Guadalcanal for the assault.

The TF 61 organization for CLEANSLATE was as follows:

CLEANSLATE ORGANIZATION – TF 61

(a)   **TG 61.1 Transport Group** – RAdm Turner

TU 61.1.1 TRANSDIV Twelve – Cmdr John D. Sweeney

Stringham (APD-6)	*Humphreys* (APD-12)
Manley (APD-1)	*Sands* (APD-13)

(Each with 4 LCP(L) and 15 LCR(L) on board.)

TU 61.1.2 Mine Group – Cmdr Stanley Leith

Hopkins (DMS-13)	*McCall* (DD-400)
Southard (DMS-10)	*Maury* (DD-401)
Trever (DMS-16)	

TU 61.1.3 TRANSDIV Dog – Cmdr Wilfrid Nyquist

Saufley (DD-465)	*Hovey* (DMS-11)
Craven (DD-382)	*Zane* (DMS-14)
*Gridley (DD-380)	

*Gridley substituted for *Hovey* in initial movement.

TU 61.1.4 TRANSDIV Easy – Cmdr Thomas J. Ryan

Wilson (DD-408)	*Lansdowne* (DD-486)
LCT-158 Lt Edgar M. Jaeger, USNR	LCT-159 Lt (jg) Frank M. Wiseman, USNR
LCT-58	LCT-156
LCT-60	LCT-369
LCT-181 Lt Ashton L. Jones, USNR	LCT-63 Lt (jg) Ameel Z. Kouri, USNR
LCT-62	LCT-323
LCT-322	LCT-367

(Each destroyer type except *Hopkins, Wilson,* and *Lansdowne* towing one LCM, one LCV, and two LCPs.)

(b) **TU 61.1.5 Service Group** – Lt James L. Foley
Bobolink (AT-131) with 1,000-ton flat top lighter in tow.

TG 61.2 Attack Group – Lt Allen H. Harris, USNR
Motor Torpedo Boat Squadron TWO (THREE)

PT-36	PT-109	PT-146
PT-40	PT-110	PT-147
PT-42	PT-144	PT-148
PT-48	PT-145	

(8 of the 11 boats in the Squadron were to be picked for the operation.)

(c) **TG 61.3 Occupation Force** – MGen Hester

TU 61.3.1 Landing Force – MGen Hester

43rd Infantry Division (less 172nd Combat Team)

3rd Marine Raider Battalion (temporarily attached)

One-third 11th Marine Defense Battalion

One platoon of Company B, 579th Aircraft Warning Battalion (Radar)

One regiment from CACTUS Force (when assigned)

TU 61.3.2 Naval Base – Cmdr Charles E. Olsen

Naval Advance Base Force

ACORN Three

One-half 35th Naval Construction Battalion

Naval Communication Units

CLEANSLATE Boat Pool (50 boats)

LCTs Ready for Action

The Landing Craft, Tank of 1942-43 was 112 feet over-all, had a 32-foot beam, and a draft of a little over three feet. It was normally expected to carry four 40-ton tanks or to load 150 to 180 tons or about 5,760 cubic feet of cargo. Its actual speed, loaded and in a smooth sea, was a bit more than six knots, although it had a designed speed of ten knots. These large tank landing craft, which shipyards in the United States started to deliver in large numbers in September and October of 1942, were the first of their kind to be used offensively in the South Pacific. (See LCT Flotilla Five profile in Volume I of this trilogy.) The first mention of the LCT in Rear Admiral Turner's Staff Log occurs on 19 December 1942, when 6 LCTs of Flotilla Five were reported at Nouméa loading for Guadalcanal.

Through the leadership efforts of RAdm George H. Fort, Turner's Chief of Staff, Capt Benton W. Decker and, after arrival in SOPAC, his senior landing craft subordinate, Capt Grayson B. Carter, the Landing Craft Flotillas, PHIBFORSOPAC, were trained under forced draft.

After only 12 months of war, the landing craft were manned to a marked extent with officers and men who had entered the Navy after the attack on Pearl Harbor. To assist in the training, Commander Landing Craft Flotillas in due time issued a comprehensive Doctrine full of instructions and information for the dozens of landing craft moving into the SOPAC command during the January to June period in 1943.[4] The LCT "Veterans" of CLEANSLATE became the nuclei for this massive training effort.

As a matter of record, the first 12 LCTs to get their bottoms crinkled in war operations in the South Pacific were LCTs 58, 60, 62, 63, 156, 158, 159, 181, 322, 323, 367, and 369.

Most of the senior officers in LCT Flot 5 (Jaeger, A.L. Jones, Kouri, and Wiseman) participated in CLEANSLATE. They got the LCTs off to a good start in the South Pacific.

The largest landing craft carried by the amphibious transports and cargo ships was the Landing Craft, Medium (LCM). The LCM could carry 30 tons or 2,200 cubic feet of cargo. Among the smaller shipborne landing craft, both the Higgins LCP (Landing Craft, Personnel) and the LCVP (Landing Craft Vehicle/Personnel) could transport 36 men or one medium tank. The WWI-vintage destroyers which had been converted into fast transports (APDs) could carry 200 troops and limited amounts of their equipment. The converted fast minesweepers (DMS) could carry somewhat fewer troops.

Spit Kit Expeditionary Force [5]

Task Force 61, in effect the Joint Expeditionary Force, consisted of the Army troops and Marines in the 9,000 Landing Force, seven destroyers (DDs *Craven, Gridley, Lansdowne, Maury, McCall, Saufley, Wilson*), four destroyer transports (*Stringham, Manley, Humphreys, Sands*), four fast minesweepers, the logistic service ship *Bobolink*, eight motor torpedo boats (PTs) of Torpedo Boat Squadron Two, and 12 LCTs of Landing Craft Tank Flotilla Five.

Of the 16 ships, 108 large and small landing craft and 8 motor torpedo boats in CLEANSLATE, only the fast minesweepers *Hopkins, Trever, Southward,* and *Zane,* and the destroyer *Wilson* of the original WATCHTOWER invasion task force shared with RAdm Turner the satisfaction of participating in the initial phase of the first forward island jumping movement of the South Pacific Area. The *Hovey* (DMS-11) lost out on this high honor when she did not arrive at Guadalcanal in time to load and the *Gridley* (DD-380) was substituted for her in the initial phase of CLEANSLATE.

In addition to the 43rd Infantry Division (less its 172nd Regimental Combat Team) the major units named to participate in the operation were the Marine 3rd Raider Battalion, anti-aircraft elements of the Marine 11th Defense Battalion, half of the 35th Naval Construction Battalion and ACORN Three, the naval unit designated to construct, operate, and maintain the planned aircraft facilities on Banika Island.

An ACORN was an airfield assembly designed to construct, operate, and maintain an advanced land plane and seaplane base and provide facilities for operation. Marine Air Group 21 and the 10th Marine Defense Battalion were enroute to the South Pacific Area and were to be assigned to the Russells upon arrival.

CLEANSLATE was also the first major amphibious island jumping operation where radar-equipped planes, "Black Cats," were used to cover all of the night movements of our own ships and craft against the approach of enemy surface and air forces.

Supporting Forces

CTF 63, COMAIRSOPACFOR, VAdm Fitch, was ordered to provide long-range air search, anti-aircraft cover, anti-submarine

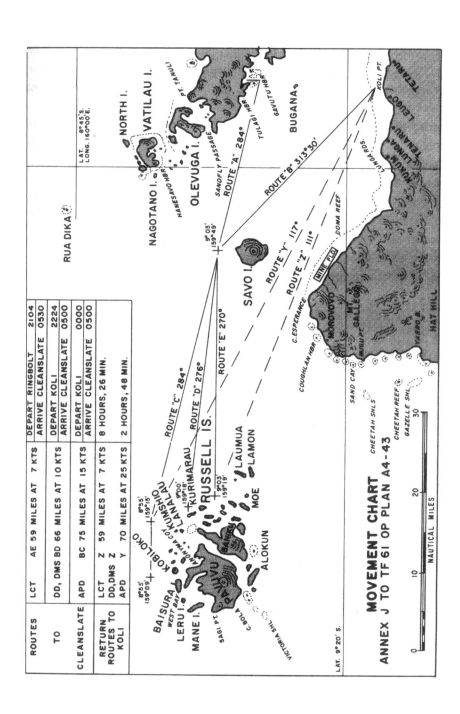

MOVEMENT CHART
ANNEX J TO TF 61 OP PLAN A4-43

ROUTES			DEPART RINGBOLT	2104
	LCT	AE 59 MILES AT 7 KTS	ARRIVE CLEANSLATE	0530
TO	DD, DMS BD	66 MILES AT 10 KTS	DEPART KOLI	2224
			ARRIVE CLEANSLATE	0500
CLEANSLATE	APD	BC 75 MILES AT 15 KTS	DEPART KOLI	0000
			ARRIVE CLEANSLATE	0500
RETURN ROUTES TO KOLI	LCT	Z 59 MILES AT 7 KTS	8 HOURS, 26 MIN.	
	DD,DMS	Z		
	APD	Y 70 MILES AT 25 KTS	2 HOURS, 48 MIN.	

screen and air strikes. If needed, he would supply direct air support during the landing and advance from the beaches.

Cruiser Division 12, commanded by Captain Aaron S. (Tip) Merrill (about to be elevated to Flag rank) was ordered to provide immediate support to TF 61, and the fast carrier task forces were ordered to be within supporting distance of the Russells on D-Day to deal with any major Japanese Naval Forces entering the lower Solomons.

The staging movement of Army troops and Marines, Seabees, and other naval personnel into Guadalcanal and Gavutu was accomplished in large transports and cargo ships, six echelons arriving before D-Day, 21 February, and four follow-up echelons moving through after the 21st.

Preliminaries

During the nine-day period between the issuance of COMSOPAC's CLEANSLATE Operation Order and the actual landing, two groups of observers from TF 61 visited the Russells and reported that the islands had recently been evacuated by the Japanese. These parties obtained detailed information in regard to landing beaches and selected camp locations and anti-aircraft gun sites. The second group remained to welcome the Task Force, and marked the landing beaches to be used. This was a task later to be taken over under more difficult and dangerous conditions by the Underwater Demolition Teams.

The main movement of the amphibians from the staging areas to the Russells was planned and completed in four major echelons. The over-water movement from Koli Point, Guadalcanal, to the Russells for the initial landings was largely carried out as planned.

During the preliminary movement when the first echelon of the 43rd Division was being staged (the 840 miles from New Caledonia to Koli Point) RAdm Turner moved with them in the *McCawley* which carried part of the amphibian troops. On 16 February 1943, he shifted his operational staff ashore to Koli Point from the *McCawley*. During the first phase of the CLEANSLATE landing operations he flew his flag in the fast minesweeper

LCTs 159 and 482 unloading men and equipment on Solomon Islands beach. Note that reefs and sandbars prevented LCTs from reaching the beach. Courtesy John McNeill.

Hopkins, and commanded the Transport Group, TG 61.1

On 19 February 1943, one task group (4 APA, 1 AO, 6 DD) carrying the second echelon of the amphibians and their logistic support from Nouméa to the Koli staging area on Guadalcanal, was subjected to a seven aircraft Japanese torpedo plane attack when about 20 miles east of the southern tip of San Cristobal Island. By radical maneuver, the transports and their destroyer escorts escaped damage, and by spirited anti-aircraft fire accounted for five Japanese aircraft lost. Otherwise, the ten-day preparation period was largely unhampered by the Japanese.

The Landings

RAdm Turner's (CTF 61) and Commander Landing Force's orders called for three simultaneous landings at dawn on 21 February 1943. These were:

1. On the north of Pavuvu Island at Pepesala Bay
2. At Renard Sound on the east coast of Banika Island
3. At Wernham Cove on the southwest coast of Banika Island.

According to RAdm Turner's Operation Order: "The landing beaches in the Russells are bad, with much coral. Every precaution will be taken to prevent damage to boats, particularly propellers."

For the initial landings totaling 4,030 officers and enlisted personnel on Pavuvu and Banika, more than 200 men were ferried on each of the seven destroyers, four destroyer transports, and four fast minesweepers. Additionally most destroyers and minesweepers towed four small landing craft: 2 LCPs and 2 LCVPs.

The four fast transports each carried, in addition to troops, four LCVPs and 15 rubber landing boats. The mighty *Bobolink* (AT-121) towed a 1,000-ton flat top lighter for use at Wernham Cove.

CLEANSLATE went off with precision, but without fanfare or publicity since it was believed that the Japanese were unaware of the preparations for the operation or its execution. So besides radio silence, there was press and public relations silence. All the ships and landing craft, except one LCT with engine trouble, departed for their return passages to Guadalcanal by 1230 on D-Day.

The 800 men of the 3rd Marine Raider Battalion, which had missed out on the WATCHTOWER Operation, were loaded onto four destroyer transports at Koli Point and at 0600 on 21 February landed on Beach Red in Pepesala Bay, Pavuvu Island, where the Japanese formerly had their main strength and where MGen Hester, Commander Landing Force, in his Operation Order expressed the opinion "definite possibilities exist that enemy patrols and small units may be located."

RAdm Turner, MGen Hester, and their operational staffs went ashore from the *Hopkins* onto Beach Yellow in Wernham Cove, Banika Island. They landed just after 800 troops from two DDs and two DMSs and additional troops ferried by eight LCTs had landed. The Naval Base Headquarters was established on the north side of Wernham Cove.

Another 800 troops from three DDs and one DMS and additional troops aboard four LCTs landed at Beach Blue, Renard South. Most of the Banika Island troops came from the 103rd Regimental Combat Team of the 43rd Infantry Division.

A follow-up landing of 800 troops from the 169th Infantry Regiment of the 43rd Division, U.S. Army, took place on the sandy beaches of Pepesala Bay in northern Pavuvu Island, early on the morning of 22 February, the day after the Marines had landed in this area. At the same time 1,400 more troops landed at Beach Yellow in Wernham Cove.

The second to fourth follow-up echelons moved on D plus 2, D plus 3 and D plus 4. The ships and larger craft continued to make most all their movements between Guadalcanal and the Russells at night so as not to alert the Japanese, while the LCTs usually made one-way passages each night. No public disclosure of the landing was immediately made and the base at CLEANSLATE maintained radio silence.

In two days 7,000 troops were landed. By 15 March, 15,500 troops were in the Russells and by 18 April when command passed to the Commanding General, Guadalcanal, 16,000 men were busy there and no less than 48,517 tons of supplies had arrived there by amphibious effort. The Japanese did not react to the occupation for 15 days. On 6 March 1943, they made the first of a series of air raids.

Commander Charles Eugene Olsen, who had successfully skippered the early base building efforts at Tongatabu, and who had

Gasoline and 500-pound bombs on Russell Island beach from an LCT in 1943. Courtesy John McNeill.

LCT-326 unloading at Banika Island (Russells) at Lever Coconut Plantation, 1943. Courtesy John McNeill.

impressed RAdm Turner when he had flown through the Tonga Islands in July 1942, was given the task of building the Advanced Naval Base in the Russell Islands. By the end of March, on Banika Island, there was a good airfield with three fighter squadrons, a motor torpedo base at Renard Sound, and a growing supply activity.

The weather and navigational hazards unhappily put three destroyer-types *(Lansdowne, Stringham, Sands)* on the beach on February 26th. The landing craft had a normal ration of unintentional groundings and breakdowns, but none of the destroyer-types became permanent additions to the Russells.

RAdm George H. Fort relieved RAdm Turner as Commander Task Force 61 on 3 March 1943 and Turner returned to Nouméa to continue his favorite chore of planning the next operation.

The CLEANSLATE Operation has been both praised and criticized. For example, *Time Magazine* said, "The operation went more smoothly [than Guadalcanal]. The Japs had evacuated." [6]

In June 1943, RAdm Turner made a simple exposition to newspaper correspondents as to why the Allies needed the Russells, before moving into the central Solomons:

> It was simply because we must have fighter coverage for Rendova...We couldn't have fighters from Guadalcanal. It's that extra little distance west that makes coverage possible for Rendova from the Russells. ...From Rendova to the Russells is 125 miles, from Guadalcanal to the Russells is 60 miles. [7]

When the Russell Islands logistical support movements were completed, COMSOPAC took note of this and smartly changed the code name of the Russells to EMERITUS.

Summary

From the point of view of both COMSOPAC and COMPHIBFORSOPAC, the Russells had two great advantages over any and all other immediately possible objectives necessary to carry out the 2 July 1942 Joint Chiefs of Staff directive. The Russells (1) were on the direct line from Guadalcanal to Rabaul and (2) they lay within COMSOPAC's command area, so that high level arrangements in regard to command did not have to be negotiated, a process usually taking weeks or months.

The amphibians had an excellent opportunity to put together the dozens of suggestions arising out of WATCHTOWER for the improvement of amphibious operations and test them under conditions far more rugged than any rear area rehearsal could provide. The Russells added not only skill but also confidence to the amphibians. As RAdm Turner pointed out:

> During the course of the operation, a technique was developed for the movement of troops and cargo from a forward base to a nearby objective without the use of APAs and AKAs. It is expected that the experience of this operation will prove useful in planning future offensives.
>
> The CLEANSLATE Operation again demonstrated that the overwater movement and landing of the first echelon of troops is only the initial step in a continuous amphibious series, all of which are integral parts of the same venture. Success of the venture depends upon the ability to deliver safely not only the first, but also the succeeding echelons of troops, engineers, ancillary units, equipment and operating and upkeep supplies and replacements. The aggregate of personnel and cargo for the later movements is far greater than that carried initially. Each movement requires protection, and losses in transit from the logistic bases to the combat position must be kept low enough to be acceptable. It is particularly true that when small vessels are used, an uninterrupted stream of them must be maintained.
>
> The first movement for the seizure of a position; the exploitation on shore of that position; the long series of succeeding movements of troops and materiel, together form a single operation. All parts must be accomplished under satisfactory condition if the whole operation is to be successful.[8]

From the period of its activation in July 1942 to the completion of its first major tasks in January 1943, the Amphibious Force, South Pacific had about the same number of ships and landing craft assigned with replacements being supplied for ships sunk or worn out in war service. But there was a steadily growing prospect of a real increase in size when the coastal transports and larger landing craft, building or training on the East and West Coasts of the United States, were finally cut loose and sailed to the South Pacific to fulfill their war assignments.

By late January 1943, the ships and landing craft assigned to the Amphibious Force South Pacific had grown sufficiently so that a new organization had to be established.

(See Appendix J for composition of Amphibious Force South Pacific [PHIBFORSOPAC] as of January 1943.)

By counting on one's fingers, it is obvious that among the large work horses of PHIBFORSOPAC there are now 18 ships (11 APAs and 7 AKAs) versus 19 ships (14 APAs and 5 AKAs) six months earlier. However, there are now 10 APDs versus four at the earlier date and a definite promise of 127 landing ships and craft versus none earlier.

Eventually, it is planned that the Landing Craft Flotillas, SOPAC, will include 127 large landing ships and craft, i.e. 37 LSTs, 36 LCIs, and 54 LCTs. However, in late January 1943, only a few of the early birds had been formed up organizationally in the United States much less trained in amphibious operations and journeyed to the South Pacific.

In addition to the list of ships and craft in Appendix J, four more APDs and 50 coastal transports (APs) were under order to report to COMPHIBFORSOPAC, but they had not even reached the stage of division and squadron assignments. When they report, the force will consist of more than 200 ships and large landing craft.[9]

It is interesting to note from this roster that the fast-learning officers of the Naval Reserve had learned enough by January 1943 to take over command of some of the destroyer transports. And it is a sad commentary on how slowly the wartime promotion system spread to Amphibious Force SOPAC. Note that a year after the Pacific War started, a fair number of the skippers of the large transports of PHIBFORSOPAC had 23 to 25 years of commissioned service but were still wearing the three stripes of a commander.

CHAPTER 5

Lull Between Storms
February – June 1943[1]

O ccupation of the Russells, following closely on the heels of the Guadalcanal victory, seemed to whet the appetite of Allied forces in the South Pacific for more showdowns with the Japanese.

In Admiral Halsey's New Caledonia headquarters, optimism and enthusiasm ran high. Singleness of purpose and a spirit of camaraderie united all representatives on ComSoPac's staff; and, charged by Halsey's impatience to get on with the war, his staff busied itself planning for the next major offensive in the Solomons. The objective: seizure of the New Georgia Group.

Adm William Halsey, Jr., COMSOPAC and MajGen Alexander A. Vandegrift, USMC, American Occupation Commander in the Solomons during a Jan. 1943 conference at Adm Halsey's headquarters. Naval Historical Center.

New Georgia, the Allies had decided, would be the target of the next offensive in the South Pacific. Munda airfield was the bull's-eye. As a military prize, it held the enemy's hopes for a re-entry into the lower Solomons and the Allied hopes for another step towards Rabaul.

USS George Clymer (APA-27) and other ships in the harbor at Nouméa, New Caledonia, 1943. National Archives.

Espiritu Santo waterfront, circa 1943-44. USNCB.

The Japanese advantage at this point was mainly one of position. Historian Morison summed it up: [2]

> The Japanese owned a nicely spaced series of airstrips beginning with four at Rabaul, going down 166 miles to Buka, thence 105 miles to Kahili in lower Bougainville, thence a 102-mile jump to Vila, with Munda and Rekata Bay (the last a seaplane base) only a little farther. Munda was very convenient for staging planes from Rabaul or Bougainville for raids on Tulagi-Guadalcanal. The bombers stopped there only long enough to refuel, and after executing their mission refueled again and returned to Rabaul, beyond Henderson Field fliers' range. Against these air tactics, the American air bombings and naval bombardments which pitted Munda Field with holes were vain. The Japanese ground crews, on the double, filled in the craters with crushed coral, and in a matter of minutes or hours the strip was again operational. Instead of rebuilding destroyed structures, the ground crews went underground.

During this so-called "lull" between Solomons campaigns there was a major build-up in Allied troops, supplies, and aircraft as well as the long-awaited revolutionary new landing ships and craft.

The South Pacific was the scene of unprecedented activity. Places which had been nothing but mud-holes during the Guadalcanal campaign were now well-organized bases. Nouméa was fast becoming a rear area. Even Espiritu Santo, which had been a jungle hell for a year, was made almost habitable for the thousands of American Army, Navy, and Marine Corps men deposited there to build a firm foundation for the structure which was to extend through the Solomons.

Guadalcanal was cleansed of snipers; the crushed coral roads from Henderson Field to Koli and Lunga were given route numbers, as in the United States. New airfields were built, on better sites than the quaking meadow where the slipshod Japanese had laid out Henderson Field. Tulagi was an advanced naval base.

The Russell Islands became the headquarters of ComLanCraFlotSoPac—a new and forbidding designation for a new and threatening officer: Commander, Landing Craft Flotillas, South Pacific.

The man who labored under this titular burden was Rear Admiral George H. Fort, a friendly and forthright officer. Into his harbors would soon appear swarms of LCTs and LCIs and occasional

LSTs. For the uninitiated, the abbreviations refer respectively to: Landing Craft, Tank; Landing Craft, Infantry; and Landing Ship, Tank.[3] These vital amphibious landing craft began to come off the shipyard assembly lines in ever-increasing numbers during the winter of 1942-43.

The Guadalcanal landings were made entirely from the large transports and the little Higgins boats. The same was true of the invasion of North Africa. The next amphibious moves in the Southwest Pacific, the South Pacific, and in Europe were to be made with the immeasurable advantage of flat-bottomed, open-bowed craft up to 2,200 tons, which could nose into the beaches and put ashore both men and equipment in a fraction of the time needed by older methods.

Most accounts of the Guadalcanal Campaign end with the final departure of the Japanese ground forces. Very little attention is paid to the ensuing months during which a great deal of enemy action made life perilous for both shipboard and land-based personnel. There was, however, some official acknowledgement on the part of the Navy for a portion of that period. A battle star was awarded for: "Consolidation of the Southern Solomons—8 February, 1943 to 20 June, 1943." We include in this chapter the two largest Japanese air raids on U.S. ships since Pearl Harbor and describe Admiral Yamamoto's final air offensive before his death.

Renard Sound, separating the two airfields on Banika. Construction of roads, airfields, and boat bases began in February, and by 15 April the first of the two airfields was ready for operation. The torpedo boat base at Lingatu (Wernham) Cove went into operation on 25 February 1943.

LCT beached while discharging Army tank.

LST underway with a piggy-backing LCT aboard.

LCI "steaming as before" during shakedown cruise.
All courtesy Naval Historical Center.

February – June 1943 Chronology

The following monthly chronologies summarize significant events during the "lull" following the bitter six-month struggle for Guadalcanal and the start of the Central Solomons campaign in the New Georgia group. It encompasses the CARTWHEEL areas of the Solomon Islands, Papua, New Guinea, and the Bismarck Archipelago, with emphasis on the Solomons and adjacent waters.

Events covered range from submarine and aerial torpedo attacks, to naval bombardments and minelaying, to day and night air raids and rescues at sea. To those of us who were there, it serves as a reminder of how little we knew about the war going on around us, largely due to the need for secrecy.

FEBRUARY 1943 Chronology [4]

1 Monday

High-speed transport *Stringham* (APD-6) and five tank landing craft (LCTs) land U.S. Army second Battalion, 132nd Infantry, at Verahue, Guadalcanal, to the rear of Japanese positions at Cape Esperance, covered by four destroyers. Although the landing itself is unopposed, three LCTs, escorted by destroyers *Nicholas* (DD-449) and *DeHaven* (DD-469), come under attack from Japanese planes about three miles south of Savo Island. *DeHaven* is sunk by three bombs, 09°09'S, 159°52'E, while *Nicholas* is damaged by near-misses. Tank landing craft LCT-63 and LCT-181, aided by SOCs (VCS Detachment RINGBOLT), rescue 146 *DeHaven* sailors, including 38 wounded. (See Author's Note.)

Light minelayers *Tracy* (DM-19), *Montgomery* (DM-17), and *Preble* (DM-20) sow 255 mines to deny the Japanese "Tokyo Express" access to the channel between Savo Island and Cape Esperance. The three ships clear the area as Japanese men-of-war are only 12,000 yards away and closing.

7 Sunday

SBDs escorted by F4Fs and P-40s from Henderson Field, attack 18 Japanese destroyers (Rear Admiral Hashimoto Shintaro) on the final mission to evacuate Japanese troops from Guadalcanal, damaging *Isokaze* and near-missing *Urakaze*.

8 Monday

Japanese destroyer force (Rear Admiral Hashimoto Shintaro) completes the evacuation of 1,796 troops from Guadalcanal.

9 Tuesday

Organized Japanese resistance on Guadalcanal ends, thus conclud-ing the bitter six-month struggle for Guadalcanal and other islands in the southern Solomons.

10 Wednesday

Japanese submarine I-21 continues pursuit of U.S. freighter *Starr King* and torpedoes her, 34°15'S, 154°20'E; there are no casualties among the merchant crew or Armed Guard. Australian destroyer HMAS *Warramunga* rescues survivors but has to abandon attempt to tow the crippled freighter when a line fouls her port screw. *Starr King,* how-ever, sinks that night.

14 Sunday

PB4Ys (VB-101) bomb and strafe Japanese ammunition ship *Hitachi Maru* off Buin, Bougainville, 06°48'S, 155°50'E.

15 Monday

Joint air command designated Aircraft, Solomons (Rear Admiral Charles P. Mason) is established with headquarters at Guadalcanal.

Submarine *Gato* (SS-212) sinks Japanese stores ship *Suruga Maru* in Bougainville Strait, 06°27'S, 156°02'E.

16 Tuesday

Submarine *Triton* (SS-201) departs Brisbane, Australia, for her sixth war patrol. She will never be seen again.

17 Wednesday

Japanese torpedo-carrying land attack planes (701st *Kokutai*) en-gage TU 62.7.2 (Captain Ingolf N. Kiland) northeast of San Cristobal, Solomons. The four transports (carrying the U.S. Army 169th Infantry to Guadalcanal) and one oiler are screened by six destroyers; the task unit suffers neither loss nor damage in turning away the attackers.

19 Friday

Submarine *Gato* (SS-212) torpedoes Japanese ammunition ship *Hibari Maru* off eastern Bougainville, 06°27'S, 156°05'E. *Hibari Maru* is beached off Buin (see 28 February).

Submarine *Grampus* (SS-207) torpedoes Japanese transport/aircraft ferry *Keiyo Maru* off coast of New Britain, 04°55'S, 152°26'E.

USAAF B17s (5th Air Force), in coordination with attack by RAAF Catalinas on Japanese airfield installations at Kahili, bomb enemy shipping off Buin, Bougainville, damaging transport *Tokai Maru*, 06°45'S, 155°50'E.

21 Sunday

Operation CLEANSLATE: Marines (Third Raider Battalion, USMC, and 10th Defense Battalion detachment) and Army troops (elements of 43rd Division) occupy Russell Islands in the inaugural movement through the central Solomons. Supported by TU 62.7.2 (Captain Ingolf N. Kiland), the landings are made with no opposition. Four light cruisers and four destroyers of TF 68 (Rear Admiral Aaron S. Merrill) and Henderson Field, Guadalcanal-based carrier *Saratoga* (CV-3) air group provide cover.

27 Saturday

SBDs, escorted by F4Fs, attack Japanese convoy off northeast coast of Vella Lavella, Solomons, damaging transport *Kirikawa Maru* despite efforts of escorting minesweeper W.22 and submarine chaser Ch 26, one of which scuttles the burning ship.

Submarine *Grampus* (SS-207) possibly damages Japanese minesweeper W.22 off Kolombangara, Solomons.

28 Sunday

TBF (VGS-11) bombs Japanese shipping at Buin, Bougainville, and completes destruction of ammunition ship *Hibari Maru,* previously damaged on 19 February.

Air-Sea Rescue near Bougainville. A downed aviator swims to a Navy PBY rescue plane, which has landed near Bougainville to pick him up. Note life jackets, life raft, and radio antennas on the PBY. Naval Historical Center.

Author's Notes

Cape Esperance End Run 1 February – For a colorful eyewitness account of this historic LCT end run around Cape Esperance, see Volume I, *The Amphibians Are Coming!*, p. 101-107.

Also In February 1943 – ComSoPac launched logistics Operation DRYGOODS, the supply part of logistic support needed to conduct the next big operation in the Central Solomons. DRYGOODS called for build-up on the Guadalcanal-Russell Islands of some 50,000 tons of supplies, 80,000 barrels of gasoline (and storage tanks to hold this amount) and tens of thousands of tons of equipment for the various units slated to participate in the next operation, which in due time would be named TOENAILS.

RAdm Turner had drafted a memorandum to ComSoPac on 14 Jan. 1943, recommending this essential logistic step for future operational success. Despite all that could be said about the inadequacy of unloading and storage facilities on Guadalcanal in the spring of 1943, VAdm Halsey gave the proposal a green light and consequently made a major contribution to the success of TOENAILS.

Since nearly every one in the United States knew by this time that Guadalcanal's code word was CACTUS, the 'Canal received the new code name MAINYARD for the DRYGOODS Operation.

1ˢᵗ Special NCB Stevedore Gang. Courtesy Claude Gulbransen.

There was also significant build-up in American air power in the South and Southwest Pacific areas, which made it increasingly difficult for the enemy to reinforce and resupply their troops.

LST-460 discharging supplies. Courtesy George Heard.

Calvertville – the Tulagi PT Boat Base named for Cmdr Allen P. Calvert, ComMTB Flot One, circa 1943. Naval Historical Center.

Radio Communications Room,
Tunnel No. 1 (Joselyn Tunnel),
Guadalcanal. USNCB.

USO Entertainer.
Courtesy Earnie Crippen,
1st Special NCB.

The show must go on! Earnie Crippen, 1st Special NCB.

Bridge building.

Crane cargo handling.

Where do we put it? All courtesy Earnie Crippen, 1ˢᵗ Special NCB.

MARCH 1943 Chronology

1 Monday

USAAF B-24 (5th Air Force) on reconnaissance flight spots Japanese convoy of eight transports and cargo vessels (with soldiers of the 51st Division embarked) in a convoy (Captain Matsumoto Kametaro), escorted by eight destroyers (Rear Admiral Kimura Masatomi, flag in *Shirayuki*), moving south-westward along the north coast of New Britain under cover of a westward-moving weather front. USAAF B-24 attacks convoy; B-17s drop flares (see 2-3 March).

Japanese submarine I-10 torpedoes U.S. tanker *Gulfwave* at 22°30'S, 174°45'E; *Gulfwave* reaches Suva, Fiji, under her own power and suffers no casualties to either her merchant crew or the Armed Guard.

2 Tuesday

Battle of Bismarck Sea opens: USAAF B-17s and B-24s (5th Air Force) carry out succession of attacks on the convoy consisting of either Japanese transports and cargo vessels (with soldiers of the 51st Division embarked), escorted by eight destroyers (Rear Admiral Kimura Masatomi, flag in *Shirayuki*), bound for Lae, New Guinea, at the northern entrance of Dampier Strait, off the southern tip of New Britain, 05°05'S, 148°28'E. Army cargo ship *Kyokusai Maru* is sunk; destroyers *Yukikaze* and *Asagumo* rescue the survivors, steam ahead to Lae to disembark them, and then rejoin the convoy. During the attacks this day, army cargo ship *Kembu Maru* and transport *Teiyo Maru* are damaged; army cargo ships *Oigawa Maru* and *Shinai Maru* are near-missed. RAAF Catalina tracks the convoy as it passes through Vitiaz Strait during the night and into the next morning (see 3-5 March).

3 Wednesday

Battle of Bismarck Sea continues: RAAF Catalina continues tracking the Japanese convoy attacked the previous day. RAAF Beaufort spots the ships at 07°10'S, 148°20'E, about 60-70 miles east-southeast of Lae, New Guinea. USAAF B-17s and B-24s (5th Air Force), escorted by P-38s, carry out high-level bombing attacks, while B-25s and A-20s and RAAF Beaufighters and Bostons carry out relentless low-level skip-and-mast-head bombing attacks and strafing runs against the enemy ships. Rear Admiral Kimura Masatomi is wounded on board his flagship, destroyer *Shirayuki*. Due to the nature of the battle, wartime analysts deemed it neither "possible from the pilots' accounts to determine which ships were hit by which bombs" nor "possible to determine exactly how and when each vessel was sunk." In any event, destroyers *Asashio, Tokitsukaze,* and *Shirayuki* are all sunk southeast of Finschhafen, 07°15'S, 148°30'E, a fourth destroyer, *Arashio,* is abandoned and left in sinking condition (see 4 March). Supply ship *Noshima,* damaged by aircraft and collision with *Arashio,* sinks southeast of Finschhafen, New Guinea, 07°15'S, 148°30'E. Army cargo vessels *Aiyo Maru, Shinai Maru, Taimei Maru,* and *Kembu Maru,* and transport *Teiyo Maru* (the latter two ships damaged the day before) are sunk by U.S. and RAAF aircraft, 07°15'S, 148°30'E; army cargo ship *Oigawa Maru* is damaged and abandoned. That night, motor torpedo boats PT-143 and PT-150, searching for damaged ships in Huon Gulf, sink *Oigawa Maru* at 06°58'S, 148°16'E (see 4-5 March).

Japanese land attack planes bomb shipping at Tulagi, Solomons; cargo ships *Carina* (AK 74) is damaged by near-misses. PB4Y sinks Japanese guardboat *Choi Maru* off Vella Lavella, Solomons.

4 Thursday

Battle of Bismarck Sea continues: USAAF B-17s and B-25s (5th Air Force) bomb and sink hulk of abandoned destroyer (most likely *Arashio,* 07°15'S, 148°30'E). The attack by B-25s on that warship terminates the efforts against the major vessels of the convoy; only strafing missions against boats and rafts remain to be carried out (see 5 March).

5 Friday

Battle of Bismarck Sea concludes: RAAF Beaufighters strafe Japanese landing barges and lifeboats crammed with survivors of the ships sunk on 3 March ("grim and bloody work for which the crews had little stomach") in Huon Gulf. U.S. motor torpedo boats destroy barges in the vicinity of those attacked by the Australian planes. Failure of the convoy to reach its destination, Japanese naval officers admit later, proves "the impossibility of surface transport in the Lae area." Of the sixteen ships that sailed for Lae, all eight transports are sunk, as are four of the escorting destroyers. Motor torpedo boats PT-143 and PT-150, patrolling 25 miles northeast of Cape Ward Hunt, New Guinea, encounter a Japanese submarine rescuing survivors of the engagement and force her down.

6 Saturday

TF 68 (Rear Admiral Aaron S. Merrill), composed of three light cruisers and seven destroyers, bombards Vila and Munda, Solomons, and sinks Japanese destroyers *Minegumo* and *Murasame* in Kula Gulf, 08°05'S, 157°15'E.

9 Tuesday

TBFs and SBDs, escorted by F4Fs, bomb Japanese installations at Munda, Solomons. Bombing of this area becomes a regular occurrence.

10 Wednesday

Motor torpedo boat PT-114, acting on intelligence that 18 Japanese in a lifeboat (survivors from the Battle of the Bismarck Sea) had drifted ashore on Kiriwina in the Trobriand Islands, captures the enemy soldiers and takes them to Milne Bay, New Guinea, the following day.

13 Saturday

Submarine *Grayback* (SS-208) damages Japanese transport *Noshiro Maru* 100 miles northwest of Bismarck Archipelago 00°10'S, 151°06'E.

15 Monday

United States Commander in Chief establishes numbered fleet system; fleets in the Pacific will have odd numbers and those in the Atlantic even.

29 Monday

Submarine *Gato* (SS-212) evacuates military and civilian people (including nine women, three nuns, and 27 children) from Teop Island, Solomons.

Author's Notes

The Battle of Bismarck Sea – This battle 2-5 March dramatically emphasized the importance of land-based air in the CARTWHEEL Campaign. The results of this running fight by Australian and American squadrons with the Japanese were so significant that General MacArthur stated:

> We have achieved a victory of such completeness as to assume the proportions of a major disaster to the enemy. Our decisive success cannot fail to have most important results on the enemy's strategic and tactical plans. His campaign, for the time being at least, is completely disrupted. [5]

Not only did the Japanese fail to get a substantial reinforcement through to the Huon Peninsula area, but the transport losses forced them to abandon large-scale reinforcement attempts altogether. Dampier Strait did not belong to the Allies yet, but Kenney's fliers made it clear that the Japanese had no clear title either. Supplies and men slated for enemy garrisons in Eastern New Guinea or the Solomons—for any base within effective range of Allied planes—were now moved forward by destroyers, whose high speed, excellent maneuverability, and anti-aircraft guns gave them a measure of protection, or by small craft hugging the island coasts.[6]

First LST Arrives in SoPac – LST-446 departed Espiritu Santo for Guadalcanal on 5 March. She arrived 8 March having cruised from San Francisco independently and unescorted, a major accomplishment considering only one member of the ship's company had ever been to sea before. LST-446, the "Lone Wolf," was the first LST to arrive in the South Pacific. On the day of arrival, the 446 crew made several demonstration landings on Guadalcanal beaches for the benefit of various amphibious commanders. Objective: to determine which 'Canal beaches would be available for future use by the remarkable new landing ships. The 446 was run hard aground several times while executing orders from "higher authority," but was always extricated by the hard and tedious labor of the ship's crew.

The CO of the 446 created quite a stir when he sent off a report a short time later to OPNAV, CinCPac, BuSHIPS, and half-a-dozen afloat commands, enumerating on the trials and tribulations of a new type of ship operating in the Southern Solomons. He objected strenuously to his ship "being loaded while the ship was beached." The CO continued, "An LST is the only ship in the world of 4,000 tons or more that is continuously rammed onto and off of coral, sand and mud."[7]

USS LST-446, the "Lone Wolf," was the first LST to arrive in the South Pacific in March 1943. Naval Historical Center.

APRIL 1943 Chronology

1 Thursday

Submarine *Gato* (SS-212) is damaged by depth charges off New Ireland, 03°08'S, 153°00'E, and is forced to terminate her patrol.

USAAF B-24s and B-17s (5th Air Force) bomb Japanese convoy off Kavieng, New Ireland, sinking freighter *Kokoko Maru*.

3 Saturday

USAAF B-17s (5th Air Force) bomb Japanese shipping off Kavieng, New Ireland, sinking transport *Florida Maru,* 02°35'S, 150°49'E, and damaging heavy cruiser *Aoba* and destroyer *Fumizuki*.

Japanese destroyer *Kazagumo* is damaged by mine, Kahili Bay, Bougainville.

5 Monday

Destroyer *O'Bannon* (DD-450) sinks Japanese submarine RO-34 near Russell Island, Solomons, 08°15'S, 158°58'E.

7 Wednesday

"I" Operation, a major Japanese air offensive is launched. Japanese Carrier bombers (VALs), supported by fighters (ZEROs), strike U.S. and Allied shipping off the east coast of Guadalcanal, off Koli Point, and off Tulagi, damaging destroyer *Aaron Ward* (DD-483) and sinking New Zealand corvette HMNZS *Moa* and damaging oilers *Kanawha* (AO-1) and *Tappahannock* (AO-43) and tank landing ship LST-449 (the latter two ships by near-misses). Submarine rescue vessel *Ortolan* (ASR-5) and tug *Vireo* (AT-144) attempt to beach *Aaron Ward*, but the destroyer sinks as the result of bomb damage at 09°10'S, 160°12'E. Destroyer *Farenholt* (DD-491) is near-missed by at least three bombs. Tug *Rail* (AT-139) is damaged by friendly fire as motor torpedo boat tender *Niagara* (AGP-1), moored alongside, fires through the former's rigging. *Rail* fire party boards abandoned *Kanawha* and, assisted by minesweeper *Conflict* (AM-85), attempts to put out the raging fires until told to withdraw. Later, *Rail,* tug *Menominee* (AT-73), and net tender *Butternut* (YN-9), tow *Kanawha* into Tulagi Harbor, where the damaged oiler is beached. *Rail* suffers further damage alongside *Kanawha* (see 8 April). Elsewhere off Tulagi, destroyer *Sterett* (DD-407) is damaged by friendly fire from adjacent ships (six men are wounded), while attack cargo ship *Libra* (AKA-12), off Lunga Point, is near-missed. *Adhara* (AK-71), loading cargo off the Tenaru River, is damaged by near-misses and suffers one dead and eight wounded. Of the freighters, two bombs land near *William Williams, Louis Joliet* is strafed, and *Dona Nati* is shaken by two near-misses; none of these three ships suffer casualties.

8 Thursday
Oiler *Kanawha* (AO-1), damaged the day before and beached off Tulagi by tugs *Rail* (AT-139) and *Menominee* (AT-73), sinks.

9 Friday
Submarine *Drum* (SS-228) attacks Japanese convoy, sinking army cargo ship *Oyama Maru* about 180 miles north-northwest of Kavieng, New Ireland, 00°32'N, 150°05'E.

17 Saturday
Japanese transport *Shinnan Maru* is sunk by mine (laid by USN TBFs on 30 March), near Buin, Bougainville, 06°50'N, 155°45'E.

18 Sunday
Admiral Isoroku Yamamoto, Commander in Chief Combined Fleet, is killed when the land attack plane (BETTY) (705th *Kokutai*) in which he is traveling is shot down by USAAF P-38s (339th Fighter Squadron) off Bougainville. Interception of Yamamoto, who is on an inspection trip of the forward areas to inspire those under his command, is brought about through signals intelligence. A second BETTY is splashed by the P-38s, but its high-ranking passenger, Vice Admiral Ugaki Matome, Yamamoto's chief of staff, survives (see 21 April).

Submarine *Drum* (SS-228) sinks Japanese ammunition ship *Nisshun Maru* about 200 miles north-northwest of Mussau Island, Bismarck Archipelago, 01°55'N, 148°24'E. Submarine chaser Ch-18 rescues survivors, including a number of Army prostitutes among them.

22 Thursday
Japanese land attack planes (NELLs) (775th *Kokutai*) commence bombing airfield at Funafuti, Ellice Islands (see 23 April).

23 Friday
Japanese land attack planes (NELLS) (775th *Kokutai*) conclude bombing attack on airfield at Funafuti, Ellice Islands; two USAAF B-24s (7th Air Force) are destroyed, five are damaged.

District patrol vessel YP-422 founders after grounding on Tumbo Reef, three miles southeast of entrance to North Bulari Passage, New Caledonia.

29 Thursday

Submarine *Gato* (SS-212) lands coastwatchers at Teop Island, Solomons, and evacuates missionaries.

30 Friday

U.S. freighter *Phoebe A. Hearst* is torpedoed and sunk by Japanese submarine I-19 about 240 miles southeast of Suva, Fiji Islands, 19°48'S, 176°44'E (see 1, 5, and 14 May).

LtGen George C. Kenney, USAAF, Commanding General of the Fifth Air Force looks over a chart with Maj Wilbur B. Beezley. U.S. Army Air Force.

Author's Notes

7 April 1943 Air Strike – Following the Bismarck Sea debacle, the Japanese decided that a strong counter-strike was needed to blunt the Allied air spearhead and to gain a respite for their own defense build-up. Tokyo assigned the task, designated *I Go* ("I" Operation), to Admiral Yamamoto and his Combined Fleet.

The combined force available for *I Go* was at least 182 fighters, 81 dive bombers, and 72 medium-range land bombers, plus a few torpedo planes.

The busy cluster of ships, large and small, including RAdm "Pug" Ainsworth's task force of 3 U.S. cruisers and 6 destroyers plus three dozen other vessels of corvette size or larger, in the vicinity of Tulagi and Guadalcanal, was the initial *I Go* target.

Near noon of 7 April, 67 enemy Val dive bombers with an escort of 110 Zeke fighters took off from staging airfields on Buka and Bougainville to make the attack. Their departure was duly noted and reported to Henderson Field by coastwatchers on Bougainville; at 1400, radar in the Russells picked up the oncoming flights and 76 interceptors, Guadalcanal's typical joint-service mixture, scrambled and tangled with the Zeke escort over the Slot. The Japanese bombers, hiding behind a blanket of heavy black clouds that covered Indispensible Strait between Malaita and Florida, headed for Tulagi.

Almost all the ships were out of Tulagi harbor when the raiders struck; only a fleet oiler *Kanawha* and New Zealand corvette *Moa* were caught in the confined waters. Both were sunk. The attack continued against the rapidly maneuvering vessels in Ironbottom Sound, but ship and shore anti-aircraft fire kept the Vals high and the bombing inaccurate. The destroyer *Aaron Ward,* attempting to protect an LST that had become the focus of enemy attention, was seriously damaged; she later sank under tow.

The bombers caused no other significant damage and drew off soon after they released their loads. The Zekes scored just as lightly as the Vals, accounting for only seven Marine fighter planes; all but one of the pilots were saved.

Yamamoto's Third Fleet planes then attacked shipping in Oro Bay near Buna on 11 April; made a mass attack on the airfields surrounding Port Moresby the following day; then attacked the ships and airfields at Milne Bay on 14 April—all Papua, New Guinea. In these three attacks, 5 Allied planes were lost, and the Japanese admitted the loss of 21 aircraft.

On 16 April, Admiral Yamamoto called off the "I" Operation, ordering the remaining *Third Fleet* planes back to Truk. He had been completely misled by the glowing reports of his pilots into believing that *I Go* had been a tremendous success. The total damage claim for the four raids was staggering: 1 cruiser, 2 destroyers, and 25 assorted transports and cargo vessels sunk, with heavy damage to 2 more transports and several smaller vessels; 134 planes shot out of the air (including 39 probables).

Matched against these totals was the actual Allied loss of 1 destroyer, 1 corvette, 2 merchantmen, and less than 20 aircraft.

It would seem that the Japanese *Third Fleet* pilots had adopted the penchant for reporting gross exaggeration of damage inflicted. Whatever the explanation for pilot error, be it willful exaggeration or wishful thinking, the premature ending of *I Go* without any significant results was chilling to Japanese hopes of delaying Allied offensive preparations. [8]

The Amphibians Are Coming! – Volume I of this trilogy, has an eyewitness account of the 7 April strike by Gunnery Officer Rogers Aston of LST-446 on pp. 136-139.

Death of Fleet Admiral Yamamoto – On 17 April, a top-secret dispatch was delivered to RAdm Marc A. Mitscher, ComAirSols, in his headquarters between Henderson Field and the Lunga River. The message outlined in detail the itinerary then being followed by Admiral Isoroku Yamamoto, Commander in Chief of the Combined Fleet, during an inspection tour of Japanese bases in the South and Southwest Pacific. It stated that he would leave Rabaul the following morning, traveling in a Betty (Mitsubishi '01 twin-engined bomber), with most of his staff in another plane of the same type, and that they would have a close escort of six Zero fighters. The eight-plane flight was due to land at Kahili airdrome at 9:45 a.m. local time. American commanders in the area concerned were directed to exert "maximum effort" to destroy Yamamoto. The message was signed by Frank Knox, Secretary of the Navy. Historian Morison:

> As had been predicted, Yamamoto and the most important members of his staff boarded two Betty bombers at Rabaul. At 0800 April 18, protected by six Zeke fighter planes, they took off for Kahili airfield, Buin. Sixteen Lightnings of the 339th Fighter Squadron from Henderson Field, led by Major John W. Mitchell, USA, were already flying low up along the west coast of New Georgia. Yamamoto arrived over Buin at 0935. So did the Lightnings.

Mitsubishi G4M1 Betty, its left engine blown away, is about to crash. Admiral Yamamoto went down in similar fashion 18 April 1943 in the jungle north of Buin, Solomon Islands. Naval Historical Center.

Exactly as planned, the plane commanded by Captain Thomas G. Lanphier, USA, flashed in under the departing Zekes just as the two bombers were about to land. Lanphier shot down the one, Lieutenant Rex T. Barber, USA, disposed of the other. The first, which carried Yamamoto, crashed in the jungle north of Buin; the other, carrying Vice Admiral Ugaki, his chief of staff, spiraled into the sea and sank. Yamamoto and five or six key staff officers were killed; Ugaki was critically injured. The American planes retired after nipping three of the Zekes and losing one P-38 piloted by Lieutenant Raymond K. Hine, USA.

Next morning there was wild if restricted elation in Nouméa. Even dour Kelly Turner 'whooped and applauded,' while Halsey sent a jubilant dispatch to Rear Admiral Mitscher at Guadalcanal: 'Congratulations to you and Major Mitchell and his hunters. Sounds as though one of the ducks in their bag might have been a peacock.' [9] At Pearl Harbor, Nimitz with a beaming smile gave the news to his immediate entourage, swearing them to secrecy. Not until 21 May was the news of Yamamoto's death in 'air combat' released by Tokyo. Until then we were not quite sure we had got the Fleet Admiral; the victim might have been someone else. [10]

Fleet Marine Force – By 30 April 1943, the Fleet Marine Force in the Pacific had reached formidable strength in comparison to the few battalions and squadrons that had been its aggregate at the outbreak of war. Over 110,000 Marines and sailors were serving in three divisions, three air wings, and a wide variety of supporting units positioned at Allied bases along a broad, sweeping arc from Midway to Australia.

The majority of combat troops were located in the South Pacific under Admiral Halsey's command, where the highest Marine ground echelon was Major General Clayton B. Vogel's I Marine Amphibious Corps (IMAC).

The senior Marine aviator, Major General Ralph J. Mitchell, wore two hats as commander of newly established area headquarters, Marine Aircraft, South Pacific (MASP), and of its principal operating component, the 1st Marine Aircraft Wing (1st MAW). Neither IMAC nor MASP had any substantial tactical function; both commands were organized primarily to serve as administrative and logistical headquarters.

From his command post at Nouméa, General Vogel controlled the 2d and 3d Marine Divisions, then in training in New Zealand, as well as a strong body of supporting troops either attached to the divisions or encamped in New Caledonia, the lower Solomons, and the New Hebrides. General Mitchell's units, all temporarily assigned to the 1st Wing, were stationed at airfields from New Zealand to the Russells. Guadalcanal was the focal point of air activity as a steady rotation of squadrons was effected to maintain maximum combat efficiency in the forward areas. Also part of MASP was Headquarters Squadron of 2d MAW, newly arrived in New Zealand to prepare for a command role in future operations.[11]

MAY 1943 Chronology

1 Saturday

PBY rescues eight survivors from U.S. freighter *Phoebe A. Hearst,* sunk by Japanese submarine I-19 the previous day (see 5 and 14 May).

2 Sunday

U.S. freighter *William Williams* is torpedoed by Japanese submarine I-19 near Suva, Fiji Islands, 20°09'S, 178°04'W. There are no casualties among the 40-man merchant crew and the 15-man Armed Guard; the latter remains on board with a fire-fighting crew to battle the blaze in two compartments (see 4 and 7 May).

4 Tuesday

Net tender *Catalpa* (YN-5) begins towing damaged U.S. freighter *William Williams,* torpedoed by Japanese submarine I-19 on 2 May (see 7 May).

5 Wednesday

Twenty-three survivors from U.S. freighter *Phoebe A. Hearst,* sunk by Japanese submarine I-19 on 30 April, reach Tofua Island; motor minesweeper YMS-89 picks them up and transfers them to Tongatabu, Tonga Islands, in the southwest Pacific (see 14 May).

7 Friday

TG 36.5, composed of light minelayers *Gamble* (DM-15), *Preble* (DM-20) and *Breese* (DM-18), covered by destroyer *Radford* (DD-446), mines Blackett Strait, western approaches to Kula Gulf, Solomons (see May 8).

Net tender *Catalpa* (YN-5), escorted by minesweeper *Dash* (AM-88), brings damaged U.S. freighter *William Williams,* torpedoed by Japanese submarine I-19 on 2 May, into Suva, Fiji Islands. *William Williams* is ultimately acquired by the Navy under bareboat charter, renamed *Venus,* and classified as cargo ship, AK-135. Converted at Sydney, Australia, she is commissioned on 26 September 1944 and serves until decommissioned on 18 April 1946.

8 Saturday

Japanese destroyer *Kuroshio* is sunk by mine laid by TG 36.5 on 7 May, Blackett Strait, Solomons; destroyer *Oyashio,* damaged by mine off Rendova is sunk by SBDs; destroyer *Kagero,* damaged by mine off Rendova, is sunk by USMC aircraft; destroyer *Michisio* is damaged by SBDs in Blackett Strait.

13 Thursday

TF 18 (Rear Admiral Walden L. Ainsworth) bombards Munda and Vila, Solomons, while minelayers (TG 36.5) sow a field across the northwestern approaches to Kula Gulf. Light cruiser *Nashville* (CL-43), 08°28'S, 158° 49'E, and destroyers *Chevalier* (DD-451) and *Nicholas* (DD-449), 08°30'S, 158° 01'E, are all damaged by gun mount explosions.

14 Friday

USMC TBFs (VMSB-143) damage Japanese army cargo ship *Houn Maru* and force her aground off Tonolei, Bougainville, 06°48'N, 155° 49'E, a total loss.

Minesweeper *Dash* (AM-88) rescues 25 survivors from U.S. freighter *Phoebe A. Hearst,* sunk by Japanese submarine I-19 on 30 April. With this recovery, all hands from the lost freighter (including the 16-man Armed Guard) are accounted for.

15 Saturday

GENERAL TRIDENT Conference begins, with President Franklin D. Roosevelt, British Prime Minister Winston S. Churchill, and the Combined Chiefs of Staff meeting in Washington, D.C.

Naval Advance Base and Naval Air Facility, Russell Islands, Solomons, are established.

16 Sunday

Submarine *Grayback* (SS-208) damages Japanese destroyer *Yugure* northwest of Kavieng, 01°00'S, 148°, 44'W.

U.S. freighter *William K. Vanderbilt* is torpedoed by Japanese submarine I-19 southwest of Suva, Fiji Islands, 18°41'S, 175°07'E, and abandoned by the 41-man merchant complement. The 16-man Armed Guard remains on board to the last, but abandons after a second torpedo splits the ship in two. I-19 then fires upon one lifeboat and two rafts, and questions the ship's master before departing; throughout the ordeal only the ship's chief engineer is killed (see 17 May).

17 Monday

Minesweeper *Dash* (AM-88) rescues 56 survivors from U.S. freighter *William K. Vanderbilt,* sunk by Japanese submarine I-19 the previous day southwest of Suva.

18 Tuesday

U.S. tanker *H.M. Storey* is torpedoed by Japanese submarine I-25 while en route from Nouméa, New Caledonia, to San Pedro, California, 17°10'S, 173°02'E, and abandoned by the 48-man civilian complement (two merchant seamen are lost when the ship is hit), two passengers, and 15-man Armed Guard. I-25 then hastens the sinking by shelling the burning ship. Destroyer *Fletcher* (DD-445) subsequently rescues *H.M. Storey's* survivors and takes them to Efate, New Hebrides.

20 Thursday

ComSoPac creates Joint Logistic Board composed of:
1. Commander Service Squadron, SoPac,
2. Commanding General, Services of Supply, SoPac, Army,
3. Commanding General, Supply Service, First Marine Amphibious Corps, and
4. Commander Aircraft, SoPac (represented by COM Fleet Air, Nouméa).

The Board was charged with keeping the appropriate departmental authorities in Washington informed of present and future service requirements, with providing inter-change of emergency logistical support within SoPac, and with recommending to Washington appropriate levels of supply within SoPac.

Ships of Task Force 18 underway in the Solomons in 1943. Photographed from USS O'Bannon (DD-450). The first three ships are destroyers Nicholas, Jenkins and Radford. National Archives.

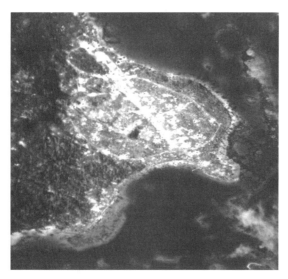

Aerial view of Munda Airfield after a heavy bombardment. National Archives.

23 Sunday

Motor torpedo boat tender *Niagara* (AGP-1), damaged by horizontal bomber while en route from Tulagi to New Guinea, is scuttled by motor torpedo boat PT-147, 11°00'S, 163°00'E.

Motor torpedo boats PT-165 and PT-173 are lost on board U.S. tanker *Stanvac Manila* when Japanese submarine I-17 torpedoes the tanker which is transporting the boats, 100 miles south of Nouméa, New Caledonia, 23°45'S, 166°30'E. (The other boats being transported on board *Stanvac Manila* — PT-167, PT-171, PT-172, and PT-174 — are damaged, but are reparable.)

25 Tuesday

GENERAL TRIDENT Conference ends. President Roosevelt and British Prime Minister Churchill reaffirm earlier decisions to accord first priority to defeating Germany; agree to step up the strategic bombing of Germany and occupied Europe as a preliminary for a cross-channel invasion; to sever Italy from the axis following the capture of Sicily (Operation HUSKY); to bomb the Ploesti (Romania) oil fields from bases in the Mediterranean; to increase aid to, and communication with, China;

Depth charge explodes astern of a speeding "Higgins" type PT boat. Naval Historical Center.

and to plan the invasion of northwestern Europe to take place on 1 May 1944 (Operation OVERLORD). General approval is accorded the U.S. plan for advancing across the Central Pacific toward Japan.

29 Saturday

Submarine chaser SC-669 sinks Japanese submarine I-178, 30 miles west of Espiritu Santo, New Hebrides, 15°35'S, 166°17'E.

Submarine *Scamp* (SS-277) sinks Japanese seaplane carrier *Kamikawa Maru* north of Kavieng, New Ireland, 01°36'S, 150°24'E, and survives attack by one of the submarine chasers escorting her, Ch-12 or Ch-37.

Morison Tours "MAINYARD" [12]

Let's take a look at Guadalcanal in the spring of 1943 prior to the New Georgia campaign. No longer known in code as "CAC-TUS," the advance base on Guadalcanal is now referred to as "MAINYARD." And a mainyard it finally was, with a thousand main-land factories and a hundred other bases funneling materiel into the supply dumps around Lunga Point. Take a tour now with RAdm Morison and the Commander of Mainyard, Captain Thomas M. Shock, as they inspect his military fiefdom:

1ˢᵗ Special NCB camp scene. Guadalcanal 1943-44. Claude Gulbranson.

To unfamiliar eyes all is a jumble; an office here, a workshop there, supply dumps everywhere. But the whole functions with the precision of the cruiser that 'Tommy' Shock lately commanded.

Here is the radio station, underground at last but damp and hot. Watch those dispatches grow on the spindle as the operators translate the whine of the high-frequency into the clatter of typewriter keys. Over there is a switchboard, the telephone exchange.

Do you wish to call the airfield? Which one? There are several now besides Henderson. Suppose you want Public Works, as almost every-body in the Navy does. Which part of Public Works—the power plant, the road gangs, the Quonset hut builders, the telephone linemen?

We ride a jeep down lanes of coconut palms, past rows of green Quonsets. This is the armory, a small part of the Ordnance Depart-ment, which also runs an ammunition depot, demolition units, mine detail, torpedo 'circus,' and defense gun batteries.

Supply Officer is another hard-worked sailor man. Food, cloth-ing, tools and stores of all kinds pass through his worried custody.

On the beach we find the Port Director installed in a hut which affords him a good view of the crowded Lunga roadstead. A cranky 'spitkit' fleet, part of which runs regular ferry service to Tulagi, is under his jurisdiction. They are the least of his worries. Scores of small craft need repairs and attention. Merchant ships anchored in the roadstead want lighters and tugs. Transport skippers scream for pilots, charts, berthing and unloading instructions. Unwanted visitors (like this writer) want transportation to Tulagi, Purvis Bay, Aola, the Russells. 'Can't send

Operations Tower and Port Director's office in Tulagi. USNCB.

you today, Commander; come 'round tomorrow.' No use arguing; he's 'fightin' the war.'

Captain of the Yard, an old Navy title that brings memories of mellowed stone buildings and green parade grounds, means something very different on this island. Here he is boss of 'boys' from Malaita, each dressed in a lava-lava with a hibiscus flower in his startling coiffure, who work on roads, tote cased supplies and build a fine mess hall out of palm leaves (much cooler than imported architecture), all for a shilling a day.

Captain of the Yard is also chief of a fire department that proves to be a necessity in spite of the prevailing damp; he runs a stockade enclosing the few Japanese prisoners; he supervises the homely services of mess cook, barber, laundryman and tailor, which are rendered under shrapnel-torn coconut palms.

The Medical Department, under a genial Harvard professor in uniform who is well-named Colonel Friend, runs the hospital, pursues 'bugs' in drinking water and mosquitoes in swamps and for morale purposes, trains a fine brass band. He wins the battle against malaria and has tropical ulcers—figuratively and literally—on the run. When our troops move up to Bougainville where the mosquitoes are even more numerous and deadly than in the 'Canal, the incidence of malaria will be reduced almost to zero.

With no more necessity to push Japanese off Guadalcanal, there have come the good and the bad of ordered life; motion pictures, daily tabloid full of jokes and gripes, Sunday services, officers' and enlisted

Takin' Five. Courtesy Earnie Crippen.

men's clubs, a police force, courts martial and boards of investigation.

Captain Shock must also deal with many units beyond his jurisdiction, although on the same island. Three hundred planes of the armed forces roost nightly on the Lunga plain; nearby are encamped hundreds of men to serve them with bombs, bullets, fuel and overhauls. Camped in cool, healthy area near Cape Esperance, the 43rd Army Infantry Division practices jungle tactics against the hour of the New Georgia landings. Not far away the 3rd Marine Division is limbering up for the next push.

Supply dumpsite. Earnie Crippen.

Pontoon dock under construction. USNCB.

Guadalcanal church built by natives and given to American servicemen. John Case.

Across Ironbottom Sound, Captain Oliver O. Kessing—better known as 'Scrappy'—gives orders and dispenses hospitality at Government House, Tulagi. The sleepy old Chinatown, abandoned by its inhabitants early in 1942, has been completely razed and a city of huts erected; the cricket pitch of the former British residents has been turned into a baseball field; the golf links have been largely covered with buildings.

Up-harbor, where there used to be a native village called Sesape, a swarm of motor torpedo boats is moored and new barracks for their crews have been built across the harbor at 'Calvertville.'

On Florida Island, behind Gavutu and Tanambogo, which were captured only last August, Seabees are completing a seaplane base.

Port Purvis, next estuary to the east, is now a fleet anchorage where 'Tip' Merrill's and 'Pug' Ainsworth's task forces may rest by day. Hard by the Lord Bishop of Melanesia's palm-leaf cathedral, a new officers' club, 'the Ironbottom Bay Club,' is being built to provide interim refreshment for these night-riding sailors.

As the sun slips under the horizon by Savo Island, we pay social calls on some of the old-timers: Colonel 'Harry the Horse' Liversedge and Lieutenant Colonel Griffith Corrigan of the Solomon Islands Native Defense Force. They dispense liquid hospitality from a battered gasoline tin. Sergeant Vouza, hero of the native constabulary, comes out of the shadows clad in GI shirt, loincloth, Silver Star and George Medal. He pays his respects to blond Sam Griffith and tells of hunting down stray Japs, a sport for which he feels proper sympathy is lacking among the newcomers (profile follows). The talk harks back to Gavutu, the Tenaru and the Bloody Ridge, 'the good old days' when we 'fit' with General Vandegrift.

Chief Scout, USMC – Jacob Charles Vouza was born in 1900 at Tasimboko, Guadalcanal, British Solomon Islands Protectorate, and educated at the South Sea Evangelical Mission School there. In 1916 he joined the Solomon Islands Protectorate Armed Constabulary, from which he retired at the rank of sergeant major in 1941 after 25 years of service.

After the Japanese invaded his home island in World War II, he returned to active duty with the British forces and volunteered to work with the Coastwatchers. Vouza's experience as a scout had already been established when the 1st Marine Division landed on Guadalcanal. On 7 August 1942 he rescued a downed naval pilot from the USS *Wasp* who was shot down inside Japanese territory. He guided the pilot to friendly lines where Vouza met the Marines for the first time.

Vouza then volunteered to scout behind enemy lines for the Marines. On 27 August he was captured by the Japanese while on a Marine Corps mission to locate suspected enemy lookout stations. Having found a small American flag in Vouza's loincloth, the Japanese tied him to a tree and tried to force him to reveal information about Allied forces. Vouza was questioned for hours, but refused to talk. He was tortured and bayoneted about the arms, throat, shoulder, face and stomach, and left to die.

He managed to free himself after his captors departed, and made his way through the miles of jungle to American lines. There he gave valuable intelligence information to the Marines about an impending Japanese attack before accepting medical attention.

After spending 12 days in the hospital, Vouza then returned to duty as the chief scout for the Marines. He accompanied Lieutenant Colonel Evans F. Carlson and the 2d Marine Raider Battalion when they made their 30-day raid behind enemy lines at Guadalcanal.

Sergeant Major Vouza was highly decorated for his World War II service. The Silver Star was presented to him personally by Major General Alexander A. Vandegrift, commanding general of the 1st Marine Division, for refusing to give information under Japanese torture. He also was awarded the Legion of Merit for outstanding service with the 2d Raider Battalion during November and

December 1942, and the British George Medal for gallant conduct and exceptional devotion to duty. He later received the Police Long Service Medal and, in 1957, was made a Member of the British Empire for long and faithful government service.

After the war, Vouza continued to serve his fellow islanders. In 1949, he was appointed district headman, and president of the Guadalcanal Council, from 1952-1958. He served as a member of the British Solomon Islands Protectorate advisory Council from 1950 to 1960.

He made many friends during his long association with the U.S. Marine Corps and through the years was continually visited on Guadalcanal by Marines. During 1968, Vouza visited the United States, where he was the honored guest of the 1st Marine Division Association. In 1979, he was knighted by Britain's Queen Elizabeth II. He died on 15 March 1984. [13]

Sergeant Major Sir Jacob Charles Vouza. Courtesy of U.S. Marine Corps.

Solomon Islands Air Force (AirSols)

AirSols was a heterogeneous mix of U.S. Army, Navy, and Marine Corps airmen as well as the New Zealand Air Force. Marine, Navy, and Army fliers flew on missions together, lived through bombing raids together, and many died together aloft or in foxholes.

Airsols' fighter planes kept guard over ships off Guadalcanal and over convoys running north of Espiritu Santo; its deep-chested Fortresses (B-29s) and Liberators (B-24s) pulverized enemy airfields; its PBY-5A "Black Cats," equipped with radar and landing wheels as well as pontoon hulls, conducted night-time scouting and anti-submarine patrols, rescue missions and bombing and gunfire spotting; its PBY "Dumbo" rescue planes picked up shipwrecked mariners and bailed-out aviators, delivered rations to beleaguered coastwatchers, and rushed spare parts to the fighting front. And, to reduce the enemy's fondness for night air attacks, night fighter squadrons of Corsairs (F4U-2) and Vega Venturas (PV-1) were added to the mix of AirSols' firepower.

Commander Aircraft Solomon Islands (ComAirSols) in June 1943 was RAdm Marc A. Mitscher, (command of Airsols rotated between the U.S. Army, Navy and Marine Corps.) By the spring of 1943, AirSols had gained the advantage in quality aloft and sometimes in numbers, too. Many changes based on combat experience were made in older models of American planes—more power, more heavily armed and armored with longer ranges. New types were the F6F-Hellcat and F4U Corsair fighters, and the B-24 Liberator, which was capable of carrying more bombs longer distances than the older B-17.

Just two of many AirSol pilots to distinguish themselves were Marine Medal of Honor winners Capt Joe Foss and Major "Pappy" Boyington. Both would become top Aces during the August 1942-April 1944 period—Foss with 26 victories and Boyington with 28. [14]

Two SBD dive bombers take off from an air strip in the Russell Islands, 1943.

Solomons Campaign, 1943. This Marine F4U "Corsair" fighter was the first U.S. plane to land at Munda Airfield after its capture and reconstruction by U.S. forces, August 1943. Pilot was Maj R.G. Owens, USMC. National Archives.

Vought F4U-1A "Corsair" Fighters of VF-17 in flight over Bougainville in early March 1944. Plane #29 is Bu# 55995, flown by Lt (jg) Ira Kepford, then the Navy's leading Ace with 16 kills. Naval Historical Center.

On 20 August. the first Marine Corps aircraft such as this F4F Grumman Wildcat landed on Henderson Field to begin comb at air operations against the Japanese. National Archives.

Photos in this AirSols' section are courtesy Dept. of Defense (USMC) unless otherwise credited.

The Vought Kingfisher two-seat observation seaplane OSU-3 flies over firing ships and landing craft which carried invading forces to the shores.

Three personalities of the Cactus Air Force pose after receiving the Navy Cross from Adm Nimitz on 30 September 1942. From left: Maj John L. Smith, Maj Robert E. Galer, and Capt Marion E. Carl. Courtesy Capt Stanley S. Nicolay.

Maj Gregory "Pappy" Boyington (at center) relaxes with some of his pilots. He became the best known Marine ace. A member of the Flying Tigers in China before WWII, he later commanded VMF-122 before taking over VMF-214.

Two aces walk with another famous aviator. Charles Lindbergh, at right, visited the Pacific Combat areas to help Army, Navy, and Marine Corps get the most from their mounts. Maj Joe Foss, left, and now-Maj Marion Carl, center, in May 1944.

Three of the Corps' top aces at Torokina in early 1944. From left: 1stLt Robert Hanson, Capt Donald M. Aldrich, and Capt Harold Spears, members of VMF-215, following the loss of Pappy Boyington. The three aviators accounted for a combined total of 60 Japanese aircraft.

An exuberant LtCol Bauer demonstrates his technique to two ground crewmen. Intensely competitive, and known as "the Coach," Bauer received the Medal of Honor, albeit posthumously, at Guadalcanal. National Archives.

Capt Joseph Foss, USMCR, in the South Pacific, 1943. In six weeks' combat out of Guadalcanal, he shot down 22 Japanese planes. National Archives.

Black Sheep pilots scramble toward their F4U-1 "birdcage" Corsairs. The early model fighters had framed cockpit canopies. The next F4U-1As and subsequent models used bubble canopies which enhanced the limited visibility from the fighter's cockpit. Courtesy of Cmdr Peter B. Mersky, USNR.

Brigadier General Roy S. Geiger, USMC

Geiger, commander of the 1st Marine Aircraft Wing, arrived on Guadalcanal on 3 Sept. 1942 to assume command of air operations emanating from Henderson Field. He was 57 years old, and had been a Marine for 35 of those years, commanded a squadron in France in WWI, served a number of tours fighting the bandits in Central America, and had served in the Philippines and China. He was designated a naval aviator in June 1917, thus becoming the fifth flyer in the Marine Corps and the 49th in the naval service. He was well equipped to assume command of I Marine Amphibious Corps (later III Amphibious Corps) for the Bougainville, Guam, Peleliu, and Okinawa operations. But it was at Guadalcanal, where his knowledge of Marine planes and pilots was so important in defeating the myth of Japanese invincibility, that he first made his mark in the Pacific War.

1st Lt Ken Walsh of VMF-124 connects his radio lead to his flight helmet before a mission in 1943. He was the first F4U pilot to be decorated with the Medal of Honor for a mission on 30 Aug. 1943, during which he shot down 4 Japanese Zeros before ditching his borrowed Corsair. National Archives.

1st Lt Robert M. Hanson of VMF-215 enjoyed a brief career in which he shot down 20 of his final total of 25 Japanese planes in 13 days. He was shot down during a strafing run on 3 Feb. 1944, a day before his 24th birthday.

On 30 Jun. 1943, 1st Lt Wilbur J. Thomas of VMF-213 shot down 4 enemy planes while providing air cover for American operations on New Georgia. Two weeks later, on 15 July, he shot down 3 or more Japanese bombers. Before he left the Pacific, his total of kills was 18 1/2.

Capt Donald N. Aldrich was a 20-kill ace with VMF-25. He had learned to fly with the Royal Canadian Air Force before the U.S. entered the war. Although he survived the war, he was later killed in a flying mishap in 1947.

1st Lt James E. Swett of VMF-221 rose in flight from Guadalcanal to challenge enemy planes on 7 Apr. 1943. In a 15-minute period, he shot down seven Japanese bombers, a performance which earned him the Medal of Honor.

New Georgia Campaign, 1943. SBD Dauntless dive bombers take off from Munda Airfield after its reconstruction for U.S. Aircraft. National Archives.

SBD bombers fly over the target area. National Archives.

Grumman TBF Avenger Aircraft during operations in the South Pacific area, January 1943. National Archives.

As most of the pre-war fighters, the Wildcat was a relatively small aircraft. Its narrow gear track is shown to advantage in this view of a VMF-121 F4F-3.

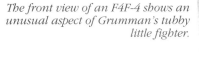

The front view of an F4F-4 shows an unusual aspect of Grumman's tubby little fighter.

The first Army Air Force's P-400 Bell Air Cobras arrived on Guadalcanal on 22 August, two days after the first Marine planes, and began operations immediately. National Archives.

TBF "Avenger." National Archives.

Fighter Strip Number One, Torokina Air Field, Bougainville. RNZAF Curtiss P 40 Fighter takes off, during April 1944. Planes in background include over twenty USAAF P-39 Fighters and one Navy TBF Avenger. Naval Historical Center.

Navy PB4Y patrol plane takes off from Carney Field, Guadalcanal, on a photographic mission in 1943. National Archives.

Army C-47 Transports on a supply mission. U.S. Army.

*USAAF P-38 "Lightning" Fighter based on Guadalcanal, 1943.
Note "Shark's Mouth" markings. National Archives.*

*One of the Patrol
Squadron 81's
Black Cat PBYs
on a mission in
the Solomons.
VP-81 was based
at Munda, New
Georgia, and
Bougainville.
National Archives.*

*PBY Catalina Amphibian Flying
Boats over U.S. invasion fleet.*

A USAAF B-24 bomber takes off from the island's airfield as Navy Seabees work to spread coral while widening the runway. Other B-24s are parked in the distance. National Archives.

The end of an A-20. A Douglas light bomber, caught by Japanese flak, goes out of control.

North American B-25 medium bombers on raid over Bougainville.

The Marine pilot of this F4U-1, Lt Donald Balch, contemplates his good fortune by the damaged tail of his Corsair fighter.

Maintenance crews service this F4U-1 at a Pacific base. Note the Corsair's bubble canopy used on the late-production -1s and subsequent models.

Marine mechanics service an early F4U Corsair, perhaps of VMF-124, on Guadalcanal in 1943. "Bubbles" is already showing effects of the harsh tropical environment as well as the constant scuffing of its keepers' boots. Note the Corsair's large gull wings and long nose which prohibited a clear view, especially during taxi and landings.

Armorers place a .50-caliber aircraft Browning machine gun M2A1 in the nose of a North American B-25 at the airfield on Betio Island as interested natives look on.

The Enemy in the Air

Allied pilots found the Japanese airmen far superior to the stereo-
types depicted by WWII U.S. journalists and cartoonists. In fact, the
first American air crews to return from combat knew they had faced
some of the world's most experienced combat pilots equipped with
formidable airplanes. Early in the war, Japanese training of airmen
was tough—reportedly far beyond the limits of U.S. Marine Corps
boot training. But by the spring of 1943, their edge wore thin as they
lost many of their most experienced pilots and flight commanders
along with their aircraft. Even the most experienced pilots eventually came up against a losing roll of the dice.

To make matters worse, every Japanese plane was highly flammable
for lack of self-sealing gas tanks. As RAdm Morison put it: "'Val' was
a slow and easy target for an American fighter plane or anti-aircraft
bullet. 'Kate,' the torpedo-bomber, lacked speed and endurance compared with the American TBF (Avenger). 'Betty,' the twin-engined
torpedo-bomber, was fast and long-winded but horribly quick to
catch fire. Japanese Army planes, seldom seen in the Solomons, were
subject to the same defects.

The enemy made no provision for pilot survival. Many an aviator
prematurely joined his ancestors because he was unprotected by
cockpit armor. There was no rescue organization similar to our
'Dumbo,' and aviators, like other Japanese fighting men, were in-
doctrinated to die rather than surrender. An air squadron was often
kept flying until completely wiped out, instead of some of the veterans being saved to instruct young aviators."[15]

*Mitsubishi G4M Betty bombers during the Solomons campaign. Probably the
best Japanese land-based bomber in the war's first two years, the G4M series
enjoyed a long range, but could burst into flames under attack, much to the
chagrin of its crews.*

While the Marines on Guadalcanal fought for their lives, their Navy compatriots far offshore also challenged the Japanese. At the Battle of Santa Cruz, October 1942, Japanese bombers hit the American ships damaging the vital carrier Enterprise as well as attacking squadrons of inexperienced Navy aircrews. The A6M2 Model 21 Zero launches from the carrier Sholalu during Santa Cruz while deck crewmen cheer on the pilot, Lt Hideki Shingo.

Zero fighter-bombers prepare to launch for a raid from their Bougainville base in late 1943. Originally an air superiority weapon, the Zero toted light bombs as required, and ended the war as one of the primary aircraft used by the Kamikaze suicide pilots.

A Japanese "Val" bomber dives toward a ship through a sky peppered with anti-aircraft fire. Naval Historical Center.

These A6M3s are from the Tainan Air Group and 106 is identified as being flown by top ace Nishizawa. The Zero's range was phenomenal, to nearly 1,600 miles, making a lengthy flight for its exhausted pilots.

Petty Officer Hiroyoshi Nishizawa in 1942. Usually considered the top Japanese ace, Navy or Army, he died while flying as a passenger in a transport caught by American Navy Hellcats in October 1944.

A rebuilt late-model Zero shows off the clean lines of the A6M series, which changed little during the production run of more than 10,000 fighters.

Petty Officer Sadamu Komachi flew throughout the Pacific War, from Pearl Harbor to the Solomons, from Bougainville to the defense of the Home Islands. His final score was 18.

Newly commissioned Ensign Junichi Sasai in May 1941. By 1942, his high scores made him one of the Gekitsui-O (Shoot-Down Kings).

LCdr Tadashi Nakajima, who led the Tainan Air Group, was typical of the more senior aviators. His responsibilities were largely administrative, but he flew missions when his schedule permitted, usually with unproductive results. It is doubtful that Nakajima scored more than 2 or 3 kills.

Lt (jg) Junichi Sasai of the Tainan Air Group. This 1942 photo shows the young combat leader (also above), now in league with such pilots as Sakai and Nishizawa, shortly before his death over Guadalcanal.

LST Flotilla Five Arrives SoPac – Captain Grayson B. Carter, USN, Commander LST Flotilla Five in LST-340 (F) arrived in Nouméa on 14 May 1943 at 1518 local time with 11 of his earlybird "chicks." (Six of his "flock" – LSTs 334, 390, 446, 447, 448 & 449 – had arrived earlier and were now on loan to ComSoWestPac.)

During the next two weeks Carter's LST crews were kept busy unloading cargo—including the LCTs which had been riding on the main decks piggy-back style the entire trip—and making repairs. Training also continued. Six men from each LST were detailed to attend anti-aircraft school for four days. Although they didn't know it at the time, they would have just four weeks to get ready for Operation TOENAILS.

Captain Grayson Birch Carter.

JUNE 1943 Chronology

5 Saturday

TBFs and SBDs, covered by F4Us and USAAF P-40s and P-38s, bomb Japanese shipping, Bougainville; army cargo ship *Shintoku Maru* is sunk southwest of Buin, 07°00'S, 155°33'E.

15 Tuesday

Eleven LST Flotilla Five ships arrive Guadalcanal 15 June at 1355 and immediately start readying ships to unload cargo in spite of pouring rain.

16 Wednesday

In the largest raid since 7 April, Japanese aircraft attack ships off Guadalcanal. While a large number of enemy planes are shot down, tank landing ship LST-340, damaged by dive bombers, is beached off Lunga Point, 09°26'S, 160°05'E; cargo ship *Celeno* (AK-76) is also damaged, 09°24'S, 160°02'E.

17 Thursday

Submarine *Drum* (SS-228) attacks Japanese convoy, sinking transport *Myoko Maru* about 175 miles east-northeast of Kavieng, New Ireland, 02°03'S, 153°44'E.

21 Monday

Fourth Raider Battalion, USMC, lands at Segi Point, New Georgia, Solomons.

23 Wednesday

Japanese submarine RO-103 sinks cargo ship *Aludra* (AK-72) and torpedoes cargo ship *Deimos* (AK-78) while both are in convoy en

LSTs arrive in the South Pacific in 1943. Note the barrage balloons used for protection. They were discarded later in 1944 in the Pacific as they gave away the position to enemy search planes. Naval Historical Center.

LST launching an LCT in 1943. Naval Historical Center.

route to Espiritu Santo, 11°26'S, 162°01'E. *Deimos,* irreparably damaged, is scuttled by destroyer *O'Bannon* (DD-450), 11°26'S, 162°01'E.

SBDs and TBFs, with F4F escort, bomb Japanese anti-aircraft positions at Rekata Bay; this attack may have been responsible for the sinking of Japanese guardboat *Nikka Maru* north of Bougainville, 05°34'N, 155°07'E. TBFs and USAAF B-25s (13th Air Force), escorted by F4Us, bomb Buki Village, Ganongga Island, New Georgia.

30 Wednesday

Beginning shortly before midnight on 29 June, four cruisers and four destroyers of TU 36.2.1 (Rear Admiral Aaron S. Merrill) bombard Vila-Stanmore on Kolombangara and Buin-Shortland, Bougainville, Solomons; TU 36.2.2—light minelayers *Preble* (DM-20), *Gamble* (DM-15), and *Breese* (DM-18) sow mines off Shortland Harbor, Bougainville, between Alu and Munda Islands. *Gamble* also lays mines off New Georgia.

Operation TOENAILS TF 31 (Rear Admiral Richmond Kelly Turner), supported by land-based aircraft (Vice Admiral Aubrey W. Fitch) and destroyer gunfire, lands New Georgia Occupation Force (Major General John H. Hester, USA). Army troops (172nd Infantry, 43rd Division) go ashore on Rendova without opposition. Marines (Fourth Raider Battalion, USMC) land on New Georgia and begin move toward Viru Harbor (see 1 July). Destroyer *Gwin* (DD-433) is damaged off Munda by Japanese shore battery. Attack transport *McCawley* (APA-4) (Rear Admiral Turner's flagship) is damaged by Japanese torpedoes from land attack planes (702nd or 705th *Kokutais*) off New Georgia. Turner transfers his flag to destroyer *Farenholt* (DD-491); destroyer *Ralph Talbot* (DD-390) removes all unnecessary crew and wounded while attack cargo ship *Libra* (AKA-12) takes the damaged transport in tow. Destroyer *McCalla* (DD-488) removes remainder of crew; tug *Pawnee* (AT-74) relieves *Libra* of tow. *McCawley,* however, is later accidentally torpedoed by U.S. motor torpedo boat and sinks, 08°25'S, 157°28'W. High-speed minesweeper *Zane* (DMS-14) is damaged by grounding off Onaiavisi Island, 08°30'S, 157°25'E, but is towed off the beach by tug *Rail* (AT-139).

Operation CHRONICLE: TF 76 (Rear Admiral Daniel E. Barbey) lands troops on Woodlark and Kiriwina Islands, off southeastern coast of New Guinea, the former from tank landing ships (LST), and the latter from infantry landing craft (LCI). Airstrip construction soon begins on Woodlark.

Author's Notes

16 June Air Strike – There were 21 air strikes against the Guadalcanal-Tulagi area between 15 May and 16 June. The June 16 raid was the second largest the enemy had mounted since their attack on Pearl Harbor. The Japanese may have suffered "total and complete defeat on Guadalcanal" as of 9 February—as General Patch radioed Admiral Halsey—but he was speaking on behalf of the ground forces. Apparently the Japanese pilots never got the word.

One more personal note: My "baptism under fire" occurred off the 'Canal during the 16 June strike, followed a week later by a submarine attack on our small Task Unit in "Torpedo Junction" southeast of San Cristobal Island.

Japanese "Zero" just before being shot down during raid. Naval Historical Center.

Japanese submarine, probably RO-100 Class, 1943, near Rabaul, New Britain. Naval Historical Center.

Bottomline: We departed Nouméa 9 June for Guadalcanal. The Task Unit consisted of four Liberty freighters: Navy AKs *Aludra, Celeno,* and *Deimos,* and merchant ship *Nathaniel Currier;* plus three escorts: destroyer *O'Bannon,* destroyer transport *Ward* and minesweeper *Skylark.*

During the 16 June raid, the *Celeno* was bombed, burned and beached. LST Flot 5 flagship LST-340 was also bombed, burned and beached that day.

On 23 June while steaming through "Torpedo Junction" en route to Espiritu Santo, *Aludra* and *Deimos* were both hit by torpedoes in the dark of night at 0443. I was in the U.S. Navy gun crew aboard the *Currier* but, because we were ordered to hightail it out of there by the Escort Commander, I never knew until fifty years later

USS Aludra (AK-72). National Archives.

USS Celeno (AK-76). Naval Historical Center.

that both ships were sunk. Furthermore, I didn't even know the names of the ships or their hull numbers. But I've never forgotten the date or place. Declassified documents supplied the missing information. Fortunately, I was able to track down and interview forty-some survivors. I don't call that living in the past; it's researching the past to update history. [16]

Volume I in this trilogy includes a moving eyewitness account of the 16 June strike by Ensign Anthony Tesori, Gunnery Officer of LST-340.

Admiral Chester W. Nimitz, CinCPAC, in his June 1943 report to the Joint Chiefs, summarized the 16 June action:

> On 16 June, the largest enemy force since 7 April attacked our shipping in the Guadalcanal area. Enemy forces consisted of at least 60 VB (bombers), screened by a like number of fighters.
>
> One hundred four U.S. fighters were scrambled in defense, and 74 made contact with enemy. There were numerous U.S. ships in the transport areas off Lunga Point and in Tulagi. The attack lasted from 1315 to 1513 (-11).

LST-340 burns off Lunga Point, 16 June 1943. Courtesy P.D. Clodfelter.

ComSoPac [RAdm Halsey] credits his VFs [fighters] and ships' A/A with the destruction of 107 enemy planes. Six of our VFs were lost, two pilots being recovered.

During this attack the LST-340 received one hit which set fire to her cargo of trucks, gas, oil, etc., completely destroying it [the cargo]. LST-340, itself, though badly damaged, was beached and later salvaged. At 1410 *Celeno* (AK) received 2 hits, and the resultant fire destroyed most of her cargo, though the ship was likewise beached and later salvaged. [17]

In Conclusion

That completes our review of the buildup of Allied Forces and the many significant events that took place during the "lull." Admiral Halsey, ComSoPac, is more than ready to get on with the war by launching the next major offensive in the Solomons: seizure of the New Georgia group of islands in the Central Solomons.

CHAPTER 6

Operation TOENAILS
The Invasion of New Georgia
21 June – 20 September 1943[1]

The Solomon Islands were taken back from the Japanese in three geographical operations between 7 August 1942 and 25 November 1943:

• The Guadalcanal-Tulagi operation, which stopped enemy advances in the South Pacific, has been described as a *defensive-offensive* campaign. It also represented a real turning point in the Pacific war.

• The New Georgia Campaign culminating in the capture of the strategically important Munda Airfield was the first large-scale land, sea, and air *offensive* in the Pacific.

• The Bougainville operation was the final phase of the Solomons' campaigns. From an airfield on Bougainville, U.S. fighters could escort bombers to Rabaul—the big, heavily de-fended Japanese base on the eastern end of New Britain Island.

The New Georgia campaign took place in two phases: phase one consisted of the landings on the islands of Rendova, New Georgia, Vangunu, and Arundel; phase two covered the invasion of Vella Lavella six weeks later.

As the fighting on Guadalcanal drew to a close in early 1943, American commanders intensified their planning for the eventual seizure of Rabaul, the primary Japanese stronghold in the South-west Pacific. This major air and naval base on the eastern end of New Britain was centrally located between New Guinea and the northwestern terminus of the Solomons. That allowed the Japa-nese to shift their air and naval support from one front to the other on short notice.

Conversely, simultaneous American advances through New Guinea and the Solomons would threaten Rabaul from two directions. With that in mind, Admiral William F. Halsey's South Pacific command prepared to drive farther up the Solomons chain, while MacArthur continued his operations along the New Guinea Coast.

The New Georgia group lying 200 miles northwest of Guadalcanal extends in a northwesterly-southeasterly direction for a distance of 150 miles. Most of the islands are mountainous and are of volcanic origin. Off their coasts barrier islands and reefs have formed lagoons which in times past were the habitat of a people known throughout Melanesia for their maritime aggressiveness.

RAdm Morison used these colorful words to describe the island of New Georgia, the largest of the like-named group: [2]

> The rain-forest green of the serrated hills, the calcimine blue of the still lagoons and the lacy foam around the reefs, as seen from the ocean, suggest a tropical paradise; and ashore there is some substance to that elusive dream. Wild orchids bloom in extravagant profusion, bird-winged butterflies fly about, nearly as large as the screaming white cockatoos which keep them company; friendly natives ply graceful canoes along the quiet shores of the lagoons.

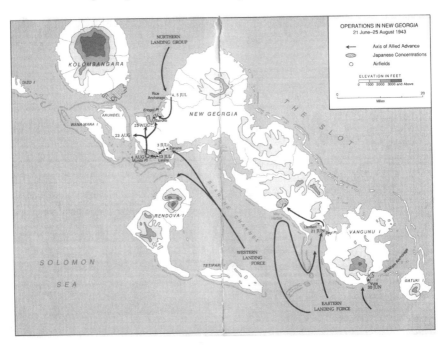

Around the turn of the century, an Australian pioneer named Norman Wheately established his headquarters at Lambeti plantation, Munda Point, on the shore of island-studded Roviana Lagoon. There he planted one of the few coconut plantations on the island; there, too, the Methodists founded a mission. And there, in 1943, Hirohito's 'flying eagles' found good level ground for their nest.

As long as Japan held Munda and had the planes, she could stop the Allies at the Russells. If, on the other hand, the Allies could base planes at Munda, they could deny everything below Bougainville to the enemy and would have another leg-up toward Rabaul.

At first the Japanese made use of numerous hideouts and dispersal anchorages and established staging points in the Central Solomons for the purpose of ferrying troops and supplies to Guadalcanal. Later, after their failure to gain command of the air over Guadalcanal in November 1942, they began to construct an airfield near Munda Point on the southwest coast of New Georgia Island. The location of Munda Point rendered it almost immune to invasion from the sea. There are only two approaches: one from the north through Diamond Narrows, a deep but very narrow channel; the other from the west across Munda Bar, which has only two fathoms of water and is therefore dangerous during a heavy sea. Shortly before the completion of the Munda airfield on 29 December, the Japanese began to build a second air base near the mouth of the Vila River on the southern tip of Kolombangara Island.

PRELIMINARY ACTIONS

The threat offered by these new Japanese bases to our position on Guadalcanal was obvious. Beginning 3 December 1942 (the day the Munda field was discovered), aircraft from Guadalcanal made repeated attacks, bombing and strafing gun emplacements, buildings, and runways. During the ensuing three months, our fliers conducted more than 80 raids. Some of these promised spectacular success; yet none interrupted Japanese use of the installations for more than a day or two.

Surface naval bombardments the nights of 4-5 January, 23-24 January, 5-6 March and 12-13 May 1943 were hardly more successful. The chief value of these operations was in neutralizing airfields and destroying enemy supplies and personnel.

Logistics Preparations

Even before the Japanese had been driven out of Guadalcanal, Naval Construction Battalions (Seabees) were at work on additional fighter strips to improve dispersion and relieve congestion on Henderson Field. Other units were constructing an additional bomber field on Koli Point. By the time that preparations had been completed for the final assault against Munda, Airsols had available four airfields on Guadalcanal and two in the Russells, all completely staffed and with maintenance units attached.[3]

During June 1943, supplies for the New Georgia campaign were moved up to the Russell Islands from the stockpiles in the Guadalcanal area. However, the primary bases for the invasion were still located at Nouméa and Espiritu Santo.

Estimated Enemy Strength

Enemy naval forces in the Solomons area were estimated at two destroyer divisions, one submarine division, and twelve non-combatant ships. Available forces in the Bismarck Archipelago were believed to consist of one light cruiser, five destroyers, seven submarines, and twenty-five non-combatant ships. Most of the Japanese naval strength was concentrated at Rabaul and brought into the Solomons by way of anchorages in the Shortlands and advanced bases on Bougainville.

Defending the New Georgia Island Group were the Southeast Detachment of Major General Noboru Sasaki and the 8th Combined Special Naval Landing Force under Rear Admiral Minoru Ota (later to die as commander of Japanese naval forces at Okinawa). Subordinate units included the 13th Infantry Regiment, 229th Infantry Regiment, Kure 6th Special Naval Landing Force, and the Yokosuka 7th Special Naval Landing Force.

New Georgia and Kolombangara, and enemy outposts on Rendova, Santa Isabel, Choiseul, and Vella Lavella, were strongly defended. The number of Japanese occupying the outlying islands was comparatively small. The forces on Kolombangara were "estimated" at 10,000 troops while those on New Georgia were figured to be between 4,000 and 5,000.

Japanese air strength in the Solomons-Bismarck area was estimated at approximately 380 planes for combat purposes. In addition, they could draw on a force of slightly less than 100 combat planes in New Guinea in order to replace combat losses in the Solomons.

In addition to the previously mentioned airfields at Munda and Vila, the enemy had fields at Buka, Kahili, Ballale, and Kieta, as well as seaplane bases at Shortland-Faisi, Rekata Bay, and Soraken. Furthermore, the fields at Lakunai, Rapopo, Vunakanau, and Kavieng in the Bismarck Archipelago and the seaplane base at Rabaul were available for staging aircraft and for air operations in the Solomons.

Plan of Attack

Plans for the New Georgia operation were discussed in conferences held on RAdm Turner's flagship, the *McCawley*, during the last two weeks of May. On 3 June, Admiral Halsey issued the basic operation plan dubbed "TOENAILS." D-day was set for 30 June.

The primary objective was to capture the Munda airfield on the island of New Georgia. Preliminary landings to support the main effort were to be made at:

- Rendova, the island separated from New Georgia by a narrow channel. It was within artillery range of Munda airfield. The 24th NCB would accompany the Army troops in the assault on Rendova and build and maintain roads over which the artillery and its ammunition could be moved.
- Segi Point, at the extreme southeast end of New Georgia. (The 47th NCB would immediately set to work constructing an air strip.)
- Viru Harbor, on New Georgia's southern coast. (The 20th NCB would build a PT-boat base.)
- Wickham Anchorage on Vangunu Island.

Possession of Viru and Wickham would protect supply lines and provide staging areas for the New Georgia operations.

The second phase of the operation consisted of invading New Georgia proper to seize Munda while a northern force secured the Bairoko-Enogai area, in order to prevent the Munda garrison from being reinforced from the north.

According to the plan, ground forces would drive the Japanese into the Munda Point area and once there, Allied air, artillery, and tanks could support the main landing.

The massive U.S. force about to converge on the New Georgia Island Group in the Central Solomons was impressive for so early in the war. RAdm Richmond Kelly Turner, Amphibious Force Commander, divided his assigned forces into two task groups:

The Western Force, which he would personally command, was to seize Rendova, Munda, and Bairoko-Enogai; the Eastern Force, under RAdm George H. Fort, also an experienced amphibious force commander, was directed to capture Wickham Anchorage, Segi Point, and Viru Harbor.

TASK ORGANIZATION [4]
Third Fleet (South Pacific Force)
Admiral William F. Halsey, at Nouméa

The TOENAILS plan provided for the following three task forces:

TF 31, the amphibious attack force, under the command of RAdm R.K. Turner. It was subdivided into two groups:

TG 31.1, the Western Force under the direct command of RAdm Turner, would conduct the operations in the Rendova-Munda area.
TG 31.3, the Eastern Force, under the command of RAdm G.H. Fort, would be responsible for the landings and subsequent operations at Viru, Segi, and Wickham Anchorage.

TF 36, the covering force, acting under the direct command of Adm Halsey, would cover the operation and furnish fire support.

TF 33, the main air support, operated under the command of VAdm A.W. Fitch (South Pacific Air Force). Its principal duties were to conduct reconnaissance and striking missions, provide direct air support during landings and on other occasions as requested, and furnish liaison and spotting aircraft. RAdm Marc A. Mitscher, as commander of aircraft in the Solomons (AirSols), had tactical command initially of that portion of the task force which operated from Henderson Field and other bases in the Solomons. (Mitscher was relieved by MGen Nathan F. Twining, USAAF, on 5 July 1943.)

The composition of U.S. Task Forces and the Ground Force Organization can be found in Appendix J. Note that most of the "earlybird" Flotilla Five LCTs, LSTs, and LCIs profiled in Volume I in this trilogy [5] were on the scene for the TOENAILS operation. We will reconnect with their crews as they fight their way up the Slot to Bougainville during the second half of 1943.

GROUND FORCE ORGANIZATION

The ground troops for all TOENAILS attack forces were designated the New Georgia Occupation Force (NGOF). Since the 43rd Division was the major ground unit slated for TOENAILS, Admiral Turner chose the division commander, MGen John H. Hester, to be the NGOF commander. Turner declined to use the XIV Corps headquarters and staff available on Guadalcanal, instead requiring the 43rd Division headquarters to perform double duty. Hester thus had to function as both division commander and NGOF commander.

From the outset General Harmon was leery of this command arrangement. On 10 June he ordered the XIV Corps commander, MajGen Oscar W. Griswold, to keep himself informed and be ready to take command should the necessity arise.

NGOF was comprised of the 43rd Infantry Division; Marine 9th Defense Battalion; the 136th Field Artillery Battalion from the 37th Infantry Division; the 24th Naval Construction Battalion; Company O of the 4th Marine Raider Battalion; the 1st Commando, Fiji Guerrillas and assigned service troops.

RAdm Fort's Eastern Force included Army Colonel Daniel H. Hundley's Army 103rd Regimental Combat Team (RCT), less a battalion with Hester; Companies N, P, and Q of the 4th Raider Battalion; elements of the 70th Coast Artillery (Anti-aircraft) Battalion; parts of the 20th Naval Construction Battalion; and service units.

Colonel Harry B. Liversedge's 1st Marine Raider Regiment (less the 2d, 3rd, and 4th Battalions) was designated ready reserve for the operation, while the Army's 37th Infantry Division (less the 129th RCT and most of the 148th RCT) was held in general reserve on Guadalcanal ready to move on five days' notice.

Hester's corps headquarters was formed by taking half of the

43rd Division staff, the rest remaining with the Assistant Division Commander, BGen Leonard F. Wing, USA.

Over 30,000 men were in the units assigned to the NGOF, the majority of which were Army troops, Marine and Seabee units, PT-boat squadrons, and naval base personnel. Marines from the 10th and 11th Defense battalions were in reserve as reinforcements.

Marine historian Charles Melson described some of the preliminary TOENAILS actions this way:

> In mid-Spring 1943, reconnaissance parties from the units slated to take part in the New Georgia campaign began patrolling in the areas designated for landings. Solomon Islanders acted as guides and scouts led by British resident administrators and Australian navy intelligence personnel, who, as Coastwatchers, hid in the hills in the enemy rear areas. From here they radioed information about Japanese troop, air, and naval sightings and movements to Allied listening stations.
>
> With the exception of two or three members from each patrol party, who remained behind to arrange for guides and to give homing signals to Allied vessels on their approach, all patrols returned to their parent units by 25 June 1943. For these individuals, the campaign was already underway.

The Solomon Islands were some of the least known and underdeveloped areas in the world. John Miller, Jr., himself a former Marine veteran of Guadalcanal, and after the war an Army historian, considered it "one of the worst possible places" to fight a war. All

Coastwatcher Capt W. F. Martin Clemens, British Solomon Islands Defence Force, poses with some of his constabulary. National Archives.

the islands had much in common and much that is common is unpleasant. The islands were mountainous, jungle-covered, pest-ridden, and possessed a hot, wet tropical climate. There were no roads, major ports, or developed facilities. New Georgia was all of these, and more.

For four days before the landings, Munda was heavily attacked by Navy bombers. On the night of 29-30 June, as a prelude to the New Georgia movement, a task group of light cruisers and destroyers (CLs of the 12th Cruiser Division, *Montpelier, Denver, Columbia,* and *Cleveland,* and DDs *Philip, Renshaw, Waller,* and *Saufley*) under the command of RAdm Aaron S. Merrill, steamed up the Slot and bombarded the Vila-Stanmore area on the south coast of Kolombangara and the Buin-Shortland area two hundred miles beyond, near the southeast end of Bougainville Island.

As a part of this operation, a mine detachment consisting of the *Preble, Gamble,* and *Breese,* led by Capt William R. Cooke, Jr., in the *Pringle,* laid 336 mines off Shortland Harbor between Alu and Munia Islands.

The purpose of this preliminary operation was to:

- Temporarily disrupt enemy surface raids out of Buin via the Shortland route during the early phases of the New Georgia operations
- Lengthen the Japanese surface routes to New Georgia
- Place a suitable surface force in position to cover the New Georgia landings
- Provide a diversion for the New Georgia movement
- Temporarily reduce enemy air strength and installations on Ballale
- Damage enemy installations in the Shortland-Faisi area.

EASTERN LANDING FORCE [6]

Segi Point Landing, 21 June 1943

Things did not go entirely according to plan. During June the Japanese used some of their reinforcements to extend their coverage of New Georgia. They ordered a battalion to Viru with instructions to clean out native forces operating in the vicinity of Segi.

The Solomon Islanders, under command of Coastwatcher Donald G. Kennedy, had repeatedly attacked enemy outposts and patrols in the area. As the Japanese battalion advanced closer to Segi Point, Kennedy requested support.

On 20 June, Admiral Turner ordered LtCol Currin and half of his 4th Raiders to move immediately from Guadalcanal to Segi. Companies O and P loaded on board APDs *Dent* and *Waters* that day and made an unopposed landing the next morning. On 22 June, two Army infantry companies and the advance party of the airfield construction unit arrived on APDs *Schley* and *Crosby* to strengthen the position.

47th Naval Construction Battalion

The Seabees, led by Cmdr J. S. Lyles, CEC, USNR, had been assigned the task of ripping an airstrip out of the jungle so that our bombers coming up from Guadalcanal to bomb Munda could have fighter protection over the target. Success of the whole operation depended on the speed with which this airstrip could be built. The first wave of the 47th began landing at Segi at 1010 on June 30, just twenty hours before the 24th began landing at Rendova.

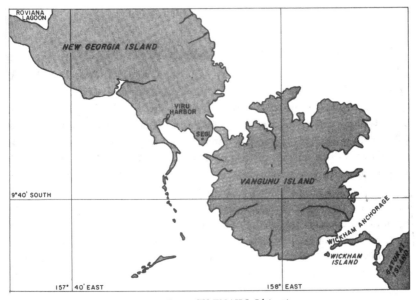

Eastern Force TOENAILS Objective.

The landing at Segi had been planned as a sneak operation. It was hoped that the battalion could get ashore unobserved by the Japanese and could get a headstart on the airstrip before being attacked. To facilitate this strategy, a Seabee scouting party led by Cmdr Wilfred L. Painter, CEC, USNR, had slipped ashore from native fishing boats on the night of June 22. The following day, Painter selected an abandoned coconut plantation overgrown with jungle as the site for the airstrip, and the party began laying out the field.

On D-Day the scouts had the field laid out, ready for work to begin and they were standing on the beach to direct the landing. When the 47th's big HD-12 bulldozers and power shovels rolled off the boats, they at once began pushing down the coconut palms, clearing the strip. From that moment the 47th battled time and the jungle around the clock. Equipment "unraveled" off the boats as needed. Supplies were unloaded and dispersed. Floodlights were ready before darkness on the first night. A bivouac area was cleared. AA guns were manned; exterior guard posted. And, above all, work proceeded on the airstrip with all possible speed.

At 0822 on July 11 the pilot of a Navy Corsair fighter brought his plane down on the strip in an emergency landing which saved both himself and his ship. He pronounced the field ready for use, and the exact time was recorded: 10 days, 22 hours, 12 minutes after the first landing boat had ground ashore! While the Seabees would restore captured Japanese fields in much less time, this stood as a world's record for converting jungle into a landing area. During the eleven days in which the 47th was setting its record, 14 inches of rain fell at Segi Point.

Here's what the speed record at Segi meant to the Munda operation: It was fighter planes from Segi which helped relieve the Jap aerial pressure on the men-in-the-mud at Rendova. The Segi fighters stood at Ready Alert, and when our bombers came up from Guadalcanal to bomb Munda, the Segi fighters roared into the air to escort the bombers over the target.

LCT-159 Voyage Continues

Ensign John McNeill and his LCT-159 crew (profiled in Volume I) were assigned to Task Unit 31.3.2 in the 4th Echelon of the Segi

Point Occupation Group. The 159 transported units of ACORN 7, an airfield construction and operations group, on D-Day 30 June 1943. McNeill:

> New Georgia is to me one of the most interesting islands on earth.... The passages between the islands and the reefs would make a yachtman's paradise, and the coral-bottomed Roviana Lagoon is probably the largest in the world.... There were several very nice coconut plantations in the area, which were abandoned by the planters with the coming of the Japanese.
>
> Segi Point at the extreme southeast part of New Georgia Island, is a low, spiky land protruding into Pango Bay and only a stone's throw from Vangunu Island. In peacetime it was the site of the fine Markham Plantation.... With the coming of the Japs, it was abandoned but never occupied by the enemy.
>
> At this point in time, along came a most remarkable man who took up residence there and assembled and trained his own army. Donald Kennedy was an Australian District Officer who had lived in the Solomons for many years. With the war approaching, he made the decision to remain in the islands and join the Coastwatchers under Eric Feldt. Kennedy had the poise and charm of an English diplomat, was an excellent organizer and disciplinarian, a mechanical genius, a handsome 'ladies' man' and a bloodthirsty killer in a fight. He converted Segi into an armed camp with about 80 well-trained natives equipped with salvaged or stolen equipment. He established a 'forbidden zone' around Segi and no Japanese who ever penetrated this zone left alive.

LCT Division approaching New Georgia escorted by Apc. John McNeill.

Kennedy supplied our forces with accurate and abundant intelligence and rescued many downed fliers and shipwrecked sailors. He hosted several reconnaissance teams who were flown in by PBY to gather specific information for 'TOENAILS.'

Finally, the Japs at Munda realized the extent of Kennedy's operations and dispatched a large force to investigate. Realizing that he could not handle such a threat, Kennedy reluctantly radioed Admiral Turner for help. This was on June 20, just ten days before the scheduled D-Day.

At dawn the next morning, Admiral Turner landed two companies of Marine Raiders from two destroyer transports, and followed the next day with some 400 more Army troops. They also brought Cmdr Bill Painter, Commander of ACORN 7, so he could begin to layout the fighter strip. He boasted, 'You can land airplanes here ten days after my equipment arrives.'

On the morning of 28 June, LCT-159 began loading equipment and material [at Guadalcanal] for the construction of the airfield at Segi Point.... She then steamed up to Renard Sound in the Russell Islands that night and joined up with LCTs 146, 156, and 322, and escort APc 29. We met on the APc and discussed plans for departure and our course through Pango Bay which was almost uncharted and known to be filled with coral heads—pinnacle-like growths of coral protruding almost to the surface.

Because of the shallow water in Pango Bay [and the constant threat of enemy air raids] the Segi operations did not use large transports....

Gasoline and ammunition going ashore at Segi. Courtesy John McNeill.

The new landing craft were specifically designed to handle tasks like this: LCIs as troop carriers and LCTs to haul cargo of all kinds. As the 159 and her sisters cleared the Russells on 1 July 1943, heavy seas and strong winds made for hard going. McNeill:

> I was able to hold my course even though visibility was very poor. The night was miserable but at dawn, we were in exactly the right spot to enter Pango Bay. We crossed this bay and beached at Segi without difficulty.
>
> The 159 was carrying a large crane near the bow which we unloaded on a solid beach and soon it was operational. It was used immediately to unload much of the materiel on our deck. All was peaceful ashore and the heavy weather kept the Japanese aircraft away.
>
> In the early afternoon after unloading, we retracted from the beach and anchored in the narrow channel between Segi and Vangunu Island.
>
> Not having slept the night before, I sat in a deck chair behind the wheelhouse where we had erected a small canvas shelter, and relaxed for a few minutes. I was facing Vangunu and saw a small group of men walking along the shore toward us. They looked rather odd so I focused my binoculars on them. They were Japanese!
>
> I ordered General Quarters and alerted a nearby LCT and the APc . We trained all of our guns on the Japs and waited to see how close they would come. Before we could see the whites of their eyes, someone on another ship opened fire and ruined our chance to annihilate them. We all opened fire and poured several hundred rounds of 20-mm shells into them. This either put them to rest or to flight, for when the smoke cleared we could not see them.
>
> I relaxed again and fell asleep in the chair. Soon I was awakened by the lookout who had sighted a native canoe approaching us from the Vangunu-Segi passage. Being ever alert for nasty Japanese tricks, I had two sailors with Tommy-Guns cover the canoe. My binoculars showed one native in the dugout canoe filled with bananas. He approached to within a few feet of our ship and I greeted him. He responded in perfect English, 'Would you like some bananas?' I thanked him and replied yes, but cautioned the crew to keep their guns on him until we could see what was under the bananas. He came alongside and began handing bunches of bananas to the sailors, and then an American aviator sat up in the canoe. This native had rescued that flyer and brought him around the Japanese lines.
>
> I correctly guessed the 'native' was the famous Harry Wickham of the Lambeti Methodist Mission, an Olympic swimmer for Australia in the late 1930s. We were all so astonished that one of the sailors exclaimed, 'Well, I'll be GD.' To this remark Mr. Wickham responded, 'If the Father above hears you, he will be on the Japs' side.' Needless to say, my opinion of foreign missions reached a new high.

We signaled for an LCVP from the beach and soon had the flyer in the hospital being erected ashore. We showered Mr. Wickham with praise and gifts and sent him on his way.

Task Unit 31.3.2 encountered full gale winds and heavy seas on their return trip to the Russells. During the storm, they received another scare: they were challenged by blinker light by RAdm Stanton "Tip" Merrill's cruiser-destroyer support group at 0200.[7] Skipper McNeill remembers that long night very well:

The only good thing was I now knew we were not in shoal water, since the cruisers were nearby. The night seemed endless, but with the dawn I could see Vangunu Island. I made my way closer and soon could recognize Oloana Bay. The other LCTs and the APc were already there—the 322 was broached on the beach.

Admiral Turner mentioned the storm in his memoirs with the comment, "Task Force 31.3.2 was dispersed by the storm on 3 July but all craft made it independently to Oloana Bay, New Georgia. LCT-322 broached and was carried high and dry on the beach, where she remained until 6 July when she was refloated by the aid of tugs."

Unloading at end of Segi fighter strip on New Georgia Island, July 1943. Courtesy John McNeill.

Ensign Bob Capeless and his LCT-62 crew were assigned to the 2^d Echelon of the Segi Point Occupation Group. Capeless remembers:

> The Segi Point landing was interesting since advance scouts had been there to mark trees to cut down for the air strip. We landed right where the air strip was to be, and in a few days they had fighter planes landing there. The Seabees were fantastic.
>
> Let me throw in one other thing with respect to the initial landing at Segi. It took us 12 hours fully loaded to go up but it took 24 hours to come back empty. That was the worst night of the war for all of us involved. The sea was so heavy that every time we climbed on top of a big wave, it washed out from under us and we went crashing down to the bottom. All I could think of was that a green crew had put those 3 sections [of our LCT] together. It was a miracle that we didn't lose any boats!

A few days later, LCT-159 and five of her Flotilla 5 sisters made another run to Segi Point with more material for the airfield. The trip holds special memories for McNeill:

> The airfield was almost finished and while we were unloading, a flight of Marine Corsairs requested emergency landing permission. They were badly shot up and almost out of fuel. Everyone turned to and quickly cleared the field of construction equipment.
>
> As the Corsairs circled the field, we could see that they were in poor condition. Each made what amounted to a crash landing, but all the pilots survived. I recognized some of the planes as members of the 'Black Sheep' Squadron.
>
> Segi never became a great air base, but it was especially valuable for many damaged planes and wounded pilots before Munda was captured. Later in the afternoon, I received permission to visit Donald Kennedy, the famous coastwatcher who had recently moved his operations to Vangunu. I had brought along a few luxury items he might like such as coffee, tea, chocolates and some Florida-type fruit. 'Bo' Gillette (LCT-369), Bob Capeless (LCT-62), Bob Carr (LCT-367) and I went by boat to Vangunu. As we came alongside the pier, we realized we were covered by several well-concealed machine guns.
>
> A uniformed native approached us and saluted, offering to be of service. We explained we would like to see Mr. Kennedy. The native asked our names and disappeared into the jungle. In a few minutes he returned and asked us to follow him.
>
> We were led up a neat trail to a beautiful building on top of a hill. Every inch of the trail was covered by gun positions manned by natives, all part of Kennedy's private army. The house was a spacious, thatch-covered island home built of bamboo with woven plants of intricate

design. Since the material was all from the jungle, there were no glass windows. Wide verandas surrounded the house and mosquito netting covered the windows.

We were met on the veranda by a native in a starched white jacket who greeted us and showed us to a parlor well-furnished with native furniture. Soon Mr. Kennedy entered and greeted us warmly. We said we had come to express our thanks for his efforts for our cause and to bring a token of appreciation. He made us comfortable as white-coated native houseboys served us tea.

We were very impressed! Indeed, I was overwhelmed. Here on an isolated island that we had never heard of, within a few miles of a major battle surrounded by an enemy he had totally confused, this world famous man was living in the style of a British diplomat. My admiration soared as he quietly discussed the military situation and questioned us about the capabilities of our ships.

He brought out a uniquely carved Japanese rifle and asked us to deliver it to the General on Guadalcanal as a gift. He explained he took it from the Commander of the Japanese force that was sent down to Segi to capture him. We all knew the story well. Kennedy and about 50 of his troops had ambushed the company and annihilated them at night before they reached Segi. Mr. Kennedy explained that he never killed a man while he slept. 'I always tap them on a shoulder before I cut their throat.'

Walter Lord, who has done extensive research on the Coastwatchers, stated that Kennedy personally killed more than 50 Japanese. I consider it a great privilege to have met this extraordinary man.

We'll rejoin the LCT Flotilla 5 crews later in this chapter.

Viru Harbor, 1 July 1943

At Viru Harbor, which RAdm Halsey wanted as a small-craft base, the landing at Viru was delayed for one day beyond the time originally planned because of the late arrival of the advance unit, which had landed at Segi on 21 June and dispatched overland to Viru.

There was good reason for the late arrival. After linking up with Coastwatcher Kennedy at Segi Point, LtCol Michael S. Currin, USMC, turned his attention to his initial goal, the seizure of the protected anchorage at Viru Harbor. He had to accomplish this prior to the arrival of the invasion force on 30 June, and on the night of 27 June, he and his 4th Marine Raiders set out by rubber boats across the mouths of the Akuru and Choi rivers for Viru.

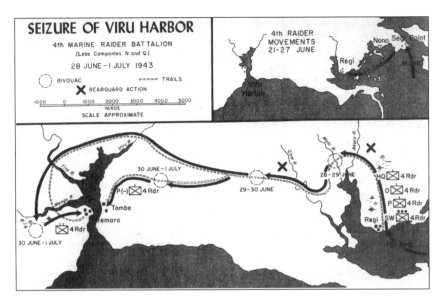

After an eight-mile paddle, the Raiders arrived at Regi Village early on 28 June. Led by native guides, Currin began the approach march to Viru Harbor. Fighting a stubborn combination of terrain, weather, and Japanese patrols, the Raiders were short of their objective on 30 June.

The Raiders launched their attack at 0900, 1 July, to seize Tetemara and Tombe Villages. Capt Walker attacked Tombe with part of his company, while the remainder attacked Tetemara with First Lieutenant Raymond L. Luckel's Company O. After six hours of fighting and a Japanese counterattack, the objectives were captured.

Meanwhile the first echelon of the Viru Harbor Occupation Unit, under the command of Cmdr Stanley Leith, arrived on schedule off Viru at 0610 on 30 June. The landing force stood off the beach after taking fire from enemy coastal defense guns. (The Viru Harbor Occupation Group, TU 31.3.1, is detailed in Appendix J.)

The directive governing the operation provided that the landing force embarked in the ships was not to land until the enemy guns guarding the entrance to the harbor had been immobilized by the advance unit attacking from the direction of Segi. It also provided that the commander of the occupation unit should disembark the landing force into boats and have it in readiness to send in at 0645.

A message was received en route, however, that the Raiders had been delayed at Choi River near Nono, New Georgia, on 28 June by enemy action. It was then decided by the task group commander that the troops should not be disembarked into the boats until there was some indication that the advance unit was attacking Viru Harbor.

A BAR man in the bow of the rubber landing craft (LCR(L) provides covering fire as the infantry men approach the beach. Courtesy U.S. Marine Corps.

Two Marines of the 4ʰ Raider Battalion at Viru Harbor with souvenir flag. Courtesy Ensign Walter "Bo" Gillette.

As soon as the task group arrived off Viru, attempts were made to establish contact with the advance unit by radio. These were continued for several hours without success.

At 1007 a dispatch was transmitted to Adm Turner by the unit commander recommending that in view of the unknown position of the Raiders and the inadvisability of attempting a frontal assault without a simultaneous land attack, the embarked troops be landed at Nono Point at the mouth of the Choi River, so that they might proceed overland to Viru. This recommendation was approved, and the troops were landed accordingly. The *Kilty, Crosby,* and *Hopkins* then returned to base.

Waiting to land at Viru Harbor, New Georgia Island, on 1 July 1943.

LCTs 134, 330, and 369 waiting to unload at Viru Harbor, 2 July 1943.

LCT Sidebar – Ensign Walter "Bo" Gillette, and his LCT-369 crew were part of the 2ᵈ Echelon of the Viru Occupation Group. During our interview, he reminded me that the Navy didn't require LCT "drivers" to keep war diaries or ship's logs. I asked Bo to explain:

> First of all, we were most all Reserves and didn't always follow regulations. For example, when we were in the final stages of preparing for the TOENAILS operation in late June of '43, we knew we would probably run into some trouble and wanted to have some spare engines

Marines near the Japanese huts at Viru Harbor, 2 July 1943.

Looking out to sea at Viru Harbor, 2 July 1943. A Japanese 3" gun was mounted on a cliff to the right. All courtesy of Ensign Walter "Bo" Gillette.

with us. But somebody in Tulagi said, 'Wait, I need to wire Washington for approval, first.' But there wasn't time for that kind of red tape, so that night one of the Flotilla 5 group commanders went in and cut the lock off the gate and loaded several spares.

As the story goes, he said 'To hell with them! We're going to a war zone, we're not going to fool with paperwork.' That happened several times.

At 1700 on 1 July the capture of Viru by the advance unit was reported and additional forces were able to land directly from seaward that night. The Marine Raiders turned the beachhead over to the Army occupation force and returned to Guadalcanal. The 4th Raider Battalion lost 13 killed and 15 wounded in this action. The Japanese defenders withdrew, with an estimated 61 dead and 100 wounded.

The first echelon of the 20th NCB accompanied the first landing having been assigned the task of building a base for PT-boats. They immediately commenced unloading operations.

The Seabees improved and extended an existing road and built a new one along the beach to provide for transferal of cargo. A sector of the main defense line was assigned to the detachment, and machine-gun emplacements and rifle pits were constructed and camouflaged. Extensive barbed-wire entanglements were strung in front of the line and fitted with booby traps.

The original plan for the establishment of a PT-boat base was abandoned because the harbor was found to be unsuitable. However, the Seabees remained at Viru Harbor until October, to carry out minor construction projects and maintenance. A marine railway was constructed for the repair of small landing craft, and an existing wharf, 50 feet by 30 feet, was rehabilitated, using earth and coral fill held by coconut-log cribbing.

Wickham Anchorage, 30 June 1943 [8]

The first landings in the Wickham Anchorage area were made at Oloana Bay at 0630 on the morning of 30 June. At 1812 on 29 June Task Group 31.3.3 under RAdm George H. Fort in the *Trevor*, left Wernham Cove in the Russell Islands and proceeded northwest toward Vangunu Island.

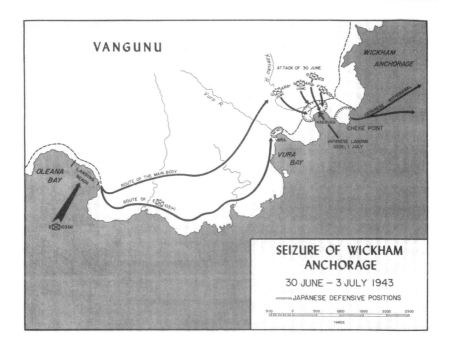

The Wickham landing demonstrated the danger of disembarking troops on strange beaches during darkness. At 0335 the Task Unit hove to off the west side of Oloana Bay. At 0345 disembarkation of the first wave commenced under extremely hazardous conditions as a result of heavy seas, low clouds, and high wind. The outline of the beach was not readily discernible at any point.

LCI-334 War Diary – Lt (jg) Al Ormston, Skipper of LCI-334 (our lead LCI historian in Volume I), confirmed the harrowing conditions that night with the following entries in the 334's *War Diary:*

JUNE 30 1943

0230 Proceeding along Southern tip of Vangunu Island toward Oloana Bay. Shore signal lights observed, and one red beach marker seen. Visibility extremely poor, weather misty, heavy swells and force 4 wind on shore. Contact with ship ahead nearly impossible.

0300 Ships astern dropped out of sight. As we received no order to beach and conditions were very bad, we stayed in formation...through heavy rain squalls, waited for daylight, and further orders.

0707 Beached in Oloana Bay and discharged troops and gear. Troops were very slow to unload gear, delaying our retraction.

Al Ormston's first command, LCI-334, at Guadalcanal. Courtesy Al Ormston.

0915 Retracted, underway.
0921 Formed up at Rendezvous, proceeded toward Russells.
1737 Anchored, Renard Sound.

The Army and Marines still faced four days of dirty jungle fighting, supported by air strikes and bombardment by destroyers *Woodworth* and *Jenkins*, before the defending force of some 300 Japanese was wiped out. Here is a brief summary of this action:

The night landing under conditions of low visibility and heavy seas turned into a fiasco. The APDs began debarkation in the wrong spot (their Higgins boats lost formation when they attempted to pass through the LCIs loaded with soldiers) and the two Raider companies ended up being scattered along seven miles of coastline.

The operation, as the official Army history candidly recounts, "was exactly what might be expected from a night landing in bad weather," with the Marines landing in "impressive disorganization." In the ensuing chaos, six landing craft became lodged on the coral reef, while others discharged troops at the wrong site and then had to reload.

When the Army units began to land after daylight, they found just 75 Marines holding the designated beachhead. A two-man patrol (one lieutenant each from the Raiders and the Army battalion) had been ashore since mid-June to reconnoiter with the aid of native scouts. They provided the exact location of the Japanese garrison, and the joint force soon headed northeast toward its objectives.

Native scouts and the handful of Marines led the way, with two Army companies (F and G) in trace. The remaining Raiders were to join up with their unit as soon as they could. All but one platoon did catch up by the time the Americans reached their line of departure a few hundred yards north of the village.

Despite a confused landing in poor conditions, by afternoon the Marines and units of the Army 2^d Battalion, 103rd Infantry reached the Kaeruka River and attacked the Japanese located there. This position was taken and then defended.

The enemy made no ground attack that night, but periodically fired mortars and machine guns at American lines. During a lull at 0200, three Japanese barges approached the beach, apparently unaware that ownership of the real estate was under dispute. As they neared shore, the Marines guarding the seaward portion of the perimeter opened up. One craft sank and the other two broached in the surf. Two Marines and one soldier died in the firefight, but the entire enemy force, estimated at 120 men, was destroyed in the water or on the beach.

The next morning Brown decided to disengage and move to Vura Village, where he could reorganize and direct fire support on the remaining enemy at Kaeruka prior to launching another attack. The Americans received only harassing fire as they withdrew.

After a day of preparatory fire by air, artillery, and naval guns, the composite battalion returned to Kaeruka on 3 July. They seized the village against minimal resistance, killed seven more Japanese and captured one. The Raiders returned to Oloana Bay by LCI later the next day.

On 9 July they made a predawn landing from an LCT on Gatukai Island southeast of Vangunu to investigate reports of a 50-man Japanese unit. The Marines found evidence of the enemy but made no contact. They returned to Oloana Bay on 10 July and departed for Guadalcanal the day after. There they joined up with LtCol Currin and the rest of the 4th Raider Battalion.

WESTERN LANDING FORCE [9]

Rendova Landing, 30 June 1943

The most important landings on 30 June were those on the north coast of Rendova Island, five miles across Blanche Channel from Munda Point on New Georgia Island. But before the first echelon of the Western Landing Force arrived at Rendova, a few preliminary steps had to be taken to secure the Onaiavisi Entrance to Roviana Lagoon.

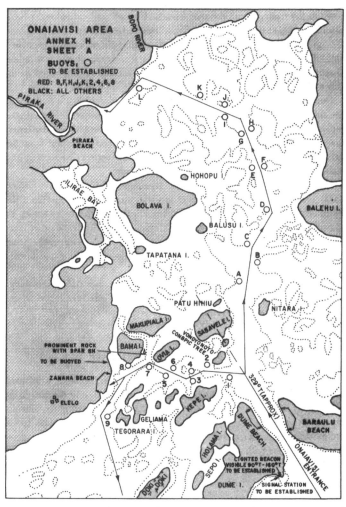

Onaiavisi Entrance and approach to Zanana Beach, New Georgia Island.

At 0230 on 30 June, APD *Talbot* and minesweeper *Zane* arrived off Onaiavisi with the Initial Landing Force and began to debark units of the 169th Infantry, 43rd Division, on Sasavele and Baraulu Islands adjacent to the entrance. At the time of arrival the visibility was very poor with no moon and persistent heavy rain squalls.

At 0257 while maneuvering on an approximate heading of 155 degrees T. the *Zane* ran aground on Dume Island. While she struggled to free herself, the troops and supplies landed without opposition and assured a protected channel into the lagoon at such time as the invasion of Munda would commence. *Zane* perched helplessly on the reef throughout the morning, luckily unmolested by enemy planes or artillery. At 1248 *Rail* pulled her off.

A second pre-dawn landing also suffered from foul weather. Destroyer-transports *Dent* and *Waters* ferried to Rendova a jungle-trained and physically-hardened advance unit, the "Barracudas" of the 172[d] Regimental Combat Team, USA. These men planned to land in Rendova Harbor at a spot marked with a light by the advance patrol that had been there for several days. The rain quenched the signal and the troops landed in the wrong spot. Since they were supposed to wipe out the Japanese garrison before the main force arrived, this meant that the major landing would be opposed.

The first ships of RAdm Turner's Task Group 31.1 Western Force appeared out in Blanche Channel at the break of dawn and edged into position off Rendova Harbor. The transports' crews and troops had been undergoing a final period of training in debarking and landing operations at Guadalcanal after their arrival from the New Hebrides.

Picking their way through the reefs, the troop transports entered the harbor and at 0642 began debarking men and materials. Two groups of destroyers were assigned the task of patrolling the two entrances of the harbor. Others screened the transports, ready to silence any shore gun which went into action. The boats leaving the *McCawley* were informed: "You are the first to land. Expect opposition." The small craft went ashore in the face of machine-gun fire from the beach. At a few minutes after 0700, the

Japanese batteries on Munda Point opened up. The first salvo registered a hit in the engine room of the *Gwin*. A near hit was also scored on the *Buchanan*. About the same time, two other batteries on Baanga Island and one or two at Lokuloku to the eastward joined in.

The *Buchanan* and the *Farenholt*, veterans of the Battle of Cape Esperance, undertook the silencing of enemy guns. Hits were obtained on the Munda Point area with the second salvo. Seven batteries in all were put out of action by the accurate gunfire of the two destroyers, which meanwhile varied their speed and heading so skillfully that the Japanese fire control problem was rendered practically insoluble. Exchange of fire between shore batteries and screening destroyers continued intermittently throughout the day.

About 0700 the 172^d Infantry began landing on Rendova. There was confusion and disorganization, but the regiment quickly overwhelmed a 120-man Japanese detachment and established a 1,000-yard-deep beachhead. All troops, including General Harmon, were ashore in half an hour.

Troops of the Western Landing Force hit the Rendova beach 30 June 1943.
Note LCM also carries tank with short gun. National Archives.

By 0730 all troops except ship working details had been landed. Within two hours from the time of initial debarkation, the newly emplaced shore batteries on Kokurana Island were shelling the enemy installations at Munda. The transports remained hove to in the debarkation area, completing their unloading. On two occasions, however, they had to get underway and move to the eastward under the threat of air attack.

Throughout the landing operations a 32-plane Combat Air Patrol (CAP) was maintained by fighters from our bases in Guadalcanal and the Russells. Twice during the forenoon these planes drove off enemy aircraft which threatened our ships. Word of an impending attack was first received at 0857, and all destroyers closed transports to form an AA screen. The task unit steamed about in Blanche Channel until the all clear was given at 0950, when all units resumed their previous stations and disembarkation was continued.

At 1105 air attack again appeared imminent, whereupon the task unit again ceased operations and proceeded into Blanche Channel until the all clear was given. In neither case did enemy

Unloading operations on the beach. Courtesy of Seabees.

planes come within range of our ships.

Unloading was completed by 1500 with a high degree of efficiency. The *McCawley* had discharged its cargo at the rate of 157 tons per hour while placing 1,100 troops on the beach.

Moving supplies off the beach quickly became the main problem. As rain turned the ground into red clay mud, heavy traffic ruined the island's single mile-long road, making it so muddy that a bulldozer sank. Inadequately marked supplies, dumped on the beach by troops wading ashore, piled up and became intermixed. So many trucks became mired in the mud that General Hester had to temporarily stop shipment to the beachhead.

Orders were now given for the various units to gather in cruising formation and stand out through Blanche Channel to the southeast for the return to Guadalcanal. Within the hour, a group of 24 to 28 Mitsubishi torpedo bombers, escorted by an unknown number of Zero fighters, was sighted coming in over the northwest corner of New Georgia Island near Munda Point. The enemy bombers circled the task group's formation, using land background, and then made very low approaches at a speed hardly less than 250 knots. About one minute before the leading attack planes reached the screen, the formation executed "Emergency Turn 9" from a base course of 139 degrees.

All vessels opened fire, and hits were immediately scored. The bombers ignored their losses and came in with great determination, releasing their torpedoes at ranges approximating 500 yards. Three planes in succession made drops off the *Farenholt's* port beam. The first torpedo broached and passed ahead. The second missed astern. The remaining plane appeared to be about to attempt a suicide dive on the ship, but the pilot finally dropped his torpedo and sheered off ahead. The *Farenholt's* commanding officer ordered full right rudder. A thud was felt on the bridge, and all hands waited for the explosion which seemed sure to follow. The seconds ticked by and nothing happened. Either the vessel had been hit by a dud or the torpedo had run too short a distance to arm.

The *McCalla* was likewise bracketed by three torpedoes, one of which passed about 25 yards ahead, another 50 yards astern, and the third apparently passed under the ship. Flank speed and full right rudder were used to bring the course parallel to the torpedo tracks.

The task group had just executed a ninety degree turn to the right and opened fire when a torpedo was seen approaching the port side of the 7,712-ton transport *McCawley*, flagship of RAdm Turner. Her rudder was put over hard right, and the starboard engine was backed full. A moment later the torpedo struck amidships in the vicinity of the engine room. The *McCawley* lurched to port but immediately righted herself, still swinging to starboard with her rudder jammed hard over and all engines stopped.

Admiral Turner ordered cargo vessel *Libra* to take the flagship in tow, and destroyers *Ralph Talbot* and *McCalla* were directed to stand by. Adm Turner and his staff then went down the ropes and boarded the *Farenholt*. RAdm Wilkinson remained aboard the *McCawley* in charge of the salvage crew.

As a result of the first explosion a hole was opened in the ship's side about 18 to 20 feet in diameter extending from about frame 87 to 93. The frames between were carried away, and shell plating

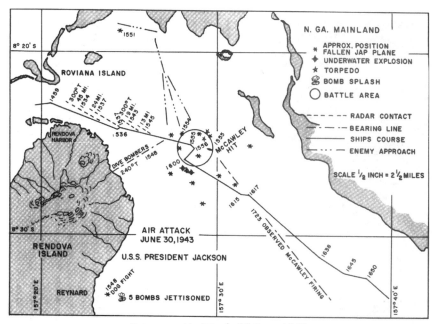

Japanese Air Attack, 30 June 1943.

was blown outward with very ragged edges. All watertight doors remained intact, however. About 30 seconds after the initial explosion, another detonation of lesser magnitude followed, probably as a result of the rupturing of the compressed air tanks used in connection with the port main engine. In spite of the efforts of damage control parties the ship continued to settle aft.

By 1558 the attack was over; the action had lasted only eight minutes. Only two enemy planes survived the attacks of our protecting fighters and the anti-aircraft fire of the ships, and they were shot down during retirement by our planes.

Loss of USS *McCawley* (APA-4)

About an hour later, the *McCawley* was attacked by a group of 12 to 15 Aichi dive bombers, which broke through the overcast at a level of about 1,000 feet. Although the ship was now dead in the water, the salvage crew manned the guns so effectively that the enemy aircraft were driven off. By this time, however, it was apparent that the *McCawley* could no longer be kept afloat, so the *McCalla* eased alongside and all hands were ordered to abandon ship.

At 2002 the *McCalla* was ordered to prepare torpedoes for sinking the *McCawley* if the settling of that vessel should warrant it. But the end came more quickly than had been expected. At 2023, the doomed transport was struck by three torpedoes; thirty seconds later she sank stern first in 340 fathoms of water. At first it was believed that she had fallen prey to an enemy submarine, but it has since been learned that the *McCawley* was sunk by friendly PT boats which mistook her for an enemy.

In spite of the loss of the *McCawley*, enemy air opposition to our landing operations at Rendova was not impressive. The first attack group consisted entirely of fighters. The main strike by coordinated dive bombers and torpedo planes did not take place until 1500. Except for the threat of strafing at 1100, our amphibious operations were unopposed from the air for nearly eight hours of daylight, and thus the early and more difficult phases of our landing and unloading operations were completed without air opposition.

Two reasons for this have been suggested. It was known that the principal Japanese striking force in this area was either maintained at or staged through Rabaul and only flown into Kahili in preparation for a major strike. There is also reason to believe that many Japanese carrier-type aircraft pilots in this theater were not trained in night takeoffs. These factors taken in combination offer the best explanation for the fact that there was a lapse of four hours between the initial sighting of our force by a Japanese search plane and the arrival of the first wave of attacking enemy planes.

The *McCawley* was the only ship other than the destroyers equipped with radar. After she was torpedoed it was necessary for the other transports to place full dependence on destroyer radars and the fighter director ship for the locations and identification of planes which could not be identified visually. The TBS circuit was particularly helpful in advising all units quickly in cases requiring prompt action before the attack was competed and afterward.

Rendova Second Echelon

The second echelon, consisting of four LSTs and five LCIs under the command of Capt Carter in LST-354, escorted by the *Farenholt, Buchanan,* and *Gwin,* arrived at Rendova Harbor the following day.

LST-397 standing off Rendova Island, July 1943. Pictured left to right: Don Connell, CSM; Don Chalfont, SM 2/c; and Jerry Valenti. (Two men on right unidentified.) Courtesy Don Connell.

The beach at Kokoruna was satisfactory, although embarkation of troops and cargo was handicapped by rains and heavy mud. However, the East Beach of Rendova Harbor proved extremely unsatisfactory. The beaching had to be made at dead slow speed, and the vessels were unable to plow their way through the mud to the beach proper. Vehicles could be operated only with difficulty because of deep mud, and many had to be abandoned. This area was finally vacated, and the LSTs were diverted to the beach section opposite Pago Pago Island.

In his report of the operation, Capt Carter observed :

"The selection of beaches for use by LSTs from air reconnaissance only cannot be satisfactory.... In planning future operations, every effort should be made to obtain reliable and actual information relative to beaches intended to be used by LSTs. Air photos are inadequate and even misleading thereby endangering the success of such an operation."

Zanana Amphibious Movement

On 2 July, a good beach was located at Zanana on the south coast of the New Georgia mainland six miles east of Munda, and a company of SoPacFor Scouts was landed there. That night the Scouts were reinforced by units of the 169th and 172[d] Infantry.

The "Green Dragon" Landing Ship, Tank. National Archives.

Assault boats from the Rendova Boat Pool, LCMs, LCVPs, and LCP(R)s, protected by PT-boats were used to convey the troops in a shore-to-shore amphibious movement from Rendova to Zanana via Onaiavisi Entrance. Combat patrols moved ashore and took up their positions along the Barike River, the Army's line of departure. By 8 July all artillery and troops were in position for the jump-off against Munda.

Marine Defense Battalions

Elements of four Marine defense battalions played an important role in the New Georgia Campaign. Here is a condensed version of their critical participation:

On 29 June, the 9th Defense Battalion commanded by LtCol William J. Scheyer was attached to XIV Corps for the duration of the New Georgia operation. The battalion was given the mission of assisting in the capture, occupation, and defense of Rendova Island, by landing on the beaches south of Renard Channel entrance. It was then to move immediately into position to provide anti-aircraft defense. A third mission was to fire 155-mm guns on the enemy installations, bivouac areas, and the airfield at Munda.

The anti-aircraft group of the 9th Defense Battalion moves ashore at Rendova. Here a TD-9 tractor pulls a 90-mm gun from an LST. The TD-9 would soon prove too light to move through the muddy terrain beyond the beach. U.S. Marine Corps.

As a fourth task, the tank platoon would support the attack on Munda Airfield. Fifth, the battalion would be prepared to repel attack by hostile surface vessels. When the Japanese forces on new Georgia Island were overrun, the battalion would then move as a whole or in part to Munda to defend the field when Allied air units moved in and began operating.

LtCol Scheyer said on leaving Guadalcanal: "The Japanese have a mistaken notion that they must die for their Emperor and our job is to help them do that just as fast as we possibly can...." At 1600 on 29 June, the 9th's first echelon, 28 officers and 641 enlisted Marines, combat-loaded on board AKs *Libra* and *Algorab*, the vessels assigned to transport the battalion, and sailed from Guadalcanal.

At 0635 the morning of 30 June, the first units of the XIV Corps' assault wave began landing on Kokorana Island and East Beach of Rendova. They were met by Coastwatcher Flight Lieutenant D.C. Horton and guides from the amphibious reconnaissance patrols. The battalion unit soon took out an enemy machine gun position. Major Robert C. Hiatt's reconnaissance party from the artillery group killed another enemy soldier, who was said to have been stripped of souvenirs before hitting the ground. The defenders withdrew inland to harass the Americans from the hills and swamps.

LCI-222 after disembarking troops on Rendova July 1943. Naval Historical Center.

Throughout the day, enemy air attacks were turned back by friendly fighters. Allied fighters over the area on 30 June reportedly destroyed over 100 enemy aircraft.

Both *Algorab* and *Libra* were unloaded with the assistance of the 24th Naval Construction Battalion. On the first day of landing, Battery E of the Anti-aircraft Group set up on Kokorana and was prepared to fire by 1645; all Special Weapons Group light anti-aircraft guns landed and were emplaced along the coast to protect the XIV Corps' beachhead; sites were located for the 155-mm and the remaining 90-mm batteries. Battery demolition crews ventured near and into enemy territory to blast out fields of fire for the gun positions.

Weather and terrain made unloading and emplacement extremely difficult. Torrential rains began on 30 June and continued almost without cessation, rendering what passed for roads impassable and causing great congestion on the beaches as men and supplies came ashore. Areas believed suitable for occupation proved to be swampy. Steel matting and corduroy roads constructed with coconut logs were utilized, but even these were ineffective. Tanks, guns and vehicles of all types mired down in the incredible mud and only the sturdiest tractors or manpower extricated them. The congestion of supplies on the beachhead

Behind a revetment of sandbags and coconut logs, this 9[b] Defense Battalion crew manning a 90-mm anti-aircraft gun keeps vigilant watch against Japanese air attacks on positions at the beach at Rendova. Courtesy U.S. Marine Corps.

rendered them and the troops moving themselves and the supplies inland vulnerable to enemy air attack.

The 9th's motor transport section performed as best it could with the resources available and until the majority of its vehicles burned out from the strain of operating in the Rendova muck. Their task was made easier by the amphibious tractors, which were the only sure means of transportation and these had troubles of their own as they threw off their tracks on uneven terrain. All tractors were damaged eventually in the Japanese air attacks that followed.

Sailors and soldiers make a corduroy road from coconut logs across an exceptionally muddy spot. Courtesy U.S. Marine Corps.

A 155-mm Long Tom is dragged through the mud of Rendova en route to a new position from which it could punish Japanese positions and defend against counterattacks. U.S. Marine Corps.

The 9th Defense Battalion's second echelon arrived in LSTs 395 and 354 and disembarked at Rendova on 1 July as Allied fighter cover continued to turn back enemy air attacks. Unloading was done quickly, 155-mm guns and their tractors soon made mud and slime which made walking around difficult to say the least. By the end of the day, Capt Henry H. Reichner's Battery A was in firing position.

A third battalion echelon arrived in LSTs 342 and 398 and disembarked on 2 July. That morning Capt Walter C. Well's Battery B was emplaced and Battery A commenced shelling enemy positions in the Munda area.

The dead had to wait to be buried until the wounded were taken care of and the battlefield was secured. In some cases it was not until after the Japanese had withdrawn or been solidly beaten that the dead Marines could be recovered.

A burial detail renders honors to those Marines who were killed in action. The firing squad is armed with Garand M-1 rifles. Courtesy U.S. Marine Corps.

At 1335, 2 July, 18 Mitsubishi G4M Betty bombers and Zeke fighter escorts entered the area from the southwest and pattern-bombed the beachhead, causing considerable damage and many casualties. Zero fighters flew over the beach area at tree-top level, strafing and bombing the beach and landing craft. Gasoline storage tanks and an explosives dump were hit and several fires were started in the area.

Battery A's Joseph J. Pratl recounted, "We saw the bombers, we assumed them to be American B-25s. We hit foxholes and the earth shook like a rubber band as three bombs fell near our battery."

On board a beached LST, Francis E. Chadwick, of Battery B, was hauling ammunition for a Navy 40-mm anti-aircraft gun when "the LST was showered in water. You could feel the heat from the bombs. The noise was deafening." The area around the landing beach became known as "Suicide Point."

Four 9th Defense Battalion men were killed, one was missing, and 22 were wounded as a result of the raid. Damage to the battalion included two 155-mm guns hit, two 40-mm guns hit, three amphibious tractors hit, one TD-18 tractor demolished, and an unknown amount of supplies and personal gear destroyed.

One bomb landed between the trail legs of one 155-mm gun in Battery A, but failed to detonate. This put the gun out of action until the bomb was excavated, pulled clear, and detonated.

That day, the battalion bomb disposal teams successfully removed or destroyed a total of 9 bombs and 65 unexploded projectiles of 105-mm or larger.

The 9th Defense Battalions's 90mm Group had four gun batteries, each with its own range finder, computer, and radar. This weapons system continued in use through the war and into the 1950s. Courtesy U.S. Marine Corps.

The damage caused by this attack was due in part to the lack of working surveillance radar and to the withdrawal of friendly fighter cover because of weather. The battalion's radars had not yet been installed.

On 3 July, both batteries of "Long Toms" fired for effect on the Munda airfield and enemy artillery positions on Baanga Island. At Munda a defender wrote, "They must be firing like the dickens. Sometimes they all come at once. I don't exactly appreciate this shelling."

Earning special credit during this period were the battalion's attached Navy corpsmen and doctors, who performed their work in the midst of enemy raids and under the most trying conditions. Besides caring for the 9th's casualties at the battalion aid station set up on the exposed East Beach of Rendova, battalion surgeon LCmdr Miles C. Krepelas treated many Navy wounded and Army troops returning from New Georgia, who could not locate their own medical detachments.

Battalion S-4 Major Albert F. Lucas was faced with the extremely difficult task of supplying the widely dispersed elements of the battalion. The preparation and delivery of food required a major effort throughout the campaign because the battalion elements were widely spread out in the target area, and the battalion had to

The first Japanese aircraft shot down from the beach was credited to this gun crew on its first day ashore. From the left: 1st Lt William A. Buckingham, PFC Francis W. O'Brien, Cpl Paul V. Duhamel, and PFC Nemo Hancock, Jr, of the 9[b] Defense Battalion. Courtesy U.S. Marine Corps.

feed all other units which did not have their own messing facilities. Hot meals were provided once a day and the artillery group's pastry cook raised morale by providing doughnuts and other baked goods during some of the more difficult periods.

Throughout July reinforcements of men and supplies were moved into Rendova on a daily schedule by the transport command. Between 30 June and 31 July, 28,748 personnel (25,556 Army, 1,547 Navy, and 1,645 Marines), 4,806 tons of rations, 3,486 tons of fuel, 9,961 tons of ammunition, 6,895 tons of vehicles, and 5,323 tons of other freight were unloaded at Rendova by the "Pacific Express."

24th Naval Construction Battalions

The first echelon of the 24th Battalion accompanied the 172d infantry in the landing on Rendova 30 June. The assault was met by Japanese fire, but bulldozers immediately set to work to cut roads into the jungle. The battle against nature, time, and the inevitable Japanese bombers was joined. Leading the Seabees was Commander H. Roy Wittaker, CEC, USNR. He described the action:

The impossible takes a little longer. USNCB.

Where we landed the soil was unbelievably marshy. The mud was deep and getting deeper. A swampy coconut grove lay just back of the beach, and we had to cut a road through there. Guns had to be transported from our beach over to West Beach so that shells could be hurled across the narrow strip of water onto the Jap positions at Munda. And still that rain poured.

All day long we sweated and swore and worked to bring the heavy stuff ashore and hide it from the Jap bombers. Our mesh, designed to 'snowshoe' vehicles over soft mud, failed miserably. Even our biggest tractors bogged down in the muck. The men ceased to look like men; they looked like slimy frogs working in some prehistoric ooze. As they sank to their knees they discarded their clothes. They slung water out of their eyes, cussed their mud-slickened hands, and somehow kept the stuff rolling ashore.

A detachment fought to clear the road at West Beach. The ground was so soft that only our biggest "Cats" could get through. The Japs were still sniping but in spite of this the men began felling the coconut palms, cutting them into 12-foot lengths and corrugating the road. Our traction-treaded vehicles could go over these logs, but the spinning wheels of a truck would send the logs flying, and the truck would bury itself. To pull the trucks out we lashed a bulldozer to a tree, then dragged the trucks clear with the 'dozer's winch.

When night came, we had unloaded six ships but the scene on the beach was dismal. More troops, Marines and Seabees had come in, but the mud was about to lick us. Fox-holes filled with water as rapidly

Road construction. USNCB.

as they could be dug. There was almost no place near the beach to set up a shelter tent, so the men rolled their exhausted, mud-covered bodies in tents and slept in the mud. As the Japs would infiltrate during the night, the Army boys holding our line in the grove would kill them with trench knives.

Next day, at 1330, without warning, the Jap planes came in with bomb bays open. All of us began firing with what guns had been set up, but most of the Seabees had to lie in the open on the beach and take it. We tried to dig trenches with our hands and noses while the Japs poured it on us.

The first bombs found our two main fuel dumps, and we had to lie there in the mud and watch our supplies burn while the Japs strafed us. One bomb landed almost under our largest bulldozer, and that big machine just reared up like a stallion and disintegrated. Then every man among us thought that his time had come. A five-ton cache of our dynamite went off, exploding the eardrums of the men nearest it. That soggy earth just quivered like jelly under us.

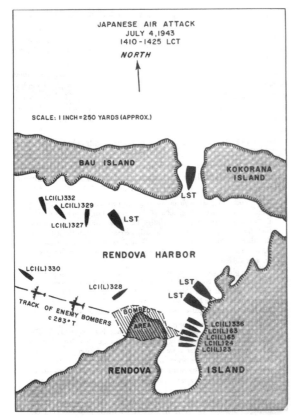

Location of LCI(L) Group 14 landing craft participating in anti-air action, 4 July 1943, Rendova Harbor.

When the Japs had exhausted their ammunition, they flew off, leaving us to put out the fires and treat our wounded. I'll never forget the scene on that beach. In our outfit, two of our best officers and 21 enlisted men were dead. Many more were wounded, others were missing, and a number were out of their heads. Our galley equipment, most of our supplies, and all the men's seabags and personal belongings were destroyed.

'Okay, men,' I yelled, 'We got nothing left but what we got on, so let's get back to work.'

All that night Doctor Duryea (LCmdr Garrett Duryea, Medical Corps, USNR) worked with our wounded. The biggest job was to get them clean. That's one thing about being a Seabee. Aboard ship you bathe, wash down with antiseptic, and put on clean clothing before an action. In the Air Force you can take a bath before you take off. But when a Seabee gets hit, he's usually on a beach in the mud. Mud seems to be our element. When we die, we die in the mud.

Next day, while we worked in relays, chaplains from the Army and Marines helped us bury our dead. Three more had died during the night. Not one of those boys would have ever thought of himself as a hero, but I felt proud to have been their commanding officer.

By the morning of the fourth day we had opened the road to West Beach, but what a road it was! We had literally snaked those big 155s through two miles of mud, and the Marines began setting them up. We were also developing a storage area some distance from the beach and were trying desperately to reduce our hazards on the beach.

The beach, as always, was a potential torch with ammunition, diesel oil and gasoline everywhere. The mud was too deep for trucks. To move the inflammable stuff back into the storage areas, the men had to emplace themselves in the mud in bucket-brigade fashion. For hours they'd work that way, passing the heavy packages back into the camouflage area and sinking deeper into the mud each time they handled a package. And still the rain poured.

Late that afternoon we got our first big thrill. From over on West Beach the Marines opened up on Munda with the 155s. Our men stopped work and cheered almost insanely. The others stationed with bulldozers and winches along the road to West Beach joined in the cheering. No group of men had ever endured more in order for guns to begin firing. It hurts American construction men down deep to have to lie in mud and be strafed by Japs; and now those 155s were giving it back to the Japs with interest. The firing was a tonic to us. The men went back to unloading furiously.

Heavy Japanese bombing attacks were daily occurrences while skirmishing and sniping continued. However, the corduroy roads permitted the Marines to move heavy artillery to points from which they could bring the Japanese stronghold at Munda Point under fire.

By August 1, the entire 24th Battalion had reached Rendova; on the 15th it moved across the channel to Munda.

While Marine anti-aircraft artillery dealt with air raids, 155-mm Long Toms were fired at targets some eight miles or more away, round-the-clock, in all weather, taking a toll of the defenders. Courtesy USMC.

A fire direction center processed target information from observation posts and air spotters, which group commander LtCol Archie E. O'Neil and executive officer Maj Robert C. Hiatt translated into firing data on Rendova. USMC.

The success of the CAP in warding off Japanese attacks over Rendova is attested to by the fact that during the entire operation only three hits were registered on U.S. ships by bombing and torpedo plane attacks, and only one horizontal bombing attack reached the objective during daylight hours.

To Sum Up

The Rendova landing surprised the Japanese commanders on Munda and Rabaul, who had no counterattack force ready. Artillery fire from Japanese batteries on Munda, therefore, was the only Japanese response until late morning when air attacks began. Three air attacks on 30 June damaged only Admiral Turner's flagship, the transport *McCawley*, which was accidentally torpedoed and sunk by American PT boats later that evening.

A Japanese air strike against Rendova two days later killed 30 men, wounded more than 200, and exploded fuel dumps. An attempted encore performance on 4 July, however, provided the Americans with more gratifying fireworks. Sixteen Japanese bombers appeared unescorted. A mere eighty-eight rounds of anti-aircraft fire brought down twelve, and waiting fighters shot down the rest.

Reinforcements, the majority splashing ashore on Rendova, continued to disembark at all four beachheads until 5 July, when virtually the entire New Georgia Occupation Force was assembled. The first phase of TOENAILS had succeeded.

During the night of 2-3 July 1943 Flotilla 5 LCIs 23, 24, 63, 65, 327, 328 (F), 329, 330, 332, 333, 334, 335 and 336 moved from Tulagi to the Russells and began loading 169th Infantry troops and gear at 1045 on 3 July. At 1650 the 13 LCIs plus 2 LSTs departed Moquiti Bay arriving Rendova Harbor at 0720 on 4 July.

At 1019 LCI-334 began debarking troops at West Beach and continued the operation during a Condition Red. At 1216 the 334 retracted and proceeded to Poko Plantation, Rendova and beached with several other LCIs.

General Quarters sounded at 1400 and for the next 90 minutes, there was plenty of July 4th fireworks. Here's the bottom line excerpted from the LCI-334 War Diary: [10]

1405 Aerial activity west of Rendova, three planes (fighters) seen shot down smoking, identity unknown.

1410 Formation of 16 bi-motored bombers passed overhead on course 080, disappearing over Rendova.

1420 Same formation of bombers reappeared over Rendova Harbor on westerly course. Bombs seen falling. Heavy anti-aircraft fire set up from Rendova Harbor; one of the first bursts striking one bomber forward directly, causing its complete disintegration in flames. A second bomber then was hit, plunging nose first smoking into Rendova Harbor, followed by a third which broke up and fell in parts inside the reef. A fourth bomber was hit and its empennage was blown off, apparently hit aft. Its wing fell off, and engines fell separately. When the fuselage struck the water, a tremendous explosion occurred. U.S. fighter planes attacked the formation as soon as it was clear of the A-A fire, and when last seen, two of the bombers were smoking badly, course 290.

1455 Retracted from beach.

1515 Re-beached in small cove around point, at Poko Plantation.

1530 Secured from General Quarters. Remained in cove, with camouflage nets and palm branches hiding ship.

Poko Plantation became a second "home" to LCI-334 and many of her sisters for the next 10 days. With the ship's stern anchor

A 40-mm gun and crew look skyward for Japanese aircraft. Landing Craft Infantry (LCIs) are run up the beach in the background, as working parties unload them by hand. Courtesy U.S. Marine Corps.

cable out and bowlines run to trees ashore, the 334 was clear of coral, yet concealed by nearby trees. During this period, the LCI crews witnessed some show: the continued shelling of Munda Point by our artillery, numerous dogfights high overhead, the bombardment of Munda and Lambeti areas by friendly destroyers and cruisers, and the constant dive bombing of Munda Airfield by friendly planes. The 334 crew was called to General Quarters 11 times over this same period but no direct air attacks were made on the ship.

WESTERN NEW GEORGIA LANDINGS

Admiral Turner restructured the Western Force for the main invasion of New Georgia, renaming the ground forces the Munda-Bairoko Occupation Force (MBOF). Commanded by Hester, the force was subdivided into two landing groups:

The Northern Landing Group, commanded by Col Harry "The Horse" Liversedge, USMC, consisted of one battalion each from the 145th and 148th Infantry, 37th Division, and the 1st Raider Battalion, 1st Marine Raider Regiment. Liversedge's mission was to invade New Georgia's northwest shore at Rice Anchorage and defeat the Japanese in the area directly north of Munda between Enogai Inlet and Bairoko Harbor, called Dragons Peninsula. This would interdict the Japanese supply line to Munda and prevent Japanese troops on nearby Kolombangara from reinforcing Munda.

The Southern Landing Group, under the command of assistant division commander BrigGen Leonard F. Wing, consisted of the 43rd Division (less one infantry battalion), the 136th Field Artillery Battalion, and elements of the 9th Marine Defense Battalion and the South Pacific Scouts. Wing's force would land some five air-miles east of Munda at Zanana beach, a site undefended by the Japanese, and attack westward.

The plan for taking Munda was not complicated. General Hester envisioned the 169th and 172d marching from Zanana to the Barike River, a distance of no more than three miles. Using the river as a line of departure, his regiments would drive west (the 169th inland, the 172d along the coast), capture the high ground, and then take the airfield.

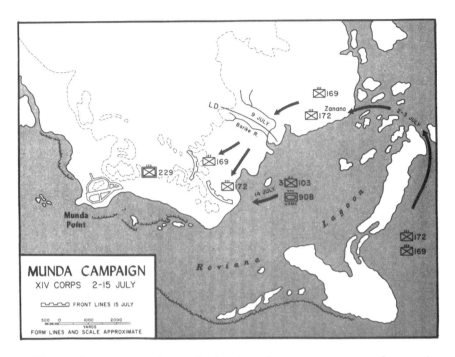

MUNDA CAMPAIGN
XIV CORPS 2-15 JULY

FRONT LINES 15 JULY

500   0   1000   2000
YARDS
FORM LINES AND SCALE APPROXIMATE

The only passage through the jungle was a narrow footpath just north of Zanana that led west. Called Munda Trail, it wound through the middle of the high ground—a series of convoluted ridges that ran inland and northwest for 3,000 yards and concealed the main Japanese defenses.

On paper, the plan seemed simple. For the green troops, however, who would be using inadequate maps to find their way through a labyrinth of coral juttings, draws, and swamps, all so densely overgrown with exotic jungle flora that visibility was measured in yards and enemy positions were invisible, the reality proved quite different.

As stated earlier, the landing at Zanana began on 2 July and both the 172ᵈ and 169th Infantry Regiments were fully ashore by 6 July. The 43rd Division was ready to advance. Meanwhile, the 9th Marine Defense Battalion consisting of a detachment of 52 men with four 40-mm guns and four .50-caliber machine guns under the command of 1st Lt John R. Wismer moved to Zanana Beach on New Georgia to provide anti-aircraft and beach defense protection for the 43rd Infantry Division.

The 172^d reached the line of departure with only minor trouble, but the 169th received a brutal introduction to jungle warfare. On 6 July the men spent an exhausting day following native guides along the narrow, vine-choked Munda Trail. That night the worn-out 3rd Battalion failed to establish proper defenses and fell prey to Japanese harassment. The tired and nervous troops spent a sleepless night firing at imagined Japanese raiding parties.

The next morning the battalion continued along Munda Trail, running into a well-camouflaged trail block established by a Japanese infantry platoon. Dug-in machine guns on high ground with supporting riflemen stopped the advance. Frontal assaults against hidden enemy positions resulted only in the loss of platoon leaders and a company commander. Finally, after the mortar platoon of the 3rd Battalion, 169th cut down trees to create fields of fire, observers crept to within thirty yards of the Japanese to direct 81-mm mortar fire on enemy positions on what was now called Bloody Hill. The battalion spent another sleepless night as the target of Japanese harassment.

Immediately after assault troops cleared the beachhead and moved inland, supplies and equipment began to litter the beach, inviting targets for enemy bombers. U.S. Marine Corps.

The 3rd Battalion stormed the Japanese position the next day and eradicated it before advancing west with the remainder of the regiment and joining the 172d on the line of departure along the Barike River. That night the 3rd Battalion, along with the rest of the regiment, endured yet another evening of Japanese torment. It was too much. Overwhelming fatigue and stress combined with imagination and anxiety to produce something resembling widespread panic.

The official Army history recounts that when the Japanese made their presence known to the three battalions, or when the Americans thought there were Japanese within their bivouacs, there was a great deal of confusion, shooting and stabbing. Some men knifed each other. Men threw grenades blindly in the dark. Some of the grenades hit trees, bounced back, and exploded among the Americans. Some soldiers fired round after round to little avail. In the morning no trace remained of the Japanese dead or wounded. But there were American casualties; some had been stabbed to death, some wounded by knives. Many suffered grenade wounds, and 50 percent of these were caused by fragments from American grenades.

Ominously, there now appeared the first large number of shaken hollow-eyed men suffering from a strange malady, later diagnosed as "combat neuroses." (Before the end of July, the 169th would suffer seven hundred such cases of battle fatigue.)

After an hour-long bombardment of suspected Japanese positions on 9 July, the offensive jumped off. Progress was slow. The difficult terrain, the absence of tactical intelligence regarding Japanese defenses, and the physical depletion of the troops all hindered the advance. Weighted down with equipment and ammunition, the men forded the rain-swollen river and its twisted tributaries. Between streams, they slogged through mangrove swamps, struggling to stay upright while trying to find their way without accurate maps.

Soldiers in the lead platoons had to cut their way through the tangles of rattan vines that knotted the jungle. Narrow trails forced units to advance in single-file columns, churning the trails into mud and allowing a few hidden Japanese to slow the advance. By the late afternoon, the 172d had gained approximately 1,100 yards.

Farther inland, the 169th made little progress, still shaken from the previous night. Advancing along Munda Trail the next day, the 169th struck the first line of the Japanese main defenses.

Despite the slow advance, both regiments soon had overextended supply lines. The primeval jungles of New Georgia, and the Solomons in general, were thankless places to build roads. The 118th Engineer Battalion spared no effort to construct a road—more accurately, a jeep trail—from Zanana to the front, but even its indefatigable exertions could not speed road building in a jungle crisscrossed with streams.

As the road's terminus gradually fell farther and farther behind the advancing troops, ammunition, food, water, and other supplies had to be hand-carried to the front and casualties carried to the rear. Half of the combat troops soon were performing such duties, and Allied cargo planes were pressed into service to parachute supplies to the troops.

General Hester recognized that logistical shortcomings were restraining his advance and decided to shorten his supply line. He ordered the 172[d] to push through the mangrove swamp behind Laiana, two miles east of Munda, and establish a new beachhead.

On 13 July, when the Army infantry units landed at Laiana Beach on new Georgia about 2 1/2 miles east of Munda Airfield, a detachment of 22 men from the 9th Marine Defense Battalion accompanied them with one 40-mm, one twin 20-mm, and two .50-cal. machine guns to defend the landing site.

Skipper John McNeill and his LCT-159 crew made several short runs between Rendova and New Georgia ferrying troops and cargo. Here are two of the most memorable:

> We steamed up to Rendova to join the assault on Munda Point. The Army was bogged down in the jungle and a reserve Division was called up to break the stalemate. Over on New Georgia, the 43rd was in trouble and our mission was to take five tanks from Rendova and land them near the front lines.
>
> As we were loading, we were attacked by a group of Val dive bombers. They had sneaked in at low level behind the mountains. They were on us before we could open fire, but luckily their aim was poor and the bombs fell in the water. However, a piece of shrapnel struck James Hunt, my Columbia classmate and skipper of LCT-134, and severed his leg...I was deeply sorry.

We stood out of Rendova, cleared the Onaiavisi Entrance and...carefully felt our way through the coral reefs by masthead navigation and aerial photographs, and approached Zanana Beach. A sniper had set up on a very small island off the beach and we contributed a drum of 20-mm shells to his destruction as we passed. The tanks were landed without problems and we returned to Rendova.

Mr. Jones [Lt Ashton L. Jones LCT Group 13 Commander] met me and said a reconnaissance was needed on the Munda Bar. This meant that a frontal assault on Munda Point was being considered and, although our artillery at Rendova was reaching this area, it was uncertain what effect it was having. An LCVP was ready with an Army and a Marine Colonel, Mr. Jones and me, plus two native guides.

We left Rendova and approached Munda Bar, which, besides the reef, consisted of some very small wooded inlets. We drew considerable machine gun fire, fortunately out of range. We went as close to Munda Point as we thought practical and made observations of water depth and coral formations. On the return across the Bay, the machine gun fire was heavier and we responded with our two 30-caliber machine guns. Returning safely, we made our report and went back to our ship.

According to Austin Volk, skipper of LCT-60, "The real action was ferrying war materiel from Rendova Harbor over to Munda Point where the fighting was taking place." Makes sense since that short run was made to order for the LCTs.

While General Hester's southern forces prepare to establish a new beachhead, let's examine the amphibious operation of the Northern Landing Group at Rice Anchorage.

Northern Landing Group, 5-19 July 1943 [11]

RAdm Turner's last minute plans called for a 4 July amphibious landing at Rice Anchorage, 15 miles north of Munda Point on the New Georgia side of Kula Gulf. The actual landing was delayed until 5 July due to a necessary troop unit shift. The tasks of the Landing Force of the Northern Landing Group were to:

- Close the back door to Munda and prevent its reinforcement from Kolombangara Island by seizing Enogai Inlet and Bairoko Harbor, and
- Prevent the escape of the Munda garrison when it was placed under heavy attack from the flank and front.

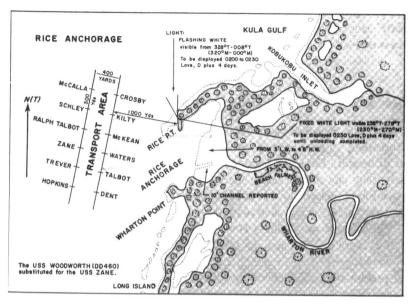

Rice Anchorage on the northwest coast of New Georgia Island.

Rice Anchorage was chosen rather than Enogai Inlet or Bairoko Harbor because Japanese troops at these two ports were closer to Munda, and hence easier to support or reinforce.

The mission of the Northern Landing Group was to embark 2,600 Marine and Army troops at Guadalcanal and land them at Rice Anchorage. The Escort Group Commander was RAdm Ainsworth, CTG 36.1, and the Landing Force Commander was Col Harry B. Liversedge, USMC. The Transport Group Commander was Cmdr Stanley Leith. CTF 31 had directed that all transports must leave the Transport Area by 0700 on 5 July, in order to reduce the chance of daylight air raids during the return to base.

During the night of 4-5 July, in preparation for these landings, a task force of cruisers (*Honolulu, Helena,* and *St. Louis*) and destroyers (*Nicholas, O'Bannon, Strong,* and *Chevalier*) under RAdm Walden L. Ainsworth, bombarded enemy positions and gun installations in the Vila-Stanmore and Bairoko Harbor areas.

During the first leg of the bombardment which opened at 0026 on 5 July, the cruisers and rear destroyers (*O'Bannon* and *Chevalier*) subjected the Vila target objectives to a heavy and extremely accurate fire. Salvos were employed at six second intervals. The bombardment plan called for firing 14 minutes without ceasing on a course of 190 degrees T., checking fire long enough to change course 100 degrees to port and then firing for six or seven minutes on targets in Bairoko Harbor. Once the bombardment had commenced, however, enemy shore batteries forced some deviation from this plan.

As the flagship changed course to the northward after completing its bombardment of Bairoko, only one destroyer ahead appeared upon the screen. Almost immediately the missing destroyer was identified as the *Strong*, and within a few moments she was located, on the starboard side of the *Honolulu*, dead in the water as a result of a torpedo hit received at 0043.

The destroyers *Chevalier* and *O'Bannon* were detailed to conduct rescue operations, during which enemy shore batteries repeatedly illuminated the whole area with star shells and the three ships were subjected to accurate and intense fire from the beach as well as to bombing by Japanese planes circling above them.

Loss of USS *Strong* (DD-467)

In going alongside the *Strong*, the *Chevalier* struck the sinking ship on her port bow, opening a hole in her own bow ten feet long and two feet wide at the level of the first platform deck. All damage was above the waterline, however, and did not seriously impair the operation of the ship.

A 6-inch manila line was passed, and every effort was made to expedite transfer of personnel from the *Strong*, as she was settling fast. Before the *Chevalier* retired she managed to rescue seven officers and 232 men during a period of nine minutes.

While the *Strong* was sinking, she was hit twice by one of the shore batteries. As she disappeared at 0123, at least four of her depth charges exploded below the forward part of the *Chevalier*, lifting that vessel nearly out of the water and rendering her radar and compasses inoperative.

Several hours later the commanding officer of the *Strong*, Cmdr Joseph H. Wellings, was picked up by one of the screening destroyers of the transport group. He was on a raft with a small number of other *Strong* survivors and was suffering from concussion caused by the depth charges. Some of the *Strong* survivors were shell-shocked, while others were blinded by fuel oil.

The source of the torpedo which sank the *Strong* is not definitely known. It may have been a submarine on the westward or northwestward side of the *Strong* or possibly two destroyers which are believed to have left Kula Gulf at high speed about 0040. Since only one ship was attacked and no other ships reported torpedo wakes, it is possible that the damage was inflicted by a two-man submarine.

In spite of the many shells which fell in the transport area there were no casualties. The *Waters* had her main truck shot away, and several of the other transports were hit by shrapnel but sustained no damage. At 0110, soon after the bombardment ceased, the landing operations began. (By this time our beachheads east of Munda were firmly established, and preparations were being made to advance on Munda Airfield.)

Rice Landing Force

The force involved in the landing operations consisted of a fast transport group made up of 7 APDs (*Dent, Talbot, Waters, McKean, Kilty, Crosby,* and *Schley*) and destroyer *McCalla*; a mine group

Marine Raiders pull away from APD in rubber boats.

composed of *Hopkins, Trevor,* and the destroyer *Ralph Talbot,* and a screening unit comprising the *Woodworth, Gwin,* and *Radford.*

As stated earlier, the Northern Landing Group, commanded by Col Harry "The Horse" Liversedge, USMC, consisted of one battalion each from the 145th and 148th Infantry, 37th Division, and the 1st Raider Battalion, 1st Marine Raider Regiment.

About 0130 on 5 July, the amphibians launched all boats in a driving rainstorm and began disembarking the Marines and Army troops. The lights on the beach were not due to be turned on until 0200, so the coxswains did not even have these feeble aids to assist them in the heavy rain when the first boats left for the beach at 0145.

In the hurry to unload the transports, some of the ships overloaded their landing boats with the result that the landing boats could not clear the reef blocking the entrance to Wharton River. These boats had to return to their transports to lighten their loads and make a second try. It was a case of "haste makes waste."

The Northern Landing Group, built around the 1st Marine Raider Regiment, landed at Rice Anchorage on 5 July and proceeded cross-country to take Enogai on Dragons Peninsula. The Marine third from the left hefts a Boys rifle used by the Raiders as an anti-tank weapon. Courtesy U.S. Marine Corps.

The Rice Anchorage beach was several miles northeast up the coast from the Bairoko-Enogai area. Shallow water and a narrow landing beach hindered the landing more than the inaccurate Japanese shelling. Liversedge planned for two companies from the 3rd Battalion, 145th Infantry, to defend the landing site, while the rest of the battalion, the 1st Marine Raider Battalion and the 3rd Battalion, 148th Infantry, moved to Dragons Peninsula.

There the 3rd Battalion, 148th, would veer southwest and take up a blocking position along the Munda-Bairoko trail. Remaining forces would clear the peninsula and take Bairoko. Because speed was so important, Liversedge's force was lightly armed and provisioned, carrying only three days' worth of rations.

Moving out early on 5 July, the men soon learned that, contrary to earlier intelligence reports, following the rough trails hacked out of the jungle by coastwatchers and native New Georgians would be exceedingly tough.

Constant rain plagued the first weeks of the campaign, making more dismal the task of struggling up and down jungle hills seemingly composed in equal parts of sharp coral and thick clinging

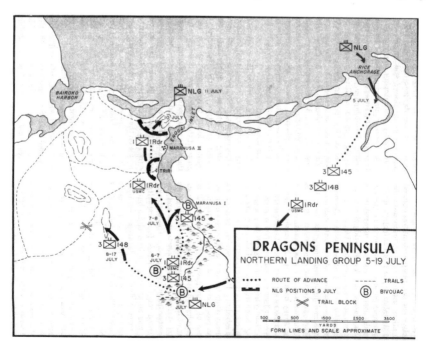

DRAGONS PENINSULA
NORTHERN LANDING GROUP 5-19 JULY

vines. The rain also added unforeseen tasks; one stream soon became a nine foot deep river to ford. The men in the 148th's weapons company, laboring under the weight of their heavy machine guns and 81-mm. mortars, were soon far to the rear.

On the night of 5-6 July, the naval Battle of Kula Gulf erupted with the resultant loss of the cruiser USS *Helena* (CL-50). This isolated the Northern Landing Group from even naval support.

On 7 July, the Marines and two companies of the 145th Infantry reached Enogai Inlet and, after heavy skirmishing, seized the village of Triri. There they spent the night and Liversedge established his command post. The next day, while the Marines made an abortive effort to march to Enogai, several companies became involved in an extended firefight south of Triri along the trail to Bairoko, which left 120 Japanese dead.

The next morning, Marines used an unguarded trail to approach Enogai. Although their afternoon assault was unsuccessful, it provided enough information about the Japanese defenses to ensure a successful attack the following day.

Despite the capture of Enogai, Liversedge's tactical situation remained difficult. Already five days behind schedule and with

During a lull in the fight, a Marine machine gunner takes a break for coffee, with his sub-machine gun on his knee and his .30-caliber light machine gun in position. Courtesy U.S. Marine Corps.

many wounded, he was so short of supplies that he was receiving resupply by air. The Marine battalion was at one-half of its effective strength. Liversedge needed to capture Bairoko to cut the Japanese line of communications to Munda.

Meanwhile the men of the 3rd Battalion, 148th Infantry, had forced their way around the southern side of a series of hills, until they reached the Bairoko-Munda trail. On 8 July they established a camouflaged blocking position along the trail about eight miles north of Munda. There they remained for nine days.

Although the battalion sustained eleven men killed and twenty-nine wounded in skirmishes, the Japanese did not make a determined attempt to eliminate the trail block. Willing to let an American battalion isolate itself deep in the jungle, they simply bypassed it by using more westerly trails to reinforce Munda.

More naval surface actions occurred the night of 12-13 July as the U.S. Navy intercepted Japanese destroyers and cruisers attempting to resupply forces on Vila and Munda. The ships' gunfire looked like a giant lightning storm followed by massive thunder and permitted little sleep for the observers ashore. More on the surface battles later in this chapter.

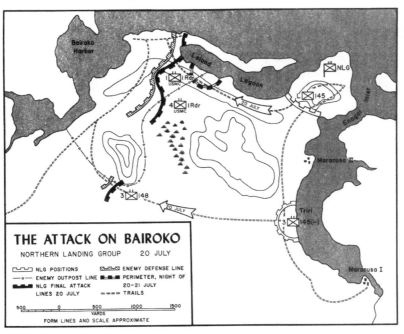

THE ATTACK ON BAIROKO

NORTHERN LANDING GROUP   20 JULY

NLG POSITIONS   ENEMY DEFENSE LINE
ENEMY OUTPOST LINE   PERIMETER, NIGHT OF
NLG FINAL ATTACK   20-21 JULY
LINES 20 JULY   TRAILS

500   0   500   1000   1500
YARDS
FORM LINES AND SCALE APPROXIMATE

The unit's severest trial was its food shortage, and here, too, supplies had to be airdropped. Finally, on 17 July, Liversedge ordered the battalion to abandon the trail block and move north to assist with the attack on Bairoko.

Three days later, Col Liversedge's force, reinforced by the 4th Marine Raider Battalion, launched a prepared attack against Bairoko's fortified positions. Lacking artillery support and tactical intelligence, outgunned by Japanese 90-mm mortars firing from across Bairoko Harbor, and unable to obtain timely close air support, the attack failed.

The failure to seize the objective and the severe American losses were plainly the result of poor logistics and a lack of firepower. A Joint Chiefs of Staff post-mortem on the operation noted that "lightly armed troops cannot be expected to attack fixed positions defended by heavy automatic weapons, mortars, and heavy artillery." The Raiders might still have won with a suicidal effort, but Bairoko was not worth it.

The 1st Raider Regiment and its assorted battalions settled into defensive positions for the rest of July. The sole action consisted of patrols toward Bairoko and nuisance raids from Japanese aircraft. In early August elements of the force took up new blocking positions on the Munda-Bairoko Trail.

Soldiers and Marines consolidate their positions and construct barbed wire obstacles on Dragons Peninsula after the attack on Bairoko. Their apparent condition, mixture of clothing, and the ever-present jungle, provide eloquent testimony to the physical demands of the campaign. U.S. Marine Corps.

On 9 August they made contact with Army troops from the Southern Landing Group. In the meantime, the main enemy force had escaped by sea and American soldiers took control of the harbor on 24 August. The Raider headquarters and both Marine battalions embarked in transports on 28 August and sailed for Guadalcanal.

The Northern Landing Group's campaign had been a costly one. Total American casualties were 49 killed, 200 wounded, and two missing—the vast majority of them suffered by the Raider battalions.

Each Marine Raider battalion had suffered battle casualties of more than 25 percent. In addition, sickness had claimed an even greater number. The 1st Raiders now had just 245 effectives; the 4th Raiders only 154.

Let's return to the Southern Landing Group and the Munda-Bairoko Occupation Force (MBOF). But first, it's time for a little break. Remember Jack Johnson, skipper of LCT-182, one of our better storytellers? He also became one of the better SOPAC "operators" according to his peers. During our interview, Jack always called a spade a spade; my kind of up-front guy. So sit back. He's got three sea stories for you.

Early in our interview, Jack said he had been accused of borrowing provisions from Major General John Hester. I asked Jack to elaborate:

> **CHICKEN CAPER** – Well, you know our LCTs congregated in Rendova Harbor. That was about 10 miles from Munda Point. Now we were supposed to put the flag up there in four days. It took us 37 days. It was such a screw-up. General Hester was Army. I had him aboard one time. He was a little fart. He wore these high lace-up boots and carried a riding crop. Vandegrift, the Marine General who had been at Guadalcanal, offered to help him and Hester turned him down. He wanted him to know it was an Army operation.
>
> Anyhow, over in Rendova, there was this big stack of canned chicken. Now, we were on Spam and hadn't had any good food in weeks. So, I went over and asked for a couple of cases for my crew and this Colonel said, 'Oh no, this is for General Hester's officers.' So I went back to our Commander Jones and he said, 'I know what you mean. Let me check into it.'

A few days later, Jones says to us over the radio—we all had nick-names like 'Storybook', 'Liberty' and 'Magazines'—'pick up your re-quested loads.' It was this canned chicken. So, we stacked it aboard. Oh hell, there was like a half a boxcar full of it. Anyway, as soon as I got through the Onaiavisi Entrance, I pulled off to the left and these 105s were all lined up. They were shooting over our heads up into the hills trying to hit the Japs and the noise was terrible, but anyway, I pulled in pretty close.

Every LCT was pulling out and I said, send a message. 'Come alongside for good chow!' They would come alongside and we'd throw off 2 or 3 cases and they would immediately stow it. We were throwing cases down into one of our storage tanks. I took probably 40 cases. I waited until right before dark then pulled in so the crew could unload them, then we pulled back off. We always anchored at night, because the Japs had these guys and they could float along and throw hand grenades up on you.

The next morning I pulled in and here's this Colonel. He says, 'I'm down here for the canned chicken that you stole.' I said, 'We unloaded last night and you had no working party here. We had to retract before dark.' With that he said, 'I'm coming aboard.' I says, 'I'm Captain, you're not coming aboard.' I pulled out my pistol and said, 'You get my permission or you get shot.' He says, 'I'm going to have you court-martialed.' I said, 'Go ahead. I been out here a couple of years. I'd welcome a trial back in the States.' He backed off then. I did get a nasty letter from the Army.

Hell, by that time the food had been consumed. I got pretty tired of eating canned chicken and biscuits. I couldn't take anymore. I think our group commander Kouri taught us how to do that. Hell, he'd steal bulldozers and everything else off the Army. There for a while, all LCTs had jeeps aboard. We would paint them as soon as they came aboard and change their looks so whenever we got ashore someplace, we could go sightseeing.

PILOT RESCUE – In the time I was down there [Solomons] my LCT-182 crew pulled, I think, five flyers out of the 'drink.' They used to spot us. Our crew would say, 'Here comes one, he's smokin',' and they would let down ahead of us, maybe 500 yards. We would lower the ramp and they would just walk off the wing. They never even got their feet wet.

One of the fellas was a Marine pilot. He didn't want me to report saving him. I had him for two weeks and finally convinced him that his folks would be getting a missing in action letter and everything, so I dumped him off in the Russells. He was enjoying a little R and R. He would fish off the stern. They had a lot of pressure on them. Later, I saw him get killed.

GAS ATTACK – I had a scare at Segi Point one time. We took an evaporator over there to make fresh water. We tied up near where the Seabees were cutting an airstrip out of the jungle. They were covering the strip with coral while we were there, and I can remember unloading that big evaporator. It was on skids and the Seabees used a bulldozer to pull it off the deck.

Anyway, we stayed there for the night. That same night the Japs bombed the runway and it blew that coral stuff all over us. We had heard that the Japs were using poison gas. Boy, I thought this is it, when that big cloud came over us. I yelled to everybody to get their masks on. We tested for gas and they all had a laugh on me. I felt sure that we were getting poison gas, but we weren't.

THE ASSAULT ON MUNDA POINT

The offensive was sputtering, and MGen Hester's superiors were upset with the lack of progress on New Georgia. General Harmon soon began pressing Admiral Halsey, over Admiral Turner's objections, to send part, if not all, of the XIV Corps headquarters to New Georgia. Recognizing that the workload of the 43rd Division staff had to be reduced—it was conducting operations on New Georgia as well as preparing for the upcoming attack on Kolombangara—Harmon flew to Halsey's headquarters on New Caledonia to press the issue. Halsey agreed.

Command Changes

Major General Oscar W. Griswold USA, arrived on Rendova with an advance section of his headquarters on 11 July and quickly assessed the situation. "Things are going badly," he radioed Harmon on the morning of 13 July. The 43rd Division looked "about to fold up." He recommended that the remainder of the 37th Division, then in reserve, and the 25th Division on Guadalcanal be committed immediately to combat. Harmon, whom Halsey recently had placed in charge of New Georgia ground operations, instructed Griswold to be prepared to assume command and promised reinforcements.

MGen Griswold relieved General Hester as Commander of XIV Corps at midnight on 15-16 July. Earlier that day there had been another command change. RAdm Turner, who in Harmon's opinion had been "inclined more and more to take active control of land operations," left to assume a new command in the Central Pacific theater. His replacement was Halsey's deputy, RAdm Theodore S. Wilkinson. General Harmon may have thought he convinced Adm Halsey to relieve VAdm Turner while he was at it, but nothing could be farther from the truth.

As early as 13 June 1943: Admiral Nimitz, CINCPAC, had proposed to Admiral King, COMINCH, that RAdm Turner be relieved by RAdm Wilkinson "after completion first stage New Georgia Operation," and be ordered to command the Amphibious Forces, Central Pacific and the Fifth Amphibious Force being formed up for the Central Pacific campaign. This future employment of RAdm Turner received a favorable nod from COMINCH, and Adm Halsey, COMSOPAC, was directed to issue the necessary orders to Turner at the appropriate time. [12]

On 24 June, COMINCH directed CINCPAC that an amphibious command with its planning staff located at Pearl Harbor "must be established at the earliest possible time," for the development and integration of amphibious plans, under VAdm Spruance's command for the Central Pacific Operation. Halsey and Turner were thus alerted that desires existed at higher levels of command for Turner's presence at Pearl Harbor at an early date.

The 9th Marine Defense Battalion's platoon of light tanks played an important role in the assault on Munda Airfield. During the next five days, the 9th's tanks spearheaded the advance knocking out enemy log bunkers, pillboxes, and other strong points. On a number of occasions during the assault on the enemy's final defense positions north of Ilanana, the tank platoon operated in the densely wooded and irregular terrain under conditions believed highly unsuitable for tank employment. For the first time, the Japanese attacked the tanks with magnetic mines and Molotov cocktails (bottles of gasoline with lit wicks.)

On the morning of 15 July, the tanks broke through the enemy's strong positions after Army infantry had repeatedly been thrown back.

Reorganize and Reinforce

Ground operations were well behind schedule and the troops worn. Griswold decided not to renew the offensive until the supply situation improved and his troops were reorganized and reinforced. To improve logistics, he designated a specific offshore island to serve as a supply dump for each division. Griswold also accelerated expansion of the Laiana beachhead, as well as the engineers' furious road-building effort, which allowed supplies to be stockpiled nearer the front line.

Reinforcements were badly needed. By 17 July the 43rd Division's casualties were 90 dead and 636 wounded. More than a thousand men had contracted diseases. Diarrhea was a common affliction, while dysentery cases and malaria relapses were prevalent. One-quarter of the men were suffering from varying degrees of skin fungus. Additionally, between fifty and one hundred men left the line each day as neuroses cases.

In the opinion of the XIV Corps surgeon, who flew in on 14 July, there was no doubt that the major reason for these "non-battle casualties" was combat fatigue—extreme exhaustion exacerbated by atrocious living conditions. Little could be done until rest camps could be built on the offshore islands. The high incidence of casualties due to disease and combat fatigue would continue throughout the campaign.

Munda Attack Stalled

While the XIV Corps attack on Munda was stalled by both the dogged resistance of the defenders and the rugged terrain, the Marines' "Murderers' Row" of 155-mm guns continued shelling the Munda Airfield, Baanga Island, and other outlying islands from Rendova. The primary targets were anti-aircraft and field artillery positions, and ammunition dumps. Directed by both ground and air observers, this firing proved very effective. "The artillery shelling's accuracy has become a real thing. We can never tell when we are to die," wrote a Munda defender.

Concurrently, the U.S. Army's 169th was involved in a savage fight to occupy the high ground north of Munda. The combat location was eerily reminiscent of World War I. More than once, infantrymen, following their artillery barrage, clambered over shattered trees and shell craters to attack Japanese machine gunners in pillboxes with only rifles and bayonets.

Also evoking echoes of the Western Front were high casualties and progress that was measured in yards. After five days of attacks, the 169th's 3rd Battalion had penetrated 500 yards into the Japanese defenses. The battalion paid for its achievement with 101 casualties in the first twenty-four hours after the penetration. There on Reincke Ridge, in the high ground south of Munda Trail, the regiment regrouped and prepared to assault the main defensive line on imposing Horseshoe Hill.

The buildup of forces on New Georgia continued with the arrival of elements of MGen J. Lawton Collins' 25th Infantry Division on 21 July and the arrival the next day of the remainder of the 37th Infantry Division. What one division failed to accomplish would now be attempted by two, the 43rd and the 37th.

After their initial daytime air losses, the Japanese relied on air attacks at night with only infrequent daylight bombings. One was mounted against the Rendova area on 20 July by six planes, one on 1 August by another six planes, and another on 7 August by a formation of 15 aircraft.

Several larger strikes were turned back by A-A fire. According to Army historians, a total of 26 enemy planes were downed over Rendova by A-A fire of the 9th Marine Defense Battalion.

USS LST-343 Bombed

On 21 July 1943, LST-343 was beached on the western side of Kukorana Island off Rendova receiving casualties to be evacuated. At 1655, the ship went to General Quarters when enemy planes were reported 25 miles southwest of Rendova Island. The 343 Action Report described the action: [13]

> At 1709 six "Val" (Aichi 99) dive bombers were sighted at an altitude of 7,000 feet coming out of a cloud southwest of the ship. They immediately dove in the ship's direction. Three headed north and passed over Bau Island, one headed east and passed over Rendova Island.
>
> Two planes came toward the ship from the starboard quarter at 1710. The planes released their bombs from about 2,000 feet. The first and third bombs of the first plane straddled the ship, the second hit the superstructure, starboard side, frame 36. The bombs from the second plane passed over the ship and landed on the beach. Both planes were shot down by this ship's 20-mm anti-aircraft guns.

The direct hit, believed to have been a 300-pound demolition bomb, penetrated the superstructure and exploded in wardroom country. Resulting casualties: one killed, one died later from wounds received, two seriously wounded, and ten received minor injuries. Capt Gendreau, USN, Pacific Fleet Medical Officer, was one of those killed.

The entire superstructure was severely damaged, surrounding decks and bulkheads buckled, the wardroom country was almost completely demolished, the radio equipment was damaged, and the steering gear was inoperative. During the next three months, the 343 would undergo repairs at Espiritu Santo.

Captain Carter, ComLSTFLOT 5, included the following observations/recommendations in his endorsement of the LST-343 Action Report of 27 July 1943:

> At the time of this attack, USS LST-472 was beached about 25 yards on the starboard beam of USS LST-343, a practice which should be definitely discouraged for obvious reasons of minimizing target presentment.
>
> That this attack was successful is believed to be due to the fact that LST is insufficiently armed to repel plane attacks. There is definite need for augmenting automatic armament of LSTs...
>
> The Group Commander, Captain, Officers, and Men of this vessel are to be commended for their conduct during this action...
>
> Excellent work was done by the Commanding Officer, Lieutenant H. H. Rightmeyer, USN, in handling the fire which developed and in readying the ship for return to Guadalcanal, and he is to be highly commended.

The Final Offensive

Griswold's Corps offensive began on 25 July with five regiments attacking abreast. The 43rd Division with two regiments in line (103rd on the coast, 172^d—later the 169th—on its right) moved along the coast. Farther inland, the 37th Division (north to south: 148th, 161st, and 145th Regiments) made the main attack, combining a frontal assault with a flanking movement designed to envelop the Japanese northern flank, take Bibilo Hill, and swoop down on Munda.

Achieving Munda would not be easy. In defense were approximately three Japanese infantry battalions in fortified positions. Also

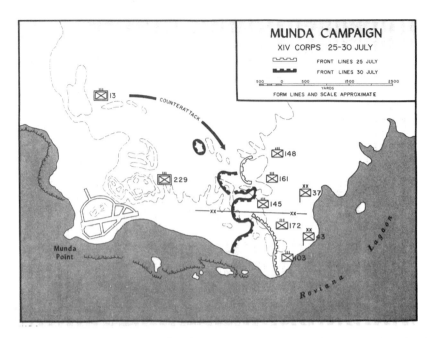

off the American right flank were survivors of a unit that had attacked the 169th Infantry during the night of 17-18 July. Driven off with heavy losses, they now lurked in the jungle awaiting an opportunity.

Most foreboding was information from the 172d Infantry, which, with the support of Marine tanks, had cleared the Laiana beachhead of Japanese during the logistic buildup. These operations revealed the nature of the main Japanese defenses: machine gunners and riflemen ensconced in sturdy pillboxes with interlocking fields of fire. The pillboxes were tough obstacles. Constructed with three or four layers of coconut logs and several feet of coral, they were largely subterranean. The few feet exposed above ground contained machine-gun and rifle firing slits, so well camouflaged that American soldiers often could not determine their locations.

When the offensive resumed, therefore, so did the demanding, draining, and deadly task of assaulting hidden Japanese positions one by one—a style of warfare that chewed up rifle companies and became all too familiar to American ground troops in the Pacific.

Because the enemy was virtually invisible in his pillboxes and rarely fired indiscriminately, reconnaissance squads and platoons frequently could not determine the extent of Japanese defenses; details of Japanese positions often remained unknown until the attack.

Once infantrymen located an enemy position, they called in artillery fire which made the position visible amidst the jungle growth, if not destroying it outright. Next, mortars with delay fuses would fire on visible positions. Finally, a platoon or company assaulted with support by whatever heavy weapons were available.

When full reconnaissance was not possible, troops had to attack the terrain, seize and occupy pieces of ground while calling in mortar fire on likely pillbox sites. A tactic of necessity, attacking the terrain could be risky against more than light opposition. The operations officer of the 145th Infantry noted, "Enemy strong points encountered in this fashion often times resulted in hasty withdrawals which were costly both in men and weapons."

Further, although they lacked anti-tank guns, the Japanese soon adopted measures to knock out tanks lacking infantry support. American troops quickly learned the importance of close infantry-armor coordination for successfully assaulting Japanese positions.

Flamethrowers in action at Munda. Courtesy U.S. Army.

Likewise, although flame-throwers proved useful in attacking pillboxes, the operator had to expose his head and torso and was likely to be shot unless supporting infantry provided suppressive fire. Just as in tank-infantry operations, troops learned that mutual cooperation and support between riflemen and flame-thrower operators were vital to success.

Once integrated with infantry, both tanks and flame-throwers were important infantry-support weapons on New Georgia, especially because the irregular shape of the front line and the poor quality of available maps often made artillery support impractical.

Over the next several days, the regiments clawed their way forward through the Japanese defenses. The gritty, vicious fighting continued as small groups of men eliminated pillboxes and their supporting foxholes, but hard-won experience now began to pay dividends, and the pace of the American advance quickened. On 29 July Harmon replaced an exhausted Hester with Maj Gen John R. Hodge, the Americal Division commander. Hodge had been the assistant division commander of the 25th Division during the fighting on Guadalcanal and was experienced in jungle warfare. Harmon told Griswold that Hodge was the "best Division Commander I have in the area for this particular job."

The Fall of Munda Airfield

Concurrent with the change in American command, the Japanese withdrew to a final defensive line in front of the airfield. They had suffered heavy casualties and, unbeknownst to the Americans, their main defenses had been shattered.

The Japanese withdrawal facilitated the XIV Corps advance, but did not make it any less dangerous. On 29 July the 172^d was attacking the last high ground protecting Munda field trying to break through the Japanese defensive line, when 1st Lt Robert S. Scott almost single-handedly blunted a Japanese counterattack. Although he was wounded in the head and had his rifle shot from his hand, Scott refused to retreat and inspired his company to seize the hill.

Two days later, a medic in the 145th Infantry, PFC Frank J. Petrarca, who had repeatedly demonstrated his commitment to treating wounded soldiers without regard for his own safety, was killed when he went to the aid of a mortar victim lying in an area swept by enemy fire. Both were awarded the Medal of Honor.

To the north, at the far right of the American line, the 148th Infantry had not encountered prepared defenses. Moving far ahead of the regiment to its left, the 148th was attacked by the Japanese lurking off the American right flank. The Japanese were too few to destroy the Americans outright, but, divided into small groups, they managed to encircle and harass the American rear areas for several days.

Slowed by the need to transport a growing number of wounded, the 148th stolidly worked back to the American line, fighting through innumerable ambushes and raids. It was in the midst of this withdrawal that a Japanese machine gun on higher ground fired on Pvt Rodger W. Young's platoon. Although wounded by the first bursts, Young attacked on his own initiative until he was killed, firing and throwing hand grenades and allowing his platoon to escape. Private Young was also awarded the Medal of Honor.

The tank platoon of the 10th Marine Defense Battalion, reinforced by five tanks from the 11th Defense Battalion and the surviving tank of the 9th Defense Battalion, led the assault on Kokengolo and Bibilo Hills. After two days of heavy fighting, they routed the defending forces and helped clear the way to the principal objective of the entire New Georgia campaign, the Munda Airfield.

In early August, John McNeill and his LCT-159 crew were ordered to transport a 90-mm gun from Kokorana, a small island off the entrance to Rendova Harbor, to an islet near Munda Point. At Kokorana, the crew put out hawsers from the bow to some coconut trees on the beach and John called for slow ahead on the engines—standard procedure. However when the tractor operator pushed the big gun down a rather steep incline, (in the rain, yet) things got complicated. The heavy gun and tractor began to slip and slide and the operator lost control. Here's McNeill:

> The gun hit the edge of the ramp and the impact snapped the beach lines and pushed the 159 off the beach. The gun, alas, dropped into 70 feet of water. I was terribly embarrassed and laid off the beach while the gun was salvaged by a mobile crane. Another gun was available

so we returned to the beach, put out extra lines, and went ahead full-speed on the engines to hold the ship securely on the beach.

The replacement 90-mm was successfully loaded along with the gun crew and several hundred rounds of ammunition. I was given a chart and an aerial photograph showing a very small islet lying about 200 yards off Munda Airfield. We were to approach the islet from the 'blind side' and land the gun and ammunition in preparation for the final assault on Munda Airfield.

We crossed Blanche Channel and slowly passed through Onaiavisi Entrance into Roviana Lagoon. Carefully moving through the coral reefs, we passed the front lines near Laiana Beach and approached within a few hundred yards of Munda Point, on which the airstrip extended to the water's edge. We couldn't see any troops, but many large artillery shells were falling on the airstrip. I sighted the islet and began our approach, keeping the islet between the 159 and Munda.

When we landed, we were able to get the ramp down properly, so a bulldozer could pull the gun ashore....We then unloaded the ammo and backed away from the islet....As we left the area, we could see the first of our troops reach the runway. However, the Japs held out at the other end for another day.

We returned to Rendova and the next day I noticed the ship was listing to starboard. I could see no visible reason for this and had the Chief sound the voids below deck. Soon he called me and reported serious trouble. He said, 'Skipper, there ain't no bottom on this ship!' He ran a sounding rod through a test plate and could not contact anything.

Alarmed, I jumped overboard and swam under the ship and discovered we had lost an entire 4 x 8 foot bottom plate, which accounted for our list. Since there were no repair facilities in the area, we continued to operate with the 32-square-foot hole in our bottom.

However, McNeill and his crew were forced to return to Tulagi for repairs about the middle of August. As McNeill put it:

Our engines were giving us trouble and were badly in need of overhaul. They now had 4,500 hours of operation, the only LCT in the Flotilla to go over 4,000 without an overhaul. One day the port engine went out and the others were smoking badly...

We got underway around dark and headed for Tulagi alone. Our speed was about 4 knots and the smoke from the exhaust was heavy...

When we arrived at Carter City, our main base, the 159 was a sorry sight. With shrapnel holes in the hull, a 10 percent list to starboard, a coat of rust and the smoking engines, we 'roared' into the harbor at about 3 knots. The crew was in about the same condition, not having slept in two nights...

After a slight "confrontation" with the repair base Chief Machinist Mate over whether LCT-159 should receive new or rebuilt engines, base personnel installed three new engines.

Several other LCT Flotilla 5 craft straggled in for repairs over the next few days including the boats of Bob Capeless (LCT-62), Bob Carr (LCT-367) and "Bo" Gillette (LCT-369).

Shortly thereafter, these illustrious pioneer skippers received a big surprise. They were relieved of their duties as Officers-in-Charge, promoted to the rank of Lieutenant (jg) and reassigned as division commanders of 6 LCTs each (numbers to be announced at a later date). They were then detailed to the Flotilla 5 staff and billeted in a quonset hut ashore. They received their orders to return to the States in October 1943 for new assignments as LCT Training Officers at the Solomons ATB in Maryland. They had come full circle!

Meanwhile back at Munda, the end came more quickly than any had foreseen. American troops reached the airfield's perimeter and encircled it on 3 August. But Sasaki's remnants were still able to charge admission to Munda Field by bitter resistance, particularly at the base of two hills. Army infantrymen and Marine tanks harried the enemy all day. Americans inundated the hills with mortar and 37-mm fire until they literally made the top of Bibilo bounce. Japanese soldiers' guns and pillboxes flew as much as 15 feet into the air, while some unfortunates, blown out of their holes, "ran around in little circles like stunned chickens," to be mowed down by machine guns.

On 5 August the Americans overran Munda, with 43rd Division infantrymen killing or driving the remaining Japanese from their bunkers, tunnels, and pillboxes. From Bibilo Hill, General Wing informed General Hodge, "Munda is yours at 1410 today." Operational within two weeks, Munda's 6,000-foot runway soon made it the most-used airfield in the Solomons.

From Bibilo Hill, General Wing informed General Hodge,
"Munda is yours at 1410 today."
— New Georgia, 4 Aug. 1943

By 1500 on 5 August all major organized resistance at Munda had ceased, two days less than a year after the first landing of the Marines at Guadalcanal and six weeks after the invasion of New Georgia.

Seabee Miracles [14] – Three weeks after the opening of the airstrip at Segi, the last Japanese had been killed at Munda. On 9 August 1943, advance platoons of the 73rd Naval Construction Battalion began work on the blasted Jap air base. The Japanese had been unable to operate the field for eight weeks, but Commander Kendrick P. Doane, CEC, USNR, leader of the 73rd Seabees, was ordered to have the field in operation by 18 August.

Naval Construction Battalions on the job. Courtesy Claude Gulbranson.

On 11 August additional units of the 73ʳᵈ NCB arrived, and Doane ordered round-the-clock operations. The weather gods smiled at last, and a full moon came out to make artificial lighting unnecessary. In just two more days the men had repaired the north and south runways, and American planes began landing at Munda on the afternoon of 13 August—four Army Curtiss P-40 Warhawks made an unscheduled landing to "christen the field."

During the night of the 13th, the battalion completed additional hardstands off the runways, and on the 14th began receiving additional air units, including VMF-123 and -124. Other Marine squadrons soon arrived, including the VMF-214 "Black Sheep" of Major Gregory "Pappy" Boyington, who reportedly became a grudging admirer of the Marines' anti-aircraft marksmanship and a source of entertainment with his radio transmissions while flying over Munda.

Supplying Enogai – On 15 August, APc 25, accompanied by LCTs 325 and 327, proceeded from Lunga Point to Enogai, via Russell Islands, Segi Point, Mongo Entrance and Visu Visu Point, arriving on 16 August. You can bet the farm Harry "The Horse" Liversedge and his Marine and Army troops were glad to see those LCTs and the supplies they had aboard!

From 2140, 15 August, when the ships were about 2 miles beyond Lever Harbor, until 0500, 16 August, when they were en route back to Lever Harbor, there was virtually continuous harassment by enemy planes. A combination of good fortune and good headwork by escorting PT Boats limited the damage to the wounding of 2 crew members of LCT-325 by flying fragments. The Motor Torpedo Boats drew the attacking planes to themselves by increasing their speed and exploding smoke charges. At one time, these smoke charges were heavily attacked by the enemy.

Seabees Build and Fight

On 15 August the 24ᵗʰ NCB, which had fought the mud battle at Rendova, arrived at Munda, and set to work to make Munda a major base.[15] The Japanese had dug an elaborate tunnel system in the coral, and many of them had died in the tunnels from our flamethrowers. The Seabees cleaned out the Japanese and converted

"Minnie" Cat and Carryall cleaning airstrip.

Road construction.

Paving operations.

Supply depot.

All courtesy U.S. Naval Construction Battalions.

the tunnels into deluxe living quarters where a man could sleep and never have to jump up and run for a foxhole.

One company of the 47th NCB, the 828th Aviation Engineers, and the 131st Army Engineers were also assigned to Munda to expedite completion of the airfield, which was ready for bomber operations before 15 October. By December 1943, the runway had been extended to 8,000 feet, and taxiways had been built along both sides. Quonset huts served for operations buildings, mess halls, and galleys; personnel were housed under canvas.

In addition to the construction of aviation facilities, the Seabees were responsible for several other projects including:

- Construction of hospitals for ACORN 8, and CUB 3, were completed in October.
- The 24th Battalion completed the erection of an aviation-gasoline tank farm of eight 1,000-barrel tanks and one 10,000-barrel tank in October.
- Housing was also provided for various naval base activities, as well as numerous steel archrib warehouses for the supply depot.
- The 73rd Battalion completed the deepening of the channel through Munda Bar to provide a 300-foot channel, 15 feet deep, for passage of LSTs and similar craft in November.

On Ondonga Island, near Munda Point, the 82d and the 37th Battalions constructed a "satellite" air and naval base with a fighter strip 4,500 feet long and 200 feet wide in 25 days, in time to provide additional coverage for the forthcoming Bougainville campaign.

The Seabees also added to the pier facilities on Roviana Lagoon. By November 1943, Companies A and D of the 9th (Special) Construction Battalion had reported to New Georgia for stevedoring operations.

In November 1943, Admiral Bill Halsey declared that Munda was the finest air base in the South Pacific. Commander Doane and his Seabees received a citation which read in part:

> Prior to commencing work at Munda there were no roads, and the airfield and taxiways were unusable due to bombardment and shelling of the area by our forces prior to its capture. In spite of shortage of personnel and equipment, and faced with a task of great magnitude,

Commander Doane was able, nevertheless, by virtue of his planning,
leadership, industry, and working "round the clock" to make service-
able the Munda Airfield on August 14th, 1943, a good four days ahead
of the original schedule.

Though subjected to shelling and bombing, both in the camp area
and on the airfield, Commander Doane and his men have expanded
the size and facilities of the airfield at a phenomenal rate....

On receipt of his citation Commander Doane commented: "It's
easy to perform construction miracles with men like the Seabees.
They are the world's finest construction men. Courage is innate
with them. They volunteered to do a job, and all they want is a
chance to finish that job as soon as possible. When we took men
like this and put them into one organization, we loaded the dice
against the Japs."

Commander Doane failed to mention one other factor which
contributed to Seabee success at Munda. He himself had built a
few airfields before he got to Munda. One of them which he helped
to plan and superintend is La Guardia Field, New York. And Commander Lyles, who set the record at Segi Point, built the Will Rogers
Airport at Oklahoma City.

The advance naval base in New Georgia was decommissioned
in March 1945. [16]

NEW GEORGIA MOP-UP

The capture of Munda Airfield on 5 August was only one phase
of the New Georgia campaign. There were still Japanese on New
Georgia, as well as on the surrounding islands of Arundel, Baanga,
Gizo, Kolombangara, and Vella Lavella. Until we controlled the
troop and supply funnels from these islands, Sasaki could threaten
the airfield. Conversely, American control of western New Georgia and the islands fringing Kula Gulf would effectively neutralize
Vila (Kolombangara). So, while Seabee battalions repaired and
improved the battered Munda Field, ground forces vanished into
the jungle for another six weeks' battling.

General Griswold had tried to prevent Japanese from escaping
during the Munda operation by encircling the airfield to prevent
withdrawals and trap Japanese troops, but this tactic proved only
partially successful.

After the Munda airstrip was captured, Griswold sent the 27th and 161st Infantry Regiments of MGen J. Lawton Collins' 25th Division in pursuit of the retreating Japanese north to Bairoko Harbor and northwest along the coast. The XIV Corps command had informed Col Harry Liversedge, USMC that Munda Point was reached and that his force should cut off the retreating Japanese near Zieta.

On 9 August, the Northern Landing Group linked up with the Southern Landing Force advancing from Munda Point and assumed control of the 1st Marine Raider Regiment.

Most Japanese moved to Arundel, Kolombangara, and Baanga, leaving behind only a small detachment to contest the American advance. U.S. troops spent two weeks eliminating these forces and finally occupied Bairoko on 25 August.

On 11 August the 169th Infantry moved onto Baanga, from where a pair of Japanese 120-mm guns had been shelling Munda Point. When the Japanese resisted strongly, the 172d also was ordered onto the small island and into the fight. The two regiments spent ten days driving the Japanese from the southern part of Baanga, losing 52 killed, 110 wounded, and 486 non-battle casualties. The remaining Japanese troops withdrew to Arundel.

Arundel Island – Adm Halsey wanted Arundel taken because of its important position. Whoever owned it controlled the Blackett Strait route from the north, and the Diamond Narrows passage from the south. Long-range artillery properly emplaced on Arundel could register on Vila or Munda.

The 172d Infantry landed

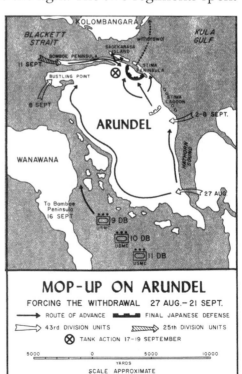

MOP-UP ON ARUNDEL

FORCING THE WITHDRAWAL   27 AUG.– 21 SEPT.

→ ROUTE OF ADVANCE ■▬■▬■ FINAL JAPANESE DEFENSE

▷ 43rd DIVISION UNITS ▷▷▷▷ 25th DIVISION UNITS

⊗ TANK ACTION 17–19 SEPTEMBER

5000   0   5000   10000

YARDS

SCALE APPROXIMATE

on 27 August, but additional troops were needed, and soon joining the 172ᵈ were the 169ᵗʰ Infantry, two battalions of the 27ᵗʰ Infantry, a 4.2-inch mortar company, plus 13 light tanks from Capt Blake's 9ᵗʰ, 10ᵗʰ, and 11ᵗʰ Marine Defense Battalions. Due to recent undetected reinforcements and because of the difficulty of its terrain—perhaps the worst in New Georgia—Japanese resistance proved stronger than expected. While combat on Arundel was viewed primarily as "mopping up small groups of Japanese," one 43ʳᵈ Division battalion commander later described the fighting on Arundel as "the most bitter combat of the New Georgia campaign." The fighting continued through the first three weeks of September, when, once again, remaining Japanese troops withdrew at night, this time to Kolombangara leaving 500 dead on Arundel Island. The Americans lost 44 dead, 256 wounded.

Marine Capt Reichner's Battery A moved to Piru Plantation on 29 August and two days later began shelling the Vila area of Kolombangara with the services of spotter aircraft. The move was made by landing craft and foot. A Japanese defender there wrote in his diary, "with the situation as it is, one just can't help but distrust the operational plans of the Imperial Headquarters."

On 15 September, General Sasaki would be ordered to evacuate his remaining 12,400 men from Kolombangara.

U.S. Marines reloading their howitzer. National Archives.

OTHER NEW GEORGIA ACTIONS

Due to space limitations, I am forced to condense the excellent information available for the following actions.

Battle of Kula Gulf 5-6 July 1943 [17]

On the afternoon of 5 July while returning from its bombardment mission of the evening before, the task group, commanded by RAdm Ainsworth in *Honolulu*, received orders to reverse course and proceed northward to the Kula Gulf area in order to intercept some 10 vessels of the Tokyo Express on its nightly run from Bougainville.

Destroyers *Radford* and *Jenkins* were assigned to the task group in place of *Strong* and *Chevalier*. Otherwise the ships were the same which had bombarded Vila-Stanmore and Bairoko on the night of 4-5 July. The composition of the task organization follows:

TASK GROUP 36.1 RAdm Walden L. Ainsworth

Crudiv 9, RAdm Ainsworth

Honolulu, Helena*, St. Louis

Screen, Capt Francis X. McInerney (ComDesRon 21)
Nicholas, O'Bannon, Radford, Jenkins

*Sunk in this action.

In compliance with this order, the task group steamed up the Slot via Indispensable Strait, picking up the *Radford* and *Jenkins* en route. This was the most direct route and would save fuel, in which all ships were low. It would also avoid the friendly ships which were expected off Guadalcanal.

The American radar picked up the enemy at 0140 July 6 at 24,700 yards but the range had dropped to 11,000 yards (nearly six miles) before Ainsworth gave the order to commence firing, but nothing happened until 0157. By then, the range was down to just over a mile, the advantage had been lost. When *Helena* opened fire, her gunfire flashes gave the Japanese all they needed. Within seconds, 16 "Long Lance" torpedoes were roaring at the Americans at 50 knots.

The Americans quickly poured out more than 2,500 rounds of 6-inch cruiser fire, but at 0203 the first torpedo hit *Helena*, quickly followed by two more. *Helena* was mortally wounded. Her bow was torn off, almost up to Turret 2.

The second torpedo hit *Helena* deep under the after stack. The final fish hit near the second one, but deeper, opening the ship's bottom. Capt Charles P. Cecil called to any who might hear, "Abandon Ship!" and in six minutes *Helena* was gone, in 2,000 feet of water.

After the first clash, Ainsworth retired with the cruisers, while the Japanese retired to reload torpedoes. American destroyers carried no reload torpedoes, but the Japanese did, and knew how to handle those 3-ton fish even on a tossing deck.

The enemy had lost one destroyer so far, *Niizuki*, smashed by the first American salvoes, even as *Helena* was receiving a death blow. At the same time, *Nagatsuki* took one 6-inch shell, but she got her troops ashore. *Niizuki* lost 300 of her men and also Admiral Akiyama.

The Japanese left *Nagatsuki* stranded on the Kolombangara shore, and American bombers set her afire that afternoon. Her magazines exploded and the final score stood one American cruiser for two Japanese destroyers.

At 0327 on 6 July the cruisers began retirement down the Slot in company with the *O'Bannon* and *Jenkins*. The *Nicholas* and *Radford* under Capt McInerney were directed to remain behind and pick up the survivors of the *Helena*. The *Nicholas* and *Radford* slowly nosed their way into the midst of the oil-soaked crew, who were scattered over an area a mile square. The men were singing and acting very much as if they were participating in a peacetime drill. Some were in life rafts; others were swimming separately; many had flashlights and were blowing whistles.

For three hours the rescue operations were carried out almost in the direct path of enemy ships returning from Kula Gulf to their bases in the Buin-Faisi area. Constant reports of torpedoes, torpedo wakes, and submarines were received. Rescue operations were interrupted at 0403, 0515, and 0605 when the two destroyers made radar contact with enemy ships and aircraft. In the latter

two cases torpedoes and gunfire were exchanged but no damage
was done.

Daylight was now breaking. A combination of factors prompted
the Squadron Commander to order the two destroyers to retire
from the area after rescuing 52 officers and 687 enlisted men:

- Submarines were likely to be in the vicinity,
- The number and size of enemy surface units still in Kula
  Gulf were unknown,
- The approach of daylight deprived Capt McInerney of
  the advantage of night fighting,
- Enemy air attack was expected soon.
  (More on *Helena* rescue operations to follow.)

Shortly after 0340, the task group commander had advised Capt
McInerney by TBS that he would request air coverage at dawn, but
this message had not been received. The four boats from the destroyers with boat crews, were left in the water near the survivors.

At 1300 on 6 July, the *Nicholas* and *Radford* arrived back at
Tulagi. Both they and the cruiser group which preceded them had
been provided with air cover, but neither had been subjected to
enemy air attack.

Comments/Conclusions – Just how the *Helena* was torpedoed
is a matter for conjecture. Capt Cecil was of the opinion that the
torpedoes which found the *Helena* came from the last destroyer in
the first enemy group, which had put on a burst of speed and closed
our line. From the plot submitted by Capt Cecil it appears that if
these torpedoes had been fired at the exact moment the U.S. ships
opened fire, they would have had to be extremely fast to reach
the *Helena* at the time she was hit. The possibility that they issued
from an enemy submarine lurking in the vicinity cannot therefore
be overlooked.

During the entire battle, none of the American ships were hit
by gunfire with the possible exception of the *Helena*, and she was
sunk by torpedoes. In its larger aspects, the action may be described as a duel between American gunfire and Japanese torpedoes. To be sure, 24 torpedoes were fired by our destroyers independently, but no coordinated attack was attempted or ordered.

The first dispatch from the task group commander stated that a minimum of six enemy ships had been sunk and one beached. It now appears that the damage inflicted on the enemy was more like two Japanese destroyers definitely sunk, one possibly sunk, and at least 5 were damaged.

Naval Bombardments of Munda, July 1943 [18]

Night of 8-9 July – At the request of the commanding general of the New Georgia Occupation Force, an hour's naval bombardment of the Munda Point area was ordered to coincide with the initial jump-off of the 43rd Division on a front along the Barike River over difficult terrain. The bombardment area was divided into four parts, and each ship was assigned a specific sector.

At 0345 a task unit of four destroyers (*Farenholt* (F), *Buchanan*, *McCalla* and *Ralph Talbot*) under the command of Capt T.J. Ryan, Jr. ComDesRon 12, entered Blanche Channel. At 0512 it commenced firing on a course of 245 degrees T. A total of 2,344 rounds of 5"/38 were fired by the four destroyers.

Night of 11-12 July – On 11 July, the 172^{d} Infantry disengaged and moved south in order to establish another beachhead at Lainana. The enemy quickly detected this movement and infiltrated between the 169th and 172^{d} regiments, severing communications between the two and creating a critical situation.

During the night of 11-12 July a second naval bombardment of Munda was undertaken. As finally constituted the task group was under the command of RAdm A.S. "Tip" Merrill and consisted of the following ships:

Bombardment Group

Cruisers: RAdm Merrill, ComCruDiv 12. *Montpelier* (FF), *Denver, Columbia, Cleveland.*

Destroyers: Capt Thomas J. Ryan, Jr. ComDesRon 12. *Farenholt* (F), *Buchanan.*

Advance Sweeping Group: Cmdr John M. Higgins, ComDesDiv 23. *Gwin* (F), *Maury, Ralph Talbot.*

Inner Screen: Capt William R. Cooke, Jr., ComDesRon 22. *Waller* (F), *Saufley, Pringle, Philip, Renshaw.*

The approach was made without incident. At 0255 the *Montpelier* took the firing course of 247 degrees T. and at 0257 commenced bombardment. She was followed at five minute intervals by the *Denver, Columbia,* and *Cleveland,* which with the *Montpelier* fired a total of 3,204 rounds of 6-inch and 4,407 rounds of 5-inch from the southeast. Ten minutes before the cruisers ceased fire, the *Farenholt* and *Buchanan* commenced bombardment from the west, steaming at 5 knots and using 12-second salvos.

At the request of the Army, the original plan was changed to move the bombardment area to the west. This left a heavily-wooded "no-man's land" about one mile wide between the advanced lines of our own troops and the eastern limit of the bombardment area, which was to be covered by artillery fire.

Spotting was conducted by ship spotters carried in two Black Cats. Communications were excellent, and the performance of the spotters was good until the target area became obscured by dust and smoke. The cruiser bombardment appeared to be very effective.

The opposition from shore batteries was negligible. However, the firing drew enemy planes to the scene, as one observer put it "like hawks over a broom-sage fire." Early in the bombardment one of them succeeded in illuminating the entire cruiser column very effectively. After the initial illumination, the screening destroyers were successful in driving off the harassing planes.

One Black Cat reported an attack by five Japanese Zeros but succeeded in evading them without damage. While searching out the reverse slope of Kokengolo, the two bombarding destroyers registered hits on a large ammunition dump which went up with a cascade of sparks and burned brilliantly with intermittent explosions long after the bombardment was over.

Battle of Kolombangara 12-13 July 1943

The night of 12-13 July, RAdm Ainsworth's Task Group 36.1 engaged another force of enemy ships off Kolombangara Island. It was a virtual facsimile of the Battle of Kula Gulf and took place in the same black waters 7 to 13 miles northwest of the island of Kolombangara. Some have called it "the last large cruiser/destroyer battle of the war, and perhaps for all time."

The composition of the task group was constituted as follows:

TASK GROUP 36.1 RAdm Walden L. Ainsworth

Destroyer Squadron 21, Capt Francis X. McInerney

Nicholas, O'Bannon, Taylor, Jenkins, Radford

Cruiser Division 9, RAdm Ainsworth

Honolulu, H.M.N.Z.S. Leander, St. Louis

Capt Thomas J. Ryan (ComDesRon 12)

*Ralph Talbot, Buchanan, Maury, Woodsworth, *Gwin*

*Sunk in this action.

The task group mission: Intercept the "Tokyo Express." The action, which involved both gunnery and torpedoes, resulted in all three of our cruisers being hit by torpedoes, but not sunk, while the destroyer *Gwin* was torpedoed during the action and sank on her way home.

The Japanese losses estimated by Commander Third Fleet were: 1CL and 1DD sunk, 2DDs possibly sunk, and 1 damaged. Except for the light cruiser *Jintsu* from which two survivor prisoners were recovered, these enemy losses were computed largely on radar evidence.

It was another big reinforcement run for Japanese RAdm Shunji Izaki in light cruiser *Jintsu*, with 10 destroyers and APDs loaded with 1,200 troops destined for Kolombangara.

The two battle lines collided shortly after 0100 13 July north of Kolombangara, with no surprise to either side. Black Cat planes spotted the Japanese as early as 0036, some 26 miles ahead of Ainsworth's force. His flagship, *Honolulu,* picked up Izaki's force on radar at 0100.

What Americans never knew until after the war was that Izaki was watching his enemy for a full hour before battle, using a radar detector. This new device could pick up radar emissions and enable the Japanese to plot back to the origin of the signals—the enemy ships.

At 0109, Ainsworth ordered his destroyers to "attack with torpedoes." Once again the Americans were too slow—perhaps a minute earlier the Japanese destroyers had launched a spread of 31 Long Lance torpedoes in the direction of the American cruisers.

Ainsworth had been holding his cruiser fire until his torpedoes got away. When he did release the cruisers, a torrent of 6-inch shells went for the big one, cruiser *Jintsu*, the Japanese flagship. Over 2,600 rounds of main battery fire were in the air and at 0117 *Jintsu* was dead in the water, disintegrating, and Admiral Izaki was dead, along with the commanding officer and 482 crewmen of the *Jintsu*. And on *Honolulu* the shout went up, "We got the cruiser." True, but the battle was far from over.

The Japanese torpedoes began to arrive and *Leander* was hit first, killing 28 of her men. (*Leander* limped all the way to Boston for rebuilding but was out of the war.) Then *Honolulu* and *St. Louis* took torpedoes within seconds. Both hit forward and mercifully no men were lost. But both American cruisers had crushed bows and all three cruisers were now heading for Tulagi, best speed, slowly.

At 0214 destroyer *Gwin* took a Long Lance square amidships, exploded, and burned fiercely. *Ralph Talbot* took off *Gwin* survivors and she lasted until 0930 when she was scuttled. In all, she lost 67 of her officers and crew. That fatal torpedo was one of the reloads the Japanese had made in a remarkably short time since their first lunge at the Americans. But the enemy never wavered from his main task; when the battle cooled, all 1,200 Japanese reinforcing troops were ashore and the enemy force was homeward bound.

Comments/Conclusions – Once more, as in the case of the Battle of Kula Gulf, the enemy chose to match torpedo against radar-controlled gunfire. The speed and accuracy of the Japanese torpedo fire was impressive. In the past the enemy had not hesitated to press home torpedo attacks at close range. In this action, however, the tactics pursued by the enemy seemed to be based on the consideration that "a torpedo which hits near the end of its run does just as much damage as one fired at closer range." He seemed fully aware that when a destroyer pushes an attack to close range, she gives her target earlier warning of the attack and hence more time to sink the attacker and turn away, than would have been the case if the salvo had been fired just inside the torpedo range.

Bottom line: The two night surface battles of 5-6 July and 12-13 July, although costly, removed the Japanese threat to our landings on the north coast of New Georgia. They also deterred them from using the Kula Gulf route to supply and reinforce their garrisons at Vila and Munda. During the remainder of the campaign, the enemy was reduced to the expedient of sending ships and barges around Vella Lavella to the west of Kolombangara and slipping them into anchorages along the south coast of that island.

Rescue of *Helena* Survivors, 16 July 1943

When *Nicholas* and *Radford* left the Kula Gulf area on the morning of 6 July, many *Helena* survivors were still in the water. They were in two general groups which became separated during the night, and by morning, were out of sight of each other:

Group one consisted of Captain C. P. Cecil and two other *Helena* officers, 78 men, plus seven men from *Nicholas* and *Radford* in three motor whaleboats and on three rafts dropped by the two destroyers. This group reached Menakasapa Island on the north coast of New Georgia about 1700 on the 6th, camped overnight, and were rescued on the morning of the 7th by destroyers *Gwin* and *Woodworth*.

Group two consisting of over 100 officers and men under Lt Cmdr Chew, had collected on life rafts, in their life jackets, or on two rubber boats dropped by friendly planes. After a harrowing experience, during which one man died and several disappeared from the rafts, they finally reached shore on Vella Lavella on the morning of the 8th. A total of 11 officers and 93 men made camp and were assisted and protected by friendly natives and Chinese.

This group, together with another two officers and 59 enlisted men camped further down the coast, were finally evacuated in the early morning of the 16th by Capt Thomas J. Ryan in *Taylor*—with *Maury, Gridley,* and *Ellet* as an escorting force for Cmdr J.D. Sweeney in *Dent* with *Waters.* Capt Francis X. McInerney in *Nicholas* with *Radford, Jenkins* and *O'Bannon* covered the operations.

The *Helena* survivors rescued from Vella Lavella totaled 160 enlisted men, 14 naval officers, and one army officer. In addition,

16 Chinese inhabitants of the island and one Japanese army POW aviator were removed. Eight *Helena* officers and 190 enlisted men were lost out of a total complement of 1,177.

Destroyer Operations 17-18 July 1943

On 17-18 July, Task Unit 36.2.3 composed of APDs *Kilty, Ward, Waters,* and *McKean* covered by DDs *Lang, Stack, Waller, Saufley,* and *Pringle* landed the 4th Marine Raiders and supplies at Enogai Inlet to reinforce Col Liversedge's troops previously landed at Rice Anchorage, and evacuated passengers, sick and wounded. Passage to Enogai was uneventful, the force arriving at 0104. The APDs were met by about 30 Higgins boats and guides, unloading proceeded without incident, and the APDs departed Enogai for Guadalcanal at 0312.

Loss of LST-342, 18 July 1943 [19]

On 18 July, LST-342, proceeding without escort for Rendova with a cargo of ammunition and 196 passengers, was torpedoed 8 miles southeast of Oloana Bay (Vangunu Island) and broke into two pieces.

As the sole surviving officer of LST-342, Ensign T. B. Montgomery filed a report on 28 July 1943 from the "Commanding Officer" to CINCPFLT via the usual channels starting with Capt Carter, ComLSTFLOT 5. Since the report is the only significant LST-342 document housed in the Washington archives, here is a condensed/paraphrased version of its contents:

> LST-342 was the LST Group 14 flagship of Cmdr Paul S. Slawson, USN. The ship departed Guadalcanal at 0100 on 17 July for the Russell Islands where she took on additional cargo, probably ammunition. Total cargo, a relatively light load of 500 tons. The 342 was also carrying 196 passengers: 4 army officers, 2 naval officers, 169 army troops, and 21 navy enlisted men.
>
> LST-342 got underway for Wernham Cove in the Russells at 1630 and, after some indecision on Cmdr Slawson's part as to whether to proceed or await an escort, departed Wernham Cove for Rendova.
>
> At 2345 on 17 July, Ensign Montgomery took over the watch as Officer-of-the-Deck. Course 284 degrees T, speed 9.5 knots. Because of rain, no one was topside except for six lookouts also serving as the nucleus for three gun crews.

Between 0100-0115 navigator Ensign Jerome J. Sobota, USNR took bearings and plotted them on the signal bridge chart, then retired below.

By 0115 on 18 July, the rain had stopped and weather conditions had improved: condition of sea-0; force of wind-0; moon-full, partly obscured by cumulus clouds which covered 90 percent of the sky; visibility-excellent. At this time, Cmdr Slawson and Rudolph J. Farley, QM 3/c, USNR, Quartermaster of the Watch, were on the signal bridge with Montgomery.

Shortly before 0130, Ensign Montgomery noticed a torpedo wake about 40 yards from the ship and started to give warning. The next thing he knew, he was being sucked under water. After fighting to get back to the surface, he heard the cries of the other LST-342 survivors and spotted some rafts which someone had cut away from the still-floating forward part of the ship.

The floating hulk was discernible in the moonlight, but due to current and wind conditions, it was impossible to close it by paddling, so the survivors drifted until daylight. At about 0630 on 18 July, all able-bodied survivors started paddling the seven rafts toward Wickham Anchorage, Vangunu Island.

Numerous friendly planes and small craft were sighted but attempts to flag them down failed. Finally, at 1700 a PBY spotted their signals and shortly thereafter, LCI-62 stood out of Wickham and rescued them. The survivors were taken to Wickham, given first aid, and returned to Guadalcanal on 20 July.

Of the 196 passengers, 147 survived. Of the ship's crew of 82, five survived. Only two of the five were quartered in the after half of the ship.

Capt Grayson Carter, ComLSTFLOT 5, in his First Endorsement to Ensign Montgomery's report, emphasized the need for adequate escort when he wrote: "...If this type of ship, with its highly vulnerable cargo of gasoline, powder, and other related material, is to stand any chance of survival, the provision of adequate escort must be had...."

However, Wilkinson, CTF 31, and Halsey, COMSOPAC defended the decision to send LST-342 up the Slot in their Third and Fourth Endorsements respectively which state in part:

"No escort was available for LST-342 at the time she sailed for Rendova. Of the six destroyers assigned to the operational control of Commander Task Force Thirty-one, four were covering the movement of five APDs which were landing reinforcements and supplies and evacuating seriously wounded of the First Marine

Raider Regiment at Enogai, New Georgia. The other two were operating with Commander Destroyer Squadron 22 north of Kolombangara against a possible Tokyo Express run. Of the eight APDs in Task Force Thirty-one, five were en route to Enogai, New Georgia, and three were at Rendova.

> *At this time, the need for ammunition at New Georgia which comprised the bulk of the load of LST-342, was so urgent that her sailing unescorted was believed warranted, particularly in view of the fact that no submarines were known to have been operating in the area, and no submarine contacts had been made along the track, or in the immediate area.*
>
> — T.S. Wilkinson

> *It is considered that the sailing of the LST-342 without escort was warranted under the circumstances.*
>
> — W.F. Halsey

In its July 1943 report, CINCPAC offered this word of caution regarding enemy submarines—albeit after-the-fact for LST-342: "As has been the rule during offensive action by our forces in the South Pacific, the enemy immediately countered with a concentration of submarines in the operating area. There were numerous reports of sightings and contacts, and a few successful attacks by and on the enemy submarines. At the same time, attacks on our more distant supply routes ceased."

On 22 July, the fixed route laid down in the original operations order was changed. The Flot 5 LSTs had been traveling the same nightly route between the 'Canal and Rendova for 22 days. Amazing!

LST-342 was torpedoed by Japanese submarine RO-106 commanded by Lieutenant Nakamura. (RO-106 was sunk at dawn on 22 May 1944 by USS *England* (DE-635) north of the Admiralty Islands.) [20]

Boatswain Mate Jim Cogswell, one of the surviving LST-342 passengers, recently shared with me his memories of that awful night 58 years ago. Here are some highlights:

> After taking treatment for malaria on Guadalcanal, I was shipped out on LST-342 for Rendova Island. On July 17, 1943, we left Guadalcanal

and put in at Russell Islands where I was assigned to a work party loading about 10 tons of explosives at the aft end of the tank deck. During this time, I remember talking to *Life Magazine* artist, McClelland Barclay, who was sketching various crew members.

Late that afternoon we left the Russells to meet a convoy at 1800. The convoy was apparently in a squall and could not be seen, so the Skipper took off for Rendova Island....

When the torpedo hit that night, I recall three distinct explosions causing the 342 to break apart at the aft end of the midship head—the break was so clean it could have been cut with a burner's torch....

As a passenger, I was berthed in the forward starboard troop compartment....By the time I reached topside, the stern section of the ship had already disappeared....I ran to the aft end of the bow section and was going to jump, when I saw water going into the bottom of the ship and then washing out. I then realized the double bottom compartments were keeping us afloat.

I started yelling at the army troops to stay aboard as I believed we would stay afloat....About this time, I spotted the periscope of a sub off our starboard beam. I rushed to the starboard bow 40-mm yelling for loader help but, as it turned out, the sub was so damn close—less than 50 yards, I'd say—we couldn't even depress the guns down on him.... He continued to circle us with only his periscope showing for one hell of a long time....

After the sub left the scene, I got two groups of passengers to go below and secure all the watertight doors between the troop compartments for added watertight integrity....

Later in the morning, we saw our planes fly over us but we couldn't attract their attention....During the afternoon, we spotted a small ship on the horizon, headed our way. As the rescue ship began to offload the survivors from the bow section of the 342, her skipper asked for a couple volunteers to stay aboard to handle a tow line and to drop anchor when we got to the beach. Since I was the only one with 'anchor detail' experience I was one of the lucky 'volunteers.' Another young sailor whose name I can't recall stayed with me.

When the ship returned—I remember it as an APc , not an LCI— the two of us handled the tow line and later, about 1930, dropped the anchor, some 18 hours after the torpedo hit.

We were returned to the 'Canal and I was transferred to the *President Hayes* (APA-20) and spent the rest of the war on her.

Gerhard Hess, one of the five lucky survivors of the 342 crew, shared a copy of the statement he gave to Navy officials on 21 July 1943. Here is a greatly condensed version of that statement:

I was on gun watch with L.F. Hedding on the forecastle....Everything was peaceful 'til a sudden jar threw us about four or five feet into the air...then back down and back up again. I grabbed my life jacket and looked around and saw the last remains of the stern fall into the water.

I told Hedding that we would have to trip the rafts...in case the submarine surfaced and shelled the remaining part of the ship. I tripped number two raft forward on the port side with the help of some soldiers....After I was in the raft...I yelled to the soldiers on deck to jump but they refused. By this time, the raft Hedding and I were on was loaded with troops who had jumped with us....

About 60 or 70 yards away from the ship we heard two voices and recognized one as Mr. Montgomery, so we paddled over and picked them out of the water. Mr. Montgomery was hanging onto wreckage when we found him. He was also injured....After that we gathered all the rafts afloat and divided them up among the men. There were seven rafts in all....

We drifted until morning and then around 0730 we saw a PBY fly over...so we started to wave our paddles but he didn't recognize us. We could also see the forward part of the ship which was still floating....

Later in the afternoon a PT boat passed us on the west side but couldn't see us, although we raised and waved our paddles. After that, a PBY came directly over us but we didn't know whether they knew we were there or not....After this, we saw a ship coming out from the island, so we started to wave our paddles and flash a mirror which they acknowledged by flashing back. They picked us up about 1700 and took us to the sickbay on the island....

From what I gather, we got one torpedo and the after magazine blew up....I still say, it doesn't pay to go unescorted into dangerous waters.

In a recent interview with Anthony ("Tony") Tesori, Gunnery Officer of LST-340 which was bombed and beached at the 'Canal on 16 June 1943 (Volume I), he informed me Ensign Montgomery was a friend of his from Gunnery School days. Tesori spent some time with "Monty" at Carter City after LST-342 was hit. Tony remembers their conversations:

Monty had volunteered to take the 'Conn' for a fellow officer who was too ill to stand his own watch that night. All in the conning tower with Monty perished including Commander Slawson and the crewmen manning the port and starboard bridge gun positions who were serving as lookouts.

I attended the ceremony held on Tulagi when the Purple Heart awards were bestowed on the men wounded at Guadalcanal on the 340 and the 342 torpedoing. Some days later, the bow section of LST-342 was recovered and towed to Tulagi and beached with the torpedoed end facing the beach for all to see, and close to the burned out hulk of LST-340. What a terrible and sad sight for us to look at each day.

Montgomery's survival was indeed a miracle in itself. He was a nervous wreck and in constant state of shock all the while he was with us on Tulagi. He couldn't remember being picked up. All he seemed able to talk about was the heavy refrigerator door he found himself under and the struggle to get out from under it. It wasn't until he finally popped to the surface that he realized that it was the door that had pinned him down. He was such a long time coming to the surface that his lungs seemed on fire and ready to burst. That door became his temporary raft. I have never seen or heard from Monty since I left Tulagi in late Sept. 1943, but I have often wondered about him.

Postscript – On 5 August 1943, Commander Naval Base Tulagi recommended that the forward half of LST-342 be made into a pier and storage warehouse for landing craft. According to a number of Flot 5 LST vets who have visited the Solomons in recent years, she is still at Lyons Point in Purvis Bay near Tulagi, a rusted wreck guaranteed to bring back memories for all who pay her a visit.

The burned out LST-340 received a reprieve and left Purvis Bay on 7 September 1943 under the tow of tug *Rail* for the States.

Bombardments of Bairoko and Lambeti Plantation, 23-25 July 1943

Bairoko – During the night of 23-24 July, the destroyers *Conway, Patterson, Taylor,* and *Ellet* (TG 31.2) under the command of Cmdr Arleigh A. Burke[21] escorted TransDiv 22 (APDs *Kilty, Crosby, Talbot,* and *Waters*) to Enogai Inlet in order to supply our beleaguered Marine force there. They were covered by a task group of cruisers and destroyers (*Montpelier, Cleveland, Waller, Pringle, Philip, Maury,* and *Gridley*) under the command of RAdm Merrill, which made a sweep to the north and west of Kolombangara without encountering opposition.

The transport group left Guadalcanal at 1452 and arrived off Enogai Inlet at 0100. The signal light which the Marines had been directed to display at Enogai Point, was delayed twenty minutes.

Thereafter unloading proceeded as planned.

At 0316 *Taylor* and *Ellet* commenced bombardment of Bairoko, and at the same time, *Conway* and *Patterson* opened fire on shore batteries off Enogai which had kept up a spasmodic fire during the unloading of the APDs. All firing ceased at 0330, the bombardment group having expended 894 rounds of 5"/38. *Conway* and *Patterson* fired another 425 rounds of 5"/38. The latter silenced 6 shore batteries. TG 31.2 retired to Guadalcanal without incident.

Lambeti Plantation – Following the second bombardment of Munda, enemy resistance to the drive on the airport was localized in two centers about a thousand yards apart astride the Munda trail just east of Roviana. A rainy period had set in, and to all the other discomforts sustained by the combatants was added that of mud.

On 17 July Gen Griswold informed Adm Wilkinson that he was planning a new drive to capture Munda and requested that a naval bombardment of the Lambeti Plantation be undertaken in advance of troop movement. Wilkinson advised Griswold that four or more destroyers would be made available for this purpose.

On the same day the 172^d Infantry pushed its way to within 200 yards of the southernmost center of enemy resistance near Lilio. On the right, the 169th Infantry facing the northern enemy strong point in more heavily wooded terrain, was unable to gain. During the day, the 161st Infantry of the 25th Division came ashore and went into position on the right in support of the 169th.

That night the Japanese made two slashing counterattacks from their southern strong point, one against the 169th and the other against the Laiana beachhead. Both were thrown back, whereupon the enemy withdrew along the Munda trail.

On 23 July, Cmdr Burke, the new Task Group 31.2 commander, accompanied an escort mission to Rendova in order to make a reconnaissance of the Munda area for the purpose of picking out possible points of aim. On the morning of 24 July, following his return, a conference was held at Koli Point, and a dispatch order for the bombardment of 25 July was prepared.

Plans were made for a 30-minute bombardment beginning at 0615 on 25 July and overlapping an aerial bombardment, which was to begin at 0630. It was tentatively decided to place a high concentration of naval gunfire in a strip approximately 1,400 yards by 400 yards, the axis of which was more or less parallel to the estimated front line positions of our troops and the eastern edge which was about 400 yards from these lines. Subsequently, at the request of the commanding general, the target area was moved several hundred yards to the west because of new front line positions on the north flank.

It was also determined that our ships would have to open fire in succession because of the small arc in which point of aim could be seen and the necessity for each ship to fire spotting salvos to make certain they were on in deflection. The shore fire control party was cautioned that in case the fall of shot came dangerously close to our troops, a signal to "lift barrage" was to be sent to the bombarding ships at once.

At 1900 on 24 July the bombardment group sailed from Tulagi and formed line of section columns, interval 4,000 yards, order from left to right:

Section 3 – Lt Cmdr Katz in *Taylor, Ellet, Patterson.*
Section 1 – Cmdr Burke (ComDesDiv 44) in *Conway, Wilson.*[22]
Section 2 – Cmdr Sims in *Maury, Gridley.*

This formation was chosen so that hunter-killer operations against submarines could be undertaken en route to Munda while at the same time only simple changes would be required in forming for bombardment. The group passed south of Savo Island and the Russells and entered Blanche Channel, assuming column formation at 0337. At 0544, the *Maury* and *Gridley,* the two leading ships, formed a screen on both bows of the *Conway.*

The plan called for the *Maury* and *Gridley* to open fire in advance of the main bombardment and subsequently to conduct counter-battery fire. At 0607 the *Maury* reported that the light was too dim and that she could not see the target. At 0609, on the basis of new instructions, she opened with indirect fire, followed by the *Conway* at 0615 and by each of the other ships in succession at two minute intervals.

Within fifteen minutes, the slight morning haze had lifted, but by this time there was considerable dust and smoke over the target area. At 0618 gun flashes from one or two shore batteries were observed. The *Maury* and *Gridley* were called upon to silence these batteries, which they did very effectively. At 0630 AirSols started bombing a beach strip to the south of the target area with fragmentation and 500 pound bombs, which added to the smoke and dust.

A total of 4,000 5"/38 projectiles were placed in the target area. The gunfire appeared to be heavy, accurate, and well controlled although its effectiveness could not be judged at the time. At 0644 the order was given to cease firing, and retirement by sections to Tulagi followed.

During and following the surface bombardment, U.S. planes carried out the largest raid yet made in this area. One hundred seventy-one bombers and torpedo planes, escorted by 79 fighters, heavily bombed targets in the Munda area.

MTB Operation 25 July – 5 August 1943

During the last two weeks of the Munda campaign, our naval operations were mainly confined to PT boat activity. Throughout this period our MTB patrol groups based on Rendova made almost nightly contacts with the enemy. The majority of their contacts were with large barges (90'-100') which the MTBs were ill-equipped to destroy. The barges were immune to torpedo attack because of their shallow draft; the 20-mm and .50 cal. guns of the PTs were likewise ineffective except against personnel. Nevertheless, the MTBs undoubtedly forced the enemy to use barges in preference to the larger and speedier destroyers and transports.

PT Motor Torpedo Boat drawing. Courtesy WWII PT Boats, Bases, Tenders Museum Archives.

Lt John F. Kennedy, USNR (far right) with other crewmen of USS PT-109, circa 1943. Naval Historical Center.

The results of their operations are indefinite, due to the fact the operations were at night and primarily radar-controlled. However it is certain they sank some barges, and damaged others.

On 18 July, they got one torpedo hit on one of six Jap DDs off western Kolombangara, and on 30 July, they sank a small auxiliary off Meresu Cove.

On 6 July, three MTBs grounded off Kunda Kunda Island and were fired on by enemy shore batteries at Munda. Though heavily damaged, they were later salvaged.

The night of 1-2 August, a Japanese destroyer struck PT-109, Lt John F. Kennedy's boat, on the starboard side about 15 feet from the bow and cut her in two.[23] The survivors succeeded in swimming to shore on a small island about four miles to the southeast of Gizo and remained there until the night of 7-8 August when they were rescued by two PTs and removed to Rendova.

Battle of Vella Gulf, 6-7 August 1943

On the night of 6-7 August, TG 31.2 engaged the Tokyo Express 6 miles off the northwest coast of Kolombangara and in a well-fought destroyer battle, annihilated the enemy force.

Summary of Action:

The night of 6-7 August, U.S. destroyers had center-stage without the cruisers. RAdm Theodore S. Wilkinson sent six of them out alone, under Cmdr Frederick Moosbrugger, to see what they could find in the Vella Gulf. It seemed about time for a Japanese reinforcement to run down the Slot. It was. Capt Kaju Sugiura, in destroyer *Jagikaze*, together with destroyers *Arashi, Kawakaze,* and *Shigure,* was en route with 1,150 troops and supplies for Kolombangara.

Moosbrugger left Savo Sound the afternoon of 6 August and took the route south of Munda to turn up into Vella Gulf west of Kolombangara, expecting action around 2300. *Dunlap, Craven* and *Maury* led the way, followed by *Lang, Sterett* and *Stack*. At 2333, *Dunlap's* SG radar picked up the enemy at 19,700 yards, just under 10 miles. Eight seconds later Moosbrugger ordered 'Fire torpedoes' and the battle was on. This time, everything went like magic for the Americans. At 2346 the rear destroyers under Cmdr Rodger W. Simpson (*Lang, Sterett* and *Stack*) opened fire with their 5"38s. The Japanese were stunned and handled their destroyers badly, perhaps showing poor training and discipline, or perhaps exhaustion from the long campaign. Within minutes, three of the destroyers were sinking, and only the *Shigure* would escape.

Only a handful of Japanese survived, and not one would surrender although the American vessels combed the crowded water offering aid. Moosbrugger and his destroyermen departed with barely a scratch and there was jubilation at Guadalcanal.

NEW GEORGIA AIR OPERATIONS

During the Munda Operation, the Solomon Islands Airforce ("AirSols") was called upon to:

- Provide cover for U.S. convoys and warships moving between Guadalcanal and Rendova.
- Maintain a patrol over the Rendova area during daylight hours to ward off attacking enemy planes.
- Strike at enemy bases and shipping.
- Carry out an on-going aerial search of the area to prevent an attack on our positions by Japanese surface units.
- Pick up targets for our striking forces.
- Provide close support for ground forces when requested.
- Protect the large amount of shipping in the Guadalcanal-Tulagi area.

Before going any further, I would like to update our profile on Airsols. I described the heterogeneous makeup of AirSols in Chapter 5 and how the command rotated between the U.S. Army, Navy and Marine Corps. I also described how AirSols had gained the quality advantage aloft by June 1943, and sometimes was experiencing a numbers advantage, too, but explained why and how the Japanese held the important advantage in their nicely spaced airstrips between Rabaul and Guadalcanal.

AirSols – With a big assist from Marine historian Charles D. Melson, here is an update on AirSols: [24]

The air war for the Central Solomons was a series of sorties—fighter sweeps and bombing runs. For aviation units, the operating area was divided into the combat area, the forward area, and the rear area. These zones shifted as the campaigns moved north towards Rabaul....

The Corsair, known as the Whistling Death to the Japanese and the Bent Wing Widow Maker to the Marines, was delivered in March 1943 in time to have eight Marine squadrons available for the New Georgia campaign. The Corsair, along with the new F6F Hellcat fighter, dominated the air-to-air battle to sweep the skies of the Japanese. This superiority was enhanced by the Army Air Corps Lockheed P-38 Lightning....

By June, Marine Aircraft Group (MAG) 21 was pounding away at Munda, but not without losses. Flying from Guadalcanal and the Russell Islands, Airsols fighter and strike aircraft covered the TOENAILS land-

The first Marines to fight in the Central Solomons campaign were the airmen based on Guadalcanal and the Russells. They flew the Douglas SBD Dauntless dive-bombers that struck at Munda and elsewhere on New Georgia, prior to the landings. In 1943 the planes were painted, from top, in sea blue, mid blue, and semi-gloss sea blue, with insignia white undersurface. U.S. Marine Corps.

ings and subsequent operations ashore. From 30 June 1943 through July, there were only two days that did not have Condition Red and dogfights with Japanese aircraft over the objective area by Allied combat air patrols.

At the same time, Japanese naval forces were located and attacked, thus forcing the Japanese to move at night by circuitous routes with landing barges alone. Bomber and Strike command aircraft ranged as far north as Ballale, Buin, Kahili, and the Shortlands in concert with Fifth Air Force strikes at the same locations.

For efficient air control for the New Georgia operation, Adm. Mitscher set up a new command, Commander Aircraft New Georgia (ComAir New Georgia), as part of the landing force and under Marine BGen Francis P. Mulcahy, who commanded the 2ᵈ Marine Aircraft Wing. ComAir New Georgia had no aircraft of his own, but controlled everything in the air above or launched from a New Georgia airfield. Mulcahy and his staff ensured command, control, and coordination of direct air support for the New Georgia Occupation Force after it had landed.

ComAir New Georgia established its command on Rendova after the assault waves landed on D-Day, 30 June 1943. From Rendova, he began to integrate the air defense and support system to provide XIV Corps with direct air support.

On 11 July, Commander Aircraft Segi under LtCol Perry O. Parmelee was established under Mulcahy's direct command....Mulcahy provided air support to the infantry advance at Munda Point and against other Japanese-held areas on New Georgia. By the end of the campaign, Mulcahy had ordered over 1,800 preplanned sorties mainly flown by SBDs and TBFs against targets at Viru, Wickham, Munda, Enogai, and Bairoko.

After the capture of Munda Point, General Mulcahy moved his command from Rendova to Munda airfield to set up strike and fighter control at Kokengolo Hill. In a Japanese-built tunnel that Navy Seabees had cleared of debris and dead personnel, Mulcahy was able to conduct round-the-clock operations.

The first fighters assigned to Munda landed at 1500 on 14 August.

The establishment of the new landing strips in the Russells and on Segi Point and Munda in the New Georgia Group corrected one outstanding deficiency: fighter escorts could now cover bombers on missions to the north even on daylight strikes.

There were numerous instances of the value of this during the campaign. For example, in a daylight strike against shipping in the Buin-Kahili area on 17 July, our fighter cover of 114 planes was so effective that we lost only one TBF, and all bombers were

The first fighter plane to land on Munda was a VMF-215 Corsair flown by Major Robert G. Owens, Jr., on 14 August 1943.

Commander Aircraft New Georgia, BGen Francis P. Mulcahy, expanded airfield operations on Munda with the construction of more secure shelters than those the Japanese left behind. A heavily sandbagged sickbay is on the left and the personnel office is in the center.

BGen Francis P. Mulcahy, Cmdr Air Solomons, at right, at his headquarters on Munda. On left, Army Air Force Col Fiske Marshall and 1st Lt Dorothy Shikoski, an Army nurse who flew with Marine transport squadrons during medical evacuations. All courtesy U. S. Marine Corps.

able to press home their attacks. Forty-six enemy planes were shot down with a loss of four U.S. fighters. One Japanese destroyer leader, two destroyers, one submarine chaser, two cargo vessels and one oiler were sunk, and one cargo vessel was damaged.

Approximately 130 separate bombing attacks were made by Allied forces on targets in the area during the five weeks of the campaign. The Munda attacks generally involved only SBDs (Dive Bombers) and TBFs (Torpedo Bombers), the former armed with 1,000-pound instantaneous fuse or daisy cutter bombs, the latter with 2,000-pound bombs. The size of the attacking forces ranged from 18 SBDs and 18 TBFs used on 30 June, to 52 TBFs and 53 SBDs employed in the coordinated assault of 25 July, when U.S. Army B-17s and B-25s also took part.

Altogether, more than 950 tons of bombs were dropped on the Munda area between 30 June and 5 August 1943. Attacks on other land positions were concentrated mainly at Vila and Kahili.

Thirty-two fighter planes were constantly on station over Rendova between 0700 and 1630 daily. Ninety-six planes were required to maintain this daily patrol with any leeway. As a result, only some 80 to 100 fighters were left to meet all other requirements of the operation. The Rendova Patrol furnished cover for most of the light bomber attacks on Munda and Vila, but additional fighter protection was required for heavy strikes on these targets.

Seabees clear a Japanese tunnel at the base of Kokengolo Hill for use in case of enemy attack. The discomfort of the cave, filled with refuse and corpses, seemed a small price to pay for the security of overhead cover from artillery and air attacks.

The enemy's airplane and pilot losses continued to mount. Consider this:

- The Japanese lost 107 planes on 16 June 1943 over Guadalcanal-Tulagi hoping to surprise the big transports commanded by Capt Paul Theiss destined for Rendova, only to learn later that the ships were still in the New Hebrides.
- The enemy lost another 125 planes on 30 June and 1 July during the first two days of the New Georgia campaign.
- The Japanese suffered another setback on 15 July when they lost 29 fighters and 15 twin-engine bombers.

The Japanese air force virtually ceased to attack our forces in daylight hours. Even in the last stages of the campaign when their

The engineering effort pushed forward and built upon the Japanese construction that remained. The work was completed 10 days after Munda was captured.

Wreckage was soon pushed aside in the rush to open the Munda field for American use. The captured airfield included aircraft such as a Zero fighter, in a coconut and coral enclosure, that could not take off after the American landing.

land forces needed all possible aid, their offensive air efforts were confined to fighter sweeps, sometimes accompanied by a small number of dive bombers, and night harassing of our land positions and task units by float planes and medium bombers.

During the New Georgia campaign alone, the U.S. Marine, Navy and Army Air Force pilots reported the destruction in combat of 259 Japanese fighters, 60 twin engine bombers, 23 dive bombers, and 16 float planes. Japanese shipping destroyed or otherwise damaged by our aircraft included one seaplane carrier, one oiler, four destroyers, nine cargo vessels, and three submarine chasers or corvettes damaged.

Airfield Construction – Allow me to end this section with a direct quote from Admiral Chester W. Nimitz, CinCPAC/POA, who pays tribute to some of the very best U.S. servicemen in WWII: [25]

> One of the outstanding features of the war in both the North and South Pacific Areas has been the ability of U.S. forces to build and use airfields, on a terrain and with a speed which would have been considered fantastically impossible in our pre-war days. The credit for this is wide-spread. It belongs to:
> • The surface craft and their personnel which carried the material and equipment and got it ashore, often on storm-lashed open coasts without piers or other aids, and in the face of air, surface, and submarine attack.
> • The Army Engineers, Navy "Seabees," and others who did the actual construction work, under conditions of unprecedented difficulty and hardship, bending their whole effort towards the earliest readiness of a runway that planes could use, to the subordination of comforts, conveniences, and conventional methods.
> • The Air Force themselves, who knew well that even the best available sites in some areas would have been considered almost murderously unsafe by pre-war standards, yet who accepted the dangers as well as the inconveniences and hardships of such fields, through their strategic necessity. Our superiority over the enemy in airfield construction has been an outstanding element of our success so far....It is not too far-fetched to say that the American bulldozer and grader deserve a place with the American ship, plane, and gun as agencies for victory.

Author's Note: Admiral Nimitz, our high leader in the Pacific, paid tribute to most of the players in the "Pacific Express," even though he had never heard of my descriptive term at the time.

NEW GEORGIA LESSONS LEARNED

Casualties – Historian Morison summarized American losses in the New Georgia Campaign with these words: [26]

> The Central Solomons campaign ranks with Guadalcanal and Buna-Gona for intensity of human tribulation. At the end of 84 days fighting, one reinforced battalion of the 172[d] Infantry had lost 777 dead, wounded and sick out of an original strength of 1,002.
> Total American losses in ground fighting were 1,136. [27]
> A few hundred Allied sailors were lost in the Battles of Kula Gulf and Kolombangara, together with cruiser *Helena*, destroyers *Strong* and *Gwin* and three cruisers damaged. The air took its toll, too.

Now we'll have VAdm Dyer, RAdm Kelly Turner's biographer,[28] sum up the lessons learned in the TOENAILS campaign.

Logistic Support – The Navy had been much condemned for its inadequacies in logistic support during the first months of WATCHTOWER. Unlike the Guadalcanal Operation, there were 1st, 2[d], 3rd, and 4th Echelon logistic support movements set up for the TOENAILS Operation and a dozen support echelons had sailed in the first 15 days.

Just as Rear Admiral Turner was leaving SOPAC, Commander Landing Craft Flotillas [RAdm G. K. Fort] made a report to him on the performance of landing craft in which was written these heartening logistic words: "It appears for the first time in modern warfare that supplies have arrived with or immediately behind the Assault Troops. A good example is the airstrip at Segi. There, bulldozers were clearing a strip forty (40) minutes after the first echelon LST had beached. The flow of supplies to the front has been greater than the Advanced Bases could handle. All have requested that the flow of supplies be reduced." [29]

Enemy action, groundings, and modified plans had forced many changes in the ships and landing craft originally designated for specific supporting echelon tasks. The important lesson from all this was that in order for logistic support to be delivered by amphibious ships and craft on time, a large excess of ships and craft is required over the computed space requirements for the total of personnel and tons of equipment to be moved.

For the TOENAILS Operation, 36 LSTs, 36 LCIs, 72 LCTs and 28 APcs had been scheduled to be available. Fortunately plans were not based on this number as only 12 LSTs, 26 LCIs, 43 LCTs and 16 APcs were in the area on 30 June 1943. This number was barely adequate. [30]

CINCPAC had preferred that the large transports not be employed for the assault landings in TOENAILS, because of the lack of strong air cover over the landing areas and a decent respect for Japanese air capabilities.

Landing Ships and Craft – The personal worry bug to be overcome by every amphibian, (coxswain, officer-in-charge, or commanding officer) was the coral shelf and the many coral heads off the few and generally narrow beaches. In due time, these coral heads would be dynamited. The beaches would be augmented with landing piers, which would be coconut log bulkheads backed up by crushed coral. But the first few days in poorly or uncharted waters were real tests.

When the first surge of TOENAILS was over, it was apparent from the reports that both landing ships and craft had turned in better than satisfactory performance. RAdm Fort:

> The LCTs had been the most useful of all types. However, low speed (6 knots) limits their daily staging in combat areas to about 100 miles per night....It is still advisable to have them underway only at night. Against a head sea, their speed is greatly reduced, sometimes to two knots....The crews and officers have been standing up well in spite of operating two out of every three days.
>
> Some LSTs have transported 400 men each for short periods....LCTs have carried as many as 250 men overnight, but in exposed positions....
>
> The LCIs carry about 170 combat troops...For unopposed short runs of a few hours, 350 men have been transported on a single LCI....They are ideal for night landings on good beaches....
>
> The APcs, besides having proved useful as escorts, have been used to transport small groups of men....
>
> The arrival of a mobile landing craft repair base unit with a floating dock has been expected for months, but has still not arrived. [31]

Night Landing Operations – Night landings on foreign shores look very good on paper and over the long history of amphibious

Rendova Commanders, from left, Brigadier General Leonard F. Wing, Admirals Wilkinson and Turner, and General Hester.

operations have been resorted to many times, e.g., the North Africa invasion on 8 November 1942.

Rear Admiral Turner took a dim view of night landings prior to TOENAILS but had not closed his mind to their use. He was willing to experiment on a small scale. So the Eastern Force scheduled a night landing at Wickham Anchorage and the Western Force scheduled night landings for the Onaiavisi Entrance Unit and for the Advance Unit on Rendova.

One lesson which Adm Turner stated he had vividly relearned during the TOENAILS Operation was the great hazard of night operations. In fact, his lack of success with them soured him on night landings for any large contingent of amphibians for the rest of the war.

Adm Turner later commented on Samuel Eliot Morison's statement about the "folly of not taking Laiana first," and added that the decision to land at Zanana Beach instead of Laiana Beach was predicated on an acceptance, at that stage of the war, of Gen Vandegrift's often repeated statement that, "Landings should not be attempted in the face of organized resistance, if, by any combination of march or maneuver it is possible to land unopposed and undetected."

Bad weather blotted out the special lights needed to guide landing craft to beaches. Special lights had been provided at Rendova, Oloana Bay and Rice Anchorage. None were visible in the manner planned.

Offshore Toeholds – During the New Georgia amphibious operation, an operational technique was developed which carried through the Central Pacific campaigns and on into the planning for the final attack on the Japanese homeland. This technique was pointed towards seizing toeholds on nearby islands close to, but not so well defended as the main objective, and making a key part of the major assault on the main objective direct from these toeholds rather than from far across the sea. They also provided a place from where artillery support could be supplied on a round-the-clock basis.

Shore Parties – The Shore Party had been much condemned for its inadequacies on 7 August 1942 at Guadalcanal. Much effort had gone into making more definite its duties and increasing the number of warm bodies to carry out these duties during the next three months. On 16 October 1942, COMPHIBFORSOPAC issued a new "trial operating procedure" for the Shore Party. But in November 1942, the Commander Transport Division Eight still wrote: "The bottleneck of unloading is still the Shore Party....At Aola Bay, the Shore Party was 800 strong (200 per ship). 400 Army, 100 Marines and 100 ACORN personnel....Unloading boats on a beach is extremely strenuous physical labor and the Shore Party must be organized into reliefs if the unloading is to extend over 12 hours."[32]

Further increases in personnel as well as cleaner command lines were again tried in TOENAILS. They paid off.

Force Requirements – There was one sobering lesson from TOENAILS which carried forward into future planning of assault and follow-up forces for the island campaigns of the Pacific. It was expressed in a COMINCH planners memorandum of 6 August 1943:

> At the termination of Japanese resistance in Munda, there were
> seven regimental combat teams, totaling more than 30,000 troops in

our assault forces. No information differing from our initial estimate of 4,000 to 5,000 troops on Munda, to which reinforcements were believed to have been added for a time, has been received.

However, of the Japanese on Munda only 1,671 are known to be dead and 28 captured. The overwhelming superiority of our forces in numbers and equipment had to be applied for 12 days despite air bombing and naval bombardment support before a force not more than one-seventh its size had been overcome. If we are going to require such overwhelming superiority at every point where we attack the Japanese, it is time for radical change in the estimate of the forces that will be required to defeat the Japanese now in the Southwest and Central Pacific.[33]

By-passing Enemy-held Islands – In view of the successes achieved and lives saved, no more popular strategical concept came out of the Pacific War than that of by-passing or leapfrogging Japanese-held islands and letting the Japanese threat "die on the vine," while our forces direct their efforts at the enemy closer to the Japanese homeland.

The popularity of this strategy has led to many claims as to who was the originator. According to VAdm George Dyer, who read thousands of dispatches relating to the Pacific War while doing research for his excellent book, the first dispatch in which he saw the expression used was in a dispatch of VAdm Halsey's (COMSOPAC's 110421 of July 1943) addressed to RAdm Turner asking for his comments and recommendations on the concept.

CHAPTER 7

Occupation of Vella Lavella
15 August – 9 October 1943[1]

T he capture of the airfield at Munda Point on 5 August 1943 ended the first phase of the Allied northward march through the New Georgia Group. Despite the fact that a total of 1,671 Japanese dead was counted and that heavy additional casualties were known to have been inflicted by Allied naval, artillery and air bombardments, many Japanese were able to withdraw to the north and effect a junction with other troops holding out at Bairoko Harbor, the last major center of Japanese resistance on New Georgia.

A few others—probably high-ranking officers for the most part—were evacuated by barges to the enemy base at Vila-Stanmore on Kolombangara. This road of escape, however, was effectively denied to the majority of the survivors by the U.S. light surface vessels, which reported intercepting and sinking several troop-carrying barges in Kula Gulf during the final stages of the fighting at Munda.

Allied use of the Munda airstrip, it was felt, would effectively neutralize the field at Vila-Stanmore, besides bringing our fighters and bombers within much closer range of the enemy's last three remaining air bases in the Solomons—Kahili, Ballale and Buka.

Even though partially neutralized, the base at Vila-Stanmore remained a stumbling block in the path of our northward drive. Indications were that the Japanese had no intention of withdrawing from the area, despite the fact that its potential usefulness had greatly diminished. It was believed, on the contrary, that the enemy intended to augment his garrison there, and to this end was preparing to move in troops and equipment from the north in barges and destroyers under cover of darkness.

The difficulty, effort, and cost involved in ejecting an estimated 5,000-10,000 Japanese from fortified jungle defenses, as on Munda, however, were not lost on Adm Halsey. Wary of Japanese strength on Kolombangara, he had no desire for another slugging match.

Strategic Considerations

There was another option. In mid-July as the advance toward Munda floundered and the Japanese reinforced Kolombangara, Halsey's staff suggested a deviation from the original TOENAILS plan: instead of Kolombangara, seize Vella Lavella, only fifteen miles northwest of Kolombangara and weakly held by the Japanese.

Halsey endorsed the idea, recognizing that it exploited both American mobility and local air and sea superiority. He would gain his objective, a better airfield nearer to Bougainville, while avoiding a costly battle. Japanese forces on Kolombangara would be left to "die on the vine."

This decision marked an important departure from the strategy hitherto followed in the South Pacific. Our advance so far had been from one enemy-occupied defended island to the next. The primary objective in both Guadalcanal and New Georgia had been an enemy airstrip. The new strategy was to by-pass the enemy defenses on Kolombangara and his airfield at Vila and advance our island perimeter many miles beyond to an island with negligible defenses and no airfield.

Lying northwest of Kolombangara, athwart the path of the supply routes of enemy bases on that island, Vella Lavella would furnish bases for more

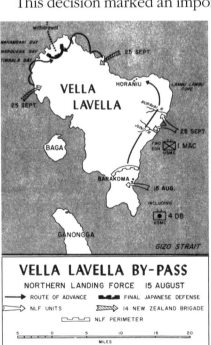

VELLA LAVELLA BY-PASS

NORTHERN LANDING FORCE   15 AUGUST

➡ ROUTE OF ADVANCE   ▬▬ FINAL JAPANESE DEFENSE

➡ NLF UNITS   ▨▨▨ 14 NEW ZEALAND BRIGADE

    ▭▭▭ NLF PERIMETER

5   0   5   10   15   20

MILES

SCALE APPROXIMATE

effective patrol of both Vella Gulf and Blackett Strait. The latter provided the favorite route for Japanese barges running supplies to the garrison at Vila. It was intended to establish a minor naval base and an airstrip on the island from which Japanese shipping and air bases of southern Bougainville might be attacked.

The coastal area of Vella Lavella is a narrow strip varying in width from 100 yards to one mile. Beyond this the ground rises abruptly toward a central ridge from 2,000 to 3,000 feet in height. Apart from the coconut plantations along the coast, usually located opposite channels giving entrance through the main reefs, the country is overgrown with heavy jungle through which it is impossible to see more than a few yards.

On the night of 21-22 July, a party of six Army, Navy and Marine officers was landed on Vella Lavella by PT boat for the purpose of making a comprehensive reconnaissance of the southern part of the island. The party investigated Liapari Island, Biloa Anchorage, landing beaches, and a site for an airstrip. Taken off six days later, along with a rescued crew of a Catalina patrol plane, the reconnaissance mission reported suitable beaches and a site for a PT base at either Liapari or Nyanga. Because of good drainage, safe approaches, suitable beaches and bivouac areas, Barakoma was selected as the site for the landing and for the

Lt to rt: Rear Admiral George W. Fort, USN; Admiral William F. Halsey, USN; and Rear Admiral Theodore S. Wilkinson, USN. Courtesy U.S. Naval Institute.

construction of an airstrip. Furthermore, the locality was not occupied by the Japanese and no opposition in force was expected.

Acting upon RAdm Theodore S. Wilkinson's recommendations, Adm Halsey designated 15 August as D-day, and authorized a force composed of Naval, Army and Marine Units for the operation.

See Appendix K for the composition of the III Amphibious Force Task Units, code-named "William."

Preliminary Operations – During the week preceding the operation, considerable enemy air strength was reported in Kahili and Rabaul, and Japanese destroyers were observed in the Buin-Shortlands area. Photographs of the Rabaul area taken on the 13th revealed 19 cargo vessels, 2 cruisers, 5 destroyers, 6 submarines, and various smaller warships. Airfields in the area held an estimated total of 271 aircraft. In the harbor were 25 floatplanes and 4 flying boats. All these hostile forces had to be taken into account in the plan of operations.

Surface forces of the Third Fleet were held in reserve to provide protection against any major enemy forces that might put in an appearance. Motor torpedo boats based on Rendova and Lever Harbor were to screen our forces by picket lines to the south, the west, and the northeast of Vella Lavella during the night of 14-15 August, returning to base at daylight on the 15th.

Shore-based aircraft from Munda were to support the operation. An attack upon Rabaul by aircraft from the Southwest Pacific Area was requested in view of the concentration at that point, but General MacArthur reported this to be impractical because of other commitments.

In spite of adverse weather through most of the week preceding the attack on Vella Lavella, Allied planes struck at enemy bases and depots in the Vila, Buin and Rekata Bay area. TBFs and SBDs dropped 36 tons of bombs on gun positions at Disappointment Cove and Kape Harbor, Kolombangara, on the 13th. On the 12th and 13th Liberators dropped a total of 49 tons of explosives on the airfield at Kahili, destroying many planes and shooting down 11 enemy fighters. The seaplane base in Rekata Bay was attacked seven times and the Vila airdrome was raided almost nightly during the week.

Advance Party 12-14 August – As a final preliminary to the action, a scouting party was landed at Barakoma on the night of 12-13 August to mark the channels and beaches to be used by landing craft and to select bivouac and dispersal areas and defense positions. Another duty assigned this advance party, which consisted of only 25 men, was to take custody of a large number of Japanese prisoners reported to be held by native sentries. Upon arrival, however, it was discovered that no prisoners were in hand, but that several hundred refugees from Kolombangara and survivors from the enemy ships sunk during the night of 6-7 August were at large. These Japanese were reported to be armed with hand grenades, clubs, and a few firearms.

Seabees – There were five Seabees of the 58th NCB in the advance party. Their job was to go ahead, survey the site for the airstrip, and mark the beach for the landing operation. The Seabee contingent consisted of Lt John L Reynolds, Lt (jg) Richard A. Currie, Warrant Officer Roy H. Smith and Chief Carpenter's Mates William H. Moss and Francis J. Dowling.

The scouting party boarded PT boats at Guadalcanal on the afternoon of 11 August for the overnight run up to Vella Lavella. It was a rough trip. Not only did the party suffer the agonies of PT seasickness, but Japanese planes spotted the wakes of the boats and bombed and strafed them for two hours.

Seabee Lt Reynolds:

> There was nothing for us to do but lie under the torpedo tubes and pray. For a while we prayed for the bombs not to hit us; then, as seasickness grew unbearable, we prayed for the bombs to hit us. But fortunately for the expedition, none of us were hurt.
>
> The party sneaked ashore on Vella Lavella just before daylight on August 12. The island was alive with Jap patrols, but in their best Indian fashion the officers began surveying the landing and airstrip sites. On the thirteenth, seeing that they were certain to be discovered by a Jap patrol, they ambushed the patrol and wiped it out to the last man. We taught those Japs a few jungle tricks, but the next thirty-six hours were uneasy ones for us. [2]

Reinforcement was immediately requested and after some delay, troops were moved in from Rendova by motor torpedo boats after dawn on the 14th.

Approach and Landing at Barakoma

First Echelon – Loading of equipment and supplies on the LSTs at Guadalcanal had begun on 12 August and was completed the following day. On the 13th troops embarked, conducted a debarkation drill, and reembarked. At 2130 that evening at Kokumbona, a single enemy plane came in low for an attack on the *Eaton*. The destroyer opened fire and observed its tracers hitting the approaching plane, which quickly ignited, whirled off to the west and crashed inland.

With the exception of one reinforced battalion of the 35th Combat Team, which embarked in the Russells, all units of the Main Body of the Task Force embarked at Guadalcanal. The three Transport Groups, each with its screen of destroyers, departed independently on 14 August on a schedule arranged to time their arrival at Barakoma on the 15th as follows:

	Depart Guadalcanal 14 August	Arrive Barakoma 15 August
Advance Transport Group (T.U. 31.5.1)	1600	0610
Second Transport Group (T.U. 31.5.2)	0800	0710
Third Transport Group (T.U. 31.5.3)	0300	0800

It was hoped thus to avoid undue exposure to air attack by giving each group full use of the beaches and cutting to a minimum the time other groups would be kept awaiting opportunity to unload.

Adm Wilkinson chose as his flagship the *Cony*, on which Gen McClure also embarked. The *Pringle* was designated primary fighter director ship with the *Conway* as relief. The *O'Bannon* and the *Taylor*, as bombardment ships, were to open fire on any shore battery, which threatened our landing craft. Screening destroyers were to maneuver to seaward of the transport area.

Let's backtrack for a moment and follow the LCIs in TU 31.5.2 as they prepare to head north. On 13 August at 0628, LCIs 332 and 334 departed Carter City for Koli Point, Guadalcanal to embark the 58th NCB Seabees. At 1930 the two LCIs anchored near the torpedo net at Kukum about 4,000 yards offshore in the vicinity of 11 other LCIs, 7 APDs and several other ships.

As all hands in the Task Unit would learn later, they were the primary target of a Jap sneak attack that night. Here's how Admiral Nimitz's staff reported the strike:[3]

> On 13 August, an unknown number of Jap VB and VT made a rather skillful 'sneak' raid on GUADALCANAL, sinking JOHN PENN (APA) with an aerial torpedo. Following in a flight of U.S. heavy bombers returning from a strike in the SHORTLAND-BUIN area, the enemy VB dropped a few bombs and flares over GUADALCANAL. With our attention thus diverted, an estimated 8 torpedo planes, flying low and fast, came in over FLORIDA Island to attack our shipping—well over 30 DDs, AKs, APs, and miscellaneous craft, either on patrol or unloading, and dispersed throughout this area.
>
> At 2034, after successive conditions 'red' at SAVO and RUSSELL Island, condition 'red' at GUADALCANAL was announced. Moon was in 3rd quarter, very bright, with surface visibility at 10,000 yards. About half an hour later, bombs and flares were seen in the vicinity of HENDERSON Field, Point CRUZ, etc. Friendly Liberators were coming in to land (some were damaged by our ship's AA). One 'Kate' launched a torpedo at *JENKINS* which avoided same by radical maneuvers and increased speed. A second 'Kate' was downed by her AA. *EATON* claims 1 VT down, as does *RALPH TALBOT.*
>
> *JOHN PENN*, however received the brunt of the attack. The 1st VT zoomed across her bow, strafing; the 2d, under fire by DDs *JENKINS* and *FULLER,* crashed off the bow. About this time, 3 planes were sighted with relative bearings of 060 degrees, 090 degrees and 170 degrees. The plane bearing 060 degrees dropped a torpedo at about 150 yards. The plane bearing 170 degrees was shot down by 20-mm and crashed on the ship near the mainmast.

The raid was no doubt triggered by the increase in shipping around the lower Solomons and the resultant increase in radio traffic. It was revealed later that the *John Penn* (AP-51) lost 98 men and another 64 were wounded. The assembled invasion force escaped untouched.

On 14 August Task Unit 31.5.2 (the Vella Lavella Second Transport Group) got underway at 0800 in compliance with CTF 31's secret operation order No. A12-13, 11 August.

LCI Unit Cmdr James M. Smith. LCIs 21, 22, 23, 61, 67, 68, 222 (F), 322, 331, 332, 333, and 334.

Destroyer Screen, Capt W.R. Cooke, Jr. (ComDesDiv 43). DDs *Waller, Philip, Saufley,* and *Renshaw.*

As the Task Unit passed abeam Rendova Island at 2345, all hands were at GQ, but permission had been granted for 50 percent of the men at a time to sleep on deck at their battle stations. (We'll revisit the LCIs later in the day.)

The weather during the approach to Barakoma was excellent, the sea calm, the sky nearly cloudless, and at night there was a brilliant moon. All Task Groups took the same course, lying south of the Russells and Rendova, thence north through Gizo Strait. Northwest of Rendova the three groups "leap-frogged." Shortly before dawn the Third Group with LSTs was slowly overhauled and passed by the Second Group with the LCIs, while almost simultaneously the Advance Group with the swift APDs overtook and passed both the slower Groups. The Units finally entered Gizo Strait in correct order. So far, but for the approach of an enemy snooper plane which apparently passed without spotting our force, the passage had been uneventful.

The Advance Group arrived off Barakoma at the break of dawn on 15 August and began unloading troops and equipment at 0615. Debarkation proceeded with dispatch, and was completed by 0715. The APDs departed on the return trip to Guadalcanal at 0730 with a screen of four destroyers.

It was with the beaching of the LCIs of the Second Group at 0715 that the schedule was broken. It was discovered that only 8 of the 12 landing craft could be accommodated at one time by the three beaches. This condition, plus an error in communications from the beach party, delayed the completion of unloading the last four LCIs until about 0900. In the meantime, the LSTs had arrived at 0800 according to schedule and were awaiting their turn to beach.

Anti-aircraft Action – Friendly aircraft from Munda were overhead by 0605. Since the landing was carried out within 90 miles of Kahili, the largest Japanese air base in the Solomons, it was no surprise when the radar of the fighter director destroyer picked up bogies at 0747. The original raiding party was considerably larger than the number of planes that succeeded in breaking through to deliver the attack. Our fighters, which successfully intercepted the attack, were credited with shooting down many planes.

At 0759 between 15 and 20 enemy fighters and dive bombers commenced an attack on the destroyers of the screen, ignoring for the moment the more vulnerable targets presented by the beached LCIs and the slow LSTs. The flagship *Cony* sustained three near hits, two within 50 yards of the ship, but there was no damage to the vessel and only one man was slightly wounded. Planes also dove on other destroyers, straddling the *Philip's* bow narrowly and bracketing LST-395 with two near hits, but without damage to either.

Anti-aircraft fire from the attacked vessels was effective in helping drive off the attack. Destroyers *Nicholas, O'Bannon, Taylor,* and *Chevalier,* still in the area during the attack, also joined in the firing.

The LCIs completed unloading by 0900 and retired with all remaining destroyers except the *Conway* and the *Eaton.* The Advance Group and the Second Group returned separately to Guadalcanal.

Now back to LCI-334. The following War Diary entries by Skipper Al Ormston, highlight the day's events as seen from the 334's perspective: [4]

August 15, 1943

0000 Underway as before. Clear sky, bright moon, visibility too good.

0250 LST formation sighted on parallel course 2 pts. on starboard bow.

0440 LST group abeam to starboard. APD group sighted astern.

0615 Vella Lavella on port bow.

0645 Kolombangara abeam to starboard.

0700 Standing by off Barakoma beach.

0710 Four LCIs proceeded toward beach. APDs having completed mission and withdrawn.

0759 AA fire and medium bomb bursts astern of us in DD area, and about four to six 'Val'-type dive-bombers seen attacking. This ship proceeded to beach and debarked troops.

0805 One enemy 'Val' came in range astern and guns 2, 3, and 4 fired; several hits were observed and the plane, still under fire from this ship and several other LCIs, disappeared smoking badly over the trees on the beach. One P-40 Warhawk drew heavy AA fire from all ships as he came out of sun in pursuit of a Jap plane; he was almost impossible to identify due to his approach angle.

Enemy planes last seen were over Shelter Island under attack by our fighters.

0840 Withdrew from beach and formed on LCI-332 column.

0910 All ships completed mission, withdrew and formed up, under way for Rendova and on to Florida Island on return course route.

0940 One of escorting DDs fired on Jap barge which was underway for western side of southern tip of Vella Lavella, demolishing it.

1115 Secured from General Quarters (total 12 hours 15 minutes).

1215 General Quarters. 25 bogies reported coming in. AA fire sighted at Vella Lavella.

1315 Secured from General Quarters.

The LCIs entered Hutchinson Creek the next morning at 0724. Before 16 August was history, the weary 334 crew were called to GQ three more times. But they would have the rest of August and then some to rest up before their next trip north.

Third Transport Group, TU 31.5.3 – Between 0900 and 0915 LSTs 354, 395, and 399 beached and began unloading. LST-395 struck a ledge of broken coral short of dry land, necessitating the construction of a ramp. This was quickly accomplished with the aid of a bulldozer that had been placed in the bow of the ship for just such a purpose.

Difficulties in clearing jungle growth for space to deposit supplies—and in keeping the unloading party working—threw the LSTs off schedules. Unloading proceeded laboriously under a burning sun and a perfectly clear sky. Visibility was so excellent that Corsairs and Kitty Hawks circling at altitudes up to 24,000 feet were clearly visible to the unaided eye.

After the attack of 0800, TU 31.5.3 remained unmolested until 1227 when the heaviest attack of the day began, continuing about 15 minutes. The Japanese planes Aichi 99 dive bombers and Mitsubishi Zeros were intercepted, but two groups consisting of 8 to 12 bombers broke through and attacked. One of these groups attacked the beached LSTs; the other two struck at the destroyers. Bombers were seen circling at 14,000 feet and starting their glides, some of which were steep, others shallow.

The first bomber to dive on the *Conway* was shot down, crashing within 50 feet of that ship. Three of its bombs burst close off the ship's starboard bow. The bombs from the second plane fell even closer on the starboard bow, one within 20 yards. The third plane was shot down and crashed 500 yards from the *Eaton*. The next three bombers sustained no apparent damage, but their bombs missed badly.

Eight bombers came in high and fast out of the sun to attack the LSTs. Near hits were scored on two of the ships. No material damage was done, although one man was seriously wounded. One LST claimed to have downed two bombers with anti-aircraft gunfire and another at least one.

Scarcely had the bomber attack been broken up when the *Conway* spotted seven Zeros and Vals, hedge-hopping over a saddle in the ridge of the island and closing in for a strafing attack on the landing area. The gun control officer of the *Conway* opened effective fire before the planes were sighted by the landing ships, and brought down one. Amply warned by the destroyer's fire, the crews of the LSTs put up a tremendous fire from small and medium weapons which completely frustrated the attack. One of the landing ships claimed three planes, another two, and the third claimed one plane shot down. Capt Grayson B. Carter, commander of the Third Transport Group, considered the repulse of this attack "the highlight of the day." In all, our forces reported they shot down ten planes in the noon attack.

Unloading was resumed and proceeded uneventfully until warning of a fourth attack came at 1724 from the Combat Air Patrol. This attack group, a large one coming in from the northwest, was intercepted and all but broken up by the Air Patrol. Only about eight single planes succeeded in getting through. They dived wildly, released bombs indiscriminately, and fled low over the water without inflicting any damage.

Shortly after this attack, the Third Transport Group completed unloading except for about 130 tons of cargo aboard two LSTs and retired at 1800 to avoid exposure to night attacks while without fighter cover.

Defense against air attacks during the day had been highly successful so far as the ships and their personnel were concerned. Ashore, however, twelve men of the landing force had been killed and forty wounded, although damage to materiel was slight.

On the return to Guadalcanal under a brilliant full moon and a clear sky, two of the three Transport Groups were subjected to repeated air attacks. From five to eight Mitsubishi 97s attacked the Second Group, consisting of 12 LCIs and four destroyers, when it was south of Rendova Island. The planes attacked singly at intervals from 2050 to 2140, dropping, it was believed, six torpedoes in all. No hits were made, however.

As in the daylight attacks, it was the Third Transport Group that took the most prolonged punishment. Between 2034 and 2330 the Group underwent six horizontal bombing attacks, and for four hours the convoy was surrounded or partially surrounded by flares and float lights dropped by the enemy. The bombs were usually dropped in patterns of eight, and each one was thought to be around 100 pounds in weight.

All three of the LSTs were sprayed with shrapnel. One reported some 200 holes punctured in bulkheads. Another reported 14 near hits from bombs within 100 feet of the vessels. The destroyers made frequent use of smoke screens. That our ships survived the attacks with only minor damage and insignificant casualties, was attributed, among other things, to "a perfectly phenomenal supply of good luck." Several officers commented on the excellence of the Japanese night search and attack.

Operations Ashore – During D-day, the three Transport Groups had landed at Barakoma a total of 4,600 troops, including 700 Naval personnel; 2,300 tons of equipment and supplies, including eight 90-mm anti-aircraft guns; 15 days' supplies of all classes, and three units of fire, except for the 90-mm guns, for which one Marine Unit (300 rounds per gun) was landed. The supplies discharged were considered sufficient to sustain the landing party well beyond the scheduled arrival of the next echelon.

The 4th Defense Battalion of the Fleet Marine Force immediately upon landing began setting up anti-aircraft guns in temporary shore positions. By 1530, sixteen .50-caliber machine guns, eight 20-mm, and eight 40-mm guns were in position. Marine gunners were credited with shooting down five enemy dive bombers during the day. By 1800 two searchlights were in readiness. During the night of 15-16 August shore installations were attacked 12 times by enemy planes, but only minor damage was inflicted.

Troops of the 35th Regimental Combat Team had landed without opposition and proceeded with their task of establishing a temporary defense perimeter. This was accomplished by noon without any Japanese resistance, and field artillery was emplaced in temporary positions by 1700. In the meantime, naval base units including the 58th NCB, commenced work upon docks, ramps, roads, airstrips, and dispersal areas.

Supplying Vella Lavella, 17 August – 3 September

The amphibious phase of the Vella Lavella campaign continued for twenty days after the initial landing and was not complete until four more echelons landed supplies, equipment, and personnel from Kokumbona and Kukum on the coral beaches of Barakoma. Although the enemy failed to oppose these operations with surface vessels, his air force did not neglect the opportunity our "Pacific Express" vessels presented while moving slowly through the narrow waters of Gizo Strait and Blanche Channel or lying beached at Barakoma.

The 35th Regimental Combat Team, concerned with establishing and maintaining a defense perimeter, had accomplished its mission without meeting any resistance. Patrols made a few contacts with small unorganized groups of Japanese who offered no resistance and kept moving northward. The military situation had therefore remained virtually unchanged since midday of 15 August.

The second echelon arrived at Barakoma at 1625 the following day. It consisted of:

Second Supply Echelon, Northern Force, Capt William R. Cooke, Jr.
    Transport Unit, Capt Cooke
        LSTs 339, 396, 460, Lt Cmdr Roy W. Lajeunesse
    Screen, DesDiv 43 (less *Renshaw*), Capt Cooke
        Waller, Saufley, Philip, SC 1266
    Landing Unit, Maj Frank G. Umstead, USMC
        Detachment 35th Combat Team; 155-mm Gun Group,
        4th Defense Battalion; Battery D (90-mm), 4th Defense
        Battalion; 1/2 Battery G (S/L), 4th Defense Battalion
        Detachment, 58th Naval Construction Battalion.

In planning the operation, it had been thought that all echelons subsequent to the initial landing group could be more safely unloaded at night. However, shortly after our fighter cover withdrew, two waves of enemy planes, one at 1850 and a second at 1910, attacked the beached vessels with bombs and strafing. Expecting the attacks to be continued through the night, BGen McClure ordered the LSTs, although still not unloaded, to withdraw from the beach and return in the direction of Rendova pending further orders.

With destroyers in screening stations, the convoy proceeded down Gizo Strait. There the third enemy plane attack began at 2110, and continued for two hours and seventeen minutes.

From the first attack at 1850 on 17 August, the convoy was under almost continuous attack by enemy planes until about 0200, 19 August. With only brief respite, men were at general quarters stations for a period of about 36 hours. During the greater part of this period no air cover was present because of darkness or unfavorable weather conditions.

At 2237, while engaging bombing and torpedo planes, the *Waller* and *Philip* collided in the narrow waters of Gizo Strait. At the moment of collision both ships were laying smoke screens and making radical changes of course at approximately 30 knots. The *Waller* was engaging one plane while the radar screen showed two more approaching. The damage was not serious enough to prevent the ships from continuing their screening duties through the night, although the following morning the *Waller's* damage was found to be more extensive than had been originally thought, and it was necessary to send her to Tulagi.

Loss of LST-396, 18 August 1943

The convoy continued toward Rendova until 0143, on 18 August when the course was reversed to return to Barakoma. At 0220 flames suddenly burst from the ventilators of LST-396. It was quickly apparent that the fire was beyond control and that the ship would have to be abandoned. The burning ship launched its only boat and threw life rafts overboard. Capt Cooke ordered the *Saufley* and SC-1266 to pick up survivors, which was accomplished without loss of a single life. The rescue was effected under hazardous exposure to exploding ammunition and falling debris.

At **0232** a heavy explosion blasted out the after section of the main deck, and subsequent explosions tore the vessel apart, sending flames hundreds of feet in the air. LST-396 sank at 0320.

The cause of the LST-396 explosions and fires is still a mystery after all these years. Let's back up for a minute and examine a condensed version of the 396 Action Report for 17-18 August by her C.O., Lt Eric White, USN: [5]

> At about **1630** on 17 August 1943, LST-396 arrived and beached at Barakoma, Vella Lavella, and commenced unloading in accordance with basic orders. At 1900, enemy planes attacked dropping two bombs and strafing the beach. No damage...was suffered by this ship...
>
> At **2030**, received orders from the Commanding General, Northern Occupation Force...to retreat from beach and retire towards Rendova.
>
> Immediately after departure...the ship was subjected to numerous air attacks by enemy dive-bombers and torpedo planes, interspersed with strafing attacks. The escorts immediately and continuously laid smoke screens and repelled these attacks with a very effective barrage.
>
> At about **2215** a torpedo wake was observed to pass under the ship from starboard to port with no apparent injury to the ship...
>
> At about **0045** the Executive Officer inspected the tank deck and cargo and reported conditions satisfactory.
>
> At about **0200**, 18 August 1943, received orders from Task Unit 31.1.6 to reverse course and return to Barakoma, on course 300 degrees T, at which time...a heavy dull explosion was felt seemingly coming from deep within the ship, or possibly beneath the ship, on the port side in the vicinity of frame #34.
>
> Two subsequent explosions followed closely. Intense heat was generated immediately after the explosions, and smoke and fire began to issue from the tank deck ventilators, followed by flames.
>
> All possible attempts were made to combat the fire. The First Lieutenant reported the tank deck a mass of flames. A series of lesser explosions began and continued. No aircraft was known to have been in the vicinity.
>
> At this time, I ordered the engine room force to set the fire and bilge pumps at maximum pressure and to abandon the engine room. I ordered the ship's boats launched. By this time, flames were shooting high above the ship and lesser explosions were occurring constantly. I then ordered the ship abandoned. The Executive Officer reported to

me that, to the best of his knowledge, everyone was off the ship, so he and I also abandoned ship.

After the first explosion and evidence of fire, I called the LST-460 by voice radio and informed them that we were on fire. They asked if they should come alongside to aid and I answered in the affirmative. After the second and third explosions, it was impossible for any ship to come alongside to help.

The remaining cargo on board was distributed as follows: gasoline, ammunition, powder charges on the forward half of the tank deck; vehicles, diesel oil and other cargo on the after half of the tank deck.

Upon questioning the officers and crew, it is the consensus of opinion that the ship had been hit by an armor-piercing, delayed-action bomb. Intense heat and acrid odor were noticeable after the explosions. One hole in the main deck on the port side in the vicinity of frame #34 was observed by members of the crew.

The first explosion seemed to occur in the port shaft alley. The access plate between the shaft alley and the main engine room was blown into the main engine room severing the main clutch service air line causing both propellers to stop. At this time, the port shaft was observed by the engine room force to be broken in two.

All hands succeeded in abandoning the ship. The USS *Saufley* picked up 94 men and SC-1266 picked up 9 men. Mulkey, Vernon Hayward, PhM 1/c, died on board the *Saufley* from injuries sustained in the explosion.

The ship broke in half as a result of the explosion, with both ends sinking. No ship's records, confidential papers, codes, ship's log, or papers were saved...

— E. W. White

Before Lieutenant White authored the Action Report, he obviously surveyed his officers and crew and the consensus was the 396 had taken a direct bomb hit. I've interviewed five of his crew for this book and all still agree with that position. In fact, they are very adamant about it. To wit:

"Sometime after midnight, on 18 August...we heard a plane quite high above us. Shortly after this, there was an explosion and fire below deck. The second bomb exploded near the tank deck a short time later."

— Jim Stackpole, QM 1/c, LST-396

"At 0218, the first bomb hit the port shaft alley knocking out the shaft, bulging the bulkhead behind the port engine and breaking an oil line…. The next bomb exploded on the tank deck which was loaded with aviation gasoline and 105- and 90-mm shells."

— Bob Hilliard, MoMM 1/c, LST-396

"The official U.S. Navy sketch lists the loss of the 396 as accidental. My personal opinion: It's a discredit to the officers and crew of LST-396. Besides being shot at off and on all day and part of the night, we were on the beach all day with bow open and ramp down, unguarded."

— Bill Leadingham, PhM 1/c, LST-396

Cmdr R.W. Lajeunesse, USN, ComLSTGRP 14 was on board LST-460 with LST-396 in column 500 yards astern during trip to Vella Lavella and observed the burning of the 396. Capt Carter, ComLSTFLOT 5 ordered him to investigate and submit a Casualty Report on the loss of LST-396. Here are some key excerpts from that report followed by relative comments excerpted from reports and endorsement letters as the report made its way up the line: [6]

> The exact cause of the fire on board this vessel cannot be determined. There has been offered the theory of a delayed action bomb and there is certain evidence and opinions of members of the crew to support this theory. This possibility cannot be denied. However, there had been no apparent attack by enemy planes for about two hours prior to the discovery of fire. Enemy planes were reported by radar within the area but no plane had been sighted nor any attack detected since just prior to midnight at 2367 Love. A plane was heard overhead passing down the column and one bomb was seen to explode in the water at a distance of about 1,500 yards on the starboard quarter of the column.
>
> It is believed that, had the LST-396 received a direct hit with a delayed action bomb at this time, the fact would have been known on board immediately. In view of the excellent manner with which the vessels of the escort gave timely radar warning of impending attacks during the movement of this echelon, it is hard to believe that a plane could have attacked the LST-396 just prior to the outbreak of the fire without having been detected by one or more ships of the formation…
>
> After passing through Gizo Straits, a head wind and sea were encountered and all the LSTs were subjected to heavy rolling. In addition to the sea, the escort vessels were zigging at high speed ahead and across the bows of the column laying protective smoke screens. The LSTs were repeatedly smashing into the high speed wakes thrown up

by the destroyers and at times rolled very heavily because of these wakes. It is believed that under these conditions some part of the cargo of the LST-396 could have fallen down or shifted in such a way as to have started a fire by spark or friction.

Gasoline and other fuel fumes are always present and are a constant menace to the safety of the LSTs and cargo. The major part of the cargo carried was extremely flammable and any fire started would spread very rapidly and be accompanied by relatively violent explosions. There is no proof that the fire was started in this manner, and is merely proposed as one of the possible theories which should be considered.

Endorsements to CO USS LST-396 Secret Letter, 22 Aug. 1943

Fifth Endorsement:

"The cause of the initial explosion which caused the loss of this vessel is as yet undetermined. The hypothesis offered in paragraph 4 of the first endorsement is tenable. The Task Force Commander is however of the opinion that it was torpedo hit from a submarine, since several D/F reports had been lately received of submarines in the SOLOMONS Sea, to the westward of the scene of the sinking."

— T. S. Wilkinson
Commander Task Force 31

Sixth Endorsement:

"The fact that the first explosion seemed to occur in the port shaft alley, as stated in paragraph 6 of basic letter, and that the access plate between the shaft alley and main engine room was blown off with considerable force, leads this command to believe that a torpedo hit as expressed in the fifth endorsement, is the most likely explanation to the cause of the explosion."

— Robt. B. Carney
Chief of Staff
W. F. Halsey
Commander South Pacific

Seventh Endorsement:

"The basic report, and endorsements thereto, offer three additional theories as to the explosion and fire: (1) that it was due to a delayed action, armor-piercing bomb, (2) a submarine torpedo, or (3) to explosive cargo having come adrift and become ignited by impact or friction. Either (2) or (3) of the foregoing appear most probable.

"The Commander in Chief, Pacific Fleet, regrets the loss of LST-396, but is gratified at the efficiency with which the ship was abandoned and her officers and crew rescued without loss of life."

— C. H. McMorris
Chief of Staff
C. W. Nimitz
Commander in Chief, U.S. Pacific Fleet

The Bureau of Ships evidently had the final word on the subject:

"The cause of the fire was not determined. No bomb hit was observed and there had been no underwater explosion. Although several theories were advanced to account for the first explosion, all the evidence indicated that a gasoline vapor explosion occurred in the port shaft alley, and that this was the origin of the fire that rapidly destroyed the ship"

— Bureau of Ships War Damage Report No. 46

Motor Mac Bob Hilliard and Quartermaster Jim Stackpole have both written articles on the subject published in *Scuttlebutt*, the National LST Association newspaper. I asked Hilliard to elaborate on his position:

> The report on the 396 sinking had it as an explosion, but it wasn't. Two Jap bombs hit us. Here's what really happened. We beached at Barakoma about 1600 on the 17th and began discharging passengers and cargo. About four hours later, we were ordered off the beach because the Japs were trying to bomb us.
>
> The Japs followed us—they were good at night torpedo and bombing attacks—and around 2200, I heard this loud thump underneath the ship. I called up to the bridge and asked them what happened. They said, 'Don't worry about it, they just fired a torpedo at us.'
>
> Early the next morning [0230 on 18 August] the first bomb hit the shaft alley and once in the shaft it disabled our engine. And then the other one hit the tank deck. I could see the hole when the hatch blew. The bomb blew up instead of down and that's when it knocked the hatch off and smashed Corpsman Mulkey's leg.

I think, in retrospect, the controversy over what happened that night can be blamed on all of the excitement and confusion during and following a night attack.

I then asked Quartermaster Stackpole to tell me what happened when the order came to abandon ship:

After an officer shouted 'Abandon Ship,' we cut the life rafts free and one by one they dropped into the ocean.... Somehow I made it to a raft already loaded with sailors and climbed aboard. Explosions were getting more numerous with fragments of the ship raining down around us. Finally, when the ship was about a half mile away, there was one tremendous explosion and the ship just disappeared.

Pharmacist Mate Bill Leadingham shared an amazing story with me:

Our medical officer, Lt David James, went into the crew area shower and pulled out pharmacist mate Vernon Mulkey. Doctor James got him into a life raft where, with the assistance of Pharmacist Mate Green, they amputated one of Mulkey's legs. Unfortunately, Mulkey died aboard the *Saufley* and was buried at sea that afternoon. Doctor James received the Silver Star for his efforts.

After completing their rescues, the *Saufley* and SC 1266 had to beat off yet another air attack before arriving at Barakoma. There they found that LSTs 339 and 460 had already beached at 0700. Before they left, enemy planes made two more bombing attacks. A near hit lifted LST-339 so high on the beach that she had difficulty in retracting. Damage inflicted upon enemy planes was impossible to assess with accuracy, but it was thought possible that four planes were shot down during the daylight attacks and two during the night attacks.

The convoy returned to Guadalcanal after unloading was completed without further attack, although the presence of bogies kept the men at general quarters until 0200, 19 August.

Third Echelon to Vella Lavella, 20 August – The third echelon departed Guadalcanal 20 August and arrived at Barakoma at 0700, 21 August. It consisted of:

Transport Unit, Capt Grayson B. Carter
    LSTs 354, 395, 399.

Screen, DesDiv 44 (less *Cony*)
   Conway, Eaton, Pringle, SC-505.
Landing Unit, Capt Burtis W. Anderson, USMC
   Detachment 35th Combat Team; Tank Platoon, 4th Defense
   Battalion; Detachment 58th Naval Construction Battalion.

En route up Gizo Strait, the formation was subjected at 0540 to torpedo, bombing and strafing attacks. Smoke screens and anti-aircraft fire were used against the attack. The *Pringle* sustained slight damage as a result of strafing that killed two men and wounded 25.

After the LSTs were beached, the destroyers retired to Rendova leaving only SC-505 for A/S screen. At 1015, sixteen Aichi 99 bombers accompanied by Zeros appeared over the beach at high altitude, having penetrated our fighter air cover. The enemy planes, after maneuvering uncertainly, apparently in search of the destroyers that had already departed, attacked the SC but retired without pressing home their attack on the LSTs.

A third air attack, developing about 1515, was pressed home with determination against the LSTs by a formation of more than 20 planes, consisting of dive bombers, torpedo bombers, and Zeros. Eight concentrated on LST-354. A few planes swerved off without dropping their bombs, and a few dropped their loads prematurely, but some ten planes dived steeply through intense anti-aircraft fire directly upon the beached vessels. Although there were no direct hits, bombs landed thickly in the area between and around the LSTs. Near hits, one within 25 feet, lifted the bow of one ship clear of the beach, knocked off a hatch cover, jammed the elevator, and knocked personnel on the main and tank decks off their feet. Bombs exploding on the beach covered the decks with coral rocks, some of them over 100 pounds in weight, knocked down gunners, and put about 50 percent of the LST batteries out of commission. A fire broke out on LST-398 but was quickly extinguished. In all, personnel casualties amounted to four killed and eleven seriously wounded.

The 58th NCB was highly commended for its zeal, not only in unloading, but in fighting. Ignoring danger, the men of this Battalion carried out the Task Group Commander's order to "go on and stay on till the job is done." They continued at their task under the hottest attack, and manned batteries when their gunners were knocked out.

Capt Grayson Carter, OTC of the Third Echelon, logged these remarks:

> Beaching was done at about the time intended, a dry ramp immediately thereafter, and as the ramp came down, aboard the ships came the shore party (of the 58th CBs) prepared to take everything LSTs had to offer. Not a second's delay was had; the party was splendidly organized; more than a sufficient number of men was on hand; and plenty of trucks and other equipment necessary to handle the load were available. The work proceeded on a basis which would brook no delay. In no instance was there any lag, and the supervision exercised by the shore party was of the very highest order. This was cooperation at its very best.

Admiral Nimitz added this comment:

> The Commander in Chief, Pacific Ocean Areas, heartily commends both the admirable courage of these Navy Seabees, who are proving themselves anything but non-combatant in spirit, and their demonstration of how the material difficulties of unloading and clearing craft from the beaches can be overcome, provided there is the proper organization and leadership.

Thanks to the Seabees, the LSTs were unloaded—except for a few tons remaining on two of the ships—and were able to withdraw at 1600. The return trip under escort was without incident.

The next two echelons were more fortunate than previous ones in their experience with enemy aircraft. Improving weather, for one thing, enabled air cover from Munda to give more effective protection, and lessons learned from previous experiences could be profitably applied.

Third Echelon to Vella Lavella, 20-22 August – LSTs 354, 395, and 398 with destroyers *Conway, Eaton,* and *Pringle*, and SC-505, departed Guadalcanal at 0305 on 20 August. This formed Task Group 31.7.

On 21 August while the Task Group was en route to Vella Lavella, the destroyers began making smoke at 0533 at the first sign of bogies. At 0545 *Pringle* had a near miss from a torpedo, a near miss from a bomb and was strafed. One man was killed and 25 wounded. Shortly thereafter, the *Conway* dodged a torpedo.

Capt Carter, Commander TG 31.7, asked for fighter cover at 0619 but received no response. At 1010 twelve enemy dive bombers and 12 Zeros attacked the subchaser patrolling in the harbor but no attempts were made on the LSTs.

At 1530 between 15 and 20 bombers dived on the LSTs while they were discharging cargo. Eight concentrated on LST-354. They all took near misses within 100 yards which covered the decks with coral dust and boulders. The boulders and shrapnel killed 4 and injured 11 on LST-398. Eighteen men were injured on LST-354.

The LSTs were happy to retract from the beach at 1614 and get underway for Guadalcanal. The LSTs shot down a total of 10 planes: LST-395 got 4; 354 splashed 2; and 398 knocked down 4. The Task Group arrived at Kukum Beach at 1800 on 22 August where they disembarked 4 dead, 49 ambulatory, 23 stretcher personnel and 13 Chinese nationals.[7]

The LST-398 crew counted some 20 holes up to 2 inches in diameter in the vicinity of the bow. One piece of shrapnel punctured the hull near the starboard ammunition locker and started a fire which was quickly extinguished after the ammo locker was flooded. Martin "Flags" Melkild (LST-398) expressed the feelings of many a weary sailor that evening with these words:

> The events of the day, coupled with the loss of dead and wounded shipmates, left one with depressed feelings. However, during the many hours on 'the long watch,' the ship's galley crew came through with coffee, soup, and sandwiches for all stations.[8]

Fourth Echelon to Vella Lavella, 25-26 August – LSTs 339, 397, and 399, loaded with twenty 21/2-ton trucks each, in addition to rations and ammunitions, were escorted to Barakoma by the *Saufley, Renshaw, Cony* and SC-733, under command of Capt Cooke. Aside from mistakenly firing upon one friendly plane at 0350 and driving off a formation of enemy planes with the assistance of friendly fighter planes at 0615, the convoy made the approach without further incident. All LSTs were beached at 0855, 26 August, and unloading proceeded with speed and efficiency, facilitated by use of the trucks aboard each vessel. This was the first echelon to escape air attack during unloading operations. The return voyage was similarly uneventful.

Fifth Echelon to Vella Lavella, 30-31 August – Capt Cooke also commanded the Fifth Echelon (TG 31.6) using the same screening destroyers in addition to the two APDs *Dent* and *McKean*, each of which carried about 175 men. LSTs 398, 341, and 353 departed with the convoy from Kokumbona at 0400, 30 August, and five LCIs with the 1st Battalion of the 145th Infantry joined the force off Munda the following morning at 0145. The night's passage was uneventful except that unidentified planes were fired upon twice.

Beaching and unloading were staggered, the *Dent* and *McKean* proceeding independently at 0600. These vessels disembarked their troops and commenced retirement independently by 0800, when the remainder of the convoy arrived. The LCIs completed disembarkation within the next hour and started to form for the return trip under escort by the three destroyers.

About this time, at 0900, enemy planes that had been under radar observation for several minutes closed for an attack on the destroyers. Nine dive bombers, apparently Aichi 99s, divided their attention among the three vessels, four attacking the *Saufley*, two the *Cony*, and three the *Renshaw*. All ships suffered near hits, and direct hits were avoided only by radical maneuvers at high speed. All three sustained superficial damage topside, and two men on the *Cony* were injured by fragments. Damage inflicted on the enemy was indeterminate, although two planes were possibly shot down.

After escorting the LCIs to a point within 15 miles of Rendova, the destroyers returned to Barakoma for the unloaded LSTs at 1400. The return passage was accomplished without mishap.

Passage of Command – The amphibious phase of the Vella Lavella operation was considered complete at midnight, 3 September 1943, when the island passed to the command of Gen McClure, New Georgia Occupation Force.

The unloading of the Fifth Echelon left the forces on Vella Lavella with approximately 40 days' rations, fuel and other supplies sufficient for 30 days, and five units of fire. During the 20 days from the initial landing at Barakoma to the passage of command, the

"Pacific Express" had delivered the following troops and supplies to Vella Lavella:

Total Troops and Supplies 15 Aug. - 3 Sept. 1943

Personnel	6,505
Rations	1,097 tons
Drummed petroleum products	843 tons
Ammunition	2,247 tons
Vehicles	2,528 tons
(263 cargo type, 190 construction type, 134 special type: 587 total vehicles)	
Other freight	1,911 tons
Total cargo	8,626 tons

Barakoma Developments 15 Aug. - 3 Sept. – In the period between 15 August and 3 September the 35th Regimental Combat Team enlarged the defense perimeter, extending it from a point north of the Barakoma River on the east to Varisi on the west coast. By the end of August, strong outposts were established at Malasova and Supato to the west and Marivari to the east. The whole southern end of the island was mopped up and patrols pushed up the east coast to Orete Cove.

Behind these lines the unhindered development of the Barakoma area went forward according to plan. The Advanced Naval Base was responsible for the immediate construction of beach points, roads and anchorages. As a means of informing units of which road connections were not available, the No. 9 Boat Pool, with its 16 LCVPs and LCMs, became indispensable. Two or three coxswains were wounded in the course of their duty when the boats were taken ashore under fire.

By 3 September the 58th NCB had succeeded in clearing ground for the airfield strip and had begun the work of grading. The establishment of an advanced base was moving forward along lines that were to establish the pattern of subsequent island operations.

The passage of command to Gen McClure supposedly signaled the end of the amphibious phase of the Vella Lavella, but I'm pretty sure the amphibians who made the next several runs to Vella would question the call. Here's a summary of the runs. Echelons eight and nine describe the loss of LSTs 167 and 448: [9]

Sixth Echelon to Vella Lavella, 6-8 September – LSTs 167 and 397, escorted by DesDiv 45, less *Stanley*, was under command of Cmdr V. K. Busck, ComLSTGRP 15. The formation departed Kukum at 0400 on 6 September for Barakoma, and returned to the 'Canal without incident on 8 September.

Seventh Echelon to Vella Lavella, 17-19 September – Task Group 31.6 consisting of LSTs 167, 448, 449, 472, and 485; LCIs 333, 332, 331, 327, 328, 330, and *Bobolink*, was escorted by *Farenholt, Woodworth, Lardner, Lansdowne, Radford, Jenkins, Dent, Waters, Talbot, Kilty, Ward,* and *Crosby*. Cmdr Burke, CTG. Cmdr V. K. Busck, ComLSTGRP 15 were in LST-485.

The convoy departed the 'Canal 17 September 0400, commenced unloading at Vella 18 September 0747, completed unloading cargo 1330, underway for return trip at 1345, and back at Purvis Bay 19 September at 1847 without incident.

Eighth Echelon to Vella, 24-26 September – Task Group 31.6 comprised of LSTs 167, 334, 448, 449, 472, and 485, Cmdr R.W. Lajeunesse, ComLSTGRP 14 aboard LST-485, and APDs *Stringham, McKean, Talbot, Waters, Dent, Kilty, Ward,* and *Crosby;* escorted by DDs *Selfridge, Ralph Talbot, McCalla, Patterson, Radford, Jenkins,* and *Converse* departed the 'Canal 24 September 0400, and commenced unloading at Sanaporo Point, Vella Lavella at 0730.

The LST-449 Deck Log recorded the morning's action:

08-12 – Beached as before continuing unloading cargo. At 1050 two flights of Bogies being tracked in from North and Northwest by fighter director. At 1100 three enemy planes observed to the North after sighting 3 bomb bursts in vicinity of LST-167. At 1109 four unidentified planes sighted bearing 280 degrees, altitude 5,000 feet. At 1110 shore batteries opened fire at planes. Ship then opened fire. Ceased firing at 1112. Expended 415 rounds of 20-mm and 38 rounds of 40-mm ammunition. At 1158 completed unloading cargo and commenced loading U.S. Army cargo.

12-16 – Beached as before loading cargo and Army personnel....At 1300 Lt (jg) William A. Ferraro, MC, USNR, Ruchalski, Chester L, PhM 2/c and Kain, Hugh C., PhM 3/c left ship to give medical aid to LST-167. At 1440 made preparation for retracting. At 1503 retracted, underway steering various courses and using various speeds conforming to channel.[10]

The Task Group, less LST-167, was back at the 'Canal 26 September at 2109.

By 1800 on 27 September, the LST-167 fire was under control but a below-deck inspection had not been made. It was thought that no underwater holes were present because the ship was floating high. The bow doors were open and bow ramp was lowered. Since the auxiliary engines were out, there was no power to effect closing. A portable generator was suggested but in case of failure, the ship could be towed stern first by *Bobolink* to Carter City.

The unhospitalized survivors of 167 were taken to Receiving Ship, Tulagi, for quartering and subsistence. The known dead were two officers and seven enlisted men. Tug *Bobolink* towed the 167 to the Russells in late September, then completed the job on 10 October when she arrived at Hutchinson Creek with LST-167 in tow. Requests were made the same day for her appraisal by COMSERONSOPAC. In the meantime, Capt Carter asked for permission to "borrow" urgently needed parts for other LSTs.

On 17 November, it was recommended that LST-167 not be towed away but that all salvageable parts be removed and the hull made into an ammunition barge at Tulagi. Finally, on 26 November, the fate of the 167 became just that, an ammo barge. LST-167, a U.S. Coast Guard-manned ship, had reported for duty with Flotilla 5 on 28 August 1943, so it was a short tour as an LST. She made just three trips up the Slot prior to her ill-fated encounter with the enemy. (She was built by Missouri Valley Bridge and Iron Co. in Evansville, Indiana and commissioned on 27 April 1943.)

LST Flotilla Five Group 13 Returns [11]

Flotilla Five Group 13 LSTs 446, 447, 448, 449, 334, and 390 reported for duty in Carter City between 6-24 September 1943 after stops in Nouméa for repairs and dry-docking in Espiritu Santo. These pioneer vessels—profiled in Volume I—had been on loan to "MacArthur's Navy" since late April 1943.

LST-446 was the first of the new landing ships to arrive in the Pacific (March 8) and made the first LST run to the Russells (March

11). The 446 departed Guadalcanal on 18 April 1943 with her three "400+" sisters, the 447, 448, and 449 and met up with newly arrived Flotilla 5 LSTs 334 and 390 in Nouméa in preparation for their trip to Townsville, Australia.

Allow me to change up for just a moment to bottomline their duty in the Amphibious Force Southwest Pacific—a.k.a. VII Amphibious Force—commanded by RAdm Daniel E. Barbey, affectionately known as "Uncle Dan the Amphibious Man."

The acute shortage of landing ships and craft in the Pacific at this early stage of the war called for cooperation between our amphibious forces. Consequently, Gen MacArthur and Adm Barbey borrowed the 6 Flot 5 LSTs plus APDs *Brooks, Gilmer, Humphreys* and *Sands* from Adm Halsey and Turner.

Rear Admirals Turner and Barbey would share the honor of launching the first forward amphibious movement to take back the Solomons and New Guinea in 1943.

Another 6 LSTs fresh from the States were soon added to Barbey's Task Force before learning what they would be expected to do.

LST-446 had a change of command on 28 May 1943. Lt Cmdr W. A. Small was detached to the U.S. Army Hospital in Townsville and was replaced by one of the ship's watch officers, Lt (jg) J.C. Adams, USNR, who received a spot promotion to Lieutenant Senior Grade.

Adm Barbey's 12 new-found LSTs formed up in Townsville for the Trobriands exercise, organized into two groups of six ships each. LST-446 became the flagship for one group commanded by Cmdr Roger Cutler, USNR, and would lead it during the second Woodlark landing, departing Townsville 27 June, arriving Woodlark 1 July 1943 under cover of darkness.

Strategically, Woodlark and Kiriwina Islands lie in the Solomon Sea, both off the southeast coast of New Guinea. Kiriwina is about 125 miles south of New Britain Island (Rabaul); Woodlark is more than 200 miles southwest of Bougainville Island. Together they would give the Allies powerful bases for staging air strikes against Rabaul, or so it was then believed.

It should also be noted that 30 June 1943 was chosen as D-day for the Woodlark and Kiriwina operations in the Trobriands to coincide with RAdm Turner's move into New Georgia in the

Solomons, and U.S. Army General Eichelberger's troop landing at Nassau Bay below Salamaua on the Papuan Peninsula of New Guinea.

On 25 June, destroyers *Mugford* and *Helm* escorted north from Townsville half of the Woodlark force, six LSTs and one subchaser.

Destroyers *Bagley* and *Henley* followed the next day with a similar force. H.M.A.S. *Benalla* (a survey ship) and two APcs set forth from Milne Bay on the 29th together with 12 LCTs, 12 LCIs and 7 LCMs screened by four destroyers, for the main landing at Kiriwina.

On Woodlark the advance party laid out markers and prepared the beaches so that unloading went forward with dispatch. Kiriwina, surrounded by a spiny necklace of coral, proved troublesome. Unloading dragged along discouragingly and a fortnight was required to unsnarl all tangles.

Three weeks elapsed, but the Japanese offered no opposition to the movement into the Trobriands because the simultaneous landings on New Georgia and New Guinea seemed more important—and, of course, they were. During this time, VII 'Phib brought

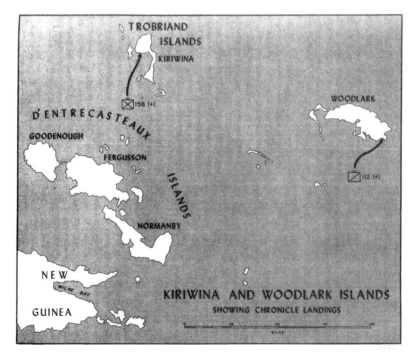

KIRIWINA AND WOODLARK ISLANDS
SHOWING CHRONICLE LANDINGS

16,000 men into the islands without the loss of a single man, ship, or boat, and the Seabees built an airstrip on Woodlark.

LST-446 completed 4 operational runs to Woodlark Island from Townsville, Australia and one from Milne Bay, New Guinea.

According to Gen MacArthur, the only value of the Trobriands lay in their position as Allied air bases to afford fighter protection and bigger payloads for bombers raiding Rabaul, Kavieng and the Northern Solomons.

Admiral Barbey also considered the operation an opportunity to test amphibious doctrine and equipment much like the Russell Islands exercise was in February 1943. Using this as a measuring stick, the bloodless occupation was a big success.

In September, the 6 wayfaring LSTs reported back for duty at Carter City, home base for LST Flotilla Five, just in time for a few Munda and/or Vella resupply "warm-ups" before the upcoming invasion of Bougainville.

Rogers Aston, LST-446 Gunnery Officer, and one of our LST historians in Volume I, has two short stories for us. Here's Aston:

> George Shaw, who became skipper [of the 446] after Cooper Adams was sent back to the States for magnificent duty was noted as close with a buck. He was popular and respected, but a buck was a buck. He decided he would solve his laundry problem.
>
> George purchased a pair of regulation khaki pants from ship's stores and tied them with a small rope so they could be dragged in the wake of the ship. We were cruising for some time when he remembered his pants being caressed by the salty brine. I went back to witness the magic as he pulled them in. Attached to the rope was a waistband and two pockets. The balance of his new pants were a few shreds and strings. This hit good old George right in the wallet, and that pained him greatly. George never conducted any more laundry experiments.

Many a sailor learned the above lesson the hard way. Shaw was lucky it was only one pair of pants. Now for the other Aston sea story:

> Doc Innis was our ship's doctor for some time. Demands on his services were not great, and Doc got really bored. He would go to the small officers' club at Lyon's Point on Florida Island. He was known to stow away a bit too much of the liquid happiness before being returned to the ship.

One time Doc was so relaxed he couldn't climb the ladder to the main deck. We secured a rope around him and hoisted him aboard. I now admit that those on the ship were also bored, so we decided to have a little fun with Doc. We brought him to his natural state of undress. We then painted his finger nails and toe nails a brilliant deep purple, a popular song at that time, with gentian violet. Using gentian violet our quiet little group also turned some more intimate parts of the sleeping doctor's anatomy purple.

Doc expressed himself quite strongly, while the guilty villains struggled to look innocent. It should be pointed out that gentian violet cannot be washed away, and it took Doc Innis some weeks before the violet nails grew out, and he was once again his own man.

Could it be that the officers we swabbies saw as "straight arrows" actually had a sense of humor, and even joked around at times?

Ninth Echelon to Vella Lavella, 30 September-2 October – Task Group 31.6 comprised of LSTs 334, 448, 449, 460, 485, and 488 and APDs *Stringham, Crosby, Ward, Talbot, McKean,* and *Kilty,* escorted by DDs *Patterson, Ralph Talbot, Converse, McCalla, Foote, Radford,* and *Jenkins,* departed the 'Canal 30 September 0400, beached at Beach Baker, Vella Lavella on 1 October and commenced discharging passengers and cargo at 0730. Cmdr V. K. Busck, Com-LSTGRP 15, aboard LST-485 was in charge of the LST unit.

At 1030, enemy dive bombers in the vicinity of LSTs 448 and 334 attacked and both ships received direct bomb hits.

Loss of LST-448, 1-5 October 1943

The LST-448 Action Report provides detailed coverage of the tragic loss of the 448. Due to space limitations, here are some condensed highlights: [12]

> **October 1, 1943** – Beached at Nargvai, Vella Lavella... Ship in Condition One; after guns trained into sun.
>
> At 0935, without a Condition "Red" having been given, sighted and commenced firing at a plane diving out of the sun, angle about 40 degrees, range about 4500 yards. General Quarters and tank deck howler were sounded. Three planes attacked from bearing 190 degrees relative.

First plane sighted began smoking, veered to starboard, jettisoned bombs to seaward of ship and passed about 500 yards to starboard. This plane definitely claimed as destroyed as ground forces later sighted crashed plane in woods behind beach.

Second plane had been sighted close behind first and was under fire. This plane continued dive although smoking and appeared as though crash diving into ship. However, plane pulled out releasing bombs, the first striking forward port corner of 3"/50 caliber gun platform, penetrating through main deck, exploding in crew's compartment, starting fire in this compartment and in commissary storeroom above after magazine. Second bomb struck main deck forward port corner of cargo hatch. Conn was enveloped in smoke and fire, apparently from exploding gas drums.

No other planes were sighted by Commanding Officer due to smoke and flames. However, another bomb was felt to strike and from information given by Lieutenant (jg) Breimyer, forward battery officer, a fourth made a near miss near port bow.

Entire attack did not last more than thirty seconds. Generators were torn from base by second bomb and Auxiliary Engine Room was flooded... Orders were given to fight fire and flood after magazine but with all power gone there was no pressure on fire main. Due to fire, we could not get near CO_2 on tank deck. Ammunition in cargo was beginning to explode and at 0950 Commanding Officer gave orders to abandon ship.

Commanding Officer, Engineer Officer, Gunnery Officer, Communications Officer, one doctor, one Pharmacist's mate and three men remained on board to evacuate wounded, who were lowered by stretcher into our personnel boat and transferred to beach about 500 yards to starboard.

About 1000 all wounded aft were off ship and Commanding Officer with officers (less Communication Officer who was ordered into boat) proceeded up starboard side to search forecastle for wounded. Two men were found badly mangled but both died on stretchers before being put over the side. At 1010 Commanding Officer gave orders for all officers and men to leave ship. We proceeded to same beach to discharge wounded...

At 1100 an alert was sounded. All officers and men ran into jungles searching for foxholes. On all clear, Commanding Officer had word passed for all hands... We arrived at [New Zealand] hospital at 1215, engineer and supply officer were ordered to check survivors and wounded. Commanding Officer attempted to contact CNB Vella Lavella by telephone but was unsuccessful. At 1315 all survivors left N.Z. hospital for Naval Base passing LST-449 unbeaching en route. At 1530 arrived at Naval Base and attempted to contact Commander LST Group Fifteen through signal station...

Ship was again bombed during afternoon of 1 October being hit by a heavy bomb on main deck almost opposite to second bomb hit. This bomb exploded on tank deck tearing a large hole in tank deck starboard bulkhead at frame #26.

At about 1300, the other ships in the task group, began retracting from the beach. At 1545 they departed Barakoma for Guadalcanal. The LST-448 able-bodied survivors had their work cut out for them. Let's rejoin them early the next morning drawing on more Action Report highlights:

October 2, 1943 – At daylight Commanding Officer, Engineering Officer, Gunnery Officer and working party returned to ship to fight fire using pump furnished by CNB Vella Lavella...

October 3, 1943 – Due to physical and mental exhaustion of survivors, working party from naval base was sent out at daylight to pump out water with pump used to fight fire...

October 4, 1943 – Commanding Officer with working party boarded ship at daylight and began pumping out water. Using a 'Cat' and relieving tackle, ramp and starboard door were closed. Towing bridle had been rigged forward. Ship was slowly settling by stern probably due to broken piping in auxiliary engine room allowing water to enter. No holes had been found in port side of hull and only a few holes well above the water line were found in starboard side. Draft aft about 16 feet...

October 5, 1943 – At 0730, *Bobolink* arrived to take ship in tow. At 1155 ship floated free settling aft until she had about three feet of freeboard...

Captain of Naval Base, Commanding Officer, and Engineering Officer proceeded to tug which continued towing LST-448 by stern. At this time, ship had settled so only one foot freeboard remained at stern. Tow was shifted to bow and ship appeared to ride easy.

Captain of Naval Base, Commanding Officer, and Engineering Officer of LST-448 returned to Naval Base at 1715. Tow was then to seaward of Barakoma, Vella Lavella on course 190 T making about six knots through water. At 1830 Love *Bobolink* reported LST-448 sank while in tow.

On 4 November 1943, Cmdr R.W. Lajeunesse, ComLSTGRP 14 would be ordered to conduct an investigation into the sinking of LST-448 by *Bobolink*. In a separate "Narrative of Events During

Attack," Lt C. E. Roeschke, the 448 C.O., had some kind words for his forward gun crews: "The crews of the two 20-mm and 40-mm guns on the foc'sle did a commendable job by remaining at their stations during the approach and fighting the fire afterwards. On the approach, the 448 was afire from frame 38 to the stern, and the ammunition ready boxes of the 20-mm, 40-mm and 3" guns were bursting at intervals throwing fragments on the bow of this vessel but not a man showed signs of leaving the foc'sle."

There were 31 casualties on the 448—17 killed and 14 wounded. As far as this writer knows, the casualty count for troops and cargo handlers was never recorded. John "Monty" La Montagne was the gunnery officer on the 448. (We met him earlier in Volume I.) As well as having his own LST command, Monty would serve on 5 LSTs before the war ended. In our interview, I asked Monty to tell me what he remembered of the 1 October enemy air strike. Here's Monty:

> We were nearly unloaded. The ships were not all together. We were probably a half mile or more apart because the beaches were so tiny. Steep coral stuff. We had our bow into the beach on our little section of land as we did every time we made a run up the Slot.
>
> This was our third, maybe fourth, time to make the Vella run. We were the target and three planes came down at us out of the sun. They let fly and some of the bombs came down on the starboard side and some down on the port side from what I could tell. The shower of coral was all over our deck. We had unloaded all of the equipment but there were still a few men aboard unloading other cargo. I know some Marines and Seabees had come aboard to help.
>
> There were bodies laying all over the place down there. I remember standing forward of the deckhouse—on the little walkway ahead of the Conn actually—and seeing these holes in their bodies with their blood actually boiling out of their bodies. This was immediately after it happened, you know. The action was so quick, as you probably know.
>
> Suddenly, I heard our guns fire because somebody had seen the Jap planes coming in. I turned around immediately and walked back inside the Conn and put my headset on. At that time, the noise was so deafening that I was hollering, 'keep firing,' and suddenly, there was dead silence. Now we had been hit at least three times. Bombs were going off on both sides, but the strange part of it is, I don't remember any sound. I don't remember hearing anything. Everybody gets a different reaction.

Harold Breimyer, our Communications Officer, was up on the bow and I was on the bridge with Mr. Hays and Charles Roeschke, the Captain. The skipper had seen the bomb go off just forward of us and he was blinded temporarily. I didn't see it because I was going back in to get my headset phones. We couldn't go down a forward ladder because of the fire and the exploding ammunition. So Hays and I took Roeschke arm in arm and led him down the aft ladder onto the boat deck, and then on down to the stern. There a bomb had gone through the after guntub before it exploded and just tore up everybody back there. Some were still alive and we were rendering first aid.

By this time, Roeschke had recovered his sight. He asked me to go forward to see what I could find. I didn't see Breimyer because he had left the ship through the bow. The Marines' 40-mm mobiles had been blown off the deck. The chief steward, the only CPO we had on board, was gone. The crew was gone except for one man by the name of Adams. I still remember his name. He was a Motor Mack. He was laying there dead and looked perfectly normal.

I asked Monty, "When you say gone, do you mean they had died, left the ship, or were maybe missing?"

They were not dead, they were gone. They weren't there. They hadn't left the ship—they'd been blown off the ship. The bomb landed right near them. The gun was gone, the whole thing. That explosion was enough to blow that weapon over the side and only one man was lying there on the deck. Up forward, the elevator cables broke and the elevator dropped and crushed some men under it. So it was a real mess. Many were wounded.

One young man, his name was Raven, had his back blown out pretty badly. Our doctor, fortunately, was with us back there in the stern. He was giving these guys morphine shots and I remember looking down on this young kid. You know these kids were 17 or 18 years old. I could see his lungs going up and down. Just his raw lung—his ribs were gone. His ribs and his whole back were gone. It's amazing to see how much lung you have in your body cavity. I think he died later.

Then I asked Monty if he could recall the 448's crew size and the number of troops on board when the Japs hit them.

We had a small crew of about 4 officers and 50-some enlisted men. Early in the war there were never enough men to go around. Later on, when they increased the weapons, we had bigger crews. Fortunately, most of the troops had disembarked by the attack, but there were still some on board helping unload, and a few volunteers. There were still more of the troops killed than there were of our people.

"It seems like you were sitting there on the beach, pretty much isolated from the other LSTs in your Task Group, when the bombs started falling. Am I right?" I asked.

> Our sister LSTs were out of sight. I think what happened was one of the three Jap pilots had us dead in his sights and his bombs did the job on us. Other bombs came down on either side of the ship. That's what I recall anyway. I know the water around us was saturated with mud after the attack.

"Sounds like you didn't get much notice the Japs were on their way," I added. "Is that true?"

> We didn't have any warning at all. We were at relaxed GQ. It was a total surprise to have those guys just appear out of nowhere. As I said, I wasn't even aware of the raid until I heard our own guns going off, and here I am the Gunnery Officer.

Here are some pertinent direct quotes from Cmdr Busck's LST Group 15 Action Report:

> At 0937 [on 1 October] LST-334 reported "Being attacked by 15 dive bombers and as many Zeros" after which he went silent. Called away boat from 485 loaded with plasma, first aid boxes previously prepared for such emergencies by LCmdr Cuttle (MC), and Lt Marquis (MC), and headed north towards pillar of smoke rising there. When passing LST-460, directed them to send small boat with medical aid.
>
> About 1000 arrived alongside 448, disembarked medical men and supplies to dressing station and made boat available for wounded. Boarded 448 by ramp. Vessel entirely deserted, nobody even near it on beach. Penetrated tank deck about 2/3 way, observing about ten bodies therein and small fire in back of cargo still loaded. Bomb explosion(s) in this area had wrecked forward elevator and trucks in after end of vessel, but no hull penetration was observed.
>
> Went topside and aft on maindeck to after elevator where I was stopped by heat and exploding ammo. Saw about ten more bodies about guns on maindeck, both forward and aft. The deckhouse structure was on fire, ammunition in ready-boxes and in the cargo below exploding, and much minor damage evident about topside, apparently from fragments of a bomb that hit and demolished the port amidships 40-mm portable mount.
>
> Ship showed evidence of having fought fire as long as possible. Hoses were led out but had proved useless as there was no pressure.

All living wounded had been removed: a quick check of bodies that could be examined revealing them to be indubitably dead. Some had received first aid and some on stretchers ready to be evacuated when death made further effort useless.

Realizing ship could easily be saved if water were available and resolute attempt made before fires gained hold, ran over to the emergency dressing station on beach to starboard of vessel to see if by any chance there was a pumper there. Found an officer from the 460 there loading wounded into his boat for transportation to the New Zealand hospital..

Directed this officer to hail his ship en route and tell C.O. I said to retract, proceed alongside 448 and extinguish fire. I then commandeered a truck to get back to the 460 by land and confirm the message.

En route, saw 460 retract and start for Barakoma, then turn back and speak to small boat and head north towards the 448. Continued on to 485 and embarked therein. Found all cargo landed, and C.O. with good grasp of situation getting N.Z. guns off and retracting. Held up retracting to receive four wounded from small boat, but after examination by Lt Marquis (MC) ordered them taken to the N.Z. hospital as they were beyond help. Four survivors also in boat declined to come on board another LST and went with the wounded.

Retracted, and saw 460 lying to off Nairovai. Sent him a dispatch by 3000 kcs "Go alongside 448 and help put out fire, also take on casualties." This was sent at 1100. At 1103 the 460 replied, "It is too dangerous to go alongside." At 1105, I then ordered 460, "Stay in vicinity and evacuate wounded," to which he replied, "Roger Wilco." Ordered Lt Stover, Commanding Officer of the 485 to lay his vessel alongside the 448 and, at 1128, as 485 was standing alongside the 488, ordered 460 to "Get under batteries at Barakoma. Await our return."

About 1130, Lt Stover, C.O. of the 485, did a magnificent job of seamanship and laid the bow of his ship alongside the starboard (windward) quarter of the 448. Seven hoses going big guns. As soon as water touched the 448 the explosions died down, and it became a routine job of fire fighting. By 1200 five of the seven hoses were in action on the stern of the 448, one pouring water down vent to the 3" magazine to keep it cool. Fire fighting hampered by periodic bursts of flame and smoke as drums of gasoline torched off on tank deck, the heat coming up through the bomb hole on centerline between the winch and the galley.

Sent the First Lieutenant of the 485 with two small gas pumpers to fight the fire back from the bow along the tank deck. As there were no men to spare, directed him to use Seabees and Marines loafing and looting up there.

Ensign Ruwitch, USNR, the First Lieutenant, did a splendid job fire fighting with what assistance he could get, driving the fire fifteen feet back along the tank deck despite bursting gasoline drums, but the lack of proper pressure hampered him. At my direction he removed bodies from tank deck and topside, and threw over scattered ammo on topside.

At 1300 the escorts returned. Asked them to send portable fire pumps to bow of 448 and suggested they escort remainder of the convoy to safety leaving one DD to escort 485 and 448 when we got her in tow. At this time fire was getting under control...

At 1400, as preparations for towing were starting, second raid came in. Fire party manned their guns... I was on top of galley using 2" hose when attack came in. Bomb hit 448 just forward of bridge and set off so much flame and smoke I was forced to jump down on fantail and abandon ship, covered by hoses still being manned on the 485. Witnessed remainder of attack from foredeck of 485 and then examined 448. As a result of the bomb hit, the 448 was flaming anew, as if diesel oil tanks were ruptured. She settled twelve inches, making towing off improbable, so at 1405 sent the following to Task Group Commander, patrolling off beach in the USS *Foote*: "ComLSTGroup 15 regrets bomb from last attack settled 448 so she cannot be towed easily X Am gathering in my fire party and abandoning her X Expect retract in half hour X Pass to CTF 31, CTG 31.1, ComLSTFlot 5."

At 1511 retracted and started back to Barakoma. Proceeded flank speed with the *Foote* in company to catch remainder of convoy, sighted steaming down through Gizo Strait at eight knots (due to damage to 334).

Having previously received signal from Lt Roeschke, USNR, C.O. of 448 that he had wounded and survivors at N.Z. hospital and that he was going to the NavBase, directed him by signal, "Remain NavBase reporting to Cmdr Wilkinson for orders X Report killed and wounded and survivors when possible X We have Lt Haynes, Evall SC1c, and Davis S1c on board here." This decision dictated by need of getting out of there, and by unwillingness of some survivors to get back on an LST.

During evening, reformed LSTs and took control, sent a fairly detailed report to Task Group Commander for transmittal to interested parties and examined 334 from close alongside for her damage. She had received two bombs, but had no fire, personnel injuries or serious derangement although she showed evident need of dry-docking to repair underwater damage from a hit that raked her port side abreast of forward elevator. By sunset everything under control, steaming at nine knots towards Munda, which was having an active bogie hunt with planes, searchlights and anti-aircraft fire. Remainder of trip back uneventful.

With the exception of the Commanding Officer, USS LST-460, whose conduct is under investigation, and certain Seabees and Marines observed looting the 448 and its dead, the conduct of all officers and men observed by the Group Commander was splendid and in full keeping with the highest traditions of the Service.

LST-448 shipmates Hap Hansen and Stan Lesus are still haunted by the memories of not being able to help their shipmates trapped below deck in the engulfing fire and explosions. However, before responding to the abandon ship order, Lesus was able to help some troops off the tank deck and Hap Hansen helped his wounded first-loader safely off the ship.

Both men were then flown to Guadalcanal and checked into Mobile Hospital 8 for treatment of shrapnel wounds. Hansen also had broken ribs and Lesus had a ruptured ear drum.

About 30 days later Lesus and Hansen were detached to LST-334. Harold Breimyer joined LST-485 and Monty La Montagne was assigned to LST-447. (Both Breimyer and La Montagne would eventually have their own commands.) Again, survivor leave proved to be a myth.

LST-334 Follow-Up – As reported earlier in "The Loss of LST-448," the 334 reported, "Being attacked by 15 dive bombers and as many Zeros" at 0935...and "suffered direct hits." However LST-334 was more fortunate than the 448 and was able to depart Vella under her own power at 1530 on 1 October for the 'Canal. She departed Tulagi on 6 October for Espiritu Santo for dry-docking, major overhaul and repair of battle damage and was back in Purvis Bay on 1 November 1943 ready for action.

Observation: After studying the preceding "Pacific Express" runs up the Slot and the short turn-around times, it's easy to see why many amphibians and their escorts experienced burnout. The constant threat of sub and air attacks kept the crews at General Quarters for long stretches making sleep hard to come by for two or three days at a time.

Vella Lavella Air Operations

On 15 August, BGen Francis P. Mulcahy, USMC, ComAir New Georgia, sent VMF-123 and -124 fighters from Munda and Segi fields to cover the Vella Lavella landings, during which they claimed 26 Japanese aircraft downed. On this day, VMF-124's First Lieutenant Kenneth A. Walsh began a streak that would eventually earn him the Medal of Honor for shooting down 21 Japanese aircraft. After accounting for three aircraft over Vella Lavella, he brought his Corsair back to Munda Field with 20-mm holes in the wings, several hydraulic lines cut, a holed vertical stabilizer, and a flat tire.

From mid-August 1943 until the establishment of airfields on Vella Lavella and Bougainville, Munda Field was the scene of intense activity as planes landed and took off to strike at Rabaul and Japanese shipping which were first trying to supply, and then evacuate, ground forces.

Captain John M. Foster, an F4U pilot, wrote about flying during this time and his first mission from Munda. "Never had I attempted to land a plane on a field as narrow and short as the Munda strip," he recalled. Rolling onto the taxiway, he was thankful for the 2,000 horsepower of the engine to "plow through the mud."

Munda Airfield was an essential element in supporting Allied air support in the battles for Vella Lavella and Bougainville.

The crews lived in tents and messed in a screen-framed, chow-hall building which the Seabees had built. The air units provided dawn to dusk coverage, with the night spent in rest and recovery, although the night's sleep was often disrupted by the appearance of "Washing Machine Charlie."

On 24 August, ComAir New Georgia at Munda was relieved by Commander Aircraft Solomons' Fighter Command, at which time General Mulcahy turned over his responsibilities to Colonel William O. Brice. Mulcahy's staff continued to coordinate liaison and spotter aircraft and strike missions launching from Munda Field until relieved of these responsibilities by ComAirSols on 24 September.

"Success in the air is a lot of little things," observed VMF-214's commander and Medal of Honor recipient, Major Gregory (Pappy) Boyington, and most of them "can be taken care of before take-off." With the Japanese air bases now within closer range of Allied aircraft, Boyington and others conducted fighter sweeps of 36 to 48 planes that were classics of their kind. Throughout this, escorted bomber and strafing attacks continued.

Pappy Boyington briefs his pilots before a mission from Espiritu Santo. Front row, left: Boyington, with paper, Stanley R. Bailey, Virgil G. Ray, Robert A. Alexander. Standing: William N. Case, Rolland N. Rinabarger, Don H. Fisher, Henry M. Bourgeois, John F. Begert, Robert T. Ewing, Denmark Groover Jr, and Burney L. Tucker.

The capture and use of Munda Field was now felt by the Japanese "in spades" observed Fighter Command, as dive bombing and strafing attacks against the enemy were daily routines.

On 28 August, First Lieutenant Alvin J. Jensen of VMF-214 was lost in a rainstorm over Kahili and when he broke through the clouds he found himself inverted over the Japanese field. Turning wings level, he proceeded to shoot up the flightline and accounted for 24 enemy aircraft on the ground. Photographs confirmed the damage and Jensen earned the Navy Cross for this work, described as "one of the greatest single-handed feats" of the Pacific War.

Air support during the Central Solomons campaign was considered of high quality by all commanders. Aviation historian and veteran Pacific War correspondent Robert Sherrod estimated that of the 358 aircraft the Japanese lost during this campaign, 187 were destroyed by Marine air. More significant were the resultant deaths of highly trained and experienced pilots and crews whom the Japanese could not replace.

Marine aviation unit casualties for operations in the Central Solomons were 34 of the 97 Allied aircraft lost.

Seabee Construction

BuDocks summarized the 1943 Advanced Base construction on Vella Lavella with these words: "Surveying and clearing of a 4,000-by-200-foot airstrip was accomplished during August; the auxiliary installations, including signal tower, operations room, aviation-gasoline tanks, and camp for operating personnel, were completed the following month. The first landing on the strip was made Sept. 24, and thereafter the field was in daily use for shuttle service." [13]

During August, the 58th Battalion also provided installations at the naval base, including a radio room, a hospital, and an LST ramp. The radio room and hospital were underground; the sides, built up with sand-filled gasoline drums, were roofed with logs and sand bags and provided with wooden decks.

The next construction undertaken was a dispensary and sick bay, the latter consisting of four underground shelters, each with a capacity of four beds, and an underground operating room. The dispensary was above ground and consisted of a wooden deck, wooden framing and a tarpaulin roof. From the end of September until late November, the second section of the 6th (Special) Battalion handled stevedoring operations.

The 77th Battalion, which had arrived on September 25, 1943, in the midst of a Japanese bombing attack, had as its major project the construction of three complete hospital units and facilities. This construction of hospital units was rushed to completion in expectation of the Bougainville invasion. Facilities for 1,000 beds, including surgery, laboratories, wards, mess facilities, administration buildings, underground surgery, and all utilities, were put in operation as scheduled.

During the next few months the channel through the reef was deepened to admit PT boats to the lagoon base. The jetty was improved by widening and the addition of an "L" section at the end. A camp was set up at the naval base, and a marine railway and boat repair locker constructed. By the end of November, considerable additions and improvements had been completed, and by December 21 an aviation-gasoline tank farm of six 1,000-barrel tanks, with a sea-loading line, was in operation.

Night Action Off Vella Lavella, 17-18 August 1943 [14]

Early in the afternoon of 17 August, a plane contact with enemy forces from Bougainville gave Adm Wilkinson's headquarters the location, disposition, course, and speed of four destroyers making up a "Tokyo Express." They were probably destined for the relief of Kolombangara or an attack on the new base at Barakoma.

Adm Wilkinson dispatched Capt Thomas J. Ryan, Jr., commanding officer of Destroyer Squadron 21, with four destroyers of Division 41, to intercept the enemy force. The Task Group consisting of destroyers *Nicholas* (F), *O'Bannon, Taylor,* and *Chevalier* departed Purvis Bay, Tulagi Island, at 1527, 17 August, and proceeded up the Slot at 32 knots, course 305 degrees T. By the time Ryan's group engaged the enemy, the night was bright moonlight, with surface visibility about 16,000 yards. The Tokyo Express consisted of four DDs, two large barges (comparable to our LCT) and several tugs or trawlers towing an undetermined number of small barges. Here are some Task Group 31.2 War Diary highlights:

2332 - Gun flashes were seen from an attack by TBFs on the enemy force, and a few minutes later TG 31.2 received an A/C report of the enemy position. At **0014**, there were several "bogies" on radar screens. These enemy planes undoubtedly broadcast our presence, because when we ultimately made contact, the enemy was formed-up. The initial radar contact was obtained at **0027**, 11 1/2 miles to northwest of our force, with enemy DDs in column, and barges and tows between us and the enemy DDs.

0039 - Several bombs were dropped nearby followed almost immediately by A/C flares. At **0047**, TG 31.2 passed several barges (two large and several tugs and tows) to port, and proceeded after the enemy destroyers. About **0057**, the enemy had crossed our bow, on course 180 degrees T. and opened fire at 14,000 yards. At least one DD broke formation and closed us, apparently to fire torpedoes.

TG 31.2 opened fire about **0058**, followed in two minutes by a half salvo of torpedoes from *Chevalier* from which one hit was obtained. There followed about ten minutes during which TG. 31.2 was dodging enemy torpedoes and reforming.

After reforming, the enemy was again taken under fire. Meanwhile the range was opening, indicating the enemy DDs were probably troop laden. This belief is substantiated by the absence of troops on the barges. *Taylor* reports two DDs retired at high speed to northwest early in the engagement. As usual there is a divergence of opinions as to the damage inflicted. The conclusion seems to be one DD was sunk and at least two DDs damaged.

TG 31.2 then swept south to pick up the enemy barges. Contact was regained about **0151**, and barges taken under fire. One and possibly two LCT-LCI-type were sunk, as were several smaller craft, including at least two tugs.

Between **0253-0440**, TG 31.2 swept Vella Gulf northeast of Vella Lavella without further contact, except at **0307** a stick of bombs fell nearby. At **0440**, TG set course for retirement to Tulagi, which was done without incident.

The reason for the enemy's precipitous desertion of his barges is a matter for speculation. The fact that no personnel were observed aboard the barges, and that when set on fire they burned furiously with periodic explosions, leads to the supposition that they were carrying supplies only. It seems probable that the combatant vessels were carrying troops. If so, this might explain their reluctance to engage and their willingness to leave the barges unprotected.

Battle of Vella Lavella, 6-7 October 1943 [15]

The final action of the New Georgia Group campaign was a naval battle on 6-7 October when U.S. Navy destroyers intercepted Japanese evacuation ships during the Battle of Vella Lavella; an all-destroyer clash—Adm Ijuin with nine destroyers bent on evacuating Japanese from Vella Lavella, and Capt Walker with only three destroyers, *Chevalier, O'Bannon* and *Selfridge*. (Three more, *Ralph Talbot, LaValette* and *Taylor*, were making 30 knots toward Walker to back him up, but would not arrive in time.)

But we are getting ahead of ourselves. While the evacuation of Kolombangara was in progress, the campaign to clear Vella Lavella of the enemy was approaching a climax.

On 18 September elements of the 3rd New Zealand Division arrived to relieve the U.S. Army's 35th Regimental Combat Team. MajGen H. E. Barrowclough, Divisional Commander, assumed command of the Northern Landing Force, and Brigadier L.S. Potter, commanding the 14th New Zealand Brigade Group, was placed in charge of the operation.

Potter decided upon a plan to pocket the Japanese in the northwest corner of the island by moving two of his Battalion Combat Teams (BCTs) simultaneously up the east and west coasts. The operation was to be semi-amphibious in nature, with the use of LCVPs and LCMs to transport personnel and supplies from bay to bay in a series of northward jumps. The plan was put into operation on 21 September. Retiring slowly to the west, the 500 to 700 Japanese were reported to be tired and poorly armed. Captured documents indicated a low state of morale and a general hope for evacuation.

By 5 October, the 35th BCT had reached Marquana Bay on the west and the 37th BCT had arrived at Warambari Bay on the east. The Japanese were hemmed in on the narrow strip of land between with fire of two field batteries, mortars, and machine guns registering in this area from both sides. A prisoner captured during the afternoon said that the 500 remaining Japanese were well organized but realized that they were trapped. They were short of food, tired of fighting, and many wished to surrender, but were prevented from doing so by their officers. Potter decided that the time had come to close the pincers.

This was the situation when on 5 October Adm Wilkinson decided to send a force to intercept the "Tokyo Express" which might be expected to complete the evacuation of Kolombangara or to evacuate the forces cornered in northwest Vella Lavella. Of the nine destroyers available to Wilkinson at the time, six were already committed to escort a convoy of LSTs and APDs to New Georgia leaving only *Selfridge* (F), *Chevalier,* and *O'Bannon* to break up the evacuation. The group was commanded by Capt Walker.

No major contacts were made that night. The following morning the same force was ordered to continue the patrol along the southern coast of Choiseul. About 1800, 6 October, more definite word regarding the Japanese evacuation forces reached RAdm Wilkinson from Admiral Halsey. This force was reported to consist of an unknown number of destroyers, 3 PTs and 6 SCs which could be off northwest of Vella Lavella by 2230.

Three U.S. destroyers were immediately detached from the convoy en route to New Georgia and ordered to rendezvous by 2300, ten miles west of Sauka Point, Vella Lavella, with Capt Walker's destroyers. This group, commanded by Cmdr Harold O. Larson, consisted of DDs *Ralph Talbot* (F)*, Taylor,* and *La Vallette.* Capt Walker, after receiving instructions regarding the rendezvous, was later informed by RAdm Wilkinson that there were possibly nine destroyers in the "Express," which was estimated to have passed through Bougainville Strait at 2000. Further information was received that Cmdr Larson's group would not arrive at the rendezvous until 2340. It was understood that if the rendezvous was delayed, Capt Walker's group was to intercept the enemy by itself.

At 2234 the *Selfridge* sighted the enemy ships on the horizon off her starboard bow. Although Cmdr Larson's destroyers would not be expected in the area for another hour, Capt Walker immediately closed with his three destroyers for an attack upon the nine enemy ships. The order of his ships in column was *Selfridge, Chevalier,* and *O'Bannon,* keeping station at a distance of 500 yards.

To summarize this naval action: The Americans were the first to fire torpedoes, Walker ordering them away at 7,000 yards (3.5 miles). The Japanese came on in seeming disarray, and the first torpedo got *Yugumo* at 3,300 yards at 2305. Four minutes earlier, a *Yugumo* torpedo had smashed *Chevalier's* port bow, setting off magazines and mortally wounding her. In the confusion, *O'Bannon* rammed *Chevalier*, and *Selfridge* took a torpedo port side.

At this point Adm Ijuin surprised the Americans by pulling out, although he had Walker three to one. *Chevalier* was abandoned, losing 51 men. *LaValette* and *Taylor* arrived in time to rescue 250 of *Chevalier's* crew and to sink her. Both *Selfridge* and *O'Bannon* limped home but *Yugumo* did not.

Only 11 1/2 minutes had elapsed from the moment the first torpedoes were fired to the torpedoing of the *Selfridge*. At the end of the action the *Chevalier* was torpedoed, rammed and sinking; the *O'Bannon* was limping with a badly damaged bow; and the *Selfridge* had her bow sheared off. Yet this crippled force of three destroyers was left in command of the field at the end of the battle. The enemy ships that had not been destroyed or disabled had been put to flight, no doubt warned by snoopers of the approach of the American supporting force.

At 2326 the *Chevalier* reported that she was unable to remain afloat. After attempting for about 20 minutes to go alongside, the *O'Bannon* gave up the attempt because of the sharp rudder effect of her damaged bow. When the ships were within 50 yards of each other, boats were lowered to take off the wounded. Remaining survivors, floating on life rafts were towed to the ship. The *O'Bannon* picked up 16 officers, and 234 living and seven dead enlisted men. Total casualties of the *Chevalier* were one officer missing, two officers (Cmdr Wilson and his Executive Officer) wounded, and 53 enlisted men dead or missing. Most of the injured had fractured legs and arms and a few suffered from fuel oil poisoning. After leaving two motor whaleboats in the water for the use of survivors who might have escaped observation, the *O'Bannon* retired alone at 0130 and arrived at Tulagi without further incident.

Later, *LaVallette,* from Cmdr Larson's group, made an unsuccessful search for more survivors. Since there appeared to be no chance of saving the *Chevalier*, the *LaVallette* was ordered to remain behind after the other vessels had retired, and sink her. After a careful search of the wreck by a boarding party, the *LaVallette* drew off to 2,100 yards and fired one torpedo. The *Chevalier* blew up with an explosion that sent a cloud of black smoke towering over 500 feet. Her severed bow was located about a mile to the west and sunk with depth charges. After a further search for survivors, the *LaVallette* headed south before dawn.

Selfridge suffered considerable damage from the torpedo attack. She was considered a total loss forward of frame 55 and considerable blast damage occurred aft. However, her engines appeared to be undamaged except for vibration and her guns were kept manned. After torpedoes and other weights were jettisoned and the forward fireroom bulkhead shored up, it appeared that she would float and could make slow speed. At 0041 *Taylor* came alongside and all survivors were transferred to her. *Selfridge* casualties: 13 dead, 36 missing, and 11 wounded.

Selfridge then proceeded at five knots, slowly working up to 16 knots as she proved capable of better speeds. She retired to the southeast, screened by *Ralph Talbot, Taylor* and later, *LaVallette*. Fighter plane cover arrived overhead by 0515. At 0715 radar contact was made with many enemy planes coming in for an attack. Skillful direction by the *Taylor's* fighter director unit prevented any planes from getting within five miles of the ships. The group reached Tulagi in safety at 1300 on 8 October.

The evidence regarding enemy vessels destroyed or damaged in this action is inconclusive. The only sinking positively established is that of the destroyer *Yugumo*. The day following the action PT boats picked up 78 Japanese survivors, all of whom said they were from this ship. According to them, she was sunk by a torpedo after severe damage by gunfire.

All reports by eye witnesses, Japanese survivors and Americans, concur that other ships were severely damaged and some possibly sunk. For example, Cmdr Larson, although arriving too late to take part in the action, saw three enemy ships burn, explode and sink.

Vella Lavella Campaign Ends – New Zealanders of the 35th and 37th Combat Teams, waiting through the night of 6-7 October to shut the jaws of their pincers upon the Japanese the following morning, plainly heard the guns of the naval battle to the north. When dawn came, they moved forward for the final mop-up around the Bay. Patrols from both Teams returned reporting no contact whatever.

It was under cover of the naval action that the evacuation of the last Japanese troops on Vella Lavella was accomplished. Some 400 men were thought to have been taken off the island during the night. A more thorough investigation of the area by patrols of both combat teams was made on the 8th, but only dead Japanese and abandoned equipment was found. At 0900 on 9 October the leading companies of each combat team met, and the commanding officer signaled headquarters that resistance had ceased and his task was completed.

Conclusions

The occupation of Vella Lavella by U.S. forces marked the close of the Central Solomons campaign. Americans had bypassed Kolombangara and now stood on the western shore of Vella Gulf, a commanding position to threaten anything left behind them. Considering the important strategic advantages gained, the cost was small.

The success of the Vella Lavella campaign can be assessed by the fact that the airstrip was in use six weeks after the original landing. Within two months it could accommodate almost 100 planes, and was in full operation against Bougainville. Thus the next campaign was opened almost simultaneously with the closing of the previous one.

Lessons Learned – Perhaps of equal or even greater importance than the strategic advantages gained by the campaign of Vella Lavella and Kolombangara were the lessons learned. The principle of seizing unoccupied territory for the development of an airfield—soon to be repeated in the Bougainville operation—was worked out in this campaign.

The success of the operation clearly demonstrated the soundness of the strategy of by-passing enemy strongholds, then blockading and starving them out. This operational pattern, later repeated so often in the Central and Southwest Pacific, was rehearsed successfully for the first time in the Central Solomons.

Sons of the Beach
(The *Real* Story of LCTs)

I had just arrived back in the States and after the excitement of reporting in and checking through customs were over, I relaxed happily in my comfortable Pullman seat. Contrary to all the rules that are supposed to govern the reactions of men returning from overseas, I was near to bursting with desire to tell every detail of my little experience. So I was quite pleased when the elderly man in the seat opposite me began to probe.

"Been back long, sailor?" he asked.

"Just a couple of days," I answered.

"Things pretty rough?"

"Not too bad, but it was sort of interesting. I remember the time when we started out from…"

"What kind of a ship were you on, son?" he interrupted.

"Well, it's not a ship; it's a boat. An LCT."

"Oh, yes, I've seen pictures of them. They're that big landing ship—I mean boat—with the doors in front that open up."

"No, sir, that's an LST, and it's a ship alright. The LCT is something like that only it doesn't have any bow doors, just a ramp, and it's much smaller."

"Oh, sure, I've seen pictures of those. They're those dinky little boats that go into the beach first."

"No, sir, that's the LCVP you're thinking about. You see, there's the LCVP, and the LCM, then the LCT, next the LCI, and last—the big one, the LST."

"Very confusing."

Very confusing, indeed, I thought. Here you are all ready to tell the stories you've been saving up for a year—exaggerating only here and there for dramatic value, of course—and you find out that they can't tell one "L" from another. Guess I'll just have to start at the beginning and give the whole story.

Official Navy publications call them Landing Craft, Tanks, Mark 5 or Mark 6, and the other pertinent information: water-line length 105', triple screw, complement of one officer and ten to twelve enlisted men, used to land vehicles and cargo during amphibious assault. They have no names but are designated by number, and there are about, well, there are a lot of them.

Back in the spring of 1942 when the Navy was beginning to think about the creation of a landing fleet, it was decided that one of the basic types would be a version of the British craft that had spearheaded the assault on Dieppe, considerably shortened in length and sectionalized so that it might hitchhike to the forward areas mounted on merchant ships, or on its big sister, the LST. So, they had a conference.

The men and officers who have served on LCTs consider that conference legendary. They insist that it was composed of a BuShips captain whose promotion to Admiral had been passed over that morning, and a British commander who had never forgotten 1776. There are also those who insist that an officer casting about for an appropriate form of transportation for particularly vicious war criminals was also present. The conference must have gone something like this …

Well, let's see, they won't have to live on these things for more than forty-eight hours at a time, so we'll just put all the eating and sleeping and sanitary arrangements in this one little compartment. They won't need any shower or refrigerator, of course, and besides, there's no room anyway. Now, we'd better put the three Alemite fittings for the propeller bearings right under each of the lower bunks, so that when the Motor Machinist gets down on his stomach every hour to reach them with his grease gun, he can awaken the man sleeping there.

By the way, that engine room is really a wonderfully devised torture chamber. No man over five feet will be able to get in there, except on all fours. Of course, the Navy's minimum height requirement won't let them escape us there.

Guns? Oh, toss on a couple 20-mm. Better reinforce them a bit since the vibration is apt to shake the mounts right down into the Skipper's quarters. Say, we've forgotten about a place for the Officer. We'll give him that bunk over in the corner, and when the men hang their peacoats on that curtain rod, he'll have a little privacy. But he needs a desk. Let's put a folding desk against that after bulkhead. When he wants the desk up, all he'll have to do is move his bunk up out of the way and lash it there with a chain. That takes care of him just fine.

Now that leaves only navigation to take care of. Well, they'll never be asked to go more than twenty miles by themselves and certainly never out of sight of land. How about giving them that little magnetic compass they mount on the dashboard of a jeep? You know, the one that's calibrated every five degrees. 'North from South' is about as fine a line as they'll ever have to draw. Okay, that finishes it. Let's get 'em rolling.

So mass production got underway. Lady welders, working with plate so thin that no respectable can opener would have failed to cut it, turned this new craft out at the rate of two a day. Lay the keel with the morning whistle and trip the launching trigger at noon. Back after lunch and another in the water by quitting time.

At the Solomons Island and Little Creek Amphibious Training bases on the Chesapeake Bay, another assembly line got into production turning out the crews to handle these craft. In August 1942, the first group of newly manufactured ensigns, their fresh minting attested to by bright gold braid, reported for duty. Their experience? "Rowboat on the Ohio River, huh." "Staten Island Ferry." "Bathtub." "None." Assign them to the LCTs!

"Hey Bo, what the devil is an LCT?"

"Boy, I was hoping to get a tin can."

"From what I hear, we've really got one! They say the casualties will be seventy percent."

"Okay, Mac, here's your crew; ten of 'em right out of boots. You can all start together."

"Alright, which one of you men can cook? Come on, somebody's gotta get chow."

"Have you ever changed a fuse? Okay, you're the electrician."

"Like to hunt? It's guns for you."

"Are you my instructor?"

"So they tell me."

"How long have you been on LCTs?"

"Oh, I just got here last week myself...."

— Jerry Finkelstein, LCT Sailor

A true "Son of the Beach" discovers that the natives are friendly. Author's Collection.

PART III

The Northern Solomons Campaigns

Part III recounts the seizure of the Treasuries, the Choiseul Diversion, the Bougainville Campaign, plus the naval battles of Empress Augusta Bay and Cape St. George.

Finally, the many valuable lessons learned during the Solomons Campaigns are summarized—ranging from logistic support and force requirements to offshore toeholds and leapfrogging. Most became doctrine in later Pacific campaigns.

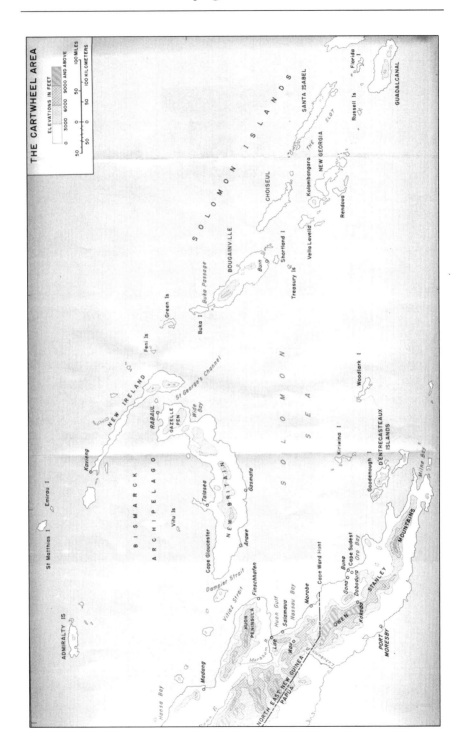

CHAPTER **8**

Bougainville Campaign
27 October – 25 November 1943[1]

Bougainville, the largest of the Solomon Islands, was invaded as the fourth and final phase of the Solomons campaign. It was part of the Allied plan—Operation CARTWHEEL—to get rid of Rabaul, the big, heavily defended Japanese base on the eastern end of New Britain Island. From an airfield on Bougainville, U.S. fighters would be close enough to the Japanese base—about 200 miles—to provide escort for Rabaul-bound bombers.

Debate about dealing with Rabaul split U.S. strategists. General Douglas MacArthur wanted to invade and overpower Rabaul. The Joint Chiefs of Staff (JCS), believing that too many U.S. troops would die in an amphibious landing, wanted to neutralize the base with continual bombing raids.

At the Quebec Conference of August 1943, President Roosevelt and Prime Minister Churchill established the strategy for the U.S. Central Pacific Campaign and made the decision about Rabaul by siding with the JCS.

Strategic Considerations

Immediately after the fall of New Georgia, Admiral Halsey and his staff in Nouméa were busily revising their initial plan to take Bougainville. Several factors dictated Halsey's scheme of maneuver for the offensive. First, he had too few transports and Marines to make a direct assault on the heavily defended enemy airfields located on the northern and southern ends of the island. Another consideration was the range of land-based fighters from bases in the Central Solomons—they could only effectively cover a landing in the southern half of Bougainville.

The planners settled on the Empress Augusta Bay-Cape Torokina region on the western side of the island. Defenses were negligible there, and Bougainville's difficult terrain would prevent any rapid reaction from enemy ground forces located elsewhere on the island. Once ashore, the invasion force would seize a defensible perimeter, build an airfield, and eventually neutralize the remainder of the island from this enclave.

A patrol, landed by submarine in late September, discovered that the areas back of the landing beaches were swampy. Aerial reconnaissance in October also discovered the construction of new defenses. Neither of these facts changed the plan, however.

General MacArthur planned to assault Cape Gloucester on the western end of New Britain. Between Bougainville and Cape Gloucester, Rabaul would have to face Allied land-based fighter aircraft coming from two directions. Air power thus could neutralize the Japanese bastion and allow it to be by-passed. The scheduled D-day for Bougainville was 1 November 1943.

Forces and Preparation – In South Pacific staff conferences in Noumea and Guadalcanal there was much grumbling about Bougainville being "Operation 'Shoestring' No. 2." Admiral Nimitz, preparing for the Gilberts invasion, the spearhead of his Central Pacific offensive, with target date 20 November, was accused of giving Halsey only the leavings, just as Operation TORCH had robbed WATCHTOWER. Nimitz, however, estimating correctly that Koga would not risk the heaviest ships of his Combined Fleet in the Solomons, thought Halsey could do with what he had.

At the start of the operation, Halsey would have only one carrier group and Merrill's Crudiv 12. Nimitz did send RAdm Laurance DuBose's new Crudiv 13 to replace Ainsworth's battered warriors, and a second carrier group, but they would not arrive on the scene before 7 November. However, South Pacific Force still had Capt Arleigh Burke's "Little Beavers" and about two more destroyer squadrons for amphibious escort duty and fire support.

In his operation plan of 12 October 1943, COMSOPAC set 1 November as D-day. Code-named GOODTIME, the plan fixed only the major objectives and assigned the major commands. RAdm Wilkinson, who was placed in command of the operation, was directed to seize and hold the Treasury Islands on D-5 day to establish there radars and minimum facilities for small craft.

On D-day he was to seize and hold a suitable site in the northern Empress Augusta Bay area, where he was to establish facilities for small craft and construct such airfields as might be directed by COMSOPAC. In addition he was to lay defensive and offensive minefields as directed.

In the same operation plan, Admiral Halsey directed Commander Aircraft, South Pacific to support the operation with land-based planes by providing defensive reconnaissance, air cover, and air support for forces engaged. He was also to provide support

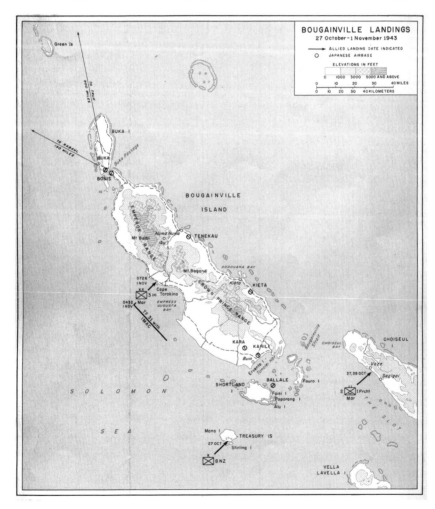

by strikes against airfields on Bougainville and against any enemy units threatening the attack force.

RAdm Frederick C. Sherman, commander of a carrier task force, was directed to be prepared to support operations of the land-based planes by strikes against enemy bases, and also to base aircraft ashore when directed. As invasion preparations proceeded, LtGen George C. Kenney's Fifth Air Force flying from New Guinea, conducted major air attacks against Rabaul.

RAdm Aaron S. Merrill, in command of a task force of cruisers and destroyers, was directed to destroy enemy surface vessels that might threaten RAdm Wilkinson's operations or the South Pacific position, and to attack enemy bases as directed by COMSOPAC.

Submarines under command of Capt James Fife, Jr., were to attack enemy shipping and surface units.

The Third Marine Division, reinforced, MajGen Allen H. Turnage commanding, was assigned the northern Empress Augusta Bay mission. These troops conducted landing exercises on beaches of the New Hebrides and Guadalcanal during the period of 17-19 October. For this operation, the 2^d and 3rd Raider Battalions were organized as the 2^d Raider Regiment. LtCol Joseph P. McCaffery took over the 2^d Raider Battalion.

The Eighth New Zealand Brigade Group, reinforced, commanded by Brigadier R. A. Row, was assigned the Treasury Islands operation and carried out landing exercises on Florida Island on 14-17 October.

The force for the Choiseul diversion was the 2^d Marine Parachute Battalion, commanded by LtCol Victor H. Krulak.

Admiral Wilkinson, Commander, Third Amphibious Force, had the responsibility for the detailed planning of the naval operations. His operation plan of 15 October, amended and elaborated by his operation order of the 18th, included plans for logistics, naval gunfire, minesweeping, minelaying, communications, and boat pools along with schedules for debarkation, ship movements and cruising dispositions for the Treasury Islands and Empress Augusta Bay operations. The ships and craft at Admiral Wilkinson's disposal for the two landings were divided into the Northern Force, for Empress Augusta Bay, and the Southern Force, for the Treasury

Islands. Admiral Wilkinson designated RAdm George H. Fort commander of the latter force, and retained command of the Northern Force himself.

Enemy Situation – Every effort was made to encourage the enemy to believe that the Allied target was the Buin-Shortland area. Enemy naval strength in the Rabaul-Solomons area as of 11 October 1943 was estimated to be 1 heavy cruiser, 1 light cruiser, 8 to 10 destroyers, 12 submarines, 21 patrol craft, plus necessary auxiliaries, numerous barges, and some PT boats. Large naval forces were at Truk.

Estimated Enemy Ground Strength as of 11 October 1943

Bougainville and Shortland Islands (including air, labor, and service troops)	35,000
Choiseul Island (including evacuees)	2,000
New Britain (Rabaul area)	56,000
New Ireland	5,500
Total	98,500

As for the troops in the Bougainville area, 5,000 were thought to be in the northern sector (Buka area); 5,000 in the eastern sector (Numa Numa-Kieta); 17,000 in the southern sector; 5,000 to 6,000 in the Shortland Islands; 3,000 in Ballale and surrounding islands; and 132 in the Treasury Islands. All indications were that the enemy considered the defense of southern Bougainville of prime importance

As of 9 October, enemy air strength was estimated to be 160 fighters, 120 medium bombers, 66 dive or light bombers, and 39 floatplanes based on Bougainville, on New Ireland, and in the vicinity of Rabaul. Approximately 72 percent of these planes were thought to be based in the Rabaul area, 20 percent in the Bougainville area, and eight percent on New Ireland.

In the vicinity of Empress Augusta Bay, the Japanese were believed to have an outpost located in the Cape Torokina area with an estimated strength of not more than 100 men and possibly some anti-aircraft machine guns. A small observation post was believed to be located near the Laruma River. Small forces were also known to be near Mawareka, with reserves, including artillery, at Mosigetta, totaling in all about 1,000 men. Large forces were known to be located in the Buka, Keita, and Kahili areas.

Neutralization of Enemy Airfields – Between our northern-most airfield at Barakoma and the proposed landing site at Cape Torokina were three enemy airfields. Kahili, a large and well-developed airfield, lay at the southern tip of Bougainville, and Kara, a new strip, lay seven miles inland from Kahili and to the north-west. Ballale airfield was on the island of Ballale, thirteen miles southeast of Kahili.

The campaign to neutralize these airfields by means of land-based aircraft bombing, was intensified on 15 October 1943. From that date through 31 October planes based at Barakoma and Munda, under ComAirNorSols, BGen Field Harris, USMC, carried out an average of four attacks a day, ranging in strength from 100 planes down to strafing attacks by a few fighters. Kahili was subjected to 18 attacks, Kara to 17, and Ballale 6 within this period. On an average day of four attacks such as 23 October, 59 tons were dropped on Kara and 68 tons on Kahili.

Enemy air activity in the South Pacific area was greatly reduced. Enemy sorties declined from 801 in September to 495 in October, while his losses increased from 148 in September to 173 in the latter month. By comparison, our aircraft in the South Pacific flew 3,259 sorties in October, with a loss of 26 planes in combat. More than 90 percent of our air effort was directed against enemy land targets—principally in the southern Bougainville area.

Naval gunfire also contributed to the discomfiture of the Japanese airfields within striking distance of Bougainville, and to the concealment of the true objective. Admiral Halsey assigned two bombardment missions to Rear Admiral Merrill's Task Force 39, comprising light cruisers *Montpelier, Cleveland, Columbia,* and *Denver,* and Destroyer Squadron 23 led by Capt Arleigh Burke, who by his actions in the next few days, was to be awarded the nickname "31-knot Burke".

Merrill's force stood out of Purvis Bay at 0230 October 31, bound for Buka Passage. After steaming 537 miles, it commenced bombarding the Buka and Bonis airfields at 0021 November 1. The task force had the benefit of spotting by two specially equipped Airsols planes; and it really plastered the airfields. Enemy planes struck back, illuminating the ships with parachute flares and harassing the force with their familiar night tactics until the third hour of 1 November, but they never scored a hit.

Merrill's force retired south some 200 miles at 30 knots before dawn 1 November to perform its second mission, the bombardment of the Shortlands.

Carrier planes also became available on D-day, when one of the fast carrier groups of Task Force 38 came down to help. This was RAdm Frederick C. Sherman's group consisting of the veteran *Saratoga* and the new light carrier *Princeton*, screened by two anti-aircraft light cruisers and ten destroyers. They steamed up the northeast coast of the Solomons and launched strikes on the two Buka Passage airfields on 1 and 2 November. After these strikes, there were few Japanese planes left to retaliate.

Altogether these strikes ensured that the enemy would have no more use of his fields, at least during the first critical week.

Seizure of Treasury Islands, 27 October - 6 November 1943

The Treasury Islands, 28 miles south of Bougainville, and about twice that distance northwest of Vella Lavella, were chosen as the site of an advance air and naval base to neutralize Japanese strongholds on New Britain, New Ireland, and Bougainville. On the night of 22-23 August, a submarine landed a reconnaissance party on Mono Island of the Treasury Group. These men were evacuated by the same means on the night of 27-28 August. Their report indicated that the best landing beach on the island was in Blanche Harbor between the Saveke River mouth and Falamai Point. This beach appeared suitable for all types of landing craft, and had an ample water supply nearby.

The reconnaissance party saw signs of enemy patrols and activities, but no Japanese were sighted. Beaches Orange One and Orange Two were therefore located by the operational orders between the mouth of Saveke River and Falamai Point. Beaches Purple One, Two, and Three were located on the north shore of Stirling Island, where no opposition was anticipated. In addition,

Beach Emerald was selected at Soanotalu, on the northern shore of Mono Island.

Admiral Wilkinson on 15 October designated RAdm George H. Fort as Commander Southern Force in command of the Treasury operation. MTBs based at Lambu Lambu, Vella Lavella and at Lever Harbor on northern New Georgia were to screen the approach by a picket line from the Shortlands to Choiseul. He also made the following ground units, under command of Brigadier Row, NZEF, available for the operation:

8th New Zealand Brigade Group (less certain detachments).

198th Combat Artillery (AA) less detachments and one provisional battalion.

Detachment Headquarters, ComAirNorSols, including Argus.[2]

2[d] Platoon, Company A, 1st Corps Signal Bn., IMAC.[3]

Advanced Naval Base: Communication Unit No. 8; and Boat Pool No. 10.

Company A, 87th Naval Construction Battalion.

1st Battalion, 14th New Zealand Brigade (in reserve).

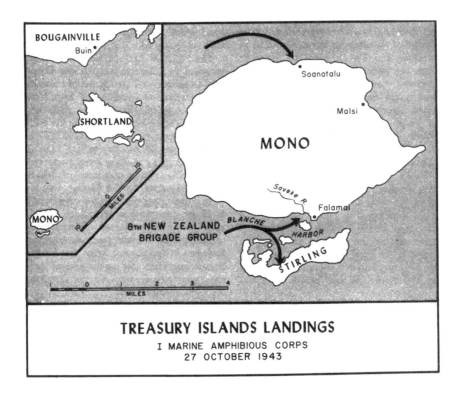

TREASURY ISLANDS LANDINGS
I MARINE AMPHIBIOUS CORPS
27 OCTOBER 1943

The New Zealanders were seasoned veterans who had participated in the campaigns of North Africa, Greece and Crete.

Admiral Halsey directed the task force commanded by RAdm
Aaron S Merrill to cover the operation from surface attack. He also
directed shore-based aircraft to support the operation by furnish-
ing air cover and support, and to neutralize enemy airfields in the
Bougainville area.

In order to obtain last minute information, a reconnaissance
party of two New Zealand noncommissioned officers and some
natives was landed by PT boat on Mono Island the night of 21-22
October. This party reported that, according to friendly natives,
the enemy had recently landed reinforcements and that his strength
was about 225 men. The reconnaissance party, evacuated the night
of 22-23 October, brought with them some Mono Island natives to
act as guides for the landing.

On the night of 25-26 October, another advance party landed
on Mono. Their mission was to cut communication lines between
the observation post at Laifa Point and the radio station just prior
to the landing.

Loading and Approach – Transport units under Admiral Fort
were divided into five groups, each with its tactical commander:

The First Transport Group, under Commander John D. Sweeney,
ComTransDiv 12, consisted of 8 APDs screened by the *Eaton, Pringle*
and *Philip.*

The Second Transport Group, under Captain Jack E. Hurff,
ComDesRon 22, was made up of 8 LCIs and two newly converted
LCI gunboats, screened by the *Waller, Cony, Saufley, Adroit, Con-
flict,* and *Daring.*

The Third Transport Group, under Commander James R. Pahl,
ComDesDiv 44, consisted of 2 LSTs screened by the *Conway,
Renshaw,* and YMs 197 and 260.

The Fourth Transport Group, under Lt (jg) Martin E. Bergstrom,
was composed of 1 APc and 3 LCTs screened by 2 PT boats.

The Fifth Transport Group, under Lt James E. Locke, consisted
of 1 APc, 6 LCMs, and 1 aircraft rescue boat.

The use of LCI(G)s for close fire support was reportedly an
invention of Capt Roy T. "Slim" Cowdrey, ship repair officer on

Halsey's staff. LCIs 22 and 23, were given additional armament consisting of two 20-mm, three 40-mm and five .50-caliber machine guns.[4] This required larger crews and sacrificed much of their troop-carrying function, but the LCI(G)s proved to be the answer for assault troops needing close-in fire support as their landing craft approached the beaches.

Flotilla Five LCIs 21, 22, 23, and 70 were the first LCIs to be converted into "Anti-Landing Craft Gunboats" in the South Pacific. They were ordered to Nouméa on 28 September 1943 in accordance with ComTransGroup secret dispatches for the conversion job, and were back in less than a month for the Bougainville/Treasury/Choiseul campaign. By 1 December LCIs 24, 67, 68, and 69 were undergoing conversion, too.[5] (The official designation LCI(G) for gunboat became effective 15 June 1944.)

The five transport groups were loaded and departed independently, timed to arrive together at Blanche Harbor on 27 October. Five days prior to the loading, the APDs and LCIs embarked troops and conducted a landing rehearsal.

The pioneer LCI Flotilla Five landing craft (Volume I) departed Carter City for Kukum, Guadalcanal at 0550 on 25 October to load troops as per CTG 31.1 Southern Force loading order of 19 October 1943.

Here are a few excerpts from the LCI-334 War Diary:[6]

LCI(G). Many LCI(L)s were converted to gunboats for close-in fire support during landing operations. ONI/226.

October 25, 1943

0755 Beached, Kukum, loaded...200 New Zealand 8th Brigade men, 15 tons equipment.

1745 Retracted, troops and gear aboard, anchored off Kukum in company with LCIs 222, 336, 24, 330, 61, 67, 69, secured.

October 26, 1943

0345 Underway for Treasury Islands, in accordance Southern Force, Task Group 31.1, Operations Order No. A16-43 with this order of ships: LCIs 222 (Cmdr J. McD. Smith, LCI Commander) 336, 24, 334, and 23 (LCI gunboat) port column; 61 (LCI guide), 67, 69, 330, 22 (LCI gunboat) in starboard column...Screened by DDs 598, 465, 466 (CTF 31.1.2) and M82, 85, 87...

1515 LCI gunboats 22, 23 took station on LCI 222's bow, 334's, quarter respectively.

October 27, 1943

0000 Underway with TG 31.1.2 as before, course 313 True.

0330 Battle stations, approaching Treasury Islands vicinity.

0400 Sighted Treasury Islands.

The next 2 1/2 hours were covered by a separate LCI-334 Action Report. We'll review it later in this chapter.

The several groups made independent passages without incident, except that a flare was dropped near the LCI gunboats between Simbo and Treasury Islands. The groups passed before dawn, as scheduled, in the area between Simbo and Treasury Islands. The covering cruiser group under Admiral Merrill, to the westward, was discovered by snoopers, and many flares and float

LCI(L) underway. ONI 226/1.

lights were dropped near the formation. "Fortunately," as Capt Arleigh A. Burke, ComDesRon 23, remarked in his report, "the bogey became so interested in playing 'hide and seek' with the [covering] task force that it is believed he did not see the landing forces coming up towards the Treasury Islands from the South."

Landing and Unloading – At 0540 on 27 October the eight APDs of the **First Transport Group** lay to 1,300 yards off Cummings Point, Stirling Island, just south of the entrance to Blanche Harbor, and commenced debarkation of troops. Sunrise was approaching, with visibility good, the sky partly cloudy, wind northeast, force 2. The *Eaton,* as fighter director ship, proceeded to her station four miles off the harbor, while the *Pringle* and *Philip* began their shore bombardment within five minutes after the transport group arrived. The air spotter was already over the targets, and at 0600 the fighter cover of 32 planes arrived on station.

The major assault was to be made on Beach Orange at Falamai, the only suitable beach on the northern coast of Mono Island. A smaller force was to land on the Purple beaches of Stirling Island where no opposition was expected. The assault wave was routed

Treasury Islands Operation, troops on the beach at Mono Island search for the Japanese pillbox that had just shot the men lying at water's edge during landings on 27 October 1943. USS LCI-24 is in the background. Naval Historical Center.

close to Stirling Island to a point just beyond Watson Island, where the boats bound for the Orange beaches turned left. Before that point was reached, the boats from the *Stringham* and *Talbot* turned right and proceeded independently to Beaches Purple 2 and 3. The New Zealand troops were landed on Stirling Island without opposition. Although the beaches were bad, no difficulty was encountered.

The assault wave hit the beach at H-hour (0626) exactly. The wave consisted of 16 LCP(R)s carrying 640 men to Orange beaches. The APDs lay in the transport area for about two hours, landing 1,600 men and at least 80 tons of stores. In the meantime, the *McKean*, which left the formation at 0430 and proceeded independently to Beach Emerald at Soanotalu on the north coast of Mono to land troops, returned to the transport area at 0708 and reported that the landing was successful and unopposed. At 0800 the APDs departed under the escort of the *Conway* and *Renshaw*.

The Second Transport Group, which included eight LCIs, completed its approach by 0630 on 27 October, and the *Cony* and *Waller* took stations as fighter director ships. The LCIs, under Cmdr J. McDonald Smith, rounded the west end of Stirling Island at 0630 in two columns: port column—222(F), 334, 24, and 336; starboard column—61, 67, 69, and 330. The landing craft were preceded by AMs (minesweepers) *Adroit, Conflict,* and *Daring.* The columns on their way up the harbor met the Higgins boats of the APDs

USS LCI-222 beaching in the Northern Solomons, 1943. Naval Historical Center.

returning from the beaches and observed shore fire converging on the gunboats accompanying the landing craft, all of which were vigorously returning the fire.

The LCIs opened fire in order of station in column as they came abreast of the enemy installations, silencing some of them. Three of the landing craft in the right column, 61, 67, and 69, swung to starboard after they were midway down the channel and proceeded to Purple beaches on Stirling Island. The remaining craft swung to port to approach the Orange beaches, on which they let go their ramps about 0647.

The LCIs were under rifle and mortar fire on the Orange beaches throughout their unloading period. Four shells exploded near the 334, and two near the stern of the 330 as she was retracting. Observers on LCI-24 spotted an active pillbox some 60 yards off her port bow, an inactive one about 20 yards off her starboard bow, and a very active pillbox some 80 yards off her starboard bow. They were all well camouflaged with netting and foliage and blended into the jungle background. Two dead men lay before one pillbox, and others lay at the water's edge. Soon two Japanese snipers tumbled from the tops of coconut trees near the beach.

The following excerpts from the LCI-334 Action Report covering the landing at Treasury Islands on 27 October, highlight the action. They confirm the "Combat Narratives" information and provide more specifics: [7]

> 1. At 0530 on 27 October, Task Unit 31.1.2 (OTC RAdm Fort CTG 31.1.1 in DD-466) in cruising formation...past point Tare...LCIs proceeded in toward Blanche Harbor. APDs were seen lying off tip of Stirling Island, and the fire support destroyers commenced shore bombardment of Falamai and Saveke area. APD boats launched and proceeding in the channel.
>
> At 0635, DD-466 left LCI formation; the sweeps, followed by LCI gunboats 22 and 23, entered Blanche Harbor; the APD boats were already in the harbor.
>
> 2. This ship [LCI-334], in the LCI formation, proceeded to enter the harbor at 0641 at full speed. Heavy machine gun tracer fire from shore was observed, and was seen hitting on or near the first returning APDs, which had unloaded. The mine sweeps and LCIs 22 and 23 returned this fire with a heavy strafing of the enemy gun nests which then ceased firing.

When the main LCI formation reached a point just north of Wilson Island, some tracer was seen coming from a nest just west of the creek at Saveke, and LCIs 222, 24, 336, and this ship all strafed the palmetto emplacement upon coming in range.

This ship ceased firing at 0643 when opposite the creek, and slowed, preparing to beach.

3. This ship beached at Orange 2 at 0646 and commenced unloading. Considerable rifle and mortar fire heard, both by our troops and the enemy, and three enemy mortar shells burst nearby, one 50 yards from our bow, on the beach, one 100 yards on port beam, and one astern 300 yards.

4. Troops completed unloading at 0719, and we retracted, with one wounded New Zealand soldier (slight head wound). At 0728 we left Blanche Harbor and formed up for return trip, passing two incoming LSTs on the way out of the channel, came to true course 131 at 0800 and proceeded in formation as before.

In spite of this opposition, the eight LCIs achieved the rather remarkable feat of debarking 1,600 troops and 150 tons of cargo within 35 minutes. LCI-330 completed the debarkation of 299 officers and men and 14 tons of heavy equipment and supplies in 14 minutes, which, according to RAdm Wilkinson "would be considered an outstanding performance even without any opposition from the beach." There were no casualties among naval personnel and no damage of consequence to the craft. By 0730 the LCIs were underway with the AMs for Guadalcanal escorted by the *Waller, Pringle,* and *Saufley.*

Flotilla 5 LCIs disembarking troops and equipment in the Northern Solomons, 1943. Courtesy Vince Robinson.

The Third Transport Group consisting of LSTs 399 and 485, stood into Blanche Harbor about 0715 on 27 October, preceded by two YMSs sweeping for all types of mines. Seeing no evidence of a beach party or beachmaster, the commanding officers selected their own landing sites and beached exactly on schedule at 0735: LST-399 at Orange 1, and 485 at Orange 2.

Five minutes later, both ships were subjected to heavy fire from 80-mm mortars, 30-mm mountain guns, and considerable small arms sniping. Within the ensuing 50 minutes, LST-399 received two direct hits.[8] One on the port side amidships tore a three-by-four-foot hole in the bulkhead and started a fire, which was quickly extinguished; another hit on the breech of a 40-mm gun destroying the gun, and killed three of its crew. LST-485 received two direct hits on the forecastle and had several near misses. These hits wounded eight men, one of whom subsequently died, but did relatively minor damage to the vessel.

LST-399 found herself in especially difficult straits. She was bracketed by a score of shells from the mortar that made the two direct hits. It was also discovered that a large, well-covered, active pillbox was located about eight yards from her port bow door, and that Japanese snipers were quite active. During a lull in the

Crew of an LST convoy alert for enemy attack en route to Northern Solomons.
U.S. Marine Corps.

firing, the ramp was lowered, but the first man off the ship was shot down, and the two who followed were dropped in their tracks. It became necessary to close the ramp for protection.

None of the LST's forward automatic weapons could be sufficiently depressed to fire on the pillbox. Personnel aboard ship opened up on the snipers and brought one down, but at that point they received orders from the beach to cease firing. At 0815, LST-399 requested permission to leave this beach, but received the reply, "Not granted." Whereupon a resourceful Seabee mounted a D-8 bulldozer and plowed the pillbox and its seven occupants under the earth. More on this now-famous story later.

LSTs 399 and 485 finally began unloading operations at 0830. In the meantime, the *Eaton,* with Adm Fort, entered the harbor in an attempt to silence the mortar fire. However, she could not locate the battery, which ceased firing when the *Eaton* approached.

Unloading from LST-399, which was the task of a detail of officers and men from the New Zealand Brigade Group, proceeded well at first, but after the mobile equipment was ashore the unloading came to "an almost abrupt halt." Many of the unloading crew were soldiers who had just come back from jungle fighting, and were not easily convinced that unloading by hand was necessary. LST-485, for lack of a bulldozer, road, or unloading area, also had to resort to unloading by hand.

At 1120 mortar fire was reopened from a new position on the hillside about 500 yards off the bow of the 399, which was bracketed and then hit on the port side. Shells continued screaming over the forecastle and striking the beach, and at 1125 another shell struck the ship on the port side, this time in the capstan control room, wrecking the capstan machinery. A few minutes later, on about the 20th salvo, the mortar (or mortars) registered a direct hit on a large ammunition dump at Falamai. A violent explosion knocked men off their feet on Beach Orange 2, fired the native village, and set off small arms dumps. Burning debris, shrapnel from exploding 90-mm shells, and exploding pyrotechnics covered the forward part of LST-399, so that the whole forecastle seemed on fire. The heat grew so intense that the forward guns had to be abandoned, and when it was noticed that the heat was blistering the paint on the starboard bow, the forward magazine was flooded. Hoses were manned up forward, by means of which several clusters of fire on the deck were extinguished. The commanding officer of LST Group 15, Cmdr Vilhelm K.Busck, then signaled LST-399 to retract and rebeach 50 yards to the west, which she promptly did.

At 1155, the *Philip* and the two LCI(G)s entered the channel in an attempt to silence the mortar fire, but by the time they had established contact with the shore party, the mortar had ceased firing. Mortar fire was never resumed.

Commander LST Group 15, after getting unloading started again on LST-485, proceeded to LST-399 where he found the unloading detail demoralized by the previous shelling. With the aid of a New Zealand officer he finally got some work under way although it went forward slowly.

At 1841, LST-485, having completely unloaded and retracted, lay off the stern of the 399 to protect her sister ship. LST-399 reported at 1902 that unloading was at a standstill, although she still had 20 tons of cargo aboard and was under orders to unload completely. Finding it impossible to resume unloading, she retracted at 1943 and both LSTs stood out of the channel, led by the *Philip* and accompanied by the two YMSs. When LST-399 was about 1,000

20-mm anti-aircraft gun crew on alert on board an LST bound for Northern Solomons, circa 1-9 November 1943. Next ship in convoy is LST-70.
Courtesy of Naval Historical Center.

yards from the beach she received reports of bogies and heard enemy planes overhead. Soon thereafter she saw the beach she had just left go up in a huge mass of flame, eight or ten bombs having been dropped.

Failure of Unloading Party – Space limitations won't allow me to expand on the trials and tribulations experienced by LSTs 399 and 485 during this landing. The full story can be found in the Action Reports. [9] Capt Carter, ComLSTFlot Five, bottom-lined the problems in his covering "First Endorsement" to Cmdr Busck's Action Report:

> The Flotilla Commander views with concern...the apparent lack of proper supervision of the shore unloading party, and lack of adequate facilities with which to unload the ships were undoubtedly responsible for much of the prolonged stay on the beach under the dangerous and trying conditions that these ships were obliged to undergo before completing the discharge of their cargo.
>
> The cooperation asked for...under "Comments And Recommendations" was apparently not had. It is thought that this vitally important phase of amphibious operations, the rapid unloading of our ships before opposed landings, is still not appreciated by shore unloading parties.
>
> On 29 October, while en route back to the 'Canal, Cmdr Busck, Commander LST Group 15, arranged for availability alongside the destroyer tender *Whitney* (AD-4) in Purvis Bay for battle damage repairs for LSTs 399 and 485. The 399 had taken 4 direct hits and the 485 two from the Jap mountain and trench mortar guns. The 399 had also taken a flare hit damaging degaussing and radio equipment during an air attack.
>
> Both LSTs were back in action in time for the Third Echelon to the Treasuries departing at 1800 on 4 November 1943.

The Fifth Transport Group, consisting of one APc, six LCMs, and an aircraft rescue boat, arrived off the western entrance of the harbor about 1830 on 27 October, and the **Fourth Transport Group**, composed of one APc, three LCTs, and a screen of two PT boats, arrived about 1850. Both groups were ordered to report to Commander Naval Base, Treasury Islands, for beaching and unloading assignments.

Air Attack – Shortly before the air attack on the LSTs, fighter director personnel on the *Cony* plotted four groups of enemy planes approaching the area. Basing their estimates on the number of raids tracked on the radar reports, fighter directors estimated that there were from 30 to 40 Val dive bombers and 50 to 60 Zeke and Hamp fighters. AirSols consisted of 16 P-38s on station divided into two groups of eight each; one at 20,000 feet and one at 25,000 feet. Airsols also had 16 P-40s, all at 10,000 feet, and eight P-39s at 10,000 feet, as well as eight P-38s and eight P-40s orbiting in the general area 15 miles northeast of the Treasury Islands. The other flights were orbiting in a general area 15 miles northwest of the islands.

The fighters were vectored out and constantly fed new plots. Three of the enemy groups were apparently intercepted. Several "tally-ho's" were heard, but no information on any of the raids was given by any of the aircraft in the 12 divisions under the *Cony's* direction. Ship's officers and men, however, reported seeing many enemy aircraft shot down. Our fighter planes claimed to have destroyed 12 enemy planes and reported no losses themselves. The attack was not turned back, however.

At 1525 the *Cony* sighted a large formation of horizontal bombers approaching from the west on a course that would take them over Blanche Harbor. Our fighters were engaging the enemy bombers and were seen to shoot down four or five of them. Seventeen enemy planes were counted as the formation closed. U.S. fighters were still engaging the bombers when they began unloading bombs, but this attack was not pressed home because of the successful interception.

A few minutes later, at 1532, a group of Vals attacked the *Cony* and *Philip* from the southwest. The planes were not intercepted before they reached their attack position. They came in out of the sun in an attack that the *Philip* described as "the best coordinated and severest this ship had experienced." The planes followed close on one another, making runs from port quarter to port bow, dropping their bombs, and leveling off to starboard. Approximately 12 bombs landed from 15 to 100 yards off the starboard side, but none of them hit the *Philip*.

Some 10 to 12 planes attacked the *Cony* in three or four waves from different sectors. Maneuvering in a series of radical turns, the *Cony* opened fire with her main battery and automatic weapons on each group. The *Cony* shot down five planes during the attack—one by 5-inch gunfire, and four by 40- and 20-mm.

About six bombs fell within 100 yards of the *Cony*. Then at 1534 two bombs struck her main deck aft abreast No. 4 gun. One of the bombs hit the starboard main deck at frame 163, one foot inboard, and exploded on contact; the other hit and penetrated to port main deck at frame 157, eight feet inboard before exploding.

As a result of the bombing, the *Cony's* after deckhouse was severely riddled and buckled, and the after engine room was flooded with oil from the ruptured after bulkhead to a level of one foot below the upper grating. A steam leak necessitated abandoning the engine room. A fire was also reported in the after living spaces and in No. 4 handling room.

Four *Cony* enlisted men were killed in the action; four others were so seriously wounded or burned that they later died. Three more men were wounded or burned seriously; seven others only slightly.

Within Blanche Harbor, LCI(G) 22 was attacked by two dive bombers. One bomb missed the craft by about 50 yards, but none struck her. Many hits from the gunboat's fire were observed on the second attacking plane, which was driven off smoking and

20-mm A.A. machine gun on board an LCI. Naval Historical Center.

probably severely damaged. The beached LSTs, however, were not attacked.

As soon as the attack ended, the *Cony* informed the *Philip* that her damage was serious; that she would begin retirement from the area at once; and that the *Philip* was to assume fighter director duties.

The *Cony*'s fires were brought under control about 1900, but continued to smolder all night. At 2000 she joined the *Waller* and proceeded in company with that ship and with tug *Apache*, which joined at 2400. She reached Purvis Bay without further incident.

In the meantime, the LSTs were being harassed on their retirement course by Japanese planes. The *Philip* was escorting and the *Saufley* later joined. At 2257, without warning from any radar-equipped vessel, a plane dropped two bombs and a float light close to the 399. The ship received several splinters of shrapnel along the port side, one of which penetrated the conning station, while another cut the forestay.

The remainder of the trip was uneventful save for the extraordinary work done by the three doctors embarked on LST-485. An operating room had been improvised in the troop quarters, and all the seriously wounded were taken aboard that ship. One doctor and two corpsmen were sent from LST-399 to LST-485, which had 45 wounded aboard. During the 30 hours en route to Guadalcanal, the three medical officers and assisting corpsmen worked without sleep or rest, performing 15 major operations and giving 120 plasma and 50 dextrose injections. All except five of the wounded were saved.

Seabee Construction – Company A and 25 men of the headquarters company of the 87th Battalion landed with the 8th New Zealand Brigade, in the first echelon making the assault on the Treasuries.

The 87th detachment was commanded by Lt Charles E. Turnbull, CEC, USNR. The assault brought distinction to Aurelio Tassone, a 28-year-old Machinist's Mate first-class from Massachusetts. Here's how Seabee historian Lt William Huie recorded the bulldozer incident made famous in the John Wayne movie, "The Fighting Seabees": [10]

The landing party had no tanks, but the Seabees had landed four bulldozers to begin clearing operations. One stubborn Jap pillbox was holding up the landing. Tassone maneuvered his bulldozer to a difficult angle of fire for the Japs, then while Lt Turnbull lay in the open and fired at the apertures in the pillbox, Tassone started a run for the Japs.

'The big machine moved slowly toward the pillbox,' Lt Turnbull reported, 'because Tassone insisted on running in low gear so that he would have power enough to crash the pillbox. He couldn't run in high gear and then shift to low gear, since that would mean bringing the bulldozer to a dead stop before the pillbox. He simply raised the blade and rolled ponderously forward. Jap machine-gun fire rattled off the blade, and it seemed that Tassone would be hit at any moment.'

At the proper second, Tassone dropped his blade and literally buried the pillbox under a ton of earth. After the island had been occupied, men of the 87th dug into the smashed pillbox and found the bodies of twelve Japs. Tassone, a slight, serious Italian-American, was awarded the Silver Star.

Please know there is another version of this famous action in which the bulldozer operator is a New Zealander. I've chosen historian Huie's version because I think Tassone's Silver Star award authenticates the story. Furthermore, the Action Report of LST-399—the ship that delivered the D-8 Bulldozer—does not specify who the operator was.

During November, the Seabee detachment with limited equipment, improved beaches for landing craft, built 21 miles of roads, established gun positions, and built a wharf for PT boats on Stirling Island. The remainder of the battalion arrived on 28 November and immediately began work on clearing and grading for the air strip. Within a month, a strip, 5,600 feet long and 200 feet wide, had been completed and had received its first fighter squadron. Construction had been carried out on a 24-hour-day basis, hindered by enemy raids and by the unexpected hardness of the coral. The 87th began clearing for taxiways and hardstands, later turning over the construction of these facilities to the 82d Battalion, which arrived during December.

The Flot 5 LCIs would make another run to the Treasuries—this time to Stirling Island—between 4-6 November with more troops and supplies. The Task Group included LCI-333 (with OTC

ComLCIGrp 13), 334, 63, and 65; LSTs 399 and 485; escorts *Conway,* *Pringle* and AMSs 82, 85, and 87. The LCIs disembarked their troops and gear at 0655 on 6 November at Purple Beach without incident; retracted and formed up for return at 0810 minus the LSTs and some of the escorts; and were back in Tulagi Harbor on 7 November at 1145.

The Choiseul Diversion, 27 October – 4 November 1943

As a diversion for the Treasury landings and for the Bougainville operation to come, a landing on Choiseul Island, of the 2[d] Marine Parachute Battalion, under command of LtCol Victor H. Krulak, was planned for midnight of D-5 day, which was the day of the landing on the Treasury Islands. The operation was to be carried out by some of the ships that participated in the Treasury landings.

TransDiv 22 and TransDiv 12 completed unloading at Treasury Islands at 0800 on 27 October and began the return to Guadalcanal. Wounded were transferred to TransDiv 12, and TransDiv 22 exchanged damaged boats for good ones.

TransDiv 22, Cmdr Robert H. Wilkinson in the *Kilty,* with the *Ward, Crosby,* and *McKean,* then left the convoy and set course

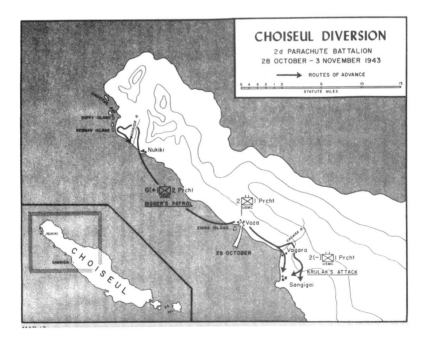

for Juno River, Vella Lavella Island, via Gizo Strait accompanied by the *Conway*. This force lay to off Juno River at 1830 on 27 October. So smooth was the planning that a large number of loaded boats were off the beach and ready to come alongside as soon as the APDs stopped. The 800 men of the 2ᵈ Marine Parachute Battalion, acting as infantry, were embarked expeditiously.

TransDiv 22, in column, fell in astern of the *Conway* as guide and proceeded across the Slot at a speed of 15 knots. The night was dark with intermittent rain squalls, sea calm, and wind force 1 and 2. The passage across the Slot was uneventful. At about 2352, a boat with a scouting party left the APDs, and at 0019 the first wave of boats followed.

The Marines were unopposed in their landing. In succeeding days they continued patrol and raiding activities along a 25-mile line, destroying enemy installations, barges, and supplies. Their swift and vigorous activity surprised the enemy and created the impression that a larger force was at work. Its mission completed, the battalion was withdrawn in LCIs at 0150 on 4 November.

U.S. losses during the entire operation were 9 killed, 2 missing, and 15 wounded, one of whom was captured. Known enemy casualties were 143 killed.

A Japanese plane plunges into the sea ahead of Columbia (CL-56) as she steams in column with other cruisers during the U.S. attack on Bougainville 1-2 Nov. 1943. Note 6"/47 gun shell casings on Columbia deck. Naval Historical Center.

Landing on Bougainville, 1 November 1943

While the preliminary air strikes and bombardments were underway, preparations for the landing at Empress Augusta Bay were carried forward. The Amphibious Force, under the command of RAdm Wilkinson for the first echelon, consisted of eight transports, four cargo ships, seven destroyers, four destroyer/minesweepers, and two fleet tugs.

These forces, called the Main Body, Northern Force, were organized around three divisions of the Transport Group, under command of Commodore Lawrence F. Reifsnider. Many subsequent echelons were transported in LSTs but, as historian Morison put it, "the 3rd Marines went up in style in twelve lightly combat-loaded transports and cargo ships."

See Appendix L for the composition of III Amphibious Force, TF 31, Main Body Northern Force, for the Empress Augusta Landings on Bougainville.

Landing Rehearsals – The period 13 to 30 October was devoted to training and rehearsal at Guadalcanal, Efate, and Espiritu Santo. The training of each transport division included a full scale debarkation and unloading of all equipment and supplies.

Much concern was felt by those responsible for operation plans regarding inaccuracies in available charts of the northern Empress Augusta Bay area and its approaches. An aerial photographic survey prior to operation disclosed the coast line of the area to be eight to ten miles out of positions indicated by Hydrographic Office charts, which were known to be approximations only.

Eleven landing beach sites were finally selected, which began at Torokina Point and extended approximately three and one-half miles up the coast, and a twelfth beach was chosen on the eastern shore of Puruata Island. There was still some apprehension concerning the condition of the beaches, about which little was known.

An advance party was landed on the night of 27 October to secure more information regarding the proposed landing area as well as enemy strength; but, unfortunately, efforts to communicate by radio were unsuccessful.

The Approach – As a precaution against alerting the enemy, operation orders postponed the merging of the three transport

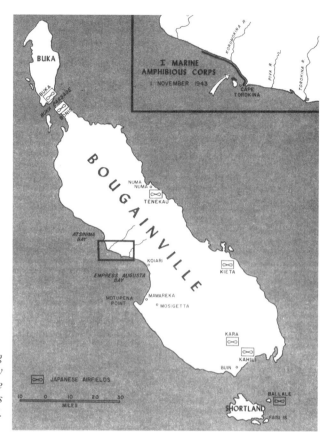

Bougainville Landing 1 November 1943 by First Marine Amphibious Corps (IMAC). USMC.

divisions until the forenoon of 31 October. TransDiv Baker departed Efate on 28 October, TransDiv Charlie left Guadalcanal the morning of 30 October and TransDiv Able departed from Espiritu Santo the afternoon of 28 October.

During the evening of 30 October, RAdm Wilkinson, commander of the task force, and Gen Vandegrift, Commanding General, First Marine Amphibious Corps, embarked in the *Clymer* off Koli Point and joined the three transport divisions at the rendezvous point the following morning at 0740. On signal from Wilkinson, Commodore Reifsnider assumed tactical command of the transport group and screen. The main body then proceeded on a northwesterly course, with transports in line of three division columns. At 1800, course was changed in the direction of the Shortland area until after dark as a possible deception associated with the seizure of Treasury Island and the diversionary landing on Choiseul.

Final arrival in the Cape Torokina transport area was set for daylight to permit visual detection of uncharted shoals believed to be offshore. H-hour was tentatively set for 0715 but was changed by signal on arrival to 0730.

Shore Bombardment – Initial shore bombardment of Cape Torokina was delivered by the *Wadsworth*, on station 7,000 yards ahead of the transport group, and the minesweeper group following the destroyer. Ships comprising the main fire support group, according to operation orders, were the *Anthony, Wadsworth, Terry,* and *Sigourney*. The fire support area assigned the *Anthony* was well to the seaward of those assigned other vessels. Opening on Puruata Island at 0603 with her 5-inch battery, the *Anthony* fired two-gun salvos at ranges from 13,300 to 11,000 yards, until 0718, with one interruption of six minutes.

The *Wadsworth* and *Terry,* as anticipated, experienced difficulty in covering the target areas assigned. One of these was at the western end of the landing beach. Another, especially critical,

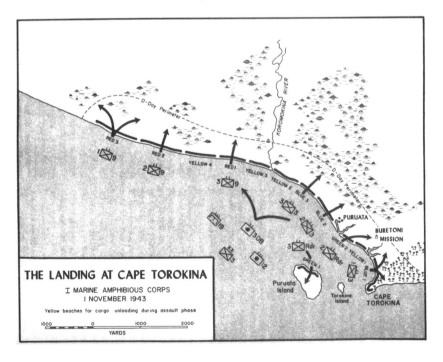

THE LANDING AT CAPE TOROKINA

I MARINE AMPHIBIOUS CORPS
I NOVEMBER 1943

Yellow beaches for cargo unloading during assault phase

Torokina airstrip on Bougainville Island, Solomon Islands. U.S. Navy.

was on the northwestern face of Torokina Point. It was known that new defenses had been constructed by the enemy in the latter area, and it was fully expected that the Marines from the *President Adams,* landing on Beach Blue One facing these defenses, would meet with resistance.

The *Sigourney* experienced no unusual difficulty in carrying out her scheduled fire mission. Shore fire control parties, which were under orders not to call for naval gunfire on targets closer than 500 yards to Allied troops, requested no supporting gunfire.

During the entrance to the transport area, the transports were to fire ranging shots on Cape Torokina and to spray Puruata Island with 20-mm gunfire. At 0615, the *Hunter Liggett*, at the head of the transport column, arrived at the turning point about 3,000 yards from Point Torokina, turned left, and opened fire on Torokina Point with her 3-inch battery for ranging in the event of any possible need for counter-battery fire. She also fired bursts of 20-mm fire at Puruata on passing abeam. Each transport in succession followed the same procedure.

Landing and Beach Conditions – Sweepers found no mines and reported sufficient depth of water for the transports which followed. The transports formed on the inshore line for debarkation, and the cargo vessels on a second line about 500 yards to seaward. By 0645 all transports were in the transport area, and the signal "land the landing force" was executed. Ships dropped anchor underfoot and the boats were "rail-loaded"—meaning the

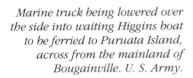

Marine truck being lowered over the side into waiting Higgins boat to be ferried to Puruata Island, across from the mainland of Bougainville. U. S. Army.

Marines took their places in the LCVPs and LCMs before the boats were lowered. Between 7,000 and 8,000 troops were landed in the first wave.

The line of departure for the boats was the line of bearing of the transports. The signal to start the first assault wave for the ship with the longest run to the beach (*President Adams* at 5,000 yards) was executed by the OTC at 0710. Simultaneously the fire support group commenced bombardment of prearranged targets. It was the responsibility of each transport to start its wave of boats at the proper time to reach assigned beaches on schedule.

Bombardment was lifted at 0721, and immediately thereafter 31 TBFs from Munda bombed and strafed the landing beaches for five minutes. The first wave from the *President Jackson* hit the beach at 0726, H-hour minus 4 minutes.

It was clear, even from the transport area, that surf on the beach was bad, but boat crews found conditions worse than anticipated. This was especially true of the four northernmost of the twelve landing beaches. The beach was very narrow and had a 12-foot bank immediately back of the surf line for a considerable part of its length. Coxswains reported that the steepness of the beach prevented proper grounding of boats along the length of their keels.

Bougainville Invasion, 1 Nov. 1943. Marines in landing craft headed for the shores of Empress Augusta Bay. Courtesy U.S. Marine Corps.

Beneath Bagana Volcano assault boats circle in Empress Augusta Bay awaiting their turn to storm the beaches. U.S. Coast Guard.

Admiral Halsey pronounced the beach and terrain conditions "worse than anything ever encountered before in the South Pacific." For more than a mile inland the terrain consisted of swamp except for two narrow corridors of land raised a few inches above swamp level. The beaches were so narrow that in most places two bulldozers could not pass abreast between jungle and sea.

What followed, according to one officer, was "almost a disaster." Bottom line: 86 boats in the transport group—64 of them LCVPs and 22 LCMs—were broached and stranded during the landing operations.

Later in the morning, when the surf grew worse, the *Crescent City, American Legion, Hunter Liggett, Alchiba,* and *Titania* were shifted to beaches assigned other ships to the east. This caused additional delay and considerable congestion, while the loss of the large number of boats proved a serious handicap. Because of intervening shoals, the tug *Sioux* was unable to get close enough to the beach to assist in salvaging stranded boats.

As anticipated, the heaviest enemy resistance was encountered by the boats from the *President Adams* on Beach Blue One. Machine-gun fire from the northern side of Puruata Island was also encountered on the way in to the beach. Our fire support group did not lift bombardment until a few minutes before H-hour, making it necessary for the first wave of boats to slow down at 500 yards from the beach to avoid shells, some of which were falling in the water approximately 100 yards offshore. Shore batteries on Torokina Point held their fire until our boats were only 50 yards offshore, then opened up with deadly accuracy.

Enemy defenses on Beach Blue One included a total of two 77-mm guns, two 90-mm mortars, and fifteen machine guns, located about ten yards from the water's edge, all well-emplaced in pillboxes.

Sgt Charles U. Wolverton of the 37th Division bites his tongue as he begins to heave a grenade at a pillbox emplacement. U.S. Army.

Wounded Marines, 3rdMarDiv, are carried aboard a Higgins boat for evacuation from Bougainville, Solomon Islands. U.S. Marine Corps.

Later examination of the defenses revealed that most of the destroyer projectiles were exploded above ground by striking palm trees, and the bombs of the TBFs fell too far back from the beach. The pillboxes containing the 77-mm mortars were untouched, despite the fact that destroyers fired some 900 rounds of 5-inch shells at this beach.

Of the eight boats in the first wave from the *President Adams*, three received direct hits. Ten other boats were damaged by gunfire to such an extent that they had to be hoisted for repair. The second wave of eight boats landed and retracted without damage or casualties. In the third wave, however, one boat received three shells through the ramp just prior to striking the beach. Five Marines were seen to climb out over the side. The remainder of the 30 aboard the boat were killed or wounded.

Salvage boats operated throughout the landing period of nine hours within easy range of enemy guns, and officers and men of the beach party repeatedly risked their lives to rescue wounded men from the water.

With 60 per cent of the Marine shore party withdrawn to press the attack against the enemy, Lt (jg) James H. Moore remained for nine hours under the most difficult conditions to organize the unloading of boats to permit the landing of 500 tons of cargo and vehicles. A determined effort was made by the enemy to disrupt unloading by means of machine gun and rifle fire.

Marines racing from landing boats across beach to the Bougainville jungle, 1 Nov 1943. U.S. Marine Corps.

Salvage Crews come to the rescue of an LCVP on Bougainville Beach. Courtesy U.S. Coast Guard.

Beach Party personnel rescue wounded men from the surf. U.S. Coast Guard.

Only light resistance was encountered from the beaches to the north of Torokina. It was estimated that there were only about 300 Japanese in all opposing the landing, but their resistance was stubborn and determined. American losses in the landing were 70 killed and missing and 124 wounded. About half the enemy force was killed, and the remaining Japanese fled inland.

Air Operations – RAdm Wilkinson's amphibious force received excellent air support. They needed all they could get with the beachhead only 210 miles from Rabaul and much nearer the Kahili strip on lower Bougainville. To neutralize these enemy airfields, Wilkinson depended on AirSols, which had shifted its headquarters from Guadalcanal to Munda on 21 October 1943 while under the command of Nathan F. Twining, USA.

By that time the new fighter strip at Barakoma, Vella Lavella, had been operational for almost a month, and three Marine fighter squadrons comprising 64 Corsairs and 108 pilots were flown in as a nucleus of the force to be based there for covering the Bougainville operation.

Since some air opposition to the Bougainville landing was to be expected, despite the heavy pounding which had been given the enemy airfields, a fighter patrol of 32 AirSols planes was stationed over Empress Augusta Bay from dawn to dusk. With the help of excellent fighter direction, this patrol drove off a number of enemy planes which attempted to enter the area. Two attacks, however, succeeded in breaking through.

Warning of the first air opposition came at 0718 when bogies were reported bearing 305 degrees T., distance 50 miles. The last boats were just leaving the transports when the latter were ordered to come to course 210 degrees by emergency turn signal and stand out from the unloading area in preparation for air attack. ComDesDiv 90 ordered the fire support group to close and screen the transports.

Three attack groups, one of torpedo planes and two of bombers, were plotted by radar. The fighter director group in *Conway* vectored out the fighter cover. Eight Kittyhawks of the patrol intercepted 30 Zekes at 0800, of which they shot down seven, with one probable, without damage to our planes. About ten minutes later, eight P-38s intercepted between 15 and 20 Zekes, shot down seven, and probably downed three more, suffering no losses themselves.

In the meantime, all ships were steaming on various courses at various speeds, maneuvering radically. Some twelve Vals broke through our fighter cover and closed for attack at 0830. A number of bombs were dropped in the transport area, but only the destroyers were seriously threatened. Six Vals glided out of the sun to divebomb the *Sigourney* and *Wadsworth*. The planes were sighted at nearer than 10,000 yards, and firing was commenced immediately. The first bombs fell near the *Sigourney*.

Several seconds later the first of six bombs to straddle the *Wadsworth* exploded 25 yards off the starboard quarter. Other bombs fell from 100 to 500 yards away, causing no damage. A near hit, 25 feet from frame 208 on the port side, however, killed two men, wounded five seriously, and four slightly. The hull and superstructure were sprayed with fragments which caused minor damage.

Four of the attacking planes were shot down by U.S. ships, two of which were claimed by the *Wadsworth* and one by the *Bennett*. The remaining planes retired after enemy fighters strafed the beaches with little effect.

At 0930, the transports returned to the transport area and resumed unloading. Several bogies were reported during the morning, but it was not until afternoon that a second attack developed. Radar warning came about 1248, and the transport group was again ordered underway. The disposition was maneuvered as before.

20-mm gunners watch a Japanese plane burn and crash. National Archives.

Planes were sighted at 1316 dropping bombs over the landing beach. They also dropped a few around the formation, but they caused no damage. At this time, the *American Legion* was still grounded on a shoal in the transport area. The *Bennett* was ordered to screen the grounded vessel, and at about 1357 she took under fire a low-flying Zero making a shallow dive at the beach directly north of the *American Legion*. Two observers believed they saw a plane crash as the result of this fire. The bombs dropped on the beach and the strafing of the same area by enemy planes caused little damage and few casualties.

Our fighter patrol was vectored out in the meantime with good results. Eight F4Us engaged six Zekes at 1345, shooting down one and severely damaging three others. A few minutes later, eight F4Us shot down one of 12 Zekes encountered over central Bougainville. All of these fights were without loss to our planes. At unspecified times during the afternoon, eight F4Us encountered 30 to 40 Zekes covering 16 Bettys. The enemy made no attempt to attack, but our planes shot down three Zekes and probably destroyed one other Zeke and one Betty.

Unloading and Retirement – By 1500 all ships had returned to the transport area and resumed unloading. Each ship provided its own shore party, except that the naval platoons for AKAs were formed from embarked personnel of the Naval base unit. The AKAs had a shore service platoon of 200, plus ship details of 20 men per hatch, and boat details of three men per LCM and two men per LCVP. The APAs had a similar complement. The total number of troops employed in the shore party for the division landed was roughly 5,700, or somewhat over one-third of the total embarked.

There were numerous causes for delay in unloading: some Marine unloading details also had combat duties; the two air attacks, during which all ships had to suspend unloading and remain underway for maneuvering; the poor beaches at the northern area which necessitated the shifting of five ships to new beaches; the consequent congestion, and the grounding of the *American Legion* for several hours; the loss of 86 landing craft by stranding, and others by enemy gunfire; and interference by enemy snipers.

These and additional deterrents made it impossible to complete the unloading of the *Liggett, Legion, Crescent City,* and *Alchiba* before dark. The eight other ships completed unloading before 1800, at which time CTF RAdm Wilkinson ordered the entire transport group to get underway and retire toward Guadalcanal along the track of the approach. All ships steamed south and east together until 2300, when Commodore Reifsnider, with the four ships that had not completed unloading, left the formation as previously directed by CTF and proceeded to return to Torokina Point. These ships were screened by DesRon 45 with the *Fullam, Guest, Hudson, Bennett,* and *Braine,* plus the *Sioux.* The remainder of the transport group proceeded to Guadalcanal, where they arrived without incident about 2400 on 2 November.

The ships under Reifsnider, which were returning to Torokina Point, steered various courses to regulate the time of their arrival, and to avoid contact with the minelayer group returning at high speed from the north. About 0250, the force sighted considerable illumination over the horizon resulting from flares and gunfire from the Battle of Empress Augusta Bay, then in progress between the American covering force of cruisers and the Japanese force it had

U.S. Coast Guardsmen and Marines hit the beach in a hurry as they go after a beachhead at Empress Augusta Bay at Bougainville. This assault was made under Japanese aerial attack. Coast Guardsmen are manning the landing barges. Courtesy U.S. Coast Guard.

intercepted. The transports changed course to the east at 0300 to avoid the battle area, which was about 35 miles distant. A few hours later the *Sioux* was directed by dispatch from CTF to proceed at best speed to take in tow the *Foote* torpedoed during the night action.

Reifsnider's transports arrived off Torokina at 0905 on 2 November and commenced unloading again with the assistance of boats from the boat pool. Numerous bogies were picked up by radar, but no attack developed. By 1500, all four ships were completely unloaded and had departed for Guadalcanal. At 1616 the *Apache* joined the formation as relief for the *Sioux*, and at 1000 the following day, 3 November, the *Nashville* and *Pringle* joined. The transports arrived at Tulagi on 4 November, at 0045, without further incident.

Mine Laying – For protection against surface bombardment, a three-row defensive minefield was laid off Cape Moltke, fifteen miles northwest of Torokina, on the night of 1-2 November. The minelaying unit, composed of the *Breese, Gamble,* and *Sicard,* with *Renshaw* as screen, completed the successful laying of the field shortly after midnight and retired southward. A second unit, composed of the *Tracy* and *Pruitt,* screened by the *Eaton,* laid an offensive, two-row minefield on the same night at the eastern entrance to the Shortland area on the south coast of Bougainville.

The Marines Attack [11]

By nightfall 1 November 1943, some 14,000 Marines and more than 6,000 tons of supplies were ashore. Considering the disastrous beach conditions, landing craft problems, and unloading delays, D-day had more than its share of challenges.

The 3rd and 9th Marines, assisted by the 2d Raider Battalion, began slogging inland through swamp and jungle soon after landing, to press their attack against the enemy by seizing a swath of the coast from Cape Torokina to the northwest. At the same time, the 3rd Raider Battalion (less company M) assaulted Puruata Island off Cape Torokina. Japanese defenses in the landing area consisted of a single company supported by a 75-mm gun. One platoon occupied Puruata and a squad held Torokina Island, while the rest of the Japanese infantry was dug in on the cape itself.

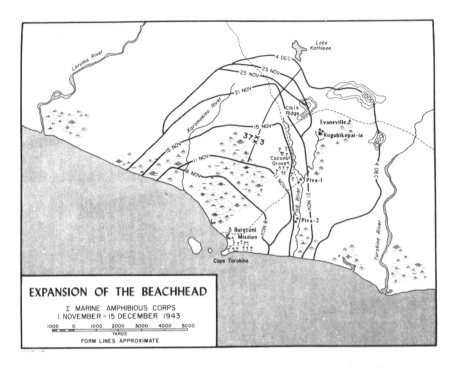

EXPANSION OF THE BEACHHEAD

I MARINE AMPHIBIOUS CORPS
I NOVEMBER – 15 DECEMBER 1943

FORM LINES APPROXIMATE

The small Japanese force gave a good account of itself. The 75-mm gun enfiladed the eastern landing beaches, while machine guns on the two small islands and the cape placed the approaches to this area in a cross fire. The result was havoc among the initial right flank assault waves, which landed in considerable disorder. The 75-mm gun destroyed four landing craft and damaged 10 others before Sergeant Robert A. Owens of the 1st Battalion, 3rd Marines silenced it. (He received a posthumous Medal of Honor for his single-handed charge against the key position.)

The 2d Raider Battalion, landing just to the left of Owens' battalion, suffered from the gun, and from mortar and machine gun fire raking the beach. LtCol Joseph P. McCaffery succeeded in reorganizing his force on the beach and in launching an attack that swept away the enemy defenses; but he fell, mortally wounded, in the process.

Other battalions farther to the west met little or no resistance, except from high surf that caused many landing craft to broach. Company M, 3rd Raiders, temporarily attached to the 2d Raider Battalion, moved out at noon and occupied a blocking position

Cpl William Coffron, USMC, fires at a sniper during landing operations in Empress Augusta Bay, Bougainville, Nov. 1943. U.S. Marine Corps.

Marine patrol crossing a river on a log "bridge" to get at Japanese snipers, soon after the Cape Torokina landings on Bougainville. Naval Historical Center.

Marine Infantry and tank in action. U.S. Marine Corps.

1,500 yards up the Piva Trail, the main avenue of approach into the beachhead. The 3rd Raiders silenced the machine guns on Puruata, and destroyed the last defenders on that island by late afternoon on 2 November. Total Raider casualties to this point were three killed and 15 wounded.

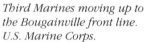

Third Marines moving up to the Bougainville front line. U.S. Marine Corps.

During two days and two nights of fierce jungle fighting on Bougainville, the Marine Raider Battalion repelled repeated attacks by overwhelming Japanese forces. Living in flooded foxholes, this machine gun team withstood each enemy attack.
Courtesy U.S. Marine Corps.

Over the next several days the Marines advanced inland to extend their perimeter. There were occasional engagements with small enemy patrols, but the greatest resistance during this period came from the terrain, which consisted largely of swampland and dense jungle once one moved beyond the beach. The thing most Marines would remember about Bougainville would be the deep, sucking mud that seemed to cover everything not already underwater.

155mm guns of Sea Coast Defense, 3rd Marine Defense, firing on Japanese positions during the perimeter attack on Bougainville.

Tents strung from trees in a jungle clearing near the Command Post on Bougainville. The trees also provided camouflage for the men. U.S. Marine Corps.

On 4 November another unit relieved the 2d Raider Battalion on the line, and both battalions of the raider regiment were attached to the 9th Marines. The raiders maintained responsibility for the roadblock and companies rotated out of the position every couple of days.

Meanwhile, the "Pacific Express" reinforcement-replenishment operation was just beginning.

Securing the Beachhead [12]

On 4 November 1943, the Second Echelon to Bougainville (but the first Echelon of LSTs) departed Guadalcanal. Capt G. B. Carter, USN, ComLSTFLOT 5 was also Commander Task Group 31.6 composed of 6 destroyers: *Eaton* (with Capt Carter aboard), *Waller* (with ComDesRon 22, Capt J. E. Hurff aboard), *Renshaw, Sigourney, Philip,* and *Saufley;* five APDs of TransDiv 12: *Stringham* (with Cmdr J. D. Sweeney, ComTransDiv 12, aboard), *Talbot, Dent, Waters,* and *McKean;* three APDs of TransDiv 22: *Kilty, Crosby,* and *Ward;* and Task Unit 31.6.1 composed of 8 LSTs: 70, 207, 339, 341, 353, 354, 395, and 488.

The primary fighter director group was aboard the *Waller* with the secondary group on board the *Eaton.*

It should be noted that trailers were employed for the first time with this trip to Bougainville. Capt Carter and Cmdr Cutler supervised the loading of the eight LSTs at Guadalcanal. All bulk cargo such as boxed or crated war materiel, field rations, and supplies, was loaded on trailers ready to roll off when the ship hit the beach. Bulldozers were loaded last so they could pull the trailers off.

The night of 4-5 November LST-488 had a near collision with one or more ships in the convoy. Boatswain's Mate Tom Byrne vividly remembers that night fifty-some years ago:

> When we sailed for Bougainville, I was the Boatswain's Mate of the watch, 1200-1400, on the conning tower above the wheelhouse. The Officer of the Deck stood his watch there also. Since we were operating under radio silence, communications from the flag commander to the rest of the ships had to be in the form of flag signals which were read with the naked eye.
>
> Sometime during my watch, the fleet commander ran up a flag signal. I knew this because our signalman on watch with us began to

attach numeral flags to the lanyards and to pull the flags up to the yardarm. He was repeating the flag signals that were visible on the ship nearest us. As I watched the process unfold, I remembered back to when I was a 'signal striker' on board the battleship *New York*.

As the flags were being run up, our Chief Quartermaster was repeating their identity and I was listening to test my memory of the flags....At one point, I didn't agree with the Chief's identification of one of the numeral flags but figured he had to be right. He's the Chief. Besides, it had been 5 years since my signal striker days. The flags continued to be hoisted until the signal was repeated in total. The flag message had to be decoded and it had to pertain to some future action....The rest of that two hour watch was filled with action and...when it was all over, I went about my regular duties.

Since I had stood the 1200-1400 watch in the afternoon, I had the 0000-0200 watch on the conning tower that night. After I had my coffee and a cigarette, I proceeded to the bridge and to the conning tower. I had to grope my way from the crew's quarters to the conning tower because we were operating under 'darken ship conditions.' When I got to my position on the conning tower, I just stood there and waited to see something. After a few minutes, I began to see. I could see the outlines of figures and knew that one of them must have been the Officer of the Deck because of the hat he was wearing. I didn't know who he was.

I stood there for a while in total darkness, thinking of home and other things. I said to myself, 'This is really total darkness.' I began to think of night blindness school. I think I'll try out what we learned there. I looked at where I thought the horizon should be and, sure enough, I saw nothing. Look above the horizon and if there's anything there, you'll see it. That's what the instructor said. I carefully scanned the horizon from the starboard bow back toward amidships. I didn't see anything. I turned back to the bow again, but this time I looked above the horizon. I immediately began to see the horizon. 'Boy, this works!' I said to myself. Suddenly I saw a black object, at least I thought I saw something. I blinked my eyes and tried to concentrate more than normal. It could be something. I can't tell you why, but I ran to the ladder leading from the conning tower, got part way down, and jumped the rest of the way to the deck below, slid down the ladder to the next deck and ran into the wardroom, turned to the passageway where Captain MacKey's cabin was located. He was asleep. I think I said something like, 'Come quick, Captain—I think I see something on the starboard bow.'

He jumped out of his bunk, half asleep, and beat me to the conning tower. He took one look at the starboard quarter and grabbed the voice tube which led to the wheelhouse just below us and yelled, 'Full left rudder!' He then yelled down to the engine room through another voice tube, 'Full speed astern!'

The ship began to vibrate as the engines began trying to overcome the forward speed and to go into reverse. Captain MacKey's big booming voice could be heard all over as he barked out orders. None of us knew exactly what was going on, even though we were right there.

When daylight arrived, we found out what happened. The Chief had misread one numeral flag. At 0100, all the other ships on the convoy made a 90-degree turn except us. That black object I saw, was another LST crossing our bow while making her turn.

The Ensign on our bow watch swears that when our bow began swinging to port, after Capt MacKey gave the orders 'full left rudder' and 'full speed astern,' he could have shaken hands with anybody standing on the port side of the LST that was passing across our bow. We were carrying a tank deck full of gasoline and explosives, and the LST we had just missed ramming was probably carrying the same type of cargo. The two ships were also carrying troops. God bless night blindness school!

Many a sailor has experienced similar close calls, but the story from Boatswain's Mate Tom Byrne illustrates the dangers of close convoy formations at night.

Bougainville Operation: Reinforcements from USS LST-353 wade ashore at Empress Augusta Bay, 6 Nov. 1943. Also present are LSTs 488 and 70. Note the barrage balloons overhead. National Archives.

Task Group 36.1 arrived at Bougainville at 0600 on 6 November. The unloading proceeded at a very slow pace and at 2000 Capt Carter notified CTF 31 he intended to have the LSTs work throughout the night to get the cargo off. The Task Group finally departed Bougainville at 0300 on 7 November and arrived at the 'Canal at 1700 on the 8th.

Working party prepares bombs for unloading from the LCT that brought them to Bougainville. These 1,000-pound bombs were stored in two layers with a level of timber between them.

A "train" of bomb carts is loaded on Bougainville. The bombs have been finned, after being unloaded from an LCT on a nearby beach. Naval Historical Center.

Here's one of those "Truth is Stranger Than Fiction" stories for you. After studying two Action Reports, and reading RAdm Morison's account of the action, I've chosen to use a direct quote from my favorite naval historian. It happened the evening of 5 November 1943 about 28 miles south of Bougainville. Morison: [13]

> LCI-70 (Lt (jg) Harry W. Frey) and PT-167 (Ensign Theodore Berlin) were escorting LCT-68 (Ensign Gordon W. Smith) back from Torokina beachhead to the Treasuries. At 1915, when about 28 miles SW of Cape Torokina, they sighted a flight of 'Kates' against the fading twilight. The wing of the leading bomber struck the PT's radio antenna and the plane splashed; but its torpedo, without hitting the water or exploding, passed through the bow of the boat leaving its entire tail assembly in the crew's head as a souvenir. A few minutes later the PT's 20-mm fire hit one of the second wave of attacking bombers and it fell in flames, so close to her port quarter that men on the stern were drenched by the splash.
>
> In the meantime, LCI-70 was having the toughest fight that any of her type had experienced. In 14 minutes, she was subjected to four low-altitude torpedo attacks and one strafing run. Owing to her shoal draft, all the torpedoes aimed at her passed harmlessly below her keel, except one that porpoised into the engine room, killing one man but not exploding; the warhead slid off into the bread locker.
>
> Fearing an explosion of the murderous torpedo, which was still smoking, Skipper Frey ordered Abandon Ship. After a decent interval had passed with no explosion, a damage-control party went on board the 'Elsie Item.' LCT-68 passed her a line and towed her back to Torokina, while PT-167 went ahead with the wounded.

Frey confirmed the accuracy of Morison's story in a recent telephone conversation.

Speaking of LCTs, while beached in a cove at Stirling Island the night of 8 November, Flotilla 5 LCT-330 took a direct hit. An extract from the skipper's log reads as follows: [14]

8 November 1943

1200 LCT beached in cove at Stirling Island with about two-thirds of craft covered by a tree.

2240 Condition red sounded.

2258 Suffered direct bomb amidships between frame #38 and frame #39; bomb passed completely through vessel and exploded. Vessel buckled at frames 38 and 39. Stern section dropped approximately fifteen degrees. Slight buckling between frames 22 and 23. Four men slightly injured.

2330 Small boats arrived from boat pool to assist in putting craft on beach broadside.

9 November 1943

0010 Beaching operation completed with lines out to beach fore and aft.

0035 Pumping operation began and continued through night.

0730 Began preparing craft for tow.

According to the Action Report submitted to A. L. Jones, Commander LCT Flotilla 5, it was probably a 100-150 pound bomb dropped by a Japanese scout plane.

"Pacific Express" Reinforces Ground Forces

On 9 November, Merrill's TF 39 left Guadalcanal with yet another echelon of reinforcements for Bougainville, eight LSTs and eight APDs.

Third Echelon to Bougainville, 9-13 November – Task Group 31.7 composed of Transport Unit (31.7.1) with TransDiv 12, TransDiv 22, LSTs 334, 390, 397, 398, 446(F), 449, and 472, Cmdr. R.W. Cutler, USN, ComLSTGRP 13, and screened by DDs *Waller, Philips, Saufley,* and *Pringle,* Capt. J. E. Hurff, USN, CTG.7 in charge, departed the 'Canal at 0700 on 9 November.

U.S. Army tank M4-A1 traveling on water off Bougainville Island. The tank is equipped with pontoons, as well as intake and exhaust extensions for emergencies while underway. Courtesy U.S. Army.

The LSTs beached at Beach #13, Cape Torokina, at 0641 on 11 November and commenced unloading troops and cargo. By 1840, TG 31.7 had completed unloading without an enemy encounter, and was underway for the 'Canal arriving there at 1159 on 13 November.

By 14 November the first four echelons had landed 33,861 Army and Marine Corps troops at Empress Augusta Bay, which had become a very busy place.

Date	Echelon	Ships	Troops	Cargo tons
1 Nov	1	8 APA, 4 AKA	14,321	6,177
6 Nov	2	8 APD, 8 LST	3,548	5,080
8 Nov	2A	4 APA, 2 AKA	5,715	3,160
11 Nov	3	8 APD, 8 LST	3,599	5,785
13 Nov	4	4 APA, 2 AKA	6,678	2,935
Total			33,861	23,137

Source: III PhibFor AR, pp 11-12.

Troops of the 149ᵗʰ Infantry push onward through the mud of Bougainville to reach their new bivouac area. Courtesy of U.S. Army.

Fifth Echelon to Bougainville, 15-19 November – The fifth echelon was comprised of LSTs 70, 207, 339, 341, 353, 395, and 488; APDs *Stringham, Ward, Dent, Waters, Kilty, Crosby, McKean,* and *Talbot,* and DD escorts *Waller, Renshaw, Pringle, Saufley, Sigourney,* and *Conway.* Capt J. E. Hurff in *Waller* was in charge of the destroyers.

Loss of USS *McKean,* 17 November 1943

Task Group 37.6 was within 20 miles of the beachhead early on the 17th when the group was jumped by a Japanese plane. *McKean* (APD-5) took an aerial torpedo at 0350 which set off a violent explosion of depth charges and ammunition in the after magazine. Within 10 minutes, skipper Lt Cmdr Ralph L. Ramey called "Abandon Ship!" and was the last man over the side.

Destroyers *Sigourney, Talbot,* and *Waller* picked up survivors. The doughty old "Green Dragon" had begun her sea life as DD-90 in 1919. She shot down the plane that had torpedoed her, and the vessels around her shot down four more that night. But that was of little solace to *McKean's* survivors who had lost 64 shipmates and 52 Marine passengers.

The remainder of TG 31.6 continued its approach to Cape Torokina with Group Commander shifting his pennant to LST-354. Beaching of LSTs was accomplished about 0600, and unloading of LSTs and APDs commenced shortly thereafter. At about 0800 the vessels of the Task Group were subjected to enemy dive bombing attacks with no damage reported.

USS Dent APD-9, the sister ship of McKean, was close aboard. First Shot Naval Vets.

At about 1425, *Talbot* and *Dent* were directed to proceed to Vella Lavella with the seriously wounded. Unloading was practically completed about 1800 by all ships, less LST-339. *Renshaw*, and *Pawnee* stood out toward Point "UNCLE," speed six knots, at which time the Group Commander shifted his pennant to *Renshaw*.

LST-339 was unable to retract from the beach, and the Group Commander directed *Pawnee* to assist, with *Renshaw* standing by. At about 2120, when *Pawnee* was unable to pull LST-339 from the beach, CTG 31.6 directed LST-399 to remain and retract at first favorable tide; thereafter, to subject herself to further orders of Commander Task Force 31. He also directed *Pawnee* to stand by LST-339.

About 2400 *Pawnee* was withdrawn from assisting LST-339, by orders of Task Force Commander, and LST-339 was left to her own devices, finally effecting retraction at about 1400 November 18th, and returning to Guadalcanal in another Task Group.

At 2120 CTG 31.6 rejoined his formation in *Renshaw* and took station ahead of LSTs, with APDs inner anti-air and submarine screen, and DDs outer screen. The formation proceeded to Guadalcanal, passage uneventful, arriving 19 November 1943, about 1030.

Down the ramp and through the surf goes a jeep with the Beach Party's assistance. U.S. Coast Guard.

Seventh Echelon to Bougainville, 21-25 November – LSTs 334, 390, 397, 398, 446(GF), 447, 448, 449, and 472 comprised the LST unit in the seventh echelon to Torokina, Bougainville. Cmdr R. W. Cutler, USNR, ComLSTGRP 13, was in charge of the LST unit. They were escorted by DDs *Waller, Renshaw, Conway,* and *Bennett.*

The morning of 22 November at 0610, a friendly Cruiser Task Force was sighted, bearing 26 degrees True, distance 15 miles. At 1100 a force of six LCIs with two destroyers were sighted on the horizon. The Slot was busy!

At 0345 on 23 November two white aircraft flares were observed resulting in a call to General Quarters. At 0355, anti-aircraft fire was observed over Cape Torokina. At 0608 the LSTs beached at Torokina. While unloading, Japanese shore batteries shelled the beached LSTs. In his "History of LST-447," Electrician's Mate Freeman Ballard described the action:

> We had beached and secured and were starting to unload our cargo around 0700 when all hell broke loose. The Japs...started shelling the whole beach area. Their spotter was located on a small island about a mile to the right of us.

A big Japanese air raid made a direct hit on a gas and oil dump at Empress Augusta Bay, Bougainville at 0200 on 19 Nov. 1943. Nearly 8,000 drums were set afire. Marines and sailors are shown fighting the flames which raged until 0800 on Nov. 20. U.S. Marine Corps.

The first shell to hit us landed on the main deck amidships. It hit the ready box for a 20-mm gun above the mess hall, which was above the auxiliary engine room, starboard side. The ready box exploded and blew a hole into the mess hall, killing two men and wounding eight others.

About eight minutes later, a second shell hit amidships, blowing a hole through the main deck into the tank deck. This hit killed one man and wounded five others. Our cargo was 280 tons of artillery shells and powder bags, along with 2,050 drums of high-octane gasoline, trucks, jeeps and food supplies. Thirteen drums of gasoline were punctured by flying shrapnel spilling gasoline all through the tank deck.

The third shell hit under the bow causing some damage but no casualties to the ship's company. The Marines suffered a lot of casualties that morning.

Two destroyers bombarded the small island to our right and the shelling was silenced in about 45 minutes.

The LSTs had completed unloading, cleared the beach by 1425, and were underway at 1429 for the 'Canal.

At 0500 on 24 November, LSTs 447 and 449 left the convoy, with escorts *Sigourney* and YP-415, and at 1253 beached at Vella Lavella to disembark Bougainville casualties. By 1456 the two LSTs were underway again, arriving at Kukum at 1458 on 25 November.

The report on the use of the experimental log ramps, built especially for the use of the LSTs in the 7th echelon by the Seabees, was very favorable. Another Carter-Cutler innovation for LST Flot 5.

USS LCT-449 loading equipment and supplies from a Guadalcanal beach for her journey north in November 1943, soon after the Marines landed. Note the LST's camouflage and truck bearing "Cub 9" markings. U.S. Marine Corps.

LST-449 Swaps Mutton for Jeep – The 449's hull number has come up several times in this chapter. It saw lots of action and had a few close calls. But, for a change of pace, here's an amusing story excerpted from "Motor Mac" Delbert Beardsley's excellent memoirs of his time aboard LST-449, a.k.a. the "Beach Lizard," during the Solomons campaign:

> Picked up our share of Australian mutton today, the 26th of November 1943. It has become a custom for us to take a supply, store it in the freezers, and when we go up the Slot, trade it to the Marines for some worn-out jeeps that have quit running. We would push and shove and generally pull the vehicle aboard. Then we would proceed to overhaul it at our convenience.
>
> The Captain and the Executive Officer would then acquire them, then put more and more restrictions on who else could use them. One morning, one of the jeeps was found sitting on the boat deck with no way of getting it down. To this day, I don't know how it got there, or who put it there. We finally had to get a big floating crane to get it off. From then on, the vehicles were used by anyone doing ship's work, going after parts, stores or anything else official.

Eighth Echelon to Bougainville, 26-30 November – LSTs 70, 207, 339, 341, 353, 354, 395, and 488 comprised the LST unit. Capt. Carter, ComLSTFLOT 5, CTG 31.7 in *Wadsworth*, plus escorts *Fullam, Hudson,* and tug *Apache.*

Task Group 31.7 departed the 'Canal at 0700 on 26 November. Several LSTs were towing barrage balloons. At 1502 on the 27th, the LSTs were attacked by a low-level bombing plane camouflaged

Heavily-loaded LSTs towing barrage balloons head for Northern Solomons. U.S. Navy.

to look like a P-39. One bomb was dropped, but no damage sustained. The plane escaped. The Task Group arrived Bougainville at 0530 on 28 November. All ships were unloaded by 1700, and the Task Group departed for Guadalcanal arriving there on 30 November.

The Flotilla Five War Diary entries for 28-30 November 1943 included the following interesting information:

> The cooperation in unloading LSTs was highly satisfactory. This was a big improvement over the other echelons. The Army pontoon bridge equipment worked very satisfactorily; also the log ramps built by the CBs. A request was made for seven more log ramps to be built. Commander LST Flotilla Five in *Wadsworth* as CTG 31.7 arrived Guadalcanal and Task Group 31.7 was dissolved. He made his report in person to Commander Task Group 31.1 at Camp Crocodile, then proceeded to Lyons Point. He was commended on his good work as Commander Task Group 31.7, and the good work of his ships.

> Commander LST Group Thirteen [R.W. Cutler, USNR] enroute continental United States. He was ordered there to have suitable trailers built for LSTs, which would be built rigidly enough to stand a rough surf. This was another step to speed up the unloading of LSTs in forward area.

> The Task Group was dissolved and LSTs went alongside LSTs of the next echelon to transfer balloons, TBY radios, and mobile 40-mm guns. The LSTs then proceeded home to Purvis Bay.

LST loaded with Marines en route to their next landing. U.S. Marine Corps.

The "Pacific Express" would continue to supply the 3rd Marines and the Army's 37th Division as well as the Seabees and the Bougainville base well into 1944. The LSTs would also continue to evacuate casualties.

LST-341 War Diary – Let's take a minute out to follow LST-341 from 29 June–30 November 1943, as she makes one trip after another up the Slot during the Central and Northern Solomons Campaigns. In just five months, LST-341 made 18 resupply/reinforcement runs: Segi Point 2, Rendova 11, Munda Point 1, Vella Lavella 1, and Bougainville 3.

In addition to trip dates and destinations, the following chart—an abstract of the 341's War Diary—lists sister Flot 5 LSTs, and other vessel types in each convoy. It also bottom lines the 341's passengers and cargo, as well as her "time outs" for an overhaul and the installation of additional armament, something all original Flot 5 LSTs gladly experienced as more guns became available.

We singled out the LST-341 (Lt F. S. Barnett, USN) for this illustration because her War Diary is one of the most complete and informative we've seen. The chart provides a glimpse into the day-to-day activities of the 'Gator sailor during the Solomons campaigns.

Soldiers of the 136th Field Artillery, 37th Division, Battery A and B, Service Company, rolling barrels of aviation gasoline ashore off LST-207 at Cape Torokina. U.S. Army.

LST-341 Slot Runs
6 June – 30 November 1943[15]

1943 Trip Dates	Destination	Amphibious Vessels	LST-341 Passengers Cargo/Activity
Jun 30-Jul 1	Segi Point	LSTs 341 and 339 traveling independently	Personnel, equipment, and supplies of 70th Coast Artillery, 132d Infantry, and 47th Naval Construction Battalion (hereafter NCB).
Jul 2-6	Rendova	LSTs 341, 339, 396, 397 plus 12 LCIs	136th Field Artillery plus other vehicles and supplies.
Jul 9-12	Segi Point	LSTs 341, 339, 396	Aviation gas and oil, .50 caliber ammo, ACORN 7 and CASU 8 equipment.
Jul 15-17	Rendova	LSTs 341 and 395	Ammo, vehicles, provisions.
Jul 20-23	Rendova	LSTs 341, 397, LCI-68 plus 2 escorts	Units of 135th Field Artillery, 155th Field Artillery, 37th Signal Co., Boat Pool 8 personnel, plus ammo and vehicles.
Jul 26-28	Rendova	LSTs 341, 397 plus 2 escorts	Passengers (not specified), ammo, vehicles, supplies.
Jul 30-31	Rendova	LSTs 341 and 472 plus 2 escorts	Units of 43rd Division, 118th Engineers, 148th Infantry, 169th Infantry, 172d Infantry, 24th NCB; vehicles, gasoline, provisions.
Aug 5-8	Rendova	LSTs 341 and 472 plus 2 escorts	Army and Navy personnel, vehicles, equipment, and provisions.
Aug 11-13	Rendova	LST-341 plus 2 escorts	Personnel of CASU 14 and ACORN 8, ordnance, aviation equipment, vehicles and equipment of CASU and ACORN.
Aug 16-18	Rendova	LSTs 341, 339, 353, 396, and 460 plus escorts DesRon 22	Army and Navy personnel; ammo, ACORN 8 equipment and supplies.
Aug 20-22	Rendova	LST-341 plus 2 escorts	Army and Navy personnel, CASU 14 oxygen tanks.
Aug 24-29	Rendova	LST-341 plus 2 escorts	Army and Navy personnel, ammo, ordnance, supplies, vehicles, oil, and grease.

1943 Trip Dates	Destination	Amphibious Vessels	LST-341 Passengers Cargo/Activity
Aug 30-Sept 1	Vella Lavella	LSTs 341, 353, 398 plus 5 escorts	Army personnel, rations, camp equipment, medical supplies, oil, gasoline, wire, and vehicles.
Sept 6-8	Rendova	LSTs 341, 460 plus 2 escorts	Army and Navy personnel, mail, provisions, medical supplies, and vehicles.
Sept 16-18	Munda	LST 341 plus 2 escorts	Army and Navy personnel, Army Quartermaster supplies, TNT, field guns, and general cargo.
Sept 21-Oct 11	Efate (New Hebrides)	LSTs 341, 339 plus 3 escorts	LST-341 alongside *Medusa* for overhaul.
Oct 12-16	Espiritu Santo	LST-341	Makes stop en route back to 'Canal to pick up cargo.
Oct 17-19	Guadalcanal	LSTs 341 and 207	
Oct 23-26	Purvis Bay	LST-341	LST-341 alongside tender *Achelous* (ARL-1) for installation of 40-mm gun on stern.
Oct 27-Nov 3	Carter City	LST-341	Transfer 40-mm mobile gun and 5-man Marine gun crew plus barrage balloons from LST-71 to LST-341.
Nov 4-9	Bougainville	LSTs 341, 339, 70, 488, 207, 353, 354, 395 plus 8 APDs and 6 escorts (Task Unit 31.6)	Various units of 3rd Marine Division, ammo, provisions, vehicles, fuel, kitchen equipment, and tents of 21st Marine Task Unit 13.
Nov 15-20	Bougainville	LSTs 341, 339, 70, 488, 207, 353, 354, 395 plus 8 APDs and 6 DD escorts (Task Unit 31.6)	Units of 3rd Marines, ammo, fuel, equipment, provisions, marston mat of 3rd BN, 21st Marines and Task Unit D.
Nov 26-30	Bougainville	LSTs 341, 70, 354, 488, 207, 339, 353, 395 plus tug Apache, plus 5 DD escorts	Units of 36th NCB, loaded vehicles, rations, sand bags, equipment for MTB Ron FIVE.

Now back to the U.S. Marines as they extend the beachhead perimeter while waiting to be relieved by the U.S. Army. On the morning of 8 November, Companies H and M were on the line and received yet another assault, the heaviest one yet. In midafternoon, Companies E and F conducted a passage of lines, counterattacked the enemy, and withdrew after two hours. The next morning, Companies I and M held the roadblock as L and F conducted another counterattack, preceded by a half-hour of artillery preparation. Japanese resistance was stubborn and elements of Companies I and M, and the 9th Marines eventually moved forward to assist.

Shortly after noon, the enemy retired from the scene. U.S. patrols soon discovered the abandoned bivouac site of the Japanese 23rd Infantry Regiment just a few hundred yards up the trail. In the midst of this action, PFC Henry Gurke of Company M covered an enemy grenade with his body to protect another Marine. (He received a posthumous Medal of Honor for his heroic act of self-sacrifice.)

Wounded Marine receives blood plasma during fighting on Bougainville. Courtesy U.S. Marine Corps.

Colonel Harry B. "Harry the Horse" Liversedge brought the 3rd Raider Battalion into existence in September 1942, then became first commander of the 1st Marine Raider Regiment upon its activation in March 1943. Here he cuts a cake for his Raiders in honor of the Marine Corps birthday on 10 November 1943. U.S. Marine Corps.

Marine Corps Celebrates Birthday – The 2d Raider Regiment (2d and 3rd Raider Battalions) celebrated the Marine Corps' birthday on 10 November by moving off the front lines and into division reserve. Other than occasional patrols and short stints on the line, the next two weeks were relatively quiet for the Raiders.

Before covering the arrival of the U.S Army's 37th Division, let's review the contributions of the "Fighting Seabees."

Seabee Construction [16] – Detachments from the 25th, 53rd, 71st and 75th Construction Battalions landed with the 3rd Marine Division on 1 November. The 75th detachment's D-day story at Torokina Point was described by Lt (jg) Robert E. Johnson, CEC, USNR, who commanded the detachment: [17]

We came in with the Marines on the USS *President Adams*; and for the landing, we divided ourselves into four units—one to unload ammunition, another to unload fuel, another to unload rations and packs, and the fourth unit manned the machine guns on Higgins boats and tank lighters.

At 0545 on D-day we went over the side and began our run for the beach. Our landing craft were ordered to pass through the narrow channel between Puruata and Torokina Islands. The Japs had machine-gun nests on the inside of both islands, and they fired heavily on our first assault boats. One boat was hit by artillery fire, and we had to unload the wounded from it under rather desperate conditions.

At the beach we encountered determined resistance. The 250 Marines and the 100 Seabees worked perfectly as a team. The Seabee gunners provided cover while the Marines advanced to erase the Japs with grenades and flame-throwers. When a Marine was shot from a crippled tractor, which was pulling in the first load of ammunition, a Seabee leaped into his place and delivered the ammo.

The Seabees dug foxholes not only for themselves but also for the Marines and for all casualties who were unable to dig their own. When a group of Marines was about to be wiped out because of lack of supplies, three Seabees managed to get through with ammunition and to bring back the wounded. Our medical officer and his corpsmen moved in to treat the front-line wounded and to handle Graves Registration.

The Seabee mission was by now quite familiar: Establish an advance air and naval base designed to facilitate attacks against Japanese positions on the island and, in this case, on New Britain and New Ireland. The major installations planned for Bougainville were airfields and a motor torpedo boat base.

The original plan of the base called for immediate installation of a small fighter strip at Torokina to provide air cover during construction of a larger bomber-fighter field (Piva Field). The construction of the fighter strip was assigned to the 71st Battalion. Torokina Field, originally planned to accommodate 35 fighter planes or light dive bombers, handled many times that number before completion of Piva Field.

Surveys for the field and clearing of the area were begun on the third day after landing, subject to continuous enemy action, with survey parties often finding themselves targets for snipers. Considerable difficulty was experienced in clearing jungle growth and removing the slimy muck to reach a suitable subgrade.

Work on the strip proceeded as energetically as conditions permitted, the tempo increasing with the arrival of each additional echelon, the last of which arrived 17 November. To meet the deadline, it was necessary to work at night. But by November 24 enough matting was laid to permit an SBD to make an emergency landing. The field was completed 10 December 1943, and the first 18 Corsair fighter planes landed on schedule.

Construction of the airstrip and facilities for aviation personnel were erected simultaneously, including two galleys and mess halls, storage buildings, a hospital with three wards and an operating room with all utilities.

NCB 36 works through the night grading the Bougainville airstrip.

36th NCB Seabees spread crushed coral over the marston mats and then regrade the bomber strip on Bougainville .

Bridge construction.

Photos courtesy of Seabees.

NCB 36 Seabees pause from their task of repairing the airstrip on Bougainville.

On 29 November 1943, the 36th Battalion, which had arrived three days earlier, began construction of the Piva bomber strip. This 8,000 x 300 foot strip, with warm-up aprons at each end, was cleared from dense jungle. The first plane landed on the strip 19 December, and on 30 December the runway was officially put into operation with the landing of ten Army transport planes. The 36th Battalion also provided the major medical facilities at Bougainville supplementing emergency installations at the various camps.

The 77th Battalion, arriving 10 December 1943, was assigned the task of completing Piva Field, and began this task the second day ashore, even working at night whenever possible. The grading of Piva strip was completed 28 December, but due to the late arrival of steel matting, final completion was delayed until 3 January. The first plane landed on 9 January.

Another critical deadline was met by the 75th Battalion in the erection of a complete tank-farm system to service the two airfields. Although all work was in marshy jungle, the tank farm, consisting of one 10,000-barrel and eighteen 1,000-barrel tanks, with tanker mooring, submarine pipe line, and 5 miles of overland pipe, was completed in time to support operations from the fields.

A PT-boat base and boat pool were set up on Puruata Island by the 75th Battalion, assisted by the 71st and 77th Battalions. Wood-pile and timber construction was used for a PT-boat pier, a crash boat pier, and a PT-fueling pier. Complete camp facilities included quarters, mess halls, an emergency hospital, with all utilities, and five prefabricated steel warehouses. Eighteen small-boat moorings, consisting of three-pile dolphins, driven and lashed, were provided,

Scene from a PT boat at Empress Augusta Bay, Bougainville Island: In the foreground is a PT aerial gunner. Transports and landing craft loaded with Marines and supplies are in the background. U.S. Marine Corps.

A sign is posted on Bougainville by Marines of the Third Marine Division, Second Raider Regiment in tribute to the Seabees. Naval Historical Center.

and LST landings installed.

Stevedoring was handled by the 6th and the 9th Battalions.

By July 1944, all major Seabee construction had been completed. The 36th Battalion, the last to leave the base, departed in August 1944. CBMU's 586 and 582, which arrived in May, took charge of mainte-nance. Roll-up of installations was accomplished early in 1945, and in June the maintenance units were ordered to forward areas.

Army's 37th Division Arrives – The 37th Division began arriv-ing in early November to reinforce the perimeter. On 23 November, the 1st Parachute Battalion came ashore and temporarily joined the Marine Raiders, now acting as corps reserve. Two days later the 2^d Raider Battalion participated in an attack extending the perimeter several hundred yards to the east, but it met little opposition.

On 29 November, Company M of the 3rd Raider Battalion rein-forced the parachutists for a predawn amphibious landing at Koiari, several miles southeast of the perimeter. The enemy reacted quickly, and pinned the Americans to the beach with heavy fire.

Landing craft, attempting to extract the forces, were twice driven off. It was not until evening that artillery, air and naval gunfire support sufficiently silenced opposition that the parachutists and raiders could get back out to sea.

During one night's action, members of a Marine patrol, trapped on a river bank, were rescued by a landing craft escorted by two PT boats, one of which was commanded by Lt John F. Kennedy, back in action after the loss of his not-yet-famous PT-109.

Army's XIV Corps Relieves Marines

Army troops continued to pour into the enlarging perimeter. On 15 December, control of the landing force passed from I Ma-rine Amphibious Corps (IMAC) to the Army's XIV Corps. The Americal Division gradually replaced the 3rd Marine Division, which had borne the brunt of the fighting.

The 3rd Marines remained on Bougainville until 11 January 1944, when the Army relieved them. The Marines boarded transports the next day and sailed for Guadalcanal. Less than a month later, the elite Raider Battalions that fought from Guadalcanal to Bougainville would be disbanded, but their legacy lives on.

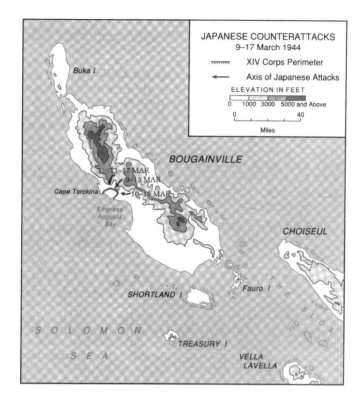

General Griswold's XIV Corps was still manning the perimeter in March 1944, when the Japanese assembled a counterattack force some 15,000 to 19,000 strong. But by this time, with a strength of approximately 62,000 men, including the Americal (Gen Hodge) and 37th (MGen Robert S. Beightler) Divisions, XIV Corps was a powerful force. Nevertheless, for two weeks, again and again the Japanese troops charged, only to be hurled back, each time suffering large losses. American manpower, combined with strong fire support, made the Japanese task hopeless.

Bottom line – By 23 March 1944, it was over for the Japanese. The enemy withdrew leaving behind their wounded and heavy equipment. They had suffered terribly, with over 5,000 men killed. In comparison, the veterans of XIV Corps, who had used their superior defenses and fought determinedly and shrewdly, lost 263 comrades killed.

For several months after major combat operations had ended, American troops patrolled and hunted for the remnants of Japanese

Army troops land on Bougainville to reinforce U.S. Marines on the island, 5 Jan. 1943. Landing craft had parent ship hull numbers blacked out for security purposes. Naval Historical Center.

Marine Raiders marching back from the point of Empress Augusta Bay near Cape Torokina, after fighting for 27 hours straight. Naval Historical Center.

units through Bougainville's vast jungles. In November 1944, command of all island operations passed from General Griswold to LtGen Sir Stanley Savige of the Australian Army, and by mid-December, Australian forces had relieved all American units in line.

During November 1943, there were several other significant actions in the Northern Solomons, all affecting the outcome of the Bougainville operation.

Battle of Empress Augusta Bay, 2 November 1943 [18]

Following the D-day landings at Cape Torokina, the DMs had laid a minefield north of the Cape, and Admiral Merrill's Task Force 39—light cruisers *Cleveland, Columbia, Denver,* and *Montpelier,* and eight destroyers—moved into position. The Japanese would have to react, and they did!

VAdm Sentaro Omori left Rabaul with two heavy cruisers, *Myoko* and *Haguro,* two lights, *Sendai* and *Agano,* and six destroyers, heading for yet another night action at the beachhead.

At 0227 on 2 November, radar on *Montpelier,* Merrill's flag, picked up Omori at 36,000 yards, approaching at 28 knots. Omori spotted the Americans via snooper at 0245, and the battle was on. Both sides launched torpedoes and opened fire, and for the next two hours, both sides expended huge amounts of shells and torpedoes. Omori lost light cruiser *Sendai* and destroyer *Hatsukaze.* Merrill had damage to cruisers *Montpelier* and *Denver,* and destroyers *Foote* and *Spence.* The battle was a clear American victory, and the Bougainville conquest was assured.

During all that action, RAdm Merrill's force took two torpedo hits. One hit destroyer *Foote* and tore her stern off around 0245, when she was making high speed. Cruiser *Cleveland* swerved sharply to avoid *Foote,* now dead in the water, and missed her by 100 yards. At the same time, *Spence* slowed to avoid *Thatcher,* and the two destroyers side-swiped with minor damage. But at 0320 *Spence* caught a shell below the waterline and one of her fuel lines began leaking.

This battle persisted until about 0800, when the Americans were certain that all the Japanese ships were sunk or headed home. Damage on the American side was minimal, considering the high volume of fire that night, much of it amazingly inaccurate. The only Japanese shots to register were three 8-inch shells that hit *Denver* forward about 0325, fortunately all duds, and two hits on *Montepelier,* which destroyed her starboard catapult and wounded one crewman.

Foote suffered the heaviest casualties that night—19 killed and 17 wounded—but a valiant crew kept her afloat and she reached Tulagi 4 November under tow of *Claxton,* one of Capt Burke's destroyers. They cheered her at Tulagi when she pulled in.

The officers and men of Adm Merrill's Task Force had the satisfaction of defeating and turning back a larger enemy force, and thereby saving the Bougainville landing force from certain disaster. It was an added satisfaction that this mission was accomplished without significant damage, other than the torpedoing of one destroyer.

Doubt, however, still hung over the final outcome of the Bougainville operation at this point in time. The enemy had six to eight heavy cruisers at Truk, from which a serious threat of surface attack developed within 48 hours. This time it was carriers to the rescue.

Air Battles and Carrier Strikes [19]

Meantime, the carriers returned to the fray, a welcome addition to the Bougainville assault campaign. The veteran *Saratoga* and the newly-commissioned *Princeton,* (first of nine *Independence* class light carriers, built on cruiser hulls), sortied 4 November from south of Guadalcanal, covered by *Atlanta* class cruisers *San Diego* and *San Juan,* plus nine destroyers under Capt Rodger Simpson in *Farenholt.*

Rabaul Strike, 5 November – The next morning off the Torokina beachhead, the U.S. carriers put up 97 planes bent on a rich target in Simpson Harbor at Rabaul—8 heavy cruisers, 20 light cruisers and destroyers.

Allied Rabaul raid, November 1943. National Archives.

The American dive bombers and torpedo bombers feasted on the target until 1300. Result: Four heavy cruisers heavily damaged. *Maya* took a bomb down the stack into her engine room and was out of service for five months. *Mogami*, the big cruiser that barely escaped from the Battle of Midway, was disabled and out of service again. *Takao* took two hits, and *Atago* survived three near misses. The Japanese, badly shaken, pulled out all of their heavy cruisers and Rabaul never again saw a Japanese heavy.

The American carriers retired untouched, but had lost 10 planes and 15 crewmen over Rabaul. Rabaul was not quite finished, but was mortally wounded. To cover this fact, the Japanese countered with propaganda bullets. They claimed the "First Air Battle of Bougainville" had cost the Americans two carriers, three cruisers, and a destroyer. Actually, 18 Japanese planes had been sent to get the carriers off Torokina, arrived about 1915 and, by mistake, engaged some small landing craft and PT boats, and lost one plane to a PT boat!

Rabaul Repeater, 11 November – For the second big air punch against Rabaul, Nimitz gave Halsey an eye-popper for the Solomons—two new *Essex* class carriers, the *Essex* and *Bunker Hill*— and one new *Independence* class, the *Independence*. But there were no cruisers available, so RAdm Alfred Montgomery, CTG 50.3, had to go with what he had—nine destroyers. Each of the big carriers was home to 80 planes, and the *Independence* added 25 for a total of 185 planes, including 23 new Helldivers (SB2Cs).

The carriers launched aircraft 160 miles east of Rabaul, plowed through a cloud of 68 Zekes and attacked the main target, the warships in Simpson Harbor. The score: light cruisers *Agano* and *Yubari* damaged; destroyer *Suzunami* sunk; *Naganami* badly crippled by a torpedo hit; and two others, *Urakaze* and *Umikaze* heavily strafed.

The American planes returned to the carriers for rearming, planning a second attack in the afternoon. But at noon, VAdm Jinichi Kusaka, commander 11th Air Fleet at Rabaul, decided to throw his full strength at the American carriers off Bougainville. He put up some 108 planes, which American radar picked up a little after 1300, over 100 miles out.

The Americans closed in a new formation—the three carriers close together, surrounded by nine destroyers, spaced out on a 4,000-yard circle. They opened fire at 1354, and the battle was on. For the next 40 minutes, the carriers and destroyers, plus, of course, their planes, banged away at full power. Midway in the mêlée, RAdm Montgomery was heard to say on the TBS, "Man your guns and shoot those bastards out of the sky!" The ships got off a huge number of salvos, including 750 rounds of 5"/38 from the two big carriers.

As usual, the Japanese at the scene made extravagant claims and Kusaka may have believed some of them, but he still sent some newly arrived cruisers and destroyers hurrying back to Truk. His air losses were bad—over 40 planes destroyed, a loss he could not replace. The very next day, all Japanese carrier planes were recalled from Rabaul. In two weeks, the Japanese had lost 85 percent of their Vals, and 90 percent of their Kates at Rabaul.

On the American side, it was all smiles. The carrier force had suffered 10 men injured, no ship damage, and 11 planes missing. For Montgomery's force, it was a memorable Armistice Day, 11 November 1943.

Surface/Air Battles – Meanwhile at Empress Augusta Bay, just at dusk on 8 November, Japanese planes had discovered RAdm Laurance DuBose's CruDiv 13 of light cruisers *Birmingham, Mobile* and *Santa Fe,* and four destroyers 25 miles offshore. In three attacks starting at 1911, the Japanese drew early blood. At 1917, *Birmingham* took a bomb skip into her plane hangar for minor damage. But at 1926, a torpedo struck her port bow, opening a 30-foot hole. At 1942, another bomb hit the face plate of Turret No. 4.

None of these stopped *Birmingham,* but a damage control measure brought her a new nickname. The deck above the port bow was cut away to relieve drag, and every time the ship took sea, a geyser shot skyward; thus the cruiser became "Old Faithful." But unloading at the beachhead never stopped, and as the empty transports left for Guadalcanal, they radioed, "Thanks for taking care of those bastards who were laying for us."

On 13 November, a cloud of Japanese Bettys picked up Adm Merrill's Task Force 39 at 0455. They boxed cruiser *Denver* with torpedoes, and one of them found her engine room. *Denver* stopped, dead in the water; 20 men were killed and 11 more wounded. She listed 12 degrees, but damage control corrected that with counterflooding, and soon the cruiser could make nearly 5 knots on her one shaft. Two destroyers stood by until daylight, when tug *Sioux* picked her up for a safe tow to Tulagi.

The Battle of Cape St. George, 25 November 1943 [20]

The Solomons campaign more or less closed out with a final naval battle, the Battle of Cape St. George, early on the morning of 25 November 1943. The fabled "31-knot Burke" and his DesRon 23 were out that night, with four new *Fletchers*, prowling west of Buka at the northern tip of Bougainville.

At 0130, Burke's destroyers—*Charles S. Ausburne, Converse, Dyson* and *Spence*—slowed to 23 knots so their wakes would not give them away. *Converse* and *Spence* took position 5,000 yards (2½ miles) from the other ships, and at 0141 picked up an enemy force 11 miles east and closing. This was Capt Koyota Kagawa and five destroyers retiring, after setting some Japanese troops ashore and making 25 knots toward Rabaul.

Capt Burke waited until the right moment, 0156, and then had three of his ships, *Ausburne, Claxton,* and *Dyson,* launch 15 torpedoes at 6,000 yards, and then turn right at flank speed to get out of the way of any enemy reply. The Japanese sighted the torpedo wakes with only 30 seconds to act. Three of them hit, and destroyers *Onami* and *Makinami* were finished. The former exploded and the latter broke in two. Both were 2,000-tonners, with less than a year in service.

The other three Japanese destroyers veered north and turned up the speed, but Burke was after them. His target split and Burke concentrated fire on one target.

Cmdr Arleigh A. Burke, USN, ComDesDiv 23, relaxing with a drink at "Cloob Des Slot," Purvis Bay, Solomons Islands, May 1943. Naval Historical Center.

This was *Yugiri*, which was plastered and sunk. The other two got away, but Burke's score was excellent—three out of five. *Converse* and *Spence* finished off the two parts of *Makinami*, and the "Little Beavers" headed for the barn.

(*Author's Note:* WWII hero "31-knot Burke" died on New Year's Day 1996, at age 94. His "Little Beavers" destroyer squadron fought numerous combat engagements in the Solomons; their high-speed dashes earned him his nickname. Burke is buried in the U.S. Naval Academy Cemetery, beneath a granite headstone engraved with 4 stars, a destroyer, and with the one-word description "Sailor" under his name.)

The destroyers now "owned" the Solomons, and roamed all around Bougainville for some weeks to protect the real estate. In December alone, the "tin cans" were out on bombardment or discovery forays on the 5th, 10th, 20th, 24th, and 27th. But the Japanese were on the run now, and in a hurry to save what they could. By early 1944 they were gone from Rabaul and Kavieng. They left behind huge stocks of weapons, ammunition, structures and harbor works at Rabaul, which Allied air power methodically destroyed in spectacular explosions and fires. The war had simply passed these Japanese outposts.

Bougainville Conclusions

By the end of November 1943, all immediate objectives had been achieved. The Japanese cruiser task force—the major threat to the landing operation—had been met, badly crippled, and routed. Enemy airfields on Bougainville, beyond and to the rear of the Allied beachhead at Torokina Point, had been neutralized or weakened to such an extent that they held no immediate threat to the Allied landing operations. American air supremacy made Japanese counter landings and reinforcements nearly impossible, while reinforcement by land routes from southern Bougainville presented grave difficulties.

In order to exploit the advantages achieved, the defense perimeter had to be expanded, airstrips completed, and an advance naval base established. Furthermore, the beachhead would have to be supplied and reinforced by "Pacific Express" echelons following a course within close range of several enemy airfields. These airfields would have to be kept neutralized, as well as constant guard maintained against enemy surface forces.

CHAPTER 9

Lessons Learned in the Solomons
August – November 1943[1]

The Amphibians had learned a good deal from the August 1942 landings at Tulagi and Guadalcanal, and they continued to learn a great deal during the long, hard six months' struggle to maintain logistic support for these two important toeholds in the Southern Solomons. By January 1943, marked changes had occurred in their thinking about the techniques of support through and over a beachhhead, and new amphibious craft were just becoming available.

RAdm G. K. Fort, Commander Landing Craft Flotillas, submitted a report to RAdm Kelly Turner following the New Georgia campaign highlighting further lessons learned in logistics support, night landings, shore party bottlenecks, force requirements, and several other areas. Capt G. B. Carter, ComLSTFLOT 5, made additional recommendations based on later combat experience in the Northern Solomons.

Space limitations prohibit a full discussion on the many lessons learned by the crews of the pioneer amphibious landing ships and craft but, suffice it to say, they paid off in spades during the remaining two years of the war. However, please know that the lessons learned that follow cover all areas of an amphibious operation—not just the new landing craft; a "checklist," if you will, that includes previously mentioned lessons as well.

Logistic Support

The Navy had been much condemned for its inadequacies in logistic support during the first months of WATCHTOWER. Unlike the Guadalcanal Operation, there were 1st, 2nd, 3rd, and 4th Echelon logistic support movements set up for the TOENAILS Operation and a dozen support echelons had sailed in the first 15 days.

Just as RAdm Turner was leaving SOPAC, RAdm G. K. Fort, Commander Landing Craft Flotillas, made a report to him on the performance of landing craft in which was written these heartening words:

> It appears for the first time in modern warfare that supplies have arrived with or immediately behind the Assault Troops. A good example is the airstrip at Segi. There, bulldozers were clearing a strip forty (40) minutes after the first echelon LST had beached. The flow of supplies to the front has been greater than the Advanced Bases could handle. All have requested that the flow of supplies be reduced.[2]

Enemy action, groundings, and modified plans had forced many changes in the ships and landing craft originally designated for specific supporting echelon tasks. The important lesson from all this was that in order for logistic support to be delivered by amphibious ships and craft on time, a large excess of ships and craft is required over the computed space requirements for the total of personnel and tons of equipment to be moved.

For the TOENAILS Operation, 36 LSTs, 36 LCIs, 72 LCTs and 28 APcs had been scheduled to be available. Fortunately, plans were not based on this number as only 12 LSTs, 26 LCIs, 43 LCTs and 16 APcs were in the area on 30 June 1943. This number was barely adequate.[3]

CINCPAC had preferred that the large transports not be employed for the assault landings in TOENAILS, because of the lack of strong air cover over the landing areas and a decent respect for Japanese air capabilities.

The Bougainville Operations again demonstrated that the overwater movement and landing of the first echelon of troops is only the initial step in a continuous amphibious series, all of which are integral parts of the same venture. Success of the venture depends upon the ability to deliver safely not only the first, but also the succeeding echelons of troops, engineers, ancillary units, equipment and operating and upkeep supplies and replacements. The aggregate of personnel and cargo for the later movements is far greater than that carried initially. Each movement requires protection, and losses in transit from the logistic bases to the combat position must be kept low enough to be acceptable. It is particularly true that when small vessels are used, an uninterrupted stream of them must be maintained.

The first movement for the seizure of a position; the exploitation on shore of that position; and the long series of succeeding movements of troops and materiel, together form a single operation. All parts must be accomplished under satisfactory condition if the whole operation is to be successful.

Landing Ships and Craft

The personal worry bug to be overcome by every amphibian, coxswain, officer-in-charge, or commanding officer, was the coral shelf and the many coral heads off the few and generally narrow beaches. In due time, these coral heads would be dynamited. The beaches would be augmented with landing piers, which would be coconut log bulkheads backed up by crushed coral. But the first few days in poorly or uncharted waters were real tests.

When the first surge of TOENAILS was over, it was apparent from the reports that both landing ships and craft had turned in better than satisfactory performances. RAdm Fort:

> The LCTs had been the most useful of all types. However, low speed (6 knots) limits their daily staging in combat areas to about 100 miles per night....It is still advisable to have them underway only at night. Against a head sea, their speed is greatly reduced, sometimes to two knots...The crews and officers have been standing up well in spite of operating two out of every three days.
>
> Some LSTs have transported 400 men each for short periods....LCTs have carried as many as 250 men overnight, but in exposed positions....
>
> The LCIs carry about 170 combat troops....For unopposed short runs of a few hours, 350 men have been transported on a single LCI....They are ideal for night landings on good beaches....
>
> The APcs, besides having proved useful as escorts, have been used to transport small groups of men....[4]

Captain Grayson B. Carter, ComLSTFLOT 5, made three innovative recommendations following the New Georgia campaign:

> Employ trailers to roll on/roll off cargo such as ammo, boxed rations, and fuel to expedite the unloading process on unfriendly beaches. Pending the procurement of the perfect trailer, Cmdr Cutler

[ComLSTGRP 13] obtained from the United States Army depot at Noumea, and brought up to Guadalcanal 22 October some 85 vehicles that would fit into LSTs without too many 'holidays.' One LST would take in 33 of these jury-rigged trailers, as Carter called them, and that gave the LST a relatively large pay load. Trailers made for quick turn-around as well, for they could be parked ashore until the soldiers got around to unloading them, and could be picked up empty later. Trailer loading was first tried in the second echelon to Bougainville with limited success; but after much practice, and with an improved model designed for such work, it became doctrine for sending LSTs into beaches where air attack was expected.

Increase the original LST armament by about 200%; e.g., replace the 3"/50 and single 40-mm guns with 40-mm quad mounts, power driven and director-controlled, supplemented with more 20-mm guns. Experience in the New Georgia campaign showed that an LST needed more armament than her original complement to repel air attack, and Carter's flotilla went up to Bougainville loaded for bear, with three to five 40-mm, eleven to eighteen 20-mm, four to eighteen .50-caliber machine guns and one three-inch 50-caliber gun apiece.

Barrage balloons for LSTs, which had been used in the Sicilian landings that summer, were introduced to the Pacific by the second echelon. This device snared one Japanese plane in early November and proved baffling to the pilots; but the balloons were finally discarded in 1944 because they gave away a task force's position to enemy search planes.

Transports and Cargo Ships

The first lesson the amphibians learned at Guadalcanal was that they were going to have to get used to being shot at. One coxswain reported:

> After getting the ramp up, we backed down as far as we could so as to keep the ramp between us and the line of fire. When we started around a little knoll, which was lined with trees, we were fired at from these trees. We spotted the flash from a gun up in one of these trees. I picked up the Marine's Risen gun and blasted the flash and the Jap fired again and I got a better bead on him, and fired again and he came tumbling down like a bird. [5]

Another coxswain reported:

> The Japs were firing at the four of us as we were cranking up the ramp and one bullet hit the winch and splattered little pieces of lead in Morgan's side along his ribs under the skin but didn't hurt him much. [6]

The *President Adams* related that:

> The boat course from the ship to shore was like the letter U...boats were under sniper fire during about the latter fourth of the trip. The final boat course was opposite to the original, this fact by itself shows the difficulty with which our boats were faced.[7]

The second lesson the big ship to shore "heavies" learned at Guadalcanal was they just had to have more people in their ships and craft. The 19 large ships of Task Force 62 that arrived at Guadalcanal-Tulagi on 7 August were not newly built ships, although most of them were relatively new to the Navy. All of the large transports and cargo ships had participated previously in some amphibious exercises with troops, equipment, and cargo to be unloaded.

But, by and large, these amphibious ships did not have enough officers and men to continuously unload over a 72-hour period. It was both good and bad fortune that the Japanese made three air raids and threatened another during the first 48 hours of unloading. For these gave many of the boat crews a breathing spell, and also supplied an urgency to the need to get the unloading job done.

Beach Troubles

The third lesson the amphibians learned at Guadalcanal was that the logistic support of the troops over the beaches in the first 24 hours had to be both beefed up and streamlined. The Captain of the *Hunter Liggett* reported:

> After dark conditions reached a complete impasse. It is estimated that nearly one hundred boats lay gunwale to gunwale on the beach, while another fifty boats waited, some of these, up to six hours for a chance to land....
>
> No small share of the blame for this delay, which prolonged by nearly twenty-four hours the period when the ships lay in these dangerous waters, would seem to rest with the Marine Corps personnel and organization. The Pioneers, whose function it was to unload the boats and keep the beach clear, were far too few in numbers. As a result much of this work was accomplished by boat crews, and stores which they landed at low water were frequently damaged or destroyed by the rising tide before the Pioneers removed them to safety. Meanwhile hundreds of Marines, many of them truck drivers, tank crews,

special weapons and support groups, whose equipment had not been landed, lounged around the beach in undisciplined idleness, shooting down coconuts or going swimming. There was no apparent reason whey these men could not have rendered valuable assistance in unloading the boats.[8]

Over at Tulagi, according to the transport *Neville's* War Diary:

> It was not until about midnight that the first word had been received to send the important food rations and ammunition ashore and from then till daylight it went slowly due to insufficient personnel to unload and conflicting orders as to where to land the stores.[9]

Not all the beach trouble was caused by inadequate Pioneer parties. Often it was the transports and cargo ships overloading the landing craft:

> A considerable number of landing boats, chiefly ramp lighters, were stranded on the beach, adding to the confusion. These ramps had been loaded too deeply by the head, and could not be driven far enough up on their particular beach to keep from filling and drowning the engine when the ramp was lowered.[10]

RAdm Turner after the landing wrote:

> There were two primary reasons for failure to completely unload. First the vast amount of unnecessary impediments taken, and second a failure on the part of the 1st Division to provide adequate and well organized unloading details at the beach.

The Shore Party had been much condemned for its inadequacies on 7 August 1942 at Guadalcanal. Much effort had gone into making more definite its duties and increasing the number of warm bodies to carry out these duties during the next three months. On 16 October 1942, COMPHIBFORSOPAC issued a new "trial operating procedure" for the Shore Party. But in November 1942, the Commander Transport Division Eight still wrote: "The bottleneck of unloading is still the Shore Party....At Aola Bay, the Shore Party was 800 strong (200 per ship); plus 400 Army, 100 Marines and 100 ACORN personnel....Unloading boats on a beach is extremely strenuous physical labor and the Shore Party must be organized into reliefs if the unloading is to extend over 12 hours."[11]

Further increases in personnel as well as cleaner command lines were again tried in TOENAILS. They paid off.

Night Landings

Night landings on foreign shores look very good on paper and over the long history of amphibious operations have been resorted to many times; e.g., the North Africa invasion on 8 November 1942.

RAdm Turner took a dim view of night landings prior to TOE-NAILS but had not closed his mind to their use. He was willing to experiment on a small scale. So the Eastern Force scheduled a night landing at Wickham Anchorage and the Western Force scheduled night landings for the Onaiavisi Entrance Unit and for the Advance Unit on Rendova.

One lesson which RAdm Turner stated he had vividly relearned during the TOENAILS Operation was the great hazard of night operations. In fact, his lack of success with them soured himon night landings for any large contingent of amphibians for the rest of the war.

RAdm Turner later commented on Samuel Eliot Morison's statement about the "folly of not taking Laiana first," and added that the decision to land at Zanana Beach instead of Laiana Beach was predicated on an acceptance, at that stage of the war, of Gen Vandegrift's often repeated statement that, "Landings should not be attempted in the face of organized resistance, if, by any combination of march or maneuver it is possible to land unopposed and undetected."

Diversionary Landings

The 7 October 1943 landing on Choiseul Island by the 2d Marine Parachute Battalion under the command of LtCol Victor Krulak as a diversion for the Treasury landings and for the Bougainville operation to come was a swift and vigorous activity that surprised the enemy while creating the impression that a much larger force was at work.

Offshore Toeholds

During the New Georgia amphibious operation, an operational technique was developed which carried through the Central Pacific campaigns and on into the planning for the final attack on the Japanese homeland. This technique was pointed towards seizing toeholds on nearby islands close to, but not so well defended as the main objective, and making a key part of the major assault on the main objective direct from these toeholds rather than from far across the sea. They also provided a place from where artillery support could be supplied on a round-the-clock basis.

Bypassing Enemy-held Islands

Perhaps of equal or even greater importance than the strategic advantages gained by the campaign of Vella Lavella and Kolombangara were the lessons learned. The principle of seizing unoccupied territory for the development of an airfield—soon to be repeated in the Bougainville operation—was worked out in this campaign.

The success of the operation clearly demonstrated the soundness of the strategy of bypassing enemy strongholds, then blockading and starving them out. This operational pattern, later repeated so often in the Central and Southwest Pacific, was rehearsed successfully for the first time in the Central Solomons. In view of the successes achieved and lives saved, no more popular strategical concept came out of the Pacific War than that of bypassing or leapfrogging Japanese-held islands and letting the Japanese threat "die on the vine," while our forces directed their efforts at the enemy closer to the Japanese homeland.

The popularity of this strategy has led to many claims as to who was the originator. According to VAdm George Dyer, who read thousands of dispatches relating to the Pacific War while doing research for his excellent book, the first dispatch in which he saw the expression used was in a dispatch of VAdm Halsey's (COMSOPAC's 110421 of July 1943) addressed to RAdm Turner asking for his comments and recommendations on the concept.

TOENAILS Weather Conditions

Bad weather can blot out the special lights needed to guide landing craft to beaches. Special lights had been provided at Rendova, Oleana Bay and Rice Anchorage. None were visible in the manner planned.[12] Later in 1943, a submarine would be stationed at Nauru (Gilbert Islands) to report the weather conditions daily there and to make special reports of bad or changing weather. Since weather moves from west to east, this would tip off the amphibians on what to expect as they approached the Gilberts.

Force Requirements

There was one sobering lesson from TOENAILS which carried forward into future planning of assault and follow-up forces for the island campaigns of the Pacific. It was expressed in a COMINCH planners memorandum of 6 August 1943:

> At the termination of Japanese resistance in Munda , there were seven regimental combat teams, totaling more than 30,000 troops in our assault forces. No information differing from our initial estimate of 4,000 to 5,000 troops on Munda, to which reinforcements were believed to have been added for a time, has been received.
>
> However, of the Japanese on Munda only 1,671 are known to be dead and 28 captured. The overwhelming superiority of our forces in numbers and equipment had to be applied for 12 days despite air bombing and naval bombardment support before a force not more than one-seventh its size had been overcome. If we are going to require such overwhelming superiority at every point where we attack the Japanese, it is time for radical change in the estimate of the forces that will be required to defeat the Japanese now in the Southwest and Central Pacific.[13]

Garrison Group Follow-Up

Out of the experience of Guadalcanal and New Georgia had come a strong conviction that the garrison troops and their logistic support must be firmly scheduled to arrive and replace the assault troops and their equipment as soon as practicable after the objectives were secured by the assault troops. The challenge this conviction frequently created was the lack of suitable naval transports and naval cargo ships to carry the "follow up," not from the lack of garrison troops or logistic support.

Neutralization of Enemy Airfields

Enemy airfields on Bougainville beyond and to the rear of the Allied beachhead at Torokina point had been neutralized or weakened to such an extent by the end of November 1943, that they held no immediate threat to the Allied landing operation. American air supremacy made Japanese counter landings and reinforcements near impossible while reinforcement by land routes from southern Bougainville presented grave difficulties. However, in order to exploit the advantages achieved, the defense perimeter had to be expanded, airstrips completed, and an advance naval base established. Furthermore, the beachhead would have to be supplied and reinforced by echelons following a course within close range of several enemy airfields. These airfields would have to be kept neutralized as well as a constant guard maintained against enemy surface forces.

Gunfire Support

WATCHTOWER and TOENAILS were poor operations for training gunfire support ships, and for bettering the judgment of either planners or operators in the fine art of first-rate gunfire support against a well-defended coral atoll. However, based on experience gained primarily during the North African invasion by the amphibious forces of the Atlantic Fleet, a completely revised chapter on Naval Gunfire in FTP 167 ("Landing Operations Doctrine") was promulgated by COMINCH on 1 August 1943 and distributed to the Fleet.

This newly issued chapter provided that the Naval Gunfire Annex to an operational order issued by a Commander Naval Attack Force would:

> ...contain the directions for furnishing naval gunfire support for the Landing Force. Its preparation is a joint function of the Staff of the Commander Attack Force and the Staff of Commander Landing Force.

The detailed instructions provided that:

> The staff of the Marine Division Commander [should] outline on the map prepared for the operation the probable target locations and probable enemy dispositions in the area to be attacked. The assignment of fire missions is a function of the Staff of the Commanding General, Marines. The Combined Staffs of the Commander Naval Attack Force and Commanding General, Marines now prepare the plan of naval gunfire. Upon approval, this plan is authenticated and issued as the Naval Gunfire Annex.

Close fire support was supplied by destroyer *Monssen* (DD-436) for steep-hilled Gavutu and Tanambogo with 92 rounds of 5-inch from 500 yards. This gunfire was particularly effective at Tanambogo the second day after a 200-round five-minute bombardment from a respectable 4,000 yards had proven ineffective the first day.[14] This close fire support by the *Monssen* was the first really "close up" use of the 5-inch naval gun from a thin-skinned naval ship to blast Japanese defenders from caves and well-prepared defense positions.

One marked improvement in gunnery did result from TOENAILS, where it had been learned that high-capacity ammunition with thinly cased shells was inadequate to pierce Japanese defense structures. However, if armorpiercing projectiles were used, an appreciable angle of fall had to be provided by increasing the gun range and reducing the powder charge, otherwise the AP projectile would ricochet without exploding.

Close Air Support

The Air Controller in the *McCawley* had radio communication with the home base, the carriers, and up and down the naval chain of command in the Guadalcanal combat area, as well as with the Marine chain of command, and with the Senior Carrier Air Group Commander and the liaison planes in the air; but, in part, it was step by step communication. He did not have direct voice communication with all ships nor with lower echelon Marine units. These Marine ground units did not have direct communication with the individual planes circling overhead.

All scheduled air strikes were delivered on time and largely on target. Some targets had not been minutely described or pinpointed and so were not recognized. The carrier pilots, not specially trained for this exacting and difficult air support chore, did not always come up to the expectations of the Marines, their own desires, or the desires of the top command.

The lack of separate radio frequencies for the Tulagi and the Guadalcanal Air Support Groups caused much radio interference at times. RAdm Turner wrote:

> ...there was a partial ground or short on the antenna of the *McCawley's*

TBS, which was not discovered and remedied until about November, 1942. The effects of the ground were to cause a rough tone to both reception and transmission, and to reduce the range of incoming and outgoing messages from the usual 20 miles to about 8 miles. For example, TBS exchanges between the *McCawley* and ships off Tulagi, 15 miles away, had to be relayed through a DD of the outer screen of the XRAY Group.[15]

The most important lesson learned in close air support in the first two days of the WATCHTOWER Operation was that it was:

> Essential that ground forces in an operation of this type have radio communication directly with the liaison planes or Air Group Commander in order that maximum support may be afforded ground personnel.[16]

The second most important lesson learned was that the Air Support Director Group should not be positioned at limit of voice radio range from any part of the forces being supported, or there will be constant delays or failures in air support operations.

Advances in Operation Planning

Vice Admiral Spruance's GALVANIC Operation Plan represented a distinct advance over the plans issued for WATCHTOWER and TOENAILS, which RAdm Turner, Commander Assault Force, previously had fought under.

Vice Admiral Spurance's plan provided the following advances in doctrine:

1. That a ship-based commander—Commander Central Pacific Force—with a determination to be in the objective area, retained immediate personal operational control over the operation.

2. For the coordination of the various Central Pacific task forces under one commander in the operating or objective area should a Japanese surface or carrier task force show up to threaten or attack the amphibious forces.

3. In advance, the conditions for the essential change of command from the Amphibious Task Force Commander to the Landing Force Commander at each assault objective.

4. In advance, the command responsibility for the development of the base facilities at the objective to be seized.

5. For support aircraft at each assault objective to be under the control of the Amphibious Task Force Commander. These aircraft had a capability for dawn or dusk search of the sea area approaches to the assault objective areas, should the need arise.

6. For the reconnaissance aircraft to be at the outer limits of their searches at sundown in lieu of arrival back at base at sundown.

The Defense Force and Shore-Based Air Force was new in concept, developing out of the experience at Guadalcanal. Its missions included defending and developing the positions captured, including the construction and activation of airfields on the atolls of Makin, Tarawa, and Apamama. All this was to be done to give air support to the Central Pacific campaign.

On 25 October 1943, CINCPAC modified his Operation Plan so that command would pass from the Commander Attack Force to

Adm Chester W. Nimitz, VAdm Raymond Spruance and MGen Holland V. Smith look over the edge of a 20-mm gun tub, while inspecting shipping at Pearl Harbor, just prior to the Gilberts operation, circa October 1943. Army BrigGen H. B. Holmes is behind them, in center, wearing Garrison cap. Naval Historical Center.

Commander Landing Force in accordance with the following procedure:

> At each atoll, as soon as the Landing Force Commander determines that the status of the landing operations permits, he will assume command on shore and report that fact to the Commander Attack Force.

This changed the previous directive under which the Commander Landing Force would announce he was ready to assume command ashore, and the Commander Attack Force would direct him to do so.

An additional change made by CINCPAC at the same time provided for an orderly change of responsibility for the defense and development of atolls or islands captured. This had been sadly lacking in the operation orders for WATCHTOWER and TOENAILS:

> Commander Central Pacific Force will determine and announce when the capture and occupation phase is completed, whereupon Commander Defense Force and Shore Based Air will assume his responsibility for the defense and development of positions captured.

This superseded the provision:

> Commander Central Pacific Force will determine when the capture and occupation phase is completed and will then direct command of all forces ashore at objectives pass from Commander Assault Force to Commander Defense Force and Shore Based Air.

RAdm Turner supported both of these changes, and inaugurated the second one. [17]

Amphibious Force Command Flagship

RAdm Turner had come out of the South Pacific with the very definite belief that the commander of an amphibious task force should be provided with a flagship which did not have to carry troops and their logistical support to the assault landing, and which had adequate working and sleeping accommodations for his staff. Additionally, the flagship had to provide adequate accommodations for the Amphibious Corps Commander, the Landing Force Commander and the Commander of the Support Aircraft and the numerous personnel of their staffs, as well as provide multiple communication facilities adequate for the escalating requirements of three or four commanders aboard the same ship during the early hours of an assault landing.

Since there was no ship currently afloat in the United States Navy to meet such requirements, a transport hull with a wholly new topside design was necessary. This ship was to be called a headquarters ship, although its official title would be Amphibious Force Command Flagship. The USS *Appalachian* (AGC-1) was the first of 15 built in 1943-1944 on Maritime Commission C-2 hulls with an average displacement of 7431 tons. (*She would arrive in the Pacific in late1943.*)

Solomons Observations and Conclusions

Now for a few final observations on the Solomons Campaigns:

- American planners would have to improve their ability to estimate the enemy's strength and defenses and the U.S. Navy would have to improve its ability to stop nighttime Japanese troop movements.

- The strategical concepts of "offshore toeholds" and "leapfrogging" would be employed in upcoming operations.

- The risk the United States incurred in the South and Southwest Pacific by dispensing its forces and conducting two strategic offenses, Solomons and New Guinea, brought substantial rewards.

- Words fail to convey the demands placed on the men who served at the front or to praise their efforts sufficiently. A special tribute is due the Seabees, Army and Marine Engineers, Marine Pioneers, and other extensions of the "Pacific Express," like the Marine's Fifth Field Depot—another logistics organization which started as the 4th Base Depot in the Solomons.

- Thanks to our newfound air supremacy and the new Allied airfields in the Central and Northern Solomons, the U.S. was now in position to drive the Japanese fleet out of Rabaul. The successful isolation of Rabaul —the ultimate objective of Operation CARTWHEEL, would be the beginning of the end.

The invasion of New Georgia signaled a new phase in the Pacific war, the beginning of an American strategic offensive. The struggle for control of the Solomons was a critical turning point in the war. It also proved—in spite of differing opinions along the way—that joint naval, land, and air operations improve with experience.

One more point. Just about every one of the one hundred plus veterans the writer has interviewed for this book has referred to the Central and Northern Solomons campaigns as "our little forgotten war," or words to that effect. And, of course, they're right. But Admiral Halsey, COMSOPAC, didn't forget. He sent the following secret Mailgram to all Task Force 31 personnel on 15 Nov. 1943 following the Treasury Islands-Bougainville landings:

The outstanding work of Task Force Thirty One has been under my personal observation during the GOODTIME dash CHERRYBLOSSOM Operations X The planning for these difficult tasks was expert and thorough X Execution was aggressive and effective X In these respects the Third Marines CMA the Thirty Seventh Army Division and the New Zealand Brigade were on a party with Task Force Thirty One X

Well done and keep the Japs on the run X **Halsey** X

Now for a few final words on the Solomons Campaigns from the Army's perspective by military historian Stephen J. Lofgren:

U.S. Army Analysis
of Northern Solomons Campaign 1943-1944

by Stephen J. Lofgren [18]

The Northern Solomons is one of the more unheralded of the U.S. Army campaigns of World War II, largely overshadowed by its predecessor, Guadalcanal, and by its more publicized successor, Leyte. Furthermore, with hindsight the campaign for the northern Solomon Islands might be described simply as bringing to bear preponderant American strength on isolated Japanese positions. Such a summary does describe accurately what American strategy skillfully achieved through sustained joint operations: the isolation and subsequent defeat in detail of Japanese forces. Nevertheless, such brevity fails to convey either the complexity or the totality of the American effort in the Solomons.

Throughout the campaign, and often under barely tolerable conditions, American soldiers, sailors, airmen, and marines of all ranks exhibited the skill, determination, and endurance that ensured victory. American forces had advantages in the Solomons Campaign, which they exploited for the greatest benefit.

There were several reasons for the American difficulties during the campaign's early stages. First the drive through the Solomons was not a top Allied priority, so Halsey's forces competed with other Allied theaters for resources. Competition prodded commanders to undertake operations as soon as possible to show that they deserved more resources. More significantly, American planners underestimated the task they faced in conquering New Georgia, miscalculating both the strength of Japanese defenses and the severe hardships that jungle fighting would impose on American troops. This grave failure to identify, and prepare for, the two most important external influences on the American ground campaign can hardly be overemphasized in explaining the ground offensive's subsequent breakdown.

Considering the earlier savage and lengthy fighting on Guadalcanal and at Buna, this seems an incomprehensible lapse. The eventual commitment of XIV Corps, with its additional combat power and administrative and logistical capabilities, underscored recognition that the original task assigned to the 43rd Division simply had been too great for its resources to accomplish.

Also contributing to the offense's woes were the overburdening of General Hester's staff, the virtual absence of useful intelligence, and, not least, the inexperience of some units like the 43rd Division. Even after these problems were surmounted, the Navy's inability to stop nighttime Japanese troop movements meant that some of the fruits of the New Georgia campaign were lost. In the Solomons, Japanese soldiers who escaped generally fought again another day.

But with hard-won experience came increased efficiency and effectiveness for American units, staffs, and commanders. Helping matters was the skill of important commanders. General Griswold inherited command at a critical moment and helped rescue a disintegrating tactical situation on New Georgia. Simultaneously, the replacement of Admiral Turner by Admiral Wilkinson brought to the fore an extremely talented amphibious commander.

At the "sharp end," troops learned to counter enemy defenses as well as reduce the jungle environment's physical and emotional toll by swiftly applying lessons learned in combat. Among those strength-sapping hardships that all soldiers endured were utter physical and mental exhaustion, malnourishment, and poor sanitation, along with a host of debilitating diseases—dysentery, malaria, and jungle rot, to name three—that flourished in the pernicious climate of the Solomons. Not for the last time, American soldiers learned that tough terrain and a determined foe make a potent combination.

There are two requirements for defeating an enemy who occupies a strong defensive position: superior firepower and men willing to go forward and attack the enemy. On New Georgia, the latter was often in greater supply than the former. Unlike the ground war in Europe, in which vast quantities of artillery often were employed at long range with devastating effect on visible targets, jungle fighting in the Solomons usually pitted small groups against a camouflaged enemy, occupying well-prepared defensive positions, at extremely close range. Irregular front-line positions often made artillery support equally dangerous to friend and foe.

Inexperienced troops, unfamiliar with the realities of Pacific island combat and the demands it placed on individual initiative and fortitude, did have difficulties. Such was the experience of the 43rd Division on New Georgia, where the untested unit suffered one of the highest rates of neuroses casualties of any American division during the war. But the division's loss of 1,500 men in a three-month period reflected most of all the extreme hardship the troops endured. Poorly prepared, ill-supplied, and surrounded by a fetid jungle that was almost as dangerous as the enemy, these men fought a grim war of attrition in the Pacific War's equivalent of World War I trenches. Acquiring their knowledge in combat, even men physically unscathed by combat paid dearly.

The risk that the United States incurred in the Pacific by dispensing its forces and conducting two strategic offensives brought substantial rewards. Especially at CARTWHEEL's operational level, the Japanese could not counter the Allied agility. Japanese efforts to use their "interior lines" in the Pacific, by shifting forces to block alternately MacArthur's and Halsey's offensives, were insufficient. Never more than a hindrance to Allied campaign progress, tactically such Japanese efforts only provided the Allies with many opportunities to inflict considerable damage on their off-balance foe. Allied forces generally made the most of these opportunities. As attrition depleted Japanese air and naval forces and interdiction of supply lines isolated ground units, the Japanese lost the initiative. Confronted with increasingly strong and aggressive Allied forces in the South and Southwest Pacific, they would never regain it. Allied destruction of Japanese men, materiel, and mobility throughout the Solomons and New Guinea left the Japanese mired in a multifront war they could not win.

During the Central and Northern Solomons Campaigns, the measure of the war with Japan changed dramatically. The invasion of New Georgia in June 1943 had signaled a new phase of the war, the beginning of a sustained American strategic offensive. Less than a year later, the failed Japanese counterattack on Bougainville and CARTWHEEL'S successful isolation of Rabaul heralded the beginning of the end—the eagerly awaited American return to the Philippines. The Solomons Campaigns constituted a major step toward that goal.

The invasion of New Georgia in June 1943 had signaled a new phase of the war, the beginning of a sustained American strategic offensive.

—Stephen J. Lofgren,
Military historian

APPENDIX A

Composition of United States South Pacific Force, Pacific Fleet – as of July 1942

Vice Admiral Robert L. Ghormley in *Argonne*

Rear Admiral Daniel J. Callaghan, Chief of Staff

TF 61 EXPEDITIONARY FORCE
Vice Admiral Frank Jack Fletcher

TG 61.1 AIR SUPPORT FORCE, Rear Admiral Leigh Noyes
Unit directly under Admiral Fletcher (old TF 11)

SARATOGA   Captain DeWitt C. Ramsey

Air Group: 1 SBD-3 (Dauntless), Commander Harry D. Felt

Squadron	Type	Commanding Officer
VF-5	34 F4F-4 (Wildcat)	LCdr Leroy C. Simpler
VB-3	18 SBD-3	LCdr Dewitt W. Shumway
VS-3	18 SBD-3	LCdr Louis J. Kirn
VT-8	16 TBF-1 (Avenger)	Lt Harold H. Larsen

Heavy Cruiser   MINNEAPOLIS   Capt Frank J. Lowry

Heavy Cruiser   NEW ORLEANS   Capt Walter S. DeLany

Destroyer Screen, Captain Samuel B. Brewer (Comdesron 1)

PHELPS	LCdr Edward L. Beck
FARRAGUT	LCdr Henry D. Rosendal
WORDEN	LCdr William G. Pogue
MACDONOUGH	LCdr Erle V. Dennett
DALE	LCdr Anthony L. Rorschach

Unit under Rear Admiral Thomas C. Kinkaid (old TF 16)
ENTERPRISE   Capt Arthur C. Davis

Air Group: 1 TBF-1 LCdr Maxwell F. Leslie

Squadron	Type	Commanding Officer
VF-6	36 F4F-4	Lt Louis H. Bauer
VB-6	18 SBD-3	Lt Ray Davis
VS-5	18 SBD-3	Lt Turner F. Caldwell Jr.
VT-3	14 TBF-1	LCdr Charles M. Jett

Battleship   NORTH CAROLINA   Capt George H. Fort

Cruisers, Rear Admiral M. S. Tisdale

Heavy Cruiser	PORTLAND	Capt Laurance T. DuBose
AA Light Cruiser	ATLANTA*	Capt Samuel P. Jenkins

Destroyer Screen, Captain Edward P. Sauer (Comdesron 6)

BALCH	LCdr Harold H. Tiemroth
MAURY	LCdr Gelzer L. Sims
GWIN	Cdr John M. Higgins
BENHAM*	LCdr Joseph M. Worthington
GRAYSON	LCdr Frederick J. Bell

Unit under Rear Admiral Noyes

WASP*	Capt Forrest P. Sherman

Air Group: 1 TBF-1, LCdr Wallace M. Beakley

VF-71	29 F4F-4	LCdr Courtney Shands
VS-71	15 SBD-3	LCdr John Eldridge Jr.*
VS-72	15 SBD-3	LCdr Ernest M. Snowden
VT-7	9 TBF-1	Lt Henry A. Romberg

Heavy Cruiser	SAN FRANCISCO	Capt Charles H. McMorris
Heavy Cruiser	SALT LAKE CITY	Capt Ernest G. Small

Destroyer Screen, Captain Robert G. Tobin (Comdesron 12)

LANG	LCdr John L. Wilfong
STERETT	Cdr Jesse G. Coward
AARON WARD	LCdr Orville F. Gregor
STACK	LCdr Alvord J. Greenacre
LAFFEY*	LCdr William E. Hank*
FARENHOLT	LCdr Eugene T. Seaward

Fueling Group

PLATTE	Capt Ralph H. Henkle
CIMARRON	Cdr Russell M. Ihrig
KASKASKIA	Cdr Walter L. Taylor
SABINE	Capt Houston L. Maples
KANAWHA	Cdr Kendall S. Reed

TF 62 SOUTH PACIFIC AMPHIBIOUS FORCE
Rear Admiral Richmond K. Turner in *McCawley*

TG 62.2 ESCORT, Rear Admiral V. A. C. Crutchley RN [1]

CA	HMAS AUSTRALIA	Capt H. B. Farncomb RAN
CA	HMAS CANBERRA*	Capt F. E. Getting RAN*
CL	HMAS HOBART	Capt H. A. Showers RAN
CA	CHICAGO*	Capt Howard D. Bode

---

* Lost during Guadalcanal operations before 10 Feb. 1943.
[1] Also second in command of TF 62.

Desron 4, Captain Cornelius W. Flynn

SELFRIDGE	LCdr Carroll D. Reynolds
PATTERSON	Cdr Frank R. Walker
RALPH TALBOT	LCdr Joseph W. Callahan
MUGFORD	LCdr Edward W. Young
JARVIS*	LCdr William W. Graham Jr.*

Desdiv 7, Cdr Leonard B. Austin

BLUE*	Cdr Harold N. Williams
HELM	LCdr Chester E. Carroll
HENLEY	Cdr Robert H. Smith [2]
BAGLEY	LCdr George A. Sinclair

TG 62.1 CONVOY[3], Captain Lawrence F. Reifsnider in *Hunter Liggett*
Major General Alexander A. Vandegrift USMC, Commander Ground Forces
Brigadier General William H. Rupertus USMC, Assistant Div. Commander

Embarking 1st and 5th Regiments 1st Marine Division, 2nd Marine Regiment
2nd Division, 1st Raider Battalion, 3rd Defense Battalion and attached
Marine Corps units; 959 officers, 18,146 enlisted men.

TRANSPORT GROUP X-RAY (for Guadalcanal), Capt Reifsnider

Transdiv A, Capt Paul S. Theiss
5th Marine Regiment (less 2nd Battalion) and attached units, Col LeRoy P. Hunt USMC

FULLER	Capt Theiss
AMERICAN LEGION	Capt Thomas D. Warner
BELLATRIX	Cdr William F. Dietrich

Transdiv B, Capt Charlie P. McFeaters
Divisional headquarters and 1st Marine Regiment, Col C. B. Cates USMC.

McCAWLEY	Capt McFeaters
BARNETT	Capt Henry E. Thornhill
GEORGE F. ELLIOTT*	Capt Watson O. Bailey
LIBRA	Cdr William B. Fletcher Jr.

Transdiv C, Capt Reifsnider
Embarking part of Support Group, HQ and Service Battery, Special Weapons Battalion,
5th Battalion 11th Marine Regiment and attached units, part of 3rd Defense Battalion.

HUNTER LIGGETT	Cdr Louis W. Perkins USCG
ALCHIBA	Cdr James S. Freeman
FOMALHAUT	Cdr Henry C. Flanagan
BETELGEUSE	Cdr Harry D. Power

---

* Lost during Guadalcanal operations before 10 Feb. 1943.
[2] Relieved by LCdr E. K. Van Swearingen 14 Aug. and became Comdesdiv 7 in *Blue*.
[3] Here arranged as organized for the landings.

Transdiv D, Capt Ingolf N. Kiland

Embarking 2nd Marine Regiment (less 1st Battalion) and attached units, Col John M. Arthur USMC.

CRESCENT CITY	Capt Kiland
PRESIDENT HAYES [4]	Cdr Francis W. Benson
PRESIDENT ADAMS [5]	Cdr Frank H. Dean
ALHENA	Cdr Charles B. Hunt

TRANSPORT GROUP YOKE (for Tulagi), Capt George B. Ashe

Transdiv E, Capt Ashe

Embarking 2nd Battalion 5th Regiment, 1st Battalion 2nd Regiment, Battery E 11th Regiment, half 3rd Defense Battalion, 1st Parachute Battalion, Company E 1st Raider Battalion and other units; Brigadier General Rupertus commanding.

NEVILLE	Capt Carlos A. Bailey
ZEILIN	Capt Pat Buchanan
HEYWOOD	Capt Herbert B. Knowles
PRESIDENT JACKSON	Cdr Charles W. Weitzel

Transdiv 12, Cdr Hugh W. Hadley

1st Raider Battalion (less Company E), LCol Merritt A. Edson USMC, embarked in Destroyer Transports:

COLHOUN*	Lt George B. Madden
LITTLE*	LCdr Gus B. Lofberg Jr.*
MCKEAN	LCdr John D. Sweeney
GREGORY*	LCdr Harry F. Bauer*

FIRE SUPPORT GROUPS

TG 62.3 Fire Support Group L, Capt Frederick L. Riefkohl

Heavy Cruiser	VINCENNES*	Capt Riefkohl
Heavy Cruiser	QUINCY*	Capt Samuel N. Moore*
Heavy Cruiser	ASTORIA*	Capt William G. Greenman

Destroyers

HULL	LCdr Richard F. Stout
DEWEY	LCdr Charles F. Chillingworth Jr.
ELLET	LCdr Francis H. Gardner
WILSON	LCdr Walter H. Price

---

* Lost during Guadalcanal operations before 10 Feb. 1943.

[4] These ships moved across the Sound on the night of 7-8 Aug. and landed their contingents Tulagi-side.

[5] Ibid.

TG 62.4 Fire Support Group M, *Rear Admiral Norman Scott

AA Light Cruiser	SAN JUAN	Capt James E. Maher
Destroyer	MONSSEN*	Cdr Roland N. Smoot
Destroyer	BUCHANAN	Cdr Ralph E. Wilson

TG 62.5 MINESWEEPER GROUP, Cdr William H. Hartt Jr.

HOPKINS	LCdr Benjamin Coe
TREVER	LCdr Dwight M. Agnew
ZANE	LCdr Peyton L. Wirtz
SOUTHARD	LCdr Joe B. Cochran
HOVEY	LCdr Wilton S. Heald

TG 62.6 Screening Group, Rear Admiral Crutchley RN
Same as TG 62.2, less Desdiv 7

TF 63 LAND-BASED AIR, SOUTH PACIFIC FORCE [6]
Rear Admiral John S. McCain

At Efate: 16 B-17s (Colonel L. G. Saunders USA), 18 Marine Corps Wildcats, 6 Scout-Observation planes (Major H. W. Bauer USMC).

In New Caledonia: 21 PBY-5s, 1 PBY-5A (Patrons 11 and 23 from Patwings 1 and 2, based on tender *Curtiss*) Army Bomron 69, Colonel Clyde Rich USA, 9 B-17s, 10 B-26s equipped with torpedoes, 38 P-39s, 16 F4F-3s, 6 RNZAF Hudsons, 3 Scout-Observation planes, 17 SBDs of Marine Corps.

In Fiji: 6 PBYs, 3 RNZAF Singapores, 12 RNZAF Hudsons, 12 Marine Corps Wildcats, 12 B-26s equipped with torpedoes, 8 B-17s, 9 RNZAF Vincents.

In Tongatabu: 6 Scout-Observation planes, 24 Marine Corps Wildcats.

In Samoa: 17 SBDs, 18 Marine Corps Wildcats, 10 Scout-Observation planes.

SOUTHWEST PACIFIC AREA
General Douglas MacArthur USA

ALLIED AIR FORCES, SOUTHWEST PACIFIC
Lt General George C. Kenney USA [7]
Northeast Area Command, Air Commodore F. W. F. Lucas RAAF
Air Command No. 2, Brigadier General Martin F. Scanlon USA

---

* Lost during Guadalcanal operations before 10 Feb. 1943.

[6] This list from Admiral Ghormley's records. The "hundreds of planes" mentioned in the O.N.I. Combat Narrative is an exaggeration.

[7] Relieved Lieutenant General Brett 4 Aug. 1942.

Available for Guadalcanal Operation
19th Bombing Group, an average of 20 B-17s operational
435th Reconnaissance Squadron component at Port Moresby

Four B-17s, 27 B-26s, 12 B-25s, a few RAF Hudsons and PBYs. 22nd Bombing Group and 3rd Bombing Group, based in Australia and staging through Port Moresby, took care of Lae and Salamaua. Two fighter squadrons of the 35th Group, with about 35 P-40s at Port Moresby. Two R.A.F. Squadrons, with about 30 P-40s in the area.

SUBMARINE FORCE SOUTHWEST PACIFIC
Rear Admiral Charles A. Lockwood Jr.

TF 42, Captain Ralph W. Christie, based at Brisbane [8]

S-38	LCdr H. G. Munson
S-39	Lt F. E. Brown
S-41	Lt I. S. Hartman
S-43	LCdr E. R. Hannon
S-44	LCdr J. R. Moore
S-46	LCdr R. C. Lynch Jr.

[8] These boats were on patrol at the time in this area. *S-38* sank *Meiyo Maru* bringing reinforcements to Guadalcanal 8 Aug. and *S-44* sank heavy cruiser *Kako* 10 Aug. 1942.

APPENDIX B

Composition of Forces for the Battle of the Eastern Solomons 24 August 1942

JAPANESE

COMBINED FLEET
Admiral Isoroku Yamamoto in BB *Yamato*
Operating near Truk with CVE TAIYO and DDs AKEBONO, USHIO, and SAZANAMI

GUADALCANAL SUPPORTING FORCES
Vice Admiral Nobutake Kondo (C. in C. Second Fleet)

ADVANCE FORCE, Vice Admiral Kondo

Main Body
Crudiv 4: ATAGO, MAYA, TAKAO
Crudiv 5 (Vice Admiral Takeo Takagi): MYOKO, HAGURO
        Screen: Desron 4, Rear Admiral Tamotsu Takama in Light Cruiser *Yura*
Destroyers ASAGUMO YAMAGUMO, KUROSH1O, OYASHIO, HAYASHIO

Support Group, C.O. of Mutsu
Battleship MUTSU, Destroyers MURASAME, HARUSAME, SAMIDARE

Seaplane Group, Rear Admiral Takaji Jojima (Comcardiv 11)
Seaplane Carrier CHITOSE (22 VSO), Destroyer NATSUGUMO

STRIKING FORCE, Vice Admiral Chuichi Nagumo (C. in C. Third Fleet)

Carrier Group
SHOKAKU (26 VF, 14 VB, 18 VT, 1 VSO), ZUIKAKU (27 VF, 27 VB, 18 VT)
Screen: DDs AKIGUMO, YUGUMO, MAKIGUMO, KAZEGUMO, SHIKINAMI, URANAMI

Vanguard Group, Rear Admiral Hiroaki Abe (Combatdiv 11)
Battleships HIEI, KIRISHIMA
Crudiv 7 (Rear Admiral Shoji Nishimura): SUZUYA, KUMANO, CHIKUMA
Screen: Desron 10, Rear Admiral Susumu Kimura in Light Cruiser *Nagara*
Destroyers AKIZUKI, HATSUKAZE, MAIKAZE, NOWAKI, TANIKAZE, YUKIKAZE

Diversionary Group, Rear Admiral Tadaichi Hara (Comcrudiv 8)
Cruiser TONE, CVL RYUJO*(16 VF, 21 VT), DDs AMATSUKAZE, TOKITSUKAZE

SOUTHEAST AREA FORCES
Vice Admiral Nishizo Tsukahara, at Rabaul

OUTER SOUTH SEAS FORCE, Vice Admiral Gunichi Mikawa (C. in C. Eighth Fleet)

Reinforcement Group, Rear Admiral Raizo Tanaka (Comdesron 2)
Escort Unit: CL JINTSU; DDs KAGERO, MUTSUKI*, YAYOI, ISOKAZE, KAWAKAZE,[1]
SUZUKAZE, UMIKAZE, UZUKI
Transport Unit: Auxiliary Cruiser KINRYU MARU, embarking 5th Yokosuka Special
Naval Landing Force, 800 men; Patrol Boats [2] Nos. 1, 2, 34 and 35, embarking 2nd
echelon Army Ichiki Detachment, 700 men

Covering Group, Vice Admiral Mikawa in CA Chokai
Crudiv 6 (Rear Admiral Aritomo Goto): AOBA, KINUGASA, FURUTAKA

Submarine Group I-121, I-123*, RO-34

LAND-BASED AIR FORCE
Vice Admiral Tsukahara (C. in C. Eleventh Air Fleet)
About 100 operational aircraft

ADVANCE EXPEDITIONARY FORCE
Vice Admiral T. Komatsu (C. in C. Sixth Fleet) in Light Cruiser *Katori* at Truk
Submarines I-9, I-11, I-15, I-17, I-19, I-26, I-31, I-174, I-175

UNITED STATES

TASK FORCE 61
Vice Admiral Frank Jack Fletcher

TF 11, Admiral Fletcher

SARATOGA	Capt DeWitt C. Ramsey

Air Group 3: 1 SBD-3 (Dauntless), Cdr Harry D. Felt

VF-5:	36 F4F-4 (Wildcat)	LCdr Leroy C. Simpler
VB-3:	18 SBD-3	LCdr Dewitt W. Shumway
VS-3:	18 SBD-3	LCdr Louis J. Kirn
VT-8:	15 TBF-1 (Avenger)	Lt Harold H. Larsen

Rear Admiral Carleton H. Wright

MINNEAPOLIS	Capt Frank J. Lowry
NEW ORLEANS	Capt Walter S. DeLany

Destroyer Screen, Captain Samuel B. Brewer (Comdesron 1)

PHELPS	LCdr Edward L. Beck

Desdiv 2, Cdr Francis X. McInerney

FARRAGUT	Cdr George P. Hunter
WORDEN	LCdr William G. Pogue
MACDONOUGH	LCdr Eric V. Dennett
DALE	LCdr Anthony L. Rorschach

---

* Sunk in this operation.
[1] These five destroyers comprised a special Bombardment Unit which shelled Henderson
Field the night of 24 August.
[2] Former destroyers *Shimakaze, Nadakaze, Suzuki,* and *Tsuta,* converted along lines
similar to U.S. Navy APDs.

TF 16, Rear Admiral Thomas C. Kinkaid
   ENTERPRISE   Captain Arthur C. Davis
  Air Group 6: 1 SBD-3, LCdr Maxwell F. Leslie

VF-6:	36 F4F-4	Lt Louis H. Bauer
VB-6:	18 SBD-3	Lt Ray Davis
VS-5:	18 SBD-3	Lt Stockton B. Strong
VT-3:	15 TBF-1	LCdr Charles M. Jett

   NORTH CAROLINA   Capt George H. Fort

Rear Admiral Mahlon S. Tisdale

   PORTLAND   Capt Laurance T. DuBose
   ATLANTA   Capt Samuel P. Jenkins

Destroyer Screen, Captain Edward P. Sauer (Comdesron 6)
   BALCH   LCdr Harold H. Tiemroth
   MAURY   LCdr Gelzer L. Sims
   BENHAM   LCdr Joseph M. Worthington
   ELLET   LCdr Francis H. Gardner

Desdiv 22, Cdr Harold R. Holcomb
   GRAYSON   LCdr Frederick J. Bell
   MONSSEN   Cdr Roland N. Smoot

TF 18, Rear Admiral Leigh Noyes

   WASP   Capt Forrest P. Sherman

Air Group 7: I F4F-4, LCdr Wallace M. Beakley

VF-71:	28 F4F-4	LCdr Courtney Shands
VS-71:	18 SBD-3	LCdr John Eldridge
VS-72:	18 SBD-3	LCdr Ernest M. Snowden
VT-7:	15 TBF-1	Lt Henry A. Romberg

Rear Admiral Norman Scott
   SAN JUAN   Capt James E. Maher
   SAN FRANCISCO   Capt Charles H. McMorris
   SALT LAKE CITY   Capt Ernest G. Small

Destroyer Screen, Captain Robert G. Tobin (Comdesron 12)
   FARENHOLT   LCdr Eugene T. Seaward
   AARON WARD   LCdr Orville F. Gregor
   BUCHANAN   Cdr Ralph E. Wilson

Desdiv 15, Captain William W. Warlick
   LANG   LCdr John L. Wilfong
   STACK   LCdr Alvord J. Greenacre
   STERETT   Cdr Jesse G. Coward

Desron 4, Captain Cornelius W. Flynn
   SELFRIDGE   Cdr Carroll D. Reynolds

APPENDIX C

Composition of Forces for the Battle of Cape Esperance
11-12 October 1942

UNITED STATES FORCES

TASK FORCE 64, Rear Admiral Norman Scott

Heavy Cruisers

SAN FRANCISCO	Capt Charles H. McMorris
SALT LAKE CITY	Capt Ernest G. Small

Light Cruisers

BOISE	Capt Edward J. Moran
HELENA	Capt Gilbert C. Hoover

Destroyers, Capt. Robert G. Tobin (Comdesron 12)

FARENHOLT	LCdr Eugene T. Seaward
BUCHANAN	Cdr Ralph E. Wilson
LAFFEY	LCdr William E. Hank
DUNCAN*	LCdr Edmund B. Taylor
McCALLA	LCdr William G. Cooper

JAPANESE FORCES

Bombardment Group, Rear Admiral Aritomo Goto* (Comcrudiv 6)

Heavy Cruisers
AOBA, KINUGASA, FURUTAKA*

Destroyers
HATSUYUKI, FUBUKI*

Reinforcement Group, Rear Admiral Takaji Joshima (Comcardiv 11)

Seaplane Carriers
CHITOSE, NISSHIN (carrying 728 Army personnel, 2 field guns,
4 howitzers, 4 tractors, 1 AA gun, ammunition, miscellaneous
equipment, medical supplies, and 6 landing craft)

Destroyers
AKIZUKI, ASAGUMO, NATSUGUMO*, YAMAGUMO, MURAKUMO*, SHIRAYUKI

* Killed or sunk in action.

APPENDIX D

Composition of Forces for the Battle of Santa Cruz Islands
26-27 October 1942

UNITED STATES

SOUTH PACIFIC FORCE
Vice Admiral William F. Halsey, at Nouméa

TASK FORCE 16, Rear Admiral Thomas C. Kinkaid

ENTERPRISE   Capt Osborne B. Hardison

Air Group 10: 1 TBF-1 (Avenger), Cdr Richard K. Gaines

VF-10:	34 F4F-4 (Wildcat)	LCdr James H. Flatley Jr.
VB-10:	18 SBD-3 (Dauntless)	LCdr James A. Thomas
VS-10:	18 SBD-3	LCdr James R. Lee
VT-10:	12 TBF-1	LCdr John A. Collett*

SOUTH DAKOTA   Capt Thomas L. Gatch

Rear Admiral Mahlon S. Tisdale (Comcrudiv 4)

PORTLAND	Capt Laurence T. DuBose
SAN JUAN	Capt James E. Maher

Destroyer Screen, Capt Charles P. Cecil (Comdesron 5)

PORTER*	LCdr David G. Roberts
MAHAN	LCdr Rodger W. Simpson

Desdiv 10, Cdr Thomas M. Stokes

CUSHING	LCdr Christopher Noble
PRESTON	LCdr Max C. Stormes
SMITH	LCdr Hunter Wood Jr.
MAURY	LCdr Gelzer L. Sims
CONYNGHAM	LCdr Henry C. Daniel
SHAW	LCdr Wilbur G. Jones

TASK FORCE 17, Rear Admiral George D. Murray

HORNET*   Capt Charles P. Mason

Air Group 8: 1 TBF-1, Cdr Walter F. Rodee

VF-72:	36 F4F-4	LCdr Henry G. Sanchez
VB-8:	18 SBD-3	Lt James E. Vose
VS-8:	18 SBD-3	LCdr William J. Widhelm
VT-6:	15 TBF-1	Lt Edwin B. Parker Jr.

* Sunk or lost in this battle.

Rear Admiral Howard H. Good (Comcrudiv 5)

NORTHAMPTON	Capt Willard A. Kitts III
PENSACOLA	Capt Frank L. Lowe
SAN DIEGO	Capt Benjamin F. Perry
JUNEAU	Capt Lyman K. Swenson

Destroyer Screen, Cdr Arnold E. True (Comdesron 2)

MORRIS	LCdr Randolph B. Boyer
ANDERSON	LCdr Richard A. Guthrie
HUGHES	LCdr Donald J. Ramsey
MUSTIN	LCdr Wallis F. Petersen
RUSSELL	LCdr Glenn R. Hartwig
BARTON	LCdr Douglas H. Fox

TASK FORCE 64, [1] Rear Admiral Willis A. Lee

WASHINGTON, SAN FRANCISCO, HELENA, ATLANTA, AARON WARD,
BENHAM, FLETCHER, LANSDOWNE, LARDNER, MCCALLA

TASK FORCE 63

Land-based Air Forces, Rear Admiral Aubrey W. Fitch

At Henderson Field: 26 F4F-4, 6 P-400, 6 P-39, 20 SBD, 2 TBF
At Espiritu Santo: 23 F4F-4, 39 B-17, 12 Hudson of RNZAF, 32 PBY, 5-OS2U
(Kingfisher); tenders CURTISS and MACKINAC
At New Caledonia: 46 P-39 (12 en route Guadalcanal), 15 P-38, 16 B-26, 13 Hudson of RNZAF

Action of 25 October in Ironbottom Sound

TREVER	LCdr Dwight M. Agnew
ZANE	LCdr Peyton L. Wirtz
SEMINOLE*	LCdr William G. Fewel
YP-284*	Lt Carl W. Rasmussen

JAPANESE

COMBINED FLEET
Admiral Isoroku Yamamoto in *Yamato* at Truk

GUADALCANAL SUPPORTING FORCES
Vice Admiral Nobutake Kondo (C. in C. Second Fleet)

ADVANCE FORCE, Vice Admiral Kondo

Crudiv 4: ATAGO, TAKAO
Crudiv 5 (Rear Admiral Sentaro Omori): MYOKO, MAYA
Screen, Rear Admiral Raizo Tanaka (Comdesron 2) in CL *Isuzu*
DDs NAGANAMI, MAKINAMI, TAKANAMI, UMIKAZE, KAWAKAZE, SUZUKAZE

---

* Sunk or lost in this battle.
[1] Operating separately. Did not engage.

Air Group, Rear Admiral Kakuji Kakuta (Comcardiv 2) [2]
JUNYO (24 VF, 21 VB, 10 VT); *Screen*: Destroyers KUROSHIO, HAYASHIO

Support Group, Vice Admiral Takeo Kurita (Combatdiv 3)
BBs KONGO, HARUNA
DDs OYASHIO, KAGERO, MURASAME, SAMIDARE, YUDACHI, HARUSAME

STRIKING FORCE, Vice Admiral Chuichi Nagumo (C. in C. Third Fleet)
   Carrier Group, Vice Admiral Nagumo (Comcardiv 1)

SHOKAKU	(18 VF, 20 VB, 23 VT)
ZUIKAKU	(27 VF, 27 VB, 18 VT)
ZUIHO	(8 VF, 6 VT)

Screen, Heavy cruiser KUMANO; Destroyers AMATSUKAZE, HATSUKAZE, TOKITSUKAZE,YUKIKAZE, ARASHI, MAIKAZE, TERUZUKI, HAMAKAZE

Vanguard Group, Rear Admiral Hiroaki Abe (Combatdiv 11)
Battleships HIEI, KIRISHIMA
Crudiv 8 (Rear Admiral Tadaichi Hara): TONE, CHIKUMA
Crudiv 7 (Rear Admiral Shoji Nishimura): SUZUYA

Screen, Rear Admiral Susumu Kimura (Comdesron 10) in CL *Nagara*
DDs KAZAGUMO, MAKIGUMO, YUGUMO, AKIGUMO, TANIKAZE, URAKAZE, ISOKAZE

Supply Group
Oilers KOKUYO MARU, TOHO MARU, TOEI MARU, KYOKUTO MARU, Destroyer NOWAKI

LAND-BASED AIR FORCE
Vice Admiral Jinichi Kusaka (C. in C. 11th Air Fleet) at Rabaul
About 220 operational planes

ADVANCE EXPEDITIONARY FORCE
Vice Admiral Teruhisa Komatsu (C. in C. Sixth Fleet) in CL *Katori* at Truk
Force "A": Submarines I-4, I-5, I-7, I-8, I-22, I-176
Force "B": Submarines I-9, I-15, I-21, I-24, I-174, I-175

OUTER SOUTH SEAS FORCE
Vice Admiral G. Mikawa in CA *Chokai* at Shortland

These ships were in Actions of 25 October in Ironbottom Sound and Indispensable Strait.

Assault Unit: Destroyers AKATSUKI, IKAZUCHI, SHIRATSUYU;
Attack (Bombardment) Unit, Rear Admiral Tamotsu Takama (Comdesron 4),
CL YURA* with DDs AKIZUKI, HARUSAME, YUDACHI, MURASAME, SAMIDARE

---

* Sunk in this action.
[2] Flagship *Hiyo* developed engine trouble on 22 October and returned to Truk with DDs Inazuma and Isonami; planes sent to Rabaul and flag transferred to *Junyo*.

APPENDIX E

Composition of Forces for the Naval Battle of Guadalcanal
12-15 November 1942

UNITED STATES
SOUTH PACIFIC FORCE
Vice Admiral William F. Halsey, at Nouméa

TASK FORCE 67
Rear Admiral Richmond K. Turner

TG 67.1 TRANSPORT GROUP, Captain Ingolf N. Kiland

MCCAWLEY	Capt Charlie P. McFeaters
CRESCENT CITY	Capt John R. Sullivan
PRESIDENT ADAMS	Cdr Frank H. Dean
PRESIDENT JACKSON	Cdr Charles W. Weitzel

Embarking 182nd Infantry (less 3rd Battalion), 4th Marine Replacement Battalion and Naval Local Defense Force personnel. This Group was escorted Nouméa -Guadalcanal by ships marked (T) in TG 67.4.

TG 67.4 SUPPORT GROUP, Rear Admiral Daniel J. Callaghan*

SAN FRANCISCO	Capt Cassin Young*

Rear Admiral Mahlon S. Tisdale (Comcrudiv 4)

PENSACOLA (E)	Capt Frank L. Lowe
PORTLAND (T)	Capt Laurance T. DuBose
HELENA	Capt Gilbert C. Hoover
JUNEAU*	Capt Lyman K. Swenson*

Destroyer Screen

BARTON (T) *	LCdr Douglas H. Fox*
MONSSEN (T) *	LCdr Charles E. McCombs

Cdr Thomas M. Stokes (Comdesdiv 10)

CUSHING*	LCdr Edward N. Parker
LAFFEY*	LCdr William E. Hank*
STERETT	Cdr Jesse G. Coward
O'BANNON (T)	Cdr Edwin R. Wilkinson
SHAW (E)	Cdr Wilbur G. Jones
GWIN (E)	LCdr John B. Fellows Jr.
PRESTON (E) *	Cdr Max C. Stormes*
BUCHANAN	Cdr Ralph E. Wilson

Ships marked (E) were detached on arrival Solomons to *Enterprise* (TF 16)
* Lost or killed in this battle.

TG 62.4 [1] Rear Admiral Norman Scott *
ATLANTA*	Capt Samuel P. Jenkins

Destroyer Screen, Captain Robert G. Tobin (Comdesron 12)
AARON WARD	Cdr Orville F. Gregor
FLETCHER	Cdr William M. Cole
LARDNER	Cdr Willard M. Sweetser
McCALLA	LCdr William G. Cooper

AKAs (Attack Cargo Ships)
BETELGEUSE	Cdr Harry D. Power
LIBRA	Cdr William B. Fletcher Jr.
ZEILIN	Capt Pat Buchanan

Embarking 1st Marine Aviation Engineer Battalion; Marine replacements;
Marine Air Wing 1 ground personnel; provisions, ammunition and materiel.
In the Night Action of 12 -13 November, the composition of TG 67.4
(Rear Admiral Callaghan*) was: SAN FRANCISCO, PORTLAND, HELENA,
ATLANTA*, JUNEAU*, CUSHING*,LAFFEY *, STERETT, O'BANNON, BARTON*,
MONSSEN*, AARON WARD, FLETCHER.

TASK FORCE 63
Land-based Aircraft, Rear Admiral Aubrey W. Fitch

At Henderson Field: 27 F4F-4, 18 P-38, 37 SBD, 9 TBF; one each of F4F-7, P-400, P-39.
At Espiritu Santo: 8 F4F-4, 13 F4F-3P, 16 TBF, 37 B-17, 5 B-26, 2 PB4Y, 5 Hudson of
RNZAF, 24 PBY, 1 PBY-5A.

TASK FORCE 16
Rear Admiral Thomas C. Kinkaid

As in air action of 14 November. Also ships marked (E) in TG 67.4.

ENTERPRISE	Capt Osborne B. Hardison

Air Group 10: 1 TBF-1 (Avenger), Cdr Richard K. Gaines
VF-10:	38 F4F-4 (Wildcat)	LCdr James H. Flatley Jr.
VB-10:	15 SBD-3 (Dauntless)	LCdr James A. Thomas
VS-10:	16 SBD-3	LCdr James R. Lee
VT-10:	9 TBF-1	Lt Albert P. Coffin

Rear Admiral Howard H. Good (Comcrudiv 5)
NORTHAMPTON	Capt Willard A. Kitts III
SAN DIEGO	Capt Benjamin F. Perry

---

* Lost or killed in this battle.
[1] Combat ships in this task group merged with TG 67.4 at Guadalcanal on 12 Nov.

Destroyer Screen, Captain Harold R. Holcomb (Comdesron 2)

CLARK	LCdr Lawrence H. Martin
ANDERSON	LCdr Richard A. Guthrie
HUGHES	Cdr Donald J. Ramsey

Desdiv 4, Commander Arnold E. True

MORRIS	LCdr Randolph B. Boyer
MUSTIN	Cdr Wallis F. Petersen
RUSSELL	Cdr Glenn R. Hartwig

TASK FORCE 64

Rear Admiral Willis Augustus Lee

(As in night action of 15 November)

WASHINGTON	Capt Glenn B. Davis
SOUTH DAKOTA	Capt Thomas L. Gatch

Destroyer Screen

WALKE*	Cdr Thomas E. Fraser*
BENHAM*	LCdr John B. Taylor
GWIN and PRESTON* (also in TG 67.4)	

JAPANESE

COMBINED FLEET

Admiral Yamamoto in *Yamato* at Truk

ADVANCE FORCE

Vice Admiral Nobutake Kondo in *Atago*

RAIDING GROUP, Vice Admiral Hiroaki Abe (Combatdiv 11)

Battleships HIEI*, KIRISHIMA*
Desron 10 Rear Admiral Susumu Kimura in light cruiser NAGARA with
destroyers AMATSUKAZE, YUKIKAZE, AKATSUKI*, IKAZUCHI,
INAZUMA, TERUZUKI

Sweeping Unit: Rear Admiral Tamotsu Takama (Comdesron 4),
destroyers ASAGUMO, MURASAME, SAMIDARE, YUDACHI*, HARUSAME
Patrol Unit: Capt Yasuhide Setoyama (Comdesdiv 27),
SHIGURE, SHIRATSUYU, YUGURE

MAIN BODY (ATTACK GROUP),[2] Vice Admiral Kondo
Bombardment Unit: heavy cruisers ATAGO, TAKAO; battleship * KIRISHIMA
Screening Unit: Rear Admiral Kimura in NAGARA with destroyers TERUZUKI,
INAZUMA, SHIRAYUKI, HATSUYUKI, ASAGUMO (Rear Admiral Takama), SAMIDARE
Sweeping Unit: Rear Admiral Shintaro Hashimoto (Comdesron 3) in light cruiser
SENDAI with destroyers URANAMI, SHIKINAMI, AYANAMI*

Late Reinforcement Unit: destroyers OYASHIO, KAGERO

CARRIER SUPPORT GROUP, Vice Admiral Takeo Kurita (Combatdiv 3)

Supporting Unit: battleships KONGO, HARUNA; heavy cruiser TONE
Air Striking Unit, Rear Admiral Kakuji Kakuta (Comcardiv 2): JUNYO (27 VF, 12 VB, 9 VT), HIYO (15 VF, 23 VB, 9 VT); four to eight destroyers [3]

OUTER SOUTH SEAS FORCE
Vice Admiral Gunichi Mikawa (C. in C. Eighth Fleet)

SUPPORT GROUP, Admiral Mikawa

Main Unit: heavy cruisers CHOKAI, KINUGASA*; light cruiser ISUZU; destroyers ASASHIO, ARASHIO
Bombardment Unit (Rear Admiral Shoji Nishimura): heavy cruisers SUZUYA, MAYA; light cruiser TENRYU; Destroyers MAKIGUMO, YUGUMO, KAZAGUMO, MICHISHIO

REINFORCEMENT GROUP, Rear Admiral Raizo Tanaka (Comdesron 2)

Escort Unit: destroyers HAYASH1O, OYASHIO, KAGERO, UMIKAZE, KAWAKAZE, SUZUKAZE, TAKANAMI, MAKINAMI, NAGANAMI, AMAGIRI, MOCHIZUKI
Transport Unit: ARIZONA MARU*, KUMAGAWA M.*, SADO M.*, NAGARA M.*, NAKO M.*, CANBERRA M.*, BRISBANE M.*, KINUGAWA M.*, HIROKAWA M.*, YAMAURA M.*, YAMATSUKI M.*

LAND-BASED AIR FORCE
Vice Admiral Jinichi Kusaka (C. in C. Eleventh Air Fleet) at Rabaul

25th and 26th Air Flotillas: about 215 operational planes

ADVANCE EXPEDITIONARY FORCE (Submarines)
Vice Admiral Teruhisa Komatsu (C. in C. Sixth Fleet), in CL *Katori* at Truk

Patrol Groups "A," "B" and "D": I-16, I-20, I-24, I-15, I-17, I-26, I-122, I-172*, I-175, RO-34
Scouting Units: I-7 (off Santa Cruz): I-9, I-21 and I-31, with seaplane, reconnoitering San Cristobal, Nouméa and Suva.

---

* Sunk, lost, or killed in this battle.
[2] This is the "emergency organization" in effect from evening of 13 Nov., incorporating certain ships from the Raiding Group and 4 destroyers originally with the Carrier Support Group and 2 destroyers from the Escort Unit, Reinforcement Group, Outer South Seas Force, which joined during the night battle of 14-15 Nov.
[3] *Hatsuyuki, Shirayuki,Uranami, Shikinami;* until 13 Nov. when they joined the Main Body (Attack Group) and were replaced by 8 survivors of the Raiding Group, several of which were also ordered to "engage in the rescue of personnel from distressed vessels." "Report on the Naval Battle of Guadalcanal" ATIS 15931.

APPENDIX F

Composition of Forces for the Battle of Tassafaronga 30 November 1942

UNITED STATES

TASK FORCE 67

Rear Admiral Carleton H. Wright

TG 67.2,   Rear Admiral Wright

MINNEAPOLIS	Capt Charles E. Rosendahl
NEW ORLEANS	Capt Clifford H. Roper
PENSACOLA	Capt Frank L. Lowe

Rear Admiral Mahlon S. Tisdale

NORTHAMTON*	Capt Willard A. Kitts
HONOLULU	Capt Robert W. Hayler

TG 67.4 (Destroyers), Commander William M. Cole

FLETCHER	Commander Cole
DRAYTON	LCdr James E. Cooper
MAURY	LCdr Gelzer L. Sims
PERKINS	LCdr Walter C. Reed

Desdiv 9, Commander Laurence A. Abercrombie

LAMSON	LCdr Philip H. Fitz-Gerald
LARDNER	LCdr William M. Sweetser

JAPANESE

DESTROYER SQUADRON 2, Rear Admiral Raizo Tanaka

DESTROYER PATROL UNIT: NAGANAMI, *TAKANAMI

TRANSPORT UNIT NO. 1, Capt Torajiro Sato: MAKINAMI, KUROSHIO, OYASHIO, KAGERO

TRANSPORT UNIT NO. 2, Capt Giichiro Nakahara: KAWAKAZE, SUZUKAZE

---

* Sunk in this action.

APPENDIX G

Composition of Task Force 18 for the Battle of Rennell Island
29-30 January 1943

Heavy Cruisers, Rear Admiral Giffen (CTF 18)

WICHITA	Capt Francis S. Low
CHICAGO*	Capt Ralph O. Davis
LOUISVILLE	Capt Charles T. Joy

Light Cruisers, Rear Admiral A. Stanton Merrill (Comcrudiv 12)

MONTPELIER	Capt Leighton Wood
CLEVELAND	Capt Edmund W. Burrough
COLUMBIA	Capt William A. Heard

Air Support Group, Captain Ben H. Wyatt

	CHENANGO	Capt Wyatt
VGF-28:	11 F4F-4	LCdr Jack I. Bandy
VGS-28:	8 SBD-3, 9 TBF-1	LCdr W.S. Butts

	SUWANNEE	Capt Frederick W. McMahon
VGF-27:	18 F4F-4	Lt Joseph F. Fitzpatrick
VGS-27:	15 TBF-1	LCdr Robert E. C. Jones

Destroyer Screen, Captain Harold F. Pullen

LA VALLETTE	Cdr Harry H. Henderson
WALLER	Cdr Laurence H. Frost
CONWAY	LCdr Nathaniel S. Prime
FRAZIER	LCdr Frank Virden

Desdiv 41, Cdr. Alvin D. Chandler

CHEVALIER	Cdr Ephraim R. McLean
EDWARDS	LCdr Paul G. Osler
MEADE	Cdr Raymond S. Lamb
TAYLOR	LCdr Benjamin Katz

* *Chicago* sank in 2000 fathoms at 11°25´30" S, 160°56´E.

APPENDIX H

Allied Air Squadrons at Henderson Field, Guadalcanal [1]
20 August 1942 – 2 February 1943

Dates following C.O.'s are of death in action when asterisked; otherwise, of relief. The number of planes in a squadron fluctuated from 1 to 19. *E* refers to Echelon or Detachment.

Commander Air South Pacific (Comairsopac)
Vice Admiral John S. McCain, *20 Sept.*
Rear Admiral Aubrey W. Fitch

Commander Air Solomons (Comaircactus)
Brigadier General Roy S. Geiger USMC, *Nov.*
Brigadier General Louis E. Woods USMC, *Nov.*
Brigadier General Francis P. Mulcahy USMC

UNITED STATES MARINE CORPS

Squadron	Type	Arrived	Commanding Officer
VMSB-232	SBD-1	20 Aug. 1942	LCol Richard C. Mangrum
VMSB-231	SBD-1	30 Aug. 1942	Maj Leo R. Smith *20 Sept.*
			Capt Ruben Iden *20 Sept.**
			Capt Elmer G. Glidden
VMSB-141	SBD-3	23 Sept. 1942	Capt Gordon A. Bell *14 Oct.**
			1st Lt W. S. Ashcroft USMCR *8 Nov.*
			1st Lt R. M. Patterson *13 Nov.*
			Maj Joseph Sailer *2 Dec.*
			Maj L. B. Robertshaw *24 Dec.*
			and Lt J. E. Kepke USMCR *25 Dec.*
			Capt C. A. Carlson *1 Jan.*
VMSB-131	TBF-1	12 Nov. 1942	Capt Jens C. Aggerbeck
VMSB-132	SBD-3	29 Oct. 1942	Maj Joseph Sailer *7 Dec.**
			Maj L. B. Robertshaw
VMSB-142	SBD-3	12 Nov. 1942	Maj Robert H. Richard
VMSB-233	SBD-4	12 Dec. 1942	Maj Clyde T. Madison *26 Dec.*
			Capt Elmer L. Gilbert
VMSB-234	SBD-4	28 Jan. 1943	Maj Otis B. Calhoun
VMF-223	F4F-4	20 Aug. 1942	Maj John L. Smith
VMF-224	F4F-4	30 Aug. 1942	Capt Robert E. Galer *31 Dec.*
			Maj Darrell D. Irwin USMCR
VMF-121	F4F-4	25 Sept. 1942	Maj Leonard K. Davis *16 Dec.*
			2nd Lt William F. Wilson *31 Dec.*
			Maj Donald K. Yost
VMF-212	F4F-4	3-16 Oct. 1942	LCol Harold W. Bauer *14 Nov.**
			Capt J. K. Little USMCR *20 Jan.*
			Capt R. F. Stout USMCR
VMF-112	F4F-4	2 Nov. 1942	Maj Paul J. Fontana

[1] The PBY and B-17 squadrons were based on various tenders or at Espiritu Santo.

UNITED STATES MARINE CORPS – *cont'd*

VMF-122	F4F-4	13 Nov. 1942	Capt Elmer E. Brackett
VMD-154 [2]	PB4Y-1	2 Dec 1942	LCol Elliott E. Bard
VMF-123	F4F-4	2 Feb. 1943	Maj Richard M. Baker

UNITED STATES ARMY AIR FORCE

Squadron	Type	Arrived	Commanding Officer
67th Fighter, *E*	P-400, P-38	22 Aug. 1942	Capt Dale D. Brannon *3 Oct.*
68th Fighter	P-40	8 Dec. 1942	Maj Robert M. Caldwell *8 Nov.*
			Lt Stanley A. Palmer *31 Dec.*
			Capt Robert B. Hubbell 27 *Jan.*
339th Fighter, *E*	P-38	3 Oct. 1942	Lt Fred V. Purnell
			Maj D. D. Brannon, *25 Nov.*
			Capt J. W. Mitchell
44th Fighter, *E*	P-40	22 Dec. 1942	Maj Kermit A. Taylor
12th Fighter, *E*	P-39	3 Jan. 1943	Maj Paul S. Bechtel *27 Jan.*
			Capt Theron J. Graves
70th Fighter, *E*	P-39, P-38	21 Dec. 1942	Maj Waldon Williams
17th Photo Recon.	F-5 [3]	17 Jan. 1943	Capt Richard T. W. Rivers
69th Bombardment	B-25, B-26	31 Dec. 1942	Maj James F. Collins
31st Bombardment	B-24	14 Jan. 1943	Maj George E. Glober

UNITED STATES NAVAL AIR ARM

Squadron	Type	Arrived	Commanding Officer
VS-5 of ENTERPRISE, *E*	SBD-3	24 Aug. 1942	Lt Turner F. Caldwell
VB-6 of ENTERPRISE, *E*	SBD-3	24 Aug. 1942	LCdr Ray Davis
VT-8 of SARATOGA, *E*	TBF-1	13 Sept. 1942	Lt Harold H. Larsen
VS-71 of WASP	SBD-3	28 Sept. 1942	Lt Porter W. Maxwell
VS-5-D14	OS2U-3	15 Oct. 1942	Lt Charles H. Franklin, USNR
VS-4-D14	OS2U-3	17 Dec. 1942	Lt John S. Farrington, USNR
VP-12 (Black Cats)	PBY-5A15	Dec. 1942	LCdr J.P. Fitzsimmons, *Dec.*
			Cdr C.O. Taff
VGS-11 [4]	F4F-4, TBF	1 Feb. 1943	LCdr Charles H. Ostrom
VGS-12	F4F-4, TBF	1 Feb. 1943	LCdr John Hulme
VGS-16	F4F-4, TBF	1 Feb. 1943	LCdr Charles E. Brunton

ROYAL NEW ZEALAND AIR FORCE

Squadron	Type	Arrived	Commanding Officer
9th Bomb Recon. *E*	Ventura	14 Nov. 1942	Sq Ldr H. M. MacFarlane
3rd Recon.	Hudson	24 Nov. 1942	Wing Cdr G. H. Fisher

[2] One photo plane of this squadron arrived 11 November. It, or another so equipped, discovered Munda Airfield 5 December 1942.

[3] P-38s equipped as photo planes.

[4] Escort Scouting Squadrons; **Avenger** torpedo planes with fighter escort.

APPENDIX I

Composition of U.S. Amphibious Force South Pacific (PHIBFORSOPAC) as of January 1943

USS *McCawley* (APA-4) FORCE FLAGSHIP

Cmdr R. H. Rodgers

TRANSPORT GROUP, SOUTH PACIFIC AMPHIBIOUS FORCE

Capt L. F. Reifsnider

COMTRANSDIV 2
    Capt I. N. Kiland
    APA-18 *President Jackson* (F)
    Cmdr C.W. Weitzel
    APA-20 *President Hayes*
    Cmdr F.W. Benson
    APA-19 *President Adams*
    Capt Frank H. Dean
    AKA-8 *Algorab*
    Capt J. R. Lannon

COMTRANSDIV 8
    Capt G.B. Ashe
    APA-17 *American Legion* (F)
    Cmdr R. C. Welles
    APA 27 *George Clymer*
    Capt A.T. Moen
    APA-21 *Crescent City*
    Capt J. R. Sullivan
    AKA-12 *Libra*
    Cmdr W.B. Fletcher
    AKA-6 *Alchiba*
    Cmdr H. R. Shaw

COMTRANSDIV 10
    Capt Lawrence F. Reifsnider
    APA-14 *Hunter Liggett* (F)
    Capt L.W. Perkins, USCG
    APA-23 *John Penn*
    Capt Harry W. Need
    AKA-9 *Alhena*
    Cmdr Howard W. Bradbury
    AKA-5 *Formalhaut*
    Cmdr Henry C. Flanagan

COMTRANSDIV 12
    Cmdr John D. Sweeney
    APD-6 *Stringham* (F)
    LCmdr Adolphe Wildner
    APD-1 *Manley*
    Lt Otto C. Schatz
    APD-5 *McKean*
    Lt Ralph L. Ramey
    APD-7 *Talbot*
    LCmdr Charles C. Morgan, USNR
    APD-8 *Waters*
    Charles J. McWhinnie, USNR
    APD-9 *Dent*
    LCmdr Ralph A. Wilhelm, USNR

COMTRANSDIV 14
    Capt Paul S. Theiss
    APA-15 *Harry T. Allen* (F)
    Capt Paul A. Stevens
    APA-7 *Fuller*
    Capt Henry E. Thornhill
    APA-4 *McCawley*
    Cmdr Robert H. Rodgers
    APA-13 *Titania*
    Cmdr Victor C. Barringer

COMTRANSDIV 16
    LCmdr James S. Willis
    APD-10 *Brooks* (F)
    LCmdr John W. Ramey
    APD-11 *Gilmer*
    LCmdr John S. Horner, USNR
    APD-14 *Humphreys*
    LCmdr Maurice J. Carley, USNR
    APD-13 *Sands*
    LCmdr John J. Branson

LANDING CRAFT FLOTILLAS

Rear Admiral George H. Fort

LST Flotilla Five

Capt Grayson B. Carter
LST Groups 13, 14, 15

LST GROUP 13	**LST GROUP 14**
Cmdr Roger W. Cutler	Cmdr Paul S. Slawson
LST Division 25	LST Division 27
LST-446	LST-166
LST-447 (FF)	LST-167
LST-448	LST-334
LST-449	LST-341
LST-460	LST-342 (GF)
LST-472	LST-390
LST Division 26	LST Division 28
LST-339	LST-71
LST-340 (FF)	LST-172
LST-395	LST-203
LST-396	LST-207
LST-397	LST-353
LST-398 (F)	LST-354

LCI Flotilla Five

Commander Chester L. Walton
LCI Groups 13, 14, 15

LCI GROUP 13 (LCI-67 Flag)	**LCI GROUP 14** (LCI-327 Flag)
LCmdr Marion M. Byrd	LCmdr Alfred V. Janotta, USNR
LCI Division 25	LCI Division 27
LCI-61 (F)	LCI-327 (F)
LCI-62	LCI-328
LCI-63	LCI-329
LCI-64	LCI-330
LCI-65	LCI-331
LCI-66	LCI-332
LCI Division 26	LCI Division 28
LCI (L)-21	LCI (L)-23
LCI (L)-22	LCI (L)-24
LCI-67 (F)	LCI-333
LCI-68	LCI-334
LCI-69	LCI-335
LCI-70	LCI-336

LCI GROUP 15

Cmdr J. McDonald Smith
LCI Division 29

LCI-222	LCI-223

LCT Flotilla Five

Lt Edgar Jaegar, USN

LCT Groups 13, 14, 15

LCT GROUP 13
Lt Ashton L. Jones
LCT Division 25
Lt A.L. Jones, USNR
LCT Division 26
Lt (jg) Ameel Z. Kouri, USNR

LCT GROUP 14
Lt Ashton L. Jones, USNR
LCT Division 27
Lt Decatur Jones, USNR
LCT Division 28
Lt (jg) Thomas B. Willard, USNR

LCT GROUP 15
Lt Laurence C. Lisle, USNR
LCT Division 29
Lt Laurence C. Lisle, USNR
LCT Division 30
Lt (jg) Frank M. Wiseman, USNR

By late January 1943 the ships and landing craft assigned to the Amphibious Force South Pacific had grown sufficiently, so that a new organization was established. However, only a few of the early birds had been formed up organizationally in the United States, much less trained in amphibious operations, before they convoyed at 8 knots or so to the South Pacific. Eventually, it was planned that the Landing Craft Flotillas, SOPAC, would include 37 LSTs, 36 LCIs, and 54 LCTs.

In addition to the ships and craft listed above, four more APDs and 50 coastal transports (APcs) were under order to report to COMPHIBFORSOPAC before they had even reached the stage of paper organization into divisions and squadrons. When they reported, the force would consist of more than 200 ships and large landing craft.*

* COMPHIBSOFORSOPAC letter, FE25/a3-1/Ser of 20 Jan. 1943, and CINCPAC's Organizational Roster dated 29 Jan. 1943.

APPENDIX J

Composition of U.S. Task Forces and Ground Force Organization for Operation TOENAILS in the Central Solomons July 1943

TF 31 AMPHIBIOUS FORCE

RAdm Richmond K. Turner in *McCawley*

(Relieved by RAdm Theodore S. Wilkinson, 15 July)

MGen John H. Hester, USA, Commander Ground Forces

(Relieved by MGen Oscar W. Griswold, USA, 15 July)

TG 31.1 WESTERN FORCE, RAdm Turner

ONAIAVISI Occupation Unit, TU 31.1.1, LCmdr Charles C. Morgan

Talbot (APD-7) and *Zane* (DMS-14) embarking 2 companies 169th Infantry, USA.
.

Rendova Advance Unit, TU 31.1.2, Cmdr John D. Sweeney

Waters (APD-8) and *Dent* (APD-9) embarking Companies C and G of 172^d Regimental Combat Team.

1st **Echelon**, TU 31.1.3 RAdm. Turner

Transport Division, TU 31.1.31: Capt Paul S. Theiss, transports, *McCawley* (APA-4), *President Jackson* (APA-18), *President Adams* (APA-19), *President Hayes* (APA-20), *Algorab* (AKA-8), and *Libra* (AKA-12), embarking 1st Echelon Western Landing Force, most of 172^d RCT.

Destroyer Screen/Fire Support

Screening Group TG 31.2 Capt T. J. Ryan Jr.

Fire Support Unit TU 31.2.1 Capt Ryan

Ralph Talbot (DD-390), *Buchanan* (DD-484), *McCalla* (DD-488), *Farenholt* (F) (DD-491)

Anti-Submarine Unit TU 31.2.2 Cmdr J. M. Higgins

Gwin (DD-433), *Radford* (DD-446), *Jenkins* (DD-447), *Woodworth* (DD-460)

MTB Squadron, TU 31.1.4 LCmdr Robert B. Kelly

MTBs 118, 151, 153, 154, 155, 156, 157, 158, 159, 160, 161, 162.

1st Echelon Western Landing Force, MGen John W. Hester

43rd Infantry Division (designated units); 9th Marine Defense Battalion; 1st Fiji Infantry (designated unit); 136th Field Artillery Battalion; and 4th Marine Raider Battalion (designated units).

Naval Base Force Capt C. E. Olsen

24th Naval Construction Battalion (less designated units)

Naval Base Units.

Headquarters: Assault Flotillas, Capt Paul S. Theiss.

Headquarters: New Georgia Air Force, BGen Francis P. Mulcahy, USMC.

2^d Echelon Movement Western Group TU 31.1.5,

Capt Grayson B. Carter in LST-354

Flot 5 LSTs 354, 395, 396, 397, and Flot 5 LCIs 61, 64, 66, 70 and 222 under Cmdr J. McDonald Smith embarking 2^d Echelon Western Landing Force, LCol Charles W. Hill, USA.

Escort Unit *Farenholt, Buchanan, Gwin*

43rd Infantry (designated units); 9th Marine Defense Battalion (designated units); and 192^d Field Artillery (designated units).

3rd Echelon Movement Western Group TU 31.1.6, Cmdr Paul S. Slawson

LST Unit, Cmdr Slawson

Flot 5 LSTs 342 (F), 353, 398, 399 embarking 3rd Echelon Western Landing Force. 24th Construction Battalion (designated units) and 9th Marine Defense Battalion (designated units).

4th Echelon Movement Western Group TU 31.1.7, Capt John S. Crenshaw

Flot 5 LSTs 343 (F), 472 and Flot 5 LCIs 61, 62, 64, 65, 66, and 222, Cmdr J. MacDonald Smith.

Reserve MTB Group TG 31.4, Cmdr Allen P. Calvert: 12 PTs.

Service Unit 31.1.8, Lt (jg) Charles H. Stedman

Tugs *Vireo* and *Rail* and two Pontoon Assembly Barges (PAB).

TG 36.1 Northern Landing Group

Escort Group: RAdm W. L. Ainsworth, Commander

Transports: Cmdr Stanley Leith

APDs *Dent, Talbot, Waters, McKean, Kilty, Crosby, Schley,* and DD *McCalla*

Screening Unit: *Woodworth, Gwin,* and *Radford*

Mine Group: *Hopkins, Trevor,* and DD *Ralph Talbot*

Landing Force: Col Harry B. Liversedge, USMC, Commander

One battalion each from 145th and 148th Infantry, 37th Division and the 1st Raider Battalion, 1st Marine Raider Regiment.

TG 31.3 Eastern Force (Group)

RAdm George H. Fort

Viru Harbor Occupation Group TU 31.3.1, Cmdr Stanley Leith

Advance Unit, LCol Michael S. Currin, USMC: 4th Marine Raider Battalion (designated companies).

1st Echelon TU 31.3.11 Cmdr Leith: *Hopkins* (DMS-13) (F), *Kilty* (APD-15), *Crosby* (APD-17).

2[d] Echelon TU 32.3.12, Lt B.F. Seligman, USNR: APc-24 and Flot 5 LCTs 134, 330, 369.

3rd Echelon TU 31.3.13, Lt. D. Mann, USNR: APcs 23, 25 and Flot 5 LCTs 139, 180, 326, 327, 351.

4th Echelon TU 31.3.14: sailed with the 3rd Echelon and are included above.

Landing Force

103rd Infantry Regiment (designated company); 20th Naval Construction Battalion (designated company); 70th Coast Artillery (designated battery); and Naval Base Units.

TU 31.3.2 Segi Point Occupation Group, Capt Benton W. Decker

1st Echelon TU 31.3.21, Capt Decker

First Section: APc-23 (F) and Flot 5 LCIs 21, 22, 67, 68, 69.

Second Section: Flot 5 LSTs 339 and 341.

2[d] Echelon TU 31.3.22, Lt W.C. Margetts, USNR: APc-27 and Flot 5/6 LCTs 58, 62, 129, 323.

3rd Echelon TU 31.3.23, Lt E.M. Jaeger, USNR: APc-28 and Flot 5 LCTs 66, 67, 128, 324.

4th Echelon TU 31.3.24, Lt (jg) E. H. George, USNR: APc-29 and Flot 5 LCTs 146, 156, 159, 322.

Landing Force

103rd Regimental Combat Team (designated units); ACORN Seven; 70th Coast Artillery (designated units); and Naval Base Units.

TU 31.3.3 Wickham Anchorage Occupation Group, RAdm Fort

1ˢᵗ Echelon TU 31.3.31, RAdm Fort

First Section: *Trevor* (DMS-16) (F), *McKean* (APD-5), *Schley* (APD-14)

Flot 5 LCIs 24, 223, 332, 333, 334, 335, 336.

Second Section: APc-35 and Flot 5 LCTs 63, 133, 482.

2ᵈ Echelon TU 31.3.32, Lt (jg) K. L. Otto, USNR

APc-36 and Flot 5/6 LCTs 60, 127, 144.

3ʳᵈ Echelon TU 31.3.33, Lt A. W. Bergstrom, USNR

APc-37 and Flots 5/6 LCTs 132, 145, 325, 367, 461.

4ᵗʰ Echelon TU 31.3.34 Lt Parker

APc-26 and Flot 5 LCTs 158, 352, 377.

Russell Islands Motor Torpedo Boat Squadron, 12 PTs, Lt Alvin P. Cluster.

Landing Force

103ʳᵈ Regimental Combat Team (designated unit); 4ᵗʰ Marine Raider Battalion (designated unit); 20ᵗʰ Naval Construction Battalion (designated unit); 70ᵗʰ Coast Artillery Battalion (designated anti-aircraft units); and 152ᵈ Field Artillery Battalion (designated unit).

TF 33 Air Force South Pacific, VAdm Aubrey W. Fitch

Solomon Islands Air Force, RAdm Marc A. Mitscher

Included in the Task Organization but not directly participating, were the following groups of combat ships organized as TF 36 covering force, under Adm Halsey's direct command: 2 Carriers, 9 Cruisers, 13 Destroyers, 4 Minelayers, 11 Submarines, plus 2 Battleship divisions, and 1 Escort Carrier division.

TOENAILS was the first major operation in the South Pacific in which the small coastal transport, the APc, participated. These small and slow woodenhulled craft were 103-feet long, displaced 258 tons, and made 10 knots with a fair breeze at their sterns.

The above listings for amphibious ships and craft were compiled from the issued revisions to the basic orders, war diaries, action reports, and dispatches by VAdm Dyer in the 1960s and are believed to be far more accurate than data published earlier.

APPENDIX K

Composition of the III Amphibious Force Task Units
For the Occupation of Vella Lavella
15 August 1943

III AMPHIBIOUS FORCE
RAdm Theodore S. Wilkinson, in *Cony*

TransDiv Twenty-two, LCmdr Robert H. Wilkinson

TASK UNIT 31.5.1
Advanced Transport Group, Capt Thomas J. Ryan, Jr.
TransDiv Twelve, Cmdr John D. Sweeney
Stringham, Waters, Dent, Talbot
TransDiv Twenty-two, LCmdr Robert H. Wilkinson
Kilty (F), *McKean, Ward*
Destroyer Screen, Capt Ryan (ComDesDiv 41)
Nicholas, O'Bannon, Taylor, Chevalier, Cony, Pringle

TASK UNIT 31.5.2
Second Transport Group, Capt William R. Cooke, Jr.
LCI Unit, Cmdr James M. Smith
LCIs 21, 22, 23, 61, 67, 68, 222 (F), 322, 330, 331, 333, 334
Destroyer Screen, Capt Cooke, Jr. (ComDesDiv 43)
Waller, Philip, Saufley, Renshaw

TASK UNIT 31.5.3
Third Transport Group, Capt Grayson B. Carter
LSTs 354, 395, 399
Screen, Cmdr James R. Pahl (ComDesDiv 44)
Conway (F), *Eaton,* SCs 760, 761

SCREEN
DesDiv 41, 43, and 44*
MTB Flotilla CAST, Cmdr Allen P. Calvert
New Georgia MTBs: 18 MTBs   Kolombangara MTBs: 8 MTBs

Northern Landing Force, BGen Robert B. McClure, USA
Troops
Headquarters Detachment
4th Marine Defense Battalion (less certain detachments)
35th Regimental Combat Team, USA (less certain detachments)
Naval Base Force, Capt George C. Kriner
58th Naval Construction Battalion (less rear echelon)
Naval Base Units including Boat Pool No. 9

Total: About 4,600 officers and men

---

* After performing convoy duty to Barakoma beach these destroyers were to form a screen
for landing operations.

APPENDIX L

Composition of the III Amphibious Force, Task Force 31 Main Body Northern Force, for the Empress Augusta Landing on Bougainville – 1 November 1943

III AMPHIBIOUS FORCE

RAdm Theodore S. Wilkinson in *George Clymer*

MAIN BODY, NORTHERN FORCE

Transport Group, Commodore Lawrence F. Reifsnider in *Hunter Liggett*
  TransDiv (Able) (APAs), Capt Anton B. Anderson
    President Jackson, (F), President Adams, President Hayes, George Clymer (FF)
  TransDiv (Baker) (APs/APAs), Capt George B. Ashe
    American Legion, (F), Hunter Liggett, Crescent City, Fuller
  TransDiv (Charlie) (AKs/AKAs), Capt Hentry E. Thornhill
    Alhena, Alchiba (F), *Libra, Titania*

Screen Group, Capt Ralph Earle, Jr. (ComDesRon 45)
    Fullam (F), *Bennett, Guest, Hudson, Conway, Anthony, Wadsworth, Terry, Braine, Sigourney, Renshaw*

Minecraft Group, Cmdr Wayne R. Loud
    Destroyer-Minesweepers: *Hopkins, Hovey, Dorsey, Southard*
    Minelayers: *Conflict, Advent, Daring, Adroit*
    Small Minesweepers: YMSs 96, 197, 238, 243
    Special Minelaying Group: *Breese, Sicard, Gamble*

Salvage Group, Fleet Tugs: *Apache* and *Sioux*

Landing Force – The initial landing force for the Cape Torokina landing at Empress Augusta Bay was the 3rd Marine Division, reinforced (less 21st RCT and a few other troops reserved for later echelons). The 3rd MarDiv was commanded by MGen A. H. Turnage, USMC.

  Other components of the landing force consisted of: 2[d] Provisional Raider Regiment; 3rd Defense Bn. (less detachments); Corps Troops assigned ComGen IMAC; Detachment Hdqtrs. ComAirNorSols, including ARGUS 5; Detachment Naval Base Unit No. 7, including Communication Unit No. 7; and Boat Pool No. 11.

  Total Personnel – 14,321

APPENDIX M
COMBATANT Ship Losses of the U.S. Navy – 1940-1945 [1]

	Total Ships[2]	Ships Lost[3]	% Ships Lost[4]
Aircraft Carriers			
-CV Fleet Aircraft Carriers	24	4	16.66%
-CVL Light Aircraft Carriers	9	1	11.11%
-CVE Escort Aircraft Carriers	77	6	7.79%
BB Battleships	25	2	8.00%
Cruisers			
-CB Large Cruisers	2	-	-
-CA Heavy Cruisers	30	6	20.00%
-CL Light Cruisers	52	3	5.77%
DD Destroyers	598	71	11.87%
DE Destroyer Escorts	421	11	2.61%
SS Submarines	321	50	15.58%
Minecraft	844	26	3.08%
Patrol Craft	1,109	31	2.79%
Motor Torpedo Boats	743	55	7.40%
U.S. Coast Guard Cutters (Cruising and Patrol)	117	5	4.27%
Additional Combatants [5]			
-AKA Attack Cargo Ships	127	-	-
-APA Attack Transports	227	2	.09%
-APD High-Speed Transports			
-Converted Destroyers (DD)	32	8	25.00%
-Converted Destroyer Escorts (DE)	95	1	1.05%
Amphibious Landing Ships & Craft [6]			
-LSV Landing Ships Vehicle	6	-	-
-LSD Landing Ships, Dock	18	-	-
-LST Landing Ships, Tank	913	41	4.49%
-LSM Landing Ships, Medium	474	9	1.90%
-LSM (R) Landing Ships, Medium (Rocket)	50	3	6.00%
-LC (FF) Landing Craft, Flotilla Flagships	49	-	-
-LCI (G) Landing Craft, Infantry (Gunboat)	218	8	3.67%
-LCI (L) Landing Craft, Infantry (Large)	905	16	1.78%
-LCI (M) Landing Craft, Infantry (Mortar)	60	-	-
-LCI (R) Landing Craft, Infantry (Rocket)	52	-	-
-LCS (L) Landing Craft, Support (Large)	130	6	4.62%
-LCT Landing Craft, Tanks (Marks V and VI)	1,435	75	5.23%
TOTALS:	9,162	440	

[1] Morison, *History of United States Naval Operations in World War II*, Vol. XV, pp. 29-74; Principle reference works cited include: *Ships Data US Naval Vessels*, editions of 1943, 1945 and 1949; *United States Naval Vessels* (ONI 222-US) 1 September 1945; Comairpac *Index of United States Fleet,* 1 Dec. 1944; and K. Jack Bauer's ms, "Ships of the United States Navy, 1775-1945."
[2] Ship counts will vary somewhat due to ship conversions and/or transfers under Lend-Lease. Note: Ship losses have not been deducted from ship totals.
[3] Number of ships lost in combat or by accident, 27 June 1940 - 2 September 1945.
[4] Percent of ships lost computed by author/editor of this book.
[5] Most sailormen we've talked too consider the vessels listed under Additional Combatants and Amphibious Landing Ships and Craft worthy of the classification, "Combatants." So do we. Consider this: On 14 March 1942, and 10 April 1942 respectively, the Amphibious Forces of the Atlantic and Pacific Fleets were created in accordance with instructions from COMINCH and in due time all amphibious units within the two Fleets were assigned to them. Organizational rosters issued close to these dates show that there were twelve APs, four AKs and two APDs in the Atlantic Fleet and six APs, two AKs and three APDs in the Pacific Fleet, when the Amphibious Forces were established as separate entities. And this was only four to five months before Guadalcanal. (The additional A for attack was not added to the designations until 1 Feb. 1943.)
[6] Sources for unnamed vessel losses include James C. Fahey's *Ships and Aircraft of the United States Fleet* and Seaweed's *Ships History – World War II Losses.*

SOURCES

I have drawn on numerous sources for this volume. The primary sources are listed below. If a reader wishes to research his or her career and any ships he or she might have served on, a complete story can be obtained by visiting or writing the places listed below. If by chance the data desired are not at these places, the capable personnel there will be able to direct you to where to look.

A. U.S. Government

1. Archives and Records Sources

a) *National Personnel Records Center (Military Personnel Records) 9700 Page Blvd., St. Louis, MO 63132-5100;* TEL: 314-538-4141 (Navy/Marine Corps/Coast Guard).

When phoning the above number you will receive a taped message. You can leave your name and address and the center will send you the proper form to fill out. You can also fax your request to 314-538-4175. Response will be made by U.S. Mail.

This Center maintains individual Personnel Records ("service records") and Medical Records (only to 16 October 1992) of Navy Commissioned officers and enlisted personnel, Marine Corps officers and enlisted personnel, U.S. Air Force Commissioned Officers and enlisted personnel and Army Commissioned Officers and enlisted personnel. The Center honors requests for information at no charge for veterans and members of their immediate families. Write and request Standard Form 180 to submit inquiry.

Author's note: If you plan to research your own story or that of an immediate relative, start here. It will give you important leads; specific dates when/where you served, on ships or shore duty.

b) *National Archives, Textual Reference Branch, 700 Pennsylvania Avenue, NW, Washington, D.C. 20408;* TEL: 202-501-5305.

This branch holds all records prior to 1 January 1941 and has no World War II material on file.

c) *National Archives II, Textual Reference Branch, 8601 Adelphi Road, College Park, MD 20740;* TEL: 301-713-7230 (textual material) or 301-713-6795 (photographic material).

The Textual Reference Branch in National Archives II maintains the deck logs of navy ships dating from 1 January 1941 through 31 December 1961.

A very large majority of all World War II War Diaries, Operational Plans, Action Reports, Damage Reports, etc. formally kept at the Operational Archives Branch, Naval Historical Center was transferred to "NATIONAL ARCHIVES II" in June 1996. This includes Action Reports from Commander-in-Chief, Pacific Fleet and Commander, Service Squadron, South Pacific Force.

d) *Department of the Navy, Naval Historical Center, Washington Navy Yard, 901 M Street, SE, Washington, DC 20374-5060;* TEL: 202-433-4132 (Navy Library), 202-433-6773 or 76 (Ships Histories Branch), 202-433-2765 (Photo Archives Section); 202-433-3224 (Operational Archives Branch).

The Deck Log Division of the Ships Histories Branch of the Naval Historical Center has control of all ships deck logs of navy ships dating from 1 January 1962 to present. For that period inquiries have to be made through that office to gain access to the logs. They are stored in the Suitland Records Center.

The Ships Histories Branch also contains data on individual ships filed alphabetically by the name. These files contain a wealth of source material other than deck logs not found in any other Archives. Copies of Citations, Action Reports, War Diaries, etc. may also be found in these files, especially those ships that served in World War II. Files are also kept on unnamed ships, such as LSTs, but these files are not complete.

The Navy Library has extensive collections of World War II publications such as the "Combat Narrative" monograph series (32 booklets), put out by the Office of Naval Intelligence shortly after the battles had been fought; the "Battle Experience" series (26 booklets), put out by Headquarters, Commander-in-Chief, Pacific Fleet and "United States Strategic Bombing Survey" Reports. While the publications are antiquated by research from World War II to the present, they are extremely useful in showing the thinking, policies, impressions, etc. of the time. In addition, they have marvelous illustrations.

Just at right angles to the building, on the right side of Leutze Oark is the Marine Corps Historical Center. Their library, while not as extensive as the Navy Library, is very good for its size and holds Marine Corps World War II publications. If research includes Marine Corps actions in the War, one should visit the library while there and stop in at the Research Branch across the floor from the library. The Research branch also holds valuable data on Marine Corps actions.

A very large majority of all World War II War Diaries, Operational Plans, Action Reports, Damage Reports, etc., formerly kept at the Operational Archives Branch, was transferred to "National Archives II." Call them to see what remains.

2. Other Sources of Information (Textual and Photographic)

a) *History Division, Photographic Section, United States Naval Institute, United States Naval Academy, 118 Maryland Avenue, Annapolis, MD 21402-5035;* TEL: 410-295-1022 or 295-1020.

This organization has a wealth of photography of U.S. Naval Ships from 1775 to present. It is easily accessible and less costly to purchase photographs from them than it is from "National Archives II." It is recommended that you try here first. A quantity of reference material is also available.

b) *Special Collections and Archives Division, Nimitz Library, United States Naval Academy, 589 McNair Road, Annapolis, MD 21402-5029;* TEL: 410-293-6903.

The Nimitz Library has a wealth of textual material covering all periods. Photographic reference material in the library is very limited. Entrance to the library is supposedly restricted to Naval Academy associated personnel. Anyone else desiring to use the library to conduct research should first write or call to get permission. This is just a formality, but required. Permission is usually given.

c) *Government Photographic Sources*

Department of the Navy, Nimitz Library Special Collections and Archives Division, United States Naval Academy, 589 McNair Road, Annapolis, MD 21402-5029; (301) 267-2220.

National Air and Space Museum, Archives Division, Smithsonian Institution, Washington, D.C. 20560; (202) 357-3133 A3.

Naval Historical Center, Photographic Section, Washington Navy Yard, Building 108, Washington, D.C. 20374-5060; (202) 433-2765. National Archives at College Park, Nontextual Division, Still Pictures Branch (NNSP), 8601 Adelphi Road, College Park, MD 20740-6001; (301) 713-6660.

d) *Veterans Associations and their Newsletters*

Additional information is available through the following newsletters:

1.   Four Stack APD Veterans. The *Four Stacker Quarterly.* Annual dues: $15. Phone: (619) 282-0971; Fax: (619) 528-0961; E-mail: apdsec@att.net. Four Stack APD Veterans, Curt Clark, Secretary. 3384 Grim Ave., San Diego, CA 92104-4654.

2.   LCT Flotillas of WWII ETO-PTO. Phone: (615) 865-0579; E-mail: hefarmer@home.com. H.E. "Bud" Farmer, Reunion Chairman. 1312 Cheshire Dr., Nashville, TN 37207-1508.

3.   Guadalcanal Campaign Veterans, *Guadalcanal Echoes.* Annual dues: $12. Phone: (708) 457-0453. Joe Micek, Editor. 4935 Frank Parkway, Norridge, IL 60706-3231.

4.   The Association of Gunner's Mates. *Guns.* Quarterly. Annual dues: $25. Phone: (219) 845-3747; E-mail: JPGUNSED@aol.com. Jack Photenhauer, Director. P.O. Box 247, Hammond, IN 46325.

5.   United States LST Association. *LST Scuttlebutt Newsletter.* Annual dues: $18. Phone: 1-800-228-5870; Fax: 1-419-693-1265; E-mail: uslst@kmbs.com. Website: www.uslst.org. Milan Gunjak, President. P.O. Box 167438, Oregon, Ohio 43616-7438.

6.   USS LCI National Association, Inc. *Elsie Item Newsletter.* Annual dues: $10. Phone: (904) 775-1521; E-mail: jet310@earthlink.net. Website: www.usslci.com. James E. Talbert, President. 147 Colburn Drive, Debary, FL 32713.

NOTES

Chapter 1. Strategic Decisions (p. 3 - 16)

1. This decision was confirmed at the "Arcadia" conference between Roosevelt and Churchill at Washington in early Jan. 1942.

2. Their planning committee even made the tentative suggestion to reevaluate the basic strategic concept of the war if the British refused to launch a European offensive in 1942, "in order to consider the possibility of concentrating U. S. offensive effort in the Pacific Area." This tentative feeler became more emphatic In June, when it looked as if the British were stalling.

3. Robert L. Ghormley, b. Portland, Oregon, 1883, Naval Academy 1906. Earlier responsibilities included C.O. *Nevada* 1935-36, on staff of C. in C. Admiral Hepburn 1936. Head of war plans division, office of C.N.O. 1938-39, Asst. Chief of Naval Operations 1939-40, special naval observer London 1940-42; died 1958.

4. Before the Guadalcanal campaign opened McCain shifted his flag to *Curtiss* and moved to Efate; later to Espiritu Santo.

5. The danger was that the Japanese 25th Air Flotilla at Rabaul would bomb the hell out of any Marines in Tulagi before we had any air base nearer to it than Townsville, Australia, about 1000 miles distant.

6. Admiral Ghormley observed in a memo to Cincpac of 1 Oct. 1942 that the original base plans of Feb.–Mar. 1942 called for Auckland to be the major and Tongatabu the minor Sopac bases, Nouméa being reserved for the Army. Consequently New Zealand, Tongatabu, Samoa, Bora Bora, Fiji and Efate had priority in base development, to the neglect of Nouméa. He had urged before leaving the U. S. that reservoirs of base materials and personnel (Cubs, Acorns, etc.) be established in New Zealand ready to be sent where the strategic situation demanded, but this was not done. The area was still dependent on shipments from the U. S. to fill urgent needs. Hence Nouméa and Espiritu Santo were suddenly overwhelmed with material for the Guadalcanal campaign, and bad unloading bottlenecks developed.

7. Nimitz also predicted a second Japanese attempt to take Port Moresby, but thought it would be made by sea like the first.

8. *Del Brazil, Electra, Lipscomb, Lykes, Alcyone, Libra, George F. Elliot, Barnet, Mizar* and *Aichiba* were the AKs.

9. Richmond Kelly Turner, b. Portland, Oregon, 1885, Naval Academy 1908 (5th in class); attained his first command, of a destroyer, in 1913 and served in *Pennsylvania, Michigan* and *Mississippi* as gunnery officer during World War I. Ordnance duty ashore for 3 years, gunnery officer on staff of Commander Scouting Fleet 1923, C.O. *Mervine* 1924-25, trained as a naval aviator, commanded aircraft squadrons Asiatic Fleet 1928 and headed plans section Buaer 1929-31. Technical adviser on naval aviation to American delegation at Geneva Disarmament Conference. "Exec." of *Saratoga* and chief of staff to Commander Aircraft Battle Force 1933-35. Took senior course at War College and served on staff. C.O. *Astoria* 1938-40. Director War Plans Division C.N.O. 1940-42, also assistant chief of staff to Admiral King 1941-42 when appointed Commander Amphibious Force South Pacific Force. At the time Admiral King became Chief of Naval Operations in March, Turner was eager for a sea command; but King, who knew his ability, had kept him in Washington as an assistant chief of staff in order to save him for the Solomons show, which might be described as a sea command plus.

Chapter 2. The Landings (p. 17 - 38)

10. This account follows closely that of the excellent O.N.I. Combat Narrative *The Landings in the Solomons,* (1943); additional details from General Vandegrift "Division Commander's Final Report on Guadalcanal Operations Phase II" 24 May 1943; Maj. John L. Zimmerman USMCR, Marine Corps historical monograph *The Guadalcanal Campaign* (I saw only the 1st preliminary draft, Sept. 1948); Action Reports of individual ships; statements by participants; personal examination of the terrain Apr. 1943.

11. East Longitude dates, Zone minus 11 time. The Japanese constantly employed Tokyo time, Zone minus 9; Allied task forces were not consistent.

12. Admiral R. K. Turner's War Diary for 18-30 July, Comsopac Op Plan No. 1 of 16 July, Task Force 62 Op Plan A3-42 of 30 July 1942.

13. The first dispatch from Tulagi notifying Rabaul of the approach of surface forces was dated 0635 and received 0725, our time.

14. In all the early reports and charts the Ilu and Tenaru Rivers are confused. The one that bordered Beach "Red" is the Tenaru; the one about 2 miles to the westward, where the battle of 21 August took place, is the Ilu. Beach "Red" was selected as lying about halfway between 2 points where the enemy was supposed to be in force; but there were none at the eastern point.

15. The North African landings began in darkness because the Army so wished it; but the Navy ran the war in the Pacific and conducted all major landings in daylight to prevent confusion.

16. Intelligence summary in Crudiv 6 Battle Report (WDC No. 160, 997).

17. Same general sources as in note 10. The Action Report of *Heywood* Capt. H.B. Knowles, is most valuable for Gavutu.

18. The numbers of these hills usually, as here, designated their height in feet above tidewater.

19. *Buchanan* and *Monssen* had stood by Gavutu and Tanambogo since the afternoon of the 7th. With the aid of Lt. G.H. Howe, RANR, who knew those waters, as pilot, they circled the islands and threaded the reefs again and again, giving most valuable fire support to the troops. Rear Admiral Scott's Action Report.

20. O.N.I. Combat Narrative *Landing in the Solomons* pp. 47-50, 59-62 for the defense; Daily War Report of 25th Air Flotilla at Rabaul (WDC No. 161,730, National Archives No. 12,264, trans. by Lt. Pineau) for the enemy. This document reveals that the Japanese bombers were also looking for our carriers but failed to locate them.

Chapter 3. The Six-Month Struggle for Guadalcanal (p. 39 - 226)

21. *The Discovery of the Solomon Islands by Alvaro de Mendaña in 1568,* ed. by Lord Amherst and Basil Thomson, a Hakluyt Society Publication of 1901, contains the best account of the early history of these Islands.

22. (1) Savo Island, 9 Aug.; (2) Eastern Solomons, 23-25 Aug.; (3) Cape Esperance, 11-12 Oct.; (4) Santa Cruz Islands, 26 Oct.; (5) Guadalcanal, 13-15 Nov.; (6) Tassafaronga, 30 Nov. 1942.

23. The Battle of Rennell Island, 29-30 Jan. 1943.

24. Alexander A. Vandegrift, b. Virginia 1887; after 2 years in the University, commissioned 2nd Lt. USMC; fought in Nicaragua, at Vera Cruz and in Haiti; assistant chief of staff, Fleet Marine Force, 1933-35; commanded Marine Embassy Guard, Pekin, two years; assistant to Commandant 1937-41; C.O. 1st Marine Div., 1 Apr. 1942; C.O. Marine Amphibious Corps with rank of Lieut. Gen., 10 July 1943; Commandant Marine Corps, 1944-47.

25. *The Coast Guard at War, the Pacific Landings,* VI (15 Mar. 1946); information from Mr. Frank R. Eldridge. Nineteen of the 23 transports and APDs in the landing force carried coastguardsmen, and several of their surfmen and coxswains distinguished themselves handling landing craft.

26. Every ship in this battle excepting *Jarvis* submitted an Action Report. Admiral Turner made none, but early in 1943 Admiral A.J. Hepburn conducted for Cominch an investigation of the facts. His "Report of Informal Inquiry into Circumstances Attending Loss of U.S.S. *Vincennes*... on Aug. 9, 1942 in the Vicinity of Savo Island" 13 May 1943 is brief; but is accompanied by a valuable Appendix, a collection of statements by about 100 officers and men. This Appendix is wanting in all but two existing copies of the Report, one of which I have used. Beginning in April 1943, I have frequently discussed the battle with key officers who participated. After the war the usual interrogations of Japanese officers were made and appear in *Inter. Jap. Off.* The Japanese after the war prepared, for ATIS, "Historical Reports, Naval Operations" 15 Mar. 1946, which include one on this battle (ATIS 15685). Several War Diaries of enemy ships are in the Washington Document Center. Concurrently with research on this chapter, Commo. R.W. Bates and Cdr. W. D. Innis were making the *War College Analysis* for the Naval War College. It is a far more thorough investigation than Admiral Hepburn could or did make in 1943, and I am more indebted to it than to any other source, although it was still incomplete when this volume went to press. Finally, in June 1949, Lt. Roger Pineau USNR of my staff went over this chapter with Admiral Mikawa, Capt. T. Omae, his chief of staff in the Battle, and Capt. Watanabe of Yamamoto's staff, who had gone to Rabaul immediately after the Battle to investigate. They made sundry suggestions which, if accepted, are incorporated here.

27. At this time numerous-troop and supply convoys were making heavy demands on Japanese destroyers. On such short notice it was impossible for Mikawa to round up more than the single destroyer. Lack of an adequate anti-submarine screen was to cost him a heavy cruiser.

28. From ships' logs of Admiral Fletcher's task force I obtain these figures of gallons fuel oil on hand at 0000 or 1200 Aug. 8 (it is not clear which); they are to the nearest thousand gallons: *Saratoga,* 1,149,000; *Enterprise,* 521,000; *Wasp* records lost; *North Carolina,* 878,000; *Balch,* 73,000; *Maury,* 70,000; *Gwin,* 88,000; *Benham,* 68,000; *Grayson,* 40,000; *Lang,* 72,000; *Sterett,* 59,000; *Stack,* 64,000; *Laffey,* 94,000; *Farenholt,* 68,000. The destroyers' daily expenditures varied from 12,000 to 24,000 and their total capacity from 127,000 to 184,000. In the *Saratoga* group *Dale* had just been topped off and was 97 per cent full; the other five averaged three quarters full. The cruisers with capacity of 618,000 to 839,000 gallons were half full or better. Thus it is idle to pretend that there was any urgent fuel shortage in this force. *War College Analysis* states that Fletcher's real reason for retirement was fear of exposing his carriers to air attack, and severely criticizes him for failure to consult with Turner by radio.

29. *Jarvis,* badly hit in the air attack of 8 August, departed Lunga Roads at midnight. Her C.O., Lt. Cdr. William W. Graham, a capable and conscientious officer, was eager to get to Sydney where destroyer tender *Dobbin* was stationed in order to obtain immediate repairs and rejoin the Fleet. He had been ordered by Admiral Turner to wait for an escort and depart by an eastern channel, but it is not clear whether he received the orders.

30. *Chicago's* story does not check with *Patterson's,* particularly as to who was illuminating what; the *War College Analysis* agrees with my guess.

31. Japanese reports of this are contradictory and incomplete. Our sources: *Campaigns of the Pacific War* (USSBS No. 255); *Inter. Jap. Off.;* Cent. Intell. Group Reports No. OOW45 (74633), OOW63 (86297). Both as to times and movements our chart reconciles discrepancies as far as possible.

32. The Navy concealed its losses in order to keep the enemy guessing until 12 Oct., when it was able at the same time to announce a victory.

33. Tabulation by Medical Statistics Division, Bureau of Medicine, Navy Dept.; *Canberra's* from her Action Report:

Ship	Killed or Died of Wounds	Wounded
CANBERRA	84	55
CHICAGO	2	21
VINCENNES	332	258
QUINCY	370	167
ASTORIA	216	186
RALPH TALBOT	11	11
PATTERSON	8	11
Total	1023	709

It is not known how many men *Jarvis* lost during the battle, since she went down with all hands—247—in an air attack later in the day.

34. Information about the Battle of Savo Island available during the last six years has been so spotty that a number of myths have grown up, which may be briefly dealt with here. (1) That placing a British admiral in command of U.S. naval vessels was responsible. Answer: Turner approved Crutchley's dispositions and C. was absent from the actual battle. (2) That the C.O.'s of *Vincennes, Chicago* and other ships knew by noon of 8 August the Japs were coming but miscalculated their speed, or were improperly informed by Turner. Answer: The information the C.O.'s had was based on the contacts with Mikawa's force on 7 August; Turner sent them the important 8 August contact report as soon as he got it. (3) That Admiral Ghormley was responsible as overall commander and was relieved as a consequence. Answer: Ghormley in Nouméa was able to exercise a general strategic direction only; he was not relieved until mid-October, and then for other reasons. (4) That during the battle *McCawley* warned the Marines ashore that Japs were landing on Beach "Red," Guadalcanal. Answer: No such messages went out or were received; there was a brief alarm of possible enemy landing craft off the shore on the night of 7-8 August which probably gave rise to the yarn.

35. Commanding General 1st Marine Division (General Vandegrift) "Final Report on Guadalcanal Operation"; Maj. John L. Zimmerman of Marine Corps Historical Division *The Guadalcanal Campaign* (seen in preliminary draft); Brig. Gen. Pedro del Valle "Marine Artillery on Guadalcanal; The Story of the 11th Marines" *Marine Corps Gazette* XXVII No. 7 (Nov. 1943), XXVIII Nos. 1, 2 (Jan., Feb. 1944) and the Army Historical Division monograph *Guadalcanal: The First Offensive* (also in preparation) by John

Miller, a former Marine, are my principal authorities for these and all other ground and land-based air operations described in this volume. Of the non-official works, John A. DeChant *Devilbirds* (1947) is the most useful.

36. Op Order A6-42; TF War Diary; sound recording by survivor M.W. Raderman, Office of Naval Records 24 Aug. 1943.

37. Originally so called, then changed to Battle of Ilu River, owing to an original error in identifying the stream; but when this volume was in press the Marine Corps officially renamed it Tenaru.

38. VMF-223 and VMSB-232. For complete list of Marine Corps and other plane squadrons at Guadalcanal, see Appendix.

39. Roy Stanley Geiger, b. Florida 1885; after graduating LL.B. Stetson 1907 enlisted in Marine Corps; 2nd Lt. 1909. One of the earliest Marines to qualify as an aviator, he served as such in World War I and later in Hispaniola and Nicaragua. Command and General Staff School, 1925; Army and Naval War College courses; C.O. 1st Marine Air Wing, 1942; Com. I 'Phib Corps 1943; Com. III 'Phib Corps 1944; and of Tenth Army at Okinawa 1945. On active duty as Lt. Gen. USMC at his death, 23 Jan. 1947.

40. Budocks *Building the Navy's Bases in World War II* (2 vols.); "History of the 6th U.S. Naval Construction Battalion" compiled by Seaman Tom O'Reilly and edited by Ens. R.H. Gedney; Summary of Construction Jobs, 6th Construction Battalion; Lt. (jg) W.B. Huie USNR *Can Do! The Story of the Seabees* (1944).

41. A flying bee wearing a sailor's cap and carrying a tommygun, a wrench and a hammer.

42. Huie *Can Do!* p. 42. In Oct. 1942 the 1st Marine Aviation Engineer Battalion came up, bringing more much-needed heavy equipment.

43. Sources: *The Campaigns of the Pacific War,* and USSBS *Inter. Jap. Off.;* Cincpac "Solomon Island Campaign-Action of 23-25 August" 24 Oct. 1942; Lt. Cdr. Salomon's notes obtained at Tokyo; action reports of ships in TFs 16 and 17; O.N.I. Combat Narrative No. 3, *Solomon Islands Campaign;* war diaries of enemy fleets and units concerned, and ATIS translation "Southeast Area Operations Part 1 (Navy)."

44. First called the Battle of the Stewart Islands; the Japanese refer to it as the Second Battle of the Solomons.

45. *Ka* is the first syllable of Guadalcanal in Japanese.

46. Battleship *Mutsu* and her destroyers were not in company with Kondo, having remained with the force oilers north of the Stewart Islands. According to a translated extract from Admiral Kondo's private diary, recently in hand, the presence of an American task force in the area was reported to Kondo as early as 20 Aug. and he proposed to seek out and attack it on the 23rd; but early that day Yamamoto ordered him to delay his attack until the position of Fletcher's carriers was positively known.

47. This and other translations in this volume from captured Japanese diaries were seen at Nouméa early in 1943 through the kindness of Colonel Julian P. Brown USMC, Admiral Halsey's Intelligence Officer.

48. Comairsopac daily Intelligence Summaries, consulted at Admiral Fitch's headquarters at Espiritu Santo, and Cincpac files and papers are most useful for day-by-day events in the Guadalcanal campaign. On the Japanese side, details are supplied by the War Diary of Japanese Naval Operations ATIS 16268, and War Diary of Desron 2.

49. YPs — district patrol vessels — small, slow craft varying in size from 50 to 175 tons' displacement; many were converted tuna fishermen from Hawaii. Wooden-hulled and slightly armed, they were not intended for combat. At Guadalcanal they were used as tugs, dispatch boats, rescue craft, troop and supply ferries, and as transports for minor amphibious assaults.

50. Clarence C. Justice and Chester M. Ellis.

51. Turner's Report "Loss of U.S.S. *Colhoun, Gregory* and *Little*," 13 Dec. 1942. *Little* lost 22 killed, 44 wounded; *Gregory*, 11 killed, 26 wounded.

52. Answers to Questionnaires on Guadalcanal Operations" ATIS 22729. Hyakutake had planned earlier to throw a whole new division into Guadalcanal but Kawaguchi, after taking Taivu, persuaded him that he had enough on hand to take Henderson Field.

53. The 105-mm howitzers alone poured out nearly 2000 rounds. "The Ridge could never have been held but for the outstanding support we had from Del Valle's artillery," wrote Col. Griffith.

54. Figures from Miller *Guadalcanal: The First Offensive*. The Japanese official report was 633 killed, 505 wounded.

55. I assume that *I-15* did the job and not *I-19*. It is possible that *I-19* was responsible, but her torpedoes would have had a mighty long run. It is known that *I-15* was in the area, because she confirmed *Wasp's* sinking. On 16 Dec. 1942 *I-15* was sunk by naval planes based on Henderson Field, about halfway between Savo and Russell Islands.

56. Position lat. 12° 25' S, long. 164°08' E, about 250 miles NW of Espiritu Santo.

57. Sources: the Zimmerman and Miller monographs; conversations with these gentlemen and with Colonel Griffith.

58. General Vandegrift's first intention was to drive the Japs beyond the Poha in order to protect Henderson Field from their artillery fire, but when advised of the impending enemy offensive, he revised his plans and decided to aim only at securing the east bank of the Matanikau. (Miller).

59. The sources of this account are the Action Reports and War Diaries of American ships and commanders, and enemy reports procured by Lt. Cdr. Salomon in Tokyo.

60. In the Pacific this term was used for that part of the Coral Sea between Espiritu Santo and the Solomons, which was patrolled by enemy submarines. Ghormley, assuming that the Japanese would take a hostile view of the passage of this regiment from Nouméa to Lunga Point, marshaled naval forces to give them constant protection and cover.

61. Norman Scott of Indianapolis, born 1889, Naval Academy 1911; outstanding service as "exec." of *Jacob Jones* when that ship was sunk by a U-boat in 1917; naval aide to the President; various C.O., gunnery and staff duties; C.O. of *Pensacola*; duty in office of C.N.O. 1941; where he "made things so miserable for everyone around him in Washington that he finally got what he wanted — sea duty" (Admiral Spruance); promoted Rear Admiral and commanded various task forces in the South Pacific, June 1942 to his death in action.

62. Japanese Naval War Diary states midget submarines were in this group for supply purposes. Diary of a Jap officer in Annex J to Marine Report indicates that 150-mm howitzers were landed from the two tenders.

63. An electronic identification system was introduced on board ships so that the radar signals of friendly vessels could be recognized.

64. "Japanese Bombardment Report" ATIS 16567-B. Capt. Watanabe, formerly of Yamamoto's staff, informed us in 1949 that the HE shells used in this bombardment had been ordered as early as Jan. 1942 in order to give profitable employment to battleships subsequent to the demonstration of their vulnerability to land-based air attack. This was the first use of the new shells, some of which were incendiaries, others fragmentation.

65. "Southeast Area Operation Part I (Navy)" Special Staff U.S. Army Historical Division pp. 31-32.

66. Comairsopac Intelligence Bulletin; Comdesdiv 22 Report, 1 Nov. 1942; account by Lt. (jg) Charles J. Bates USNR in Navy "History of *Meredith*." Cdr. Frederick J. Bell (of *Grayson*) *Condition Red* (1943) pp. 121-152 gives the story of the rescue and that of the medical officer of *Meredith*.

67. O.N.I. Combat Narrative *Miscellaneous Actions in the South Pacific* p. 40. A far more serious supply-train casualty, although it cost but two lives, was the total loss of the big army transport *President Coolidge* at Segond Channel, Espiritu Santo, on 25 October. She was carrying the 172nd Infantry 43rd Division. Her merchant skipper, although repeatedly warned by patrol craft and shore blinker, blundered into a protective mine field and she sank. All the troops' equipment and their heavy weapons were destroyed and their reinforcement of the Guadalcanal garrison was delayed for weeks. Earlier, on 4 Aug., destroyer *Tucker* had run into the same mine field with the same result.

68. The writer believes that Admiral Ghormley did as well as anyone could have done; that he was the victim of circumstances. His health was excellent. He believed that he was relieved on account of the question of reinforcement; frequently he demanded troops from the West Coast but was always told that there were none ready, and that he must "roll up" the garrisons of his rear areas, Fiji and Samoa. That he refused to do, because he feared denuding these islands of defense forces would tempt the enemy to attack them. An unfortunate concomitant of his relief was the fact that Halsey, unlike Nimitz, brought his own staff, to the detriment of his old flagship *Enterprise* and replaced many of Ghormley's experienced staff, four of whom were killed at the Battle of Guadalcanal.

69. Rear Admiral Aubrey W. Fitch relieved Vice Admiral J. S. McCain as Comairsopac 20 Sept. 1942, retaining the same headquarters at Segond Channel, Espiritu Santo.

70. The message, partly written by Harry Hopkins, is reproduced in Robert E. Sherwood *Roosevelt and Hopkins* (1948) p. 624; it is undated, but the J.C.S. records show that it was presented 24 Oct.

71. An expressive nautical phrase; a ship singles-up her doubled mooring lines before getting under way. The Marines used it to describe the attenuation of defensive lines when half the defenders are withdrawn and the other half have to spread out.

72. O.N.I. Combat Narrative *Miscellaneous Actions in the South Pacific;* Action Reports of American ships concerned; and conversation with Cdr. Amos T. Hathaway, former navigator of *Zane*; translations of Japanese "Combat Report No. 13, Comdesron 4" USSBS files; "Merit Report of Various Naval Units" (WDC No. 161,011).

73. Relieved 7 Nov. as Commander Aircraft Guadalcanal by his First Wing chief of staff, Brig. Gen. Louis E. Woods USMC, Geiger returned to Espiritu Santo, where First Wing had set up headquarters on 14 Sept.

74. Originally called "Third Battle of Savo Island," although fought nowhere near it. Sources similar to those for Cape Esperance—plus Cincpac's Report "Solomon Islands Campaign, Battle of Santa Cruz;" individual ships' Action Reports; Japanese report "Battle of Santa Cruz" ATIS 15687; Desron 10 Combat Report No. 2 (WDC No. 160,985).

75. These remarks about Capt. Gatch are based on conversations with several officers who served under him. They were all somewhat puzzled by Gatch's extraordinary power over his men. Some said it was due to his religion; he revived the old Navy practice of reading the lesson at divine service, and always urged his men to make their peace with God before going into action. Others said it was because, as a close student of the Civil War, Gatch had reached the conclusion that taut, spic-and-span units never fought well; so he let the men wear anything or nothing— "they looked like a lot of wild men." He let the ship get abominably dirty and directed all his men's energies to perfecting their shooting. Whatever the reason, Capt. Gatch was adored by his men and received a splendid ovation when he returned to duty after his wound. There is a good article on him by Capt. J.V. Claypool, the ship's chaplain, in *Chicago Tribune* 13 May 1944.

76. Desron 2 War Diary, Enclosure B to Cincpac "Orange Naval Task Force Operations, 10-30 Oct. 1942" 17 Jan. 1943.

77. Earlier called "Battle of the Solomons" or "Third and Fourth Battles of Savo Island." The sources, other than the Action Reports of vessels and commands concerned and the personal experiences of Cdr. James C. Shaw in *Atlanta*, are Cincpac Report "Solomon Islands Campaign—Battle of the Solomons, 11-15 November 1942" 18 Feb. 1943; Allied Translator and Interpreter Section of General Headquarters (General MacArthur's Command) "Naval Battle of Guadalcanal" ATIS 15931, prepared in Japan under the direction of Lt. Cdr. Henry Salomon USNR; Commander Amphibious forces South Pacific "Report of Operations of TF 67 and TG 62.4, Nov. 8-15 1942 and Summary of Third Battle of Savo," 3 Dec. 1942.

78. Daniel Judson Callaghan, b. San Francisco 1890, Naval Academy 1911. During World War I in *New Orleans* on convoy duty; asst. fire control officer of *Idaho* 1920-3; 1st Lt. *Colorado* 1925-6; engineer officer *Mississippi* 1926-7; U. of Calif. 1933-5; exec. *Portland* and staff Cdr. Cruisers' Scouting Force 1936-8; Naval Aide to President 1938-41; C.O. *San Francisco* May 1941–May 1942; chief of staff to Admiral Ghormley June–Oct. 1942.

79. Distance between types 800 yards; between cruisers 700 yards; between destroyers, 500 yards.

80. "Report on the Naval Battle of Guadalcanal" ATIS 15931. The Americans did not then have flashless powder for major-caliber guns. The advantage it gave the Japs was the subject of much comment in actions reports.

81. This order added to the confusion, in ships which could not see or bear on targets on their designated sides but did see targets on the opposite side, and it took no account of variations in gun caliber between ships.

82. "Engagement with Japanese Surface Forces off Guadalcanal Night of 12-13 Nov. 1942, and Loss of U.S.S. *Atlanta*" 20 Nov. 1942; personal recollections.

83. "Report of Engagement off Savo Island on Nov. 13, 1942 and Destruction of the U.S.S. *Cushing*" 20 Nov. 1942.

84. *O'Bannon* and *Sterett* Action Reports 20 Nov. 1942.

85. *San Francisco* Action Report 16 Nov. 1942 with chronological log of battle.

86. This conjecture was strengthened by the presence of scattered projectile fragments with *San Francisco* green dye color later found on *Atlanta* decks. Lt. Cdr. Bruce McCandless of *San Francisco* stated to the writer, 2 Nov. 1945, that his ship was not firing at *Atlanta* but at a Japanese ship beyond *Atlanta,* and that the short-range flat trajectory resulted in shells passing through *Atlanta.*

87. Buships *Summary of War Damage to U.S. Battleships, Carriers, Cruisers and Destroyers, 17 Oct. 1941 to 7 Dec. 1942,* 15 Sept. 1943; recordings in Office of Naval Records and Library by Lt. (jg) Charles Wang USNR; Lt. R.W. O'Neill and L. E. Zook SMr, in Jan. 1943.

88. *O'Bannon* Action Report. Luck, ably assisted by a spirited and capable crew, enabled her to come through the entire war unscathed by enemy action.

89. *Helena* Action Report. Text of message: *Juneau* torpedoed and disappeared lat. 10 32' S, long. 161 2' E at 1109. Survivors in water. Report Comsopac."

90. Report on sinking of *Juneau* 22 Nov. 1942; reports of other ships present, and Office of Naval Records recordings.

91. Admiral Halsey remarked after the Battle of Santa Cruz that he would never again permit Yamamoto to "suck" his carriers into waters north of San Cristobal.

92. Transports sunk on 14 Nov. were *Arizona, Shinanogawa, Sado, Canberra, Nako, Nagara* and *Brisbane*—all *Marus.*

93. Willis Augustus Lee of Natlee, KY, b. 1888; Naval Academy of 1908; at Vera Cruz 1914; World War I Atlantic destroyer duty; U.S. Olympic rifle team prizewinner; C.O. of destroyers *Fairfax, W.B. Preston* and *Larner;* student at Naval War College; "exec." *Pennsylvania;* C.O. *Concord;* staff of Cdr. Cruisers Battle Force; director of fleet training; asst. chief of staff to Cominch. In Aug. 1942 became Combatdiv 6. He served in various task forces during the remainder of the war, dying just at its close when engaged in research to counteract the kamikaze menace.

94. The flag radio log merely states that Lee established his identity with Base "Cactus" at 2240. What Lee said became legendary in a very short time. An officer in *Washington* told me that the Admiral replied in rhyme: "This is Chung Ching Lee — you mustn't fire 'fish' at me!" and I have since heard five or six different versions.

95. Cincpac "Solomons Islands Campaign—Battle of the Solomons, 11-15 Nov. 1942," 18 Feb. 1943. Cincpac criticized the presence of planes on board, remarking that they should have been flown off. Admiral Lee had considered sending the planes to Tulagi to stand by for possible night use, but he doubted that Tulagi had facilities for them.

96. The others were Battle of Calabria, 27 June 1940, Battle of Suriago Strait, 25 Oct. 1944, and the sinking of *Bismarck* where *Prince of Wales* fired a decisive shot. *Massachusetts* against immobile *Jean Bart* was not a sea action.

97. *Washington,* despite an enviable war record, received less publicity than any other capital ship in the U.S. Navy. The reasons for this are: undamaged by the enemy, she furnished no "drama," and *South Dakota* by going home grabbed all the publicity for this action, as *Boise* had for Cape Esperance. I cannot here refrain from calling attention to the presumptuous mendacity of Mr. William B. Huie who, in the *Reader's Digest* for Dec. 1948, says of the 15 U.S. battleships that operated in World War II, "They were manned by thousands of scarce men. The Navy spent millions on propaganda for them. Yet no super-battleship ever sank an enemy ship; not one of them ever fired a justifying shot."

98. "Southeast Area Operations, Part I (Navy)" Special Staff U.S. Army Historical Div. No. 851-100 p. 45.

99. Robert E. Sherwood *Roosevelt and Hopkins* p. 656.

100. Cincpac Action Report on the Solomons.

101. Also called "4th," "5th" and "6th Battle of Savo I." and "Battle of Lunga Point." Principal sources: Cincpac "Solomon Islands Campaign, 5th Battle of Savo — 30 Nov. 1942;" Action Reports of U.S. ships and commands involved; 1st Marine Division "Final Report on Guadalcanal Operation;" Capt. Toyama in *Inter Jap. Off.* I,254; Allied Japanese Report "Battle of Tassafaronga" ATIS 16086; Henry Salomon Jr. notes taken in Japan.

102. Conversations with Capt. A. E. Roberts USAMC, statistical officer of 101st Regiment, 1 May 1943; Sanitary Survey by Col. Dale G. Friend USAMC in Report to Surgeon General 1 Mar. 1943. Average sick rate American Division on Guadalcanal 15 Nov. 1942 –15 Mar. 1943 was 7 per 1,000; battle casualties only 0.3 per 1,000. Incidence of malaria 15 Nov. average 8.7 per 1,000 per day, and in some units that rejected atabrine (owing to a rumor that it impaired virility), rose as high as 20. But by 15 March, it had fallen to 1.7.

103. Maj John L. Zimmerman USMCR *The Guadalcanal Campaign*. Carlson's Raiders arrived on the island 4 Nov. 1942.

104. Admiral Halsey's endorsement on Wright's Action Report indicates extreme displeasure with the van destroyers on two accounts: (1) shooting torpedoes at excessive range; (2) retiring to the northwest without assisting the cruisers.

105. Walden Lee Ainsworth, b. Minneapolis 1886, Naval Academy 1910, served successively in *Idaho, Prairie* and *Florida* before 1917. During World War I gunnery officer on transports. Ordnance duty ashore for 3 years, "exec." *Hancock* and *Birmingham, C.O. Marcus,* ordnance and Navy Yard duties 1923-25. Asiatic Fleet for 2 years, instructor Naval Academy 3 years, navigator *Idaho* and *Pensacola* 1931-33. In Panama 1934-35; senior War College course; "exec." *Mississippi* 2 years; Comdesron 2 1940-41; C.O. *Mississippi* first half of 1942.

106. John Miller *Guadalcanal: The First Offensive* (Historical Division, Dept. of the Army), a vol. in the Pacific series of K.R. Greenfield (ed.) *U.S. Army in World War II* becomes increasingly valuable toward the close of the campaign; the author kindly allowed us to use it in advance of printing.

107. Salomon Tokyo Notes, confirmed by ATIS trans. of "Southeast Area Operations Part I (Navy)."

108. During December the U.S. Army in Guadalcanal included two regiments (164th and 182nd) of the American Division and the 147th Infantry. The 25th Division was on its way from Hawaii direct to Guadalcanal, remaining units of the American were soon to arrive, and the 6th Marine Regiment of the 2nd Marine Division arrived 4 January.

109. Brigadier General Alphonse DeCarre USMC was acting commander of the 2nd Marine Division; Major General John Marston USMC, the division commander, had to remain in New Zealand because he was senior to General Patch.

110. So called from their rough resemblance to these animals in aerial photographs.

111. Comsopac Op Plans 3-43 and 4-43, 27 Jan. 1943; Action Reports of American ships and commands involved; Cincpac "Solomon Islands Campaign—Fall of Guadalcanal, period 25 Jan. to 10 Feb. 1943"; O.N.I. Combat Narrative No. 8, *Japanese Evacuation of Guadalcanal;* "War Diary of Japanese Naval Operations" ATIS 16268; conversations with Admiral Halsey's operations officer and Admiral Giffen's chief of staff.

112. Cincpac "Solomon Islands Campaign—Fall of Guadalcanal" 17 Apr. 1943; Action Reports of ships and commands involved; Records of 2nd Destroyer Squadron (WDC No. 161,711); "Japanese Naval War Diary" ATIS 16268; Cdr R. J. Buckley's PT History.

113. Cincpac "Fall of Guadalcanal." Withdrawal figures from Japanese Naval War Diary.

114. Naval casualties during the Guadalcanal campaign (including shipboard Marine detachments) totaled 5,041 killed and 2,953 wounded. Source: Bureau of Personnel, WWII Casualty List, Books 2 and 3, Naval Historical Center, Washington, DC, as cited by Richard B. Frank in *Guadalcanal* pp. 637-644.

Chapter 4. Amphibious Rehearsals in the Russells (p. 229 - 244)

1. Unless otherwise noted, the material in this chapter is largely derived from Vice Admiral Dyer's *Amphibians Came to Conquer,* pp. 457-479. Other sources include: *ComSoPac Jan.-Apr. 1943 WarDs*; ComPhibSoPac Rept of Occupation of the Russell Islands (CLEANSLATEOp) 21 Feb.-17 Apr. 1943, dtd 21 Apr. 1943; 43rd InfDiv FO No. 2, dtd 15 Feb. 1943; 3d RdrBn Rpt of the Russell Islands (CLEANSLATEOp), dtd 9 Apr. 1943; Russell Islands Det. 11th DefBn Jnl; LtCol E. S. Watson, G-3, 43rd InfDiv, "Movement of a Task Force by Small Landing Craft," dtd 17 Apr. 1943; Morrison, *Breaking the Bismarcks Barrier;* Shaw and Kane, *Isolation of Rabaul.*

2. Based on the recommendations RAdm Turner received from all commands in TF 62, he made proposals for revisions in Fleet Training Publication (FTP) 167, the *Amphibians' Bible* as it was on the basis of these recommendations and those coming in from the Atlantic Fleet after the North African Landings that COMINCH issued on 18 January 1943, *Ship to Shore Movement U.S. Fleet* FTP 211. It expanded markedly the Naval Platoon of the Shore Party, and more clearly defined its duties during the crucial early hours of logistic support of an assault landing.

3. CINCPAC, *Command Summary,* Book Three, 23 Jan. 1943, p. 1342.

4. Commander Landing Craft Flotillas, PHIBFORSOPAC Doctrine, May 1943.

5. "Spit Kits" was an all-encompassing term for small auxiliary craft such as yard tugs, rescue vessels, landing craft and coastal transports.

6. *Time Magazine,* 31 Jan. 1944.

7. Joseph Driscoll, *Pacific Victory 1945,* p. 66.

8. COMPHIBFORSOPAC CLEANSLATE Report, 21 Apr. 1943, p. 14.

9. COMPHIBFORSOPAC letter, FE25/A3-1/Ser 007 of 20 Jan. 1943, subj: Organization and Staff of Amphibious Force, South Pacific, FE25/A3-1/Ser of 20 Jan. 1943, and CINCPAC's Organizational Roster dated 29 Jan. 1943.

Chapter 5. Lull Between Storms (p. 245 - 302)

1. Unless otherwise noted the material in this chapter is derived from Morison, *Breaking the Bismarcks Barrier;* Dyer, *The Amphibians Came to Conquer;* Hutchinson, *Bluejacket, In Harms Way From Guadalcanal to Tokyo;* and Cressman, *The Official Chronology of the U.S. Navy in WWII.*

2. Morison, *Breaking the Bismarcks Barrier,* p. 90.

3. Volume I in this trilogy profiles the Earlybird Flotilla Five LCTs, LSTs and LCIs and their crews—from landing craft design and construction to amphibious training and crew and flotilla formations, to on-the-job warfare training in the southern Solomons—in preparation for their first invasion of enemy-held territory, Operation TOENAILS.

4. The chronological events in this chapter have been derived from many sources including formerly classified documents and translated enemy records. We have also drawn on Robert J. Cressman's, *The Official Chronology of the U.S. Navy in WWII* sponsored by the Naval Historical Center.

5. Quoted in MajGen Charles A. Willougby and John Chamberlin, *MacArthur 1941-1951* (New York: McGraw Hill Book Co., 1954), p. 112.

6. USSBS, *Campaigns,* p. 174.

7. *The Amphibians Are Coming!,* pp. 133-134.

8. The material in this section is derived from Morison, *Breaking the Bismarcks Barrier;* Craven and Cate, *Guadalcanal to Saipan;* and Japanese Monograph No. 32, *SE Area AirOps; SE Area NavOps-11.*

9. *Admiral Halsey's Story,* p. 157.

10. *Breaking the Bismarcks Barrier,* pp. 128-129; 13th Fighter Command Detachment Action Report 21 Apr. 1943; Japanese and American communiqués.

11. CMC AnRept to SecNav for the Fiscal Year Ending 30 June 43.

12. RAdm Samuel Eliot Morison, *Breaking The Bismarcks Barrier,* pp. 100-103.

13. Henry I. Shaw, Jr., *First Offensive,* p. 22.

14. Cdr Peter B. Mersky, *Time of the Aces,* pp. 14-30.

15. Ibid.

16. William L. McGee, *Bluejacket Odyssey,* pp. 99-178, details the tragic voyage of TU 32.4.4.

17. CinCPOA's "Operations in Pacific Areas – June 1943."

Chapter 6. Operation TOENAILS (p. 303 - 414)

1. For the most part this chapter is based on War Diaries and Action Reports. The CINCPAC "Operations in Pacific Ocean Areas" summaries and the Office of Naval Intelligence "Combat Narratives-Solomon Islands Campaign" have been of inestimable value, as have several publications of the U.S. Navy and Marine Corps Historical Centers and the U.S. Army Center of Military History. Other valuable sources include *Breaking the Bismarcks Barrier* by RAdm Samuel Eliot Morison, *Amphibians Came to Conquer* by VAdm George C. Dyer, and *Building the Navy's Bases in WWII* by the Bureau of Yards and Docks.

2. Samuel Eliot Morison, *Breaking The Bismarcks Barrier*, p. 147.

3. The four airfields at Guadalcanal were (1) Henderson Field, a base for all light and some heavy bombers and most short range search planes, (2) Fighter No I, the main base for fighter aircraft (principally Marine and Navy fighter planes), (3) Fighter No. 2, the main base for Army and New Zealand fighter planes, (4) Carney Field, used principally for heavy and medium bombers and long range search planes. North Field in the Russells was used as a base for both light bombers and fighters; South Field was limited to fighters.

4. *Combat Narratives Operation in the New Georgia Area, 21 June - 5 August 1943,* Office of Naval Intelligence, U. S. Navy, 1944. Hereafter "*Combat Narratives.*"

5. *The Amphibians Are Coming! Emergence of the 'Gator Navy and its Revolutionary Landing Craft* by William L. McGee.

6. *Up The Slot: Marines in the Central Solomons,* Marine Corps Historical Center (hereafter, "*Up the Slot*"), *Building the Navy's Bases in WWII,* Bureau of Yards and Docks (hereafter, "*Building The Navy's Bases*"), and *Can Do! The Story of the Seabees* by William Huie (hereafter, "*Can Do*").

7. All times are Zone L (local) unless otherwise specified.

8. Sources: a) "*Combat Narratives,*" b) "*Up the Slot,*" c) *Northern Solomons,* U.S. Army Center of Military History, (hereafter "*Northern Solomons*"), d) *From Makin To Bougainville: Marine Raiders in the Pacific War* (hereafter "*From Makin to Bougainville*"), Marine Corps Historical Center, e) "*AmphibiansCame to Conquer.*"

9. Sources: a) "*Combat Narratives,*" b) "*Amphibians Came to Conquer,*" c) "*Up the Slot,*" d) "*Can Do!*"

10. LCI-334 War Diary.

11. Sources: a) "*Amphibians Came to Conquer,*" b) "*Combat Narratives,*" c) "*From Makin to Bougainville,*" e) "*Northern Solomons.*"

12. Sources: (a) CINCPAC to COMINCH, 130507 Jun. 1943; (b) BUPERS to CINCPAC and COMSOPAC 140833 Jun. 1943.

13. Sources: a) LST-343 Action Report 27 July 1943; b) History of USS LST-343.

14. "*Building the Navy's Bases*" and "*Can Do.*"

15. Of the 24th NCB, BGen A.P. Howard, USMC, said: "It is the most bombed Seabee battalion of the entire Pacific."

16. The opening chapter of *Pacific Express,* next and final volume in W. L. McGee's amphibious trilogy, is devoted to the amazing accomplishments of the Seabees and Combat Engineers who built the advance bases in the Pacific.

17. Sources: a) *"Combat Narratives,"* b) CinCPAC Operations in Pacific Ocean Areas July 1943, c) *"U.S. Cruisers."*

18. Ibid.

19. Sources: a) Report of Torpedoing of LST-342—0130 Love, 18 July 1943, by Ensign T.B. Montgomery, 28 July 1943; b) CINCPAC/POA Operations In Pacific, July 1943; c) LST Flotilla Five War Diary, July 1943.

20. *The Japanese Submarine Force and WWII,* 1995.

21. Cmdr Burke in the *Conway* arrived at Guadalcanal on 20 July and relieved Capt T. J. Ryan, Jr., as commander of destroyer task group TF-31. The *Conway* replaced *Ralph Talbot.* Cmdr Burke would earn the sobriquet "31-knot Burke" for his high-speed destroyer tactics as commander of DesRon 23 known as the "Little Beavers." Also known as a sailor's sailor, he was appointed Chief of Naval Operations in 1955 at age 53.

22. The *Wilson* had reported to CTF 31 for duty on 23 July.

23. John F. Kennedy was elected to Congress from Massachusetts in 1946 and to the Senate in 1952. He ran successfully for President in 1960.

24. *"Up the Slot."*

25. CinCPAC Operations in Pacific Ocean Areas, July 1943, Annex D. paragraph 42.

26. *Breaking the Bismarcks Barrier,* p. 224.

27. Killed: Army 957, Marine Corps and Navy 189; Wounded: Army 3646, Marine Corps and Navdy 494; Captured and missing: 23. Monthly Progress Report, Army Service Forces, *Health* 31 May 1945. These are for ground forces only; the airforce, surface Navy and submarine casualties have not yet been compiled. Capt Ohmae estimates that total Japanese casualties in the Munda campaign were 12,000, but this seems excessive.

28. VAdm George Carroll Dyer, *Amphibians Came to Conquer: The Story of Admiral Richmond Kelly Turner,* pp. 587-596.

29. Commander Landing Craft Flotillas, letter, 13 Jul. 1943.

30. CTG 31.1 Loading Order 14-43, 12 Jul. 1943.

31. Commander Landing Craft Flotillas, letter, 13 Jul. 1943.

32. COMTRANSDIV Eight to COMPHIBFORSOPAC, letter, Nov. 1942.

33. Capt Clarence Olsen, USN, to ACS (Plans), memo, 6 Aug. 1943.

Chapter 7. Occupation of Vella Lavella (p. 415 - 466)

1. Unless otherwise noted, the material in this Chapter is derived from: a) *CinCPAC/ POA, Operations in Pacific Ocean Areas,* Oct 43 dtd 20 Jan 44; b) *Combat Narratives: Solomon Islands Campaign XI, Kolombangara and Vella Lavella* 6 August - 7 October 1943; c) CominCh Rept of *SoPac Action;* d) *ComSoPac Aug-Sept 43 WarDs;* e) Com III PhibFor AR, 16-19 Aug 43, dtd 20 Dec 43; f) Com III PhibFor Rept of Occupation of Vella Lavella, 12 Aug-3 Sept 43, dtd 20 Sept 43; g) CTF 31 OpO A12-43, dtd 11 Aug 43; h) *New Georgia Campaign: NGOF Account,* NDF FO No. 1, dtd 11 Aug 43; i) *Seventeenth Army Ops—I;* j) *SE Area NavOps—II;* k) Frankel, *37ᵗʰ InfDivHist.*

2. *"Can Do!"*

3. CINCPAC/POA Operations in Pacific Ocean Areas, August 1943.

4. LST-334 War Diary.

5. USS LST-396 Action Report, August 1943.

6. ComLSTGRP 14 Casualty Report of USS LST-396, 31 August 1943.

7. LST Flotilla Five War Diary August 1943.

8. *"USS LST-398 and LST Flot 5."*

9. a) LST Flotilla Five War Diary, September-November 1943; b) LST-449 Deck Log, September-November 1943.

10. a) LST-448 Action Report, 9 October 1943; b) Action Report, LSTs of TG 31.6, 1 October 1943; c) LST Flotilla 5 War Diary, September/October 1943; d) Author interviews with LST-448 survivors.

11. Sources: a) LST Flotilla Five War Diary; b) LST-446 History; c) *Breaking the Bismarcks Barrier.*

12. a) LST-448 Action Report 9 October 1943; b) Action Report, LSTs of TG 31.6, 1 October 1943; c) LST Flotilla 5 War Diary, September/October 1943; d) Author interviews with LST-448 survivors.

13. *"Building the Navy's Bases."*

14. *"Operations in POA,"* August 1943, and *"Combat Narratives."*

15. *"Combat Narratives"* and *U.S. Cruisers."*

Chapter 8. Bougainville Campaign (p. 469 - 542)

1. Sources: *Combat Narratives Solomon Islands Campaign*, ONI; *Operations in Pacific Ocean Areas*; Jon T. Hoffman, *From Makin to Bougainville*; Stephen J. Lofgren, *Northern Solomons*; *Building the Navy's Bases*; Shaw and Kane, *Isolation of Rabaul*; Isely and Crowl, *Marines and Amphibious War*; Arthur and Cohlmia, *3ᵈ MardivHist*; Henderson, *Naval Gunfire Support*; Rentz, *Bougainville and the Northern Solomons*; Miller, *Reduction of Rabaul*; Morison, *Breaking the Bismarcks Barrier*; ComSoPac Oct-Nov 43 WarDs; Third Flt NarrRept; IMAC AR-I; IMAC C-2 Repts, 27 Oct-13 Dec 43; IMCA C-2 Jnl, 27 Oct-27 Nov 43; 8(NZ) BrigGru Rept on Ops, Treasury Is (Op GOODTIME), dtd 30 Nov 43; IIIPhibFor AR; IIIPhibFor Nov 43 WarD; ComTransGru, IIIPhibFor, Rept of LandingOps, Empress Augusta Bay, Bougainville Island, 1-2 Nov 43, dtd 22 Dec 43; 3ᵈ MarDiv, Combat Rept of the 3ᵈ MarDiv in the BougainvilleOps, 1 Nov-28 Dec 43, dtd 21 Mar 44; 3ᵈ MarDiv D-2 SAR, Empress Augusta Bay Ops dtd 1 Feb 44.

2. The complement of an Argus unit is approximately 20 officers and 178 men. Its purpose has been described as follows: To provide, during the development stage of a United States Naval Base, a comprehensive air warning, surface warning, and fighter direction organization which will coordinate all radar operations under the Area Cmdr.

3. First Marine Amphibious Corps.

4. ComLCI Flotilla 5 War Diary, November 1943.

5. LCI Flotilla Five War Diary, 26 September-1 December 1943.

6. LCI-334 War Diary, October 1943.

7. USS LCI-334 Action Report A16-3/(81), 29 October 1943.

8. USS LST-399 Action Report covering initial landing on Mono Island, 26-28 October 1943.

9. ComLSTGRP 15 Action Report, Seizure of Treasury Islands, 27 October 1943; LST Flot 5 War Diary, October/November 1943.

10. *"Can Do!"*

11. *"From Makin to Bougainville."*

12. Ibid.

13. *"Breaking the Bismarck Barrier,"* p. 329; Gunnery Officer LCI-70 Report on AA Action 5 November 1943; Officer-in-Charge LCT-68 Report of 5 November 1943 AA Attack.

14. Extract from ship's log LCT-330, Lt (jg) Leon Douglas, USNR, Officer in Charge.

15. USS LST-341 War Diary, 29 June-30 November 1943.

16. *"Building the Navy's Bases."*

17. *"Can Do!"*

18. *Combat Narratives*; *"U.S. Cruisers;" "Breaking the Bismarcks Barrier."*

19. Ibid.

20. Ibid.

Chapter 9. Lessons Learned in the Solomons (p. 543 - 562)

1. Unless otherwise noted, the material in this chapter is largely derived from Vice Admiral Dyer's *Amphibians Came to Conquer*, Commander Landing Craft Flotillas War Diaries; ComLSTFlot 5 War Diaries and Action Reports; Stephen J. Lofgren, *Northern Solomons 1943-44*.

2. Commander Landing Craft Flotillas to COMPHIBFORSOPAC FE 25-2/A3/Ser 002 of 13 Jul. 1943, subj: Performance of Landing Craft.

3. CTG 31.1 Loading Order 14-43 12 Jul. 1943.

4. Commander Landing Craft Flotillas, letter, 13 Jul. 1943.

5. *USS President Adams* Action Report, 25 Aug. 1942, Encl. (A), Report of G.I.D. Sporhase, BM2c.

6. Ibid., Encl. (B), Report of B.W. Hensen, BM2c.

7. Ibid., CO's Report, 15 Aug. 1942.

8. *Hunter Liggett* War Diary, 7 Aug. 1942.

9. *Neville* War Diary, 9 Aug. 1942.

10. *Hunter Liggett* War Diary, 8 Aug. 1942.

11. COMTRANSDIV Eight to COMPHIBFORSOPAC, letter, Nov. 1942.

12. CTF 31 Op Order A9-43, 15 Jun. 1943.

13. Captain Clarence E. Olsen, USN, to ACS (Plans), memorandum, 6 Aug. 1943.

14. USS *Monssen* War Diary, 7 Aug. 1942.

15. RKT to DCNO Admin., enclosure to letter of 20 Aug. 1950, p. 18.

16. *Wasp* Action Report, 14 Aug. 1942, encl. (B), p. 4.

17. COMFIFTHPHIBFOR, letter, OSA/A16-3/Ser 0023 of 19 Sept. 1943, with endorsements thereon by COMCENPACFOR and CINCPAC, subj: Recommended changes in command arrangements, CINCPAC Operation Plan 13-43.

18. *Northern Solomons* by Stephen J. Lofgren, U.S. Army Military History, GPO, pp. 32-35.

BIBLIOGRAPHY

Bibliographic Note

This volume is based primarily upon the official records of the Joint Chiefs of Staff and records of the U.S. Navy, Marine Corps, Army and Army Air Corps plus Japanese records. Other important sources include published World War II books, especially the histories frequently cited; interviews and correspondence with veterans who were there; and several privately published memoir manuscripts.

A. Government Publications

Allard, Dean C.; Crawley, Martha L.; and Edmison, Mary W.: *US Naval History Sources in the United States* (US Naval History Division), Washington, D.C., 1979.

Allied Landing Craft and Ships, U.S. Navy Division of Naval Intelligence Publications. ONI/226 1944 and ONI/1945. Washington, D.C.

Building the Navy's Bases in WWII, Two Vols. Bureau of Yards and Docks, Washington: GPO, 1947.

Dictionary of American Naval Fighting Ships. Naval Historical Center, Washington, D.C.

Dyer, VAdm George C. *The Amphibians Came to Conquer: The Story of Admiral Richmond Kelly Turner.* 2 Vols. Washington: GPO, 1971.

Hoffmann, Major Jon T. *From Makin to Bougainville,* (a USMC monograph), Washington, D.C. GPO 1951.

Hough, LCol Frank O. USMCR, Maj Verle E. Ludwig, USMC, and Henry I. Shaw Jr. *Pearl Harbor to Guadalcanal –History of U.S. Marine Corps Operations in World War II.* Historical Branch, G-3 Division, Headquarters, U.S. Marine Corps, Washington: GPO (no date).

Landing Craft and the War Production Board – April 1942-May 1944. War Production Board, Special Study No. 11 Washington, D.C.

Melson, Major Charles D., USMC (Ret.). *Up The Slot: Marines in the Central Solomons,* a pamphlet in World War II Commemorative Series, (Washington, D.C.: Marine Corps Historical Center, 1993).

Mersky, Cmdr Peter B. USNR. *Time Of The Aces: Marine Pilots in the Solomons,* 1942-1944, A pamphlet in World War II Commemorative Series, (Washington, D.C.: Marine Corps Historical Center, 1993).

Miller, John Jr. *Guadalcanal: The First Offensive, WWII.* U.S. Army Center of Military History. Washington, D.C., 1949.

Official Navy Department Bulletin: "The Indomitable LCTs Never Miss an Invasion," July 1944.

B. Interviews and Correspondence

LCTs:

Carl M.	Barrett,	LCT-322	Jack E. "Cookie"	Johnson,	LCT-182	
Edward H.	Burtt,	LCT-68	Ken	Keller,	LCT-158	
Robert T.	Capeless,	LCT-62	Thomas J.	McGann,	LCT-377	
Robert	Carr,	LCT-367	John A.	McNeill,	LCT-159	
Walter B. "Bo"	Gillette,	LCT-369	John	Morais,	LCT-481	
Robert	Gordier,	LCT-67	Robert B.	Sahlberg,	LCT-67	
			Austin N.	Volk,	LCT-60	

LSTs:

Douglas S.	Adams,	LST-447	William	Jayne,	LST-339
Charles J.	Adams, Jr.,	LST-281	Jack	Jordan,	LST-397
Herbert A.	Alhgren,	LST-446	Hugh	Kane,	LST-449
Robert	Allen,	LST-339	Ruben	Kemper,	LST-447
Rogers	Aston,	LST-446	Andrew	Kresnocky,	LST-334
James	Baird,	LST-353	John	La Montagne,	LST-448
Freeman A.	Ballard,	LST-447	John	Lapp,	LST-460
Delbert E.	Beardsley,	LST-449	William	Leadingham,	LST-396
Harold F.	Breimyer,	LST-448	Theron	MacKay,	LST-342
Dwight	Burt,	LST-460	Harry	Mansfield,	LST-460
Robert	Busch,	LST-851	Martin	Melkild,	LST-398
Tom	Byrne,	LST-460	Robert	Menzel,	LST-472
James	Cogswell	LST-342	Homer	Mitchell,	LST-446
John	Columbo,	LST-396	Ben	Owen	LST-339
Hugh	Comer,	LST-446	Thad	Rogers,	LST-399
Don	Connell,	LST-397	Lester	Rutter,	LST-396
Charles	Crane,	LST-472	Ed	Sargent,	LST-353
Richard	Daspit,	LST-447	Frank	Sawyer,	LST-398
Elmer	Froewiss,	LST-472	Joe	Schmits,	LST-398
Harold	Hansen,	LST-448	Miner B. "James"	Stackpole,	LST-396
George T.	Heard,	LST-460	Don	Sterling,	LST-340
Gerhard R.	Hess,	LST-342	Bill	Sutton,	LST-398
Bob	Hilliard,	LST-396	Anthony P.	Tesori,	LST-340
Gerhard	Hines,	LST-397	Robert	Thorpe,	LST-339
Tucker	Hughbanks,	LST-354	Joe	Volcik,	LST-398
Dick	Insley,	LST-460	William E.	Walsh,	LST-447
			Richard	Wilson,	LST-398

LCIs:

John	Barry,	LCI-66	Dale B.	Kirkham,	LCI-222
William A.	Bertsch,	LCI-64	Thomas	Littel,	LCI-334
Frank	Brady,	LCI-23	Fred	Moshure,	LCI-73
Donald L.	Brown,	LCI-336	Thomas P.	Mulligan,	LCI-334
Bill	Brown,	LCI-327	Alfred J.	Ormston,	LCI-334
John	Bryne,	LCI-24	Elmo	Pucci,	LCI-329
Read	Dunn, Jr.,	LCI-335	Bob	Rosenberg,	LCI-331
Ed	Fincham,	LCI-223	Homer	Reighard,	LCI-62
Harry	Frey,	LCI-70	Vince	Robinson,	LCI-336
Jack	Higgins,	LCI-67	Mike	Scalpi,	LCI-66
Ed	Korpinen,	LCI-332	Bill	Stark,	LCI-23
			Stephen A.	Wiercinski,	LCI-336

APDs/Others:

Harry Denni, Kansas City Structural Steel

Curtis G.   Clark,   APD-7

Art Zuehlke, Manitowoc Shipbuilding Corp.

C. World War II Books

Alexander, Joseph H. *Edson's Raiders, The 1st Marine Raider Battalion in World War II*. Annapolis: Naval Institute Press, 2001.

Barbey, Daniel E. *MacArthur's Amphibious Navy*. Annapolis: Naval Institute Press, 1969.

Barger, Mel. *Large Slow Target,* Vol. 3. *A History of the Landing Ships (LST) and the Men Who Sailed On Them*. Carrolton: Taylor Publishing Company, 1994.

Bartlett, LtCol Merrill L. USMC (Ret) Ed. *Assault From the Sea, Essays on the History of Amphibious Warfare*. Annapolis: Naval Institute Press, 1983.

Bruce, Colin John. *Invaders, British and American Experience of Seaborne Landings 1939-1945*. Annapolis: Naval Institute Press, 1999.

Buell, Thomas B. *Master of Sea Power: A Biography of Fleet Admiral Ernest J. King*. Boston: Little, Brown, 1980.

Clark, Curt; McDonald, Johnny; and Witherspoon, Bob, Historians /Collaborators, *The Famed Green Dragons—The Four Stack APDs*. Paducah: Turner Publishing Company, 1998.

Cook, Capt Charles. *The Battle of Cape Esperance*. Annapolis: Naval Institute Press, 1968.

Coombe, Jack D. *Derailing the Tokyo Express*. Harrisburg: Stackpole Books, 1991.

Cravan, W. F. and J. L. Cate. *The Army Air Forces in World War II*. Volume 4. *The Pacific: Guadalcanal to Saipan (August 1942-July 1944)*. Chicago: University of Chicago Press, 1950.

Cressman, Robert J. *The Official Chronology of the U.S. Navy in World War II*. Annapolis: Naval Institute Press, 2000.

Frank, Richard B. *Guadalcanal, The Definitive Account of the Landmark Battle*. New York: Penguin Books, 1992.

Gailey, Harry A. *Bougainville, The Forgotten Campaign, 1943-1945*. Louisville: University Press of Kentucky, 1991.

Garnett, Griffin T. *Sandscrapers, A Forgotten Navy*. Lively: Brandywine Publishers, 1995.

Grace, James W. *Naval Battle of Guadalcanal:* Night Action 13 November 1942. Annapolis: Naval Institute Press, 1999.

Griffith, BGen Samuel B. II. *The Battle for Guadalcanal*. Philadelphia: J. P. Lippincott, 1963.

Halsey, FAdm William F. and LCmdr J. Bryan, III. *Admiral Halsey's Story*. New York and London: McGraw-Hill, 1976.

Hammel, Eric. *Guadalcanal: Decision at Sea, The Naval Battle of Guadalcanal, November 13-15, 1942*. Pacifica: Pacifica Press, 1998.

Hayes, Grace Person. *The History of the Joint Chiefs of Staff in World War II: The War Against Japan*. Annapolis: Naval Institute Press, 1982.

Hixon, Carl K. *Guadalcanal, An American Story.* Annapolis: Naval Institute Press, 1999.

Hoyt, Edward P. *How They Won the War in the Pacific: Nimitz and His Admirals.* New York: Weybright and Tally, 1970.

King, Adm Ernest J. & Cmdr Walter Whitehill. *Fleet Admiral King.* New York: W.W. Norton, 1952.

Koburger, Jr., Charles W. *Pacific Turning Point: The Solomons Campaign, 1942-1943.* Westport: Praeger Publishers, 1995.

Krulak, Lieutenant General Victor H., USMC (Ret). *First to Fight: An Inside View of the U.S. Marine Corps.* Annapolis, 1984.

Lane, Fredrick C. *Ships for Victory: A History of Shipbuilding Under the U.S. Maritime Commission in World War II.* Baltimore, 1951.

Lewin, Ronald. *The American Magic: Codes, Ciphers and the Defeat of Japan.* New York: Farrar Straus Giroux, 1982.

Lorelli, John A. *To Foreign Shores – U.S. Amphibious Operations in WWII.* Annapolis: Naval Institute Press, 1995.

Lundstrom, John B. *The First Team and the Guadalcanal Campaign.* Annapolis: Naval Institute Press, 1994.

Mason, John T., Jr. *The Pacific War Remembered.* Annapolis: Naval Institute Press, 1986.

McGee, William L. *Bluejacket Odyssey – Guadalcanal to Bikini, 1942-1946.* Santa Barbara: BMC Publications, 2000.

Mercer, Bill and others. *USS LCI, Landing Craft Infantry, Vol. II.* Paducah: Turner Publishing Company, 1995.

Miller, Nathan. *The U.S. Navy, A History.* Annapolis: Naval Institute Press, 1997.

_____. *War at Sea, A Naval History of WWII.* New York: Scribner, 1995.

Miller, Thomas G., Jr. *The Cactus Air Force.* New York: Harper & Row, 1969.

Morison, RAdm Samuel Eliot. *History of United States Naval Operations in World War II,* Boston: Little, Brown, 1947-1990.

_____. Vol. III. *The Rising Sun in the Pacific, 1931-April 1942.*

_____. Vol. IV. *Coral Sea, Midway and Submarine Actions, May 1942-August 1942.*

_____. Vol. V. *The Struggle for Guadalcanal, August 1942-February 1943.*

_____. Vol. VI. *Breaking the Bismarcks Barrier, 22 July 1942-1 May 1944.*

_____. Vol. XV. *Supplement and General Index.*

Potter, E.B. *Bull Halsey.* Annapolis: Naval Institute Press, 1985.

_____. *Nimitz.* Annapolis: Naval Institute Press, 1976.

Sakaida, Henry. *Imperial Japanese Navy Aces 1937-1945.* Botley: Oxford Osprey Publishing, Ltd., 1999.

Smith, General Holland M., USMC (Ret). *Coral and Brass.* New York, 1949.

Strahan, Jerry E. *Andrew Jackson Higgins and the Boats that Won World War II.* Baton Rouge: LSU Press, 1994.

Tregaskis, Richard. *Guadalcanal Diary.* New York: Random House, Inc., 1943.

Twining, General Merrill B., USMC (Ret). *No Bended Knee, The Battle For Guadalcanal.* Navato: Presidio Press, 1996.

Walton, Francis. *Miracle of World War II: How American Industry Made Victory Possible.* Macmillan: New York, 1956.

Warner, Dennis and Peggy with Sadao Seno. *Disaster in the Pacific: New Light on the Battle of Savo Island.* Annapolis: Naval Institute Press, 1992.

Wittar, Robert. *Small Boats and Large Slow Targets,* Missoula, Pictorial Histories Publishing Co., 1998.

D. Periodicals

Barger, Mervin D. "Getting the Goods to the Beach." *Surface Warfare.* January/February 1980.

Hearde, Basil. "The Tim Armada: Sage of the LCT," *Challenge WWII Special* Vol. 1, No. 2, 1994.

McDonald, Johnny. "Green Dragons Deliver The Goods," *Traditions,* July/August 1996.

E. Miscellaneous

Clark, Curtis G., *World War II Battle History of APDs in the Solomons, Four Stack APD Veterans Assn.* Privately published, 1996.

Dunn Jr., Read, *Remembering.* Privately published autobiography, 1994.

Jordan, Mark H. and others. *Saga of the Sixth, A History of the Sixth U.S. Naval Construction Battalion, 1942-1945.* Privately published, 1986.

Mackay, Theron N. USN (Ret), *The Tragic Loss of USS LST-342,* Privately published, 1999.

Mason, John T. Jr., "Reminiscences of John C. Niedermair, Architect, Bureau of Ships." Oral History. Annapolis: U.S. Naval Institute, 1978.

McNeill, John A., *The Voyage of the 159,* Whiteville, NC. Privately published, 1995.

Melkild, Martin "Flags." "Landing Ship Tank USS LST-398 and LST Flot Five Pacific Theater, World War II." Privately published, 1985.

Murphy, Timothy Jr., *A Ninety Day Wonder, The Making of a U.S. Navy Officer in WWII:* LCT-84. Privately published, 1990.

Swanson, Ron, and Noel, Larry, and Joe Suozzo, *LCT History.* 3 Vols. Nashville: Privately published by LCT Flotillas of World War II, 2000. Contact: Bud Farmer, 1312 Cheshire Drive, Nashville, TN 37207.

Tesori, Anthony P., *Personal Memoirs of World War II,* Rockledge, FL. Privately published, 1994.

INDEX

Introductory Notes

1. Names of ships and numbered vessels such as PTs, LSTs and I-boats are all in *italics*.
2. Ships and craft listed in the Appendix sections are included in the Index, as are the Allied Air Squadrons at Henderson Field, Guadalcanal. However, only the names of Flag Officers in the Appendix sections are indexed.
3. Since references to Air Attacks, Aircraft, Marine and Army troops would include almost every page in this volume, only principal operations and types of planes are indexed.
4. Page references in **boldface** indicate maps, illustrations, or photographs. Page references in *italics* indicate information contained in tables or figures.

/

∎BMC PUBLICATIONS "History In The First Person"

ORDER FORM

If you are unable to obtain a BMC title through your local bookstore or Amazon.com, you may place your order directly with BMC. Please complete this Order Form and mail it along with your check payable to "BMC Publications" to:

BMC Publications
98 Main Street, #337
Tiburon, CA 94920

QTY	Title	Price	Total
	Bluejacket Odyssey 1942-1946	$35.00	$
	AMPHIBIOUS OPERATIONS IN THE SOUTH PACIFIC IN WWII SERIES The Amphibians Are Coming! Volume I	$29.95	$
	The Solomons Campaigns, Volume II	$39.95	$
	Pacific Express, Volume III (For Release 2008)	$	$
	The Amphibians Are Coming! Volume I and The Solomons Campaigns, Volume II Order both volumes and save 20%	$55.95	$
		SUB TOTAL	$
		California residents include 7.75% sales tax	$
		Shipping and handling for first title	$ 5.00
		S&H per each additional title, $2.00	$
		TOTAL	$

Please ship to:

Name _____

Address _____

City _____ State _____ Zip _____

Daytime Phone ( ) _____ (if there's a question about your order)

❏ I would like the author(s) to sign my book(s).

All domestic orders shipped via U.S. Media Mail. Please allow 14 days for delivery.

BMC Publications, 98 Main Street, #337, Tiburon, CA 94920
email: BMCpublications@aol.com
www.BMCpublications.com
Tel: 415-435-1883
THANK YOU FOR YOUR ORDER

BMC PUBLICATIONS